MICROSOFT
Access 2000
Comprehensive Concepts and Techniques

Gary B. Shelly
Thomas J. Cashman
Philip J. Pratt

Contributing Author
Mary Z. Last

COURSE TECHNOLOGY
ONE MAIN STREET
CAMBRIDGE MA 02142

Thomson Learning™

SHELLY
CASHMAN
SERIES®

Australia • Canada • Denmark • Japan • Mexico • New Zealand • Philippines
Puerto Rico • Singapore • South Africa • Spain • United Kingdom • United States

MICROSOFT

Access 2000
Comprehensive Concepts and Techniques

C O N T E N T S

Microsoft Access 2000

● PROJECT 3

MAINTAINING A DATABASE USING THE DESIGN AND UPDATE FEATURES OF ACCESS

● WEB FEATURE

PUBLISHING TO THE INTERNET USING DATA ACCESS PAGES   AW 1.1

● PROJECT 4

REPORTS, FORMS AND COMBO BOXES

● PROJECT 7

CREATING A REPORT USING DESIGN VIEW

● PROJECT 8

CUSTOMIZING FORMS USING VISUAL BASIC FOR APPLICATIONS (VBA), CHARTS, AND PIVOTTABLE OBJECTS

● PROJECT 9

ADMINISTERING A DATABASE SYSTEM

Preface

The Shelly Cashman Series® offers the finest textbooks in computer education. We are proud of the fact that our *Microsoft Access 2*, *Microsoft Access 7*, and *Microsoft Access 97* textbooks have been the most widely used database books in education. Each edition of our Access textbooks has included innovations, many based on comments made by the instructors and students who use our books. The *Microsoft Access 2000* books continue with the innovation, quality, and reliability that you have come to expect from the Shelly Cashman Series.

In our *Microsoft Access 2000* books, you will find an educationally sound and easy-to-follow pedagogy that combines a step-by-step approach with corresponding screens. All projects and exercises in this book are designed to take full advantage of the Access 2000 enhancements. The popular Other Ways and More About features offer in-depth knowledge of Access 2000. The project openers provide a fascinating perspective of the subject covered in the project. The project material is developed carefully to ensure that students will see the importance of learning Access 2000 for future coursework.

Objectives of This Textbook

Microsoft Access 2000: Comprehensive Concepts and Techniques is intended for a three-unit course that presents Microsoft Access 2000. No experience with a computer is assumed, and no mathematics beyond the high school freshman level is required. The objectives of this book are:

- To teach the fundamentals of Microsoft Access 2000
- To expose students to practical examples of the computer as a useful tool
- To acquaint students with the proper procedures to create, query, and maintain databases suitable for coursework, professional purposes, and personal use
- To develop an exercise-oriented approach that allows learning by example
- To encourage independent study, and help those who are working alone
- To demonstrate the proposed Expert level skill set for the Microsoft Office User Specialist Exam

Approved by Microsoft as Courseware for the Microsoft Office User Specialist Program – Proposed Expert Level

This book has been approved by Microsoft as courseware for the Microsoft Office User Specialist (MOUS) program. After completing the projects and exercises in this book, students will be prepared to take the proposed Expert level examination for the Microsoft Office User Specialist Exam for Microsoft Access 2000. By passing the certification exam for a Microsoft software application, students demonstrate their proficiency in that application to employers. This exam is offered at participating centers, participating corporations, and participating employment agencies. See Appendix D for additional information on the MOUS program and for a table that includes the Microsoft Access 2000 MOUS skill sets for both Core level and the proposed Expert level and corresponding page numbers where a skill is discussed in the book, or visit the Web site www.mous.net.

The Shelly Cashman Series Microsoft Office User Specialist Center Web page (Figure 1) has more than fifteen Web pages you can visit to obtain additional information on the MOUS Certification program. The Web page (www.scsite.com/off2000/cert.htm) includes links to general information on certification, choosing an application for certification, preparing for the certification exam, and taking and passing the proposed certification exam.

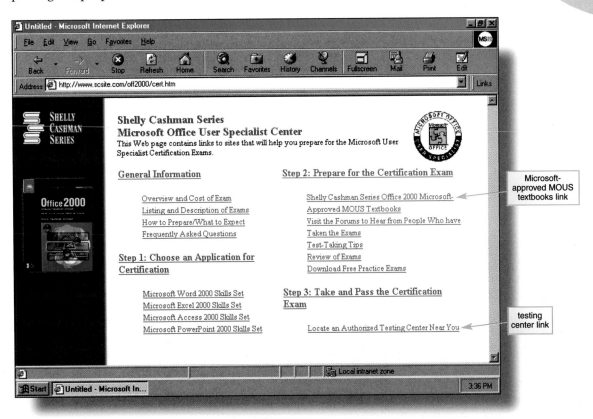

FIGURE 1

The Shelly Cashman Approach

Features of the Shelly Cashman Series *Microsoft Access 2000* books include:

- Project Orientation: Each project in the book presents a practical problem and complete solution in an easy-to-understand approach.

- Step-by-Step, Screen-by-Screen Instructions: Each of the tasks required to complete a project is shown using a step-by-step, screen-by-screen approach. The screens are shown in full color.

- Thoroughly Tested Projects: Every screen in the book is correct because it is produced by the author only after performing a step, resulting in unprecedented quality.

- Other Ways Boxes and Quick Reference Summary: Access 2000 provides a variety of ways to carry out a given task. The Other Ways boxes displayed at the end of most of the step-by-step sequences specify the other ways to do the task completed in the steps. Thus, the steps and the Other Ways box make a comprehensive reference unit. A Quick Reference Summary, available in the back of this book and on the Web, summarizes the way specific tasks can be completed.

- More About Feature: These marginal annotations provide background information that complements the topics covered, adding depth and perspective.

- Integration of the World Wide Web: The World Wide Web is integrated into the Access 2000 learning experience by (1) More Abouts that send students to Web sites for up-to-date information and alternative approaches to tasks; (2) a MOUS information Web page and a MOUS map Web page so students can better prepare for the Microsoft Office Use Specialist (MOUS) Certification examinations; (3) an Access 2000 Quick Reference Summary Web page that summarizes the ways to complete tasks (mouse, menu, shortcut menu, and keyboard); and (4) project reinforcement Web pages in the form of true/false, multiple choice, and short answer questions, and other types of student activities.

Other Ways

1. Click Analyze button arrow on Database window toolbar, click Analyze Table

More About

Control Wizards

Wizards are associated with many of the controls. The wizards lead you through a series of dialog boxes that assist you in creating the control. To use the wizards, the Control Wizards button must be recessed. If not, you will need to specify all the details of the control without any assistance.

Organization of This Textbook

Microsoft Access 2000: Comprehensive Concepts and Techniques provides detailed instruction on how to use Access 2000. The material is divided into nine projects, a Web Feature, two Integration Features, four appendices, and a Quick Reference Summary.

Project 1 – Creating a Database Using Design and Datasheet Views In Project 1, students are introduced to the concept of a database and shown how to use Access 2000 to create a database. Topics include creating a database; creating a table; defining the fields in a table; opening a table; adding records to a table; closing a table; and previewing and printing the contents of a table. Other topics in this project include using a form to view data; using the Report Wizard to create a report; and using Access Help. Students also learn how to design a database to eliminate redundancy.

Project 2 – Querying a Database Using the Select Query Window In Project 2, students learn to use queries to obtain information from the data in their databases. Topics include creating queries; running queries; and printing the results. Specific query topics include displaying only selected fields; using character data in criteria; using wildcards; using numeric data in criteria; using various comparison operators; and creating compound criteria. Other related topics include sorting; joining tables; and restricting records in a join. Students also use calculated fields, statistics, and grouping.

Project 3 – Maintaining a Database Using the Design and Update Features of Access In Project 3, students learn the crucial skills involved in maintaining a database. These include using Datasheet view and Form view to add new records, to change existing records, to delete records, and to locate and filter records. Students also learn the processes of changing the structure of a table; adding additional fields; changing characteristics of existing fields; creating a variety of validation rules; and specifying referential integrity. Students perform mass changes and deletions using queries, create single-field and multiple-field indexes, and use subdatasheets to view related data.

Web Feature – Publishing to the Internet Using Data Access Pages In the Web Feature, students learn to create a data access page to enable users to access the data in a database via the Internet. Topics include creating a data access page using the Page Wizard; previewing a data access page from within Access 2000; and using a data access page.

Project 4 – Reports, Forms, and Combo Boxes In Project 4, students learn to create custom reports and forms. Topics include creating queries for reports; using the Report Wizard; modifying a report design; saving a report; printing a report; creating a report with groups and subtotals; removing totals from a report; and changing the characteristics of items on a report. Other topics include creating an initial form using the Form Wizard; modifying a form design; moving fields; and adding calculated fields and combo boxes. Students learn how to change a variety of field characteristics such as font styles, formats, and colors.

Project 5 – Enhancing Forms with OLE Fields, Hyperlinks, and Subforms In Project 5, students learn to use date, memo, OLE, and hyperlink fields. Topics include incorporating these fields in the structure of a database; updating the data in these fields and changing table properties; creating a form that uses a subform to incorporate a one-to-many relationship between tables; manipulating subforms on a main form; incorporating date, memo, OLE, and hyperlink fields in forms; and incorporating various visual effects in forms. Students also learn to use the hyperlink fields to access Web pages and to use date and memo fields in a query.

Project 6 – Creating an Application System Using Macros, Wizards, and the Switchboard Manager In Project 6, students learn how to create a switchboard system, a system that allows users easily to access tables, forms, and reports simply by clicking buttons. Topics include creating and running macros; creating and using Lookup Wizard fields; using the Input Mask wizard; and creating and using a switchboard system.

Integration Feature – Integrating Excel Worksheet Data into an Access Database In the Integration Feature, students learn how to embed an Excel worksheet in an Access database and how to link a worksheet to a database. Topics include embedding worksheets; linking worksheets; and using the resulting tables.

Project 7 – Creating a Report Using Design View In Project 7, students learn to use Design View to create complex reports involving data from queries that join multiple tables. Topics include relating multiple tables; creating a Lookup Wizard field that uses a separate table; changing join properties in a query; changing field properties in a query; filtering a query's Recordset; creating and running a parameter query; including a subreport in a report; adding a date and page number to a report; and creating and printing mailing labels.

Project 8 - Customizing Forms Using Visual Basic for Applications (VBA), Charts, and PivotTable Objects In Project 8, students learn ways to enhance forms to make them more useable and also how to create forms using Design View. Topics include adding command buttons to forms; modifying VBA code associated with a command button; adding a combo box that will be used for searching to a form; modifying the properties of the combo box, using the combo box to search; creating a form using Design View; adding a subform control to a form; adding charts to a form; and creating and using a PivotTable form.

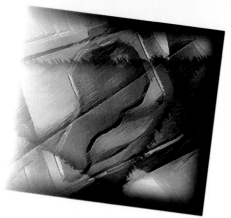

Project 9 – Administering a Database System In Project 9, students learn the issues and techniques involved in administering a database system. Topics include converting a database to an earlier version of Access; using the Table Analyzer, Performance Analyzer, and Documenter; creating a custom input mask; specifying referential integrity options; setting startup options; setting a password; encrypting a database; creating a grouped data access page; creating and using a replica; synchronizing a Design Master and a replica; and creating and running SQL commands.

Integration Feature – Using Access Data in Other Applications In the Integration Feature, students learn how to prepare Access data for use in other applications. Topics include using the Export command to export database data to an Access worksheet; using drag-and-drop to export data to a Word document; and using the proposed Export command to create a snapshot of a report.

Appendices

Appendix A presents a detailed step-by-step introduction to the Microsoft Access Help system. Students learn how to use the Office Assistant and the Contents, Answer Wizard, and Index sheets in the Access Help window. Appendix B describes how to publish Access Web pages to a Web server. Appendix C shows students how to reset the menus and toolbars. Appendix D introduces students to the Microsoft Office User Specialist (MOUS) Certification program and includes a MOUS map that lists a page number in the book for each of the MOUS activities for Core level and the proposed Expert level.

Quick Reference Summary

In Access, you can accomplish a task in a number of ways, such as using the mouse, menu, shortcut menu, and keyboard. The Quick Reference Summary at the back of this book provides a quick reference to the different ways to complete each task presented in this textbook. The Quick Reference Summary also is available on the Web at www.scsite.com/off2000/qr.htm.

End-of-Project Student Activities

A notable strength of the Shelly Cashman Series *Microsoft Access 2000* books is the extensive student activities at the end of each project. Well-structured student activities can make the difference between students merely participating in a class and students retaining the information they learn. The activities in the Shelly Cashman Series *Access 2000* books include the following.

- **What You Should Know** A listing of the tasks completed within a project together with the pages where the step-by-step, screen-by-screen explanations appear. This section provides a perfect study review for students.

- **Project Reinforcement on the Web** Every project has a Web page (www.scsite.com/off2000/reinforce.htm). The Web page includes true/false, multiple choice, and short answer questions, and additional project-related reinforcement activities that will help students gain confidence in their Access 2000 abilities. The Project Reinforcement exercises also are included on the Shelly Cashman Series Teaching Tools CD-ROM.

- **Apply Your Knowledge** This exercise requires students to open and manipulate a file on the Data Disk. To obtain a copy of the Data Disk, follow the instructions on the inside back cover of this book.

- **In the Lab** Three in-depth assignments per project require students to apply the knowledge gained in the project to solve problems on a computer.

- **Cases and Places** Up to seven unique case studies that require students to apply their knowledge to real-world situations.

Shelly Cashman Series Teaching Tools

A comprehensive set of Teaching Tools accompanies this textbook in the form of a CD-ROM. The CD-ROM includes an Instructor's Manual and teaching and testing aids. The CD-ROM (ISBN 0-7895-4636-1) is available through your Course Technology representative or by calling one of the following telephone numbers: Colleges and Universities, 1-800-648-7450; High Schools, 1-800-824-5179; Career Colleges, 1-800-477-3692; Canada, 1-800-268-2222; and Corporations and Government Agencies, 1-800-340-7450.

- **Instructor's Manual** The Instructor's Manual is made up of Microsoft Word files. The files include lecture notes, solutions to laboratory assignments, and a large test bank. The files allow you to modify the lecture notes or generate quizzes and exams from the test bank using your own word processing software. Where appropriate, solutions to laboratory assignments are embedded as icons in the files. When an icon appears, double-click it and the application will start and the solution will display on the screen. The Instructor's Manual includes the following for each project: project objectives; project overview; detailed lesson plans with page number references; teacher notes and activities; answers to the end-of-project exercises; test bank of 110 questions for every project (25 multiple-choice, 50 true/false, and 35 fill-in-the-blank) with page number references; and transparency references. The transparencies are available through the Figures in the Book. The test bank questions are numbered the same as in Course Test Manager. Thus, you can print a copy of the project test bank and use the printout to select your questions in Course Test Manager.

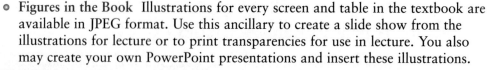

- **Figures in the Book** Illustrations for every screen and table in the textbook are available in JPEG format. Use this ancillary to create a slide show from the illustrations for lecture or to print transparencies for use in lecture. You also may create your own PowerPoint presentations and insert these illustrations.

- **Course Test Manager** Course Test Manager is a powerful testing and assessment package that enables instructors to create and print tests from the large test bank. Instructors with access to a networked computer lab (LAN) can administer, grade, and track tests online. Students also can take online practice tests, which generate customized study guides.

- **Course Syllabus** Any instructor who has been assigned a course at the last minute knows how difficult it is to come up with a course syllabus. For this reason, sample syllabi are included for each of the Access 2000 products that can be customized easily to a course.

- **Lecture Success System** Lecture Success System files are for use with the application software, a personal computer, and projection device to explain and illustrate the step-by-step, screen-by-screen development of a project in the textbook without entering large amounts of data.

- **Instructor's Lab Solutions** Solutions and required files for all the In the Lab assignments at the end of each project are available.

- **Lab Tests/Test Outs** Tests that parallel the In the Lab assignments are supplied for the purpose of testing students in the laboratory on the material covered in the project or testing students out of the course.

- **Project Reinforcement** True/false, multiple choice, and short answer questions, and additional project-related reinforcement activities for each project help students gain confidence in their Access 2000 abilities.

- **Student Files** All the files that are required by students to complete the Apply Your Knowledge exercises are included.

- **Interactive Labs** Eighteen hands-on interactive labs that take students from ten to fifteen minutes each to step through help solidify and reinforce mouse and keyboard usage and computer concepts. Student assessment is available.

- **WebCT Content** This ancillary includes book-related content that can be uploaded to your institution's WebCT site. The content includes a sample syllabus, practice tests, a bank of test questions, a list of book-related links, and lecture notes from the Instructor's Manual.

Acknowledgments

The Shelly Cashman Series would not be the leading computer education series without the contributions of outstanding publishing professionals. First, and foremost, among them is Becky Herrington, director of production and designer. She is the heart and soul of the Shelly Cashman Series, and it is only through her leadership, dedication, and tireless efforts that superior products are made possible. Becky created and produced the award-winning Windows series of books.

Under Becky's direction, the following individuals made significant contributions to these books: Doug Cowley, production manager; Ginny Harvey, series specialist and developmental editor; Ken Russo, senior Web designer; Mike Bodnar, associate production manager; Stephanie Nance, graphic artist and cover designer; Mark Norton, Web designer; Meena Mohtadi, production editor; Marlo Mitchem, Chris Schneider, Hector Arvizu, Kenny Tran, Kathy Mayers, and Dave Bonnewitz, graphic artists; Jeanne Black and Betty Hopkins, Quark experts; Nancy Lamm, Lyn Markowicz, Margaret Gatling, and Laurie Sullivan, copyeditors; Marilyn Martin, Kim Kosmatka, Cherilyn King, Mary Steinman, and Pat Hadden, proofreaders; Cristina Haley, indexer; Sarah Evertson of Image Quest, photo researcher; and Susan Sebok and Ginny Harvey, contributing writers.

Special thanks go to Richard Keaveny, managing editor; Jim Quasney, series consulting editor; Lora Wade, product manager; Erin Bennett, associate product manager; Francis Schurgot, Web product manager; Scott Wiseman, online developer; Rajika Gupta, marketing manager; and Erin Runyon, editorial assistant

Gary B. Shelly
Thomas J. Cashman
Philip J. Pratt

Shelly Cashman Series – Traditionally Bound Textbooks

For more information, see your Course Technology representative, call 1-800-648-7450, or visit Shelly Cashman Online at **www.scseries.com**

COMPUTERS	
Computers	Discovering Computers 2000: Concepts for a Connected World, Web and CNN Enhanced
	Discovering Computers 2000: Concepts for a Connected World, Web and CNN Enhanced Brief Edition
	Teachers Discovering Computers: A Link to the Future, Web and CNN Enhanced
	Discovering Computers 98: A Link to the Future, World Wide Web Enhanced
	Discovering Computers 98: A Link to the Future, World Wide Web Enhanced Brief Edition
	Exploring Computers: A Record of Discovery 2e with CD-ROM
	Study Guide for Discovering Computers 2000: Concepts for a Connected World
	Essential Introduction to Computers 3e (32-page)
	Discovering Computer Certification: Planning, Prerequisites, Potential
	Discovering Internet Companies: Doing Business in the New Millennium

WINDOWS APPLICATIONS	
Microsoft Office	Microsoft Office 2000: Essential Concepts and Techniques (5 projects)
	Microsoft Office 2000: Brief Concepts and Techniques (9 projects)
	Microsoft Office 2000: Introductory Concepts and Techniques (15 projects)
	Microsoft Office 2000: Advanced Concepts and Techniques (11 projects)
	Microsoft Office 2000: Post Advanced Concepts and Techniques (11 projects)
	Microsoft Office 97: Introductory Concepts and Techniques, Brief Edition (6 projects)
	Microsoft Office 97: Introductory Concepts and Techniques, Essentials Edition (10 projects)
	Microsoft Office 97: Introductory Concepts and Techniques, Enhanced Edition (15 projects)
	Microsoft Office 97: Advanced Concepts and Techniques
Microsoft Works	Microsoft Works 4.5[1]
Windows	Microsoft Windows 98: Essential Concepts and Techniques (2 projects)
	Microsoft Windows 98: Introductory Concepts and Techniques (3 projects)
	Microsoft Windows 98: Introductory Concepts and Techniques Web Style Edition (3 projects)
	Microsoft Windows 98[2]: Complete Concepts and Techniques (6 projects)
	Microsoft Windows 98: Comprehensive Concepts and Techniques (9 projects)
	Introduction to Microsoft Windows NT Workstation 4
	Microsoft Windows 95: Introductory Concepts and Techniques (2 projects)
	Introduction to Microsoft Windows 95 (3 projects)
	Microsoft Windows 95[1]: Complete Concepts and Techniques (6 projects)
Word Processing	Microsoft Word 2000[2] • Microsoft Word 97[1] • Microsoft Word 7[1]
	Corel WordPerfect 8 • Corel WordPerfect 7 • WordPerfect 6.1[1]
Spreadsheets	Microsoft Excel 2000[2] • Microsoft Excel 97[1] • Microsoft Excel 7[1] • Microsoft Excel 5[1] • Lotus 1-2-3 97[1]
Database	Microsoft Access 2000[2] • Microsoft Access 97[1] • Microsoft Access 7[1]
Presentation Graphics	Microsoft PowerPoint 2000[2] • Microsoft PowerPoint 97[1] • Microsoft PowerPoint 7[1]
Desktop Publishing	Microsoft Publisher 2000[1]
Graphic Design	Microsoft PhotoDraw 2000: Essential Concepts and Techniques

PROGRAMMING	
Programming	Microsoft Visual Basic 6: Complete Concepts and Techniques[1]
	Microsoft Visual Basic 5: Complete Concepts and Techniques[1]
	QBasic • QBasic: An Introduction to Programming • Microsoft BASIC
	Structured COBOL Programming, Second Edition

INTERNET	
Browser	Microsoft Internet Explorer 5: An Introduction • Microsoft Internet Explorer 4: An Introduction
	Netscape Navigator 4: An Introduction
Web Page Creation	HTML: Complete Concepts and Techniques[1] • Microsoft FrontPage 2000: Complete Concepts and Techniques[1] • Microsoft FrontPage 98: Complete Concepts and Techniques[1] • Netscape Composer • JavaScript: Complete Concepts and Techniques[1]

SYSTEMS ANALYSIS/DATA COMMUNICATIONS	
Systems Analysis	Systems Analysis and Design, Third Edition
Data Communications	Business Data Communications: Introductory Concepts and Techniques, Second Edition

[1]Also available as an Introductory Edition, which is a shortened version of the complete book

[2]Also available as an Introductory Edition, which is a shortened version of the complete book and also as a Comprehensive Edition, which is an extended version of the complete book

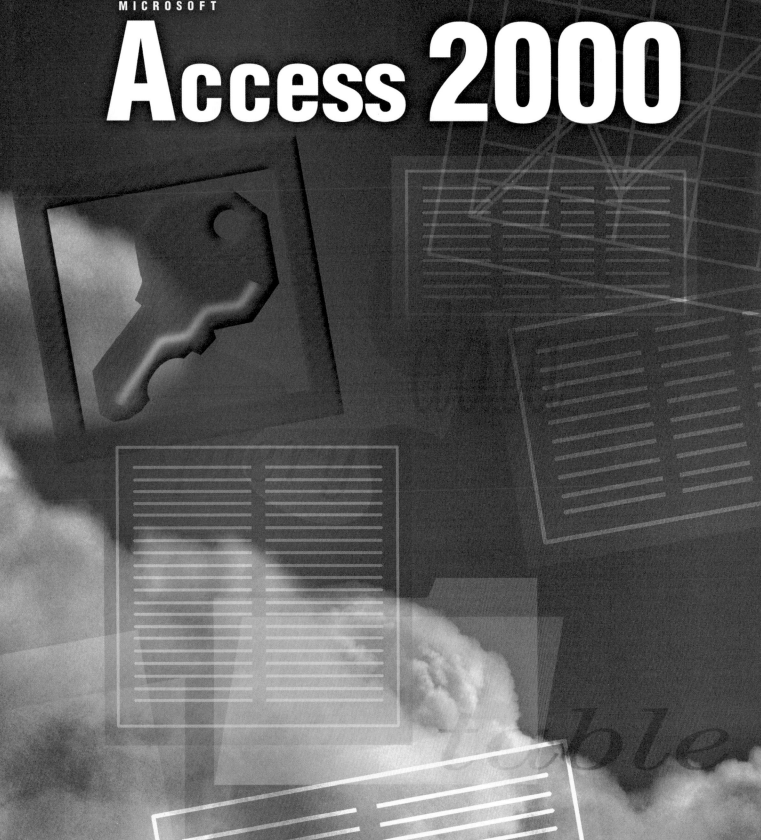

MICROSOFT

Access 2000

Microsoft **Access 2000**

Microsoft Access 2000

Creating a Database Using Design and Datasheet Views

PROJECT 1

OBJECTIVES

You will have mastered the material in this project when you can:

- Describe databases and database management systems
- Start Access
- Describe the features of the Access screen
- Create a database
- Create a table
- Define the fields in a table
- Open a table
- Add records to an empty table
- Close a table
- Close a database and quit Access
- Open a database
- Add records to a nonempty table
- Print the contents of a table
- Use a form to view data
- Create a custom report
- Use Microsoft Access Help
- Design a database to eliminate redundancy

A Match Made in Computer Heaven

Mentoring Unites Experts and Schools

Educational issues dominate the airwaves and print media. From decorum in the classroom to equal access to the Internet, school-related topics are broadcast on the evening news and published in the morning newspapers. Then discussions take place around family dinner tables and at study sessions. Often these dialogues focus on improving the classroom experience by strengthening the relationship among educators, students, community members, and funding sources.

One effective way of enriching the learning process is to involve various groups in education. For example, college students are earning federal work-study funds by helping students in elementary grades learn to read and do math in the America Reads and the America Counts programs. More than 900 public schools have received grants in the 21st Century Community Learning Centers program to provide safe places for children to gather. Business leaders critique middle school students' writing samples as part of the National School Network Exchange, a

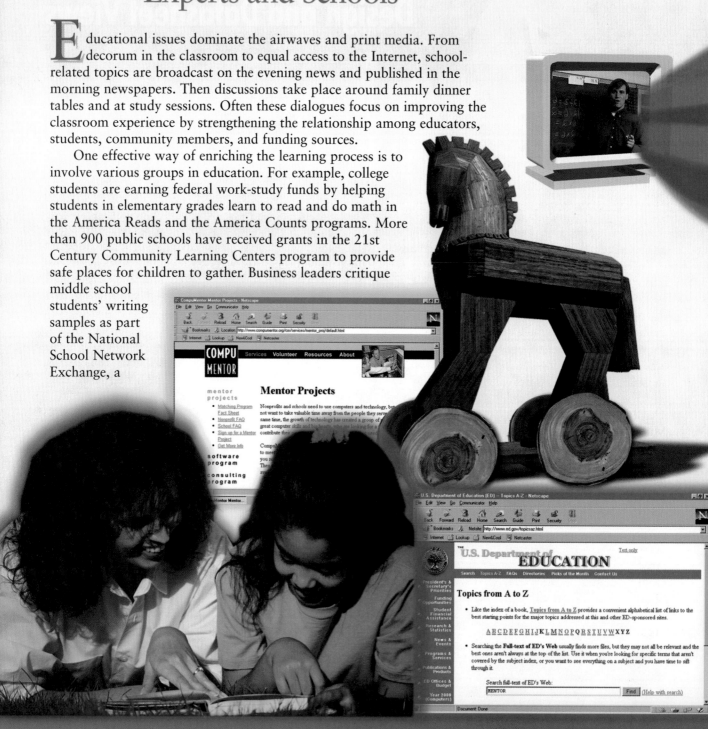

grant-funded program that links more than 500 schools, companies, museums, and governmental agencies via the Internet.

In mythology, Mentor advised Odysseus, who lead the Greeks in the Trojan War. In today's world, mentors advise people needing direction and coaching. These partnerships are common in the computer field. For example, network experts collaborate with a culturally diverse school district to network classrooms throughout the region. Technology buffs develop a distance education program for students living in remote areas. Software experts install donated copies of Microsoft Office in computer labs and then train teachers.

Building these partnerships requires superb technological and organizational skills, strong marketing, and dedicated staff members. Various local, regional, and national organizations have the right mix of technology expertise and qualified personnel to meet these requirements. The nation's largest nonprofit computerization assistance center, CompuMentor, is one of these successful partnering organizations. CompuMentor has linked its staff with more than 6,000 schools and other nonprofit organizations since 1987.

The heart of its success is matching computer experts with the appropriate school or organization. Some mentors volunteer long term, while others agree to work intensively for a few days, particularly in telecommunications areas. Potential mentors complete an application at CompuMentor's Web site (www.compumentor.org) by entering specific information in boxes, called fields, pertaining to their knowledge of operating systems, networking, and hardware repair. They give additional information about their available working hours, training experience, and special skills in office and accounting applications, databases, and desktop publishing.

This information structures records in the CompuMentor database. The staff then can search these records to find a volunteer whose skills match the school's or organization's needs. Similarly, in Project 1, you will use the Access database management system to enter records in the Bavant Marine Services database so the marina staff can match service technicians with boat owners whose vessels need repairs.

Uniting schools with appropriate experts increases awareness of educational issues and ultimately improves the learning process. For more information on building mentoring relationships, visit the U.S. Department of Education Web site (www.ed.gov) or call 1-800-USA-LEARN.

Microsoft Access 2000

Creating a Database Using Design and Datasheet Views

PROJECT 1

CASE PERSPECTIVE

With the popularity of water sports increasing, the number of recreational boaters has risen dramatically! Boats come in all shapes and sizes and are often stored at a marina.

Larger, full-service marinas typically have a service department. The department performs the requested work, such as engine repair, and bills the owner's account. Smaller marinas usually cannot provide on-site service departments, but can offer the same convenience to boat owners by contracting with Bavant Marine Services. A boat owner requiring service notifies the marina, which then contacts Bavant. Bavant sends a technician to perform the required labor and bills the marina.

To ensure operations run smoothly, Bavant Marine Services needs to maintain data on its technicians and their assigned marinas. Bavant wants to organize the data in a database, managed by a database management system such as Access. In this way, Bavant can keep its data current and accurate while management can analyze the data for trends and produce a variety of useful reports. Your task is to help Bavant Marine Services in creating and using their database.

What Is Microsoft Access 2000?

Microsoft Access 2000 is a powerful database management system (DBMS) that functions in the Windows environment and allows you to create and process data in a database. Some of the key features are:

▶ **Data entry and update** Access provides easy mechanisms for adding data, changing data, and deleting data, including the ability to make mass changes in a single operation.
▶ **Queries** (questions) Using Access, it is easy to ask complex questions concerning the data in the database and receive instant answers.
▶ **Forms** In Access, you can produce attractive and useful forms for viewing and updating data.
▶ **Reports** Access contains a feature to allow you to easily create sophisticated reports for presenting your data.
▶ **Web Support** Access allows you to save objects (reports, tables) in HTML format so they can be viewed using a browser. You also can create data access pages to allow real-time access to data in the database via the Internet.

Project One — Bavant Marine Services Database

Creating, storing, sorting, and retrieving data are important tasks. In their personal lives, many people keep a variety of records such as names, addresses, and telephone numbers of friends and business associates, records of investments, records of expenses for tax purposes, and so on. These records must be arranged for quick access. Businesses also must be able to store and access information quickly and easily. Personnel and inventory records, payroll information, client records, order data, and accounts receivable information all are crucial and must be available readily.

The term **database** describes a collection of data organized in a manner that allows access, retrieval, and use of that data. A database management system, such as Access, allows you to use a computer to create a database; add, change, and delete data in the database; sort the data in the database; retrieve data in the database; and create forms and reports using the data in the database.

In Access, a database consists of a collection of tables. Figure 1-1 shows a sample database for Bavant Marine Services. It consists of two tables. The Marina table contains information about the marinas that Bavant Marine Services provides service for. Each marina is assigned to a specific technician. The Technician table contains information about the technicians to whom these marinas are assigned.

fields

marinas of technician Trista Anderson

Marina table

MARINA NUMBER	NAME	ADDRESS	CITY	STATE	ZIP CODE	WARRANTY	NON-WARRANTY	TECH NUMBER
AD57	Alan's Docks	314 Central	Burton	MI	49611	$1,248.00	$597.75	23
AN75	Afton's Marina	21 West 8th	Glenview	MI	48121	$1,906.50	$831.25	36
BL72	Brite's Landing	281 Robin	Burton	MI	49611	$217.00	$0.00	36
EL25	Elend Marina	462 River	Torino	MI	48268	$413.50	$678.75	49
FB96	Fenton's Boats	36 Bayview	Cavela	MI	47926	$923.20	$657.50	23
FM22	Fedder Marina	283 Waterfront	Burton	MI	49611	$432.00	$0.00	36
JB92	JT Boat Club	28 Causeway	Torino	MI	48268	$0.00	$0.00	36
NW72	Nelson's Wharf	27 Lake	Masondale	MI	49832	$608.50	$520.00	23
SM72	Solton's Marine	867 Bay Ridge	Glenview	MI	48121	$462.50	$295.00	49
TR72	The Reef	92 East Bay	Woodview	MI	47212	$219.00	$0.00	36

records

Technician table

TECH NUMBER	LAST NAME	FIRST NAME	ADDRESS	CITY	STATE	ZIP CODE	HOURLY RATE	YTD EARNINGS
23	Anderson	Trista	283 Belton	Port Anton	MI	47989	$24.00	$17,862.00
36	Nichols	Ashton	978 Richmond	Hewitt	MI	47618	$21.00	$19,560.00
49	Gomez	Teresa	2855 Parry	Ashley	MI	47711	$22.00	$21,211.50

technician Trista Anderson

FIGURE 1-1

Databases in Access 2000

In some DBMS's, every table, query, form, or report is stored in a separate file. This is not the case in Access 2000, in which a database is stored in a single file on disk. The file contains all the tables, queries, forms, reports, and programs that you create for this database.

The rows in the tables are called **records**. A record contains information about a given person, product, or event. A row in the Marina table, for example, contains information about a specific marina.

The columns in the tables are called fields. A **field** contains a specific piece of information within a record. In the Marina table, for example, the fourth field, City, contains the city where the marina is located.

The first field in the Marina table is the Marina Number. This is a code assigned by Bavant Marine Services to each marina. Like many organizations, Bavant Marine Services calls it a *number* although it actually contains letters. The marina numbers have a special format. They consist of two uppercase letters followed by a two-digit number.

These numbers are unique; that is, no two marinas will be assigned the same number. Such a field can be used as a **unique identifier**. This simply means that a given marina number will appear only in a single record in the table. Only one record exists, for example, in which the marina number is BL72. A unique identifier also is called a **primary key**. Thus, the Marina Number field is the primary key for the Marina table.

The next eight fields in the Marina table are Name, Address, City, State, Zip Code, Warranty, Non-warranty, and Tech Number. The Warranty field contains the amount billed to the Marina that should be covered by the boat owner's warranty. The Non-warranty field contains the amount that is not covered by warranty.

For example, marina AD57 is Alan's Docks. It is located at 314 Central in Burton, Michigan. The zip code is 49611. The marina has been billed $1,248.00 that should be covered by warranty and $597.75 that will not be covered by warranty.

Each marina is assigned to a single technician. The last field in the Marina table, Tech Number, gives the number of the marina's technician.

The first field in the Technician table, Tech Number, is the number assigned by Bavant Marine Services to the technician. These numbers are unique, so Tech Number is the primary key of the Technician table.

The other fields in the Technician table are Last Name, First Name, Address, City, State, Zip Code, Hourly Rate, and YTD Earnings. The Hourly Rate field gives the technician's hourly billing rate, and the YTD Earnings field contains the total amount that has been paid to the technician for services so far this year.

For example, Technician 23 is Trista Anderson. She lives at 283 Belton in Port Anton, Michigan. Her zip code is 47989. Her hourly billing rate is $24.00 and her YTD earnings are $17,862.00.

The tech number displays in both the Marina table and the Technician table. It is used to relate marinas and technicians. For example, in the Marina table, you see that the tech number for marina AD57 is 23. To find the name of this technician, look for the row in the Technician table that contains 23 in the Tech Number field. Once you have found it, you know the marina is assigned to Trista Anderson. To find all the marinas assigned to Trista Anderson, on the other hand, look through the Marina table for all the marinas that contain 23 in the Tech Number field. Her marinas are AD57 (Alan's Docks), FB96 (Fenton's Boats), and NW72 (Nelson's Wharf).

Together with the management of Bavant Marine Services, you have determined the data that must be maintained in the database is that shown in Figure 1-1 on page A 1.7. You first must create the database and the tables it contains. In the process, you must define the fields included in the two tables, as well as the type of data each field will contain. You then must add the appropriate records to the tables. You also must print the contents of the tables. Finally, you must create a report with the Marina Number, Name, Warranty, and Non-warranty fields for each marina served by Bavant Marine Services. Other reports and requirements for the database at Bavant Marine Services will be addressed with the Bavant Marine Services management in the future.

Starting Access and Creating a New Database

In Access, all the tables, reports, forms, and queries that you create are stored in a single file called a database. Thus before creating any of these objects, you must first start Access and create the database that will hold them. To start Access, first make sure that Windows is running. Once you have done so, perform the following steps to start Access, create a new database, and save the database on a floppy disk.

More About

Creating a Database

Access 2000 includes a Database Wizard that can guide you by suggesting some commonly used databases. If you already know the tables and fields you need, however, you simply create the database yourself. For more information, visit the Access 2000 More About Web page (www.scsite.com/ac2000/more.htm) and then click Database Wizard.

 To Start Access

1 **Place a formatted floppy disk in drive A, click the Start button, and then point to New Office Document on the Start menu.**

The Start menu displays (Figure 1-2).

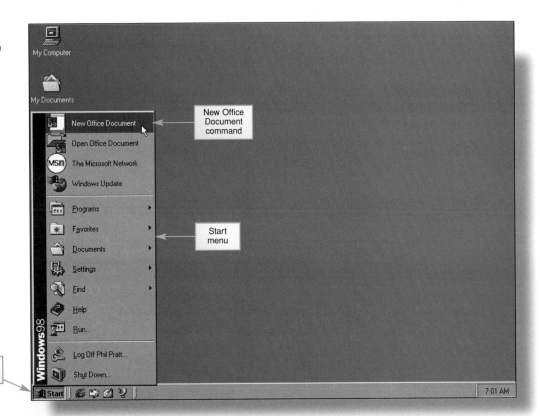

FIGURE 1-2

2 **Click New Office Document. If the General tab is not selected, that is, if it does not display in front of the other tabs, click the General tab. Click the Blank Database icon and then point to the OK button.**

The New Office Document dialog box displays (Figure 1-3). The Blank Database icon is selected.

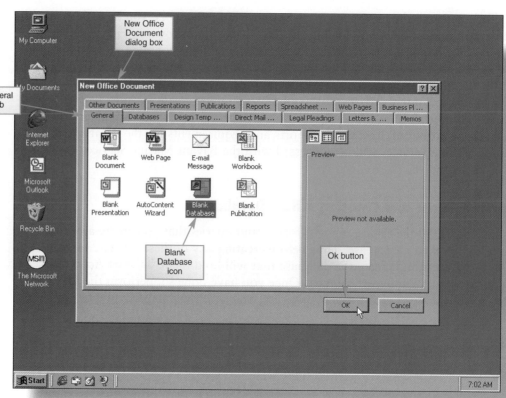

FIGURE 1-3

3 **Click the OK button and then point to the Save in box arrow.**

The File New Database dialog box displays (Figure 1-4).

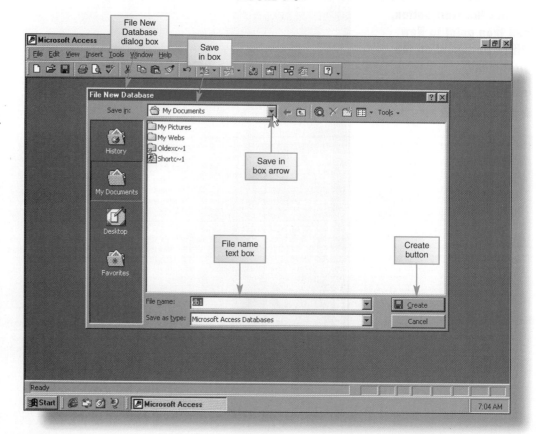

FIGURE 1-4

4 Click the Save in box arrow and then point to 3½ Floppy (A:).

The Save in list displays (Figure 1-5).

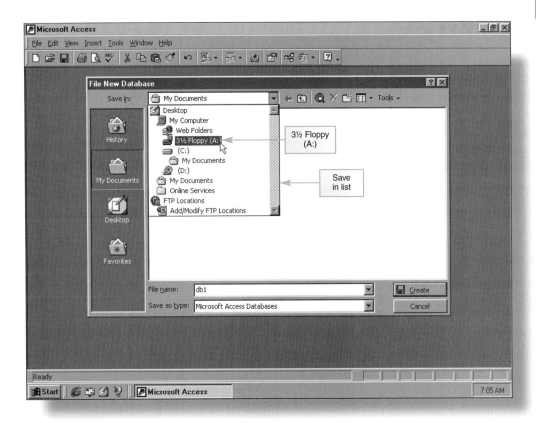

FIGURE 1-5

5 Click 3½ Floppy (A:). Click the File name text box. Repeatedly press the BACKSPACE key to delete db1 (your number may be different) and then type Bavant Marine Services as the file name. Point to the Create button.

The file name is changed to Bavant Marine Services (Figure 1-6).

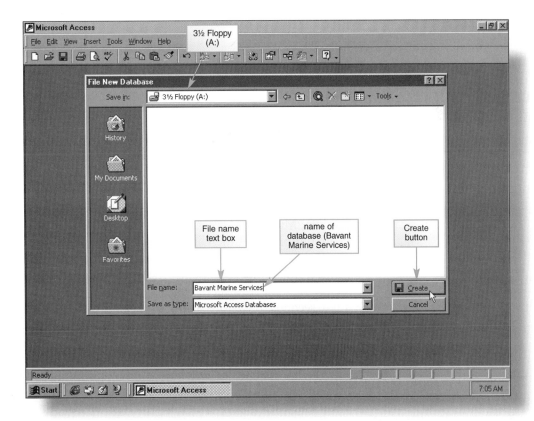

FIGURE 1-6

6 **Click the Create button to create the database. If the Office Assistant displays, right-click the Office Assistant and then point to Hide on the shortcut menu.**

The Bavant Marine Services database is created. The Bavant Marine Services : Database window displays on the desktop (Figure 1-7). The Office Assistant, a tool you can use to obtain help while working with Microsoft Access may display. (You will see how to use the Office Assistant later in this project.)

7 **If necessary, click Hide on the shortcut menu.**

The Office Assistant no longer displays.

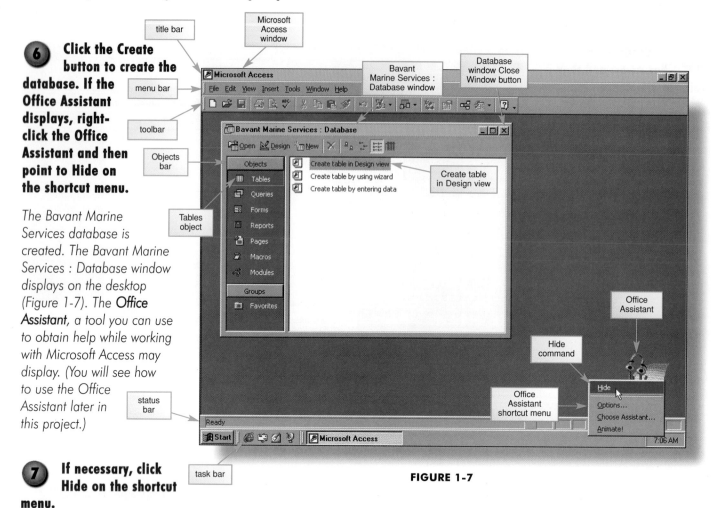

FIGURE 1-7

Toolbars

Normally, the correct Access 2000 toolbar automatically will display. If it does not, click View on the menu bar, and then click Toolbars. Click the toolbar for the activity in which you are engaged. See Appendix C for additional details.

The Access Desktop and the Database Window

The first bar on the desktop (Figure 1-7) is the **title bar**. It displays the title of the product, Microsoft Access. The button on the right is the **Close button**. Clicking the Close button closes the window.

The second bar is the **menu bar**. It contains a list of menu names. To open a menu from the menu bar, click the menu name. Initially a personalized version of the menu, one that consists of commands you have selected most recently, displays. After a few seconds, the entire menu displays. If the command you wish to select is on the personalized menu, you can select it immediately. If not, wait a few seconds to view the entire menu. (The menus shown throughout this book are the full menus, the ones that display after a few seconds.)

The third bar is the **Database window toolbar**. The Database window toolbar contains buttons that allow you to perform certain tasks more quickly than using the menu bar. Each button contains a picture, or **icon**, depicting its function. The specific buttons on the Database window toolbar will vary, depending on the task on which you are working.

The **taskbar** at the bottom of the screen displays the Start button, any active windows, and the current time.

Immediately above the Windows taskbar is the **status bar** (Figure 1-7). It contains special information that is appropriate for the task on which you are working. Currently, it contains the word, Ready, which means Access is ready to accept commands.

The **Database window**, referred to in Figure 1-7 as the Bavant Marine Services : Database window, is a special window that allows you to access easily and rapidly a variety of objects such as tables, queries, forms, and reports. To do so, you will use the various components of the window.

Creating a Table

An Access database consists of a collection of tables. Once you have created the database, you must create each of the tables within it. In this project, for example, you must create both the Marina and Technician tables shown in Figure 1-1 on page A 1.7.

To create a table, you describe the **structure** of the table to Access by describing the fields within the table. For each field, you indicate the following:

1. **Field name** — Each field in the table must have a unique name. In the Marina table (Figure 1-8), for example, the field names are Marina Number, Name, Address, City, State, Zip Code, Warranty, Non-warranty, and Tech Number.

Structure of Marina table

FIELD NAME	DATA TYPE	FIELD SIZE	PRIMARY KEY?	DESCRIPTION
Marina Number	Text	4	Yes	Marina Number (Primary Key)
Name	Text	20		Marina Name
Address	Text	15		Street Address
City	Text	15		City
State	Text	2		State (Two-Character Abbreviation)
Zip Code	Text	5		Zip Code (Five-Character Version)
Warranty	Currency			Current Warranty Amount
Non-warranty	Currency			Current Non-warranty Amount
Tech Number	Text	2		Number of Marina's Technician

Data for Marina table

MARINA NUMBER	NAME	ADDRESS	CITY	STATE	ZIP CODE	WARRANTY	NON-WARRANTY	TECH NUMBER
AD57	Alan's Docks	314 Central	Burton	MI	49611	$1,248.00	$597.75	23
AN75	Afton's Marina	21 West 8th	Glenview	MI	48121	$1,906.50	$831.25	36
BL72	Brite's Landing	281 Robin	Burton	MI	49611	$217.00	$0.00	36
EL25	Elend Marina	462 River	Torino	MI	48268	$413.50	$678.75	49
FB96	Fenton's Boats	36 Bayview	Cavela	MI	47926	$923.20	$657.50	23
FM22	Fedder Marina	283 Waterfront	Burton	MI	49611	$432.00	$0.00	36
JB92	JT Boat Club	28 Causeway	Torino	MI	48268	$0.00	$0.00	36
NW72	Nelson's Wharf	27 Lake	Masondale	MI	49832	$608.50	$520.00	23
SM72	Solton's Marine	867 Bay Ridge	Glenview	MI	48121	$462.50	$295.00	49
TR72	The Reef	92 East Bay	Woodview	MI	47212	$219.00	$0.00	36

FIGURE 1-8

More About

Data Types (General)

Different database management systems have different available data types. Even data types that are essentially the same can have different names. The Access 2000 Text data type, for example, is referred to as Character in some systems and Alpha in others.

More About

Data Types (Access 2000)

Access 2000 offers a wide variety of data types, some of which have special options associated with them. For more information on data types, visit the Access 2000 More About Web page (www.scsite.com/ac2000/more.htm) and then click Data Types.

2. **Data type** — Data type indicates to Access the type of data the field will contain. Some fields can contain letters of the alphabet and numbers. Others contain only numbers. Others, such as Warranty and Non-warranty, can contain numbers and dollar signs.
3. **Description** — Access allows you to enter a detailed description of the field.

You also can assign field widths to text fields (fields whose data type is Text). This indicates the maximum number of characters that can be stored in the field. If you do not assign a width to such a field, Access assumes the width is 50.

You also must indicate which field or fields make up the **primary key**; that is, the unique identifier, for the table. In the sample database, the Marina Number field is the primary key of the Marina table and the Tech Number field is the primary key of the Technician table.

The rules for field names are:

1. Names can be up to 64 characters in length.
2. Names can contain letters, digits, and spaces, as well as most of the punctuation symbols.
3. Names cannot contain periods, exclamation points (!), or square brackets ([ ]).
4. The same name cannot be used for two different fields in the same table.

Each field has a **data type**. This indicates the type of data that can be stored in the field. The data types you will use in this project are:

1. **Text** — The field can contain any characters.
2. **Number** — The field can contain only numbers. The numbers either can be positive or negative. Fields are assigned this type so they can be used in arithmetic operations. Fields that contain numbers but will not be used for arithmetic operations usually are assigned a data type of Text. The Tech Number field, for example, is a text field because the tech numbers will not be involved in any arithmetic.
3. **Currency** — The field can contain only dollar amounts. The values will be displayed with dollar signs, commas, decimal points, and with two digits following the decimal point. Like numeric fields, you can use currency fields in arithmetic operations. Access assigns a size to currency fields automatically.

The field names, data types, field widths, primary key information, and descriptions for the Marina table are shown in Figure 1-8. With this information, you are ready to begin creating the table. To create the table, use the following steps.

 ## Steps | To Create a Table

1 **Right-click Create table in Design view and then point to Open on the shortcut menu.**

The shortcut menu for creating a table in Design view displays (Figure 1-9).

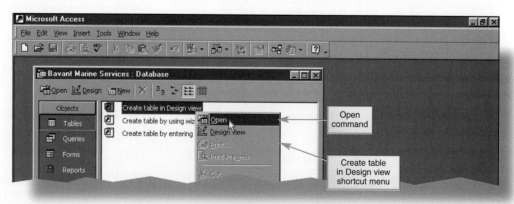

FIGURE 1-9

2 **Click Open.**

The Table1 : Table window displays (Figure 1-10).

3 **Click the Maximize button for the Table1 : Table window.**

A maximized Table1 : Table window displays.

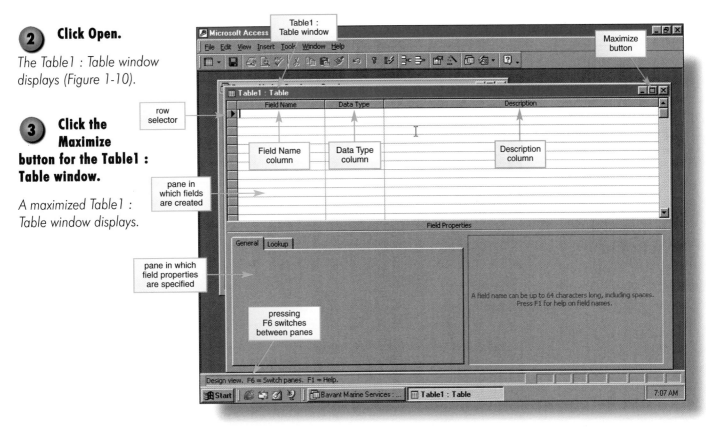

FIGURE 1-10

Defining the Fields

The next step in creating the table is to define the fields by specifying the required details in the Table window. Make entries in the Field Name, Data Type, and Description columns. Enter additional information in the Field Properties box in the lower portion of the Table window. Press the F6 key to move from the upper **pane** (portion of the screen), the one where you define the fields, to the lower pane, the one where you define field properties. Enter the appropriate field size and then press the F6 key to return to the upper pane. As you define the fields, the row selector (Figure 1-10) indicates the field you currently are describing. The **row selector** is a small box or bar that, when clicked, selects the entire row. It is positioned on the first field, indicating Access is ready for you to enter the name of the first field in the Field Name column.

Perform the steps on the next page to define the fields in the table.

1. Click New Object: AutoForm button arrow on Database window toolbar, click Table
2. On Insert menu click Table
3. Double-click Create table in Design view
4. Press ALT+N

More About

Primary Keys

In some cases, the primary key consists of a combination of fields rather than a single field. For more information on determining primary keys in such situations, visit the Access 2000 More About Web page (www.scsite.com/ac2000/more.htm) and then click Primary Key.

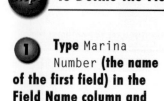

To Define the Fields in a Table

1 **Type** Marina Number **(the name of the first field) in the Field Name column and then press the TAB key.**

The words, Marina Number, display in the Field Name column and the insertion point advances to the Data Type column, indicating you can enter the data type (Figure 1-11). The word, Text, one of the possible data types, currently displays. The arrow in the Data Type column indicates a list of data types is available by clicking the arrow.

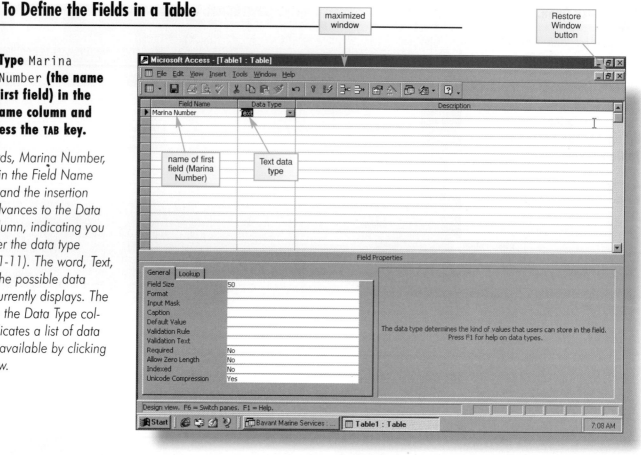

FIGURE 1-11

2 **Because Text is the correct data type, press the TAB key to move the insertion point to the Description column, type** Marina Number (Primary Key) **as the description and then point to the Primary Key button on the Database window toolbar.**

A ScreenTip, which is a description of the button, displays partially obscuring the description of the first field (Figure 1-12).

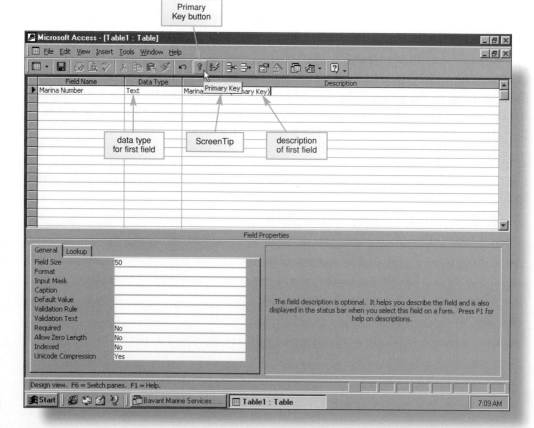

FIGURE 1-12

3 Click the Primary Key button to make **Marina Number** the primary key and then press the **F6** key to move the insertion point to the Field Size text box.

The Marina Number field is the primary key as indicated by the key symbol that displays in the row selector (Figure 1-13). The current entry in the Field Size text box (50) is selected.

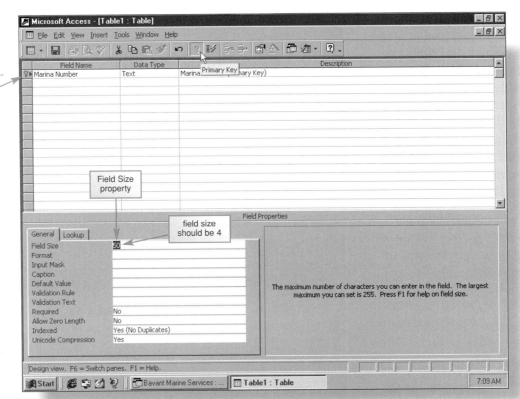

FIGURE 1-13

4 Type **4** as the size of the Marina Number field. Press the **F6** key to return to the Description column for the Marina Number field and then press the **TAB** key to move to the Field Name column in the second row.

The row selector moves to the second row just below the field name Marina Number (Figure 1-14).

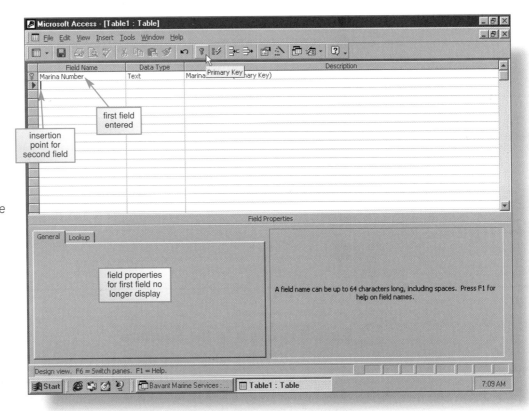

FIGURE 1-14

5 Use the techniques illustrated in Steps 1 through 4 to make the entries from the Marina table structure shown in Figure 1-8 on page A 1.13 up through and including the name of the Warranty field. Click the Data Type column arrow and then point to Currency.

The additional fields are entered (Figure 1-15). A list of available data types displays in the Data Type column for the Warranty field.

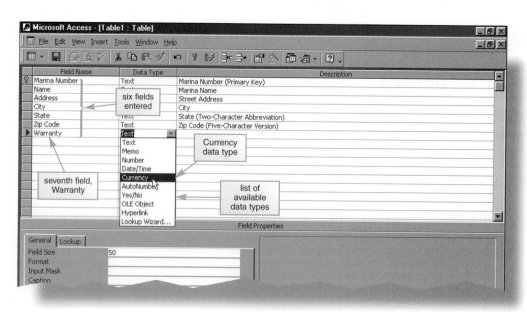

FIGURE 1-15

6 Click Currency and then press the TAB key. Make the remaining entries from the Marina table structure shown in Figure 1-8.

The fields are all entered (Figure 1-16).

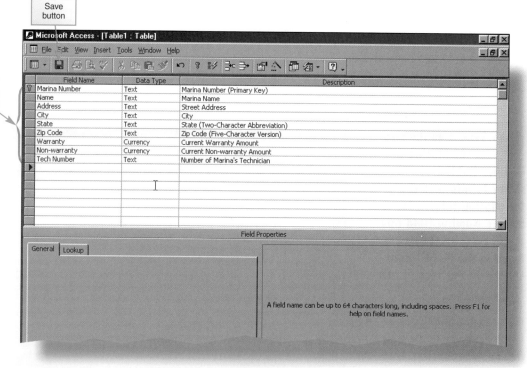

FIGURE 1-16

Correcting Errors in the Structure

When creating a table, check the entries carefully to ensure they are correct. If you make a mistake and discover it before you press the TAB key, you can correct the error by repeatedly pressing the BACKSPACE key until the incorrect characters are removed. Then, type the correct characters. If you do not discover a mistake until later, you can click the entry, type the correct value, and then press the ENTER key.

If you accidentally add an extra field to the structure, select the field by clicking the row selector (the leftmost column on the row that contains the field to be deleted). Once you have selected the field, press the DELETE key. This will remove the field from the structure.

If you forget a field, select the field that will follow the field you wish to add by clicking the row selector, and then press the INSERT key. The remaining fields move down one row, making room for the missing field. Make the entries for the new field in the usual manner.

If you made the wrong field a primary key field, click the correct primary key entry for the field and then click the Primary Key button on the Database window toolbar.

As an alternative to these steps, you may want to start over. To do so, click the Close button for the Table1 : Table window and then click No. The original desktop displays and you can repeat the process you used earlier.

Saving a Table

The Marina table structure now is complete. The final step is to save the table within the database. At this time, you should give the table a name.

Table names are from one to 64 characters in length and can contain letters, numbers, and spaces. The two table names in this project are Marina and Technician.

To save the table, complete the following steps.

Steps To Save a Table

1 **Click the Save button on the Database window toolbar (see Figure 1-16 on page A 1.18). Type** Marina **as the name of the table in the Table Name text box and then point to the OK button.**

The Save As dialog box displays (Figure 1-17). The name of the table displays in the Table Name text box.

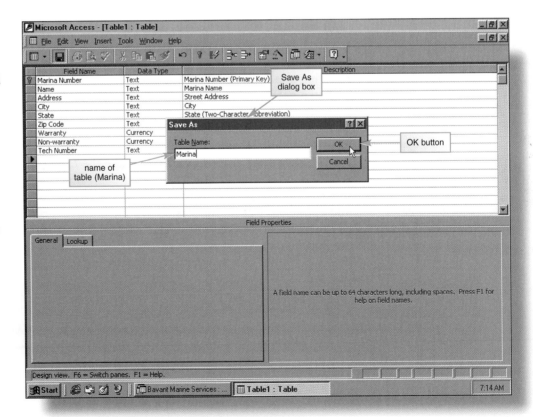

FIGURE 1-17

2 Click the OK button and then point to the Close Window button for the Marina : Table window.

The table is saved on the floppy disk in drive A. The name of the table is now Marina as indicated on the title bar (Figure 1-18).

3 Click the Close Window button for the Marina : Table window. (Be sure not to click the Close button on the Microsoft Access title bar, because this would close Microsoft Access.)

The Marina : Table window no longer displays.

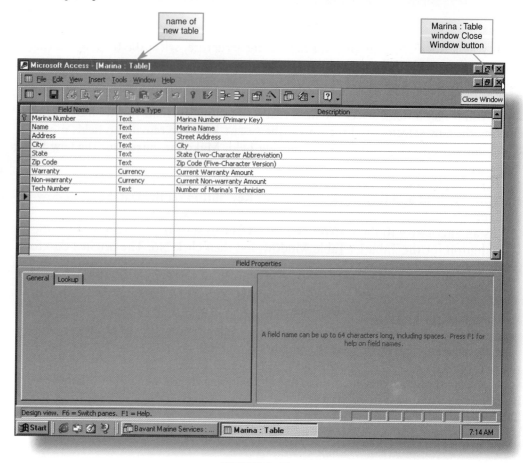

FIGURE 1-18

Other Ways

1. On File menu click Save
2. Press CTRL+S

More About

Adding Records

As soon as you have entered or modified a record and moved to another record, the original record is saved. This is different from other tools. The rows entered in a spreadsheet, for example, are not saved until the entire spreadsheet is saved.

Adding Records to a Table

Creating a table by building the structure and saving the table is the first step in a two-step process. The second step is to add records to the table. To add records to a table, the table must be open. To open a table, right-click the table in the Database window and then click Open on the shortcut menu. The table displays in Datasheet view. In **Datasheet view**, the table is represented as a collection of rows and columns called a **datasheet**. It looks very much like the tables shown in Figure 1-1 on page A 1.7.

You often add records in phases. You may, for example, not have enough time to add all the records in one session. To illustrate this process, this project begins by adding the first two records in the Marina table (Figure 1-19). The remaining records are added later.

Marina table (first 2 records)

MARINA NUMBER	NAME	ADDRESS	CITY	STATE	ZIP CODE	WARRANTY	NON-WARRANTY	TECH NUMBER
AD57	Alan's Docks	314 Central	Burton	MI	49611	$1,248.00	$597.75	23
AN75	Afton's Marina	21 West 8th	Glenview	MI	48121	$1,906.50	$831.25	36

FIGURE 1-19

To open the Marina table and then add records, use the following steps.

Steps: To Add Records to a Table

1 Right-click Marina in the **Bavant Marine Services : Database window and then point to Open on the shortcut menu.**

The shortcut menu for the Marina table displays (Figure 1-20). The Bavant Marine Services : Database window is maximized because the previous window, the Marina : Table window, was maximized. (If you wanted to restore the Database window to its original size, you would click the Restore Window button.)

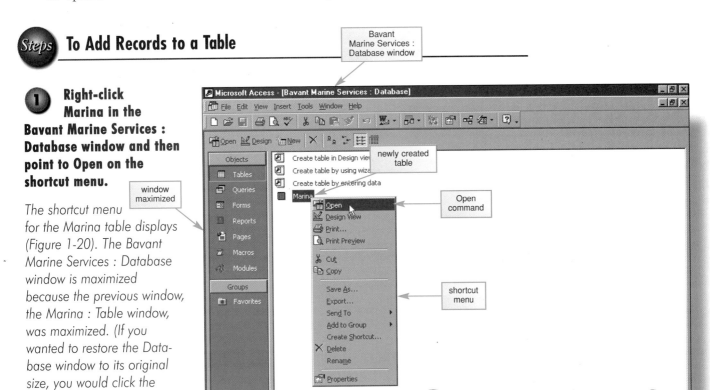

FIGURE 1-20

2 Click Open on the shortcut menu.

The Marina : Table window displays (Figure 1-21). The window contains the Datasheet view for the Marina table. The **record selector** is positioned on the first record. The record selector is the small box or bar to the left of the record. The status bar at the bottom of the window also indicates that the record selector is positioned on record 1.

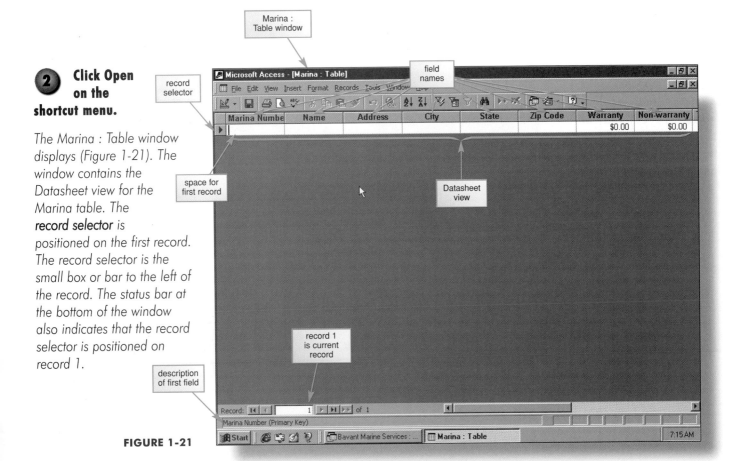

FIGURE 1-21

3 If your window is not already maximized, click the Maximize button to maximize the window containing the table. Type AD57 as the first marina number, as shown in Figure 1-19. Be sure you type the letters in uppercase, because that is the way they are to be entered in the database.

The marina number is entered, but the insertion point is still in the Marina Number field (Figure 1-22).

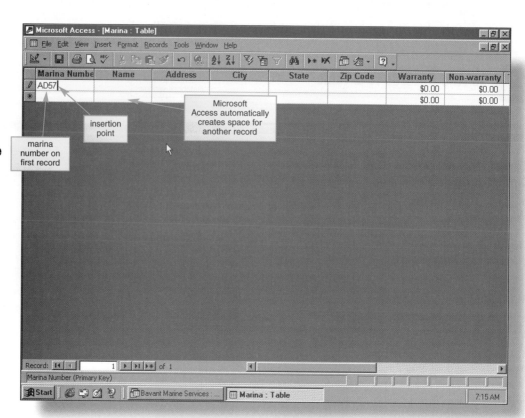

FIGURE 1-22

4 Press the TAB key to complete the entry for the Marina Number field. Type the following entries, pressing the TAB key after each one: Alan's Docks as the name, 314 Central as the address, Burton as the city, MI as the state, and 49611 as the zip code.

The Name, Address, City, State, and Zip Code fields are entered (Figure 1-23).

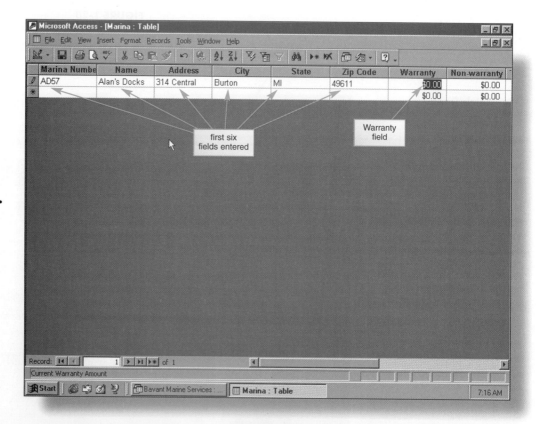

FIGURE 1-23

5 Type 1248 **as the warranty amount and then press the TAB key. (You do not need to type dollar signs or commas. In addition, because the digits to the right of the decimal point were both zeros, you did not need to type the decimal point.) Type** 597.75 **as the non-warranty amount and then press the TAB key. Type** 23 **as the tech number to complete the record.**

The fields have shifted to the left (Figure 1-24). The Warranty and Non-warranty values display with dollar signs and decimal points. The insertion point is positioned in the Tech Number field.

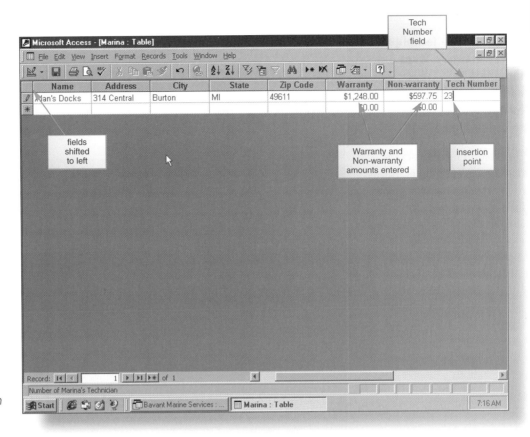

FIGURE 1-24

6 Press the TAB **key.**

The fields shift back to the right, the record is saved, and the insertion point moves to the marina number on the second row (Figure 1-25).

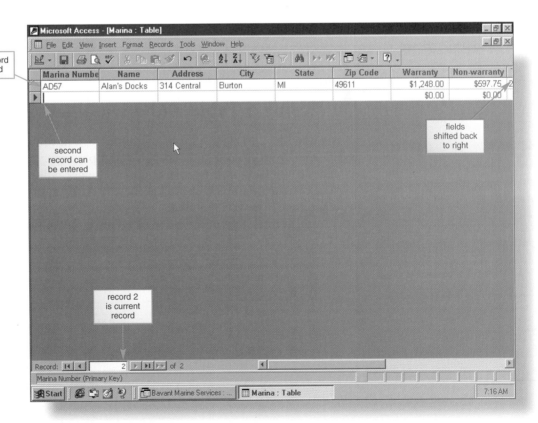

FIGURE 1-25

7 **Use the techniques shown in Steps 3 through 6 to add the data for the second record in Figure 1-19.**

The second record is added and the insertion point moves to the marina number on the third row (Figure 1-26).

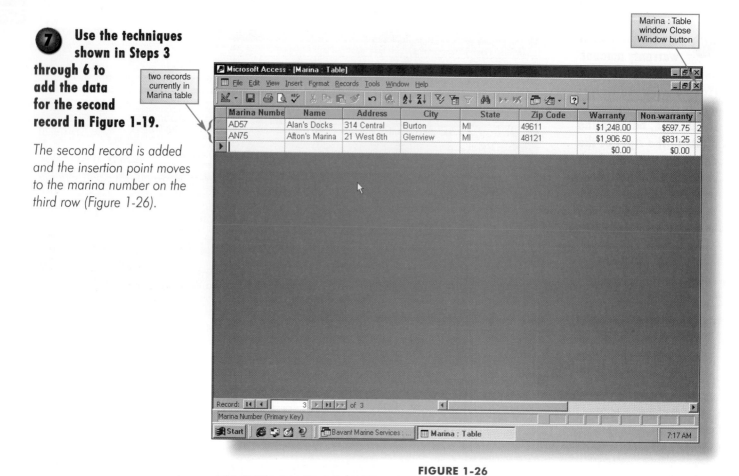

FIGURE 1-26

Closing a Table and a Database and Quitting Access

It is a good idea to close a table as soon as you have finished working with it. It keeps the screen from getting cluttered and prevents you from making accidental changes to the data in the table. If you no longer will work with the database, you should close the database as well. With the creation of the Marina table complete, you can quit Access at this point.

Perform the following steps to close the table and the database and then quit Access.

To Close a Table and Database and Quit Access

1 **Click the Close Window button for the Marina : Table window (see Figure 1-26 on page A 1.24).**

The datasheet for the Marina table no longer displays (Figure 1-27).

2 **Click the Close button for the Bavant Marine Services : Database window (see Figure 1-27).**

The Bavant Marine Services : Database window no longer displays.

3 **Click the Close button for the Microsoft Access window.**

The Microsoft Access window no longer displays.

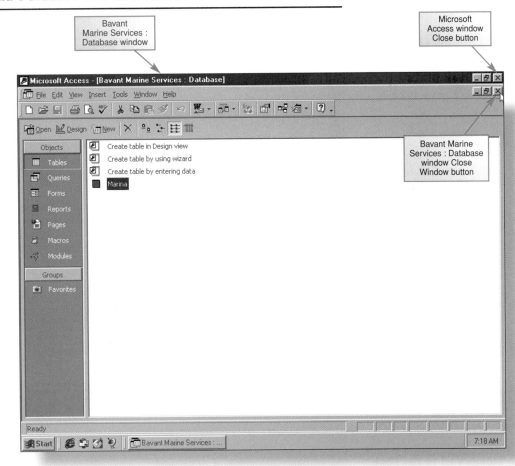

FIGURE 1-27

Opening a Database

To work with any of the tables, reports, or forms in a database, the database must be open. To open a database from the Windows desktop, click Open Office Document on the Start menu by performing the following steps. (The Other Ways box indicates ways to open a database from within Access.)

Steps To Open a Database

1 **Click the Start button and then point to Open Office Document (Figure 1-28).**

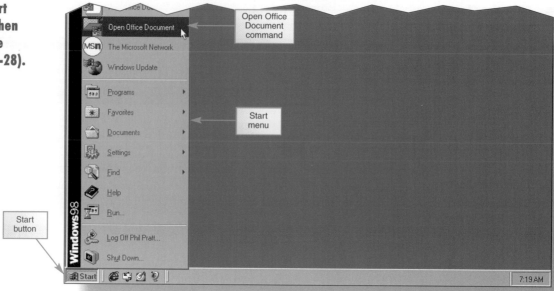

FIGURE 1-28

2 **Click Open Office Document. If necessary, click the Look in box arrow and then click 3½ Floppy (A:) in the Look in box. If it is not already selected, click the Bavant Marine Services database name. Point to the Open button.**

The Open Office Document dialog box displays (Figure 1-29). The 3½ Floppy (A:) folder displays in the Look in box and the files on the floppy disk in drive A display. Your list may be different.

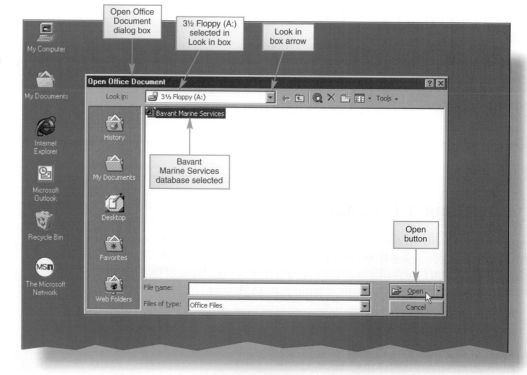

3 **Click the Open button.**

The database opens and the Bavant Marine Services : Database window displays.

FIGURE 1-29

Other Ways

1. Click Open button on Database window toolbar
2. On File menu click Open
3. Press CTRL+O

Adding Additional Records

You can add records to a table that already contains data using a process almost identical to that used to add records to an empty table. The only difference is that you place the insertion point after the last data record before you enter the additional data. To do so, use the **Navigation buttons** found near the lower-left corner of the screen. The purpose of each of the Navigation buttons is described in Table 1-1.

Table 1-1	Navigation Buttons in Datasheet View
BUTTON	PURPOSE
First Record	Moves to the first record in the table
Previous Record	Moves to the previous record
Next Record	Moves to the next record
Last Record	Moves to the last record in the table
New Record	Moves to the end of the table to a position for entering a new record

Complete the following steps to add the remaining records (Figure 1-30) to the Marina table.

Marina table (last 8 records)

MARINA NUMBER	NAME	ADDRESS	CITY	STATE	ZIP CODE	WARRANTY	NON-WARRANTY	TECH NUMBER
BL72	Brite's Landing	281 Robin	Burton	MI	49611	$217.00	$0.00	36
EL25	Elend Marina	462 River	Torino	MI	48268	$413.50	$678.75	49
FB96	Fenton's Boats	36 Bayview	Cavela	MI	47926	$923.20	$657.50	23
FM22	Fedder Marina	283 Waterfront	Burton	MI	49611	$432.00	$0.00	36
JB92	JT Boat Club	28 Causeway	Torino	MI	48268	$0.00	$0.00	36
NW72	Nelson's Wharf	27 Lake	Masondale	MI	49832	$608.50	$520.00	23
SM72	Solton's Marine	867 Bay Ridge	Glenview	MI	48121	$462.50	$295.00	49
TR72	The Reef	92 East Bay	Woodview	MI	47212	$219.00	$0.00	36

FIGURE 1-30

Steps ## To Add Additional Records to a Table

1 Right-click Marina
in the Bavant
**Marine
Services :
Database**
window and then click
Open on the shortcut menu.

When the Marina
table displays,
maximize the window by
clicking the Maximize
button. Point to the New
Record button.

*The datasheet displays
(Figure 1-31).*

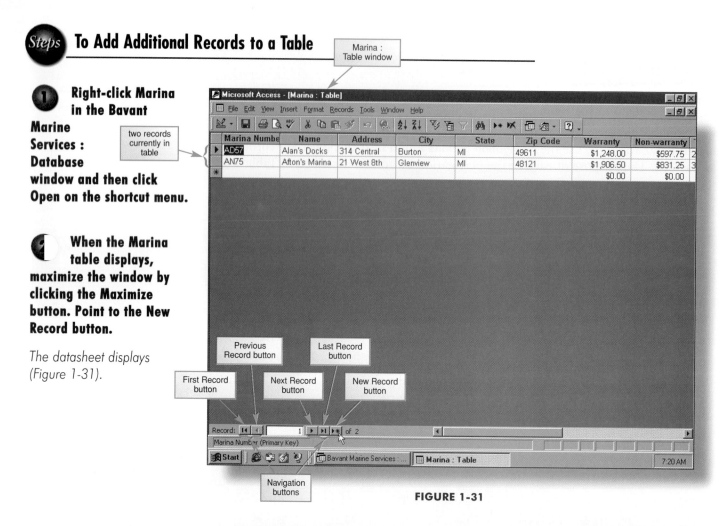

FIGURE 1-31

Click the New
Record button.

*Access places the insertion
point in position to enter a
new record (Figure 1-32).*

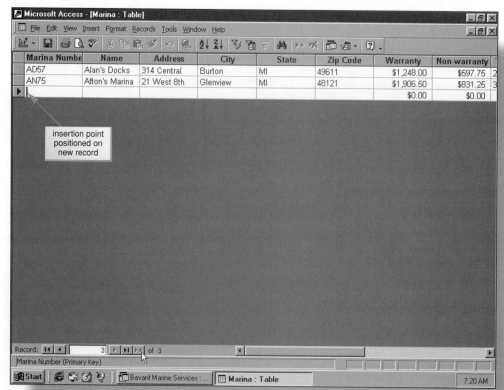

FIGURE 1-32

4 **Add the remaining records from Figure 1-30 on page A 1.27 using the same techniques you used to add the first two records. Point to the Close Window button.**

The additional records are added (Figure 1-33).

5 **Click the Close Window button.**

The window containing the table closes.

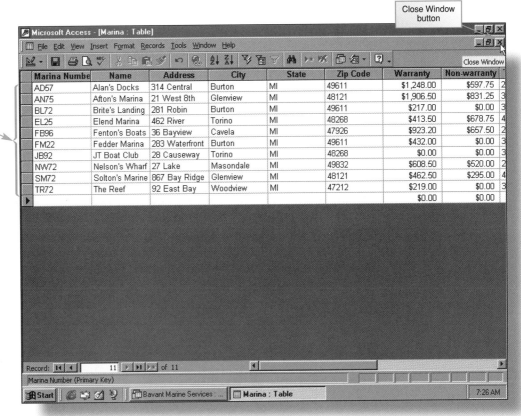

FIGURE 1-33

Other Ways

1. Click New Record button on Database window toolbar
2. On Insert menu click New Record

Correcting Errors in the Data

Check your entries carefully to ensure they are correct. If you make a mistake and discover it before you press the TAB key, correct it by pressing the BACKSPACE key until the incorrect characters are removed and then typing the correct characters.

If you discover an incorrect entry later, correct the error by clicking the incorrect entry and then making the appropriate correction. If the record you must correct is not on the screen, use the Navigation buttons (Next Record, Previous Record, and so on) to move to it. If the field you want to correct is not visible on the screen, use the horizontal scroll bar along the bottom of the screen to shift all the fields until the one you want displays. Then make the correction.

If you add an extra record accidentally, select the record by clicking the record selector that immediately precedes the record. Then, press the DELETE key. This will remove the record from the table. If you forget a record, add it using the same procedure as for all the other records. Access will place it in the correct location in the table automatically.

If you cannot determine how to correct the data, you are, in effect, stuck on the record. Access neither allows you to move to any other record until you have made the correction, nor allows you to close the table. If you encounter this situation, simply press the ESC key. Pressing the ESC key will remove from the screen the record you are trying to add. You then can move to any other record, close the table, or take any other action you desire.

Printing the Contents of a Table

You can change the paper size, paper source, or the printer that will be used to print the report. To change any of these, select the Page sheet in the Page Setup dialog box.

Previewing and Printing the Contents of a Table

When working with a database, you often will need to print a copy of the table contents. Figure 1-34 shows a printed copy of the contents of the Marina table. (Yours may look slightly different, depending on your printer.) Because the Marina table is wider substantially than the screen, it also will be wider than the normal printed page in portrait orientation. **Portrait orientation** means the printout is across the width of the page. **Landscape orientation** means the printout is across the length of the page. Thus, to print the wide database table, use landscape orientation. If you are printing the contents of a table that fits on the screen, you will not need landscape orientation. A convenient way to change to landscape orientation is to **preview** what the printed copy will look like by using Print Preview. This allows you to determine whether landscape orientation is necessary and, if it is, to change easily the orientation to landscape. In addition, you also can use Print Preview to determine whether any adjustments are necessary to the page margins.

Marina   9/7/2001

Marina Number	Name	Address	City	State	Zip Code	Warranty	Non-warranty	Tech Number
AD57	Alan's Docks	314 Central	Burton	MI	49611	$1,248.00	$597.75	23
AN75	Afton's Marina	21 West 8th	Glenview	MI	48121	$1,906.50	$831.25	36
BL72	Brite's Landing	281 Robin	Burton	MI	49611	$217.00	$0.00	36
EL25	Elend Marina	462 River	Torino	MI	48268	$413.50	$678.75	49
FB96	Fenton's Boats	36 Bayview	Cavela	MI	47926	$923.20	$657.50	23
FM22	Fedder Marina	283 Waterfront	Burton	MI	49611	$432.00	$0.00	36
JB92	JT Boat Club	28 Causeway	Torino	MI	48268	$0.00	$0.00	36
NW72	Nelson's Wharf	27 Lake	Masondale	MI	49832	$608.50	$520.00	23
SM72	Solton's Marina	867 Bay Ridge	Glenview	MI	48121	$462.50	$295.00	49
TR72	The Reef	92 East Bay	Woodview	MI	47212	$219.00	$0.00	36

Page 1

FIGURE 1-34

Perform the following steps to use Print Preview to preview and then print the Marina table.

 To Preview and Print the Contents of a Table

① **Right-click Marina and then point to Print Preview on the shortcut menu.**

The shortcut menu for the Marina table displays (Figure 1-35).

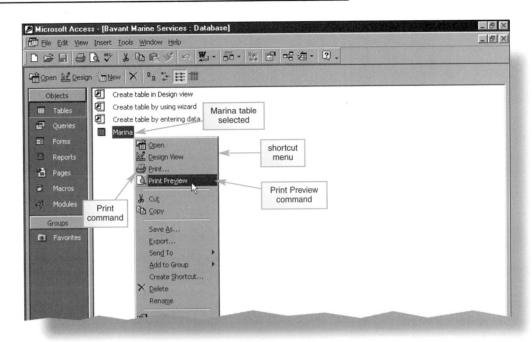

FIGURE 1-35

② **Click Print Preview on the shortcut menu. Point anywhere in the upper-right portion of the report.**

The preview of the report displays (Figure 1-36).

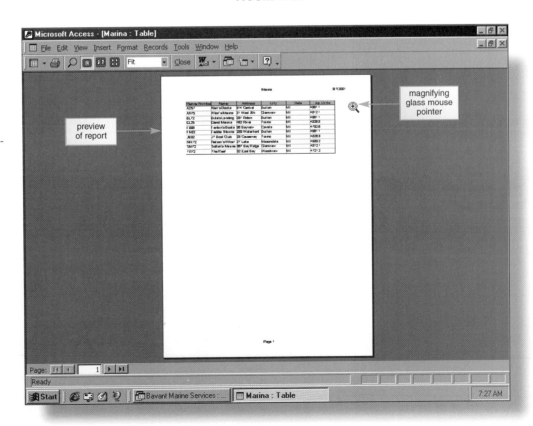

FIGURE 1-36

3 Click the magnifying glass mouse pointer in the approximate position shown in Figure 1-36.

The portion surrounding the mouse pointer is magnified (Figure 1-37). The last field that displays is the Zip Code field. The Warranty, Non-warranty, and Tech Number fields do not display. To display the additional fields, you will need to switch to landscape orientation.

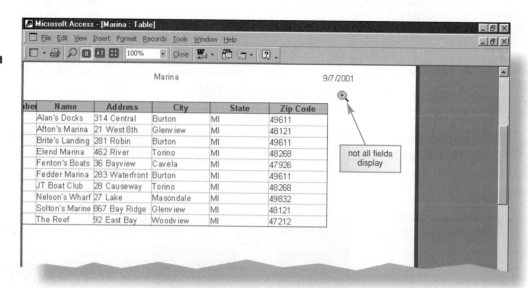

FIGURE 1-37

4 Click File on the menu bar and then point to Page Setup. (Remember that you might have to wait a few seconds for the entire menu to display.)

The File menu displays (Figure 1-38).

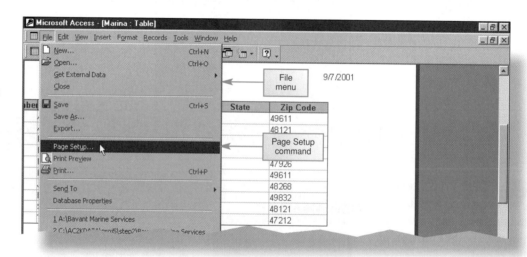

FIGURE 1-38

5 Click Page Setup and then point to the Page tab.

The Page Setup dialog box displays (Figure 1-39).

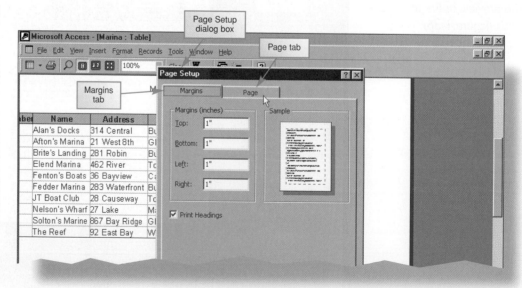

FIGURE 1-39

6 Click the Page tab and then point to the Landscape option button.

*The Page sheet displays (Figure 1-40). The Portrait option button currently is selected. (**Option button** refers to the round button that indicates choices in a dialog box. When the corresponding option is selected, the button contains within it a solid circle. Clicking an option button selects it, and deselects all others.)*

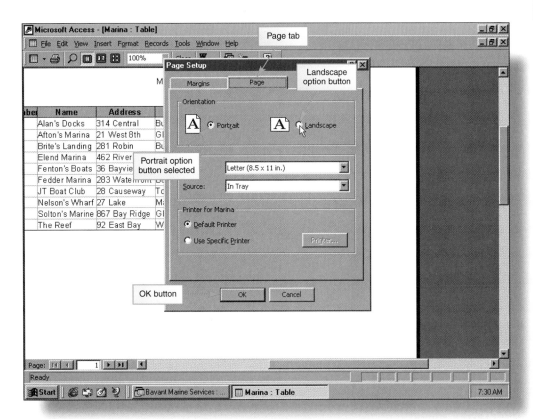

FIGURE 1-40

7 Click Landscape and then click the OK button. Click the mouse pointer anywhere within the report to view the entire report.

The orientation is changed to landscape as shown by the report that displays on the screen (Figure 1-41). The characters in the report are so small that it is difficult to determine whether all fields currently display. To zoom in on a portion of the report, click the desired portion of the report.

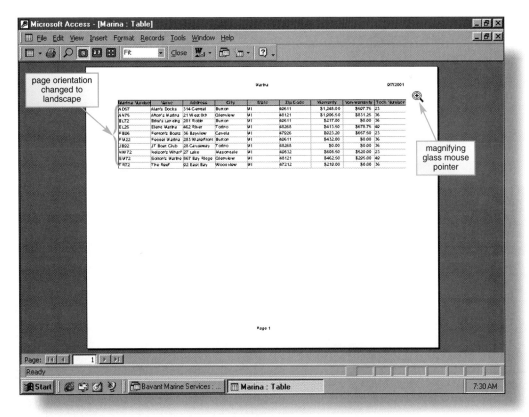

FIGURE 1-41

8 **Click the magnifying glass mouse pointer in the approximate position shown in Figure 1-41.**

The portion surrounding the mouse pointer is magnified (Figure 1-42). The last field that displays is the Tech Number field, so all fields currently display. If they did not, you could decrease the left and right margins; that is, the amount of space left by Access on the left and right edges of the report.

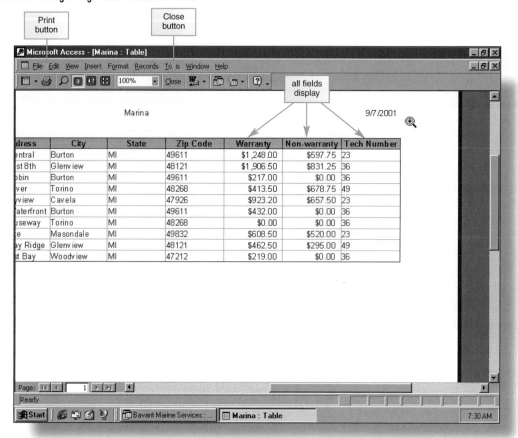

FIGURE 1-42

9 **Click the Print button to print the report. Click the Close button when the report has been printed to close the Print Preview window.**

The Print Preview window no longer displays.

Creating Additional Tables

A database typically consists of more than one table. The sample database contains two, the Marina table and the Technician table. You need to repeat the process of creating a table and adding records for each table in the database. In the sample database, you need to create and add records to the Technician table. The structure and data for the table are given in Figure 1-43. The steps to create the table follow.

Structure of Technician table

FIELD NAME	DATA TYPE	FIELD SIZE	PRIMARY KEY?	DESCRIPTION
Tech Number	Text	2	Yes	Technician Number (Primary Key)
Last Name	Text	10		Last Name of Technician
First Name	Text	8		First Name of Technician
Address	Text	15		Street Address
City	Text	15		City
State	Text	2		State (Two-Character Abbreviation)
Zip Code	Text	5		Zip Code (Five-Character Version)
Hourly Rate	Currency			Hourly Rate of Technician
YTD Earnings	Currency			YTD Earnings of Technician

FIGURE 1-43

Data for Technician table

TECH NUMBER	LAST NAME	FIRST NAME	ADDRESS	CITY	STATE	ZIP CODE	HOURLY RATE	YTD EARNINGS
23	Anderson	Trista	283 Belton	Port Anton	MI	47989	$24.00	$17,862.00
36	Nichols	Ashton	978 Richmond	Hewitt	MI	47618	$21.00	$19,560.00
49	Gomez	Teresa	2855 Parry	Ashley	MI	47711	$22.00	$21,211.50

FIGURE 1-43 (continued)

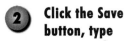 **To Create an Additional Table**

1. **Make sure the Bavant Marine Services database is open. Right-click Create table in Design view and then click Open on the shortcut menu. Enter the data for the fields for the Technician table from Figure 1-43. Be sure to click the Primary Key button when you enter the Tech Number field. Point to the Save button on the Database window toolbar after you have entered all the fields.**

The entries display (Figure 1-44).

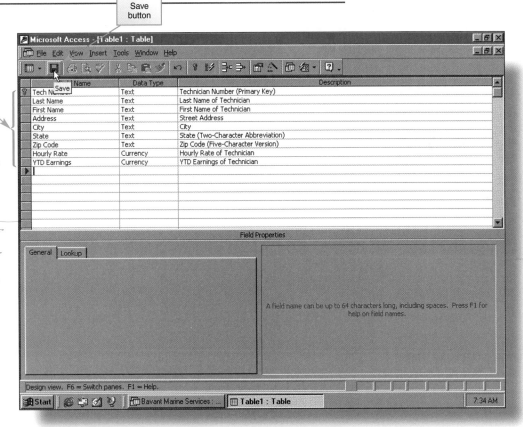

FIGURE 1-44

2. **Click the Save button, type** Technician **as the name of the table, and then click the OK button. Click the Close Window button.**

The table is saved in the Bavant Marine Services database. The Technician : Table window no longer displays.

Adding Records to the Additional Table

Now that you have created the Technician table, use the steps on the next page to add records to it.

Steps **To Add Records to an Additional Table**

1 **Right-click Technician and point to Open on the shortcut menu.**

The shortcut menu for the Technician table displays (Figure 1-45).

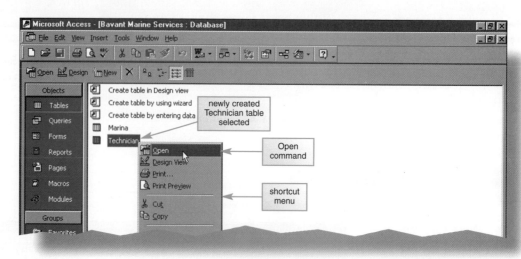

FIGURE 1-45

2 **Click Open on the shortcut menu and then enter the Technician data from Figure 1-43 on page A 1.34 into the Technician table.**

The datasheet displays with three records entered (Figure 1-46).

3 **Click the Close Window button for the Technician : Table window.**

Access closes the table and removes the datasheet from the screen.

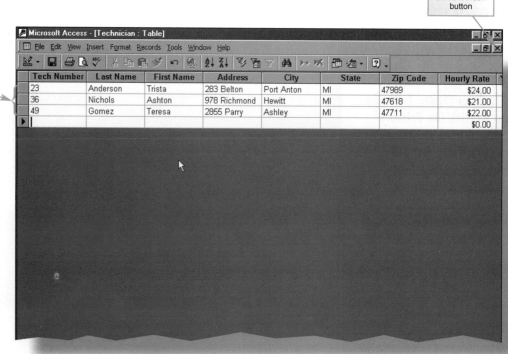

FIGURE 1-46

Using a Form to View Data

In creating tables, you have used Datasheet view; that is, the data on the screen displayed as a table. You also can use **Form view**, in which you see a single record at a time.

The advantage with Datasheet view is you can see multiple records at once. It has the disadvantage that, unless you have few fields in the table, you cannot see all the fields at the same time. With Form view, you see only a single record, but you can see all the fields in the record. The view you choose is a matter of personal preference.

Creating a Form

To use Form view, you first must create a form. The simplest way to create a form is to use the New Object: AutoForm button on the Database window toolbar. To do so, first select the table for which the form is to be created in the Database window and then click the New Object: AutoForm button. A list of available objects displays. Click AutoForm in the list to select it.

Perform the following steps using the New Object: AutoForm button to create a form for the Marina table.

More About

Forms

Attractive and functional forms can improve greatly the data entry process. Forms are not restricted to data from a single table, but can incorporate data from multiple tables as well as special types of data like pictures and sounds. A good DBMS like Access 2000 furnishes an easy way to create sophisticated forms.

 To Use the New Object: AutoForm Button to Create a Form

1 **Make sure the Bavant Marine Services database is open, the Database window displays, and the Marina table is selected. Point to the New Object: AutoForm button arrow on the Database window toolbar (Figure 1-47).**

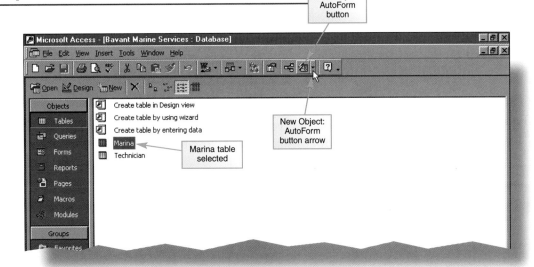

FIGURE 1-47

2 **Click the New Object: AutoForm button arrow and then point to AutoForm.**

A list of objects that can be created displays (Figure 1-48).

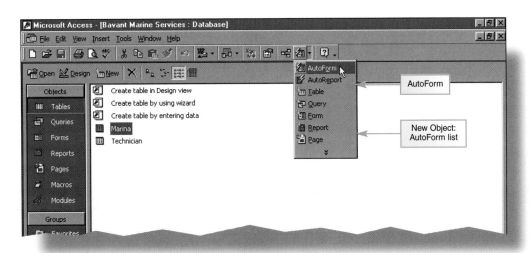

FIGURE 1-48

3 Click AutoForm in the New Object: AutoForm list.

The form displays (Figure 1-49). An additional toolbar, the Formatting toolbar, also displays. (When you close the form, this toolbar no longer displays.)

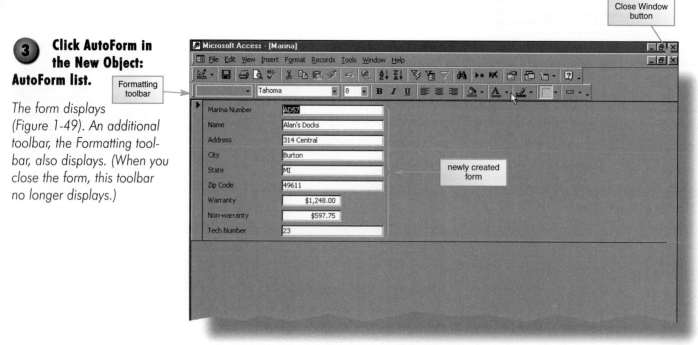

FIGURE 1-49

Closing and Saving the Form

Closing a form is similar to closing a table. The only difference is that you will be asked if you want to save the form unless you previously have saved it. Perform the following steps to close the form and save it as Marina.

 To Close and Save a Form

1 Click the Close Window button for the Marina window (see Figure 1-49). Point to the Yes button.

The Microsoft Access dialog box displays (Figure 1-50).

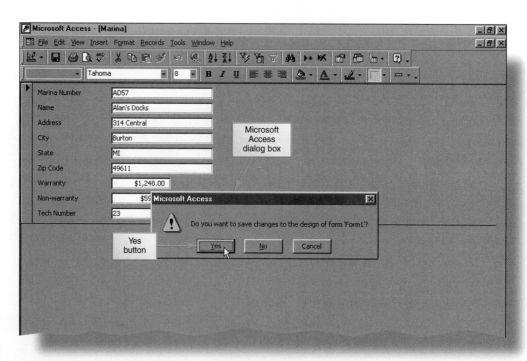

FIGURE 1-50

② Click the Yes button and then point to the OK button.

The Save As dialog box displays (Figure 1-51). The name of the table (Marina) becomes the name of the form automatically. This name can be replaced with any name.

③ Click the OK button in the Save As dialog box.

The form is saved as part of the database and is removed from the screen. The Bavant Marine Services : Database window again displays.

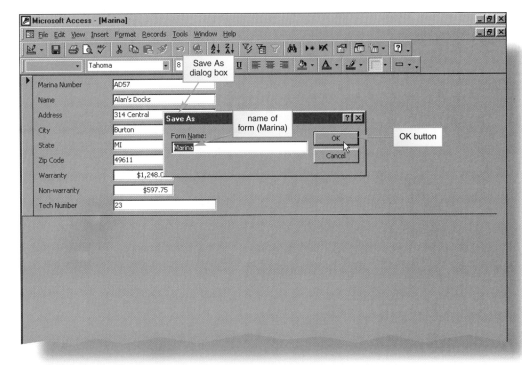

FIGURE 1-51

Other Ways

1. On File menu click Close

Opening the Saved Form

Once you have saved a form, you can use it at any time in the future by opening it. Opening a form is similar to opening a table; that is, make sure the form to be opened is selected, right-click, and then click Open on the shortcut menu. Before opening the form, however, the Forms object, rather than the Tables object, must be selected.

Perform the following steps to open the Marina form.

 To Open a Form

① With the Bavant Marine Services database open and the Database window on the screen, point to Forms on the Objects bar (Figure 1-52).

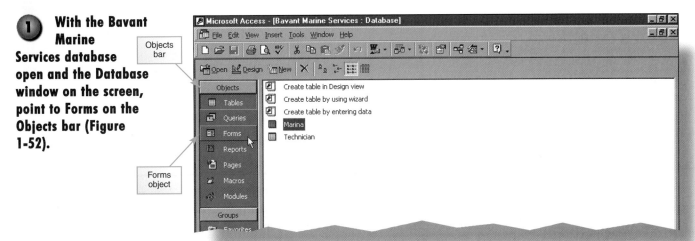

FIGURE 1-52

Click Forms, right-click Marina, and then point to Open on the shortcut menu.

The Forms object is selected and the list of available forms displays (Figure 1-53). Currently, the Marina form is the only form. The shortcut menu for the Marina form displays.

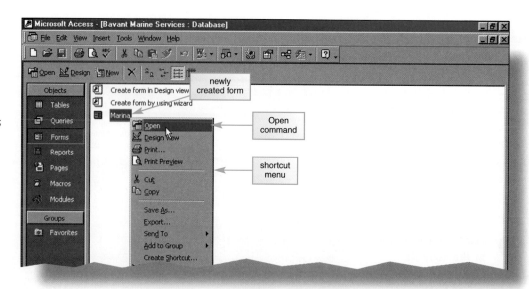

FIGURE 1-53

Click Open on the shortcut menu.

The Marina form displays (Figure 1-54).

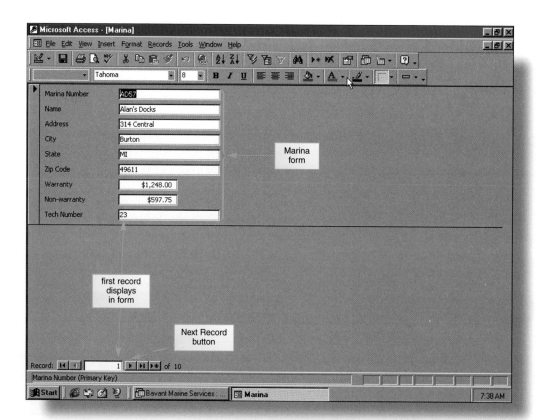

FIGURE 1-54

Other Ways

1. Click Forms object, double-click desired form
2. Click desired form, click Open button
3. Click desired from, press ALT+O

Using the Form

You can use the form just as you used Datasheet view. You use the Navigation buttons to move between records. You can add new records or change existing ones. To delete the record displayed on the screen, after selecting the record by clicking its record selector, press the DELETE key. Thus, you can perform database operations using either Form view or Datasheet view.

Because you can see only one record at a time in Form view, to see a different record, such as the fifth record, use the Navigation buttons to move to it. To move from record to record in Form view, perform the following step.

Steps **To Use a Form**

1 **Click the Next Record button four times.**

The fifth record displays on the form (Figure 1-55).

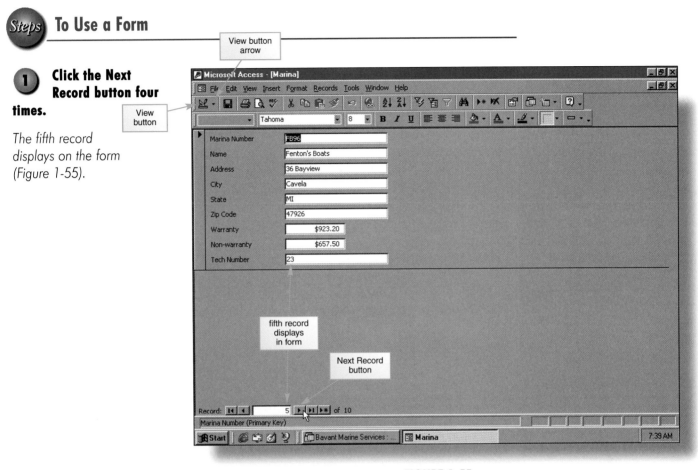

FIGURE 1-55

Switching Between Form View and Datasheet View

In some cases, once you have seen a record in Form view, you will want to move to Datasheet view to again see a collection of records. To do so, click the View button arrow on the Database window toolbar and then click Datasheet View in the list that displays.

Perform the steps on the next page to switch from Form view to Datasheet view.

To Switch from Form View to Datasheet View

 Click the View button arrow on the Database window toolbar (see Figure 1-55) and then point to Datasheet View.

The list of available views displays (Figure 1-56).

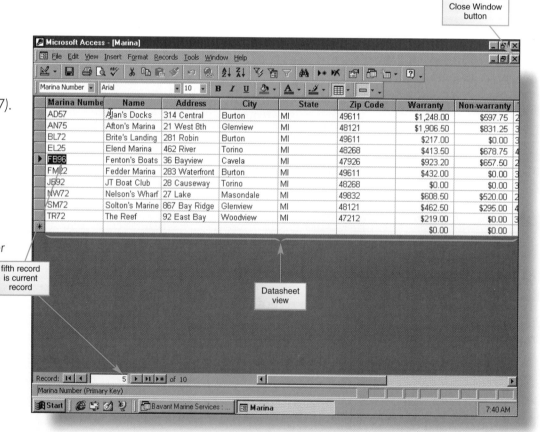

FIGURE 1-56

Close Window button

 Click Datasheet View.

The table displays in Datasheet view (Figure 1-57). The record selector is positioned on the fifth record.

 Click the Close Window button.

The Marina window closes and the datasheet no longer displays.

fifth record is current record

Datasheet view

FIGURE 1-57

 Other Ways

1. On View menu click Datasheet View

Creating a Report

Earlier in this project, you printed a table using the Print button. The report you produced was shown in Figure 1-34 on page A 1.30. While this type of report presented the data in an organized manner, it was not very flexible. It included all the fields, but in precisely the same order in which they occurred in the table. A way to change the title was not presented; it remained Marina.

In this section, you will create the report shown in Figure 1-58. This report features significant differences from the one in Figure 1-34 on page A 1.30. The portion at the top of the report in Figure 1-58, called a **page header**, contains a custom title. The contents of this page header display at the top of each page. The **detail lines**, which are the lines that are printed for each record, contain only those fields you specify and in the order you specify.

Perform the following steps to create the report in Figure 1-58.

More About

Reports

Custom reports represent one of the more important ways of presenting the data in a database. Reports can incorporate data from multiple tables and can be formatted in a wide variety of ways. The ability to create sophisticated custom reports is one of the major benefits of a DBMS like Access 2000.

Billing Summary Report

Marina Number	Name	Warranty	Non-warranty
AD57	Alan's Docks	$1,248.00	$597.75
AN75	Afton's Marina	$1,906.50	$831.25
BL72	Brite's Landing	$217.00	$0.00
EL25	Elend Marina	$413.50	$678.75
FB96	Fenton's Boats	$923.20	$657.50
FM22	Fedder Marina	$432.00	$0.00
JB92	JT Boat Club	$0.00	$0.00
NW72	Nelson's Wharf	$608.50	$520.00
SM72	Solton's Marina	$462.50	$295.00
TR72	The Reef	$219.00	$0.00

FIGURE 1-58

Steps To Create a Report

1 **Click Tables on the Objects bar. Make sure the Marina table is selected. Click the New Object: AutoForm button arrow on the Database window toolbar.**

The list of available objects displays (Figure 1-59).

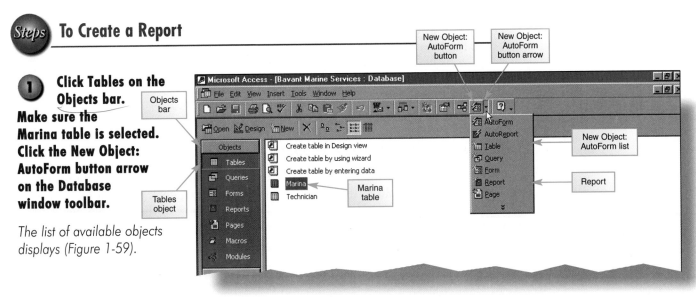

FIGURE 1-59

2 **Click Report and then point to Report Wizard.**

The New Report dialog box displays (Figure 1-60).

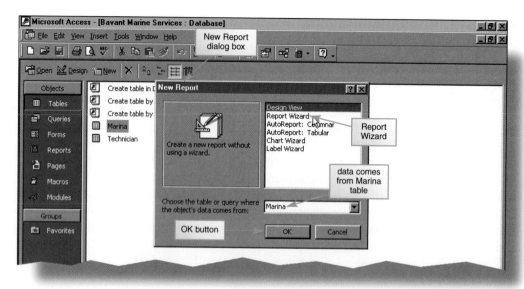

FIGURE 1-60

3 **Click Report Wizard and then click the OK button. Point to the Add Field button.**

The Report Wizard dialog box displays (Figure 1-61).

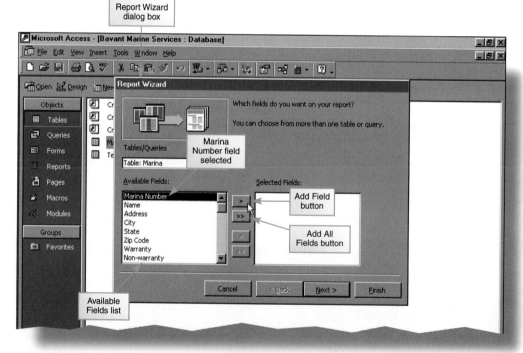

FIGURE 1-61

1. On Insert menu click Report
2. On Objects bar click Reports, click New

Selecting the Fields for the Report

To select a field for the report; that is, to indicate the field is to be included in the report, click the field in the Available Fields list. Next, click the Add Field button. This will move the field from the Available Fields box to the Selected Fields box, thus including the field in the report. If you wanted to select all fields, a shortcut is available simply by clicking the Add All Fields button.

To select the Marina Number, Name, Warranty, and Non-warranty fields for the report, perform the following steps.

 **To Select the Fields for a Report**

1 **Click the Add Field button to add the Marina Number field. Add the Name field by clicking it and then clicking the Add Field button. Add the Warranty and Non-warranty fields just as you added the Marina Number and Name fields.**

The fields for the report display in the Selected Fields box (Figure 1-62).

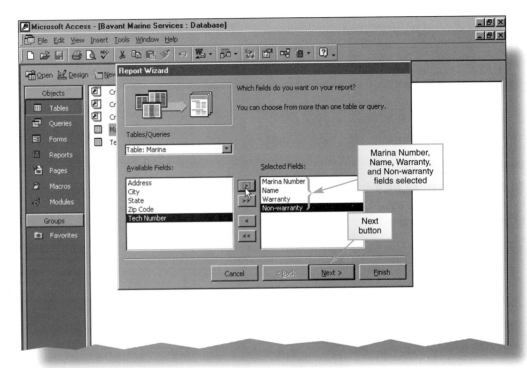

FIGURE 1-62

2 **Click the Next button.**

The Report Wizard dialog box displays (Figure 1-63).

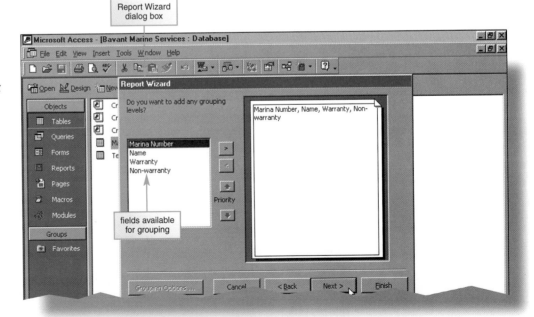

FIGURE 1-63

Other Ways

1. Double-click field

Completing the Report

Several additional steps are involved in completing the report. With the exception of changing the title, the Access selections are acceptable, so you simply will click the Next button.

Perform the following steps to complete the report.

 To Complete a Report

1 Because you will not specify any grouping, click the Next button in the Report Wizard dialog box (see Figure 1-63). Click the Next button a second time because you will not need to make changes on the screen that follows.

The Report Wizard dialog box displays (Figure 1-64). In this dialog box, you can change the layout or orientation of the report.

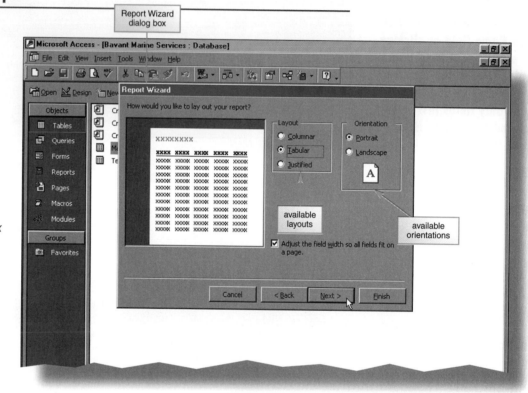

FIGURE 1-64

2 Make sure that Tabular is selected as the layout and Portrait is selected as the orientation and then click the Next button.

The Report Wizard dialog box displays (Figure 1-65). In this dialog box, you can select a style for the report.

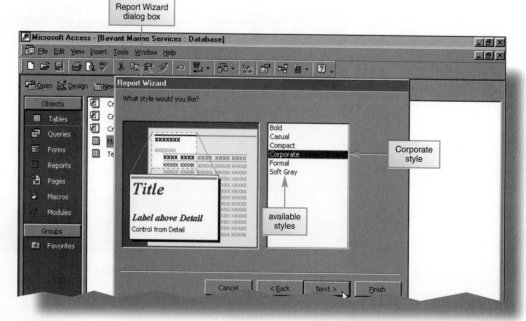

FIGURE 1-65

3 Be sure that the Corporate style is selected and then click the Next button.

The Report Wizard dialog box displays (Figure 1-66). In this dialog box, you can specify a title for the report.

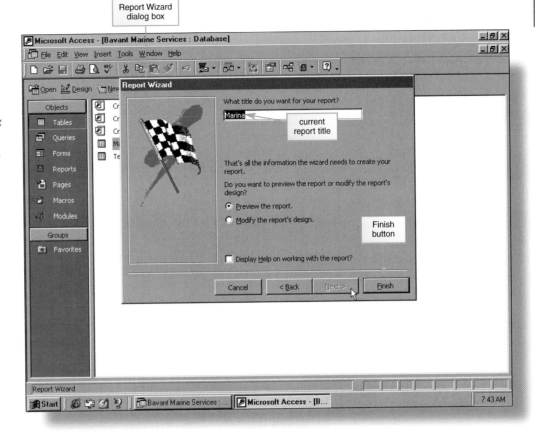

FIGURE 1-66

4 Type Billing Summary Report as the new title and then click the Finish button.

A preview of the report displays (Figure 1-67). Yours may look slightly different, depending on your printer.

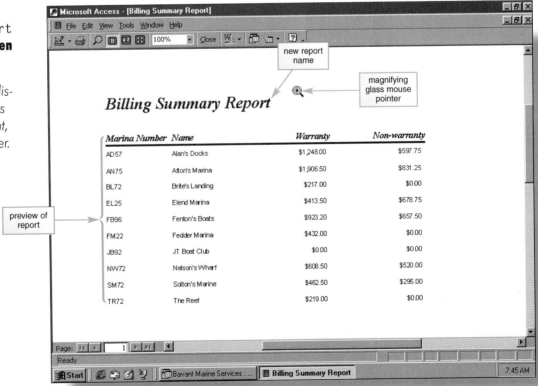

FIGURE 1-67

⑤ Click anywhere within the report to see the entire report.

The entire report displays (Figure 1-68).

⑥ Click the Close Window button in the Billing Summary Report window.

The report no longer displays. It has been saved automatically using the name Billing Summary Report.

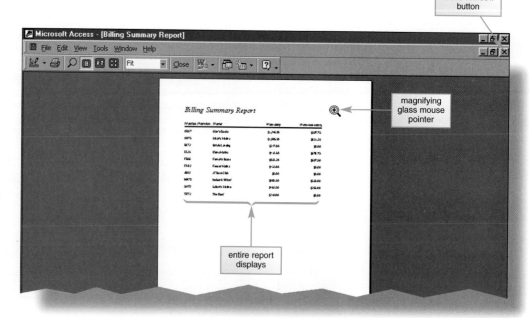

FIGURE 1-68

Printing the Report

To print a report from the Database window, first right-click the report. Then click Print on the shortcut menu to print the report or click Print Preview on the shortcut menu to see a preview of the report on the screen.

Perform the following steps to print the report.

To Print a Report

① If necessary, click Reports on the Objects bar in the Database window, right-click Billing Summary Report, and then point to Print on the shortcut menu.

The shortcut menu for the Billing Summary Report displays (Figure 1-69).

② Click Print on the shortcut menu.

The report prints. It should look similar to the one shown in Figure 1-58 on page A 1.43.

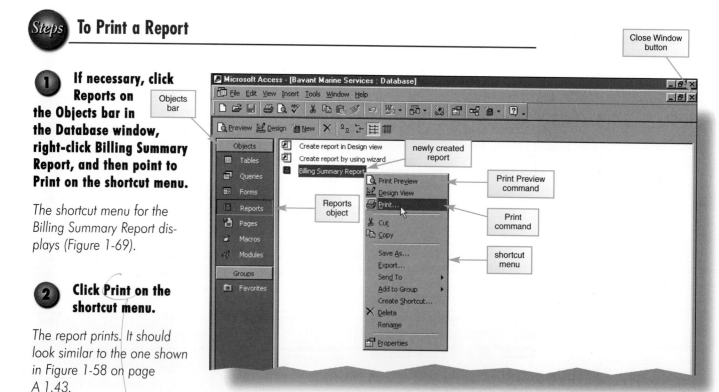

FIGURE 1-69

Closing the Database

Once you have finished working with a database, you should close it. The following step closes the database by closing its Database window.

TO CLOSE A DATABASE

 Click the Close Window button for the Bavant Marine Services : Database window.

Access Help System

At any time while you are using Access, you can get answers to questions by using the **Access Help system**. Used properly, this form of online assistance can increase your productivity and reduce your frustrations by minimizing the time you spend learning how to use Access. Table 1-2 on page A 1.51, summarizes the eight categories of help available to you. Because of the way the Access Help system works, please review the rightmost column of Table 1-2 if you have difficulties activating the desired category of help.

The following section shows how to get answers to your questions using the Office Assistant. For additional information on using the Access Help system, see Appendix A.

Using the Office Assistant

The **Office Assistant** answers your questions and suggests more efficient ways to complete a task. With the Office Assistant active, for example, you can type a question, word, or phrase in a text box and the Office Assistant provides immediate help on the subject. Also, as you create a database, the Office Assistant accumulates tips that suggest more efficient ways to do the tasks you completed while creating a database, such as printing and saving. This tip feature is part of the **IntelliSense™ technology** built into Access, which understands what you are trying to do and suggests better ways to do it. When the light bulb displays above the Office Assistant, click it to see a tip.

The steps on the next page show how to use the Office Assistant to obtain information on setting and changing the primary key.

More About 2000

Quick Reference

For a table that lists how to complete the tasks covered in this book using the mouse, menu, shortcut menu, and keyboard, visit the Shelly Cashman Series Office Web page (www.scsite.com/off2000/qr.htm), and then click Microsoft Access 2000.

Steps To Obtain Help Using the Office Assistant

1 **If the Office Assistant does not display, click Show the Office Assistant on the Help menu. With the Office Assistant on the screen, click it. Type** how do i set the primary key **in the What would you like to do? text box in the Office Assistant balloon. Point to the Search button (Figure 1-70).**

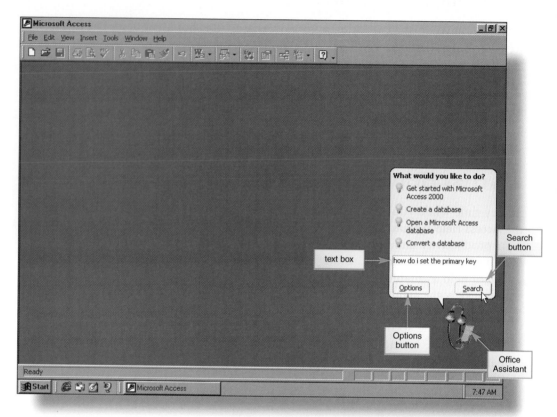

FIGURE 1-70

2 **Click the Search button. Point to the topic Set or change the primary key.**

The Office Assistant displays a list of topics relating to the question, "how do i set the primary key." (Your list may be different.) The mouse pointer changes to a hand (Figure 1-71).

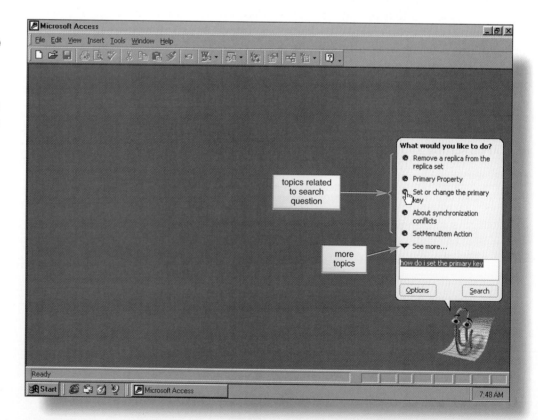

FIGURE 1-71

Click Set or change the primary key.

The Office Assistant displays a Microsoft Access Help window that provides Help information on setting or changing the primary key (Figure 1-72).

Click the Close Window button on the Microsoft Access Help window title bar.

The Microsoft Access Help window closes.

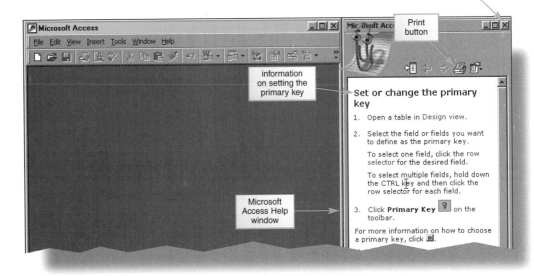

FIGURE 1-72

Table 1-2 summarizes the eight categories of Help available in Access 2000.

Table 1-2	Access Help System		
TYPE	**DESCRIPTION**	**HOW TO ACTIVATE**	**TURNING THE OFFICE ASSISTANT ON AND OFF**
Answer Wizard	Similar to the Office Assistant in that it answers questions that you type in your own words.	Click the Microsoft Access Help button on the Database window toolbar. If necessary, maximize the Help window by double-clicking its title bar. Click the Answer Wizard tab.	If the Office Assistant displays, right-click it, click Options, click the Use the Office Assistant check box, and click the OK button.
Contents sheet	Groups Help topics by general categories. Use when you know only the general category of the topic in question.	Click the Microsoft Access Help button on the Database window toolbar. If necessary, maximize the Help window by double-clicking its title bar. Click the Contents tab.	If the Office Assistant displays, right-click it, click Options, click the Use the Office Assistant check box, and then click the OK button.
Detect and Repair	Automatically finds and fixes errors in the application.	Click Detect and Repair on the Help menu.	
Hardware and Software Information	Shows Product ID and allows access to system information and technical support information.	Click About Microsoft Access on the Help menu and then click the appropriate button.	
Index sheet	Similar to an index in a book; use when you know exactly what you want.	Click the Microsoft Access Help button on the Database window toolbar. If necessary, maximize the window by double-clicking its title bar. Click the Index tab.	If the Office Assistant displays, right-click it, click Options, click the Use the Office Assistant check box, and then click the OK button.
Office Assistant	Answers questions that you type in your own words, offers tips, and provides Help for a variety of Access features.	Click the Microsoft Access Help button on the Database window toolbar.	If the Office Assistant does not display, close the Microsoft Access Help window and then click Show the Office Assistant on the Help menu.
Office on the Web	Used to access technical resources and download free product enhancements on the Web.	Click Office on the Web on the Help menu.	
Question Mark button and What's This? command	Used to identify unfamiliar items on the screen.	Click the Question Mark button and click an item in the dialog box. Click What's This? on the Help menu, and then click an item on the screen.	

Database Design (Normalization)

There is a special technique for identifying and eliminating redundancy, called **normalization**. For more information on normalization, visit the Access 2000 More About Web page (www.scsite.com/ac2000/more.htm) and then click Normalization.

Designing a Database

Database design refers to the arrangement of data into tables and fields. In the example in this project, the design is specified, but in many cases, you will have to determine the design based on what you want the system to accomplish.

With large, complex databases, the database design process can be extensive. Major sections of advanced database textbooks are devoted to this topic. Often, however, you should be able to design a database effectively by keeping one simple principle in mind: Design to remove redundancy. **Redundancy** means storing the same fact in more than one place.

To illustrate, you need to maintain the following information shown in Figure 1-73 on the next page. In the figure, all the data is contained in a single table. Notice that the data for a given technician (number, name, and so on) occurs on more than one record.

Marina table

MARINA NUMBER	NAME	ADDRESS	CITY	STATE	ZIP CODE	WARRANTY	NON WARRANTY	TECH NUMBER	LAST NAME	FIRST NAME
AD57	Alan's Docks	314 Central	Burton	MI	49611	$1,248.00	$597.75	23	Anderson	Trista
AN75	Afton's Marina	21 West 8th	Glenview	MI	48121	$1,906.50	$831.25	36	Nichols	Ashton
BL72	Brite's Landing	281 Robin	Burton	MI	49611	$217.00	$0.00	36	Nichols	Ashton
EL25	Elend Marina	462 River	Torino	MI	48268	$413.50	$678.75	49	Gomez	Teresa
FB96	Fenton's Boats	36 Bayview	Cavela	MI	47926	$923.20	$657.50	23	Anderson	Trista
FM22	Fedder Marina	283 Waterfront	Burton	MI	49611	$432.00	$0.00	36	Nichols	Ashton
JB92	JT Boat Club	28 Causeway	Torino	MI	48268	$0.00	$0.00	36	Nichols	Ashton
NW72	Nelson's Wharf	27 Lake	Masondale	MI	49832	$608.50	$520.00	23	Anderson	Trista
SM72	Solton's Marine	867 Bay Ridge	Glenview	MI	48121	$462.50	$295.00	49	Gomez	Teresa
TR72	The Reef	92 East Bay	Woodview	MI	47212	$219.00	$0.00	36	Nichols	Ashton

FIGURE 1-73

duplicate technician names

Database Design (Design Method)

There are a variety of methods that have been developed for designing complex databases given a set of input and output requirements. For more information on database design methods, visit the Access 2000 More About Web page (www.scsite.com/ac2000/more.htm) and then click Database Design.

Storing this data on multiple records is an example of redundancy, which causes several problems, including:

1. Redundancy wastes space on the disk. The address of technician 23 (Trista Anderson), for example, should be stored only once. Storing this fact several times is wasteful.

2. Redundancy makes updating the database more difficult. If, for example, Trista Anderson moves, her address would need to be changed in several different places.

3. A possibility of inconsistent data exists. Suppose, for example, that you change the address of Trista Anderson on marina FB96's record to 146 Valley, but do not change it on marina AD57's record. In both cases, the tech number is 23, but the addresses are different. In other words, the data is inconsistent.

The solution to the problem is to place the redundant data in a separate table, one in which the data will no longer be redundant. If, for example, you place the data for technicians in a separate table (Figure 1-74), the data for each technician will appear only once.

technician data
is in separate
table

Technician table

TECH NUMBER	LAST NAME	FIRST NAME	ADDRESS	CITY	STATE	ZIP CODE	HOURLY RATE	YTD EARNINGS
23	Anderson	Trista	283 Belton	Port Anton	MI	47989	$24.00	$17,862.00
36	Nichols	Ashton	978 Richmond	Hewitt	MI	47618	$21.00	$19,560.00
49	Gomez	Teresa	2855 Parry	Ashley	MI	47711	$22.00	$21,211.50

Marina table

MARINA NUMBER	NAME	ADDRESS	CITY	STATE	ZIP CODE	WARRANTY	NON-WARRANTY	TECH NUMBER
AD57	Alan's Docks	314 Central	Burton	MI	49611	$1,248.00	$597.75	23
AN75	Afton's Marina	21 West 8th	Glenview	MI	48121	$1,906.50	$831.25	36
BL72	Brite's Landing	281 Robin	Burton	MI	49611	$217.00	$0.00	36
EL25	Elend Marina	462 River	Torino	MI	48268	$413.50	$678.75	49
FB96	Fenton's Boats	36 Bayview	Cavela	MI	47926	$923.20	$657.50	23
FM22	Fedder Marina	283 Waterfront	Burton	MI	49611	$432.00	$0.00	36
JB92	JT Boat Club	28 Causeway	Torino	MI	48268	$0.00	$0.00	36
NW72	Nelson's Wharf	27 Lake	Masondale	MI	49832	$608.50	$520.00	23
SM72	Solton's Marine	867 Bay Ridge	Glenview	MI	48121	$462.50	$295.00	49
TR72	The Reef	92 East Bay	Woodview	MI	47212	$219.00	$0.00	36

FIGURE 1-74

Notice that you need to have the tech number in both tables. Without it, no way exists to tell which technician is associated with which marina. All the other technician data, however, was removed from the Marina table and placed in the Technician table. This new arrangement corrects the problems of redundancy in the following ways:

1. Because the data for each technician is stored only once, space is not wasted.
2. Changing the address of a technician is easy. You have only to change one row in the Technician table.
3. Because the data for a technician is stored only once, inconsistent data cannot occur.

Designing to omit redundancy will help you to produce good and valid database designs.

CASE PERSPECTIVE SUMMARY

In Project 1, you assisted Bavant Marine Service in their efforts to place their data in a database. You created the database that Bavant will use. Within this database, you created the Marina and Technician tables by defining the fields within them. You then added records to these tables. Once you created the tables, you printed the contents of the tables. You also used a form to view the data in the table. Finally, you used the Report Wizard to create a report containing the Marina Number, Name, Warranty, and Non-warranty fields for each marina served by Bavant Marine Services.

Project Summary

In Project 1, you learned about databases and database management systems. You learned how to create a database and how to create the tables within a database. You saw how to define the fields in a table by specifying the characteristics of the fields. You learned how to open a table, how to add records to it, and how to close it. You also printed the contents of a table. You created a form to view data on the screen and also created a custom report. You learned how to use Microsoft Access Help. Finally, you learned how to design a database to eliminate redundancy.

What You Should Know

Having completed this project, you now should be able to perform the following tasks:

▶ Add Additional Records to a Table *(A 1.27)*
▶ Add Records to a Table *(A 1.20)*
▶ Add Records to an Additional Table *(A 1.35)*
▶ Close a Database *(A 1.49)*
▶ Close a Table and Database and Quit Access *(A 1.24)*
▶ Close and Save a Form *(A 1.38)*
▶ Complete a Report *(A 1.46)*
▶ Create a Report *(A 1.43)*

▶ Create a Table *(A 1.13)*
▶ Create an Additional Table *(A 1.34)*
▶ Define the Fields in a Table *(A 1.15)*
▶ Obtain Help Using the Office Assistant *(A 1.50)*
▶ Open a Database *(A 1.25)*
▶ Open a Form *(A 1.39)*
▶ Preview and Print the Contents of a Table *(A 1.30)*
▶ Print a Report *(A 1.48)*
▶ Save a Table *(A 1.19)*
▶ Select the Fields for a Report *(A 1.45)*
▶ Start Access *(A 1.9)*
▶ Switch from Form View to Datasheet View *(A 1.41)*
▶ Use a Form *(A 1.36)*
▶ Use the New Object: AutoForm Button to Create a Form *(A 1.37)*

More About

Microsoft Certification

The Microsoft Office User Specialist (MOUS) Certification program provides an opportunity for you to obtain a valuable industry credential — proof that you have the Access 2000 skills required by employers. For more information, see Appendix D or visit the Shelly Cashman Series MOUS Web page at www.scsite.com/off2000/cert.htm.

Apply Your Knowledge

Project Reinforcement at www.scsite.com/off2000/reinforce.htm

1 Changing Data and Creating Reports

Instructions: Start Access. Open the Sidewalk Scrapers database from the Access Data Disk. See the inside back cover for instructions for downloading the Access Data Disk or see your instructor for information on accessing the files required for this book. Sidewalk Scrapers is a snow removal service that was started by two high school juniors looking for ways to earn money for college. Sidewalk Scrapers provides snow removal to residences and businesses in a city that receives lots of snow during the winter months. The business has expanded rapidly and now employs high school and college students to shovel sidewalks, steps, and driveways. Sidewalk Scrapers has a database that keeps track of its workers and customers. The database has two tables. The Customer table contains data on the customers who use the services of Sidewalk Scrapers. The Worker table contains data on the students employed by Sidewalk Scrapers. The structure and data are shown for the Customer table in Figure 1-75 and for the Worker table in Figure 1-76.

Structure of Customer table

FIELD NAME	DATA TYPE	FIELD SIZE	PRIMARY KEY?	DESCRIPTION
Customer Number	Text	4	Yes	Customer Number (Primary Key)
Name	Text	20		Customer Name
Address	Text	15		Street Address
Telephone	Text	8		Telephone Number (999-9999 Version)
Balance	Currency			Amount Owed by Customer
Worker Id	Text	2		Id of Customer's Worker

Data for Customer table

CUSTOMER NUMBER	NAME	ADDRESS	TELEPHONE	BALANCE	WORKER ID
AL25	Arders, Lars	205 Norton	555-2050	$45.00	03
AT43	Atari Cleaners	147 Main	555-7410	$80.00	10
BH81	Bond, Laura	407 Scott	555-0704	$0.00	10
CH65	Chan's Bootery	154 Main	555-0504	$70.00	14
CI05	Cinco Gallery	304 Secord	555-1304	$29.00	03
JB51	Jordach, Ben	203 Norton	555-0213	$60.00	10
LK44	Lee, Kim	605 Thurston	555-5061	$0.00	10
MD60	Martinez, Dan	410 Orange	555-4110	$95.00	03
ME02	Meat Shoppe	75 Edgewater	555-7557	$0.00	14
ST21	Styling Salon	406 Secord	555-6454	$40.00	10

FIGURE 1-75

(continued)

Apply Your Knowledge

Project Reinforcement at www.scsite.com/off2000/reinforce.htm

Changing Data and Creating Reports (continued)

Structure of Worker table

FIELD NAME	DATA TYPE	FIELD SIZE	PRIMARY KEY?	DESCRIPTION
Worker Id	Text	2	Yes	Worker Identification Number (Primary Key)
Last Name	Text	15		Last Name of Worker
First Name	Text	10		First Name of Worker
Address	Text	20		Street Address
Telephone	Text	8		Telephone Number (999-9999 Version)
Pay Rate	Currency			Hourly Pay Rate

Data for Worker table

WORKER ID	LAST NAME	FIRST NAME	ADDRESS	TELEPHONE NUMBER	PAY RATE
03	Carter	Chris	467 Norton	555-7641	$4.50
10	Lau	John	56 Parker	555-5656	$4.25
14	Sanchez	Elena	211 Thurston	555-1122	$4.75

FIGURE 1-76

Perform the following tasks.

1. Open the Worker table in Datasheet view and add the following record to the table:

07	Ferrens	Louis	24 Scott	555-2442	4.25

   Close the Worker table.

2. Open the Worker table again. Notice that the record you just added has been moved. It is no longer at the end of the table. The records are in order by the primary key, Worker Id.

3. Print the Worker table.

4. Open the Customer table.

5. Change the Worker Id for customer LK44 to 07.

6. Print the Customer table.

7. Create the report shown in Figure 1-77 for the Customer table.

8. Print the report.

Balance Due Report

Customer Number	Name	Balance
AL25	Arders, Lars	$45.00
AT43	Atari Cleaners	$80.00
BH81	Bond, Laura	$0.00
CH65	Chan's Bootery	$70.00
CI05	Cinco Gallery	$29.00
JB51	Jordach, Ben	$60.00
LK44	Lee, Kim	$0.00
MD60	Martinez, Dan	$95.00
ME02	Meat Shoppe	$0.00
ST21	Styling Salon	$40.00

FIGURE 1-77

In the Lab

1 Creating the School Connection Database

Problem: The Booster's Club at the local high school raises money by selling merchandise imprinted with the school logo to alumni. The Booster's Club purchases products from vendors that deal in school specialty items. The database consists of two tables. The Item table contains information on items available for sale. The Vendor table contains information on the vendors.

Instructions: Perform the following tasks.

1. Create a new database in which to store all the objects related to the merchandise data. Call the database School Connection.

2. Create the Item table using the structure shown in Figure 1-78. Use the name Item for the table.

3. Add the data shown in Figure 1-78 to the Item table.

4. Print the Item table.

5. Create the Vendor table using the structure shown in Figure 1-79. Use the name Vendor for the table.

6. Add the data shown in Figure 1-79 on the next page to the Vendor table.

7. Print the Vendor table.

8. Create a form for the Item table. Use the name Item for the form.

Structure of Item table

FIELD NAME	DATA TYPE	FIELD SIZE	PRIMARY KEY?	DESCRIPTION
Item Id	Text	4	Yes	Item Id Number (Primary Key)
Description	Text	25		Description of Item
On Hand	Number	Long Integer		Number of Units On Hand
Cost	Currency			Cost of Item
Selling Price	Currency			Selling Price of Item
Vendor Code	Text	2		Code of Item Vendor

Data for Item table

ITEM ID	DESCRIPTION	ON HAND	COST	SELLING PRICE	VENDOR CODE
BA02	Baseball Cap	15	$12.50	$15.00	AL
CM12	Coffee Mug	20	$3.75	$5.00	GG
DM05	Doormat	5	$14.25	$17.00	TM
OR01	Ornament	25	$2.75	$4.00	GG
PL05	Pillow	8	$13.50	$15.00	TM
PN21	Pennant	22	$5.65	$7.00	TM
PP20	Pen and Pencil Set	12	$16.00	$20.00	GG
SC11	Scarf	17	$8.40	$12.00	AL
TT12	Tie	10	$8.90	$12.00	AL
WA34	Wastebasket	3	$14.00	$15.00	GG

FIGURE 1-78

(continued)

In the Lab

Creating the School Connection Database *(continued)*

Structure of Vendor table

FIELD NAME	DATA TYPE	FIELD SIZE	PRIMARY KEY?	DESCRIPTION
Vendor Code	Text	2	Yes	Vendor Code (Primary Key)
Name	Text	30		Name of Vendor
Address	Text	20		Street Address
City	Text	20		City
State	Text	2		State (Two-Character Abbreviation)
Zip Code	Text	5		Zip Code (Five-Character Version)
Telephone Number	Text	12		Telephone Number (999-999-9999 Version)

Data for Vendor table

VENDOR CODE	NAME	ADDRESS	CITY	STATE	CODE	TELEPHONE NUMBER
AL	Alum Logo Inc.	1669 Queen	Aurora	WI	53595	608-555-9753
GG	GG Gifts	5261 Stream	Brisbane	NM	88061	505-555-8765
TM	Trinkets 'n More	541 Maple	Kentwood	VA	20147	804-555-1234

FIGURE 1-79

9. Create and print the report shown in Figure 1-80 for the Item table.

Inventory Report

Item Id	Description	On Hand	Cost
BA02	Baseball Cap	15	$12.50
CM12	Coffee Mug	20	$3.75
DM05	Doormat	5	$14.25
OR01	Ornament	25	$2.75
PP20	Pen and Pencil Set	12	$16.00
PN21	Pennant	22	$5.65
PL05	Pillow	8	$13.50
SC11	Scarf	17	$8.40
TT12	Tie	10	$8.90
WA34	Wastebasket	3	$14.00

FIGURE 1-80

In the Lab

2 Creating the City Area Bus Company Database

Problem: Like many urban transportation companies, the City Area Bus Company sells advertising. Local firms buy advertising from ad sales representatives who work for the bus company. Ad sales representatives receive a commission based on the advertising revenues they generate. The database consists of two tables. The Advertiser table contains information on the organizations that advertise on the buses. The Sales Rep table contains information on the representative assigned to the advertising account.

Instructions: Perform the following tasks.

1. Create a new database in which to store all the objects related to the advertising data. Call the database City Area Bus Company.
2. Create the Advertiser table using the structure shown in Figure 1-81. Use the name Advertiser for the table.
3. Add the data shown in Figure 1-81 to the Advertiser table.

Structure of Advertiser table

FIELD NAME	DATA TYPE	FIELD SIZE	PRIMARY KEY?	DESCRIPTION
Advertiser Id	Text	4	Yes	Advertiser Id (Primary Key)
Name	Text	20		Name of Advertiser
Address	Text	15		Street Address
City	Text	15		City
State	Text	2		State (Two-Character Abbreviation)
Zip Code	Text	5		Zip Code (Five-Character Version)
Balance	Currency			Amount Currently Owed
Amount Paid	Currency			Amount Paid Year-to-Date
Sales Rep Number	Text	2		Number of Advertising Sales Representative

Data for Advertiser table

ADVERTISER ID	NAME	ADDRESS	CITY	STATE	ZIP CODE	BALANCE	AMOUNT PAID	SALES REP NUMBER
AC25	Alia Cleaners	223 Michigan	Crescentville	MA	05431	$85.00	$585.00	24
BB99	Bob's Bakery	1939 Jackson	Richmond	MA	05433	$435.00	$1,150.00	29
CS46	Cara's Salon	787 Ottawa	Cheltenham	CT	06470	$35.00	$660.00	29
FS78	Franz and Sons	3294 Campeau	Richmond	MA	05434	$185.00	$975.00	31
GR75	G's Restaurant	1632 Shue	Manyunk	CT	06471	$0.00	$1,500.00	24
HC11	Hilde's Cards	3140 Main	Crescentville	MA	05431	$250.00	$500.00	29
MC34	Mom's Cookies	1805 Broadway	Crescentville	MA	05431	$95.00	$1,050.00	29
NO10	New Orient	2200 Lawrence	Manyunk	CT	06471	$150.00	$350.00	24
PJ24	Pajama Store	13 Monroe	Cheltenham	CT	06470	$0.00	$775.00	31
TM89	Tom's Market	39 Albert	Richmond	MA	05433	$50.00	$500.00	24

FIGURE 1-81

(continued)

In the Lab

Creating the City Area Bus Company Database (continued)

4. Print the Advertiser table.
5. Create the Sales Rep table using the structure shown in Figure 1-82. Use the name Sales Rep for the table. Be sure that the field size for the Comm Rate field is Double.
6. Add the data shown in Figure 1-82 to the Sales Rep table.
7. Print the Sales Rep table.
8. Create a form for the Advertiser table. Use the name Advertiser for the form.

Structure of Sales Rep table

FIELD NAME	DATA TYPE	FIELD SIZE	PRIMARY KEY?	DESCRIPTION
Sales Rep Number	Text	2	Yes	Advertising Sales Rep Number (Primary Key)
Last Name	Text	15		Last Name of Advertising Sales Rep
First Name	Text	10		First Name of Advertising Sales Rep
Address	Text	15		Street Address
City	Text	15		City
State	Text	2		State (Two-Character Abbreviation)
Zip Code	Text	5		Zip Code (Five-Character Version)
Comm Rate	Number	Double		Commission Rate
Commission	Currency			Year-to-Date Total Commissions

Data for Sales Rep table

SALES REP NUMBER	LAST NAME	FIRST NAME	ADDRESS	CITY	STATE	ZIP CODE	COMM RATE	COMMISSION
24	Chou	Peter	34 Second	Crescentville	MA	05431	0.09	$7,500.00
29	Ortiz	Elvia	45 Belmont	Cheltenham	CT	06470	0.09	$8,450.00
31	Reed	Pat	78 Farmwood	Richmond	MA	05433	0.08	$7,225.00

FIGURE 1-82

9. Open the form you created and change the address for Advertiser Number HC11 to 340 Mainline.
10. Change to Datasheet view and delete the record for Advertiser Number GR75.
11. Print the Advertiser table.
12. Create and print the report shown in Figure 1-83 for the Advertiser table.

Advertiser Status Report

Advertiser Id	Name	Balance	Amount Paid
AC25	Alia Cleaners	$85.00	$585.00
BB99	Bob's Bakery	$435.00	$1,150.00
CS46	Cara's Salon	$35.00	$660.00
FS78	Franz and Sons	$185.00	$975.00
HC11	Hilde's Cards	$250.00	$500.00
MC34	Mom's Cookies	$95.00	$1,050.00
NO10	New Orient	$150.00	$350.00
PJ24	Pajama Store	$0.00	$775.00
TM89	Tom's Market	$50.00	$500.00

FIGURE 1-83

In the Lab

3 Creating the Resort Rental Database

Problem: A real estate company located in an ocean resort community provides a rental service for apartment/condo owners. The company rents units by the week to interested tourists and "snowbirds" (people who spend their winters in warmer climates). The database consists of two tables. The Rental Unit table contains information on the units available for rent. The Owner table contains information on the owners of the rental units.

Instructions: Perform the following tasks.

1. Create a new database in which to store all the objects related to the rental data. Call the database Resort Rentals.

2. Create the Rental Unit table using the structure shown in Figure 1-84. Use the name Rental Unit for the table. Note that the table uses a new data type, Yes/No for the Pool and Ocean View fields.

3. Add the data shown in Figure 1-84 to the Rental Unit table.

Structure of Rental Unit table

FIELD NAME	DATA TYPE	FIELD SIZE	PRIMARY KEY?	DESCRIPTION
Rental Id	Text	3	Yes	Rental Id (Primary Key)
Address	Text	20		Street Address of Rental Unit
City	Text	20		City
Bedrooms	Number			Number of Bedrooms
Bathrooms	Number			Number of Bathrooms
Sleeps	Number			Maximum Number that can sleep in rental unit
Pool	Yes/No			Does the rental unit have a pool?
Ocean View	Yes/No			Does the rental unit have an ocean view?
Weekly Rate	Currency			Weekly Rental Rate
Owner Id	Text	4		Id of Rental Unit's Owner

Data for Rental Unit table

RENTAL ID	ADDRESS	CITY	BED-ROOMS	BATH-ROOMS	SLEEPS	POOL	OCEAN VIEW	WEEKLY RATE	OWNER ID
101	521 Ocean	Hutchins	2	1	4	Y	Y	$750.00	ML10
103	783 First	Gulf Breeze	3	3	8	Y		$1,000.00	FH15
105	684 Beach	San Toma	1	1	3		Y	$700.00	PR23
108	96 Breeze	Gulf Breeze	1	1	2		Y	$650.00	PR23
110	523 Ocean	Hutchins	2	2	6	Y		$900.00	LD45
112	345 Coastal	Shady Beach	2	2	5		Y	$900.00	LD45
116	956 First	Gulf Breeze	2	2	6	Y	Y	$1,100.00	ML10
121	123 Gulf	San Toma	3	2	8	Y	Y	$1,300.00	FH15
134	278 Second	Shady Beach	2	1	4		Y	$1,000.00	FH15
144	24 Plantation	Hutchins	1	1	2	Y		$650.00	PR23

FIGURE 1-84

(continued)

In the Lab

Creating the Resort Rental Database *(continued)*

4. Use Microsoft Access Help to learn how to resize column widths in Datasheet view and then reduce the size of the Rental Id, Bedrooms, Bathrooms, Sleeps, Pool, Ocean View, Weekly Rate, and Owner Id columns.

5. Print the Rental Unit table.

6. Create the Owner table using the structure shown in Figure 1-85. Use the name Owner for the table.

7. Add the data shown in Figure 1-85 to the Owner table.

8. Print the Owner table.

Structure of Owner table

FIELD NAME	DATA TYPE	FIELD SIZE	PRIMARY KEY?	DESCRIPTION
Owner Id	Text	4	Yes	Owner Id (Primary Key)
Last Name	Text	15		Last Name of Owner
First Name	Text	10		First Name of Owner
Address	Text	15		Street Address
City	Text	15		City
State	Text	2		State (Two-Character Abbreviation)
Zip Code	Text	5		Zip Code (Five-Character Version)
Telephone	Text	12		Telephone Number (999-999-9999 Version)

Data for Owner table

OWNER ID	LAST NAME	FIRST NAME	ADDRESS	CITY	STATE	ZIP CODE	TELEPHONE NO
FH15	Franco	Hilda	1234 Oakley	Middleville	PA	19063	610-555-7658
LD45	Lakos	Daniel	45 Fanshawe	Grenard	MI	49441	616-555-9080
ML10	Manuel	Larry	78 Unruh	Dalute	CA	95518	916-555-8787
PR23	Peoples	Rita	5489 South	Johnson	LA	58345	504-555-9845

FIGURE 1-85

9. Create a form for the Rental Unit table. Use the name Rental Unit for the form.

10. Open the form you created and change the weekly rate for Rental Id 144 to $675.00.

11. Print the Rental Unit table.

12. Create and print the report shown in Figure 1-86 for the Rental Unit table.

Available Rental Units Report

Rental Id	Address	City	Weekly Rate
101	521 Ocean	Hutchins	$750.00
103	783 First	Gulf Breeze	$1,000.00
105	684 Beach	San Toma	$700.00
108	96 Breeze	Gulf Breeze	$650.00
110	523 Ocean	Hutchins	$900.00
112	345 Coastal	Shady Beach	$900.00
116	956 First	Gulf Breeze	$1,100.00
121	123 Gulf	San Toma	$1,300.00
134	278 Second	Shady Beach	$1,000.00
144	24 Plantation	Hutchins	$675.00

FIGURE 1-86

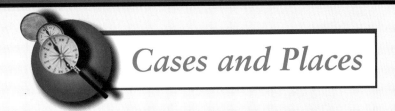

Cases and Places

The difficulty of these case studies varies:
▶ are the least difficult; ▶▶ are more difficult; and ▶▶▶ are the most difficult.

1 ▶ As a fund-raising project, the local college's Computer Science Club sells small computer accessories to students. Disks, disk cases, and mouse pads are some of the items that the club sells from a small kiosk in the student computer lab. The club has asked you to create a database that keeps track of their inventory and suppliers. The current inventory is shown in Figure 1-87.

Design and create a database to store the club's inventory. Then create the necessary tables, enter the data from Figure 1-87, and print the tables.

ITEM ID	DESCRIPTION	UNITS ON HAND	COST	SELLING PRICE	SUPPLIER CODE	SUPPLIER NAME	SUPPLIER TELEPHONE
1663	Antistatic Wipes	30	$0.15	$0.25	ER	Ergonomics Ltd.	517-555-3853
1683	CD Wallet	12	$3.45	$4.00	HI	Human Interface	317-555-4747
2563	Desktop Holder	4	$3.85	$4.75	ER	Ergonomics Ltd.	517-555-3853
2593	Disks	175	$0.20	$.75	HI	Human Interface	317-555-4747
3923	Disk Cases	12	$2.20	$2.75	HI	Human Interface	317-555-4747
3953	Mouse Holder	10	$0.80	$1.00	MT	Mouse Tracks	616-555-9228
4343	Mouse Pad	25	$2.25	$3.00	MT	Mouse Tracks	616-555-9228
5810	PC Tool Kit	9	$7.80	$9.00	ER	Ergonomics Ltd.	517-555-3853
5930	Wrist Rest	3	$2.90	$3.25	ER	Ergonomics Ltd.	517-555-3853

FIGURE 1-87

2 ▶ Sci-Fi Scene is a local bookstore that specializes in Science Fiction. The owner has asked you to create and update a database that she can use to keep track of the books she has in stock. You gather the information shown in Figure 1-88.

Design and create a database to store the book data. Then create the necessary tables, enter the data from Figure 1-88, and print the tables.

Cases and Places

BOOK CODE	TITLE	AUTHOR	UNITS ON HAND	PRICE	YEAR PUBLISHED	PUBLISHER CODE	PUBLISHER NAME
0488	Robot Wars	H Brawley	1	$5.95	1997	SI	Simpson-Ivan
0533	Albert's Way	H Brawley	2	$4.75	1999	SI	Simpson-Ivan
1019	Stargaze	G Chou	3	$5.50	1996	BB	Bertrand Books
128X	Comet Dust	R Eaton	2	$5.95	2000	PB	Peabody Books
1668	Android	E Dearling	3	$6.95	1999	VN	VanNester
3495	Dark Wind	G Chou	4	$4.95	1998	BB	Bertrand Books
3859	Infinity	R Torres	1	$4.75	1997	VN	VanNester
4889	The Galaxy	E Dearling	2	$6.75	2000	VN	VanNester
6517	Strange Alien	R Eaton	2	$9.95	1998	PB	Peabody Books
7104	Secret City	R Torres	1	$5.75	1997	VN	VanNester

FIGURE 1-88

3 ▶▶ The marching band director of your school has asked you to create a database of band members. He wants to keep track of the following data on each band member: name, address, telephone number, age, sex, emergency contact name, emergency telephone number, type of band instrument, band instrument number, whether the student owns or leases the instrument, and number of years in the band.

Design and create a database to meet the band director's needs. Create the necessary tables, enter some sample data, and print the tables to show the director.

4 ▶▶ You have been hired as an intern by the local humane society. The humane society would like you to computerize their adoption files. Currently, they keep all the information about animals that are placed for adoption on index cards. The cards include information on the family, for example, name, address, telephone number, number of children, any previous animal adoptions, and other family pets. Information on the animal also is kept, for example, type of animal, sex, age, name, and any medical problems.

Design and create a database to meet the humane society's needs. Create the necessary tables, enter some sample data, and print the tables to show the director of the humane society.

5 ▶▶▶ The Intramural Sports Club has decided that a good way to make money and help students would be to set up a used sports equipment co-operative similar to the secondhand sporting goods stores. As a member of the club, you are asked to create a database that can store data related to the sports equipment and the students who wish to sell their items.

Determine the type of data you will need, then design and create a database to meet the club's needs. Create the necessary tables, enter some sample data, and print the tables.

Microsoft **Access 2000**

PROJECT

2

Microsoft Access 2000

Querying a Database Using the Select Query Window

You will have mastered the material in this project when you can:

OBJECTIVES

- State the purpose of queries
- Create a new query
- Use a query to display all records and all fields
- Run a query
- Print the answer to a query
- Close a query
- Clear a query
- Use a query to display selected fields
- Use text data in criteria in a query
- Use wildcards in criteria
- Use numeric data in criteria
- Use comparison operators
- Use compound criteria involving AND
- Use compound criteria involving OR
- Sort the answer to a query
- Join tables in a query
- Restrict the records in a join
- Use calculated fields in a query
- Calculate statistics in a query
- Use grouping with statistics
- Save a query
- Use a saved query

Where Have All the Children Gone?

National Database Helps Search for Missing Youngsters

All parents fear this situation: One minute their children are within eyesight; the next minute they have vanished, never to be seen again.

Nearly 4,600 children are abducted by non-family members each year, according to the U.S. Justice Department. Another 438,200 children are lost, injured, or otherwise missing. Yet, thousands of these children's records appear in a database maintained by the National Center for Missing and Exploited Children (NCMEC). Through this organization, the children, while they may be missing physically, appear in photo images.

NCMEC was created in 1984 as a public and private partnership to help the public search for missing children. Since the nonprofit Center opened, more than 1.3 million calls have been channeled through its national hotline (1-800-THE-LOST). In addition, NCMEC has partnered with the U.S. Department of

Justice's Office of Juvenile Justice and Delinquency Prevention (www.ncjrs.org) to promote and raise public awareness of this crime.

Since its inception, NCMEC has evolved into a high-tech resource for family, friends, and loved ones of missing and abused children. With nearly 114,600 attempted abductions reported each year, such a resource desperately is needed. Because of these alarming rates, NCMEC has established sophisticated databases that contribute to recovery rates, which are termed child case completions. Currently, the completion rate is 90 percent, dramatically up from 66 percent, which was the norm in 1989. Through partnerships with Intel, IBM, and Tektronix, to name a few, NCMEC has grown into a solid force for solving child cases.

One example of the advanced technology utilized by NCMEC is a database that contains photographs of missing children. Investigators and Web users are able to open the database and create a precise query based on such fields as the child's name, age, eye color, and weight. Then they run the query, and within a matter of seconds they have answers to the requested information. You can create queries and view some of

these images at the NCMEC Web site (www.ncmec.org). Similarly, you will query the Bavant Marine Services Database in this project to obtain answers to questions regarding warranty amounts and marina names and locations.

Moreover, NCMEC's imaging specialists can alter a child's photograph to show how he might appear many years after he has disappeared. Subsequently, these images are stored in corresponding fields in the computerized imaging database. Many children who may not have been located otherwise have been found using this enhancement technology.

A recent technological development is the Multimedia Kiosk Program, which IBM donated to NCMEC. In this program, 50 kiosks have been placed in high pedestrian traffic areas such as LaGuardia Airport in New York and in large shopping malls throughout the country. They provide a functional database for the general public to learn about missing children and a means to transfer information quickly to affected friends and family.

Through the efforts of NCMEC, the nation now has a solid weapon and resource for the fight against child endangerment.

Querying a Database Using the Select Query Window

2

C A S E   P E R S P E C T I V E

Now that Bavant Marine Services has created a database with marina and technician data, the management and staff of the organization hope to gain the benefits they expected when they set up the database. One of the more important benefits is the capability of easily asking questions concerning the data in the database and rapidly obtaining the answers. Among the questions they want answered are the following:

1. What are the warranty and non-warranty amounts for marina EL25?

2. Which marinas' names begin with Fe?

3. Which marinas are located in Burton?

4. What is the total amount (warranty amount plus non-warranty amount) for each marina?

5. Which marinas of technician 36 have warranty amounts of more than $1,000?

Your task is to assist Bavant Marine Services in obtaining answers to these questions as well as any other questions they deem important.

Introduction

A database management system such as Access offers many useful features, among them the capability of answering questions such as those posed by the management of Bavant Marine Services (Figure 2-1). The answers to these questions, and many more, are found in the database, and Access can find the answers quickly. When you pose a question to Access, or any other database management system, the question is called a query. A **query** is simply a question represented in a way that Access can understand.

Thus, to find the answer to a question, you first create a corresponding query using the techniques illustrated in this project. Once you have created the query, you instruct Access to run the query; that is, to perform the steps necessary to obtain the answer. When finished, Access will display the answer to your question in the format shown at the bottom of Figure 2-1.

Project Two — Querying the Bavant Marine Services Database

You must obtain answers to the questions posed by the management of Bavant Marine Services. These include the questions shown in Figure 2-1, as well as any other questions that the management deems important.

What are the warranty and non-warranty amounts of marina EL25?

Which marina s names begin with Fe?

Which marinas are located in Burton?

What is the total amount (warranty + non-warranty) of each marina?

Which marinas of technician 36 have a warranty amount of more than 1,000.00?

Marina table

MARINA NUMBER	NAME	ADDRESS	CITY	STATE	ZIP CODE	WARRANTY	NON-WARRANTY	TECH NUMBER
AD57	Alan's Docks	314 Central	Burton	MI	49611	$1,248.00	$597.75	23
AN75	Afton's Marina	21 West 8th	Glenview	MI	48121	$1,906.50	$831.25	36
BL72	Brite's Landing	281 Robin	Burton	MI	49611	$217.00	$0.00	36
EL25	Elend Marina	462 River	Torino	MI	48268	$413.50	$678.75	49
FB96	Fenton's Boats	36 Bayview	Cavela	MI	47926	$923.20	$657.50	23
FM22	Fedder Marina	283 Waterfront	Burton	MI	49611	$432.00	$0.00	36
JB92	JT Boat Club	28 Causeway	Torino	MI	48268	$0.00	$0.00	36
NW72	Nelson's Wharf	27 Lake	Masondale	MI	49832	$608.50	$520.00	23
SM72	Solton's Marine	867 Bay Ridge	Glenview	MI	48121	$462.50	$295.00	49
TR72	The Reef	92 East Bay	Woodview	MI	47212	$219.00	$0.00	36

MARINA NUMBER	NAME
FB96	Fenton's Boats
FM22	Fedder Marina

MARINA NUMBER	NAME
AN75	Afton's Marina

MARINA NUMBER	NAME	ADDRESS
AD57	Alan's Docks	314 Central
BL72	Brite's Landing	281 Robin
FM22	Fedder Marina	283 Waterfront

MARINA NUMBER	NAME	TOTAL AMOUNT
AD57	Alan's Docks	$1,845.75
AN75	Afton's Marina	$2,737.75
BL72	Brite's Landing	$217.00
EL25	Elend Marina	$1,092.25
FB96	Fenton's Boats	$1,580.70
FM22	Fedder Marina	$432.00
JB92	JT Boat Club	$0.00
NW72	Nelson's Wharf	$1,128.50
SM72	Solton's Marine	$757.50
TR72	The Reef	$219.00

MARINA NUMBER	NAME	WARRANTY	NON-WARRANTY
EL25	Elend Marina	$413.50	$678.75

FIGURE 2-1

Opening the Database

Before creating queries, first you must open the database. The following steps summarize the procedure to complete this task.

TO OPEN A DATABASE

1 Click the Start button on the taskbar.

2 Click Open Office Document and then click 3½ Floppy (A:) in the Look in box. Make sure the database called Bavant Marine Services is selected.

3 Click the Open button in the Open dialog box. If the Tables object is not already selected, click Tables on the Objects bar.

The database is open and the Bavant Marine Services : Database window displays.

Creating a New Query

You create a query by making entries in a special window called a **Select Query window**. Once the database is open, the first step in creating a query is to select the table for which you are creating a query in the Database window. Next, using the New Object: AutoForm button on the Database window toolbar, you will design the new query. The Select Query window will display. It typically is easier to work with the Select Query window if it is maximized. Thus, as a standard practice, maximize the Select Query window as soon as you have created it.

Perform the following steps to begin creating a query.

Steps To Create a Query

1 Be sure the Bavant Marine Services database is open, the Tables object is selected, and the Marina table is selected. Click the New Object: AutoForm button arrow on the Database window toolbar. Point to Query on the New Object: AutoForm menu.

The list of available objects displays (Figure 2-2).

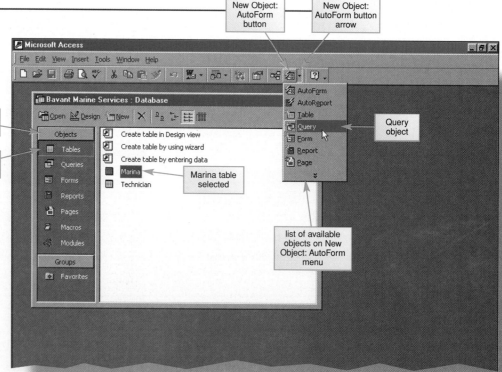

FIGURE 2-2

2 **Click Query. Be sure Design View is selected and point to the OK button.**

The New Query dialog box displays (Figure 2-3).

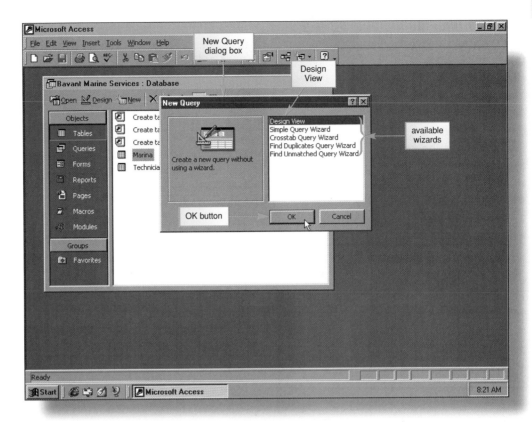

FIGURE 2-3

3 **Click the OK button.**

The Query1 : Select Query window displays (Figure 2-4). The Query Design toolbar has replaced the Database window toolbar.

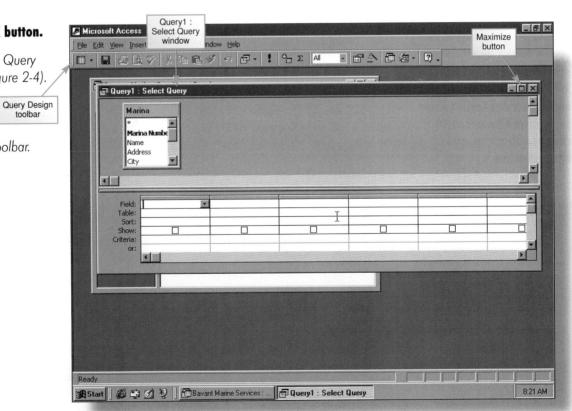

FIGURE 2-4

4 **Maximize the Query1 : Select Query window by clicking its Maximize button, and then point to the dividing line that separates the upper and lower panes of the window. The mouse pointer will change shape to a two-headed arrow with a horizontal bar.**

The Query1 : Select Query window is maximized (Figure 2-5). The upper pane contains a field list for the Marina table. The lower pane contains the **design grid**, which is the area where you specify fields to be included, sort order, and the criteria the records you are looking for must satisfy.

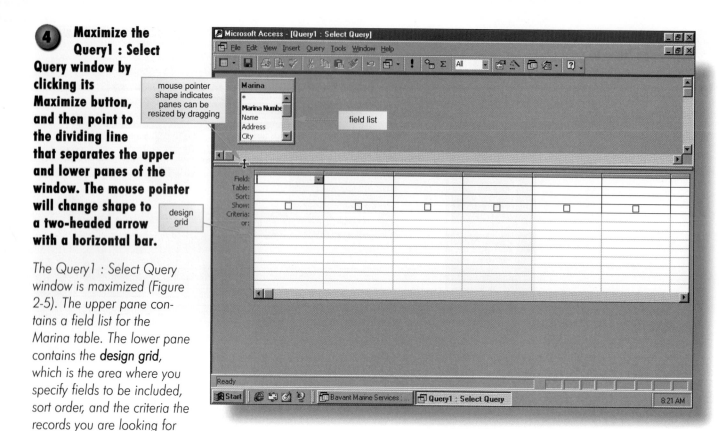

FIGURE 2-5

5 **Drag the line down to the approximate position shown in Figure 2-6 and then move the mouse pointer to the lower edge of the field box so it changes shape to a two-headed arrow.**

The two panes have been resized.

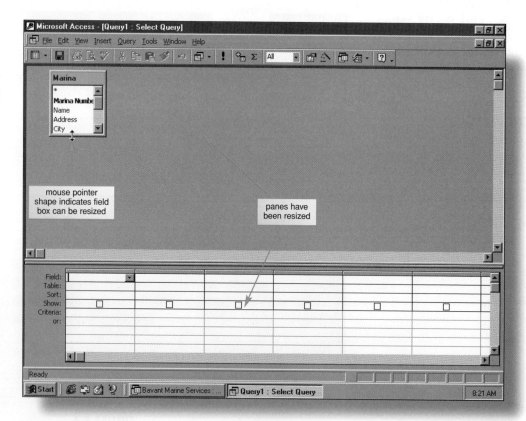

FIGURE 2-6

6 Drag the lower edge of the field box down far enough so all fields in the Marina table are visible.

All fields in the Marina table display (Figure 2-7).

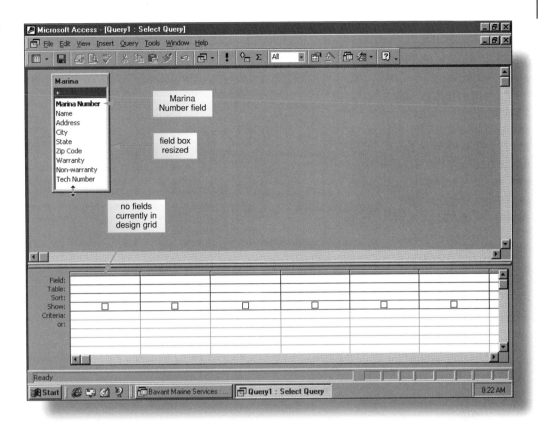

FIGURE 2-7

Using the Select Query Window

Once you have created a new Select Query window, you are ready to create the actual query by making entries in the design grid in the lower pane of the window. You enter the names of the fields you want included in the Field row in the grid. You also can enter criteria, such as the fact that the marina number must be EL25, in the Criteria row of the grid. When you do so, only the record or records that match the criterion will be included in the answer.

Displaying Selected Fields in a Query

Only the fields that appear in the design grid will be included in the results of the query. Thus, to display only certain fields, place only these fields in the grid, and no others. If you place the wrong field in the grid inadvertently, click Edit on the menu bar and then click Delete to remove it. Alternatively, you could click Clear Grid to clear the entire design grid and then start over.

The steps on the next page create a query to show the marina number, name, and technician number for all marinas by including only those fields in the design grid.

To Include Fields in the Design Grid

1 Make sure you have a maximized Query1 : Select Query window containing a field list for the Marina table in the upper pane of the window and an empty design grid in the lower pane (see Figure 2-7 on page A 2.9).

2 Double-click the Marina Number field to include the Marina Number field in the query.

The Marina Number field is included as the first field in the design grid (Figure 2-8).

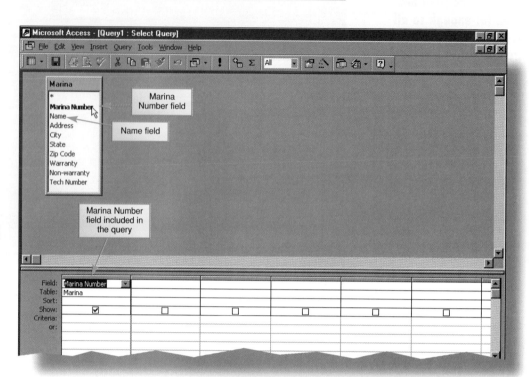

why call exclamation mark "run" button

FIGURE 2-8

3 Double-click the Name field to include it in the query. Include the Tech Number field using the same technique. Point to the Run button on the Query Design toolbar.

The Marina Number, Name, and Tech Number fields are included in the query (Figure 2-9).

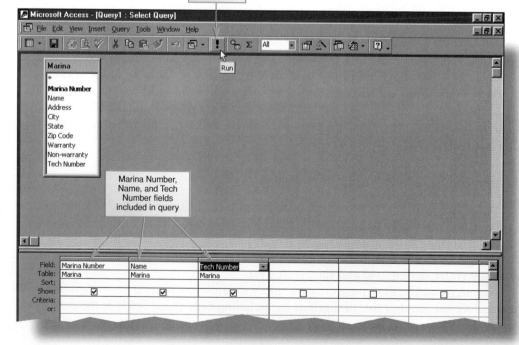

FIGURE 2-9

Other Ways

1. Drag field from field list to design grid
2. Click column in grid, click arrow, click field

Running a Query

Once you have created the query, you need to run the query to produce the results. To do so, click the Run button. Access then will perform the steps necessary to obtain and display the answer. The set of records that makes up the answer will be displayed in Datasheet view. Although it looks like a table that is stored on your disk, it really is not. The records are constructed from data in the existing Marina table. If you were to change the data in the Marina table and then rerun this same query, the results would reflect the changes.

  To Run the Query

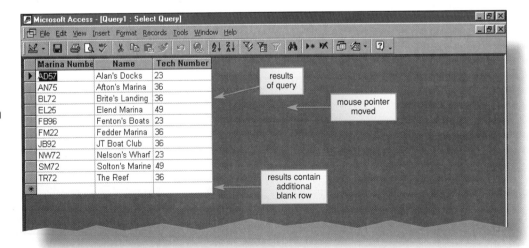 **Queries: SQL**

The most widespread of all the query languages is a language called SQL. Many database management systems, including Access, offer SQL as one option for querying databases. For more information, visit the Access 2000 More About Web page (www.scsite.com/ ac2000/more.htm) and click SQL.

1 **Click the Run button.**

The query is executed and the results display (Figure 2-10). The Query Datasheet toolbar replaces the Query Design toolbar. The Sort Ascending button on the Query Datasheet toolbar now occupies the position of the Run button. If you do not move the mouse pointer after clicking a button, the Screen-Tip for the button may obscure a portion of the first record, such as the ScreenTip for the Sort Ascending button. Moving the mouse pointer away from the toolbar after running the Query eliminates this problem.

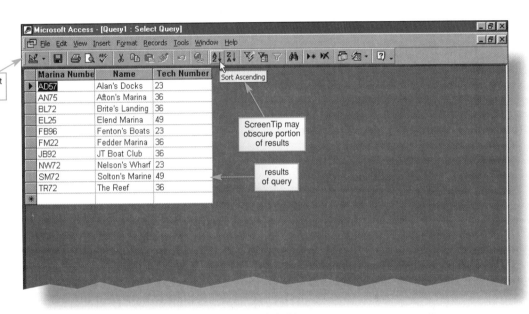

FIGURE 2-10

2 **Move the mouse pointer to a position that is outside of the data and is not on the Query Datasheet toolbar.**

The data displays without obstruction (Figure 2-11). Notice that an extra blank row, marking the end of the table, displays at the end of the results.

FIGURE 2-11

 Other Ways

1. On Query menu click Run
2. On View menu click Datasheet View

In all future examples, after running a query, move the mouse pointer so the table displays without obstruction.

Printing the Results of a Query

To print the results of a query, click the Print button on the toolbar. Complete the following steps to print the query results that currently display on the screen.

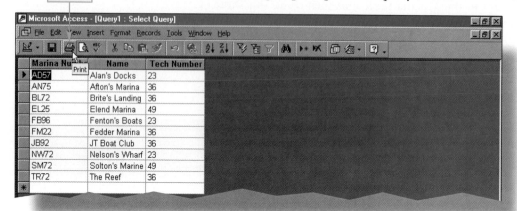

FIGURE 2-12

TO PRINT THE RESULTS OF A QUERY

1 Ready the printer and then point to the Print button on the Query Datasheet toolbar (Figure 2-12).

2 Click the Print button.

The results print.

If the results of a query require landscape orientation, switch to landscape orientation before you click the Print button as indicated in Project 1 on page A 1.30.

Returning to Design View

You can examine the results of a query on your screen to see the answer to your question. You can scroll through the records, if necessary, just as you scroll through the records of any other table. You also can print a copy of the table. In any case, once you are finished working with the results, you can return to Design view to ask another question. To do so, use the View button arrow on the Query Datasheet toolbar as shown in the following steps.

 To Return to Design View

1 **Point to the View button arrow on the Query Datasheet toolbar (Figure 2-13).**

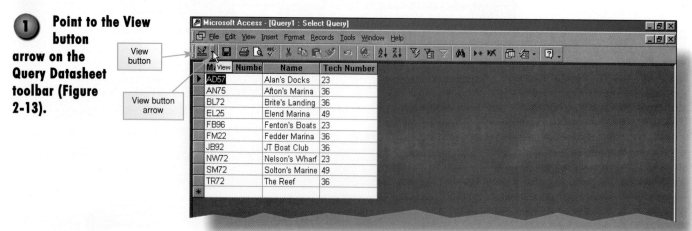

FIGURE 2-13

2 Click the View button arrow and then point to Design View.

The View button menu displays (Figure 2-14).

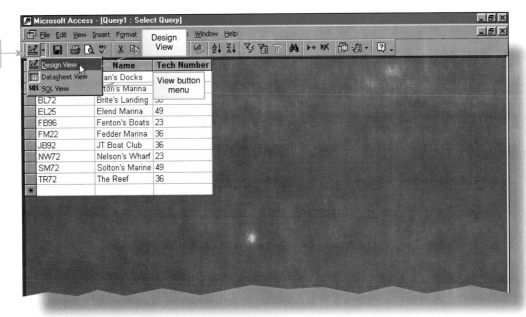

FIGURE 2-14

3 Click Design View.

The Query1 : Select Query window displays (Figure 2-15).

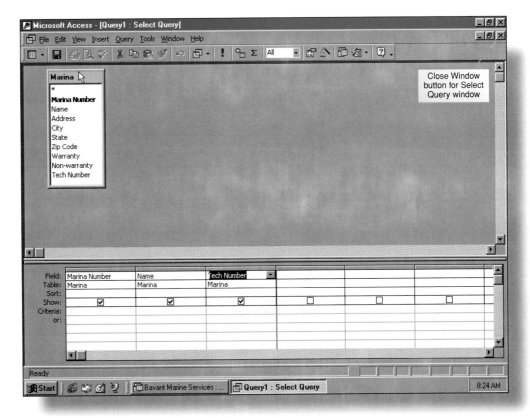

FIGURE 2-15

Other Ways

1. On View menu click Design View

Because Design View is the first command on the View button menu, you do not have to click the View button arrow and then click Design View. You simply can click the View button itself.

Closing a Query

To close a query, close the Select Query window. When you do so, Access displays the Microsoft dialog box asking if you want to save your query for future use. If you think you will need to create the same exact query often, you should save the query. For now, you will not save any queries. You will see how to save them later in the project. The following steps close a query without saving it.

 To Close the Query

1 **Click the Close Window button for the Query1 : Select Query window. (See Figure 2-15 on page A 2.13.)**

The Microsoft Access dialog box displays (Figure 2-16). Clicking the Yes button saves the query and clicking the No button closes the query without saving.

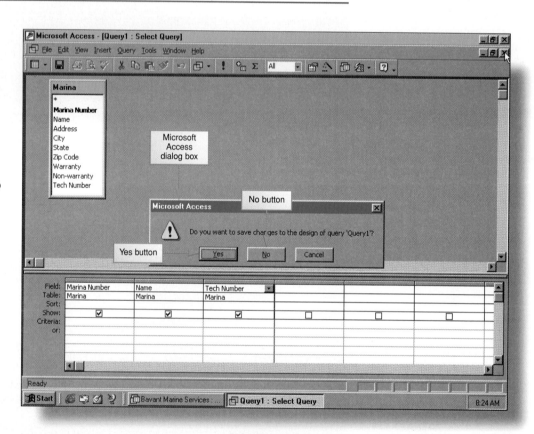

FIGURE 2-16

2 **Click the No button in the Microsoft Access dialog box.**

The Query1 : Select Query window closes and is removed from the desktop.

 Ways

1. On File menu click Close

Including All Fields in a Query

If you want to include all fields in a query, you could select each field individually. A more simplified way exists to include all fields, however. By selecting the **asterisk (*)** in the field list, you are indicating that all fields are to be included. Complete the following steps to use the asterisk to include all fields.

Steps | **To Include All Fields in a Query**

1 Be sure you have a maximized Query1 : Select Query window containing a field list for the Marina table in the upper pane and an empty design grid in the lower pane. (See Steps 1 through 6 on pages A 2.6 through A 2.9 to create the query and resize the window.) Point to the asterisk at the top of the field list.

A maximized Query1 : Select Query window displays (Figure 2-17). The two panes have been resized.

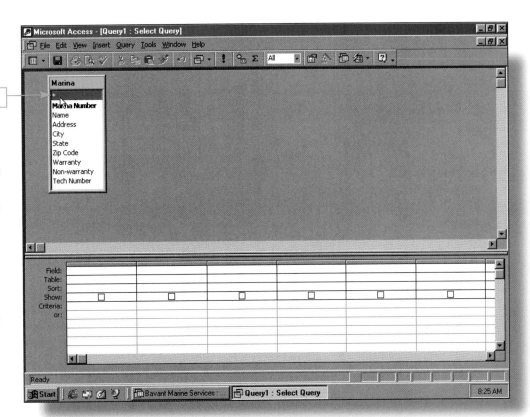

FIGURE 2-17

2 Double-click the asterisk in the field list and then point to the Run button on the Query Design toolbar.

The table name, Marina, followed by a period and an asterisk is added to the design grid (Figure 2-18), indicating all fields are included.

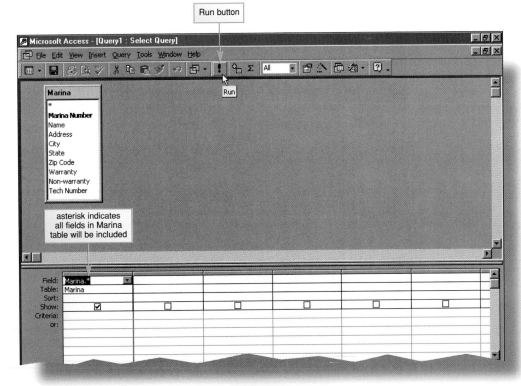

FIGURE 2-18

3 Click the Run button.

The results display and all fields in the Marina table are included (Figure 2-19). The Tech Number field does not display, because it does not fit on the screen.

4 Click the View button on the Query Datasheet toolbar to return to Design view.

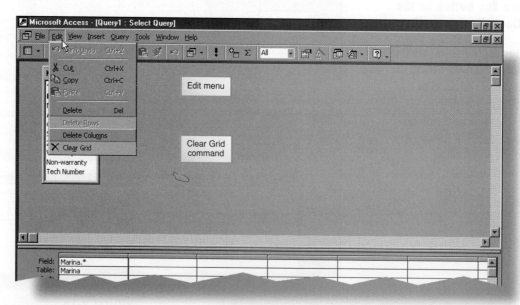

Marina Number	Name	Address	City	State	Zip Code	Warranty	Non-warranty
AD57	Alan's Docks	314 Central	Burton	MI	49611	$1,248.00	$597.75
AN75	Afton's Marina	21 West 8th	Glenview	MI	48121	$1,906.50	$831.25
BL72	Brite's Landing	281 Robin	Burton	MI	49611	$217.00	$0.00
EL25	Elend Marina	462 River	Torino	MI	48268	$413.50	$678.75
FB96	Fenton's Boats	36 Bayview	Cavela	MI	47926	$923.20	$657.50
FM22	Fedder Marina	283 Waterfront	Burton	MI	49611	$432.00	$0.00
JB92	JT Boat Club	28 Causeway	Torino	MI	48268	$0.00	$0.00
NW72	Nelson's Wharf	27 Lake	Masondale	MI	49832	$608.50	$520.00
SM72	Solton's Marine	867 Bay Ridge	Glenview	MI	48121	$462.50	$295.00
TR72	The Reef	92 East Bay	Woodview	MI	47212	$219.00	$0.00
*						$0.00	$0.00

View button

all fields included

FIGURE 2-19

Other Ways

1. Drag asterisk from field list to design grid
2. Click column in grid, click arrow, click Marina.

Clearing the Design Grid

If you make mistakes as you are creating a query, you can fix each one individually. Alternatively, you simply may want to **clear the query**; that is, clear out the entries in the design grid and start over. One way to clear out the entries is to close the Select Query window and then start a new query just as you did earlier. A simpler approach, however, is to click Clear Grid on the Edit menu.

 To Clear a Query

1 Click Edit on the menu bar.

The Edit menu displays (Figure 2-20).

2 Click Clear Grid.

Access clears the design grid so you can enter your next query.

Microsoft Access - [Query1 : Select Query]

File   Edit   View   Insert   Query   Tools   Window   Help

Can't Undo	Ctrl+Z
Cut	Ctrl+X
Copy	Ctrl+C
Paste	Ctrl+V
Delete	Del
Delete Rows	
Delete Columns	
Clear Grid	

Edit menu

Clear Grid command

Non-warranty
Tech Number

Field: Marina.*
Table: Marina

FIGURE 2-20

Entering Criteria

When you use queries, usually you are looking for those records that satisfy some criterion. You might want the name, warranty, and non-warranty amounts of the marina whose number is EL25, for example, or of those marinas whose names start with the letters, Fe. To enter criteria, enter them on the Criteria row in the design grid below the field name to which the criterion applies. For example, to indicate that the marina number must be EL25, you would type EL25 in the Criteria row below the Marina Number field. You first must add the Marina Number field to the design grid before you can enter the criterion.

The next examples illustrate the types of criteria that are available.

Using Text Data in Criteria

Some database systems require that text data must be enclosed in quotation marks. For example, to find customers in Michigan, "MI" would be entered as the criterion for the State field. In Access this is not necessary, because Access will insert the quotation marks automatically.

Using Text Data in Criteria

To use **text data** (data in a field whose type is text) in criteria, simply type the text in the Criteria row below the corresponding field name. The following steps query the Marina table and display the marina number, name, warranty amount, and non-warranty amount of marina EL25.

Steps To Use Text Data in a Criterion

1 One by one, double-click the Marina Number, Name, Warranty, and Non-warranty fields to add them to the query. Point to the Criteria row for the first field in the design grid.

The Marina Number, Name, Warranty, and Non-warranty fields are added to the design grid (Figure 2-21). The mouse pointer on the Criteria entry for the first field (Marina Number) has changed shape to an I-beam.

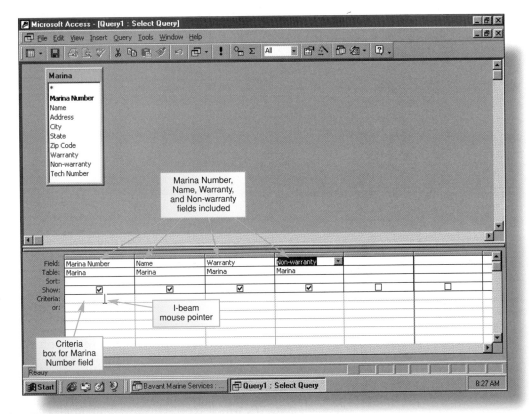

FIGURE 2-21

Click the Criteria row, type EL25 **as the criterion for the Marina Number field.**

The criterion is entered (Figure 2-22).

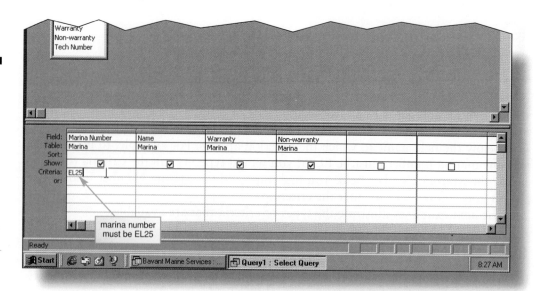

FIGURE 2-22

 Click the Run button to run the query.

The results display (Figure 2-23). Only marina EL25 is included. (The extra blank row contains $0.00 in the Warranty and Non-warranty fields. Unlike text fields, which are left blank, number and currency fields in the extra row contain 0. Because the Warranty and Non-warranty fields are currency fields, the values display as $0.00.)

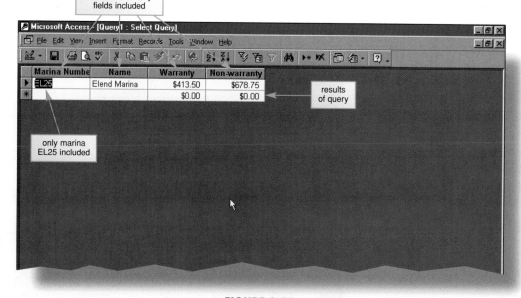

FIGURE 2-23

Using Wildcards

Two special wildcards are available in Microsoft Access. **Wildcards** are symbols that represent any character or combination of characters. The first of the two wild-cards, the **asterisk (*)**, represents any collection of characters. Thus Gr* represents the letters, Gr, followed by any collection of characters. The other wildcard symbol is the **question mark (?)**, which represents any individual character. Thus t?m represents the letter, T, followed by any single character followed by the letter, m, such as Tim or Tom. To use a wildcard, begin the criterion with the special word LIKE.

The following steps use a wildcard to find the number, name, and address of those marinas whose names begin with Fe. Because you do not know how many characters will follow the Fe, the asterisk is appropriate.

Steps To Use a Wildcard

1 Click the View button to return to Design view. Click the Criteria row under the Marina Number field and then use the DELETE or BACKSPACE key to delete the current entry (EL25). Click the Criteria row under the Name field. Type LIKE Fe* as the entry.

The criterion is entered (Figure 2-24).

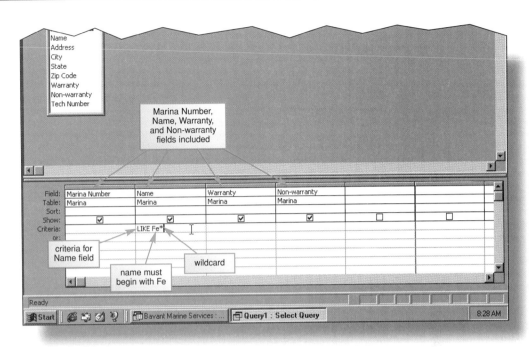

Marina Number, Name, Warranty, and Non-warranty fields included

criteria for Name field

name must begin with Fe

wildcard

FIGURE 2-24

2 Click the Run button.

The results display (Figure 2-25). Only the marinas whose names start with Fe are included.

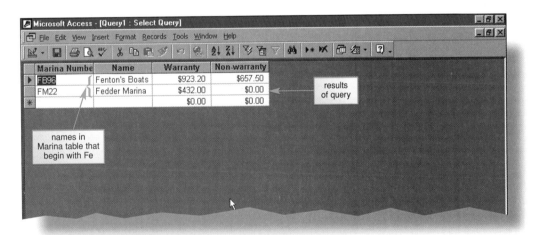

names in Marina table that begin with Fe

results of query

FIGURE 2-25

Criteria for a Field Not in the Result

In some cases, you may have criteria for a particular field that should not appear in the results of the query. For example, you may wish to see the marina number, name, address, and warranty amounts for all marinas located in Burton. The criteria involve the City field, which is not one of the fields to be included in the results.

To enter a criterion for the City field, it must be included in the design grid. Normally, this also would mean it would appear in the results. To prevent this from happening, remove the check mark from its Show check box in the Show row of the grid. The following steps illustrate the process by displaying the marina number, name, and warranty amounts for marinas located in Burton.

To Use Criteria for a Field Not Included in the Results

1 **Click the View button to return to Design view. On the Edit menu, click Clear Grid.**

Access clears the design grid so you can enter the next query.

2 **Include the Marina Number, Name, Address, Warranty, and City fields in the query. Type** Burton **as the criterion for the City field and then point to the City field's Show check box.**

The fields are included in the grid, and the criterion for the City field is entered (Figure 2-26).

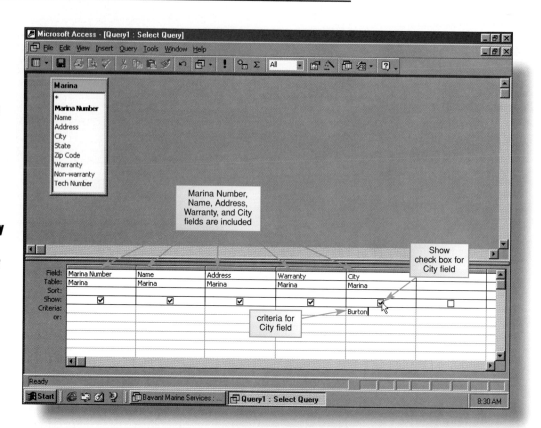

FIGURE 2-26

3 **Click the Show check box to remove the check mark.**

The check mark is removed from the Show check box for the City field (Figure 2-27), indicating it will not show in the result. Access has added quotation marks before and after Burton automatically.

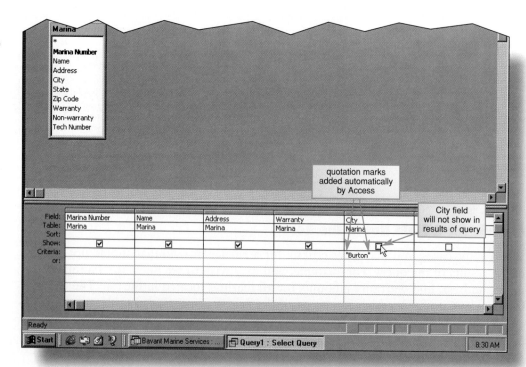

FIGURE 2-27

Run the query by clicking the Run button.

The results display (Figure 2-28). The City field does not display. The only marinas included are those located in Burton.

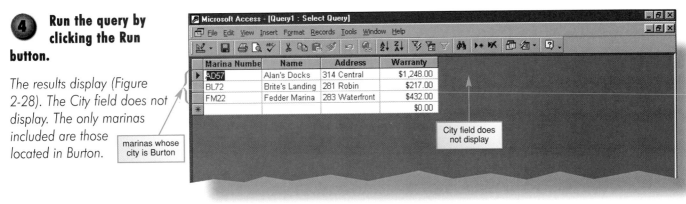

FIGURE 2-28

Using Numeric Data in Criteria

To enter a number in a criterion, type the number without any dollar signs or commas. Complete the following steps to display all marinas whose non-warranty amount is $0.00. To do so, you will need to type a 0 (zero) as the criterion for the Non-warranty field.

Steps **To Use a Number in a Criterion**

1 **Click the View button to return to Design view. On the Edit menu, click Clear Grid.**

Access clears the design grid so you can enter the next query.

2 **Include the Marina Number, Name, Warranty, and Non-warranty fields in the query. Type 0 as the criterion for the Non-warranty field. You need not enter a dollar sign or decimal point in the criterion.**

The fields are selected and the criterion is entered (Figure 2-29).

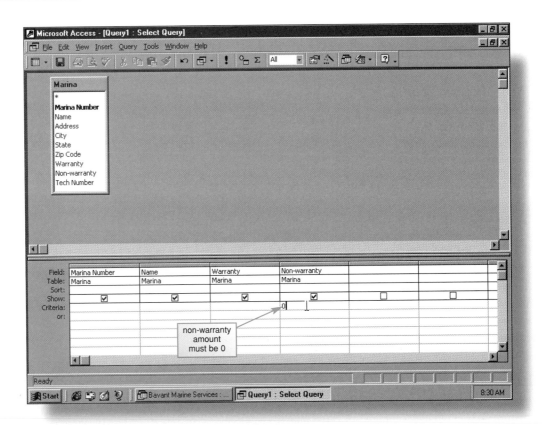

FIGURE 2-29

3 **Run the query by clicking the Run button.**

The results display (Figure 2-30). Only those marinas that have a non-warranty amount of $0.00 are included.

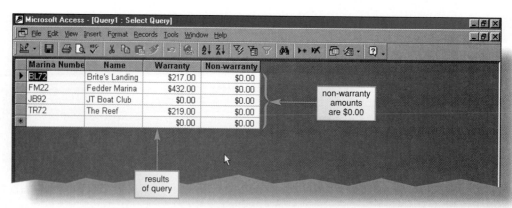

FIGURE 2-30

Using Comparison Operators

Unless you specify otherwise, Access assumes that the criteria you enter involve equality (exact matches). In the last query, for example, you were requesting those marinas whose non-warranty amount is equal to 0 (zero). If you want something other than an exact match, you must enter the appropriate **comparison operator**. The comparison operators are > (greater than), < (less than), >= (greater than or equal to), <= (less than or equal to), and NOT (not equal to).

Perform the following steps to use the > operator to find all marinas whose warranty amount is more than $1,000.

Steps **To Use a Comparison Operator in a Criterion**

1 **Click the View button to return to Design view. On the Edit menu, click Clear Grid.**

Access clears the design grid so you can enter the next query.

2 **Include the Marina Number, Name, Warranty, and Non-warranty fields in the query. Type >1000 as the criterion for the Warranty field.**

The fields are selected and the criterion is entered (Figure 2-31).

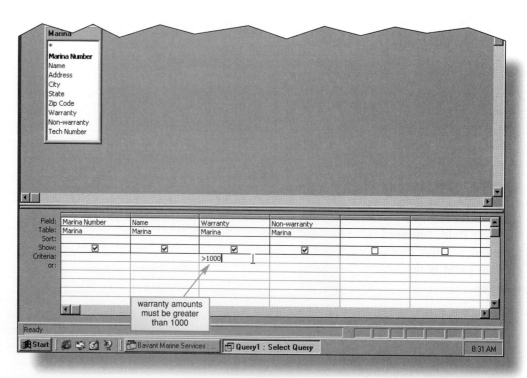

FIGURE 2-31

3 **Run the query.**

The results display (Figure 2-32). Only those marinas that have a warranty amount greater than $1,000 are included.

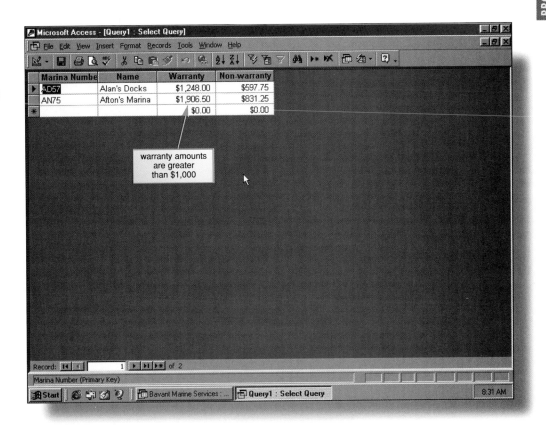

warranty amounts are greater than $1,000

FIGURE 2-32

Using Compound Criteria

Often you will have more than one criterion that the data for which you are searching must satisfy. This type of criterion is called a **compound criterion**. Two types of compound criteria exist.

In **AND criterion**, each individual criterion must be true in order for the compound criterion to be true. For example, an AND criterion would allow you to find those marinas that have a warranty amount greater than $1,000 and whose technician is technician 36.

Conversely, an **OR criterion** is true provided either individual criterion is true. An OR criterion would allow you to find those marinas that have a warranty amount more than $1,000 or whose technician is technician 36. In this case, any marina whose warranty amount is greater than $1,000 would be included in the results whether or not the marina's technician is technician 36. Likewise, any marina whose technician is technician 36 would be included whether or not the marina had a warranty amount greater than $1,000.

Using AND Criteria

To combine criteria with AND, place the criteria on the same line. Perform the following steps to use an AND criterion to find those marinas whose warranty amount is greater than $1,000 and whose technician is technician 36.

To Use a Compound Criterion Involving AND

1 **Click the View button to return to Design view. Include the Tech Number field in the query. If necessary, click the Criteria entry for the Warranty field, and then type >1000 as the criterion for the Warranty field. Click the Criteria entry for the Tech Number field and then type 36 as the criterion for the Tech Number field.**

Criteria have been entered for the Warranty and Tech Number fields (Figure 2-33).

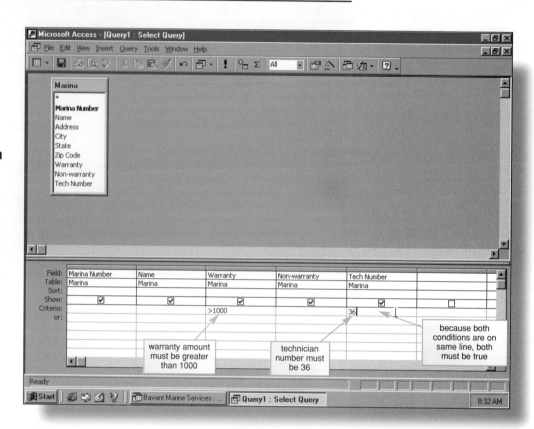

FIGURE 2-33

2 **Run the query.**

The results display (Figure 2-34). Only the single marina whose warranty amount is greater than $1,000.00 and whose technician number is 36 is included.

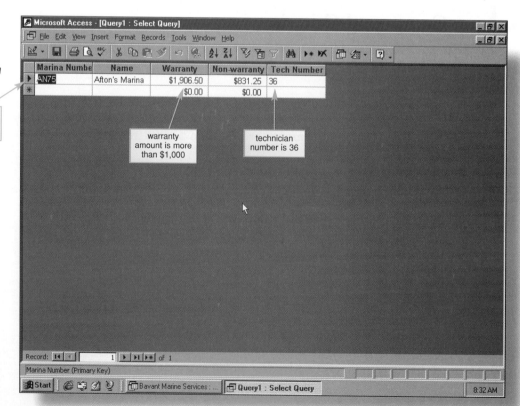

FIGURE 2-34

Using OR Criteria

To combine criteria with OR, the criteria must go on separate lines in the Criteria area of the grid. The following steps use an OR criterion to find those marinas whose warranty amount is greater than $1,000.00 or whose technician is technician 36 (or both).

To Use a Compound Criterion Involving OR

1 **Click the View button to return to Design view.**

2 **Click the Criteria entry for the Tech Number field. Use the BACKSPACE key to delete the entry ("36"). Click the or row (below the Criteria row) for the Tech Number field and then type 36 as the entry.**

The criteria are entered for the Warranty and Tech Number fields on different lines (Figure 2-35).

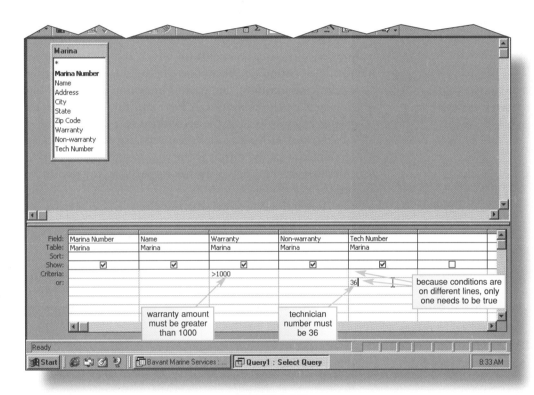

FIGURE 2-35

3 **Run the query.**

The results display (Figure 2-36). Only those marinas whose warranty amount is greater than $1,000.00 or whose technician number is 36 are included.

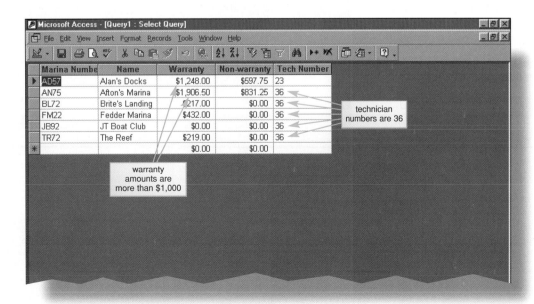

FIGURE 2-36

Sorting Data in a Query

In some queries, the order in which the records are displayed really does not matter. All you need be concerned about are the records that appear in the results. It does not matter which one is first or which one is last.

In other queries, however, the order can be very important. You may want to see the cities in which marinas are located and would like them arranged alphabetically. Perhaps you want to see the marinas listed by technician number. Further, within all the marinas of any given technician, you would like them to be listed by warranty amount.

To order the records in the answer to a query in a particular way, you **sort** the records. The field or fields on which the records are sorted is called the **sort key**. If you are sorting on more than one field (such as sorting by warranty amount within technician number), the more important field (Tech Number) is called the **major key** (also called the **primary sort key**) and the less important field (Warranty) is called the **minor key** (also called the **secondary sort key**).

To sort in Microsoft Access, specify the sort order in the Sort line of the design grid below the field that is the sort key. If you specify more than one sort key, the sort key on the left will be the major sort key and the one on the right will be the minor key.

The following steps sort the cities in the Marina table.

Compound Criteria

Access to compound criteria is precisely the approach that was proposed for Query-by-Example. (Placing criteria on the same line indicates they are connected by the word AND. Placing them on separate lines indicates they are connected by the word OR.)

To Sort Data in a Query

1 **Click the View button to return to Design view. On the Edit menu, click Clear Grid.**

2 **Include the City field in the design grid. Click the Sort row below the City field, and then click the Sort row arrow that displays.**

The City field is included (Figure 2-37). A list of available sort orders displays.

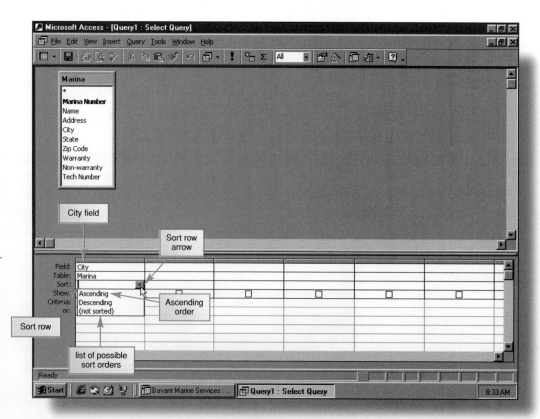

FIGURE 2-37

3 **Click Ascending.**

Ascending is selected as the order (Figure 2-38).

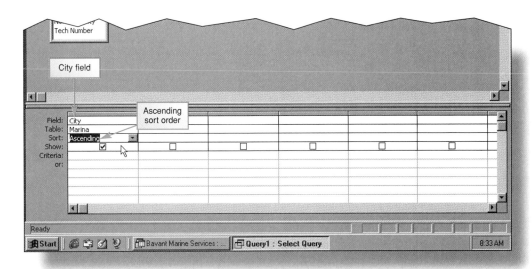

FIGURE 2-38

 4 **Run the query.**

The results contain the cities from the Marina table (Figure 2-39). The cities display in alphabetical order. Duplicates, that is, identical rows, are included.

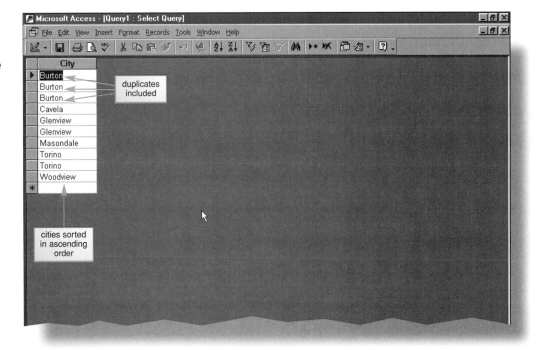

FIGURE 2-39

Sorting on Multiple Keys

The next example lists the number, name, technician number, and warranty amount for all marinas. The data is to be sorted by descending warranty amount (high to low) within technician number, which means that the Tech Number field is the major key and the Warranty field is the minor key. It also means that the Warranty field should be sorted in descending order.

The following steps accomplish this sorting by specifying the Tech Number and Warranty fields as sort keys and by selecting Descending as the sort order for the Warranty field.

Steps: To Sort on Multiple Keys

1 Click the View button to return to Design view. On the Edit menu, click Clear Grid.

2 Include the Marina Number, Name, Tech Number, and Warranty fields in the query in this order. Select Ascending as the sort order for the Tech Number field and Descending as the sort order for the Warranty field (Figure 2-40).

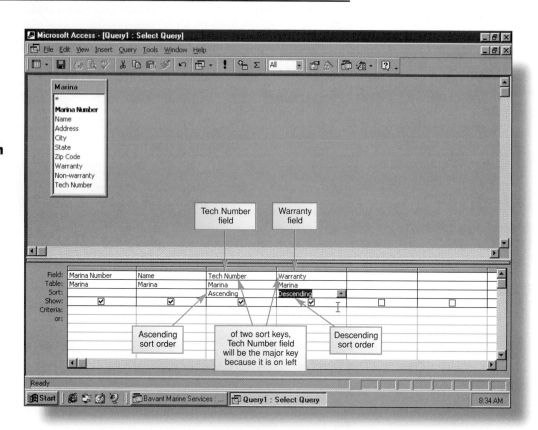

FIGURE 2-40

3 Run the query.

The results display (Figure 2-41). The marinas are sorted by technician number. Within the collection of marinas having the same technician, the marinas are sorted by descending warranty amount.

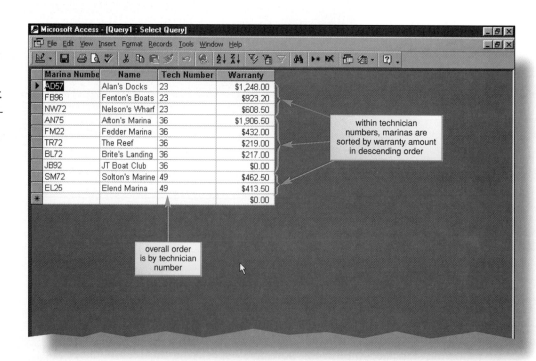

FIGURE 2-41

It is important to remember that the major sort key must appear to the left of the minor sort key in the design grid. If you attempted to sort by warranty amount within technician number, but placed the Warranty field to the left of the Tech Number field, your results would be incorrect.

Omitting Duplicates

As you saw earlier, when you sort data, duplicates are included. In Figure 2-39 on page A 2.27, for example, Glenview appeared twice, Burton appeared three times, and Torino appeared twice. If you do not want duplicates included, use the Properties command and change the Unique Values property to Yes. Perform the following steps to produce a sorted list of the cities in the Marina table in which each city is listed only once.

More About

Sorting Data in a Query

When sorting data in a query, the records in the underlying tables (the tables on which the query is based) are not actually rearranged. Instead, the DBMS will determine the most efficient method of simply displaying the records in the requested order. The records in the underlying tables remain in their original order.

 ## To Omit Duplicates

1 **Click the View button to return to Design view. On the Edit menu, click Clear Grid.**

2 **Include the City field, click Ascending as the sort order, and right-click the second field in the design grid (the empty field following City). (You must right-click the second field or you will not get the correct results.)**

The shortcut menu displays (Figure 2-42).

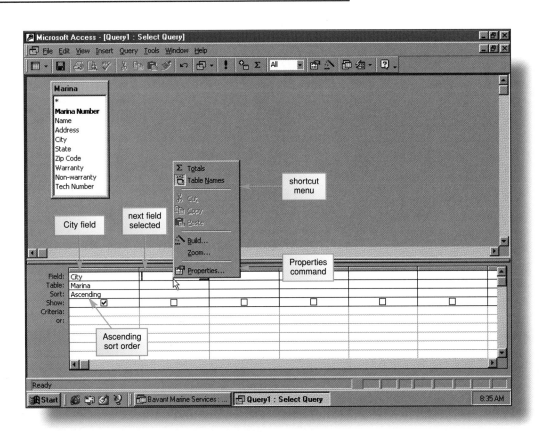

FIGURE 2-42

3 **Click Properties on the shortcut menu.**

The Query Properties sheet displays (Figure 2-43). (If your sheet looks different, you right-clicked the wrong place. Close the sheet that displays and right-click the second field in the grid.)

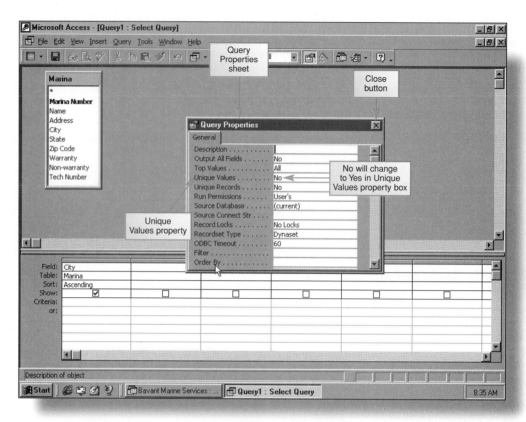

FIGURE 2-43

4 **Click the Unique Values property box, and then click the arrow that displays to produce a list of available choices for Unique Values. Click Yes and then close the Query Properties sheet by clicking its Close button. Run the query.**

The results display (Figure 2-44). The cities are sorted alphabetically. Each city is included only once.

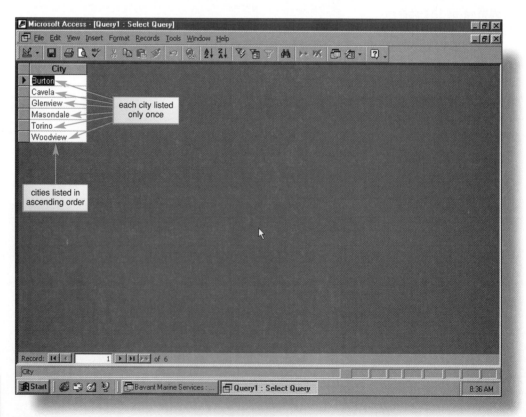

FIGURE 2-44

Other Ways

1. Click Properties button on toolbar
2. On View menu click Properties

Joining Tables

Bavant Marine Services needs to list the number and name of each marina along with the number and name of the marina's technician. The marina's name is in the Marina table, whereas the technician's name is in the Technician table. Thus, this query cannot be satisfied using a single table. You need to **join** the tables; that is, to find records in the two tables that have identical values in matching fields (Figure 2-45). In this example, you need to find records in the Marina table and the Technician table that have the same value in the Tech Number fields.

give me the number and name of each Marina along with the number and name of the marina's technician

Marina table

MARINA NUMBER	NAME	. . .	TECH NUMBER
AD57	Alan's Docks	. . .	23
AN75	Afton's Marina	. . .	36
BL72	Brite's Landing	. . .	36
EL25	Elend Marina	. . .	49
FB96	Fenton's Boats	. . .	23
FM22	Fedder Marina	. . .	36
JB92	JT Boat Club	. . .	36
NW72	Nelson's Wharf	. . .	23
SM72	Solton's Marine	. . .	49
TR72	The Reef	. . .	36

Technician table

TECH NUMBER	LAST NAME	FIRST NAME	. . .
23	Anderson	Trista	. . .
36	Nichols	Ashton	. . .
49	Gomez	Teresa	. . .

MARINA NUMBER	NAME	. . .	TECH NUMBER	LAST NAME	FIRST NAME	. . .
AD57	Alan's Docks	. . .	23	Anderson	Trista	. . .
AN75	Afton's Marina	. . .	36	Nichols	Ashton	. . .
BL72	Brite's Landing	. . .	36	Nichols	Ashton	. . .
EL25	Elend Marina	. . .	49	Gomez	Teresa	. . .
FB96	Fenton's Boats	. . .	23	Anderson	Trista	. . .
FM22	Fedder Marina	. . .	36	Nichols	Ashton	. . .
JB92	JT Boat Club	. . .	36	Nichols	Ashton	. . .
NW72	Nelson's Wharf	. . .	23	Anderson	Trista	. . .
SM72	Solton's Marine	. . .	49	Gomez	Teresa	. . .
TR72	The Reef	. . .	36	Nichols	Ashton	. . .

FIGURE 2-45

To join tables in Access, first you bring field lists for both tables to the upper pane of the Select Query window. Access will draw a line, called a **join line**, between matching fields in the two tables indicating that the tables are related. You then can select fields from either table. Access will join the tables automatically.

The first step is to add an additional table, the Technician table, to the query. A join line will display connecting the Tech Number fields in the two field lists. This join line indicates how the tables are related; that is, linked through these matching fields. (If you fail to give the matching fields the same name, Access will not insert the line. You can insert it manually, however, by clicking one of the two matching fields and dragging the mouse pointer to the other matching field.)

The following steps add the Technician table and then select the appropriate fields.

Steps To Join Tables

① Click the View button to return to Design view. On the Edit menu, click Clear Grid.

② Right-click any open area in the upper pane of the Query1 : Select Query window.

The shortcut menu displays (Figure 2-46).

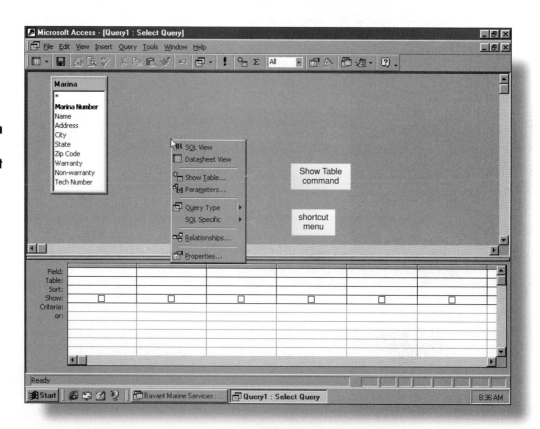

FIGURE 2-46

3 **Click Show Table on the shortcut menu.**

The Show Table dialog box displays (Figure 2-47).

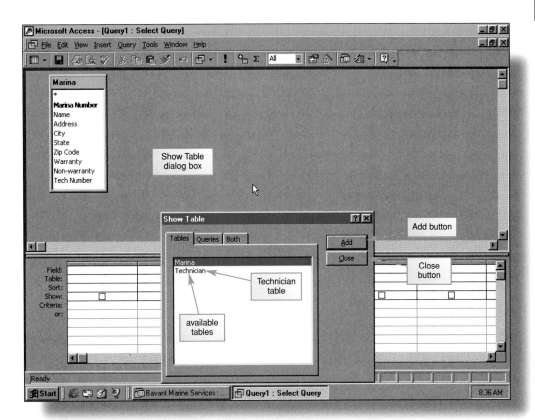

FIGURE 2-47

4 **Click Technician to select the Technician table and then click the Add button. Close the Show Table dialog box by clicking the Close button. Expand the size of the field list so all the fields in the Technician table display. Include the Marina Number, Name, and Tech Number fields from the Marina table and the Last Name and First Name fields from the Technician table.**

The fields from both tables are included (Figure 2-48).

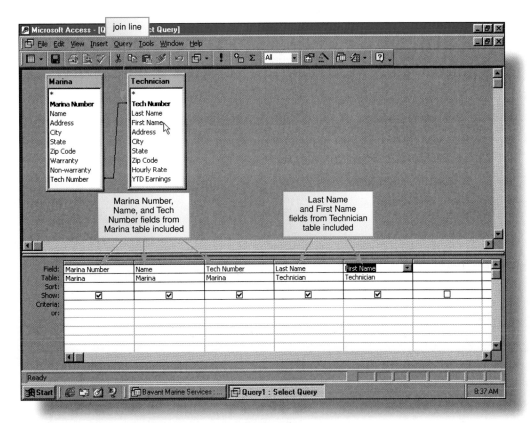

FIGURE 2-48

Run the query.

The results display (Figure 2-49) and contain data from both the Marina and the Technician tables.

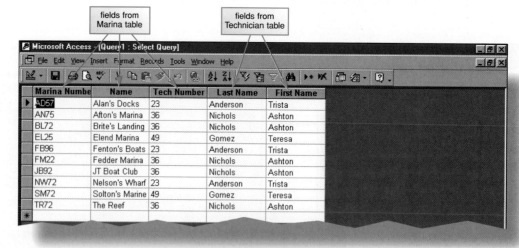

FIGURE 2-49

 Other Ways

1. Click Show Table button on toolbar
2. On Query menu click Show Table

Restricting Records in a Join

Sometimes you will want to join tables, but you will not want to include all possible records. In such cases, you will relate the tables and include fields just as you did before. You also will include criteria. For example, to include the same fields as in the previous query, but only those marinas whose warranty amount is more than $1,000, you will make the same entries as before and then also type >1000 as a criterion for the Warranty field.

The following steps modify the query from the previous example to restrict the records that will be included in the join.

Steps **To Restrict the Records in a Join**

① **Click the View button to return to Design view. Add the Warranty field to the query. Type >1000 as the criterion for the Warranty field and then click the Show check box for the Warranty field to remove the check mark.**

The Warranty field displays in the design grid (Figure 2-50). A criterion is entered for the Warranty field and the Show check box is empty, indicating that the field will not display in the results of the query.

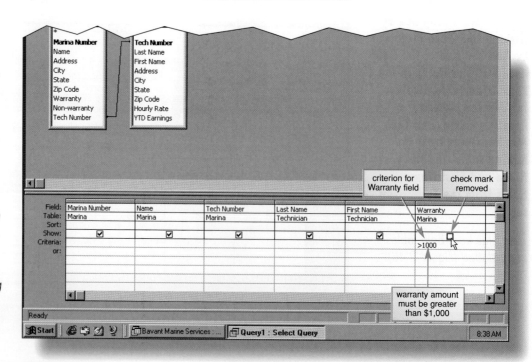

FIGURE 2-50

② **Run the query.**

The results display (Figure 2-51). Only those marinas with a warranty amount greater than $1,000 display in the result. The Warranty field does not display.

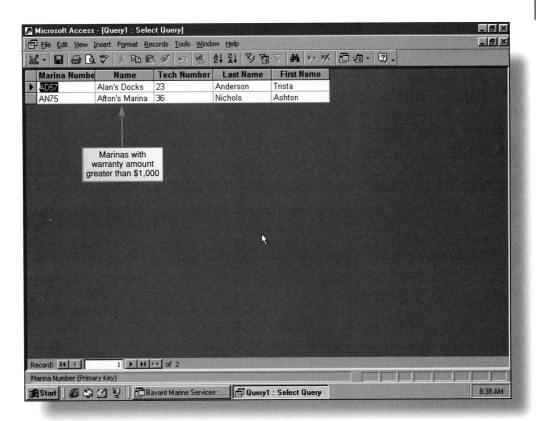

FIGURE 2-51

Using Calculated Fields in a Query

It is important to Bavant Marine Services to know the total amount for each marina; that is, the warranty amount plus the non-warranty amount. This poses a problem because the Marina table does not include a field for total amount. You can calculate it, however, because the total amount is equal to the warranty amount plus the non-warranty amount. Such a field is called a **calculated field**.

To include calculated fields in queries, you enter a name for the calculated field, a colon, and then the expression in one of the columns in the Field row. Any fields included in the expression must be enclosed in square brackets ([ ]). For the total amount, for example, you will type Total Amount:[Warranty]+[Non-warranty] as the expression.

You can type the expression directly into the Field row. You will not be able to see the entire entry, however, because the Field row is not large enough. The preferred way is to select the column in the Field row, right-click to display the shortcut menu, and then click Zoom. The Zoom dialog box displays where you can type the expression.

You are not restricted to addition in calculations. You can use subtraction (-), multiplication (*), or division (/). You also can include parentheses in your calculations to indicate which calculations should be done first.

Perform the following steps to remove the Technician table from the query (it is not needed), and then use a calculated field to display the number, name, and total amount of all marinas.

Calculated Fields

Because it is easy to compute values in a query, there is no need to store calculated fields, also called computed fields, in a database. There is no need, for example, to store the total amount (the warranty amount plus the non-warranty amount), because it can be calculated whenever it is required.

To Use a Calculated Field in a Query

1 **Click the View button to return to Design view. Right-click any field in the Technician table field list.**

The shortcut menu displays (Figure 2-52).

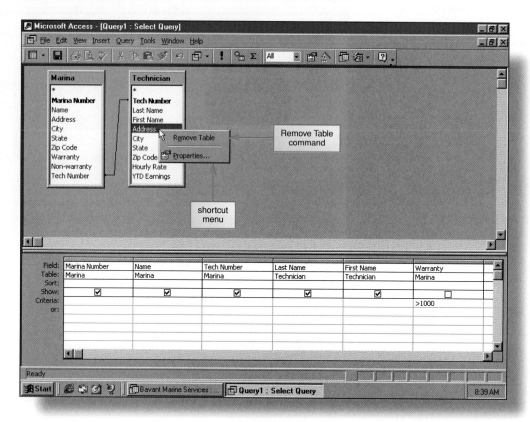

FIGURE 2-52

2 **Click Remove Table to remove the Technician table from the Query1 : Select Query window. On the Edit menu, click Clear Grid.**

3 **Include the Marina Number and Name fields. Right-click the Field row in the third column in the design grid and then click Zoom on the shortcut menu. Type** `Total Amount:[Warranty]+[Non-warranty]` **in the Zoom dialog box that displays.**

The Zoom dialog box displays (Figure 2-53). The expression you typed displays within the dialog box.

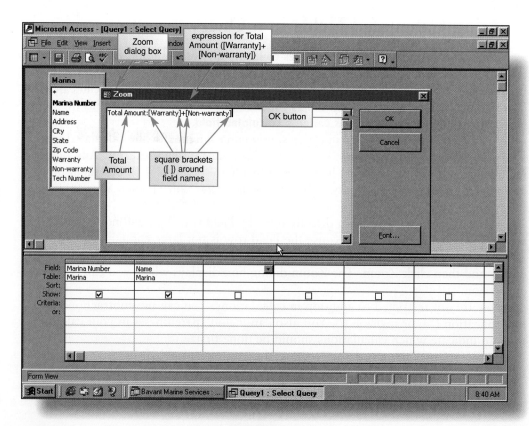

FIGURE 2-53

4 **Click the OK button.**

The Zoom dialog box no longer displays (Figure 2-54). A portion of the expression you entered displays in the third field in the design grid.

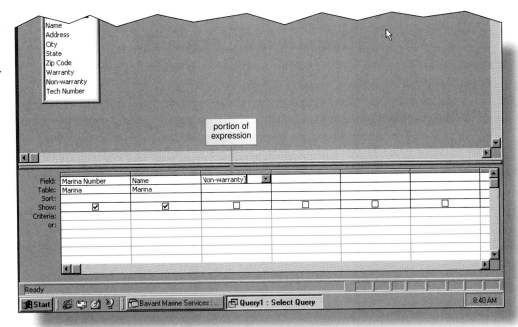

FIGURE 2-54

5 **Run the query.**

The results display (Figure 2-55). Microsoft Access has calculated and displayed the total amounts.

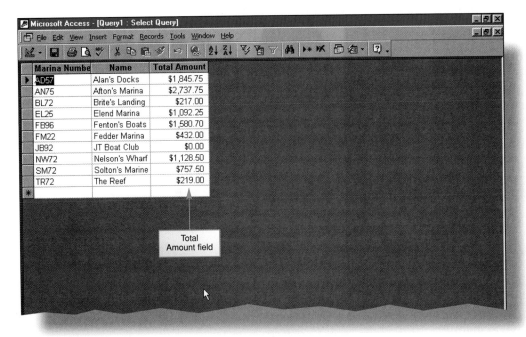

FIGURE 2-55

Rather than clicking Zoom on the shortcut menu, you can click Build. The Build dialog box then will display. This dialog box provides assistance in creating the expression. If you know the expression you will need, however, it usually is easier to enter it using Zoom.

Other Ways

1. Press SHIFT+F2

Calculating Statistics

Virtually all database management systems support the basic set of statistical calculations: sum, average, count, maximum, and minimum as part of their query feature. Some systems, including Access, add several more, such as standard deviation, variance, first, and last.

Calculating Statistics

Microsoft Access supports the built-in **statistics:** COUNT, SUM, AVG (average), MAX (largest value), MIN (smallest value), STDEV (standard deviation), VAR (variance), FIRST, and LAST. To use any of these in a query, you include it in the Total row in the design grid. The Total row routinely does not appear in the grid. To include it, right-click the grid, and then click Totals on the shortcut menu.

The following example illustrates how you use these functions by calculating the average warranty amount for all marinas.

 To Calculate Statistics

Click the View button to return to Design view. On the Edit menu, click Clear Grid.

Right-click the grid.

The shortcut menu displays (Figure 2-56).

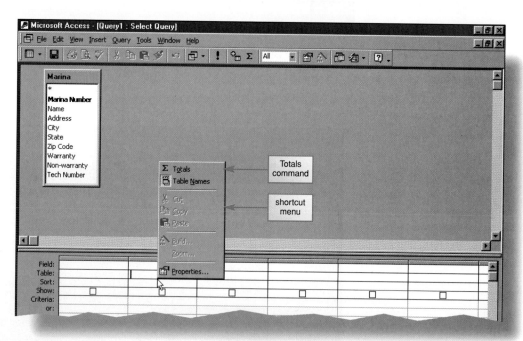

FIGURE 2-56

Click Totals on the shortcut menu and then include the Warranty field. Point to the Total row in the Warranty column.

The Total row now is included in the design grid (Figure 2-57). The Warranty field is included, and the entry in the Total row is Group By. The mouse pointer, which has changed shape to an I-beam, is positioned on the Total row under the Warranty field.

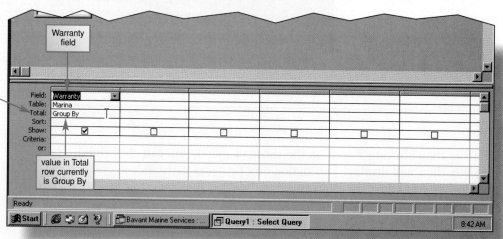

FIGURE 2-57

4 **Click the Total row in the Warranty column, and then click the arrow that displays.**

The list of available selections displays (Figure 2-58).

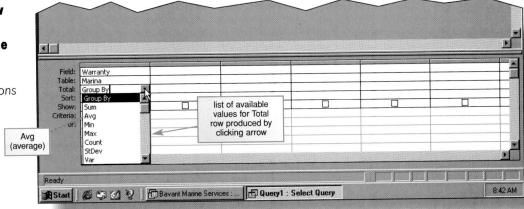

FIGURE 2-58

5 **Click Avg.**

Avg is selected (Figure 2-59).

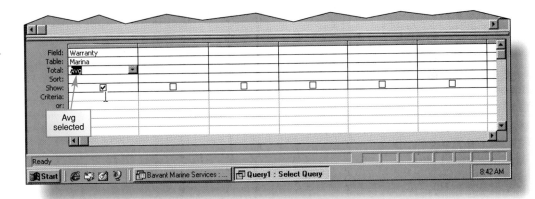

FIGURE 2-59

6 **Run the query.**

The result displays (Figure 2-60), showing the average warranty amount for all marinas.

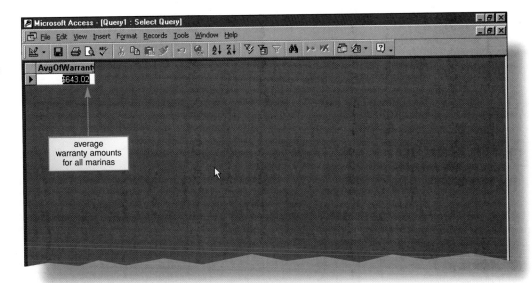

FIGURE 2-60

Other Ways

1. Click Totals button on toolbar
2. On View menu click Totals

Using Criteria in Calculating Statistics

Sometimes calculating statistics for all the records in the table is appropriate. In other cases, however, you will need to calculate the statistics for only those records that satisfy certain criteria. To enter a criterion in a field, first you select Where as the entry in the Total row for the field and then enter the criterion in the Criteria row. The following steps use this technique to calculate the average warranty amount for marinas of technician 36.

 To Use Criteria in Calculating Statistics

1 **Click the View button to return to Design view.**

2 **Include the Tech Number field in the design grid. Produce the list of available options for the Total row entry just as you did when you selected Avg for the Warranty field. Use the vertical scroll bar to move through the options until the word, Where, displays.**

The list of available selections displays (Figure 2-61). The Group By entry in the Tech Number field may not be highlighted on your screen depending on where you clicked in the Total row.

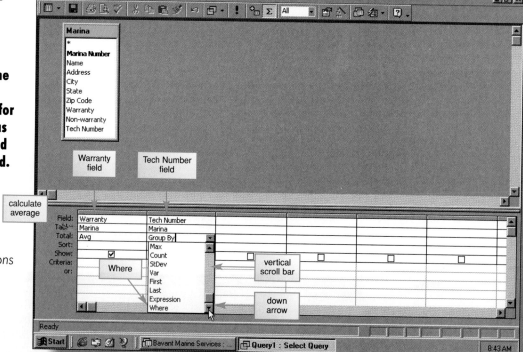

FIGURE 2-61

3 **Click Where. Type 36 as the criterion for the Tech Number field.**

Where is selected as the entry in the Total row for the Tech Number field (Figure 2-62) and 36 is entered as the Criterion.

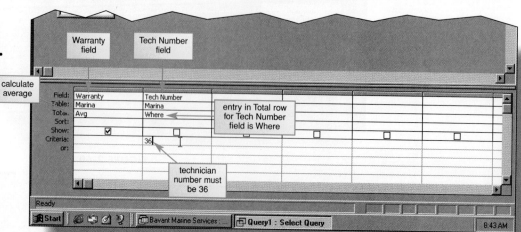

FIGURE 2-62

Run the query.

The result displays (Figure 2-63), giving the average warranty amount for marinas of technician 36.

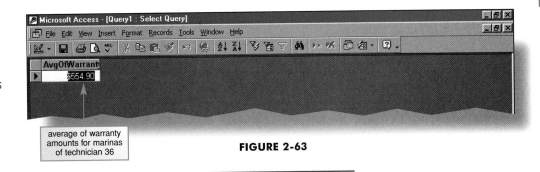

average of warranty amounts for marinas of technician 36

FIGURE 2-63

Grouping

Another way statistics often are used is in combination with grouping; that is, statistics are calculated for groups of records. You may, for example, need to calculate the average warranty amount for the marinas of each technician. You will want the average for the marinas of technician 23, the average for marinas of technician 36, and so on.

Grouping means creating groups of records that share some common characteristic. In grouping by Tech Number, for example, the marinas of technician 23 would form one group, the marinas of technician 36 would be a second, and the marinas of technician 49 form a third. The calculations then are made for each group. To indicate grouping in Access, select Group By as the entry in the Total row for the field to be used for grouping.

Perform the following steps to calculate the average warranty amount for marinas of each technician.

More *About*

Quick Reference

For a table that lists how to complete the tasks covered in this book using the mouse, menu, shortcut menu, and keyboard, visit the Office 2000 Web page (www.scsite.com/off2000/qr.htm), and then click Microsoft Access 2000.

Steps **To Use Grouping**

 Click the View button to return to Design view. On the Edit menu, click Clear Grid.

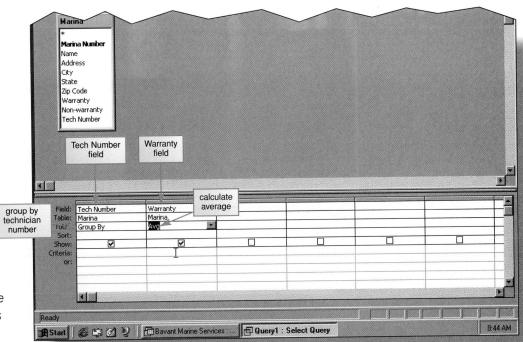

② Include the Tech Number field. Include the Warranty field, and then select Avg as the calculation in the Total row.

The Tech Number and Warranty fields are included (Figure 2-64). Group By currently is the entry in the Total row for the Tech Number field, which is correct; thus, it was not changed.

FIGURE 2-64

3 **Run the query.**

The result displays (Figure 2-65), showing each technician's number along with the average warranty amount for the marinas of that technician.

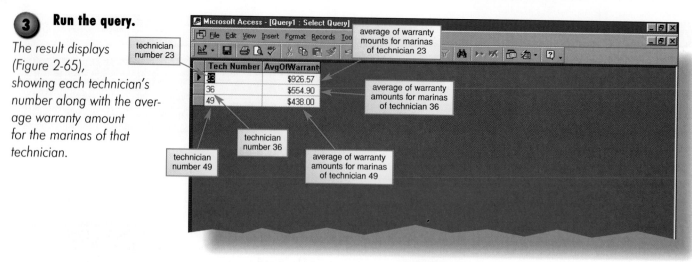

FIGURE 2-65

Saving a Query

In many cases, you will construct a query you will want to use again. By saving the query, you will eliminate the need to repeat all your entries. The following steps illustrate the process by saving the query you just have created and assigning it the name Average Warranty Amount by Technician.

 To Save a Query

1 **Click the View** ~~File~~ **button and then click the Save button. Type** Average Warranty Amount by Technician **and then point to the OK button.**

The Save As dialog box displays with the query name you typed (Figure 2-66).

2 **Click the OK button to save the query, and then close the query by clicking the Query window's Close Window button.**

Access saves the query and closes the Query1 : Select Query window.

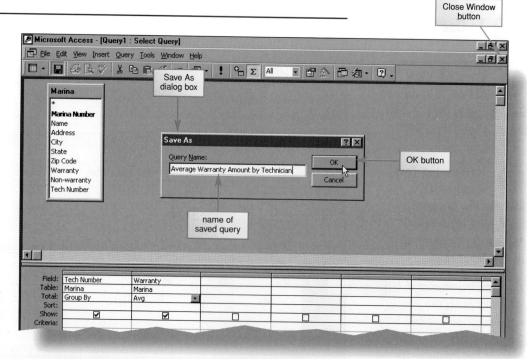

FIGURE 2-66

Once you have saved a query, you can use it at any time in the future by opening it. Opening a query produces the same results as running the query from Design view. To open a saved query, click the Queries object in the Database window, right-click the query, and then click Open on the shortcut menu. You then could print the results by clicking the Print button. If you wish to change the design of the query, you would click Design View on the shortcut menu rather than Open. If you wanted to print it *without first opening it*, you would click Print on the shortcut menu.

The query is run against the current database. Thus, if changes have been made to the data since the last time you ran it, the results of the query may be different.

More About

Microsoft Certification

The Microsoft Office User Specialist (MOUS) Certification program provides an opportunity for you to obtain a valuable industry credential — proof that you have the Access 2000 skills required by employers. For more information, see Appendix D or visit the Shelly Cashman Series MOUS Web page at www.scsite.com/off2000/cert.htm.

Closing a Database

The following step closes the database by closing its Database window.

TO CLOSE A DATABASE

 Click the Close Window button for the Bavant Marine Services : Database window.

CASE PERSPECTIVE SUMMARY

You have been successful in assisting the management of Bavant Marine Services by creating and running queries to obtain answers to important questions. You used various types of criteria in these queries. You joined tables in some of the queries. Some Bavant Marine Services queries used calculated fields and statistics. Finally, you saved one of the queries for future use.

Project Summary

In Project 2, you created and ran a variety of queries. You learned how to select fields in a query. You used text data and wildcards in criteria. You also used comparison operators in criteria involving numeric data. You combined criteria with both AND and OR. You learned how to sort the results of a query, how to join tables, and how to restrict the records in a join. You created computed fields and calculated statistics. You learned how to use grouping as well as how to save a query for future use.

What You Should Know

Having completed this project, you now should be able to perform the following tasks:

- Calculate Statistics (A 2.38)
- Clear a Query (A 2.16)
- Close the Database (A 2.43)
- Close a Query (A 2.14)
- Create a Query (A 2.6)
- Include All Fields in a Query (A 2.15)
- Include Fields in the Design Grid (A 2.10)
- Join Tables (A 2.32)
- Omit Duplicates (A 2.29)
- Open a Database (A 2.6)
- Print the Results of a Query (A 2.12)
- Restrict the Records in a Join (A 2.34)
- Return to the Design View (A 2.12)
- Run the Query (A 2.11)
- Save a Query (A 2.42)
- Sort Data in a Query (A 2.26)
- Sort on Multiple Keys (A 2.28)
- Use a Comparison Operator in a Criterion (A 2.22)
- Use a Compound Criterion Involving AND (A 2.24)
- Use a Compound Criterion Involving OR (A 2.25)
- Use a Calculated Field in a Query (A 2.36)
- Use a Number in a Criterion (A 2.21)
- Use a Wildcard (A 2.18)
- Use Criteria for a Field Not Included in the Results (A 2.20)
- Use Criteria in Calculating Statistics (A 2.40)
- Use Grouping (A 2.41)
- Use Text Data in a Criterion (A 2.17)

Apply Your Knowledge

✚ Project Reinforcement at www.scsite.com/off2000/reinforce.htm

1 Querying the Sidewalk Scrapers Database

Instructions: Start Access. Open the Sidewalk Scrapers database from the Access Data Disk. See the inside back cover for instructions for downloading the Access Data Disk or see your instructor for information on accessing the files required for this book. Perform the following tasks.

1. Create a new query for the Customer table.
2. Add the Customer Number, Name, and Address fields to the design grid.
3. Restrict retrieval to only those records where the customer has an address on Secord.
4. Run the query and print the results.
5. Return to Design view and clear the grid.
6. Add the Customer Number, Name, Telephone, and Balance fields to the design grid.
7. Restrict retrieval to only those records where the balance is greater than $50.
8. Run the query and print the results.
9. Return to Design view and clear the grid.
10. Add the Customer Number, Name, Address, and Worker Id fields to the design grid.
11. Restrict retrieval to only those records where the Worker Id is either 03 or 07.
12. Run the query and print the results.
13. Return to Design view and clear the grid.
14. Join the Customer and Worker tables. Add the Customer Number, Name, and Worker Id fields from the Customer table and the First Name and Last Name fields from the Worker table.
15. Sort the records in ascending order by Worker Id.
16. Run the query and print the results.

In the Lab

1 Querying the School Connection Database

Problem: The Booster's Club has determined a number of questions they want the database management system to answer. You must obtain answers to the questions posed by the club.

Instructions: Use the database created in the In the Lab 1 of Project 1 for this assignment. Perform the following tasks.

1. Open the School Connection database and create a new query for the Item table.
2. Display and print the Item Id, Description, and Selling Price fields for all records in the table as shown in Figure 2-67.
3. Display all fields and print all the records in the table.

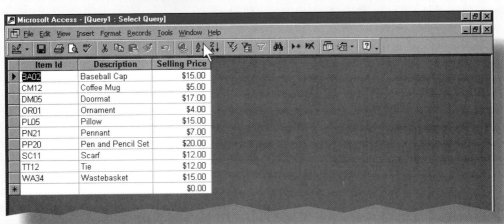

FIGURE 2-67

4. Display and print the Item Id, Description, Cost, and Vendor Code fields for all items where the Vendor Code is TM.

5. Display and print the Item Id and Description fields for all items where the Description begins with the letters, Pe.

6. Display and print the Item Id, Description, and Vendor Code fields for all items with a cost greater than $10.

7. Display and print the Item Id and Description for all items that have a selling price of $10 or less.

8. Display and print all fields for those items with a cost greater than $10 and where the number on hand is less than 5.

9. Display and print all fields for those items that have a vendor code of TM or have a selling price less than $10.

10. Join the Item table and the Vendor table. Display the Item Id, Description, Cost, Name, and Telephone Number fields. Run the query and print the results.

11. Restrict the records retrieved in task 10 above to only those items where the number on hand is less than 10. Display and print the results.

12. Remove the Vendor table and clear the design grid.

13. Include the Item Id and Description fields in the design grid. Calculate the on-hand value (on hand * cost) for all records in the table. Display and print the results.

14. Display and print the average selling price of all items.

15. Display and print the average selling price of items grouped by vendor code.

16. Join the Item and Vendor tables. Include the Vendor Code and Name fields from the Vendor table. Include the Item Id, Description, Cost, and On Hand fields from the Item table. Save the query as Vendors and Items. Run the query and print the results.

 *In the Lab*

2 Querying the City Area Bus Company Database

Problem: The advertising sales manager has determined a number of questions that he wants the database management system to answer. You must obtain answers to the questions posed by the manager.

Instructions: Use the database created in the In the Lab 2 of Project 1 for this assignment. Perform the following tasks.

1. Open the City Area Bus Company database and create a new query for the Advertiser table.
2. Display and print the Advertiser Id, Name, Balance, and Amount Paid fields for all the records in the table.
3. Display and print the Advertiser Id, Name, and Balance fields for all advertisers where the sales rep number is 24.
4. Display and print the Advertiser Id, Name, and Balance fields for all advertisers where the balance is greater than $200.
5. Display and print the Advertiser Id, Name, and Amount Paid fields for all advertisers where the sales rep number is 29 and the amount paid is greater than $1,000.
6. Display and print the Advertiser Id, Name, and City fields of all advertisers where the city begins with C.
7. Display and print the Advertiser Id, Name, and Balance fields for all advertisers where the sales rep number is 29 or the balance is less than $50.
8. Include the Advertiser Id, Name, City, and State fields in the design grid. Sort the records in ascending order by city within state. Display and print the results. The City field should display in the result to the left of the State field. (*Hint:* Use Microsoft Access Help to solve this problem.)
9. Display and print the cities in ascending order. Each city should display only once.
10. Display and print the Advertiser Id, Name, Balance, and Amount Paid fields from the Advertiser table and the First Name, Last Name, and Comm Rate fields from the Sales Rep table.
11. Restrict the records retrieved in task 10 above to only those advertisers that are in MA. Display and print the results.
12. Clear the design grid and add the First Name, Last Name, and Comm Rate fields from the Sales Rep table to the grid. Add the Name and Balance fields from the Advertiser table. Calculate the pending commission (balance * comm rate) for the Sales Rep table. Sort the records in ascending order by last name and format pending commission as currency. (*Hint:* Use Microsoft Access Help to solve this problem.) Run the query and print the results.
13. Display and print the following statistics: the total balance and total amount paid for all advertisers; the total balance for advertisers of sales rep 29; and the total amount paid for each sales rep.
14. Display and print the Sales Rep Number, Last Name, First Name, Advertiser Id, Name, Balance, and Amount Paid fields. Save the query as Sales Reps and Advertisers.

3 Querying the Resort Rentals Database

Problem: The real estate company has determined a number of questions that they want the database management system to answer. You must obtain answers to the questions posed by the company.

Instructions: Use the database created in the In the Lab 3 of Project 1 for this assignment. Perform the following tasks.

1. Open the Resort Rentals database and create a new query for the Rental Unit table.

In the Lab

2. Display and print the Rental Id, Address, City, and Owner Id fields for all the records in the table as shown in Figure 2-68.

Rental Id	Address	City	Owner Id
101	521 Ocean	Hutchins	ML10
103	783 First	Gulf Breeze	FH15
105	684 Beach	San Toma	PR23
108	96 Breeze	Gulf Breeze	PR23
110	523 Ocean	Hutchins	LD45
112	345 Coastal	Shady Beach	LD45
116	956 First	Gulf Breeze	ML10
121	123 Gulf	San Toma	FH15
134	278 Second	Shady Beach	FH15
144	24 Plantation	Hutchins	PR23

FIGURE 2-68

3. Display and print the Rental Id, Address, City, and Weekly Rate fields for all units that rent for less than $1,000 per week.
4. Display and print the Rental Id, Address, and Weekly Rate fields for all units that sleep more than four people and have a pool.
5. Display and print the Rental Id, Address, City, and Weekly Rate fields for all units that are either in Hutchins or Gulf Breeze, have more than one bedroom and an ocean view. (*Hint:* Use Microsoft Access Help to solve this problem.)
6. Display and print the Rental Id, Address, and City fields of all units where the city begins with S.
7. Display and print the Rental Id, Address, and Weekly Rate fields for all units that have more than one bedroom and more than one bathroom.
8. Include the Rental Id, Address, City, Bedrooms, Sleeps, and Weekly Rate fields in the design grid. Sort the records in descending order by bedrooms within sleeps. The Bedrooms field should display in the result to the left of the Sleeps field. Display and print the results. (*Hint:* Use Microsoft Access Help to solve this problem.)
9. Display and print the weekly rates in descending order. Each rate should display only once.
10. Display and print the Rental Id, Address, City, and Weekly Rate fields from the Rental Unit table and the First Name, Last Name, and Phone Number fields from the Owner table.
11. Restrict the records retrieved in task 10 above to only those units that rent for more than $1,000 per week. Display and print the results.
12. Clear the design grid and remove the Owner table from the query. Owner ML10 offers a 15% discount on the weekly rate if renters rent for more than one week at a time. What is the discounted weekly rental rate for his units? Display the rental id, address, city, and discounted weekly rate in your result. Format the discounted weekly rate as currency. (*Hint:* Use Microsoft Access Help to solve this problem.) Run the query and print the results.
13. Display and print the average weekly rate for each owner.
14. Display and print the Owner Id, First Name, Last Name, Rental Id, Address, City, and Weekly Rate fields. Save the query as Owners and Rental Units.

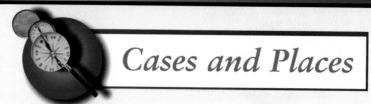

Microsoft **Access 2000**

Cases and Places

The difficulty of these case studies varies:
▶ are the least difficult; ▶▶ are more difficult; and ▶▶▶ are the most difficult.

1 ▶ Use the Computer Accessories database you created in Case Study 1 of Project 1 for this assignment. Perform the following: (a) The Computer Science Club has been unhappy with the supplier, Mouse Tracks. Display and print the description, units on hand, and cost of all items supplied by Mouse Tracks. (b) The club is considering raising the selling price of items costing less than one dollar. Find the current profit (selling price – cost) of these items and display and print the item id, description, cost, selling price, and current profit. (c) The faculty advisor for the club needs to know the on-hand value of the club's inventory. Display and print the item id, description, and on-hand value (units on hand * cost) for all items. (d) The club needs to replenish its stock. Display and print the item id, description, units on hand, supplier name, and supplier telephone for all items where there are less than 10 items on hand. (e) The club would like to display a list of items for sale. Display and print the description and selling price. Sort the list in ascending order by selling price.

2 ▶ Use the Bookstore database you created in Case Study 2 of Project 1 for this assignment. The owner of the bookstore has put together a list of the most common type of questions she would like to ask the database. She wants to know if the database you created can answer these questions. Perform the following: (a) Display and print the book code, title, price, and year published for all books written by H Brawley. (b) Display and print the authors in ascending order. List each author only once. (c) Display and print a count of the books grouped by author. (d) Display and print the book code, title, author, and price for all books published in the year 2000. (e) Display and print the book code, title, units on hand, price, and on-hand value (units on hand * price) for all books. (f) Display and print the book code, title, price, and publisher name for all books where the number of units on hand is less than two.

3 ▶▶ Use the Band database you created in Case Study 3 of Project 1 for this assignment. Perform the following: (a) The band director would like a telephone list of all band members. List the name and telephone number of all band members. (b) The band is going to a marching band competition this weekend and it is important that school officials be able to reach a parent/guardian in case of emergency. List the name and emergency contact information for all band members. (c) The local college is offering a special weekend camp for clarinet players. Identify all band members that play the clarinet. (d) Students who have been band members for two years or more are eligible for special recognition. List the name, age, sex, band instrument, and number of years in the band for these band members. (e) The school has just negotiated a new lease arrangement with a local music store. List the name, telephone number, and type of band instrument for those band members that lease their instrument. (f) The band needs an updated directory. List the band instrument type, member name, age, sex, and years in band for each member. The list should be in order by last name within band instrument type.

4 ▶▶ Use the Humane Society database you created in Case Study 4 of Project 1 for this assignment. Display and print the following: (a) The name, address, and telephone number of all families that have adopted pets. (b) A list of all animals that have been adopted. The list should include the animal's name, type, age, and sex. (c) A list of all adoptions. The list should include the name of the family, telephone number, the animal's name and type. (d) The average number of other pets owned by families that have adopted animals. (e) A list of the different types of animals that have been adopted. Each animal type should display only once.

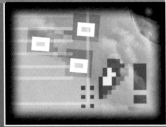

Microsoft **Access 2000**

PROJECT 3

Maintaining a Database Using the Design and Update Features of Access

You will have mastered the material in this project when you can:

OBJECTIVES

- Open a database
- Add, change, and delete records in a table
- Locate records
- Filter records
- Change the structure of a database
- Restructure a table
- Change field characteristics
- Add a field
- Save the changes to the structure
- Update the contents of a single field
- Make changes to groups of records
- Delete groups of records
- Specify a required field
- Specify a range
- Specify a default value
- Specify legal values
- Specify a format
- Save rules, values, and formats
- Update a table with validation rules
- Specify referential integrity
- Use subdatasheets
- Order records
- Create single-field and multiple-field indexes
- Close a database

Database Upkeep

An Ounce of Maintenance Is Worth a Pound of Restoration

Early on the morning of April 13, 1992, the Chicago River crashed through the roof of an abandoned railroad tunnel built in the 1800s. Water from Lake Michigan roared into the basements of Chicago's downtown office buildings, ruining computers, irreplaceable paper files, and environmental equipment. Due to lack of maintenance, what started as a small crack grew into a hemorrhage that city workers desperately tried to shore up while officials sent out for competitive bids. Unfortunately, the river would not wait the several months required for the bid process. If the city had acted immediately, a repair job estimated at $75,000 could have saved the ultimate $1 billion loss. In another, more recent example, the quality of a $44 million seismic retrofit on the freeway overpasses in San Diego came into question because of faulty welds.

Individuals are seldom faced with problems that have such massive financial impact. Unlike the Maytag repairman, however, people must contend with maintenance issues on a regular basis: cars, homes, dental

work, even personal computers. All are issues important to health, safety, and well-being. How a person handles these can make the difference between a happy life and a trying one. Likewise, for many business people, scientific researchers, and self-employed individuals, professional survival depends on maintaining their computer databases.

Information flows in today's world like the waters of all the rivers combined. From telephone lines, customer service terminals, satellite feeds, the mail, and so on, literally billions of pieces of data enter daily into the databases of entities such as insurance companies, banks, mail-order firms, astronomical observatories, medical research labs, doctors' offices, automobile dealerships, home-based businesses, and multitudes of others. Based on the content of this information, decisions are made and actions taken, often triggering a corresponding flow of information to other interested users. The process of handling this data — the lifeblood of today's information-based society — is known as database maintenance.

Microsoft Access 2000 is a powerful tool that facilitates designing the database and then maintaining it with ease. Effective design and update features in Access allow you to add, change, and delete records in a table, change the size of or add new fields to the database, and then quickly update the restructured database. In this project, you will learn the techniques to maintain any type of database with which you might work in your academic or professional life.

During college, you may use a personal database to organize and maintain information such as names, addresses, and telephone numbers of friends, family, and club members, or possessions such as a CD or tape collection, videos, or books. As a club member, you may be asked to design, update, and maintain a database of club members and information.

Your first use for a database may come when you start your search for the right graduate school or as you begin your mailing campaign for future employment opportunities. Once employed, you will be exposed to the use of databases in all facets of business. Learning the important skills associated with database maintenance will pave the way for opportunity in the workplace.

Maintenance might seem mundane, but certainly, an ounce of maintenance is worth a pound of restoration.

Microsoft Access 2000

Microsoft Access 2000

Maintaining a Database Using the Design and Update Features of Access

PROJECT 3

C A S E   P E R S P E C T I V E

Bavant Marine Services now has created and loaded their database. The management and staff have received many benefits from the database, including the ability to ask a variety of questions concerning the data in the database. They now face the task of keeping the database up to date. They must add new records as they take on new marinas and technicians. They must make changes to existing records to reflect additional billings, payments, changes of address, and so on. Bavant Marine Services also found that it needed to change the structure of the database in two specific ways. The management decided they needed to categorize the marinas by the type of storage they offer, so they need to add a Marina Type field to the Marina table. They also discovered the Name field was too short to contain the name of one of the marinas so they need to enlarge the field. In addition, they wish to establish rules for the data entered in the database to ensure that users only can enter valid data. Finally, they determined they want to improve the efficiency of certain types of processing, specifically sorting and retrieving data. Your task is to help Bavant Marine Services in all these activities.

Introduction

Once a database has been created and loaded with data, it must be maintained. **Maintaining the database** means modifying the data to keep it up to date, such as adding new records, changing the data for existing records, and deleting records. **Updating** can include **mass updates** or **mass deletions**; that is, updates to, or deletions of, many records at the same time.

In addition to adding, changing, and deleting records, maintenance of a database periodically can involve the need to **restructure** the database; that is, to change the database structure. This can include adding new fields to a table, changing the characteristics of existing fields, and removing existing fields. It also can involve the creation of **indexes**, which are similar to indexes found in the back of books and used to improve the efficiency of certain operations.

Figure 3-1 summarizes some of the various types of activities involved in maintaining a database.

FIGURE 3-1

Project Three — Maintaining the Bavant Marine Services Database

You are to make the changes to the data in the Bavant Marine Services database as requested by the management of Bavant Marine Services. You must restructure the database to meet the current needs of Bavant Marine. This includes adding an additional field as well as increasing the width of one of the existing fields. You must modify the structure of the database in a way that prevents users from entering invalid data. Finally, management is concerned that some operations, for example, those involving sorting the data, are taking longer than they would like. You are to create indexes to attempt to address this problem.

Opening the Database

Before carrying out the steps in this project, first you must open the database. To do so, perform the following steps.

TO OPEN A DATABASE

1. Click the Start button on the taskbar.

2. Click Open Office Document and then click 3½ Floppy (A:) in the Look in box. If necessary, click the Bavant Marine Services database name.

3. Click the Open button.

The database opens and the Bavant Marine Services : Database window displays.

More About 2000

Maintaining a Database: Backup

Before making changes to the database, it is a good idea to make a copy of the database (called a **backup** or a **save** copy). To do so, use the copy features in Windows to copy the database to another file with a different name (for example, Bavant Marine Backup).

Adding, Changing, and Deleting Records in a Table

Keeping the data in a database up to date requires three tasks: adding new records, changing the data in existing records, and deleting existing records.

Adding Records in a Table

In Project 1, you added records to a database using Datasheet view; that is, as you were adding records, the records were displayed on the screen in the form of a datasheet, or table. When you need to add additional records, you can use the same techniques.

In Project 1, you used a form to view records. This is called **Form view**. You also can use Form view to update the data in a table. To add new records, change existing records, or delete records, you will use the same techniques you used in Datasheet view. To add a record to the Marina table with a form, for example, use the following steps. These steps use the Marina form you created in Project 1.

Steps: To Use a Form to Add Records

1. **With the Bavant Marine Services** database open, point to Forms on the Objects bar (Figure 3-2).

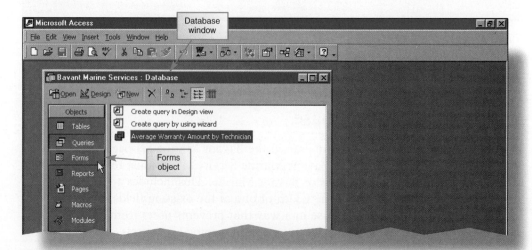

FIGURE 3-2

② Click Forms. Right-click Marina.

The shortcut menu displays (Figure 3-3).

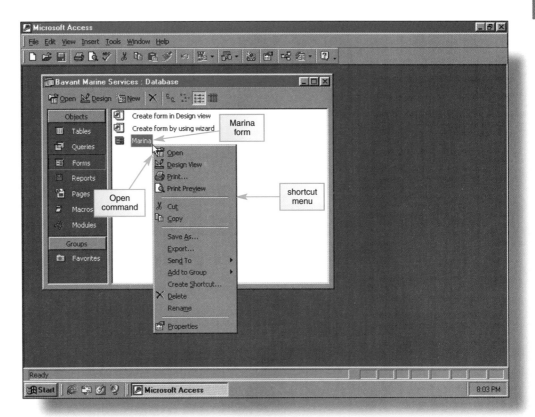

FIGURE 3-3

③ Click Open on the shortcut menu.

The form for the Marina table displays (Figure 3-4).

④ Click the New Record navigation button at the bottom of the Form view window.

The contents of the form are erased in preparation for a new record.

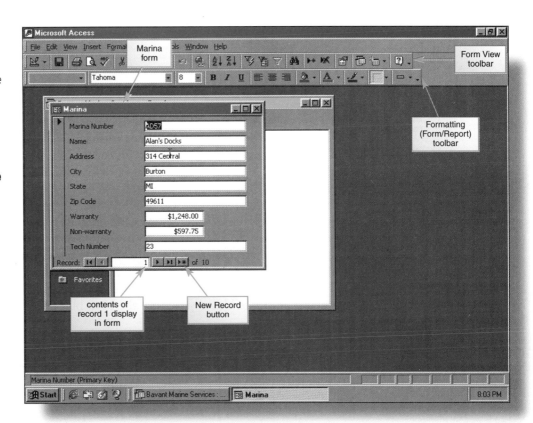

FIGURE 3-4

Using Figure 3-5, type the data for the new record. Press the TAB key after typing the data in each field, except after typing the final field (Tech Number).

The record displays.

 Press the TAB key.

The record now is added to the Marina table and the contents of the form erased.

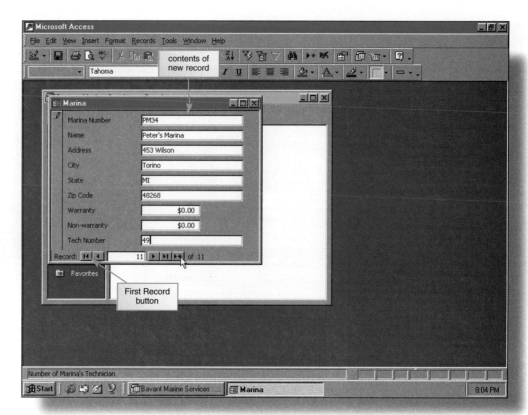

FIGURE 3-5

Other Ways

1. Click New Record button on the Form View toolbar
2. On Insert menu click New Record

Maintaining a Database: Recovery

If a problem occurs that damages either the data in the database or the structure of the database, the database is recovered by copying the backup copy over it. To do so, use the copy features of Windows to copy the backup version (for example, Bavant Marine Backup) over the actual database (for example, Bavant Marine Services). This will return the database to the state it was in when the backup was made.

Searching for a Record

In the database environment, **searching** means looking for records that satisfy some criteria. Looking for the marina whose number is FM22 is an example of searching. The queries in Project 2 also were examples of searching. Access had to locate those records that satisfied the criteria.

A need for searching also exists when using Form view or Datasheet view. To update marina FM22, for example, first you need to find the marina. In a small table, repeatedly pressing the Next Record button until marina FM22 is on the screen may not be particularly difficult. In a large table with many records, however, this would be extremely cumbersome. You need a way to be able to go directly to a record just by giving the value in some field. This is the function of the **Find button** on the Form View toolbar. Before clicking the Find button, select the field for the search.

Perform the following steps to move to the first record in the file, select the Marina Number field, and then use the Find button to search for the marina whose number is FM22.

To Search for a Record

1 **Make sure the form for the Marina table displays. Click the First Record navigation button at the lower-left corner of the Form view window (see Figure 3-5 on page A 3.8) to display the first record. If the Marina Number field currently is not selected, select it by clicking the field name. Point to the Find button on the Form View toolbar.**

The first record displays in the form (Figure 3-6).

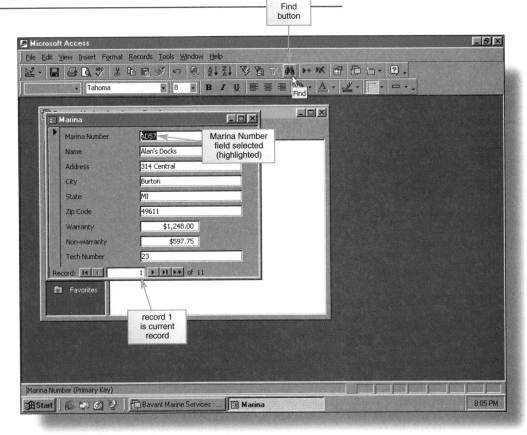

FIGURE 3-6

2 **Click the Find button on the toolbar. Type FM22 in the Find What text box in the Find and Replace dialog box.**

The Find and Replace dialog box displays (Figure 3-7). The Find What text box contains the entry, FM22.

3 **Click the Find Next button and then click the Close button.**

Access locates the record for marina FM22.

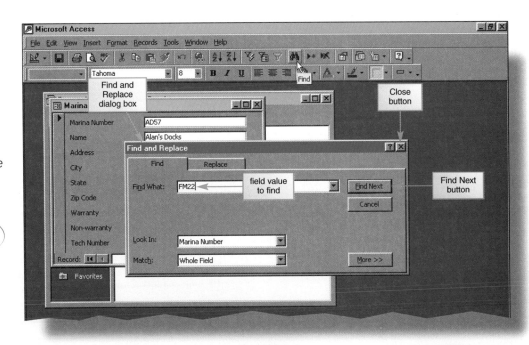

FIGURE 3-7

Why the word "Next"?

Other Ways

1. On Edit menu click Find
2. Press CTRL+F

In some cases, after locating a record that satisfies a criterion, you might need to find the next record that satisfies the same criterion. For example, if you have just found the first marina whose technician number is 23, you then may want to find the second such marina, then the third, and so on. To do so, repeat the same process. You will not need to retype the value, however.

Changing the Contents of a Record

After locating the record to be changed, select the field to be changed by clicking the field. You also can repeatedly press the TAB key. Then make the appropriate changes. (Clicking the field automatically produces an insertion point. If you use the TAB key, you will need to press F2 to produce an insertion point.)

Normally, Access is in **Insert mode**, so the characters typed will be inserted at the appropriate position. To change to **Overtype mode**, press the INSERT key. The letters, OVR, will display near the bottom right edge of the status bar. To return to Insert mode, press the INSERT key. In Insert mode, if the data in the field completely fills the field, no additional characters can be inserted. In this case, you would need to increase the size of the field before inserting the characters. You will see how to do this later in the project.

Perform the following steps to use Form view to change the name of marina FM22 to Fedder's Marina by inserting an apostrophe (') and the letter, s, after Fedder. Sufficient room exists in the field to make this change.

More About

Changing the Contents of a Record

To change data within a field, click within the field to display the insertion point. To replace the entire value, move the pointer to the leftmost part of the field until it changes into the plus pointer and then click. Type the new entry to replace the previous entry.

Steps **To Update the Contents of a Field**

1 **Position the mouse pointer in the Name field text box for marina FM22 after the word, Fedder.**

The mouse pointer shape is an I-beam (Figure 3-8).

2 **Click to produce an insertion point and then type 's to correct the name.**

The name is now Fedder's Marina.

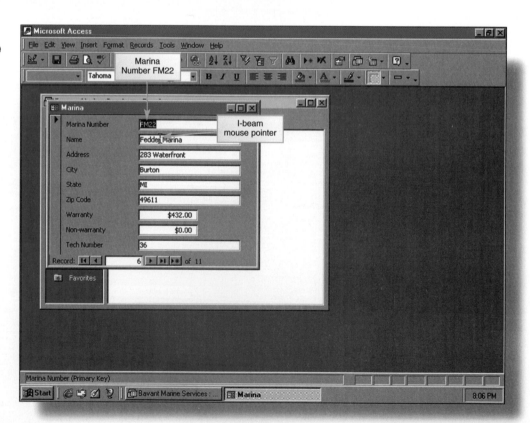

FIGURE 3-8

Switching Between Views

Sometimes, after working in Form view where you can see all fields, but only one record, it would be helpful to see several records at a time. To do so, switch to Datasheet view by clicking the View button arrow on the Form View toolbar and then clicking Datasheet View. Perform the following steps to switch from Form view to Datasheet view.

More About

The View Button

You can use the View button to easily transfer between viewing the form (Form view) and reviewing the design of the form (Design view). To move to Datasheet view, you must click the down arrow, and then click Datasheet view in the drop-down list that displays.

Steps | **To Switch from Form View to Datasheet View**

1 **Point to the View button arrow on the Form View toolbar toolbar (Figure 3-9).**

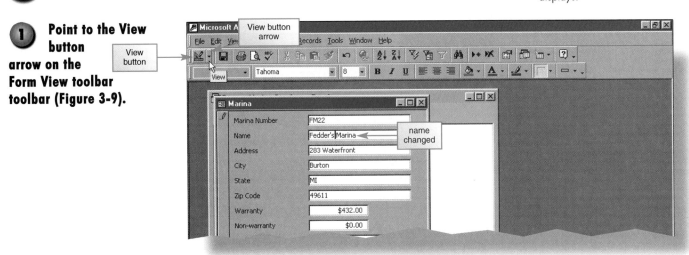

FIGURE 3-9

2 **Click the View button arrow on the toolbar. Point to Datasheet View in the list.**

The View list displays (Figure 3-10).

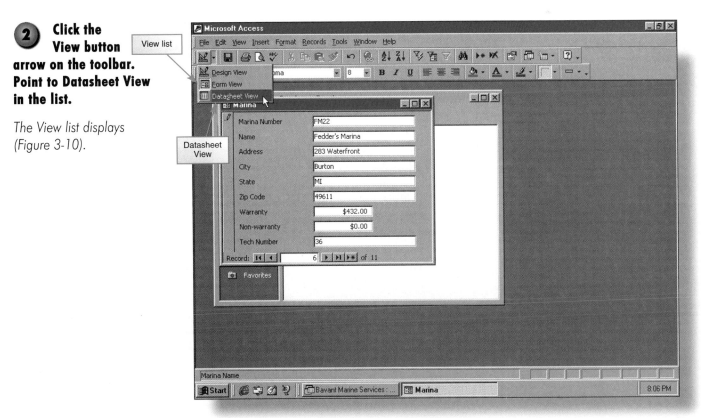

FIGURE 3-10

3 **Click Datasheet View, and then maximize the window containing the datasheet.**

The datasheet displays (Figure 3-11). The position in the table is maintained. The current record selector points to marina FM22, which is the marina that displayed on the screen in Form view. The Name field, the field in which the insertion point is displayed, is selected. The new record for marina PM34 is the last record in the table. When you close the table and open it later, marina PM34 will be in its appropriate location.

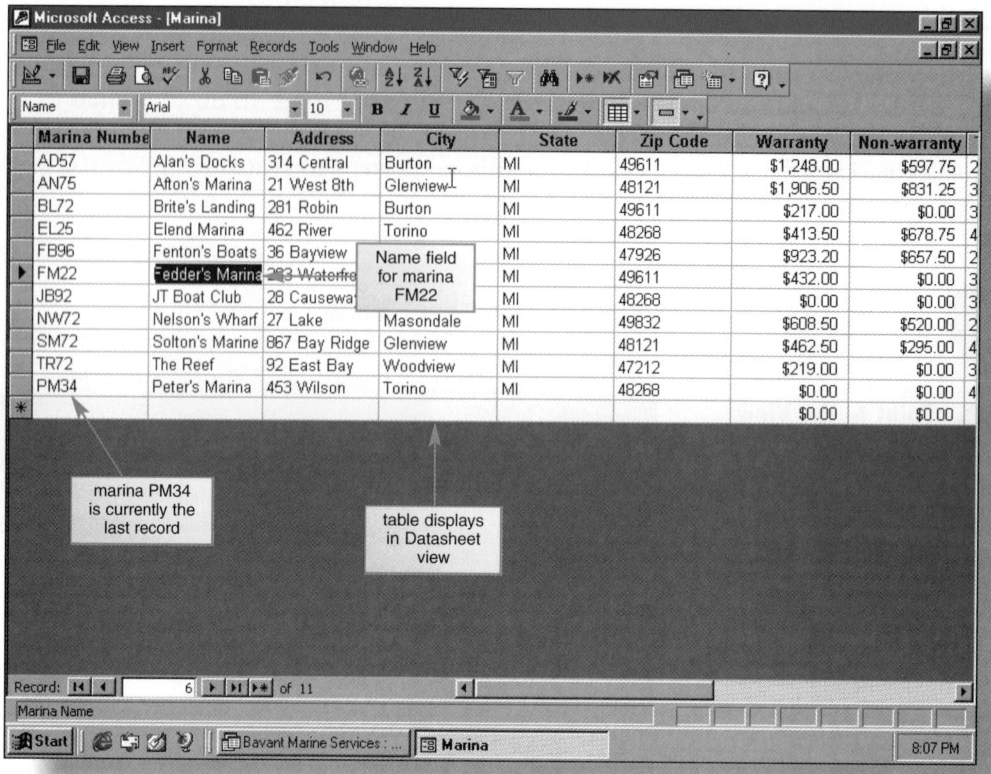

FIGURE 3-11

More About

Filters: Filter by Form

If you want to filter records based on values in more than one field, click the Filter by Form button rather than the Filter by Selection button. You will then be able to fill in values in as many fields as you want. Once you are finished, click the Apply Filter button. Only those records containing all the values you entered will display. For more information, visit the Access 2000 Project 3 More About page (www.scsite.com/ac2000/more.htm) and click Filters.

If you wanted to return to Form view, you would use the same process. The only difference is that you would click Form View instead of Datasheet View.

Filtering Records

You can use the Find button to locate a record quickly that satisfies a criterion (for example, the Marina Number is FM22). All records display, however, not just the record or records that satisfy the criterion. To have only the record or records that satisfy the criterion display, use a filter. The simplest type of filter is called **filter by selection**. To use filter by selection, give Access an example of the data you want by selecting the data within the table and then clicking the Filter By Selection button on the Form View toolbar. For example, if only the record or records on which the marina name is Fedder's Marina are to be included, you would select the Name field on the record for marina FM22, because the name on that record is Fedder's Marina. The following steps use filter by selection to display only the record for Fedder's Marina.

Steps To Filter Records

1 Make sure the name for marina FM22 (Fedder's Marina) is selected and then point to the Filter By Selection button on the Form View toolbar (Figure 3-12).

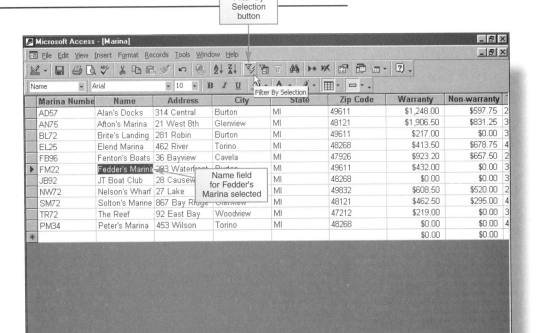

FIGURE 3-12

2 Click the Filter By Selection button on the toolbar.

Only the marina whose name is Fedder's Marina display (Figure 3-13).

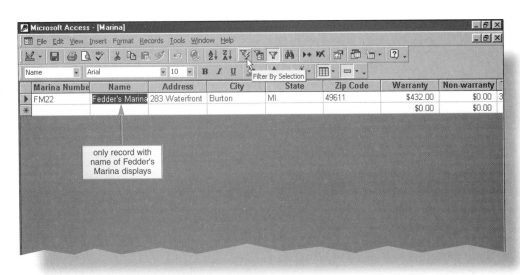

FIGURE 3-13

Because there only is one marina in the database with the name Fedder's Marina, only one marina displays. If you had instead selected the City field on the same record (Burton) before clicking the Filter By Selection button, three marinas would display, because there are currently three marinas located in Burton (marinas AD57, BL72, and FM22).

In order to have all records once again display, remove the filter by clicking the Remove Filter button on the Form View toolbar as in the following steps.

To Remove a Filter

1 Point to the Remove Filter button on the Form View toolbar (Figure 3-14).

The Remove Filter button is recessed because there currently is a filter applied to the table.

2 Click the Remove Filter button on the toolbar.

All records once again will display.

1. On Records menu click Filter, then click Filter By Selection

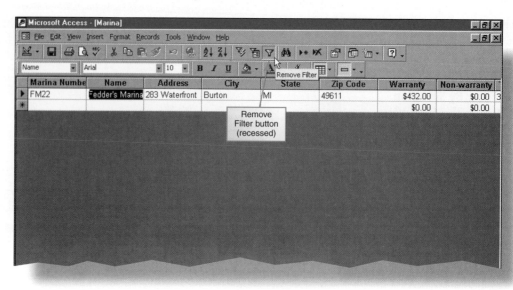

FIGURE 3-14

Deleting Records

When records are no longer needed, **delete the records** (remove them) from the table. If, for example, marina JB92 is no longer in business and already has settled its final bill, that marina's record should be deleted. To delete a record, first locate it and then press the DELETE key. Complete the following steps to delete marina JB92.

To Delete a Record

1 With the datasheet for the Marina table open, position the mouse pointer on the record selector of the record in which the marina number is JB92 (Figure 3-15).

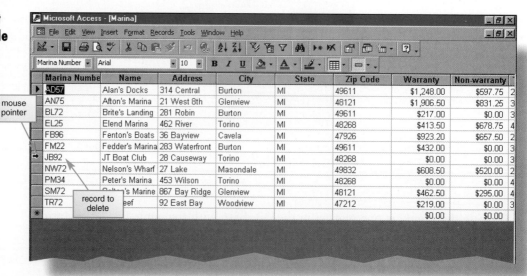

FIGURE 3-15

2 **Click the record selector to select the record, and then press the DELETE key to delete the record.**

The Microsoft Access dialog box displays (Figure 3-16). The message indicates that one record will be deleted.

3 **Click the Yes button to complete the deletion. Close the window containing the table by clicking its Close button on the title bar.**

The record is deleted and the Marina table window closes.

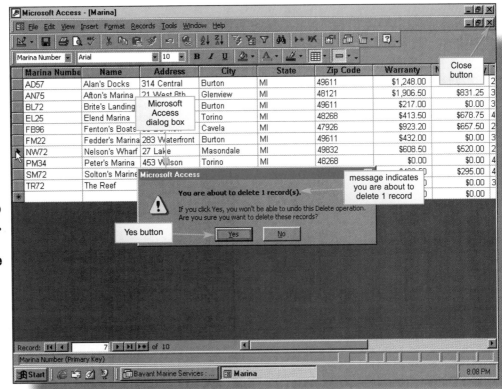

FIGURE 3-16

Changing the Structure of a Database

When you initially create a database, you define its **structure**; that is, you indicate the names, types, and sizes of all the fields. In many cases, the structure you first defined will not continue to be appropriate as you use the database. A variety of reasons exist why the structure of a table might need to change. Changes in the needs of users of the database may require additional fields to be added. In the Marina table, for example, if it is important to store a code indicating the marina type, you need to add such a field.

Characteristics of a given field may need to change. For example, the marina Alan's Docks's name is stored incorrectly in the database. It actually should be Alan s Docks Boat Works. The Name field is not large enough, however, to hold the correct name. To accommodate this change, you need to increase the width of the Name field.

It may be that a field currently in the table no longer is necessary. If no one ever uses a particular field, it is not needed in the table. Because it is occupying space and serving no useful purpose, it should be removed from the table. You also would need to delete the field from any forms, reports, or queries that include it.

To make any of these changes, click Design View on the shortcut menu.

Changing the Size of a Field

The steps on the next page change the size of the Name field from 20 to 25 to accommodate the change of name from Alan's Docks to Alan's Docks Boat Works.

More About

Changing the Structure

A major advantage of using a full-featured database management system is the ease with which you can change the structure of the tables that make up the database. In a non-database environment, changes to the structure can be very cumbersome, requiring difficult and time-consuming changes to many programs.

Steps: To Change the Size of a Field

1 With the Database window open, click Tables on the Objects bar, and then right-click Marina.

The shortcut menu displays (Figure 3-17).

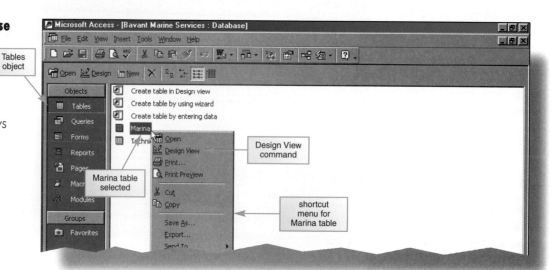

FIGURE 3-17

2 Click Design View on the shortcut menu and then point to the row selector for the Name field.

The Marina : Table window displays (Figure 3-18).

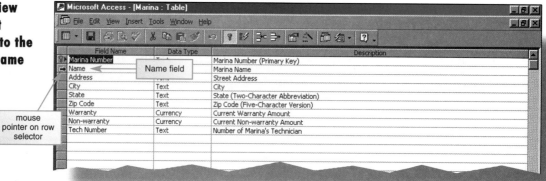

FIGURE 3-18

3 Click the row selector for the Name field.

The Name field is selected (Figure 3-19).

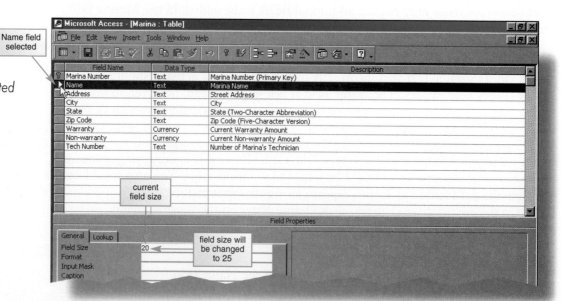

FIGURE 3-19

4 Press F6 to select the field size, type 25 as the new size, and press F6 again.

The size is changed (Figure 3-20).

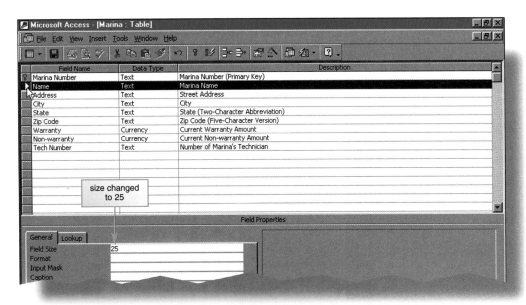

FIGURE 3-20

Adding a New Field

The management of Bavant decided they needed to categorize the marinas by the type of storage they offer. (Some marinas only support storing boats in the water. Others offer only rack storage where each boat is stored in a rack. When the owner wishes to use it, the marina places the boat in the water. As soon as the owner is done, the marina places the boat back on the rack. Still others offer both in-water and rack storage.)

To be able to store the marina type, the following steps add a new field, called Marina Type, to the table. The possible entries in this field are BIR (both in-water and rack storage), IWO (in-water only), and RSO (rack storage only). The new field will follow the zip code in the list of fields; that is, it will be the seventh field in the restructured table. The current seventh field (Warranty) will become the eighth field, Non-warranty will become the ninth field, and so on. Complete the following steps to add the field.

More About

Adding a New Field

Tables frequently need to be expanded to include additional fields for a variety of reason. Users needs can change. The field may have been omitted by mistake when the table was first created. Government regulations may change in such a way that the organization needs to maintain additional information.

 ## To Add a Field to a Table

1 Point to the row selector for the Warranty field (Figure 3-21).

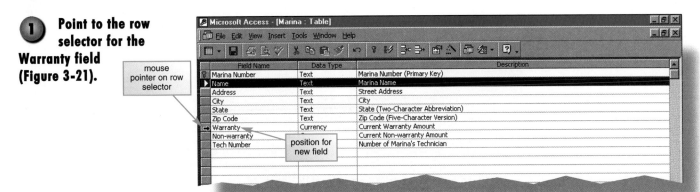

FIGURE 3-21

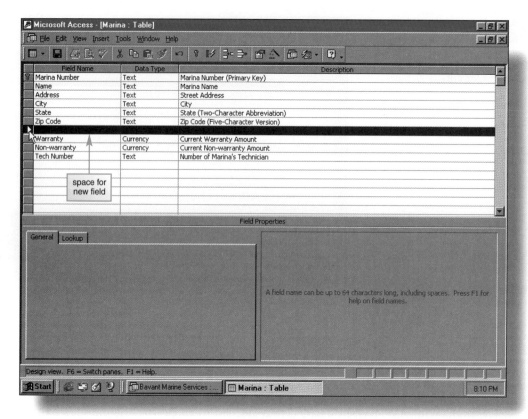

2 Click the row selector for the Warranty field and then press the INSERT key to insert a blank row.

A blank row displays in the position for the new field (Figure 3-22).

FIGURE 3-22

3 Click the Field Name column for the new field. Type Marina Type as the field name and then press the TAB key. Select the Text data type by pressing the TAB key. Type Marina Type (BIR, IWO, or RSO) as the description. Press F6 to move to the Field Size text box, type 3 (the size of the Marina Type field), and then press F6 again.

The entries for the new field are complete (Figure 3-23).

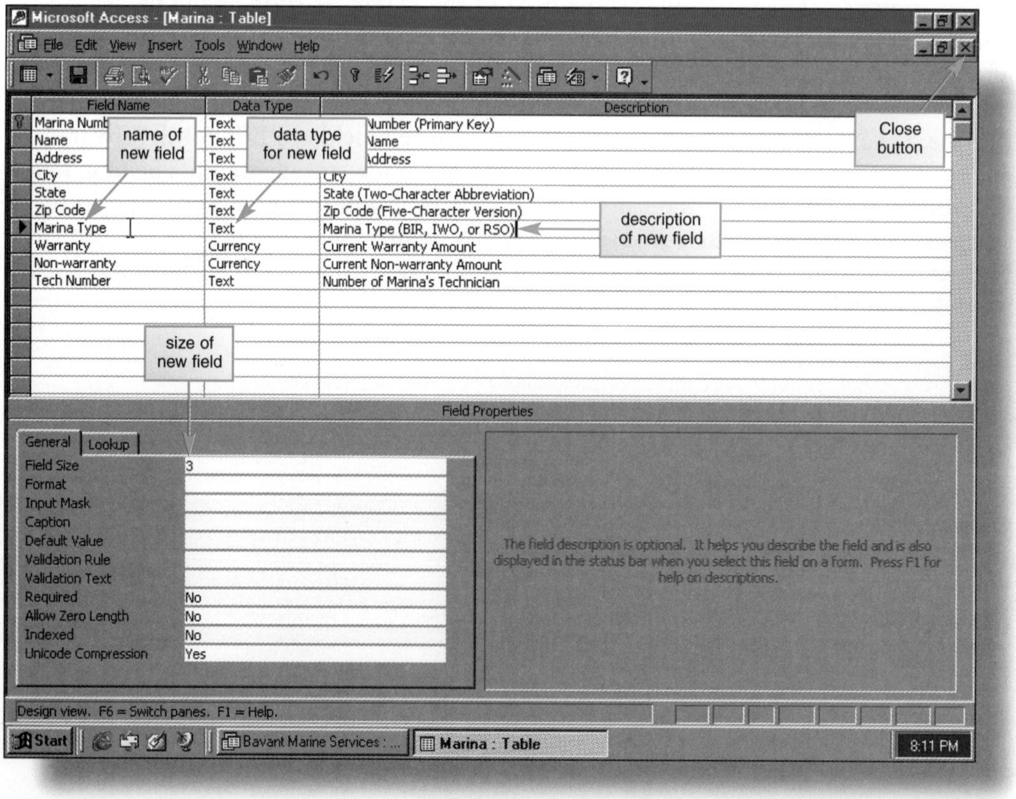

FIGURE 3-23

4 **Close the Marina : Table window by clicking its Close button on the title bar.**

The Microsoft Access dialog box displays (Figure 3-24) asking whether or not to save changes to the table s design.

5 **Click the Yes button to save the changes.**

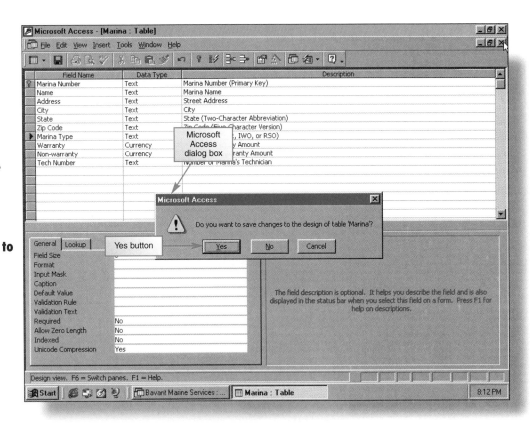

FIGURE 3-24

Deleting a Field from a Table

It is possible to find that a field in one of your tables is no longer needed. It may no longer serve a useful purpose or it may have been included by mistake. In such a case, you should delete the field. To do so, you first would open the table in Design view and then click the row selector for the field to select it. You then would press the DELETE key to delete the field. Access would request confirmation that you do indeed wish to delete the field. If you click the Yes button and then save your changes, the field will be removed from the table.

Updating the Restructured Database

Changes to the structure are available immediately. The Name field is longer, although it does not display that way on the screen, and the new Marina Type field is included.

To make a change to a single field, such as changing the name from Alan's Docks to Alan's Docks Boat Works, click the field to be changed, and then type the new value. If the record to be changed is not on the screen, use the Next Record or Previous Record navigation button to move to it. If the field to be corrected simply is not visible on the screen, use the horizontal scroll bar along the bottom of the screen to shift all the fields until the correct one displays. Then make the change.

Perform the steps on the next page to change the name of Alan's Docks to Alan's Docks Boat Works.

To Update the Contents of a Field

1 With the Bavant Marine Services : Database window open, right-click Marina. Click Open on the shortcut menu. Position the I-beam mouse pointer to the right of the second s in Alan's Docks (marina AD57).

The datasheet displays (Figure 3-25).

2 Click immediately to the right of the second s in Alan's Docks, press the spacebar, and then type Boat Works to change the name.

The name is changed from Alan's Docks to Alan's Docks Boat Works.

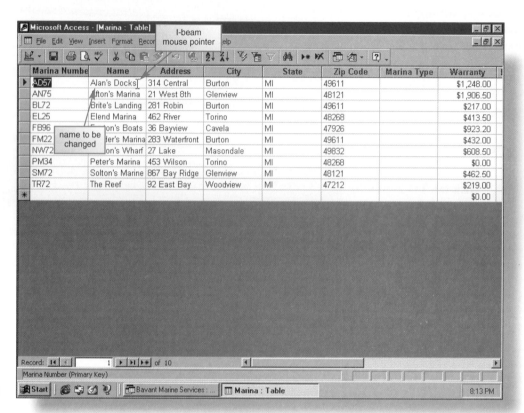

FIGURE 3-25

Resizing Columns

When you change the size of a field, the forms you previously created will not reflect your changes. If you used the AutoForm command, you can change the field sizes by simply recreating the form. To do so, right-click the form, click Delete, and create the form as you did in Project 1.

Resizing Columns

The default column sizes provided by Access do not always allow all the data in the field to display. You can correct this problem by **resizing the column** (changing its size) in the datasheet. In some instances, you actually may want to reduce the size of a column. The City field, for example, is short enough that it does not require all the space on the screen that is allotted to it.

Both types of changes are made the same way. Position the mouse pointer on the right boundary of the column's **field selector** (the line in the column heading immediately to the right of the name of the column to be resized). The mouse pointer will change to a two-headed arrow with a vertical bar. You then can drag the line to resize the column. In addition, you can double-click in the line, in which case Access will determine the best size for the column.

The following steps illustrate the process for resizing the Name column to the size that best fits the data.

Steps **To Resize a Column**

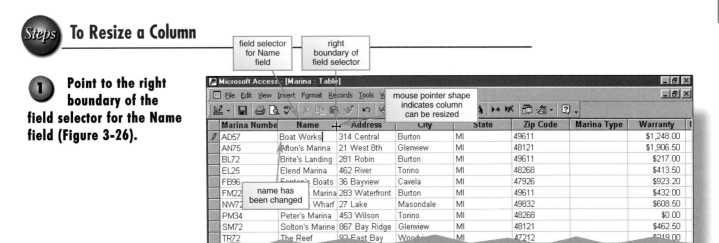

1 Point to the right boundary of the field selector for the Name field (Figure 3-26).

FIGURE 3-26

2 Double-click the right boundary of the field selector for the Name field.

The Name column has been resized (Figure 3-27).

FIGURE 3-27

3 Use the same technique to resize the Address, City, State, Zip Code, and Warranty field columns to best fit the data.

The columns have been resized (Figure 3-28).

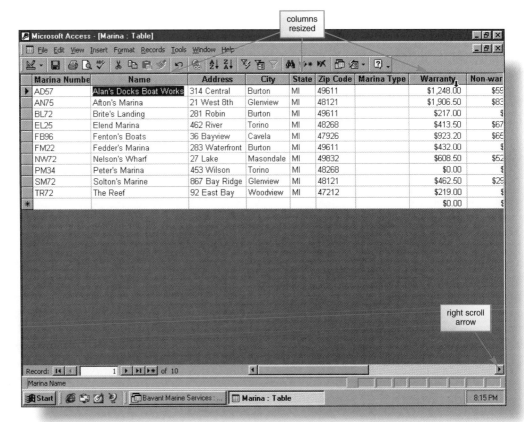

FIGURE 3-28

4 Click the right scroll arrow to display the Non-warranty and Tech Number field columns, and then resize the Non-warranty and Tech Number field columns to best fit the data.

All the columns have been resized (Figure 3-29).

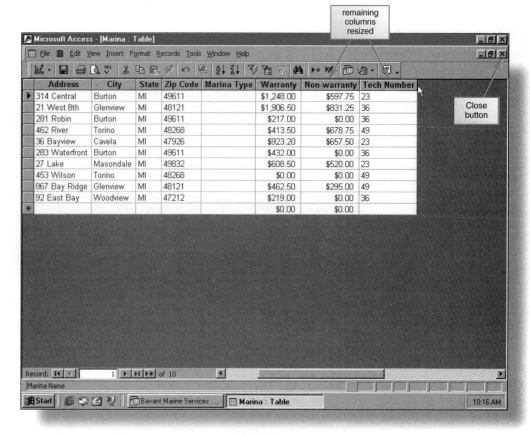

FIGURE 3-29

5 Close the Marina : Table window by clicking its Close button on the title bar.

The Microsoft Access dialog box displays (Figure 3-30) asking whether or not to save changes to the table's layout.

6 Click the Yes button.

The changes are saved. The next time the datasheet displays, the columns will have the new widths.

Other Ways

1. On Format menu click Column Width

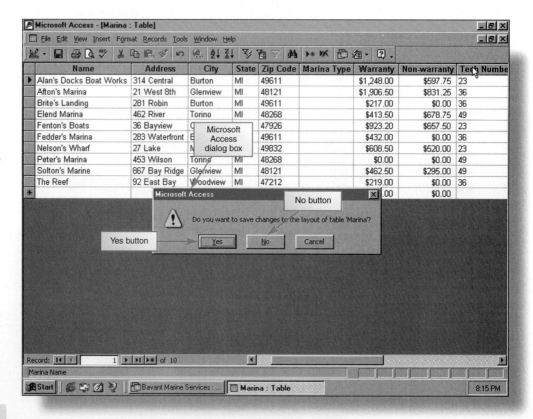

FIGURE 3-30

Using an Update Query

The Marina Type field is blank on every record. One approach to entering the information for the field would be to step through the entire table, assigning each record its appropriate value. If most of the marinas have the same type, a simpler approach is available.

At Bavant, for example, most marinas are type BIR. Initially, you can set all the values to BIR. To accomplish this quickly and easily, you use a special type of query called an **update query**. Later, you can change the type for those marinas that only offer in-water storage (IWO) or only offer rack storage (RSO).

The process for creating an update query begins the same as the process for creating the queries in Project 2. After selecting the table for the query, right-click any open area of the upper pane, click Query Type on the shortcut menu, and then click Update Query on the menu of available query types. An extra row, Update To:, displays in the design grid. Use this additional row to indicate the way the data will be updated. If a criterion is entered, then only those records that satisfy the criterion will be updated.

Perform the following steps to change the value in the Marina Type field to BIR for all the records. Because all records are to be updated, no criterion will be entered.

Update Queries

Any full-featured database management system will offer some mechanism for updating multiple records at a time, that is, for making the same change to all the records that satisfy some criterion. Some systems, including Access, accomplish this through the query tool by providing a special type of query for this purpose.

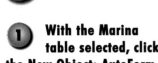 **To Use an Update Query to Update All Records**

1 **With the Marina table selected, click the New Object: AutoForm button arrow on the Database window toolbar.**

The New Object: AutoForm list displays (Figure 3-31).

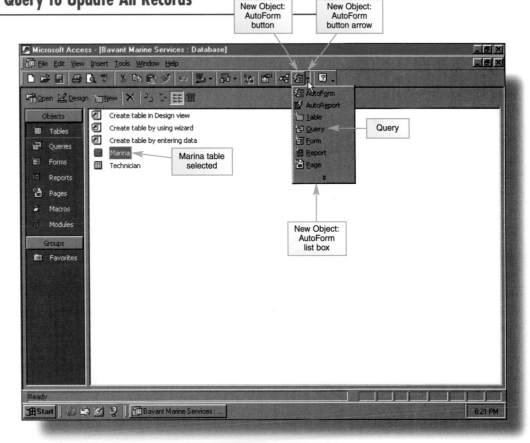

FIGURE 3-31

2 **Click Query in the list.**

The New Query dialog box displays (Figure 3-32). Design View is selected.

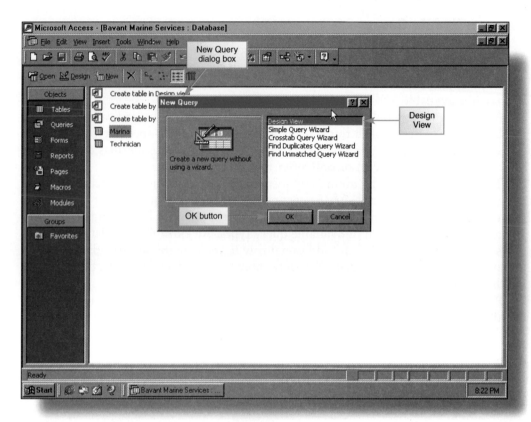

FIGURE 3-32

3 **Click the OK button, and then be sure the Query1 : Select Query window is maximized. Resize the upper and lower panes of the window as well as the Marina field list box so all fields in the Marina table field list display (see page A 2.9 in Project 2). Right-click the upper pane and point to Query Type on the shortcut menu.**

The shortcut menu displays (Figure 3-33). The Query Type submenu displays, showing available query types.

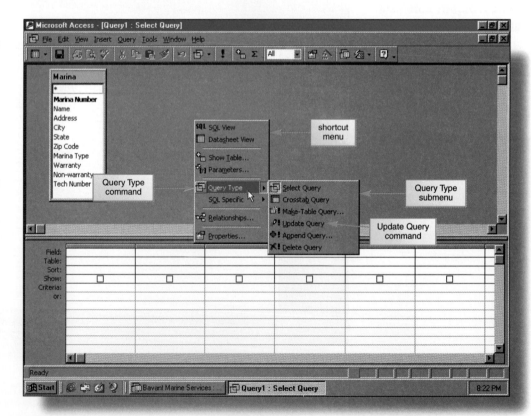

FIGURE 3-33

4 Click Update Query on the submenu, double-click the Marina Type field in the Marina table field list to select the field, click the Update To text box in the first column of the design grid, and then type BIR as the new value.

The Marina Type field is selected (Figure 3-34). In an Update Query, the Update To row displays in the design grid. The value to which the field is to be changed is entered as BIR. Because no criteria are entered, the Marina Type value on every row will be changed to BIR.

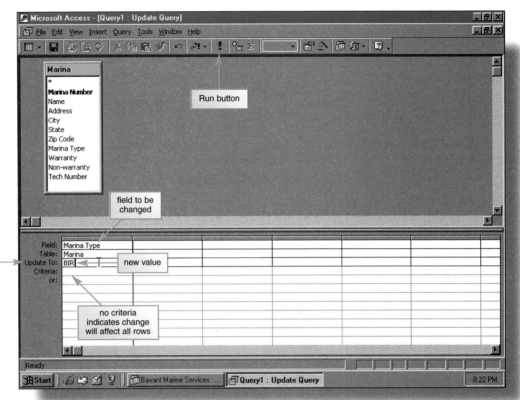

FIGURE 3-34

5 Click the Run button on the Query Design toolbar.

The Microsoft Access dialog box displays (Figure 3-35). The message indicates that 10 rows will be updated by the query.

6 Click the Yes button.

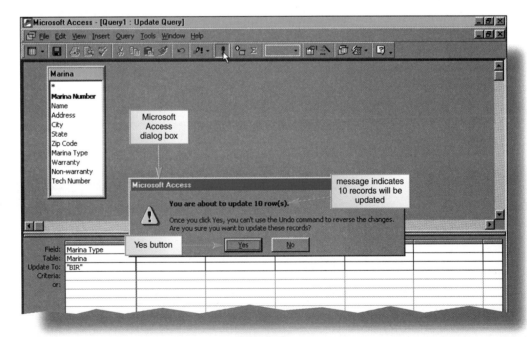

FIGURE 3-35

1. Click Query Type button arrow on Query Design toolbar, click Update Query
2. On Query menu click Update Query

Delete Queries

Any full-featured database management system will offer some means of deleting multiple records at one time, that is, deleting all the records that satisfy a given criterion. Access accomplishes this by providing a special type of query for this purpose.

Using a Delete Query to Delete a Group of Records

In some cases, you may need to delete several records at a time. If, for example, all marinas in a particular zip code are to be serviced by another firm, the marinas with this zip code can be deleted from the Bavant Marine Services database. Instead of deleting these marinas individually, which could be very cumbersome, you can delete them in one operation by using a **delete query**, which is a query that will delete all the records satisfying the criteria entered in the query.

Perform the following steps to use a delete query to delete all marinas whose zip code is 48121.

 To Use a Delete Query to Delete a Group of Records

1 **Click Edit on the menu bar and then click Clear Grid to clear the grid. Right-click the upper pane and then point to Query Type on the shortcut menu.**

The shortcut menu displays (Figure 3-36). The Query Type submenu displays the available query types.

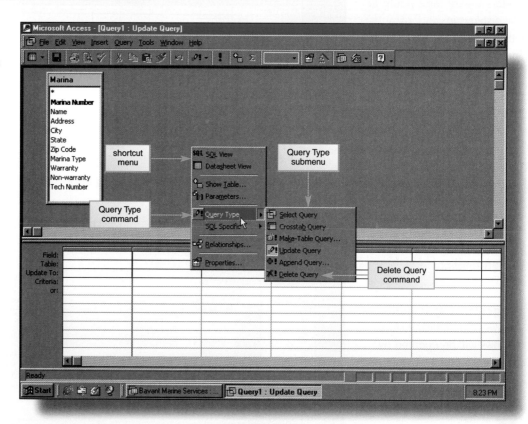

FIGURE 3-36

2 Click Delete Query on the submenu, double-click the Zip Code field in the Marina table field list to select the field, and then click the Criteria entry. Type 48121 as the criterion.

The criterion is entered in the Zip Code field (Figure 3-37). In a Delete Query, the Delete row displays in the design grid.

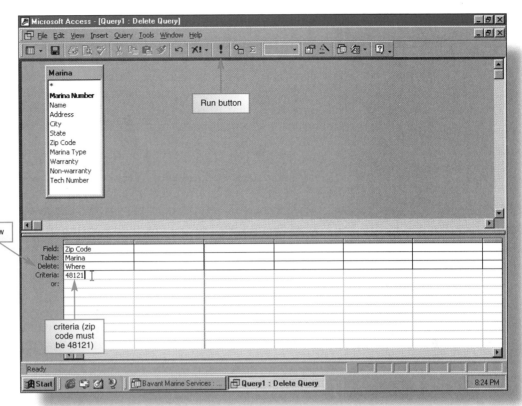

FIGURE 3-37

3 Click the Run button on the Query Design toolbar to run the query.

The Microsoft Access dialog box displays (Figure 3-38). The message indicates the query will delete 2 rows (records).

4 Click the Yes button. Close the Query window by clicking its Close button on the title bar. Do not save the query.

The two marinas with zip code 48121 have been removed from the table.

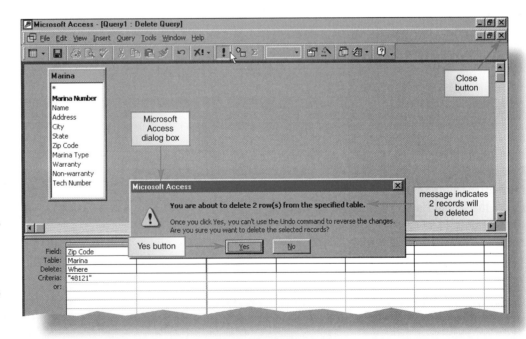

FIGURE 3-38

Other Ways

1. Click Query Type button arrow on Query Design toolbar, click Delete Query
2. On Query menu click Delete Query

Creating Validation Rules

You now have created, loaded, queried, and updated a database. Nothing you have done so far, however, ensures that users enter only valid data. To do so, you create **validation rules**; that is, rules that the data entered by a user must follow. As you will see, Access will prevent users from entering data that does not follow the rules. The steps also specify **validation text**, which is the message that will be displayed if a user violates the validation rule.

Validation rules can indicate a **required field**, which is a field in which the user actually must enter data. For example, by making the Name field a required field, a user actually must enter a name (that is, the field cannot be blank). Validation rules can make sure a user's entry lies within a certain **range of values**; for example, that the values in the Warranty field are between $0.00 and $10,000.00. They can specify a **default value**; that is, a value that Access will display on the screen in a particular field before the user begins adding a record. To make data entry of marina numbers more convenient, you also can have lowercase letters displayed automatically as uppercase letters. Finally, validation rules can specify a collection of acceptable values; for example, that the only legitimate entries for the Marina Type field are BIR, IWO, and RSO.

Specifying a Required Field

To specify that a field is to be required, change the value in the Required text box from No to Yes. The following steps specify that the Name field is to be a required field.

To Specify a Required Field

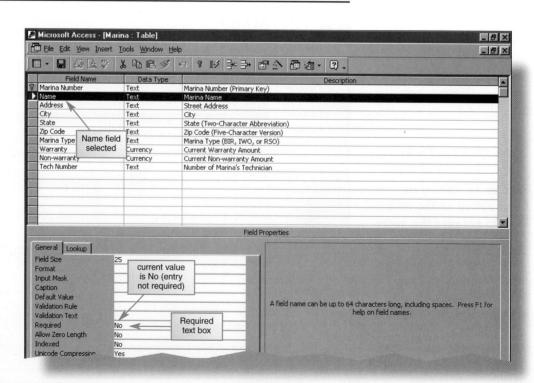

1 **With the Database window open and the Tables object selected, right-click Marina. Click Design View on the shortcut menu, and then select the Name field by clicking its row selector. Point to the Required text box.**

The Marina : Table window displays (Figure 3-39). The Name field is selected.

FIGURE 3-39

2   **Click the Required text box in the Field Properties pane, and then click the down arrow that displays. Click Yes in the list.**

The value in the Required text box changes to Yes (Figure 3-40). It now is required that the user enters data into the Name field when adding a record.

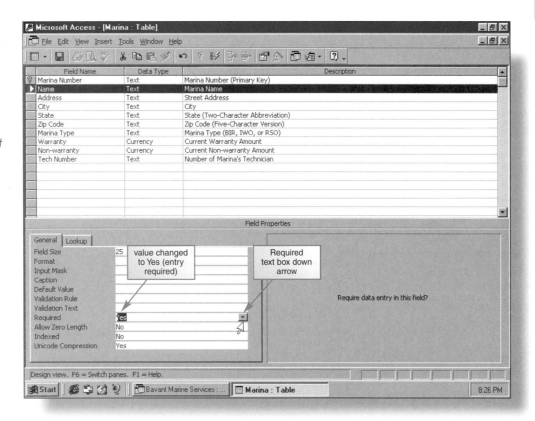

FIGURE 3-40

Specifying a Range

The following step specifies that entries in the Warranty field must be between $0.00 and $10,000.00. To indicate this range, you will enter a condition that specifies that the warranty amount must be both >= 0 (greater than or equal to zero) and <= 10000 (less than or equal to 10000).

To Specify a Range

1 **Select the Warranty field by clicking its row selector. Click the Validation Rule text box in the Field Properties pane to produce an insertion point, and then type** >=0 and <=10000 **as the rule. Click the Validation Text text box in the Field Properties pane to produce an insertion point, and then type** Must be between $0.00 and $10,000.00 **as the text. You must type all the text, including the dollar signs in this text box.**

The validation rule and text are entered (Figure 3-41). In the Validation Rule text box, Access automatically changed the lowercase letter, a, to uppercase in the word, and.

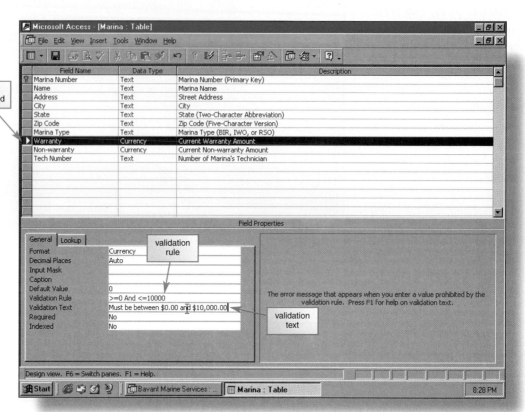

FIGURE 3-41

Users now will be prohibited from entering a warranty amount that either is less than $0.00 or greater than $10,000.00 when they add records or change the value in the Warranty field.

Specifying a Default Value

To specify a default value, enter the value in the Default Value text box in the Field Properties pane. The following step specifies BIR as the default value for the Marina Type field. This simply means that if users do not enter a marina type, the type will be BIR.

To Specify a Default Value

1 **Select the Marina Type field by clicking its row selector. Click the Default Value text box in the Field Properties pane and then type** =BIR **as the value.**

The Marina Type field is selected. The default value is entered in the Default Value text box (Figure 3-42).

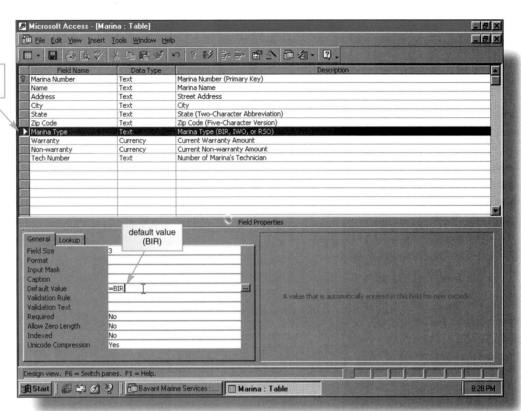

FIGURE 3-42

From this point on, if users do not make an entry in the Marina Type field when adding records, Access will set the value to BIR.

Specifying a Collection of Legal Values

The only **legal values** for the Marina Type field are BIR, IWO, and RSO. An appropriate validation rule for this field can direct Access to reject any entry other than these three possibilities. Perform the step on the next page to specify the legal values for the Marina Type field.

To Specify a Collection of Legal Values

1 **Make sure the Marina Type field is selected. Click the Validation Rule text box in the Field Properties pane and then type** =BIR or =IWO or =RSO **as the validation rule. Click the Validation Text text box in the Field Properties pane and then type** Must be BIR, IWO, or RSO **as the validation text.**

The Marina Type field is selected. The validation rule and text have been entered (Figure 3-43). In the Validation Rule text box, Access automatically inserted quotation marks around the BIR, IWO, and RSO values and changed the lowercase letter, o, to uppercase in the word, or.

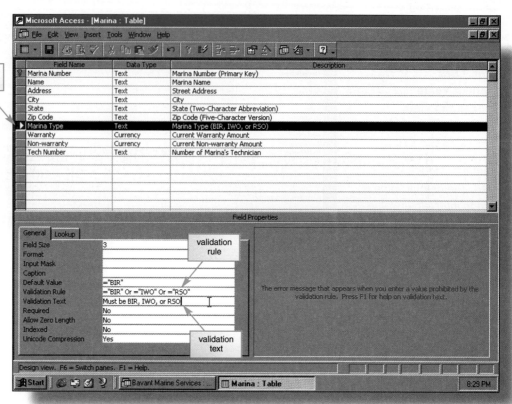

FIGURE 3-43

Users now will be allowed to enter only BIR, IWO, or RSO in the Marina Type field when they add records or make changes to this field.

Using a Format

To affect the way data is displayed in a field, you can use a **format**. To use a format, you enter a special symbol, called a **format symbol**, in the field's Format text box in the Field Properties pane. The following step specifies a format for the Marina Number field in the Marina table. The format symbol used in the example is >, which causes Access to display lowercase letters automatically as uppercase. The format symbol < would cause Access to display uppercase letters automatically as lowercase.

To Specify a Format

1 **Select the Marina Number field by clicking its row selector. Click the Format text box in the Field Properties pane and then type > (Figure 3-44).**

all lower case → become uppercase

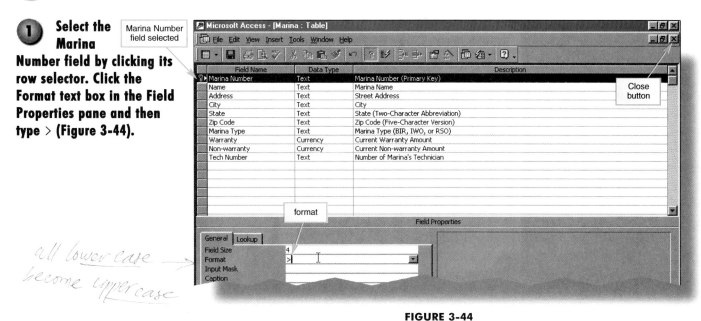

FIGURE 3-44

From this point on, any lowercase letters will be displayed automatically as uppercase when users add records or change the value in the Marina Number field.

Saving Rules, Values, and Formats

To save the validation rules, default values, and formats, perform the following steps.

 To Save the Validation Rules, Default Values, and Formats

1 **Click the Close button on the Marina: Table window title bar to close the window.**

The Microsoft Access dialog box displays, asking if you want to save your changes (Figure 3-45).

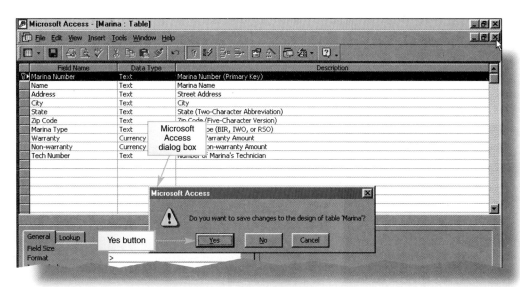

FIGURE 3-45

Click the Yes button to save the changes.

The Microsoft Access dialog box displays (Figure 3-46). This message asks if you want the new rules applied to current records. If this were a database used to run a business or to solve some other critical need, you would click Yes. You would want to be sure that the data already in the database does not violate the rules.

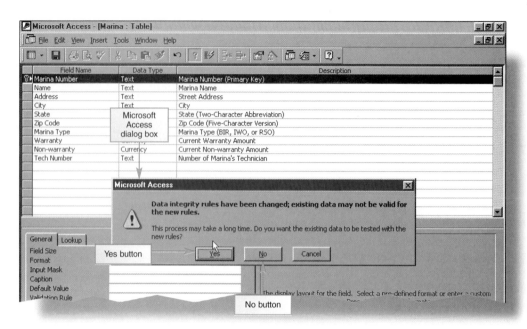

FIGURE 3-46

Click the No button.

The changes are made.

Updating a Table that Contains Validation Rules

When updating a table that contains validation rules, Access provides assistance in making sure the data entered is valid and formatted correctly. Access also will not accept invalid data. Entering a number that is out of the required range, for example, or entering a value that is not one of the possible choices, will produce an error message in the form of a dialog box. The database will not be updated until the error is corrected.

If the marina number entered contains lowercase letters, such as es21 (Figure 3-47), Access will display the data automatically as ES21 (Figure 3-48).

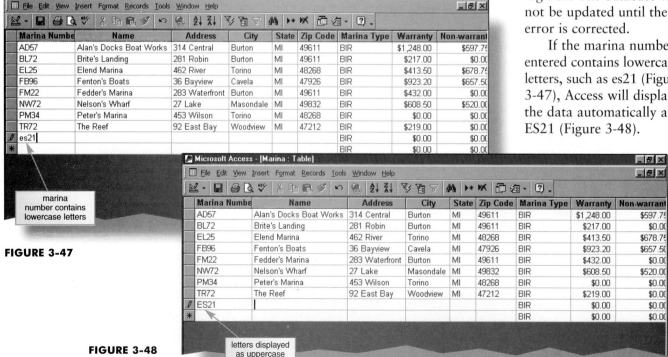

FIGURE 3-47

FIGURE 3-48

Instead of the Marina Type field initially being blank, it now contains the value BIR, because BIR is the default value. Thus, for any marina whose type is BIR, it is not necessary to enter the value. By pressing the TAB key, the value BIR is accepted.

If the marina type is not valid, such as ABX, Access will display the text message you specified (Figure 3-49) and not allow the data to enter the database.

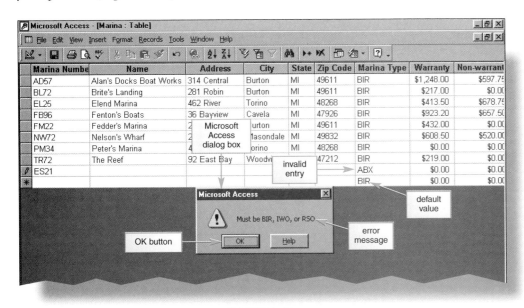

FIGURE 3-49

If the Warranty value is not valid, such as 22500, Access also displays the appropriate message (Figure 3-50) and refuses to accept the data.

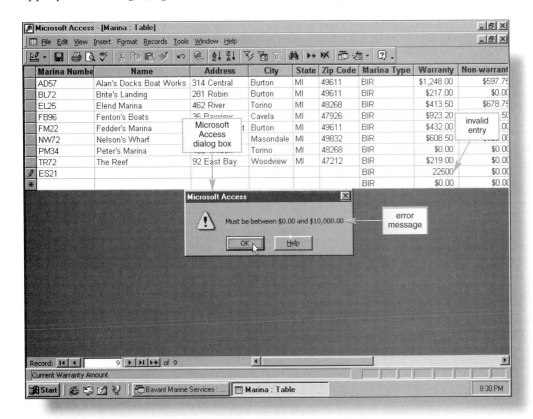

FIGURE 3-50

If a required field contains no data, Access indicates this by displaying an error message as soon as you attempt to leave the record (Figure 3-51). The field must contain a valid entry before Access will move to a different record.

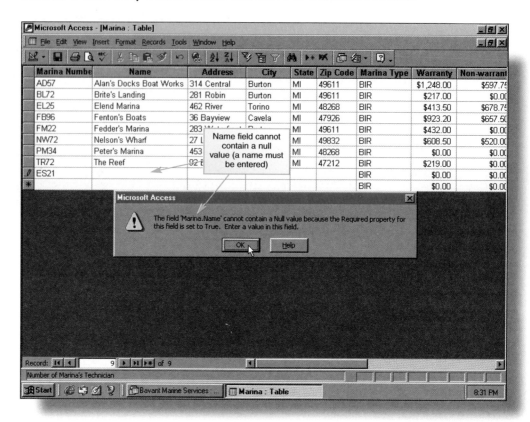

FIGURE 3-51

Take care when creating validation rules as you may come to an impasse where you neither can leave the field nor close the table because you have entered data into a field that violates the validation rule. It may be that you cannot remember the validation rule you created or it was created incorrectly.

First, try to type an acceptable entry. If this does not work, repeatedly press the BACKSPACE key to erase the contents of the field and then try to leave the field. If you are unsuccessful using this procedure, press the ESC key until the record is removed from the screen. The record will not be added to the database.

Should the need arise to take this drastic action, you probably have a faulty validation rule. Use the techniques of the previous sections to correct the existing validation rules for the field.

Making Individual Changes to a Field

Earlier, you changed all the entries in the Marina Type field to BIR. You now have created a rule that will ensure that only legitimate values (BIR, IWO, or RSO) can be entered in the field. To make a change, click the field to be changed to produce an insertion point, use the BACKSPACE or DELETE key to delete the current entry, and then type the new entry.

Complete the following steps to change the Marina Type value on the second and eighth records to IWO and on the fifth record to RSO.

Steps To Make Individual Changes

1 **Make sure the Marina table displays in Datasheet view (Figure 3-52).**

FIGURE 3-52

2 **Click to the right of the BIR entry in the Marina Type field on the second record to produce an insertion point. Press the BACKSPACE key three times to delete BIR and then type** IWO **as the new value. In a similar fashion, change the BIR entry on the fifth record to** RSO **and on the eighth record to** IWO **(Figure 3-53).**

3 **Close the Marina : Table window by clicking its Close button on the title bar.**

The Marina Type field changes now are complete.

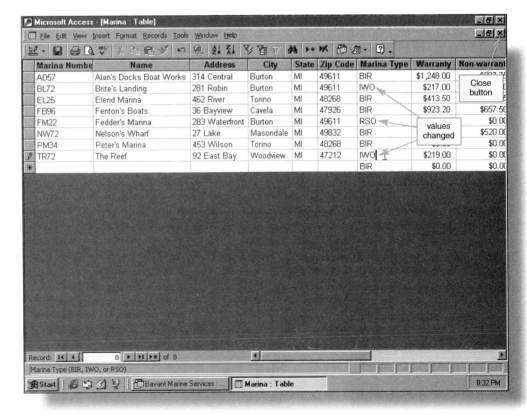

FIGURE 3-53

Referential Integrity

Referential integrity is an essential property for databases, but providing support for it proved to be one of the most difficult tasks facing the developers of relational database management systems. For more information, visit the Access 2000 Project 3 More About page (www.scsite.com/ac2000/more.htm) and click Referential Integrity.

Specifying Referential Integrity

The property that ensures that the value in a foreign key must match that of another table's primary key is called **referential integrity**. A **foreign key** is a field in one table whose values are required to match the *primary key* of another table. In the Marina table, the Tech Number field is a foreign key that must match the primary key of the Technician table; that is, the technician number for any marina must be a technician currently in the Technician table. A marina whose technician number is 02, for example, should not be stored because technician 02 does not exist.

In Access, to specify referential integrity, you must define a relationship between the tables by using the Relationships command. Access then prohibits any updates to the database that would violate the referential integrity. Access will not allow you to store a marina with a technician number that does not match a technician currently in the Technician table. Access also will prevent you from deleting a technician who currently has marinas. Technician 36, for example, currently has several marinas in the Marina table. If you deleted technician 36, these marinas technician numbers would no longer match anyone in the Technician table.

The type of relationship between two tables specified by the Relationships command is referred to as a **one-to-many relationship**. This means that *one* record in the first table is related to (matches) *many* records in the second table, but each record in the second table is related to only *one* record in the first. In the Bavant Marine database, for example, a one-to-many relationship exists between the Technician table and the Marina table. *One* technician is associated with *many* marinas, but each marina is associated with only a single technician. In general, the table containing the foreign key will be the *many* part of the relationship.

The following steps use the Relationships command to specify referential integrity by specifying a relationship between the Technician and Marina tables.

 To Specify Referential Integrity

1 **Close any open datasheet by clicking its Close button on the title bar. Then point to the Relationships button on the Database window toolbar (Figure 3-54).**

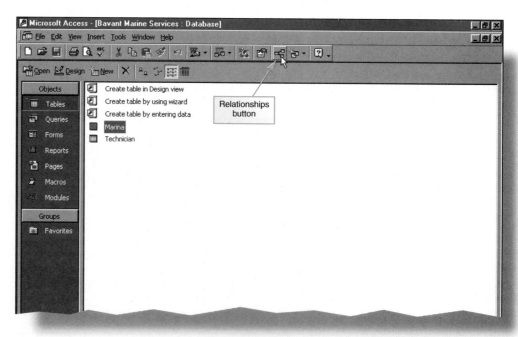

FIGURE 3-54

2 Click the Relationships button on the toolbar.

The Show Table dialog box displays (Figure 3-55).

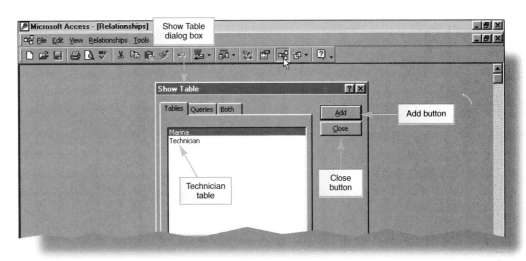

FIGURE 3-55

3 Click the Technician table, click the Add button, click the Marina table, click the Add button again, and then click the Close button. Resize the field list boxes that display so all fields are visible. Point to the Tech Number field in the Technician table field list.

Field list boxes for the Technician and Marina tables display (Figure 3-56). The list boxes have been resized so all fields are visible.

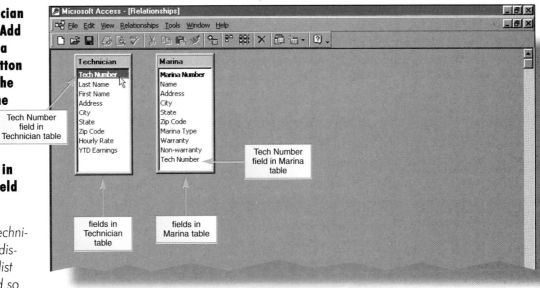

FIGURE 3-56

4 Drag the Tech Number field in the Technician table field list to the Tech Number field in the Marina table field list.

The Edit Relationships dialog box displays (Figure 3-57). The correct fields (the Tech Number fields) have been identified as the matching fields.

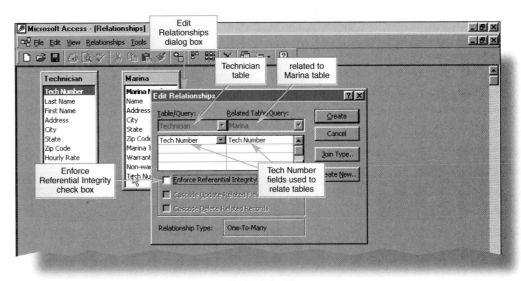

FIGURE 3-57

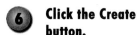

5 **Click Enforce Referential Integrity.**

Enforce Referential Integrity is selected (Figure 3-58). With Enforce Referential Integrity selected, Access will reject any update that would violate referential integrity.

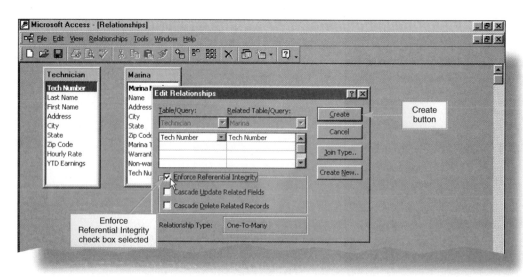

FIGURE 3-58

6 **Click the Create button.**

*Access creates the relationship and displays it visually with the **relationship line** joining the two Tech Number fields (Figure 3-59). The number 1 at the top of the relationship line close to the Tech Number field in the Technician table indicates that the Technician table is the one part of the relationship. The infinity symbol at the other end of the relationship line indicates that the Marina table is the many part of the relationship.*

7 **Close the Relationships window by clicking its Close button on the title bar. Click the Yes button to save your work.**

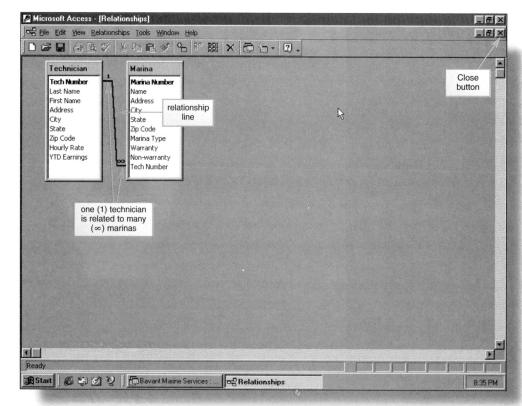

FIGURE 3-59

1. On Tools menu click Relationships

Access now will reject any number in the Tech Number field in the Marina table that does not match a technician number in the Technician table. Trying to add a marina whose Tech Number field does not match would result in the error message shown in Figure 3-60.

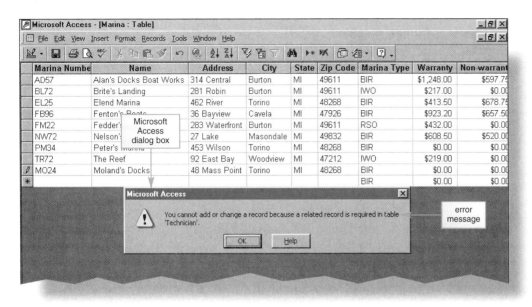

FIGURE 3-60

More About

Relationships: Printing Relationships

You can obtain a printed copy of your relationships within a database once you have created them. To do so, first click the Relationships button to display the relationships. Next, click File on the menu bar and then click Print Relationships. When the Print Preview window displays, click the Print button on the Print Preview toolbar.

A deletion of a technician for whom related marinas exist also would be rejected. Attempting to delete technician 36 from the Technician table, for example, would result in the message shown in Figure 3-61.

FIGURE 3-61

Using Subdatasheets

Now that the Technician table is related to the Marina table, it is possible to view the marinas of a given technician when you are viewing the datasheet for the Technician table. The marinas for the technician will display right under the technician in a **subdatasheet**. The fact that such a subdatasheet is available is indicated by a plus symbol that displays in front of the rows in the Technician table. To display the subdatasheet, click the plus symbol. The steps on the next page display the subdatasheet for technician 36.

Steps: To Use a Subdatasheet

1 With the Database window open and the Tables object selected, right-click Technician. Click Open on the shortcut menu. Point to the plus symbol in front of the row for technician 36 (Figure 3-62).

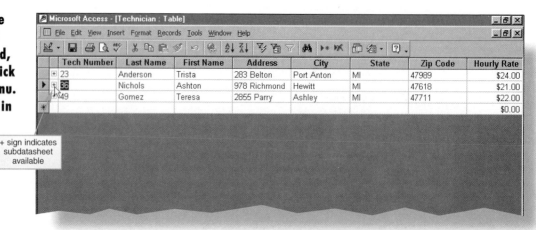

FIGURE 3-62

2 Click the plus symbol in front of the row for technician 36.

The subdatasheet displays (Figure 3-63). It contains only those marinas that are assigned to technician 36.

3 Click the minus symbol to remove the subdatasheet and then close the datasheet for the Technician table by clicking its Close button on the title bar.

The datasheet no longer displays.

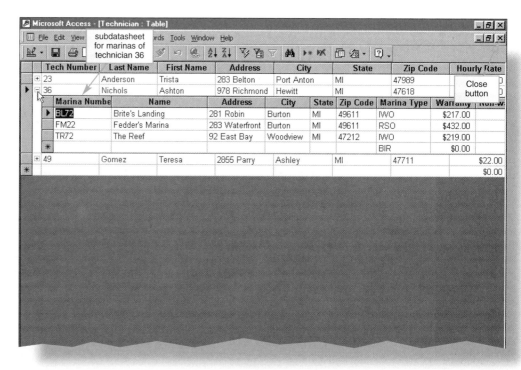

FIGURE 3-63

Ordering Records

Recall from previous discussions that Access sequences the records by marina number whenever listing them because the Marina Number field is the primary key. To change the order in which records display, use the Sort Ascending or Sort Descending buttons on the Table Datasheet toolbar. Either button reorders the records based on the field in which the insertion point is located.

Perform the following steps to order the records by marina name using the Sort Ascending button.

Steps | To Use the Sort Ascending Button to Order Records

1 **Open the Marina table in Datasheet view, and then click the Name field on the first record (any other record would do as well). Point to the Sort Ascending button on the Table Datasheet toolbar (Figure 3-64).**

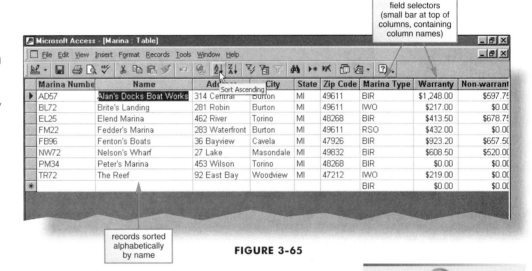

FIGURE 3-64

2 **Click the Sort Ascending button on the toolbar.**

The rows now are ordered by name (Figure 3-65).

FIGURE 3-65

If you wanted to sort the data in reverse order, you would click the Sort Descending button on the Table Datasheet toolbar instead of the Sort Ascending button.

Ordering Records on Multiple Fields

Just as you are able to sort the answer to a query on multiple fields, you also can sort the data that displays in a datasheet on multiple fields. To do so, the major and minor keys must be next to each other in the datasheet with the major key on the left. (If this is not the case, you can drag the columns into the correct position. Instead of dragging, however, usually it will be easier to use a query that has the data sorted in the desired order.)

Given that the major and minor keys are in the correct position, select both fields and then click the Sort Ascending button on the Table Datasheet toolbar. To select the fields, click the **field selector** for the first field (the major key). Next, hold down the SHIFT key and then click the field selector for the second field (the minor key). A **field selector** is the small bar at the top of the column that you click to select an entire field in a datasheet.

Other Ways

1. On Records menu click Sort, then click Sort Ascending

Order records on the combination of the Marina Type and Warranty fields using the Sort Ascending button on the Table Datasheet toolbar by completing the following steps.

Steps To Use the Sort Ascending Button to Order Records on Multiple Fields

1 Click the field selector at the top of the Marina Type field column to select the entire column. Hold down the SHIFT key and then click the field selector for the Warranty field column. Release the SHIFT key. Click the Sort Ascending button on the Table Datasheet toolbar.

The rows are ordered by marina type (Figure 3-66). Within each group of marinas of the same type, the rows are ordered by the warranty amount.

2 Close the Marina : Table window by clicking its Close button on the title bar. Click the No button to abandon changes.

The next time the table is open, the records will display in their original order.

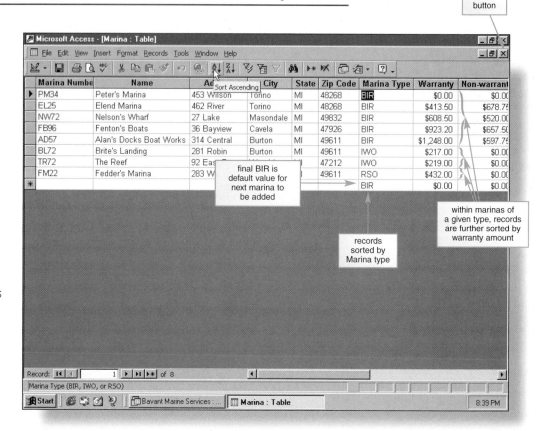

FIGURE 3-66

Creating and Using Indexes

You already are familiar with the concept of an index. The index in the back of a book contains important words or phrases together with a list of pages on which the given words or phrases can be found. An **index** for a table is similar. Figure 3-67, for example, shows the Marina table along with an index built on names. In this case, the items of interest are names instead of keywords or phrases as is the case in the back of this book. The field or fields on which the index is built is called the **index key**. Thus, in Figure 3-67, the Name field is the index key.

Index on Name		Marina Table							
NAME	RECORD NUMBER	RECORD NUMBER	MARINA NUMBER	NAME	ADDRESS	CITY	STATE	ZIP CODE	...
Alan's Docks Boat Works	1	1	AD57	Alan's Docks Boat Works	314 Central	Burton	MI	49611	...
Brite's Landing	2	2	BL72	Brite's Landing	281 Robin	Burton	MI	49611	...
Elend Marina	3	3	EL25	Elend Marina	462 River	Torino	MI	48268	...
Fedder's Marina	5	4	FB96	Fenton's Boats	36 Bayview	Cavela	MI	47926	...
Fenton's Boasts	4	5	FM22	Fedder's Marina	283 Waterfront	Burton	MI	49611	...
Nelson's Wharf	6	6	NW72	Nelson's Wharf	27 Lake	Masondale	MI	48268	...
Peter's Marina	7	7	PM34	Peter's Marina	453 Wilson	Torino	MI	48268	...
The Reef	8	8	TR72	The Reef	92 East Bay	Woodview	MI	47212	...

FIGURE 3-67

Each name occurs in the index along with the number of the record on which the corresponding marina is located. Further, the names appear in the index in alphabetical order. If Access were to use this index to find the record on which the name is Fenton's Boats, for example, it could scan rapidly the names in the index to find Fenton's Boats. Once it did, it would determine the corresponding record number (4) and then go immediately to record 4 in the Marina table, thus finding this marina more quickly than if it had to look through the entire Marina table one record at a time. Indexes make the process of retrieving records very fast and efficient. (With relatively small tables, the increased efficiency associated with indexes will not be apparent readily. In practice, it is common to encounter tables with thousands, tens of thousands, or even hundreds of thousands, of records. In such cases, the increase in efficiency is dramatic. In fact, without indexes, many operations in such databases would simply not be practical. They would take too long to complete.)

Because no two marinas happen to have the same name, the Record Number column contains only single values. This may not always be the case. Consider the index on the Zip Code field shown in Figure 3-68 on the next page. In this index, the Record Number column contains several values, namely all the records on which the corresponding zip code displays. The first row, for example, indicates that zip code 47212 is found only on record 8; whereas, the fourth row indicates that zip code 49611 is found on records 1, 2, and 5. If Access were to use this index to find all marinas in zip code 49611, it could scan rapidly the zip codes in the index to find 49611. Once it did, it would determine the corresponding record numbers (1, 2, and 5) and then go immediately to these records. It would not have to examine any other records in the Marina table.

Indexes

The most common structure for high-performance indexes is called a B-tree. It is a highly efficient structure that supports very rapid access to records in the database as well as a rapid alternative to sorting records. Virtually all systems use some version of the B-tree structure. For more information, visit the Access 2000 Project 3 More About page (www.scsite.com/ac2000/more.htm) and click B-tree.

Index on Zip Code			Marina Table							
ZIP CODE	RECORD NUMBER		RECORD NUMBER	MARINA NUMBER	NAME	ADDRESS	CITY	STATE	ZIP CODE	...
47212	8		1	AD57	Alan's Docks Boat Works	314 Central	Burton	MI	49611	...
47926	4		2	BL72	Brite's Landing	281 Robin	Burton	MI	49611	...
48268	3, 7		3	EL25	Elend Marina	462 River	Torino	MI	48268	...
49611	1, 2, 5		4	FB96	Fedder's Landing	36 Bayview	Cavela	MI	47926	...
49832	6		5	FM22	Fedder's Boasts	283 Waterfront	Burton	MI	49611	...
			6	NW72	Nelson's Wharf	27 Lake	Masondale	MI	48268	...
			7	PM34	Peter's Marina	453 Wilson	Torino	MI	48268	...
			8	TR72	The Reef	92 East Bay	Woodview	MI	47212	...

FIGURE 3-68

Another benefit of indexes is that they provide an efficient way to order records. That is, if the records are to display in a certain order, Access can use an index instead of physically having to rearrange the records in the database file. Physically rearranging the records in a different order, which is called **sorting**, can be a very time-consuming process.

To see how indexes can be used for alphabetizing records, look at the record numbers in the index (see Figure 3-67 on page A 3.45) and suppose you used these to list all marinas. That is, simply follow down the Record Number column, listing the corresponding marinas. In this example, first you would list the marina on record 1 (Alan's Docks Boat Works), then the marina on record 2 (Brite's Landing), then the marina on record 3 (Elend Marina), then the marina on record 5 (Fedder's Marina), then the Marina on record 4 (Fenton's Boats), and so on. The marinas would be listed alphabetically by name without actually sorting the table.

To gain the benefits from an index, you first must create one. Access automatically creates an index on the primary key as well as some other special fields. If, as is the case with both the Marina and Technician tables, a table contains a field called Zip Code, for example, Access will create an index for it automatically. You must create any other indexes you feel you need, indicating the field or fields on which the index is to be built.

Although the index key usually will be a single field, it can be a combination of fields. For example, you may want to sort records by warranty within marina type. In other words, the records are ordered by a combination of fields: Marina Type and Warranty. An index can be created for this purpose by using a combination of fields for the index key. In this case, you must assign a name to the index. It is a good idea to assign a name that represents the combination of fields. For example, an index whose key is the combination of the Marina Type and Warranty fields, might be called TypeWarranty.

How Does Access Use an Index?

Access creates an index whenever you request that it do so. Access takes care of all the work in setting up and maintaining the index. In addition, Access will use the index automatically.

If you request that data be sorted in a particular order and Access determines that an index is available that it can use to make the process efficient, it will do so. If no index is available, it still will sort the data in the order you requested; it will just take longer.

Similarly, if you request that Access locate a particular record that has a certain value in a particular field, Access will use an index if an appropriate one exists. If not, it will have to examine each record until it finds the one you want.

In both cases, the added efficiency provided by an index will not be apparent readily in tables that have only a few records. As you add more records to your tables, however, the difference can be dramatic. Even with only 50 to 100 records, you will notice a difference. You can imagine how dramatic the difference would be in a table with 50,000 records.

When Should You Create an Index?

An index improves efficiency for sorting and finding records. On the other hand, indexes occupy space on your disk. They also require Access to do extra work. Access must maintain all the indexes that have been created up to date. Thus, both advantages and disadvantages exist to using indexes. Consequently, the decision as to which indexes to create is an important one. The following guidelines should help you in this process.

Create an index on a field (or combination of fields) if one or more of the following conditions are present:

1. The field is the primary key of the table (Access will create this index automatically)
2. The field is the foreign key in a relationship you have created
3. You frequently will need your data to be sorted on the field
4. You frequently will need to locate a record based on a value in this field

Because Access handles condition 1 automatically, you only need to concern yourself about conditions 2, 3, and 4. If you think you will need to see marina data arranged in order of warranty amounts, for example, you should create an index on the Warranty field. If you think you will need to see the data arranged by warranty within technician number, you should create an index on the combination of the Tech Number field and the Warranty field. Similarly, if you think you will need to find a marina given the marina s name, you should create an index on the Name field.

Creating Single-Field Indexes

A **single-field index** is an index whose key is a single field. In this case, the index key is to be the Name field. In creating an index, you need to indicate whether to allow duplicates in the index key; that is, two records that have the same value. For example, in the index for the Name field, if duplicates are not allowed, Access would not allow the addition of a marina whose name is the same as the name of an existing marina in the database. In the index for the Name field, duplicates will be allowed. Perform the following steps to create a single-field index.

More About

Microsoft Certification

The Microsoft Office User Specialist (MOUS) Certification program provides an opportunity for you to obtain a valuable industry credential - proof that you have the Access 2000 skills required by employers. For more information, see Appendix D or visit the Shelly Cashman Series MOUS Web page at www.scsite.com/off2000/cert.htm.

Steps To Create a Single-Field Index

1 **Right-click Marina. Click Design View** on the shortcut menu, and then, if necessary, maximize the Marina : Table window. Click the row selector to select the Name field. Click the Indexed text box in the Field Properties pane. Click the Indexed text box down arrow.

The Indexed list displays (Figure 3-69). The items in the list are No (no index), Yes (Duplicates OK) (create an index and allow duplicates), and Yes (No Duplicates) (create an index but reject (do not allow) duplicates).

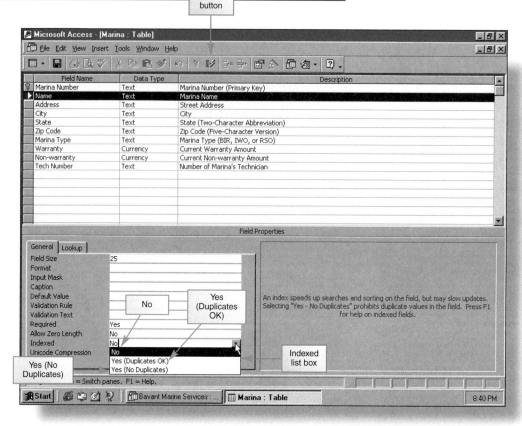

FIGURE 3-69

2 **Click the Yes (Duplicates OK) item** in the list.

The index on the Name field now will be created and is ready for use as soon as you save your work.

Creating Multiple-Field Indexes

Creating **multiple-field indexes**, that is, indexes whose key is a combination of fields, involves a different process than creating single-field indexes. To create multiple-field indexes, you will use the **Indexes button** on the Table Design toolbar, enter a name for the index, and then enter the combination of fields that make up the index key. The following steps create a multiple-field index with the name TypeWarranty. The key will be the combination of the Marina Type field and the Warranty field.

Quick Reference

For a table that lists how to complete the tasks covered in this book using the mouse, menu, shortcut menu, and keyboard, visit the Office 2000 Web page (www.scsite.com/off2000/qr.htm), and then click Microsoft Access 2000.

To Create a Multiple-Field Index

1 Point to the Indexes button on the Table Design toolbar (Figure 3-70).

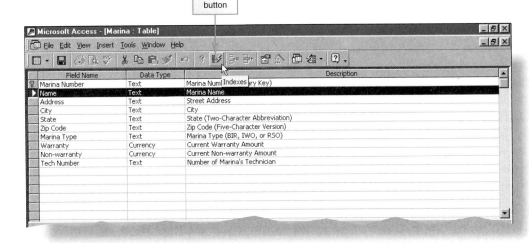

FIGURE 3-70

2 Click the Indexes button on the toolbar. Click the blank row (the row following Name) in the Index Name column in the Indexes: Marina window. Type `TypeWarranty` as the index name and then press the TAB key. Point to the down arrow in the Field Name column.

The Indexes: Marina dialog box displays. It shows the indexes that already have been created and allows you to create additional indexes (Figure 3-71). The index name has been entered as TypeWarranty. An insertion point displays in the Field Name column. The index on the Marina Number field is the primary index and was created automatically by Access. The index on the Name field is the one just created. Access created other indexes (for example, on the Zip Code field) automatically. In this dialog box, you can create additional indexes.

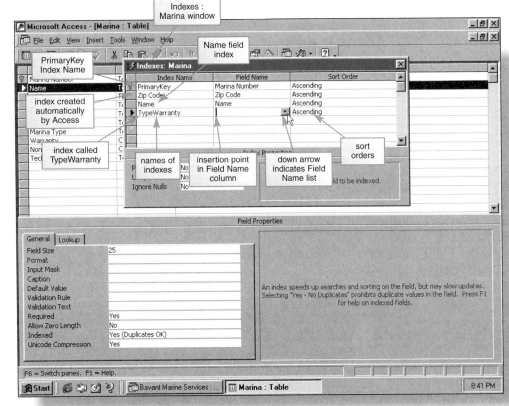

FIGURE 3-71

(3) **Click the down arrow in the Field Name column to produce a list of fields in the Marina table, scroll down the list, and then select the Marina Type field . Press the TAB key three times to move to the Field Name column on the following row. Select the Warranty field in the same manner as the Marina Type field.**

Marina Type and Warranty are selected as the two fields for the TypeWarranty index (Figure 3-72). The absence of an index name on the row containing the Warranty field indicates that it is part of the previous index named, TypeWarranty.

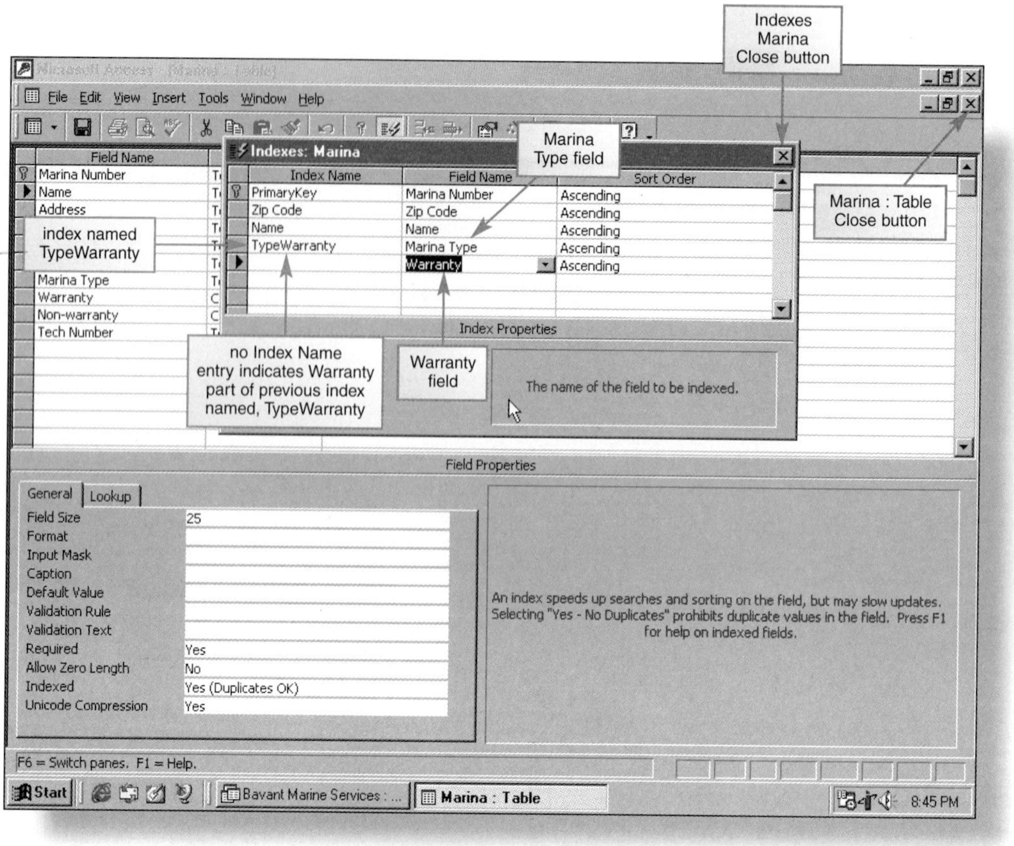

FIGURE 3-72

(4) **Close the Indexes: Marina dialog box by clicking its Close button on the title bar, and then close the Marina : Table window by clicking its Close button on the title bar. When the Microsoft Access dialog box displays, click the Yes button to save your changes.**

The indexes are created and the Database window displays.

1. On View menu click Indexes

Closing the Database

The following step closes the database by closing the Database window.

TO CLOSE A DATABASE

(1) Click the Close button on the Bavant Marine Services : Database window title bar.

The database closes.

The indexes now have been created. Access will use them automatically whenever possible to improve efficiency of ordering or finding records. Access also will maintain them automatically. That is, whenever the data in the Marina table is changed, Access will make appropriate changes in the indexes automatically.

CASE PERSPECTIVE SUMMARY

In Project 3, you assisted Bavant Marine Service in the maintenance of the database. You used Form view to add a record to the database and searched for a record satisfying a criterion. You used a filter so you could view only the record you needed. You changed and deleted records. You changed the structure of the Marina table in the Bavant Marine Services database, created validation rules, and specified referential integrity. You used a subdatasheet to view the marinas assigned to a technician while viewing technician data. You made mass changes and created indexes to improve performance.

Project Summary

In Project 3, you learned how to maintain a database. You saw how to use Form view to add records to a table. You learned how to locate and filter records. You saw how to change the contents of records in a table and how to delete records from a table. You restructured a table, both by changing field characteristics and by adding a new field. You saw how to make changes to groups of records and how to delete groups of records. You learned how to create a variety of validation rules to specify a required field, specify a range, specify a default value, specify legal values, and specify a format. You examined the issues involved in updating a table with validation rules. You also saw how to specify referential integrity. You learned how to view related data by using subdatasheets. You learned how to order records. Finally, you saw how to improve performance by creating single-field and multiple-field indexes.

What You Should Know

Having completed this project, you now should be able to perform the following tasks:

▶ Add a Field to a Table *(A 3.17)*
▶ Change the Size of a Field *(A 3.16)*
▶ Close a Database *(A 3.50)*
▶ Create a Multiple-Field Index *(A 3.49)*
▶ Create a Single-Field Index *(A 3.48)*
▶ Delete a Record *(A 3.14)*
▶ Filter Records *(A 3.13)*
▶ Make Individual Changes *(A 3.36)*
▶ Open a Database *(A 3.6)*
▶ Remove a Filter *(A 3.14)*
▶ Resize a Column *(A 3.21)*
▶ Save the Validation Rules, Default Values, and Formats *(A 3.33)*
▶ Search for a Record *(A 3.9)*
▶ Specify a Collection of Legal Values *(A 3.32)*
▶ Specify a Default Value *(A 3.31)*

▶ Specify a Format *(A 3.33)*
▶ Specify a Range *(A 3.30)*
▶ Specify a Required Field *(A 3.28)*
▶ Specify Referential Integrity *(A 3.38)*
▶ Switch from Form View to Datasheet View *(A 3.11)*
▶ Update the Contents of a Field *(A 3.10, A 3.20)*
▶ Use a Delete Query to Delete a Group of Records *(A 3.26)*
▶ Use a Form to Add Records *(A 3.6)*
▶ Use a Subdatasheet *(A 3.42)*
▶ Use an Update Query to Update All Records *(A 3.23)*
▶ Use the Sort Ascending Button to Order Records *(A 3.43)*
▶ Use the Sort Ascending Button to Order Records on Multiple Fields *(A 3.44)*

Apply Your Knowledge

➕ Project Reinforcement at www.scsite.com/off2000/reinforce.htm

1 Maintaining the Sidewalk Scrapers Database

Instructions: Start Access. Open the Sidewalk Scrapers database from the Data Disk. See the inside back cover of this book for instructions for downloading the Data Disk or see your instructor for information on accessing the files required for this book. Perform the following tasks.

1. Open the Customer table in Design view as shown in Figure 3-73.

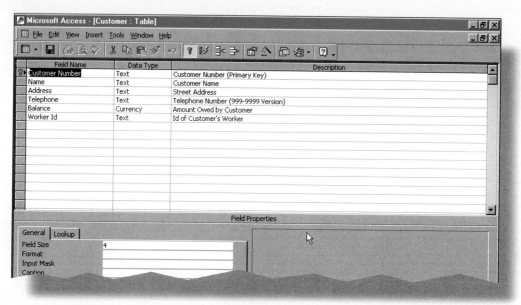

FIGURE 3-73

2. Increase the size of the Name field to 25.
3. Format the Customer Number field so any lowercase letters display in uppercase.
4. Make the Name and Address fields required fields.
5. Specify that Balance amounts must be less than or equal to $125.00. Include validation text.
6. Create an index that allows duplicates for the Name field.
7. Save the changes to the structure.
8. Open the Customer table in Datasheet view.
9. Change the name of customer ST21 to Styling Salon and Tanning.
10. Resize the Name column so the complete name for customer ST21 displays. Resize the Telephone, Balance, and Worker Id field columns to the best size.
11. Close the table and click Yes to save the changes to the layout of the table.
12. Print the table.
13. Open the Customer table and use Filter by Selection to find the record for customer BH81. Delete the record.
14. Print the table.
15. Sort the data in descending order by balance.
16. Print the table. Close the table. If you are asked to save changes to the design of the table, click the No button.
17. Establish referential integrity between the Worker table (the one table) and the Customer table (the many table). Print the relationships window by making sure the relationships window is open, clicking File on the menu bar, and then clicking Print Relationships.

In the Lab

1 Maintaining the School Connection Database

Problem: The Booster's club would like to make some changes to the School Connection database structure. They need to increase the size of the Description field and add an additional index. Because several different individuals update the data, the club also would like to add some validation rules to the database. Finally, some new items must be added to the database.

Instructions: Use the database created in the In the Lab 1 of Project 1 for this assignment. Perform the following tasks.

1. Open the School Connection database and open the Item table in Design view as shown in Figure 3-74.

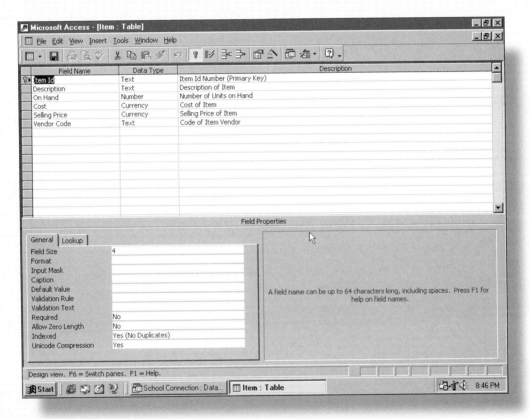

FIGURE 3-74

2. Create an index for the Description field. Be sure to allow duplicates.
3. Create and save the following validation rules for the Item table. List the steps involved on your own paper.
   a. Make the Description field a required field.
   b. Ensure that any lowercase letters entered in the Item Id field are displayed as uppercase.
   c. Specify that the on hand units must be between 0 and 50. Include validation text.
4. Save the changes.
5. Open the Item form you created in Project 1, and then add the following record to the Item table:

MN04	Mouse Pad	5	$9.10	$11.00	AL

(continued)

In the Lab

Maintaining the School Connection Database *(continued)*

6. Switch to Datasheet view and sort the records in ascending order by description.

7. Print the table. Close the table. If you are asked to save changes to the design of the table, click the No button.

8. Create a new query for the Item table.

9. Using a query, delete all records in the Item table where the description starts with the letter T. (*Hint*: Use online Help to solve this problem.) Close the query without saving it.

10. Print the Item table.

11. Open the Vendor table in Design view, and add a new field to the end of the table. Name the field, Fax Number. This new field has the same data type and length as Telephone Number. Enter the same comment as Telephone Number but replace Telephone with Fax. Save the change to the table design.

12. Open the Vendor table in Datasheet view, and then add the following data to the Fax Number field.

AL	608-555-6574
GG	505-555-8766
TM	804-555-1235

13. Resize the Vendor Code, City, State, Zip Code, Telephone Number, and Fax Number columns to the best size.

14. Print the table. If necessary, change the margins so the table prints on one page in landscape orientation. Save the change to the layout of the table.

15. Specify referential integrity between the Vendor table (the one table) and the Item table (the many table). Print the Relationships window by making sure the Relationships window is open, clicking File on the menu bar, and then clicking Print Relationships.

In the Lab

2 Maintaining the City Area Bus Company Database

Problem: The Advertising Sales Manager of the City Area Bus Company would like to make some changes to the database structure. Another field must be added to the database, and the size of the First Name field must be increased. Because several different individuals update the data, the manager also would like to add some validation rules to the database. Finally, some additions and deletions are to be made to the database.

Instructions: Use the database created in the In the Lab 2 of Project 1 for this assignment. Perform the following tasks.

1. Open the City Area Bus Company database and open the Advertiser table in Design view as shown in Figure 3-75.

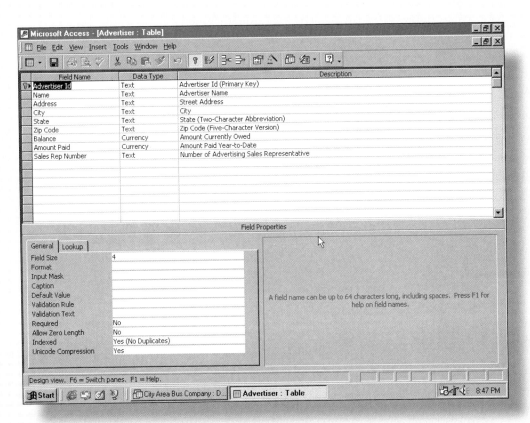

FIGURE 3-75

2. Create an index for the Name field. Be sure to allow duplicates. Create an index on the combination of the State and Zip Code fields. Name the index Statezip. Save these changes.
3. Display the Advertiser table in Datasheet view and order the records by zip code within state.
4. Print the table. If necessary, change the margins so the table prints on one page in landscape orientation. Close the table. If you are asked to save changes to the design of the table, click the No button.
5. Open the Advertiser table in Design view and change the field width of the Name field to 22.

(continued)

In the Lab

Maintaining the City Area Bus Company Database (*continued*)

6. Add the field, Ad Type, to the Advertiser table. Define the field as Text with a width of 3. Insert the Ad Type field after the Zip Code field. This field will contain data on the type of advertising account. Advertisers are classified as retail (RET), service (SER), and dining (DIN).

7. Save these changes and display the Advertiser table in Datasheet view.

8. Change the name of account HC11 to Hilde's Cards & Gifts.

9. Resize the Name column to fit the changed entry. Adjust the width of the remaining columns to best fit the size of the data.

10. Print the table. If necessary, change the margins so the table prints on one page in landscape orientation. Close the table. Save the layout changes to the table.

11. Using a query, change all the entries in the Ad Type column to RET. This will be the type of most accounts. Do not save the query.

12. Open the Advertiser table and order the records in descending order by balance. Print the table and then close the table. If you are asked to save changes to the design of the table, click the No button.

13. Create the following validation rules for the Advertiser table and save the changes to the table. List the steps involved on your own paper.
    a. Make the Name field a required field.
    b. Specify the legal values RET, SER, and DIN for the Ad Type field. Include validation text.
    c. Ensure that any letters entered in the Advertiser Id and State fields are displayed as uppercase.
    d. Specify that balance must be less than or equal $450.00. Include validation text.

14. You can use either Form view or Datasheet view to add records to a table. To use Form view, you must replace the form you created in Project 1 with a form that includes the new field, Ad Type. With the Advertiser table selected, click the New Object: AutoForm button arrow on the Database Window toolbar. Click AutoForm. Use this form that contains ad type to add the following record:

PP24	Pia's Pizza	113 Main	Richmond	MA	05434	DIN	$50.00	$0.00	31

15. Close the form. Click the Yes button when asked if you want to save the form. Save the form as Advertiser. Click the Yes button when asked if you want to replace the Advertiser form you created in Project 1.

16. Open the Advertiser form and locate the advertiser with advertiser NO10 and then change the ad type for the record to DIN. Change the ad type for advertisers AC25 and CS46 to SER.

17. Change to Datasheet view and print the table.

18. Use Filter by Form to find all records in the table where the account has the ad type of RET and a zip code of 05434. Delete these records. (*Hint:* Read the More About on page A 3.12 to solve this problem.)

19. Print the Advertiser table. Specify referential integrity between the Sales Rep table (the one table) and the Advertiser table (the many table). Print the Relationships window by making sure the Relationships window is open, clicking File on the menu bar, and then clicking Print Relationships.

In the Lab

3 Maintaining the Resort Rentals Database

Problem: The real estate company has determined that some changes must be made to the database structure. Another field must be added and the size of the Name field must be increased. Because several different individuals update the data, the company also would like to add some validation rules to the database. Finally, some additions and deletions are required to the database.

Instructions: Use the database created in the In the Lab 3 of Project 1 for this assignment. Perform the following tasks.

1. Open the Resort Rentals database and open the Rental Unit table in Design view as shown in Figure 3-76.

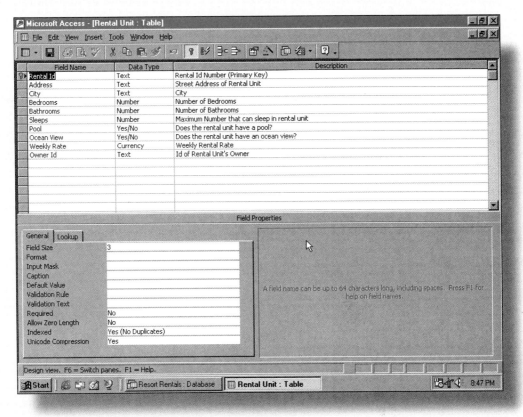

FIGURE 3-76

2. Create an index for the City field. Be sure to allow duplicates. Create an index on the combination of the Bedrooms and Bathrooms fields. Name the index Bedbath. Create an index on the combination of the Pool and Ocean View fields. Name the index PoolView. Save these changes.

3. Display the Rental Unit table and order the records by bathrooms within bedrooms.

4. Print the table and then close the table. If you are asked to save changes to the design of the table, click the No button.

5. Add the field, For Sale, to the Rental Unit table. Define the field as a Yes/No field. Insert the field after the Weekly Rate field. This field will indicate whether or not the rental unit is for sale.

6. Save these changes and display the Rental Unit table in Datasheet view.

(continued)

In the Lab

Maintaining the Resort Rentals Database *(continued)*

7. Units 101, 108, and 134 are for sale. Update the records for these rental units. Decrease the width of the For Sale column.

8. Print the table. If necessary, change the margins so the table prints on one page in landscape orientation. Close the table. Save the layout changes to the table.

9. Create the following validation rules for the Rental Unit table and save the changes to the table. List the steps involved on your own paper.

    a. Make the Address, City, Bedrooms, Bathrooms, and Sleeps fields required fields.

    b. Assign a default value of 1 to the Bedrooms and Bathrooms fields. Assign a default value of 2 to the Sleeps field.

    c. Specify that the Bedrooms and Bathrooms fields must be at least one and the Sleeps field must be at least 2. Include validation text.

    d. Specify that weekly rate must be between $500 and $2,000. Include validation text.

10. The real estate office has just received a new listing from Rita Peoples. The unit has been assigned the id 148. It is located at 123 Second in San Toma. The unit sleeps 10, has 3 bedrooms, 3 bathrooms, a pool but no ocean view. The weekly rate is $1,400 and the owner is interested in selling the unit. Add this record to the database. Remember that you can use either Form view or Datasheet view to add records to a table. If you use Form view, you must replace the form you created in Project 1 with a form that includes the new field, For Sale.

11. If necessary, close the form. Click Yes when asked if you want to save the form. Save the form as Rental Unit. Click the Yes button when asked if you want to replace the Rental Unit you created in Project 1.

12. Change to Datasheet view and print the table.

13. Using a query, delete all records in the table where the rental unit is in Gulf Breeze and has one bedroom.

14. Print the Rental Unit table.

15. Specify referential integrity between the Owner table (the one table) and the Rental Unit table (the many table). Print the Relationships window by making sure the Relationships window is open, clicking File on the menu bar, and then clicking Print Relationships.

Cases and Places

The difficulty of these case studies varies:
▶ are the least difficult; ▶▶ are more difficult; and ▶▶▶ are the most difficult.

1 ▶ Use the Computer Science Club database you created in Case Study 1 of Project 1 for this assignment. Execute each of these tasks and then print the results:

(a) Antistatic Wipes are now called Antistatic Cloths.
(b) The club has sold all the desktop holders and decided to delete this item from inventory.
(c) Mouse Tracks has increased the cost of their items by 10%. The club also has raised the selling price by 10% for these items.
(d) The club sold 25 disks.
(e) Human Interface has a new telephone number, 317-555-5847.
(f) The description for item 4343 should really be Mouse Pad with Logo.
(g) Specify referential integrity between the two tables in the database.

2 ▶ Use the Sci-Fi Scene database you created in Case Study 2 of Project 2 for this assignment. Execute each of these tasks and then print the results:

(a) The bookstore has added a used book section. The owner would like to add these books to the database but she must know whether a book is used or new. Add a field to the database to indicate whether a book is used or new. All books currently in the database are new books.
(b) The title for book 0533 is really Albert s Truth & Way.
(c) Add the used book, Martian Politics to the database and use 9867 as the book code. Martian Politics was written by E Dearling in 1995. It was published by VanNester and will sell for $2.50.
(d) Dark Wind was published in 1996.
(e) The owner sold the last copy of Infinity and the book is now out of print.
(f) Specify referential integrity between the two tables in the database.

3 ▶▶ Use the band database created in Case Study 3 of Project 1 for this assignment:

(a) Determine and create the appropriate validity checks for the sex, number of years in band, own or lease instrument, and age fields.
(b) Ensure that data always is entered in the name, telephone number, emergency contact name, and emergency contact number fields.
(c) Add three records to the database.

Cases and Places

4 ▶▶ Use the humane society database created in Case Study 4 of Project 1 for this assignment:

(a) Add a field to the database to store the date the pet was adopted and enter some sample data for this field.

(b) Determine and create appropriate validity checks for the fields in your database.

(c) Add two records to the database.

(d) Determine and create appropriate indexes for your database. Use the indexes to sort the data.

(e) Analyze the database and determine if you have a one-to-many relationship between any tables. If so, specify referential integrity between the one table and the many table.

5 ▶▶▶ Use the Intramural Sports Club database you created in Case Study 5 of Project 1 for this assignment:

(a) Analyze the database and determine if you need any additional fields. Do you have a field for the date you received a sports item? Do you have e-mail addresses for each student? Add any fields that you now think would be useful to the database.

(b) Determine and create appropriate validity checks for the fields in your database.

(c) Add two records to the database.

(d) Determine and create appropriate indexes for your database. Use the indexes to sort the data.

(e) Analyze the database and determine if you have a one-to-many relationship between any tables. If so, specify referential integrity between the one table and the many table.

Microsoft Access 2000

Publishing to the Internet Using Data Access Pages

CASE PERSPECTIVE

Bavant Marine Services is pleased with all the work you have done for them thus far. They appreciate the database you have created and the ease with which they can query the database. They find the default values, the validation rules, the validation text, and the relationships you created to be useful in ensuring that the database contains only valid data. They also find the report you created for them in Project 1 to be very useful. They are also very pleased with the form you created for them in Project 1. They have used it to view and update marina data. They would like to use a web page that would be similar to this form in order to view and/or update marina data over the Internet. They would like you to develop a sample of such a Web page for their review. If satisfactory, they will instruct the network administrator to make both the database and your Web page accessible on the Internet.

Introduction

Microsoft Access 2000 supports data access pages. A **data access page** is an HTML (hypertext markup language) document that can be bound directly to data in the database. The fact that it is an **HTML (hypertext markup language) document** means that it can be run on the Internet. Data access pages can be run only in the Microsoft Internet Explorer browser. The fact that it is bound directly to the database means that it can access data in the database directly.

Figure 1 on the next page shows a sample data access page run in the Internet Explorer browser. Notice that it is similar to the form created in Project 1 (see page A 1.38). Although running in the browser, the data access page is displaying data from the Bavant Marine Services database. Furthermore, the page can be used to change this data. You can use it to change the contents of existing records, to delete records, and to add new records.

More About 2000

Publishing to the Internet: Saving Other Objects

You also can publish other objects such as reports and datasheets to the Internet. To publish a datasheet or a report to the Internet, save the object as a Web page in HTML format. To do so, select the name of the object in the Database window, click File on the menu bar, and then click Export. In the Save As Type box, click HTML Documents.

Microsoft Access 2000

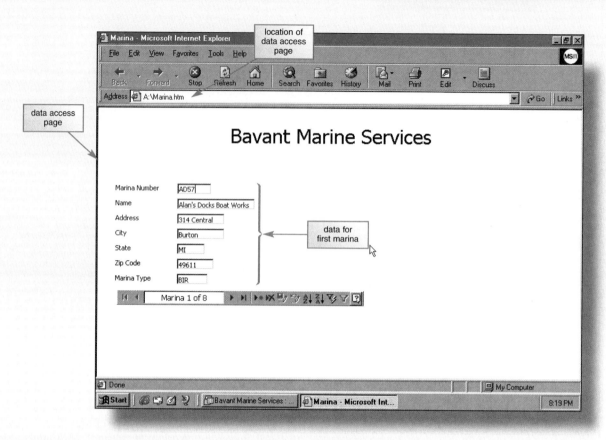

FIGURE 1

In this project, you will create the data access page shown in Figure 1. (This data access page is located on the Data Disk. The database it accesses also is located on the Data Disk. In order to use this page on the Internet, both the page and the database would need to be located on a server that would be available to the Internet. A **server** is a computer that shares its resources with other computers on the Internet. The address entered in the browser would be changed to reflect the true location of the page.)

Opening the Database

Before carrying out the steps in this project, you first must open the database. To do so, perform the following steps.

TO OPEN A DATABASE

1 Click the Start button on the taskbar.

2 Click Open Office Document and then click 3½ Floppy (A:) in the Look in box. If necessary, click the Bavant Marine Services database name in the list.

3 Click the Open button.

The database opens and the Bavant Marine Services : Database window displays.

Creating a Data Access Page

To create a data access page, use the Page Wizard as shown in the following steps.

Steps To Create a Data Access Page

1 **With the Marina table selected, click the New Object: AutoForm button arrow on the Database window toolbar.**

The list of available objects displays (Figure 2).

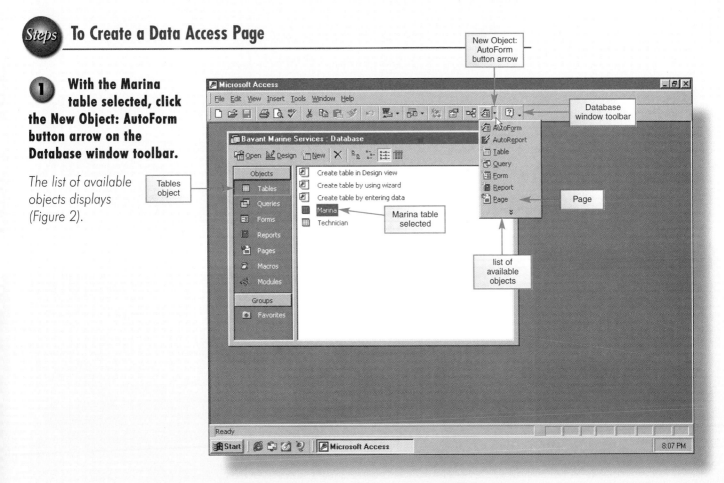

FIGURE 2

2 **Click Page. When the New Data Access Page dialog box displays, click Page Wizard and then point to the OK button.**

The New Data Access Page dialog box displays with Page Wizard selected (Figure 3).

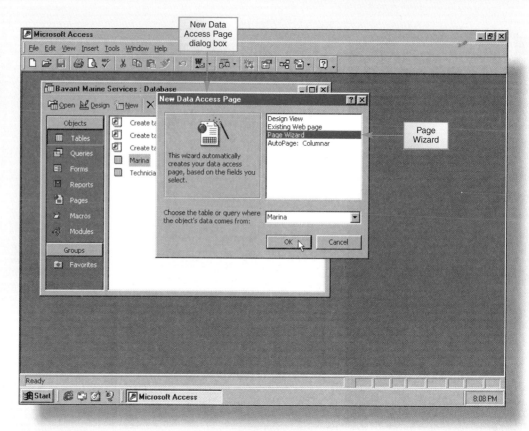

FIGURE 3

3 **Click the OK button. Point to the Add Field button.**

The Page Wizard dialog box displays (Figure 4). The fields in the Marina table display in the Available Fields box. The Marina Number field currently is selected.

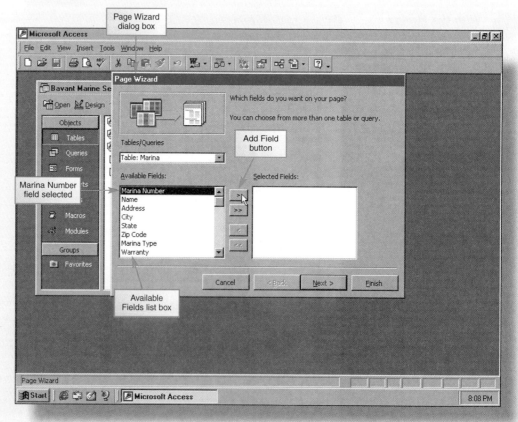

FIGURE 4

④ Click the Add Field button to add the Marina Number field to the Selected Fields box. Click the Add Field button six more times to add the Name, Address, City, State, Zip Code, and Marina Type fields. Point to the Next button.

The Marina Number, Name, Address, City, State, Zip Code, and Marina Type fields are added to the Selected Fields box (Figure 5).

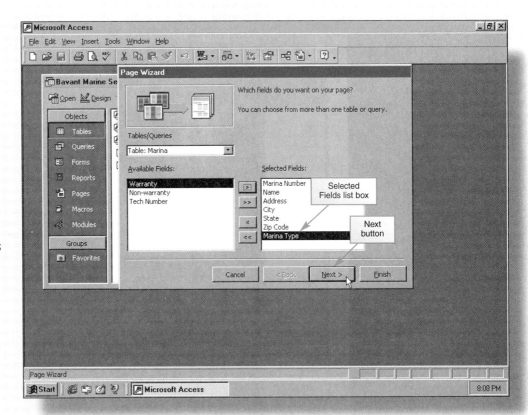

FIGURE 5

⑤ Click the Next button.

The next Page Wizard dialog box displays (Figure 6).

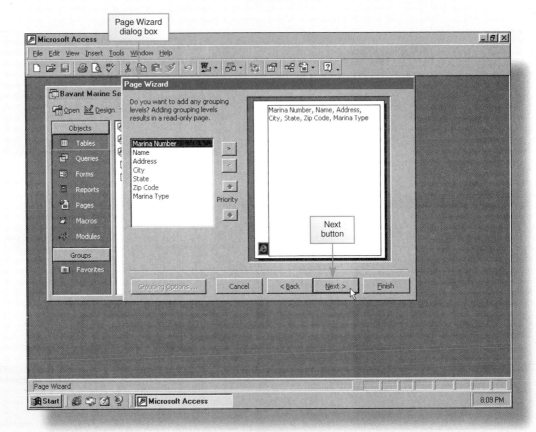

FIGURE 6

6 **Click the Next button because no grouping levels are needed. Click the Next button a second time because no changes are needed to the sort order. Point to the Finish button.**

The next Page Wizard dialog box displays (Figure 7).

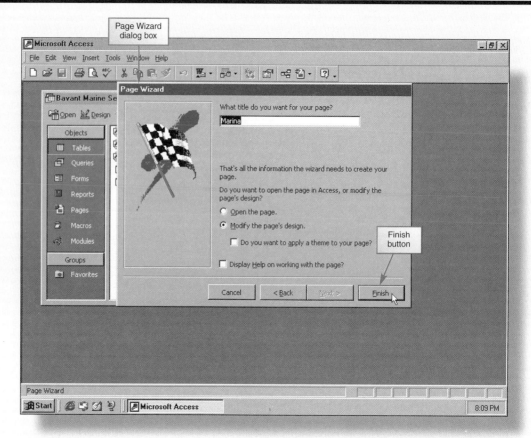

FIGURE 7

7 **Click the Finish button.**

The Page1: Data Access Page displays (Figure 8). The process of creating a data access page may take several seconds.

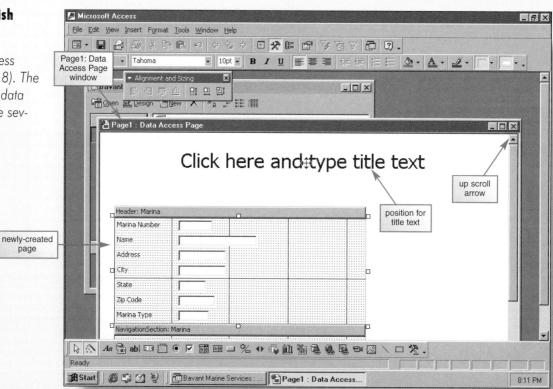

FIGURE 8

8 If necessary, click the up arrow on the vertical scroll bar to display the top of the screen. Click anywhere on the portion of the screen labeled "Click here and type title text" and then **type** Bavant Marine Services **as the title text.**

The data access page displays (Figure 9). The title is changed to Bavant Marine Services.

9 Click the Close button on the Page1: Data Access Page title bar to close the window. When the Save As Data Access Page dialog box displays, type Marina as the name of the page and click Save. If necessary, click 3½ Floppy (A:) in the Save in box to save your page to the same location as your database.

The data access page is created and saved as Marina.

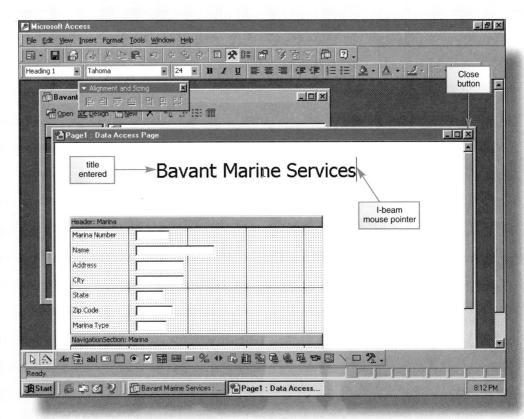

FIGURE 9

More About

Microsoft Certification

The Microsoft Office User Specialist (MOUS) Certification program provides an opportunity for you to obtain a valuable industry credential - proof that you have the Access 2000 skills required by employers. For more information, see Appendix D or visit the Shelly Cashman Series MOUS Web page at www.scsite.com/off2000/cert.htm.

Previewing the Data Access Page

While in Access, you can preview what the page will look like in the browser by using Web Page Preview on the shortcut menu. The following steps preview the data access page that was just created.

 To Preview the Data Access Page

1 **With the Database window open, click the Pages object. Point to Marina.**

The data access page objects display (Figure 10).

2 **Right-click Marina and then click Web Page Preview on the shortcut menu.**

The page displays in the maximized Internet Explorer window, similarly to Figure 1 on page AW 1.2.

3 **Click the Close button on the Internet Explorer window title bar to quit Internet Explorer. Click the Close button on the Microsoft Access window title bar to quit Access.**

The page no longer displays. The database is closed.

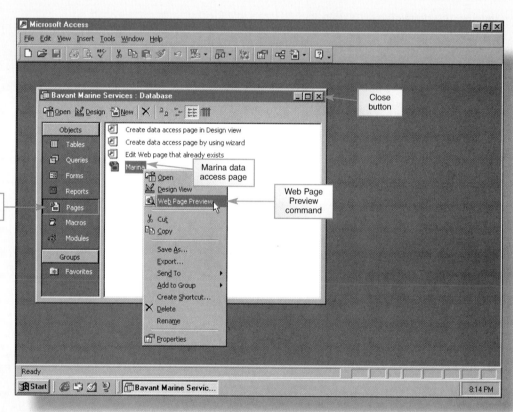

FIGURE 10

Using the Data Access Page

To use the data access page, start Internet Explorer, type the location of the data access page (for example, a:\marina.htm if you created the page on your Data Disk), and then press the ENTER key. The page then will display (Figure 11). To ensure that the data displays in marina number order, click the Sort Ascending button on the record navigation toolbar.

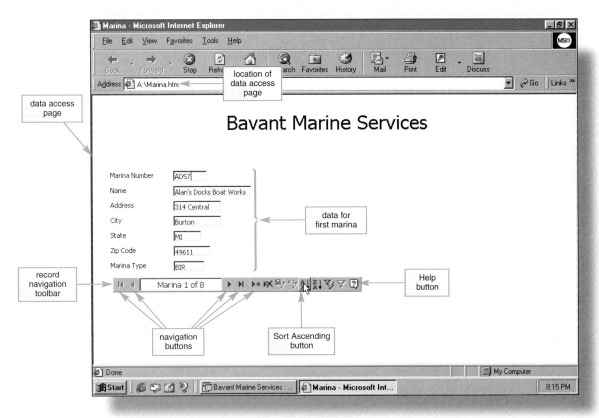

FIGURE 11

You can use the navigation buttons just as you do when viewing a datasheet or a form in Access. You can get help on the way you use the page by clicking the Help button (see Figure 11). Details concerning the use of the page then will display (Figure 12 on the next page). Clicking the plus symbol (+) in front of a category will change the plus symbol to a minus symbol (-) and display all the topics within the category. Clicking the question mark symbol (?) in front of a topic will display details concerning the topic. In Figure 12 on the next page, the plus symbol that was originally in front of the Working with Data access pages category has been changed to a minus symbol and the Data Access pages: What they are and how they work Help information displays. In addition, the Microsoft Access Data Pages Help window has been maximized, which makes it easier to read the help information.

More About

Quick Reference

For a table that lists how to complete the tasks covered in this book using the mouse, menu, shortcut menu, and keyboard, visit the Shelly Cashman Series Office site (www.scsite.com/off2000/qr.htm), and then click the application name.

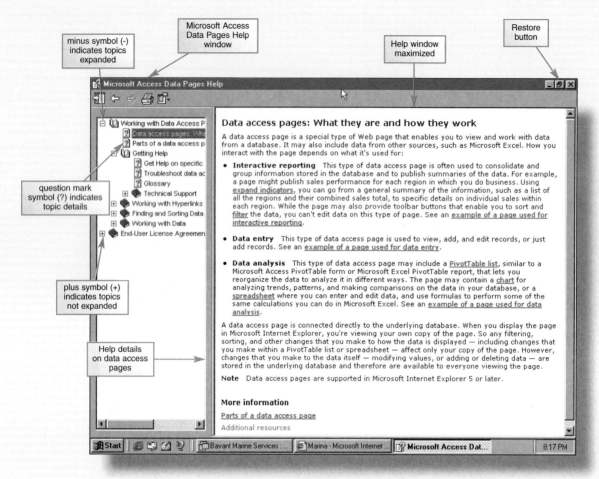

FIGURE 12

CASE PERSPECTIVE SUMMARY

In this Web Feature, you created a data access page for the Marina table in the Bavant Marine Services database. This page will enable Bavant to access their database using the Internet.

Web Feature Summary

In this Web Feature, you learned how to create a data access page to enable users to access the data in a database via the Internet. You worked with the Page Wizard to create such a page. You then previewed the data access page from within Access. Finally, you saw how to use the data access page.

What You Should Know

Having completed this Web Feature, you now should be able to perform the following tasks:

▶ Create a Data Access Page *(AW 1.3)*
▶ Open a Database *(AW 1.3)*
▶ Preview the Data Access Page *(AW 1.8)*
▶ Use a Data Access Page *(AW 1.9)*

In the Lab

1 Creating a Data Access Page for the Sidewalk Scrapers Database

Instructions: Start Access. Open the Sidewalk Scrapers database from the Data Disk. See the inside back cover of this book for instructions for downloading the Data Disk or see your instructor for information on accessing the files required for this book. Perform the following tasks.

1. Create a data access page for the Worker table (Figure 13).

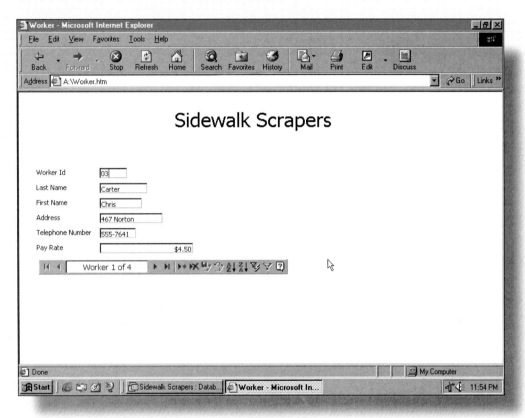

FIGURE 13

2. Print the data access page. To print the page, preview the page, click File on the menu bar, and then click Print.

In the Lab

2 Using a Data Access Page

Instructions: Make sure the Data Disk containing the Sidewalk Scrapers database and the data access page you created in In the Lab 1 is in drive A. Perform the following tasks.

1. Start Internet Explorer and then open the Worker data access page.
2. Use the data access page to add yourself as a new record to the Worker table. Use 99 as the worker id number and $7.00 as the hourly pay rate. Refer to Figure 1-76 on page A 1.56 for the maximum field sizes for the remaining fields.
3. Quit Internet Explorer and then start Access. Open the Worker table in Datasheet view. You now should have 5 records. Print the table and then quit Access.
4. Start Internet Explorer and then open the Worker data access page.
5. Use the data access page to delete the record you just added and then quit Internet Explorer.
6. Start Access and then open the Worker table in Datasheet view. Print the table and then quit Access.

Microsoft Access 2000

Reports, Forms and Combo Boxes

PROJECT 4

OBJECTIVES

You will have mastered the material in this project when you can:

- Create a query for a report
- Use the Report Wizard to create a report
- Use the Report window to modify a report design
- Move between Design view and Print Preview
- Recognize sections in a report
- Save a report
- Close a report
- Print a report
- Create a report with grouping and subtotals
- Change headings in a report
- Move and resize controls on a report
- Use the Form Wizard to create an initial form
- Use the Form window to modify a form design
- Move fields on a form
- Place a calculated field on a form
- Change the format of a field on a form
- Place a combo box on a form
- Place a title on a form
- Change colors on a form
- View data using a form

Navigation Systems

GPS Databases Help You Arrive

The age-old navigation nightmare — getting lost. This traveling torment, however, has become a thing of the past. Automakers and mobile electronics manufacturers have developed onboard navigation systems to help point drivers in the right direction. These pocket-sized navigation system computers use databases that cover the Earth's surface.

These computers collect radio signals emitted from government satellites and calculate the user's position and altitude. Then, they interface with commercial databases and display such useful information as where the closest automated teller machine is located or how long it will take to get to the campground.

The technology is the offspring of once-secret military Cold War technology. The Department of

Defense spent an estimated $10 billion developing the Global Positioning Satellite (GPS) system during the 1970s and launched its first satellite in 1978. Now, 24 GPS satellites orbit high above the Earth.

Expanding on the military's technological successes using the GPS system for bombing missions and navigating during the Gulf War, enterprising engineers developed civilian satellite-navigation systems that use mapped data from databases to guide users in a variety of applications.

Advanced mobile GPS technology allows these systems to map out a route to any known destination on a small color screen positioned near the dashboard and track the precise location of a vehicle as it moves along that route. The systems recalibrate if a motorist makes a wrong turn, and some supply audio directions in addition to the in-dash visual display. The OnStar® system, available with many makes and models, has an emergency function that can be used at the touch of a single button on the OnStar handset. The GPS automatically calculates the vehicle's location and display it on the Advisor' screen so the information can be relayed to an emergency provider with the request for assistance.

In another system, GPS technology in airplanes helps pilots save time and fuel. Databases contain information on airport locations and radio frequencies, and they interact with the satellite signals to compute the aircraft's precise location, direct route to an airport, time enroute, airspeed, and ground speed.

Hikers and boaters benefit from hand held GPS navigating technology. Databases for hikers contain details on popular campgrounds, fishing holes, and hiking trails, and the computer can calculate current position, walking speed, direction to these sites, and estimated time of arrival. GPS systems for boaters display the course traveled, distance to go, miles off course, latitude and longitude, and speed.

Entrepreneurial developers have engineered systems for trucking companies to track the location of their vehicles on the roads, farmers to analyze their crops, police to track drug dealers, and scientists to check movements of the San Andreas fault.

These portable computers and extensive databases are the most important advances in the ancient art of navigation. As they gain acceptance in sporting and traveling activities, they may certainly put an end to the folded maps, detours, stops for directions, and the familiar phrase, "Excuse me, could you tell me how to get to...?"

Microsoft Access 2000

Reports, Forms, and Combo Boxes

P R O J E C T

4

C A S E   P E R S P E C T I V E

Bavant Marine Services has realized several benefits from its database of marinas and technicians. The management and staff of Bavant Marine Services greatly appreciate, for example, the ease with which they can query the database. They hope to realize additional benefits using two custom reports that meet their specific needs. The first report includes the number, name, address, city, state, zip code, and total amount (warranty amount plus non-warranty amount) of each marina. The second report groups the records by technician number. Subtotals of the warranty and non-warranty amounts display after each group, and grand totals display at the end of the report. They also want to improve the data entry process by using a custom form. In addition to a title, the form will contain the fields arranged in two columns and display the total amount, which will be calculated automatically by adding the warranty and non-warranty amounts. To assist users in entering the correct marina type, users should be able to select from a list of possible marina types. To assist users in entering the correct technician number, users should be able to select from a list of existing technicians. Your task is to help Bavant Marina Services with these tasks.

Introduction

This project creates two reports and a form. The first report is shown in Figure 4-1. This report includes the number, name, address, city, state, zip code, and total amount (warranty plus non-warranty) of each marina. It is similar to the one produced by clicking the Print button on the toolbar. It has two significant differences, however.

First, not all fields are included. The Marina table includes a Marina Type field (added in Project 3), a Warranty field, a Non-warranty field, and a Tech Number field, none of which appears on this report. Second, this report contains a Total Amount field, which does not display in the Marina table.

The second report is shown in Figure 4-2 on page A 4.6. It is similar to the report in Figure 4-1 but contains an additional feature, grouping. **Grouping** means creating separate collections of records sharing some common characteristic. In the report shown in Figure 4-2, for example, the records have been grouped by technician number. There are three separate groups: one for technician 23, one for technician 36, and one for technician 49. The appropriate technician number appears before each group, and the total of the warranty and non-warranty amounts for the marinas in the group (called a **subtotal**) displays after the group. At the end of the report is a grand total of the warranty and non-warranty amounts for all groups.

Marina Amount Report

Marina Number	Name	Address	City	State	Zip Code	Total Amount
AD57	Alan's Docks Boat Works	314 Central	Burton	MI	49611	$1,845.75
BL72	Brite's Landing	281 Robin	Burton	MI	49611	$217.00
EL25	Elend Marina	462 River	Torino	MI	48268	$1,092.25
FB96	Fenton's Boats	36 Bayview	Cavela	MI	47926	$1,580.70
FM22	Fedder's Marina	283 Waterfront	Burton	MI	49611	$432.00
NW72	Nelson's Wharf	27 Lake	Masondale	MI	49832	$1,128.50
PM34	Peter's Marina	453 Wilson	Torino	MI	48268	$0.00
TR72	The Reef	92 East Bay	Woodview	MI	47212	$219.00

FIGURE 4-1

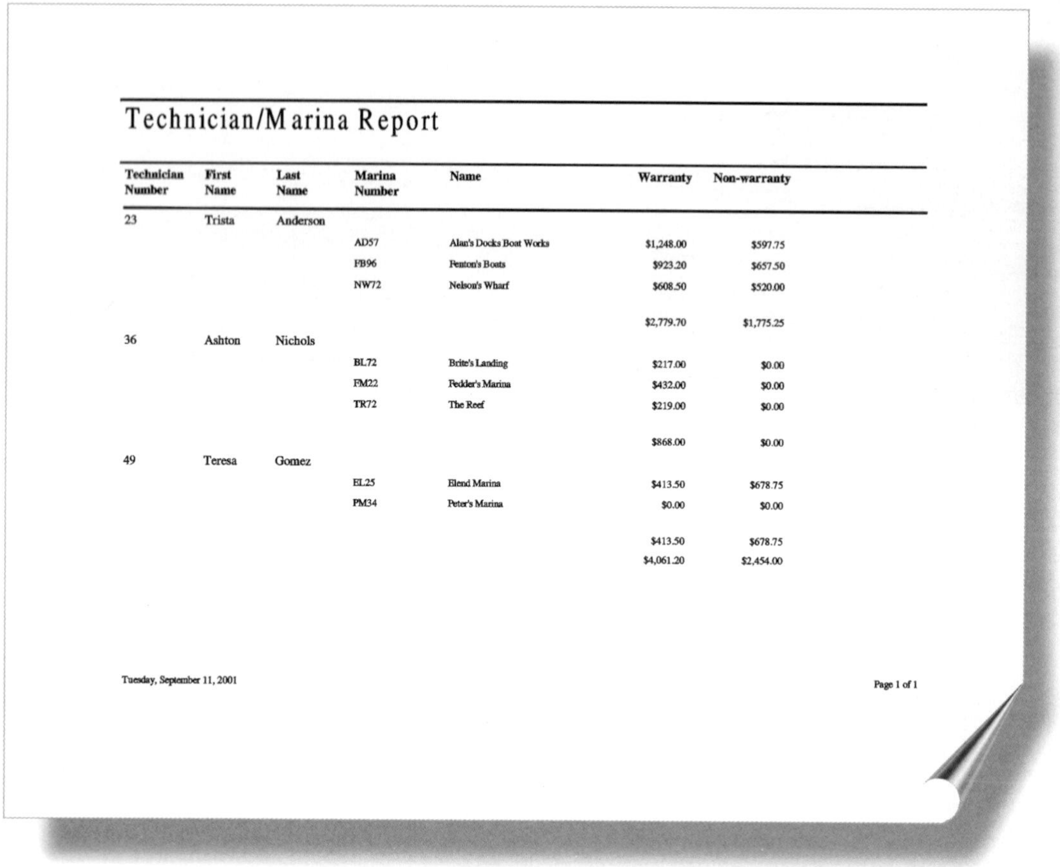

Technician/Marina Report

Technician Number	First Name	Last Name	Marina Number	Name	Warranty	Non-warranty
23	Trista	Anderson				
			AD57	Alan's Docks Boat Works	$1,248.00	$597.75
			FB96	Fenton's Boats	$923.20	$657.50
			NW72	Nelson's Wharf	$608.50	$520.00
					$2,779.70	$1,775.25
36	Ashton	Nichols				
			BL72	Brite's Landing	$217.00	$0.00
			FM22	Fedder's Marina	$432.00	$0.00
			TR72	The Reef	$219.00	$0.00
					$868.00	$0.00
49	Teresa	Gomez				
			EL25	Elend Marina	$413.50	$678.75
			PM34	Peter's Marina	$0.00	$0.00
					$413.50	$678.75
					$4,061.20	$2,454.00

Tuesday, September 11, 2001

Page 1 of 1

FIGURE 4-2

The **custom form** to be created is shown in Figure 4-3. Although similar to the form created in Project 1, it offers some distinct advantages. Some of the differences are merely aesthetic. The form has a title and the fields have been rearranged in two columns. In addition, two other major differences are present. This form displays the total amount and will calculate it automatically by adding the warranty and non-warranty amounts. Second, to assist users in entering the correct marina type and technician, the form contains **combo boxes**, which are boxes that allow you to select entries from a list. An arrow displays in the Technician Number field, for example. Clicking the arrow causes a list of the technicians in the Technician table to display as shown in the figure. You then can either type the desired technician number or click the desired technician.

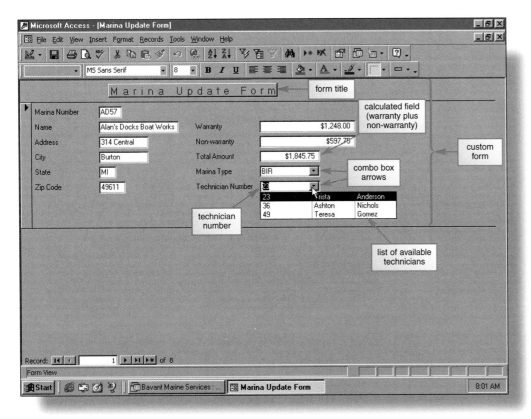

FIGURE 4-3

You are to create the reports requested by the management of Bavant Marine Services. You also must create the form the management deems to be important to the data-entry process.

Opening the Database

Before you create the reports or forms, you must open the database. Perform the following steps to complete this task.

TO OPEN A DATABASE

1 Click the Start button.

2 Click Open Office Document on the Start menu and then click 3½ Floppy (A:) in the Look in box. Make sure the database called Bavant Marine Services is selected.

3 Click the Open button.

The database is open and the Bavant Marine Services : Database window displays.

Report Creation

The simplest way to create a report design is to use the **Report Wizard**. For some reports, the Report Wizard can produce exactly the desired report. For others, however, you must first use the Report Wizard to produce a report that is as close as possible to the desired report. Then use the **Report window** to modify the report and transform it into the correct report. In either case, once the report is created and

More About

Creating a Report

There are two alternatives to using the Report Wizard to create reports. You can use AutoReport to create a very simple report that includes all fields and records in the table or query. Design View also allows you to create a report from scratch.

Using Queries for Reports

Records in a report will appear in the specified order if you have sorted the data in the query. You also can enter criteria in the query to specify that only those records that satisfy the criteria will be included in the report. Reports based on queries open faster than those based on tables.

saved, you can print it at any time. Access will use the current data in the database for the report, formatting and arranging it in exactly the way you specified when the report was created.

If a report uses only the fields in a single table, use the table as a basis for the report. If the report uses extra fields (such as Total Amount), however, the simplest way to create the report is to create a query using the steps you learned in Project 2. The query should contain only the fields required for the report. This query forms the basis for the report.

Creating a Query

The process of creating a query for a report is identical to the process of creating queries for any other purpose. Perform the following steps to create the query for the first report.

 To Create a Query

1 **In the Database window, click Tables on the Objects bar, if necessary, and then click Marina. Click the New Object: AutoForm button arrow on the Database window toolbar. Click Query. Be sure Design View is selected, and then click the OK button. Maximize the Query1 : Select Query window. Resize the upper and lower panes and the Marina field box so that all the fields in the Marina table display.**

2 **Double-click Marina Number. Select Ascending as the sort order for the field. Double-click the names of the fields to include the Name, Address, City, State, and Zip Code fields in the design grid. Right-click in the Field row of the column for the additional field (the field after the Zip Code field). Point to Zoom on the shortcut menu.**

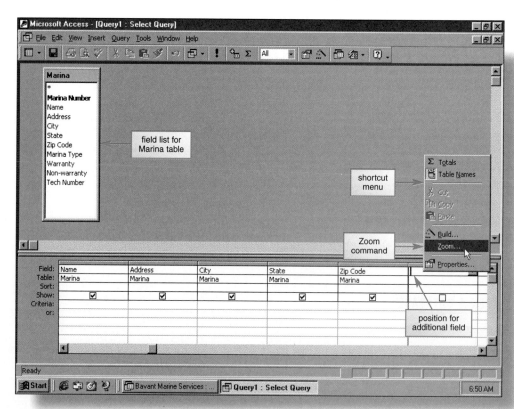

FIGURE 4-4

The shortcut menu for the extra field displays (Figure 4-4).

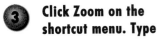 **Click Zoom on the shortcut menu. Type**
Total Amount:
[Warranty]+[Non-
warranty] **in the Zoom dialog box and point to the OK button (Figure 4-5).**

 Click the OK button. Click the Close button for the Select Query window and then click the Yes button.

(5) Type Marina Amount Query **as the name of the query and then click the OK button.**

The query is saved, and the Select Query window closes.

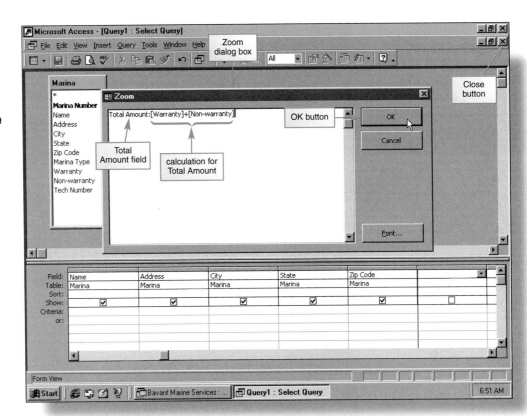

FIGURE 4-5

Creating a Report

Next, you will create a report using the Report Wizard. Access leads you through a series of choices and questions and then creates the report automatically. Perform the following steps to create the report shown in Figure 4-1 on page A 4.5.

Steps **To Create a Report**

(1) In the Database window, click Queries on the Objects bar, if necessary, and then click Marina Amount Query. Click the New Object: AutoForm button arrow on the Database window toolbar and then point to Report (Figure 4-6).

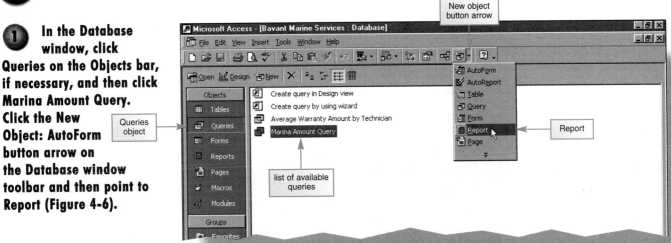

FIGURE 4-6

Microsoft **Access 2000**

2 **Click Report. Click Report Wizard. If necessary, click the Choose the table or query where the object's data comes from down arrow, and then click Marina Amount Query. Point to the OK button.**

The New Report dialog box displays and the Marina Amount Query is selected (Figure 4-7).

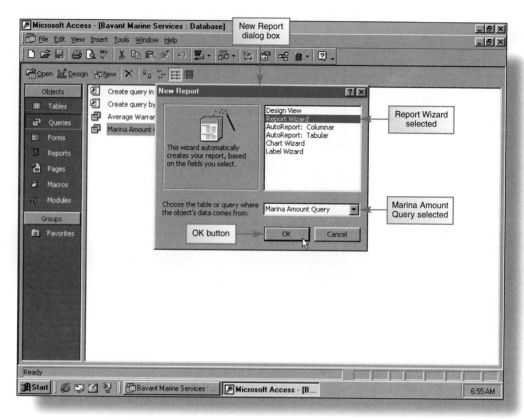

FIGURE 4-7

3 **Click the OK button and then point to the Add All Fields button.**

The Report Wizard dialog box displays, requesting the fields for the report (Figure 4-8). To add the selected field to the list of fields on the report, use the Add Field button. To add all fields, use the Add All Fields button.

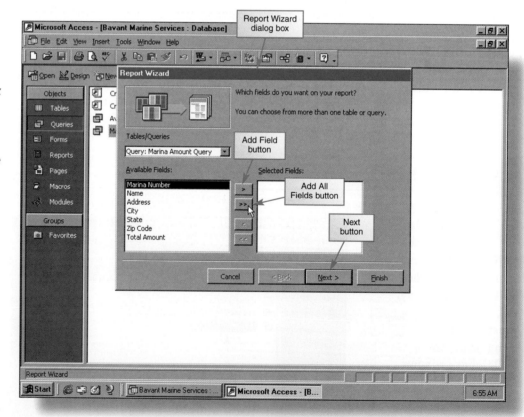

FIGURE 4-8

4 Click the Add All Fields button to add all the fields, and then click the Next button.

The next Report Wizard dialog box displays, requesting the field or fields for grouping levels (Figure 4-9). This report will not include grouping levels.

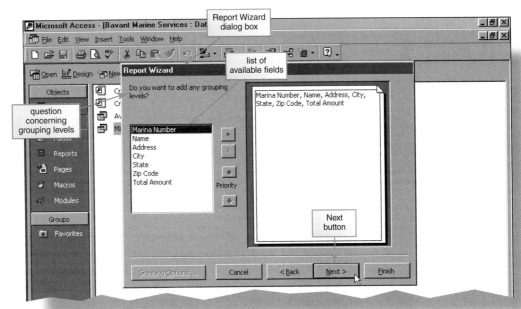

FIGURE 4-9

5 Click the Next button. The next Report Wizard dialog box displays, requesting the sort order for the report (Figure 4-10). The query already is sorted in the appropriate order, so you will not need to specify a sort order.

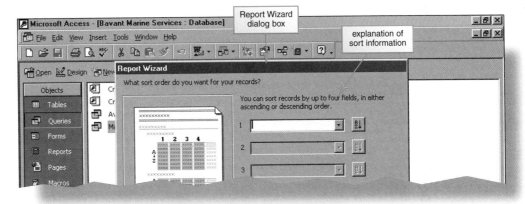

FIGURE 4-10

6 Click the Next button. The next Report Wizard dialog box displays, requesting your report layout preference (Figure 4-11).

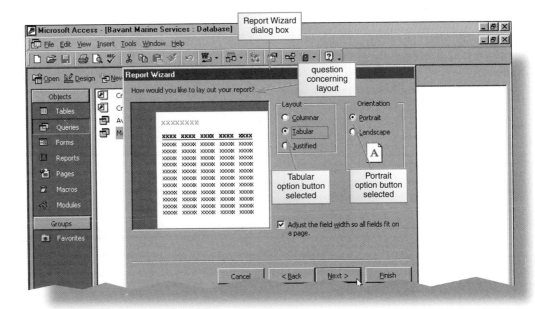

FIGURE 4-11

7 Be sure the options selected in the Report Wizard dialog box on your screen match those shown in Figure 4-11, and then click the Next button. If Formal is not already selected, click Formal to select it. Point to the Next button.

The next Report Wizard dialog box displays, requesting a style for the report (Figure 4-12). The Formal style is selected.

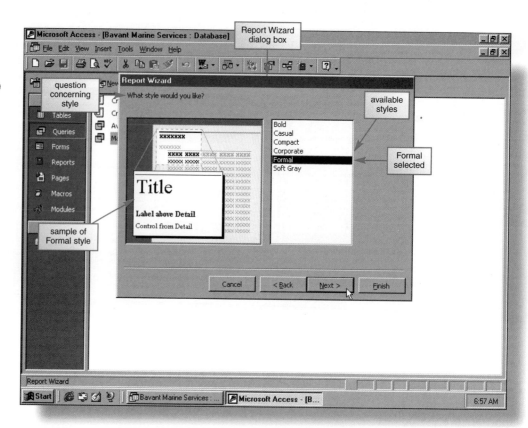

FIGURE 4-12

8 Click the Next button and then type Marina Amount Report as the report title. Point to the Finish button.

The next Report Wizard dialog box displays, requesting a title for the report (Figure 4-13). Marina Amount Report is entered as the title.

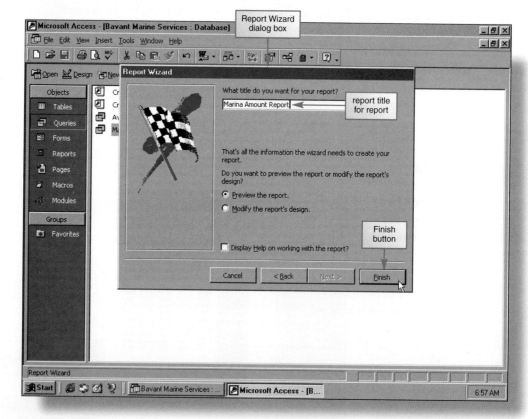

FIGURE 4-13

*Tag 3-4 trayle', Whistr diennay se
ikior fixed*

9 Click the Finish button.

The report design is complete and displays in Print Preview (Figure 4-14). (If your computer displays an entire page of the report, click the portion of the report displaying the mouse pointer.)

10 Click the Close button of the window containing the report to close the report.

The report no longer displays.

Microsoft Access - [Marina Amount Report]

File Edit View Tools Window Help

100% Close

portion of name does not display

Close button

preview of report

Marina Amount Report

Marina Number	Name	Address	City	State	Zip Code	Total Amount
AD57	Alan's Docks Boat Wor	314 Central	Burton	MI	49611	$1,845.75
BL72	Brite's Landing	281 Robin	Burton	MI	49611	$217.00
EL25	Elend Marina	462 River	Torino	MI	48268	$1,092.25
FB96	Fenton's Boats	36 Bayview	Cavela	MI	47926	$1,580.70
FM22	Fedder's Marina	283 Waterfron	Burton	MI	49611	$432.00
NW72	Nelson's Wharf	27 Lake	Masondale	MI	49832	$1,128.50
PM34	Peter's Marina	453 Wilson	Torino	MI	48268	$0.00

FIGURE 4-14

Because of the insufficient amount of space allowed in the report shown in Figure 4-14, some of the data does not display completely. The final portion of the name of Alan's Docks Boat Works does not display, for example. You will need to correct this problem.

Moving to Design View and Docking the Toolbox

Within the Report window, the different possible views are Design view and Print Preview. Use **Design view** to modify the design (layout) of the report. Use **Print Preview** to see the report with sample data. To move from Design view to Print Preview, click the Print Preview button on the Report Design toolbar. To move from Print Preview to Design view, click the button labeled Close on the Print Preview toolbar.

Within Print Preview, you can switch between viewing an entire page and viewing a portion of a page. To do so, click somewhere within the report (the mouse pointer will change shape to a magnifying glass).

In Design view, you can modify the design of the report. A **toolbox** is available in Design view that allows you to create special objects for the report. The toolbox also can obscure a portion of the report. You can use the Toolbox button on the Report Design toolbar to remove it and then return it to the screen when needed. Because you use the toolbox frequently when modifying report and form designs, it is desirable to be able to leave it on the screen, however. You can move the toolbar to different positions on the screen using a process referred to as **docking**. To dock the toolbox in a different position, simply drag the title bar of the toolbox to the desired position. The bottom of the screen usually is a good position for it.

Perform the steps on the next page to move to Design view. You will also remove the **field box** that displays, because you will not need it.

Other Ways

1. On Objects bar click Reports, click New button, and then click Report Wizard to create report
2. On Objects bar click Reports, Create report by using wizard
3. On Insert menu click Report, click Report Wizard to create report

More About

Previewing a Report

You can view two pages at the same time when previewing a report by clicking the Two Pages button on the Print Preview toolbar. You can view multiple pages by clicking View on the menu bar, clicking Pages, and then clicking the number of pages to view.

To Move to Design View and Dock the Toolbox

1 Click the Reports object in the Database window, right-click Marina Amount Report, and then click Design View on the shortcut menu. If a field box displays, click its Close button.

The report displays in Design view (Figure 4-15).

2 If necessary, click the Toolbox button on the Report Design toolbar to display the toolbox. If the toolbox is not docked at the bottom of the screen as in Figure 4-15, dock it there by dragging its title bar to the bottom of the screen.

The field box no longer displays, and the toolbar is docked at the bottom of the screen.

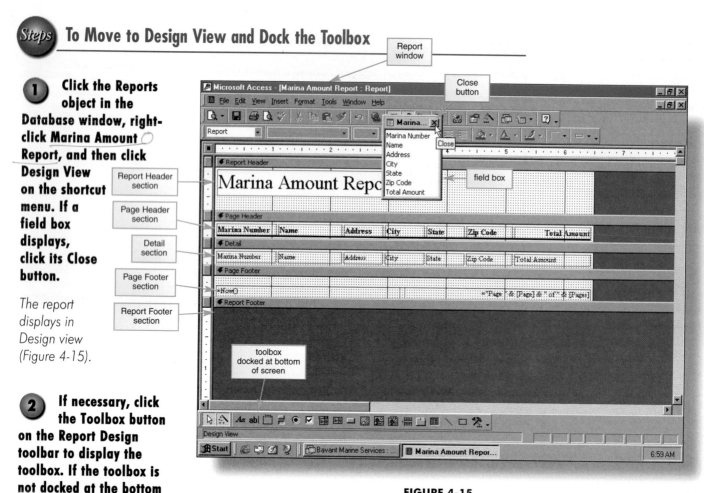

FIGURE 4-15

More About

Report Sections

Another common term for the sections in a report is band. The term, band-oriented, applied to a report tool means that the tool is very similar to the report design feature in Access; that is, you design a report by simply modifying the contents of the various sections (bands).

Report Sections

Each portion of the report is described in what is termed a **section**. The sections are labeled on the screen (see Figure 4-15). Notice the following sections: Report Header section, Page Header section, Detail section, Page Footer section, and Report Footer section.

The contents of the **Report Header section** print once at the beginning of the report. The contents of the **Report Footer section** print once at the end of the report. The contents of the **Page Header section** print once at the top of each page, and the contents of the **Page Footer section** print once at the bottom of each page. The contents of the **Detail section** print once for each record in the table.

The various rectangles displaying in Figure 4-15 (Marina Amount Report, Marina Number, Name, and so on) are called **controls**. All the information on a report or form is contained in the controls. The control containing Marina Amount Report displays the report title; that is, it displays the words, Marina Amount Report. The control in the Page Header section containing Name displays the word, Name.

The controls in the Detail section display the contents of the corresponding fields. The control containing Name, for example, will display the marina's name. The controls in the Page Header section serve as **captions** for the data. The Marina

Number control in this section, for example, will display the words, Marina Number, immediately above the column of marina numbers, thus making it clear to anyone reading the report that the items in the column are, in fact, marina numbers.

To move, resize, delete, or modify a control, click it. Small squares called **sizing handles** display around the border of the control. Drag the control to move it, drag one of the sizing handles to resize it, or press the DELETE key to delete it. Clicking a second time produces an insertion point in the control in order to modify its contents.

Changing Properties

Some of the changes you may make will involve using the property sheet for the control to be changed. The **property sheet** for each control is a list of properties that can be modified. By using the property sheet, you can change one or more of the control's properties. To produce the property sheet, right-click the desired control and then click Properties on the shortcut menu.

The problem of the missing data in the report shown in Figure 4-14 on page A 4.13 can be corrected in several ways.

1. Move the controls to allow more space in between them. Then, drag the appropriate handles on the controls that need to be expanded to enlarge them.
2. Use the Font Size property to select a smaller font size. This will allow more data to print in the same space.
3. Use the Can Grow property. By changing the value of this property from No to Yes, the data can be spread over two lines, thus allowing all the data to print. The name of customer AD57, for example, will have Alan's Docks Boat on one line and Works on the next line. Access will split data at natural break points, such as commas, spaces, and hyphens.

The first approach will work, but it can be cumbersome. The second approach also works but makes the report more difficult to read. The third approach, changing the Can Grow property, is the simplest method to use and generally produces a very readable report. Perform the following steps to change the Can Grow property for the Detail section.

guy fix car number field p A 4.13

 To Change the Can Grow Property

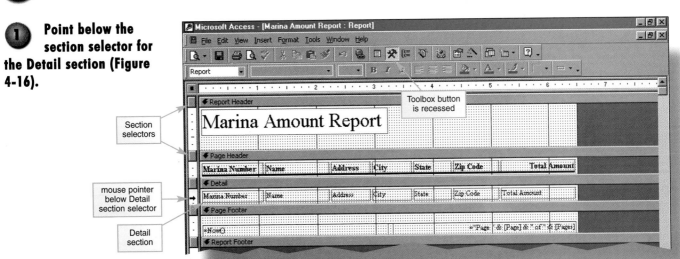

Point below the section selector for the Detail section (Figure 4-16).

FIGURE 4-16

2 **Right-click and then point to Properties on the shortcut menu.**

The shortcut menu displays (Figure 4-17). All the controls in the Detail section are selected.

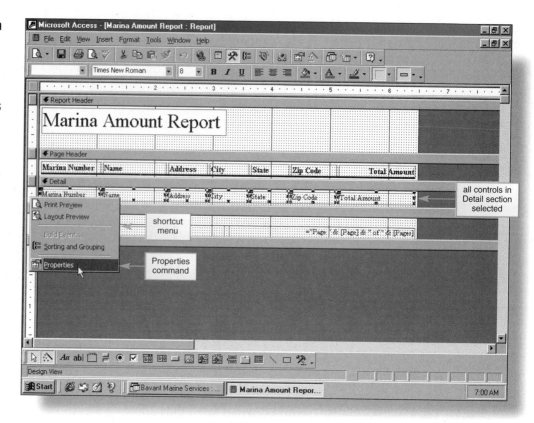

FIGURE 4-17

3 **Click Properties and then click the All tab, if necessary, to ensure that all available properties display. Click the Can Grow property, click the Can Grow box arrow, and then click Yes in the list that displays.**

The Multiple selection property sheet displays (Figure 4-18). All the properties display on the All sheet. The value for the Can Grow property has been changed to Yes.

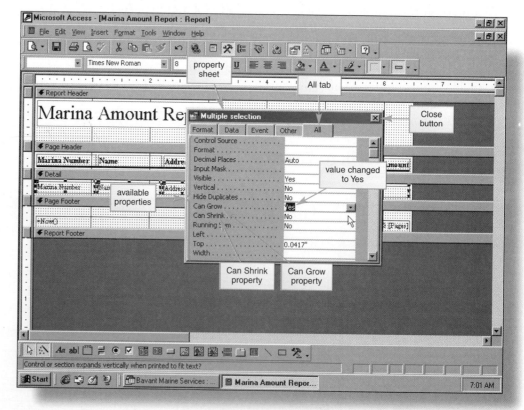

FIGURE 4-18

4 **Close the property sheet by clicking its Close button, and then point to the Print Preview button on the Report Design toolbar (Figure 4-19).**

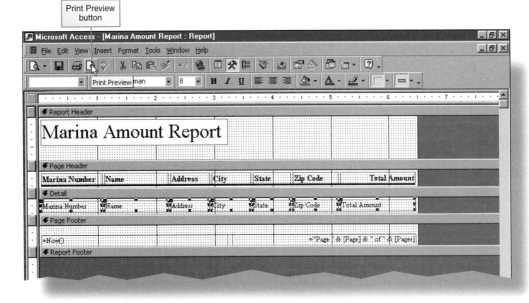

FIGURE 4-19

5 **Click the Print Preview button.**

A portion of the report displays (Figure 4-20). The names now display completely by extending to a second line. (If your computer displays an entire page, click the portion of the report displaying the mouse pointer in the figure.)

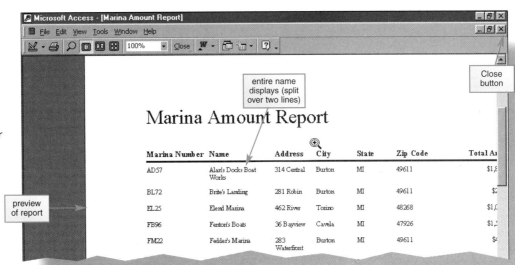

FIGURE 4-20

1. On File menu click Close

Closing and Saving a Report

To close a report, close the window using the window's Close button in the upper-right corner of the window. Then indicate whether or not you want to save your changes. Perform the following step to close the report.

TO CLOSE AND SAVE A REPORT

 Close the Report window and then click the Yes button to save the report.

Printing a Report

To print a report, right-click the report in the Database window, and then click Print on the shortcut menu. Perform the steps on the next page to print the Marina Amount Report.

To Print a Report

1 **In the Database window, if necessary, click the Reports object. Right-click Marina Amount Report. Point to Print on the shortcut menu.**

The shortcut menu for the Marina Amount Report displays (Figure 4-21).

2 **Click Print.**

The report prints. It should look like the report shown in Figure 4-1 on page A 4.5.

Cliekxong tó may liên print Co

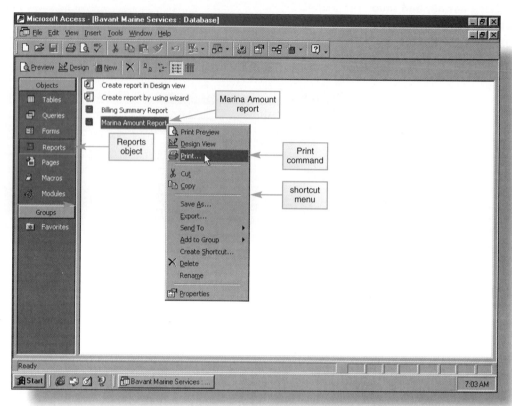

FIGURE 4-21

Grouping in a Report

Grouping arranges the records in your report. When records are grouped in a report, separate collections of records are created from those that share a common characteristic. In the report shown in Figure 4-2 on page A 4.6, for example, the records are grouped by technician number. Three separate groups were formed, one for each technician.

In grouping, reports typically include two additional types of sections: a group header and a group footer. A **group header** is printed before the records in a particular group are printed, and a **group footer** is printed after the group. In Figure 4-2, the group header indicates the technician number and name. The group footer includes the total of the warranty and non-warranty amounts for the marinas assigned to that technician. Such a total is called a **subtotal**, because it is a subset of the overall total.

Creating a Second Report

As you did when you created the first report, you will use the Report Wizard to create the second report. This time, however, you will select fields from two tables. To do so, you will select the first table (for example, Technician) and then select the fields from this table you would like to include. Next, you will select the second table (for example, Marina) and then select the fields from the second table. Perform the following steps to create the report shown in Figure 4-2 on page A 4.6.

More About

Grouping in a Report

To force each group to begin on a new page of the report, change the value of the Force-NewPage property for the group header section from None to Before Section. You can change the ForceNew-Page property for any section except the page header and page footer.

To Create a Second Report

1 **In the Database window, click the Reports object and then right-click Create report by using wizard. Click Design View on the shortcut menu. When the Report Wizard dialog box displays, click the Tables/Queries arrow and select Technician. Point to the Add Field button.**

The Report Wizard dialog box displays, requesting the fields for the report (Figure 4-22). Fields from the Technician table display. The Tech Number field is selected.

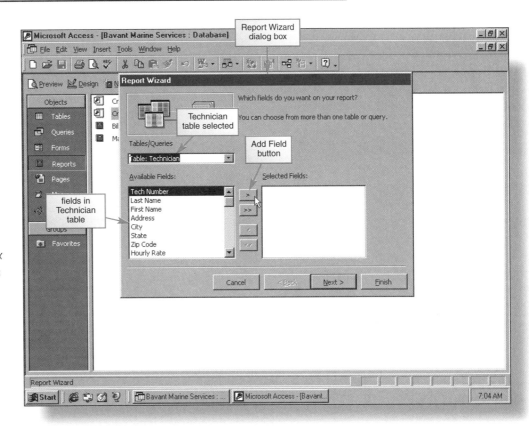

FIGURE 4-22

2 **Click the Add Field button to add the Tech Number field. Add the First Name field by clicking it and then clicking the Add Field button. Add the Last Name field in the same manner. Select the Marina table in the Tables/Queries list box and then point to the Add Field button.**

The Tech Number, First Name, and Last Name fields are selected (Figure 4-23). The fields from the Marina table display in the Available Fields box.

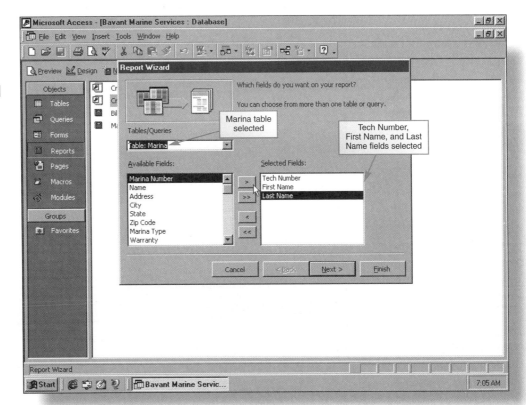

FIGURE 4-23

3 Add the Marina Number, Name, Warranty, and Non-warranty fields by clicking the field and then clicking the Add Field button. Click the Next button.

The next Report Wizard dialog box displays (Figure 4-24). Because the Technician and Marina tables are related, the wizard is asking you to indicate how the data is to be viewed; that is, the way the report is to be organized. The report may be organized by Technician or by Marina.

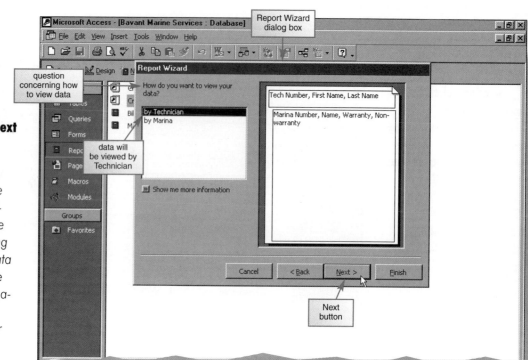

FIGURE 4-24

4 Because the report is to be viewed by technician and by Technician already is selected, click the Next button. Because no additional grouping levels are required, click the Next button a second time. Click the box 1 arrow and then click the Marina Number field. Point to the Summary Options button.

The next Report Wizard dialog box displays, requesting the sort order for detail records in the report; that is, the way in which records will be sorted within each of the groups (Figure 4-25). The Marina Number field is selected for the sort order, indicating that within the group of marinas of any technician, the marinas will be sorted by marina number.

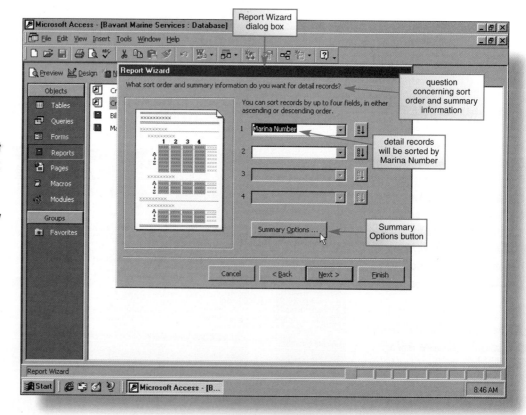

FIGURE 4-25

5 Click the Summary Options button. Point to the Sum check box in the row labeled Warranty.

The Summary Options dialog box displays (Figure 4-26). This dialog box allows you to indicate any statistics you want calculated in the report by clicking the appropriate check box.

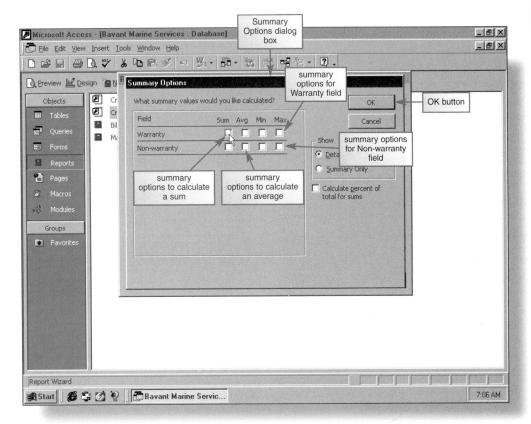

FIGURE 4-26

6 Click the Sum check box in the Warranty row and the Sum check box in the Non-warranty row. Click the OK button in the Summary Options dialog box, and then click the Next button. Click the Landscape option button.

The next Report Wizard dialog box displays, requesting your report layout preference (Figure 4-27). The Stepped layout, which is the correct one, already is selected. To see the effect of any of the others, click the appropriate option button. Landscape orientation is selected.

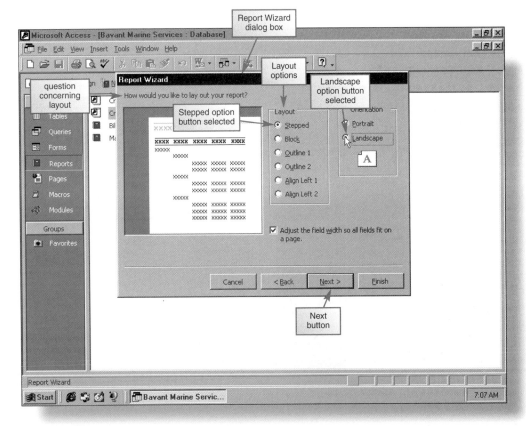

FIGURE 4-27

7 Be sure the options selected in the Report Wizard dialog box on your screen match those shown in Figure 4-27, and then click the Next button. If necessary, click Formal to select it.

The next Report Wizard dialog box displays, requesting a style for the report. The Formal style is selected (Figure 4-28).

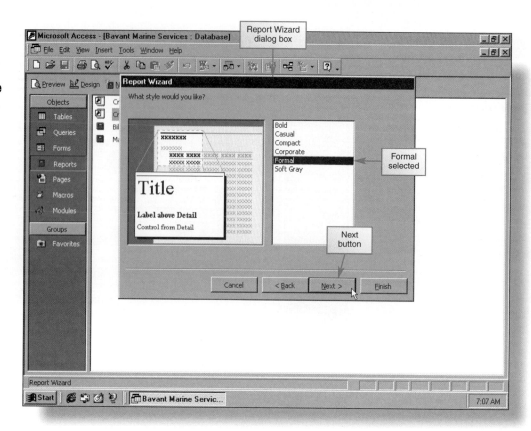

FIGURE 4-28

8 Click the Next button and then type Technician/Marina Report as the report title. Point to the Finish button.

The next Report Wizard dialog box displays, requesting a title for the report (Figure 4-29). Technician/Marina Report is typed as the title.

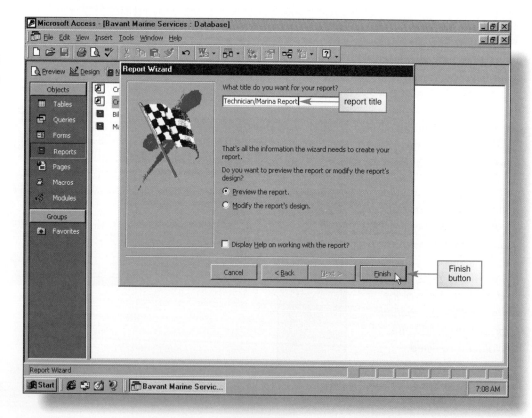

FIGURE 4-29

9 Click the Finish button.

The report design is complete and displays in the Print Preview window (Figure 4-30).

10 Close the report by clicking the Close button for the window containing the report.

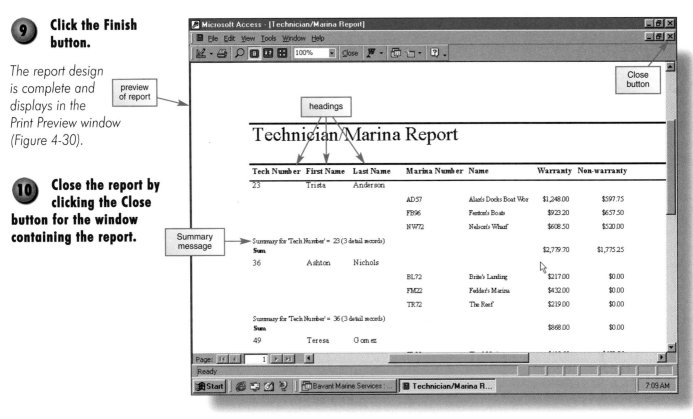

FIGURE 4-30

Reviewing the Report Design

You will find three major differences between the report shown in Figure 4-30 and the one illustrated in Figure 4-2 on page A 4.6. The first is that all the column headings in Figure 4-30 are on a single line, whereas they extend over two lines in the report in Figure 4-2. The first column heading in Figure 4-2 is Technician Number, instead of Tech Number. The second difference is that the report in Figure 4-2 does not contain the message that begins, Summary for Tech Number. There are other messages found on the report in Figure 4-30 that are not on the report in Figure 4-2, but they are included in a portion of the report that does not display. The third difference is that the marina name for Alan's Docks Boat Works does not display completely.

To complete the report design, you must change the column headings and remove these extra messages. In addition, you will move the Warranty and Non-warranty fields to make room for enlarging the Name field. You will then enlarge the Name field so the values display completely.

Removing Unwanted Controls

To remove the extra messages, or any other control, first click the control to select it. Then press the DELETE key to remove the unwanted control. Perform the steps on the next page to remove the unwanted controls from the report.

Steps: To Remove Unwanted Controls

1 Be sure the Reports object is selected in the Database window, right-click Technician/Marina Report, and then click Design View on the shortcut menu. If a field box displays, click its Close button. Point to the control that begins, ="Summary for " (Figure 4-31).

FIGURE 4-31

2 Click the control to select it, and then press the DELETE key to delete it. In a similar fashion, delete the control below that states Sum, and then delete the control that begins with the word, Grand.

The controls have been removed (Figure 4-32).

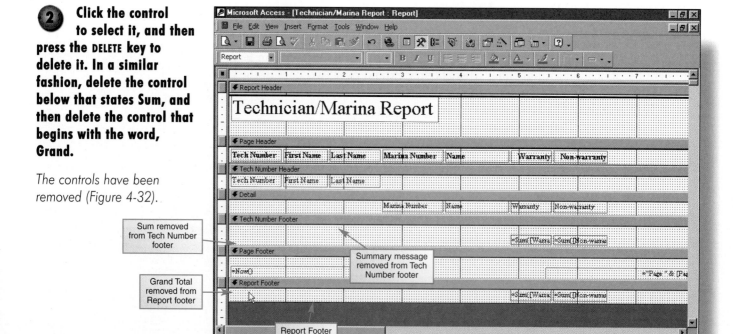

FIGURE 4-32

Enlarging the Page Header Section

The current Page Header section is not large enough to encompass the desired column headings because several of them extend over two lines. Thus, before changing the column headings, you must **enlarge** the Page Header. To do so, drag the bottom border of the Page Header section down. A bold line in the Page Header section immediately below the column headings also must be dragged down.

Perform the following steps to enlarge the Page Header section and move the bold line.

Steps: To Enlarge the Page Header Section

1 Point to the bottom border of the Page Header section (Figure 4-33). The mouse pointer shape changes to a two-headed vertical arrow with a crossbar.

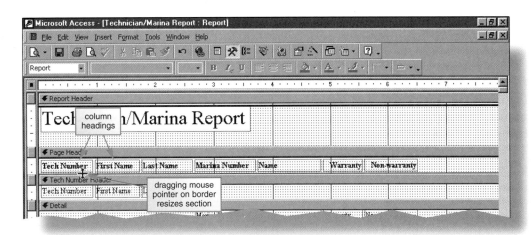

FIGURE 4-33

2 Drag the mouse pointer down to enlarge the size of the Page Header section to that shown in Figure 4-34 and then drag the bold line in the Page Header section down to the position shown in the figure.

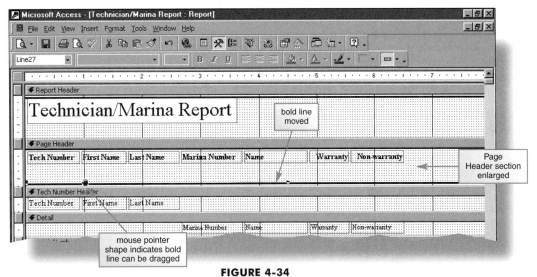

FIGURE 4-34

Changing Column Headings

To change a column heading, point to the position where you would like to display an insertion point. Click once to select the heading. Handles will display around the border of the heading after clicking. Then, click a second time to display the insertion point. Then you can make the desired changes. To delete a character, press the DELETE key to delete the character following the insertion point, or press the BACKSPACE key to delete the character preceding the insertion point. To insert a new character, simply type the character. To move the portion following the insertion point to a second line, press the SHIFT+ENTER keys.

If you click the second time too rapidly, Access will assume that you have double-clicked the heading. Double-clicking a control is another way to produce the control's property sheet. If this happens, simply close the property sheet and begin the process again.

Perform the following steps to change the column headings.

Steps: To Change the Column Headings

1 **Point immediately in front of the N in Number in the heading for the first field. Click the column heading for the first field to select it. Click it a second time to produce an insertion point in front of the N, and then press the SHIFT+ENTER keys. Click immediately after the h in Tech and then type** nician **to complete the word, Technician, on the first line.**

The heading is split over two lines, and the heading has been changed to Technician Number (Figure 4-35).

2 **Use the same technique to split the headings for the First Name, Last Name, and Marina Number fields over two lines.**

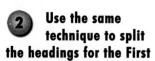

FIGURE 4-35

The changes to the header now are complete.

Moving and Resizing Controls

To move, resize, delete, or modify a single control, click it. Sizing handles display around the border of the control. To move the control, point to the boundary of the control, but away from any sizing handle. The mouse pointer changes shape to a hand. You then can drag the control to move it. To resize the control, drag one of the sizing handles.

You can move or resize several controls at the same time by selecting all of them before dragging. This is especially useful when controls must line up in a column. For example, the Warranty control in the Page Header should line up above the Warranty control in the Detail section. These controls also should line up with the controls in the Tech Number Footer and Report Footer sections that will display the sum of the warranty amounts.

To select multiple controls, click the first control you wish to select. Then hold down the SHIFT key while you click each of the others. The following steps first will select the controls in the Page Header, Detail, Tech Number Footer, and Report Footer sections that relate to the Warranty amount. You then will move and resize all these controls at once. Next, you will use the same technique to move and resize the controls that relate to the Non-warranty amount. Finally, to ensure enough room for complete names, you will enlarge the Name controls in the Page Header and Detail sections.

 Steps **To Move and Resize Controls**

① **Click the Non-warranty control in the Page Header section to select it. Hold down the SHIFT key and click the Non-warranty control in the Detail section, the control for the sum of the Non-warranty amounts in the Tech Number Footer section, and the control for the sum of the Non-warranty amounts in the Report Footer section. Release the SHIFT key. Point to the border of the Non-warranty control in the Page Header section but away from any handle. The mouse pointer shape should change to a hand.**

Multiple controls are selected, and the mouse pointer changes to a hand (Figure 4-36).

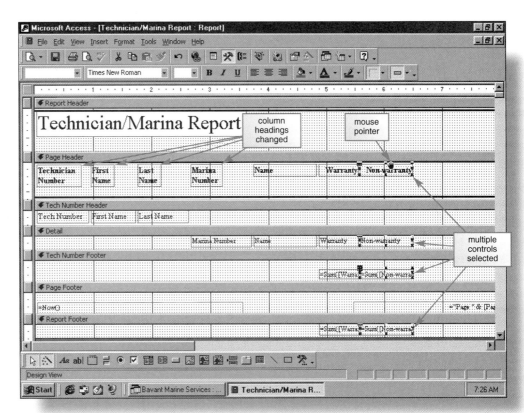

FIGURE 4-36

2 Drag the Non-warranty control in the Page Header section to the position shown in Figure 4-37. Drag the right sizing handle of the Non-warranty control in the Page Header section to change the size of the control to the one shown in the figure. You need not be exact.

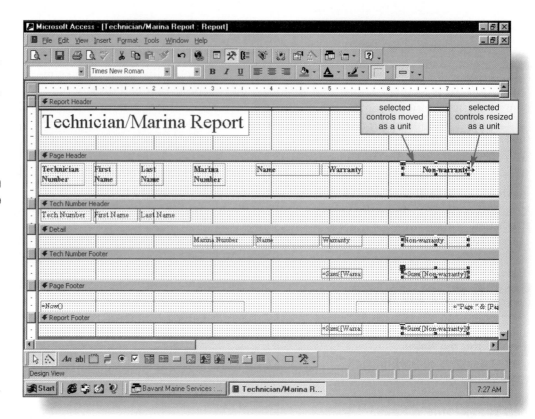

FIGURE 4-37

3 Use the same technique to move the controls for the Warranty field to the position shown in Figure 4-38 and change the size of the controls to those shown in the figure. Use the same technique to change the size of the controls for the Name field to those shown in the figure. Again, you need not be exact.

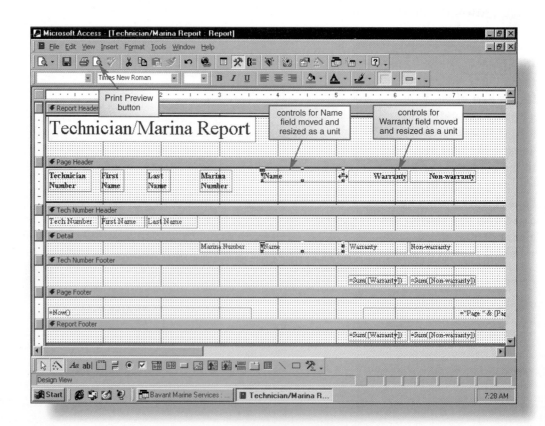

FIGURE 4-38

Previewing a Report

To see what the report looks like with sample data, preview the report by clicking the Print Preview button on the Report Design toolbar as illustrated in the following step.

TO PREVIEW A REPORT

 Click the Print Preview button on the Report Design toolbar. If the entire width of the report does not display, click anywhere within the report.

A preview of the report displays (Figure 4-39). The extra messages have been removed. The column headings have been changed and now extend over two lines.

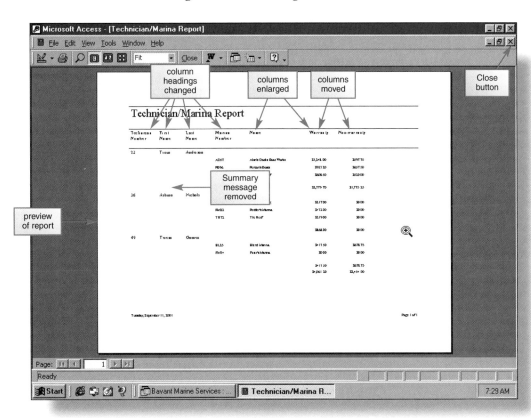

FIGURE 4-39

Closing and Saving a Report

To close a report, close the window using the window's Close button. Then, indicate whether you want to save your changes. Perform the following step to close and save the report.

TO CLOSE AND SAVE A REPORT

 Click the window's Close button to close the window. Click the Yes button to save the design of the report.

Printing a Report

To print the report, right-click the report name in the Database window, and then click Print on the shortcut menu as shown in the step on the next page.

TO PRINT A REPORT

① Make sure that the Reports object is selected in the Database window. Right-click Technician/Marina Report and then click Print on the shortcut menu.

The report prints. It should look like the report shown in Figure 4-2 on page A 4.6.

Report Design Considerations

When designing and creating reports, keep in mind the following guidelines.

1. The purpose of any report is to provide specific information. Ask yourself if the report conveys this information effectively. Are the meanings of the rows and columns in the report clear? Are the column captions easily understood? Are all abbreviations used in the report clear to those looking at the report?
2. Be sure to allow sufficient white space between groups. If you feel the amount is insufficient, add more space by enlarging the group footer.
3. You can use different fonts and sizes by changing the appropriate properties. It is important not to overuse them, however. Consistently using several different fonts and sizes often gives a cluttered and amateurish look to the report.
4. Be consistent when creating reports. Once you have decided on a general style, stick with it.

Creating and Using Custom Forms

Thus far, you have used a form to add new records to a table and change existing records. When you did, you created a basic form using the New Object: AutoForm button. Although the form did provide some assistance in the task, the form was not particularly pleasing. The standard form stacked fields on top of each other at the left side of the screen. This section covers custom forms that you can use in place of the basic form created by the Form Wizard. To create such a form, first use the Form Wizard to create a basic form. Then modify the design of this form, transforming it into the one you want.

Beginning the Form Creation

To create a form, click the Tables object and select the table. Click the New Object button arrow and then Form. Next, use the Form Wizard to create the form. The Form Wizard will lead you through a series of choices and questions. Access then will create the form automatically.

Perform the steps on the next page to create an initial form. This form later will be modified to produce the form shown in Figure 4-3 on page A 4.7.

Report Design

Proper report design is critical because users judge the value of information based on the way it is presented. Many organizations have formal rules governing the design of printed documents. For more information, visit the Access 2000 Project 4 More About page (www.scsite.com/ac2000/more.htm) and click Report Design.

Creating Forms

There are two alternatives to using the Form Wizard to create forms. You can use AutoForm to create a very simple form that includes all fields in the table or query. You also can use Design View to create a form from scratch.

Steps To Begin Creating a Form

1 **Make sure the Tables object is selected and then click Marina. Click the New Object button arrow, click Form, and then click Form Wizard. Click the OK button and then point to the Add Field button.**

The Form Wizard dialog box displays (Figure 4-40). The Marina Number field is selected.

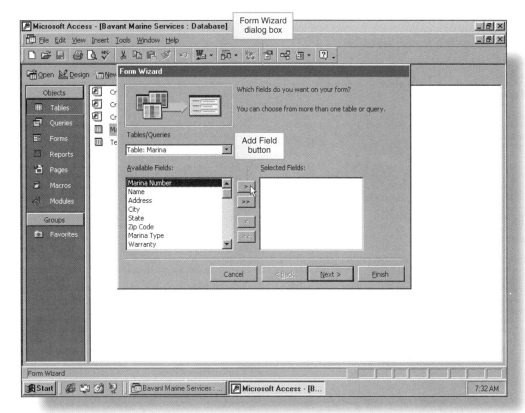

FIGURE 4-40

2 **Use the Add Field button to add all the fields except the Marina Type and Tech Number fields. Then click the Next button. When asked for a layout, be sure Columnar is selected, and then click the Next button again.**

The Form Wizard dialog box displays, requesting a form style (Figure 4-41).

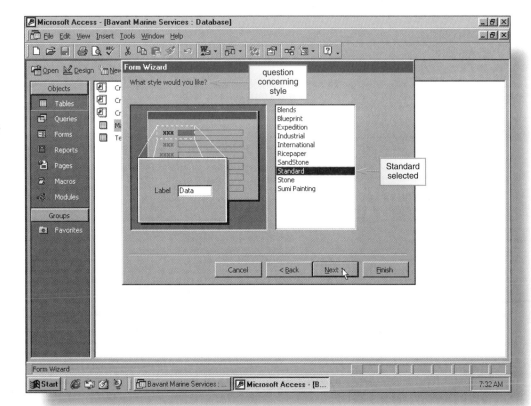

FIGURE 4-41

3 Be sure Standard is selected, click the Next button, and then type Marina Update Form **as** the title for the form. Click the Finish button to complete and display the form.

The form displays (Figure 4-42).

4 Click the Close button for the Marina Update Form window to close the form.

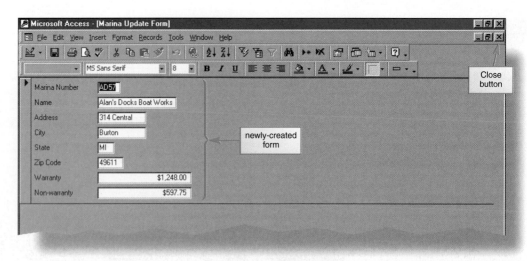

FIGURE 4-42

1. On Objects bar click Forms, click New button, and then click Form Wizard
2. On Objects bar click Forms, click Create form by using wizard
3. On Insert menu click Form, click Form Wizard

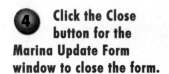

Attached Labels

You can remove an attached label by clicking the label and then pressing the DELETE key. The label will be removed, but the control will remain. To attach a label to a control, create the label, click the Cut button, click the Control, and then click the Paste button.

Modifying the Form Design

To modify the design of an existing form, right-click the form in the Database window, and then click Design View on the shortcut menu. At this time, you can modify the design. The modifications can include moving fields, adding new fields, and changing field characteristics. In addition, you can add special features, such as combo boxes and titles and change the colors used.

Just as with reports, the various items on a form are called **controls**. The three types are bound controls, unbound controls, and calculated controls. **Bound controls** are used to display data that comes from the database, such as the marina number and name. Bound controls have attached labels that typically display the name of the field that furnishes the data for the control. The **attached label** for the Marina Number field, for example, is the portion of the screen immediately to the left of the field. It contains the words, Marina Number.

Unbound controls are not associated with data from the database and are used to display such things as the form's title. Finally, **calculated controls** are used to display data that is calculated from other data in the database, such as the Total Amount, which is calculated by adding the warranty and non-warranty amounts.

To move, resize, delete, or modify a control, click it. Clicking a second time produces an insertion point in the control to let you modify its contents. When a control is selected, handles display around the border of the control and, if appropriate, around the attached label. If you point to the border of the control, but away from any handle, the pointer shape will change to a hand. You then can drag the control to move it. If an attached label displays, it will move along with the control. If you wish to move the control or the attached label separately, drag the large handle in the upper-left corner of the control or label. To resize the control, drag one of the sizing handles; and to delete it, press the DELETE key.

Just as with reports, some of the changes you wish to make to a control will involve using the property sheet for the control. You will use the property sheet of the Total Amount control, for example, to change the format that Access uses to display the contents of the control.

Perform the steps on the next page to modify the design of the Marina Update Form and dock the toolbox at the bottom of the screen, if necessary.

Steps | **To Modify the Form Design**

1 **In the Bavant Marine Services Database window, click the Forms object. Right-click Marina Update Form and then click Design View on the shortcut menu. Maximize the window, if necessary. If a field box displays, click its Close button. Be sure the toolbox displays and is docked at the bottom of the screen. (If it is not, drag the title bar of the toolbox below the scroll bar at the bottom of the screen and release the left mouse button.)**

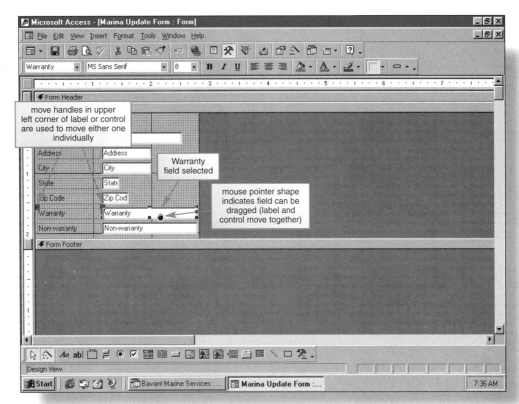

FIGURE 4-43

2 **Click the control for the Warranty field, and then move the mouse pointer until the shape changes to a hand. (You will need to point to the border of the control but away from any handle.)**

Move handles display, indicating the field is selected (Figure 4-43). The shape of the mouse pointer changes to a hand.

3 **Drag the Warranty field to the approximate position shown in Figure 4-44. The form will expand automatically in size to accommodate the new position for the field.**

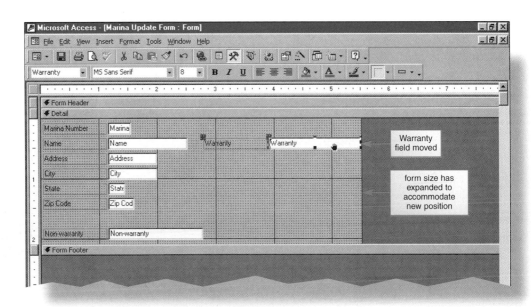

FIGURE 4-44

4 Use the same steps to move the Non-warranty field to the position shown in Figure 4-45.

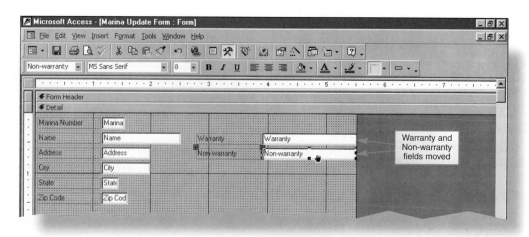

FIGURE 4-45

Adding a New Field

To add a new field, use the Text Box button in the toolbox to add a field. After clicking the Text Box button, click the position for the field on the form, and then indicate the contents of the field. Perform the following steps to add the Total Amount field to the form.

Steps To Add a New Field

1 Point to the Text Box button in the toolbox (Figure 4-46).

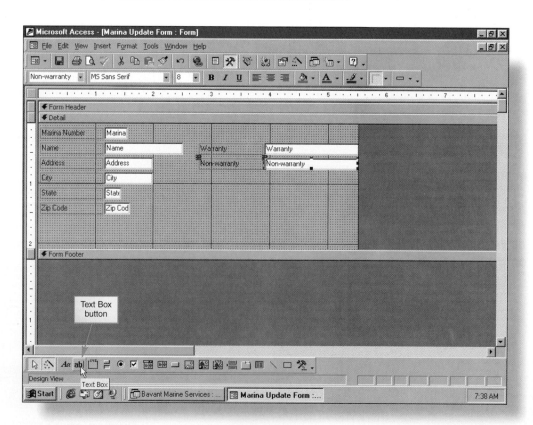

FIGURE 4-46

2 Click the Text Box button in the toolbox, and then move the mouse pointer, which has changed shape to a small plus symbol accompanied by a text box, to the position shown in Figure 4-47.

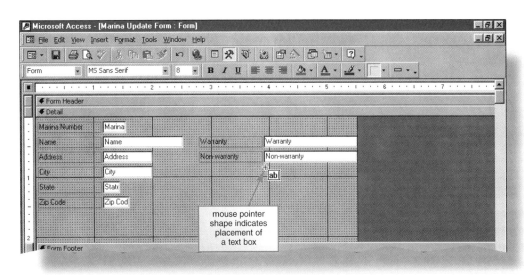

mouse pointer shape indicates placement of a text box

FIGURE 4-47

3 Click the position shown in Figure 4-47 to place a text box. Click inside the text box and type =[Warranty]+ [Non-warranty] as the expression in the text box. Click the field label (the *But Not Doubl Click* box that contains the word Text) twice, once to select it and a second time to display an insertion point. Use the DELETE key or the BACKSPACE key to delete the current entry. Type Total Amount as the new entry.

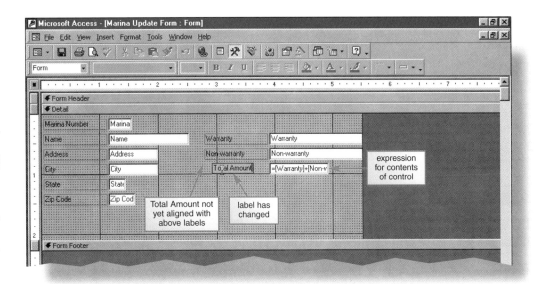

Total Amount not yet aligned with above labels

label has changed

expression for contents of control

FIGURE 4-48

The expression for the field has been entered and the label has been changed to Total Amount (Figure 4-48).

4 Click outside the Total Amount control to deselect it. Then, click the control to select it once more. Handles will display around the control. Move the label portion so its left edge lines up with the labels for the Warranty and Non-warranty fields by dragging the move handle in its upper-left corner. Click outside the control to deselect it.

Changing the Format of a Field

Access automatically formats fields from the database appropriately because it knows their data types. Usually, you will find the formats assigned by Access to be acceptable. For calculated fields, such as Total Amount, however, Access just assigns a general format. The value will not display automatically with two decimal places and a dollar sign.

Adding a Field

You can receive assistance in entering the expression for a field you are adding by using the Expression Builder. To do so, click the Control Source property on the control's property sheet and then click the Build button. The Expression Builder dialog box will then display.

To change to a special format, such as Currency, which displays the number with a dollar sign and two decimal places, requires using the field's property sheet to change the Format property. Perform the following steps to change the format for the Total Amount field to Currency.

 To Change the Format of a Field

1 **Right-click the control for the Total Amount field (the box containing the expression) to produce its shortcut menu and then click Properties on the shortcut menu. Click the All tab, if necessary, so all the properties display, and then click the Format property. Point to the Format box arrow.**

The property sheet for the field displays in the Text Box window (Figure 4-49).

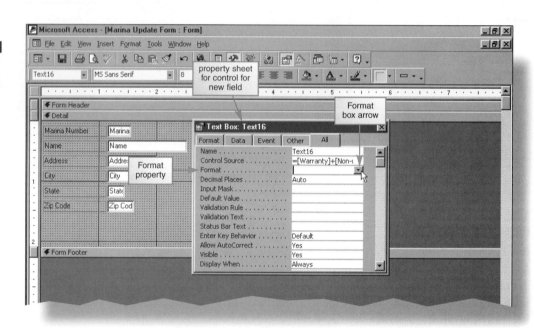

FIGURE 4-49

2 **Click the Format box arrow to produce a list of available formats. Scroll down so Currency displays and then click Currency. Close the property sheet by clicking its Close button.**

The values in the Total Amount field will display in Currency format, which includes a dollar sign and two decimal places.

Changing a Format

Access assigns formats to database fields, but these formats can be changed by changing the Format property of the fields. The specific formats that are available depend on the data type of the field. The Format list also contains samples of the way the data will display using the various formats.

Combo Boxes

When entering a value for the marina type, there are only three legitimate values: BIR, IWO, and RSO. When entering a technician number, the value must match the number of a technician currently in the technician table. To assist the users in entering this data, the form will contain combo boxes. With a **combo box**, the user can type the data, if that is convenient. Alternatively, the user can click the combo box arrow to display a list of possible values and then select an item from the list.

To place a combo box in the form, use the Combo Box button in the toolbox. If the **Control Wizards button** in the toolbox is recessed, you can use a wizard to guide you through the process of creating the combo box. Perform the steps on the next page to place a combo box for the Marina Type field on the form.

To Place a Combo Box that Selects Values from a List

1 Make sure the Control Wizards button in the toolbox is recessed. Point to the Combo Box button in the toolbox (Figure 4-50).

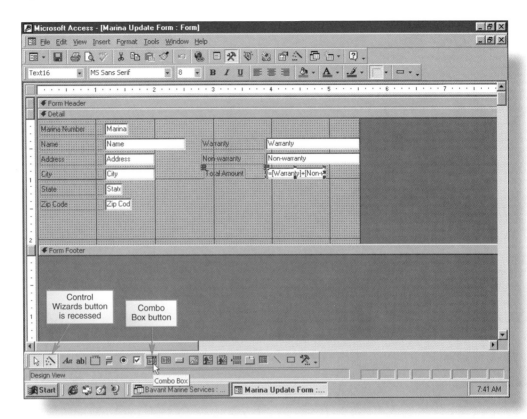

FIGURE 4-50

2 Click the Combo Box button in the toolbox, and then move the mouse pointer, whose shape has changed to a small plus symbol accompanied by a combo box, to the position shown in Figure 4-51.

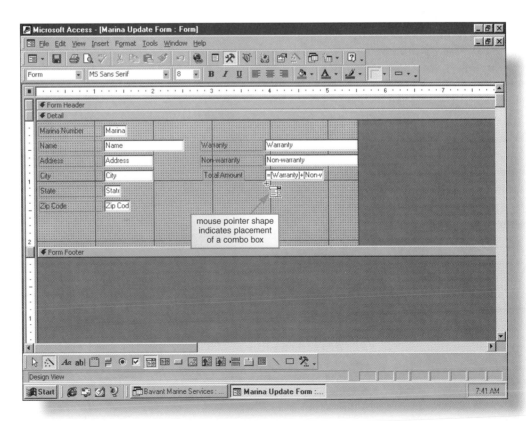

FIGURE 4-51

Microsoft Access 2000

3 **Click the position shown in Figure 4-51 to place a combo box.**

The Combo Box Wizard dialog box displays, requesting that you indicate how the combo box is to receive values for the list (Figure 4-52).

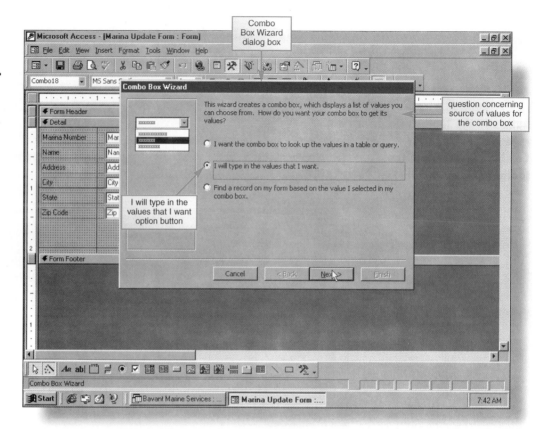

FIGURE 4-52

4 **If necessary, click I will type in the values that I want option button to select it as shown in Figure 4-52. Click the Next button in the Combo Box Wizard dialog box, click the first row of the table (under Col1) and then type** BIR**. Press the DOWN ARROW key and then type** IWO**. Press the DOWN ARROW key again and then type** RSO**. Point to the Next button.**

The list of values for the combo box is entered (Figure 4-53).

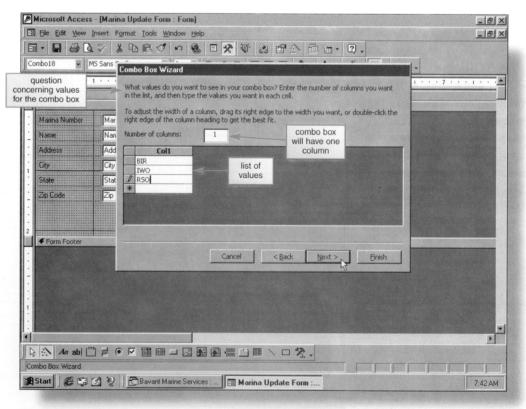

FIGURE 4-53

5 Click the Next
button. Click Store
that value in this field.
Click the Store that value
in this field box arrow, and
then click Marina Type.
Point to the Next button.

*The Store that value in this
field option button is
selected, and the Marina
Type field is selected (Figure
4-54).*

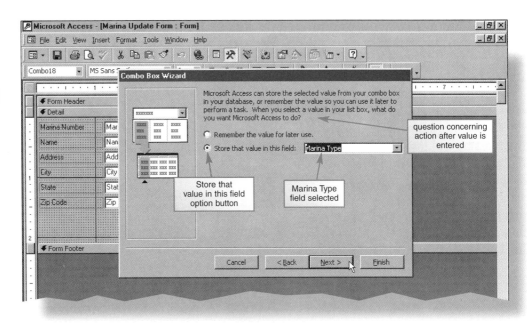

FIGURE 4-54

6 Click the Next
button. Type
`Marina Type` as the label
for the combo box and
point to the Finish button.

*The label is entered (Figure
4-55).*

7 Click the Finish
button. Click the
label for the combo box,
and then move the label so
that its left edge aligns
with the left edge of the
labels for the Warranty,
Non-warranty, and Total
Amount fields. Select the
label and then expand it by
double-clicking the handle
on its right edge so the
entire Marina Type label
displays.

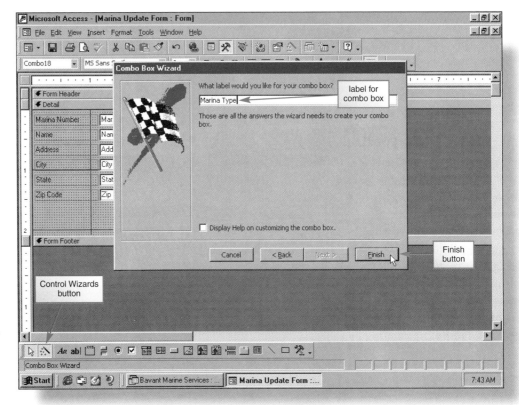

FIGURE 4-55

The steps for placing a combo box to select values from a table are similar to those for placing a combo box to select values from a list. The only difference is the source of the data. Perform the steps on the next page to place a combo box for the Tech Number field on the form.

To Place a Combo Box that Selects Values from a Related Table

1 With the Control Wizards button in the toolbox recessed, click the Combo Box button in the toolbox, and then move the mouse pointer, whose shape has changed to a small plus symbol accompanied by a combo box, to the position shown in Figure 4-56.

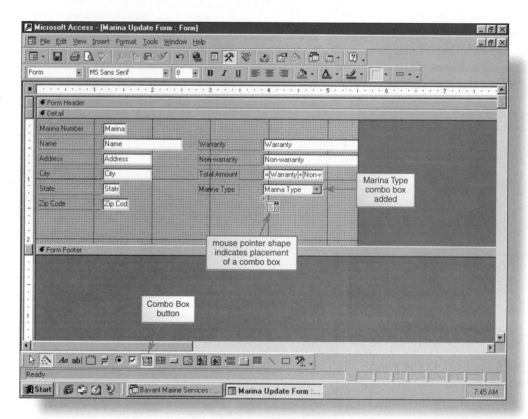

FIGURE 4-56

2 Click the position shown in Figure 4-56 to place a combo box. In the Combo Box wizard, click I want the combo box to look up the values in a table or query if it is not already selected. Click the Next button, click the Technician table, and then point to the Next button.

The Technician table is selected as the table to provide values for the combo box (Figure 4-57).

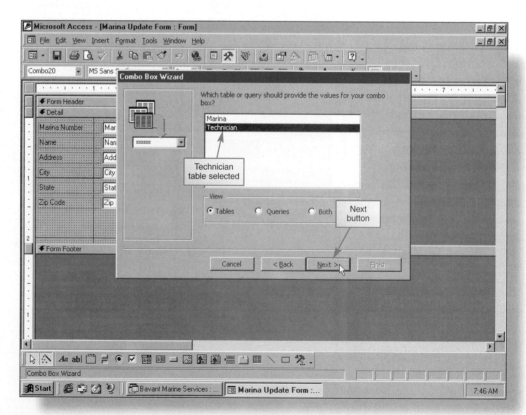

FIGURE 4-57

3 Click the Next button. Click the Add Field button to add the Tech Number as a field in the combo box. Click the First Name field and then click the Add Field button. Click the Last Name field and then click the Add Field button. Point to the Next button.

The Tech Number, First Name, and Last Name fields are selected for the combo box (Figure 4-58).

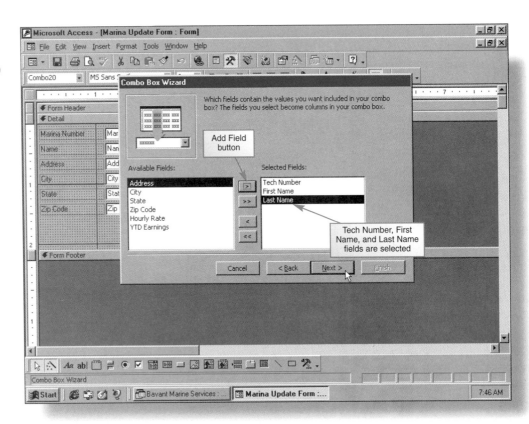

FIGURE 4-58

4 Click the Next button. Point to the Hide key column (recommended) check box.

The next Combo Box Wizard dialog box displays (Figure 4-59). You can use this dialog box to change the sizes of the fields. You also can use it to indicate whether the key field, in this case the Tech Number field, should be hidden.

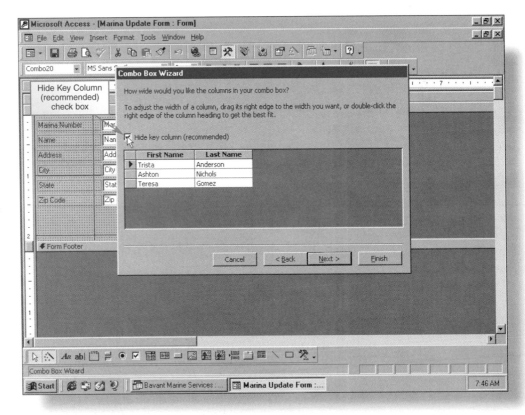

FIGURE 4-59

5 Click **Hide key column (recommended)** to remove the check mark to ensure the Tech Number field displays along with the First Name and Last Name fields. Resize each column to best fit the data by double-clicking the right-hand border of the column heading. Click the **Next** button.

The Combo Box Wizard dialog box displays, asking you to choose a field that uniquely identifies a row in the combo box (Figure 4-60). The Tech Number field, which is the correct field, is already selected.

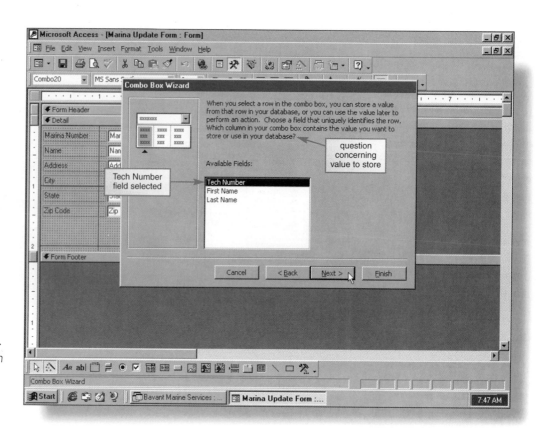

FIGURE 4-60

6 Click the **Next** button. Click **Store that value in this field.** Click the **Store that value in this field** box arrow, scroll down, and then click **Tech Number.** Click the **Next** button. Type `Technician Number` as the label for the combo box.

7 Click the **Finish** button. Click the label for the combo box, and then move the label so its left edge aligns with the left edge of the Marina Type, Warranty, Non-warranty, and Total Amount fields. Select the label and then expand it by double-clicking the handle on its right edge so the entire Technician Number label displays. Click anywhere outside the label to deselect the label.

Adding a Title

The form in Figure 4-3 on page A 4.7 contains a title, Marina Update Form, that displays in a large, light blue label at the top of the form. To add a title, first expand the Form Header to allow room for the title. Next, use the Label button in the toolbox to place the label in the Form Header. Finally, type the title in the label. Perform the following steps to add a title to the form.

To Add a Title

1 Point to the bottom border of the Form Header. The mouse pointer changes shape to a two-headed vertical arrow with a crossbar as shown in Figure 4-61.

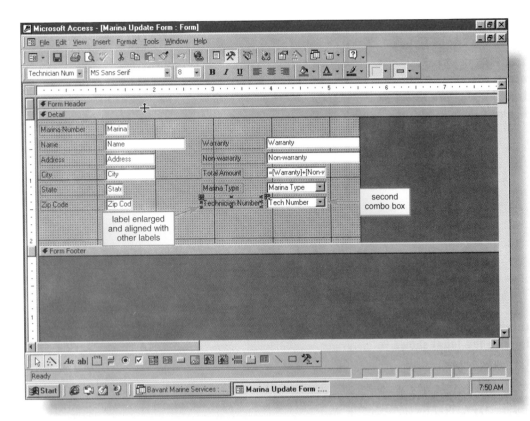

FIGURE 4-61

2 Drag the bottom border of the Form Header to the approximate position shown in Figure 4-62, and then point to the Label button in the toolbox.

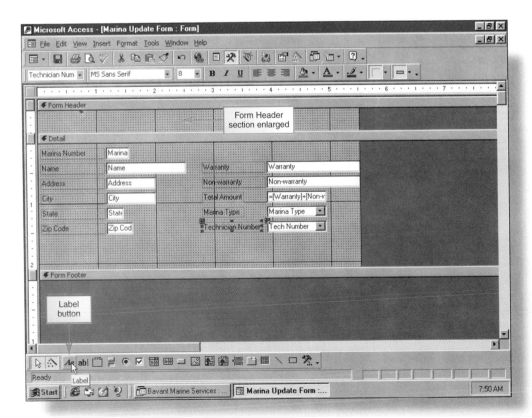

FIGURE 4-62

3 **Click the Label button in the toolbox and move the mouse pointer, whose shape has changed to a small plus symbol accompanied by a label, into the position shown in Figure 4-63.**

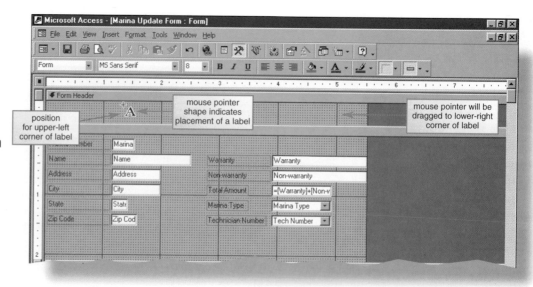

FIGURE 4-63

4 **Drag the pointer to the opposite corner of the Form Header to form the label shown in Figure 4-64.**

5 **Type** Marina Update Form **as the form title.**

The title is entered.

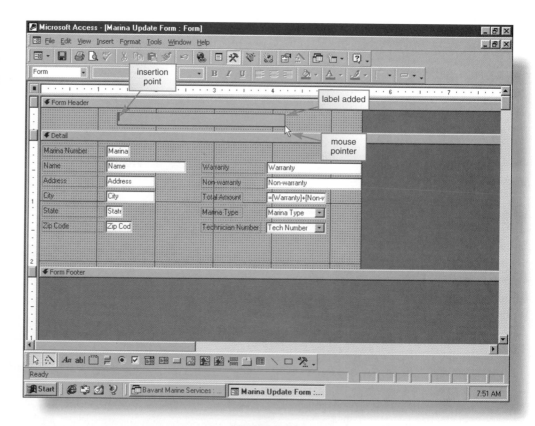

FIGURE 4-64

Enhancing a Title

The form now contains a title. You can enhance the appearance of the title by changing various properties of the label containing the title. The steps on the next page change the color of the label, make the label appear to be raised from the screen, change the font size of the title, and change the alignment of the title within the label.

To Enhance a Title

1 **Click somewhere
outside the label
containing the title to
deselect the label.
Deselecting is required
or right-clicking the
label will have no
effect. Next, right-click the
label containing the title.
Point to Properties on the
shortcut menu.**

*The shortcut menu for the
label displays (Figure 4-65).*

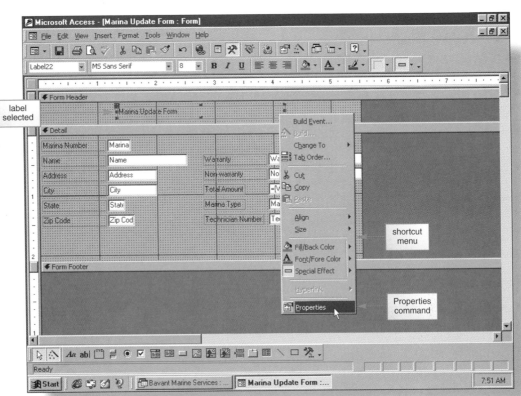

FIGURE 4-65

2 **Click Properties. If
necessary, click the
All tab on the property
sheet. Click Back Color and
then point to the Build
button (the button with the
three dots).**

*The property sheet for the
label displays. The insertion
point displays in the Back
Color property (Figure 4-66).*

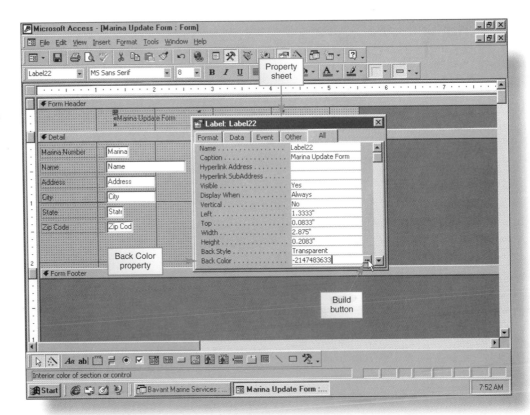

FIGURE 4-66

3 Click the Build button and then point to the color light blue in the Color dialog box that displays (Figure 4-67).

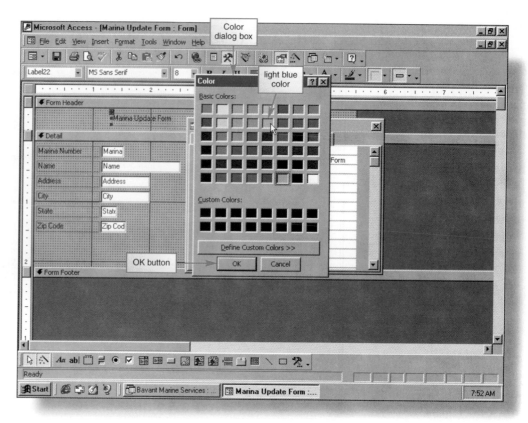

FIGURE 4-67

4 Click the color light blue, and then click the OK button. Scroll down the property sheet, click the Special Effect property, and then click the Special Effect box arrow.

The list of available values for the Special Effect property displays (Figure 4-68).

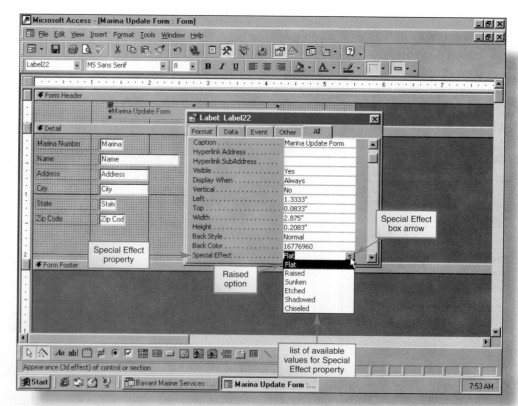

FIGURE 4-68

5 **Click Raised. Scroll down the property sheet and then click the Font Size property. Click the Font Size box arrow. Click 14 in the list of font sizes that displays. Scroll down and then click the Text Align property. Click the Text Align box arrow.**

The list of available values for the Text Align property displays (Figure 4-69).

6 **Click Distribute. Close the property sheet by clicking its Close button. If necessary, use the sizing handles to resize the label so that the entire title displays. Click outside the label to deselect it.**

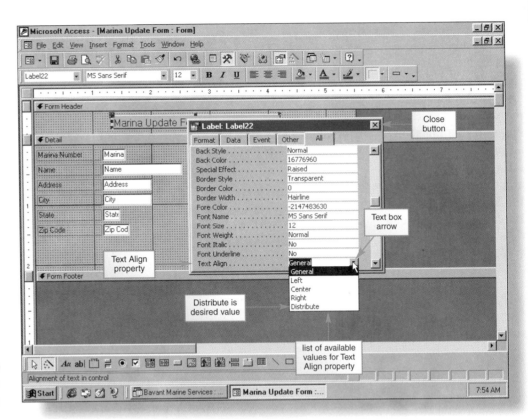

FIGURE 4-69

The enhancements to the title now are complete.

Changing Tab Stops

Users cannot change the value for the total amount. Instead, it will be recalculated automatically whenever the warranty or non-warranty amounts change. Consequently, if users repeatedly press the TAB key to move through the controls on the form, the Total Amount control should be bypassed. In order to force this to happen, change the Tab Stop property for the control from Yes to No as illustrated in the steps on the next page.

Microsoft Certification

The Microsoft Office User Specialist (MOUS) Certification program provides an opportunity for you to obtain a valuable industry credential - proof that you have the Access 2000 skills required by employers. For more information, see Appendix D or visit the Shelly Cashman Series MOUS Web page at www.scsite.com/off2000/cert.htm.

Nếu Access consider cái field "Total Amount" như là một "Label" chứ không phải là "Text" thì tìm trong properties box ở thẻ mục "Tab Stop". Lúc này ta phải switch thuộc tính của field này về "Text" bằng cách click "abl" rồi click "Total Amount"

Steps **To Change a Tab Stop**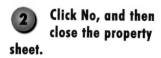

1 **Right-click the Total Amount control, and then click Properties on the shortcut menu. Click the down scroll arrow until the Tab Stop property displays, click the Tab Stop property, click the Tab Stop box arrow, and then point to No (Figure 4-70).**

2 **Click No, and then close the property sheet.**

The modifications to the control are complete. With this change, tabbing through the controls on the form will bypass the total amount.

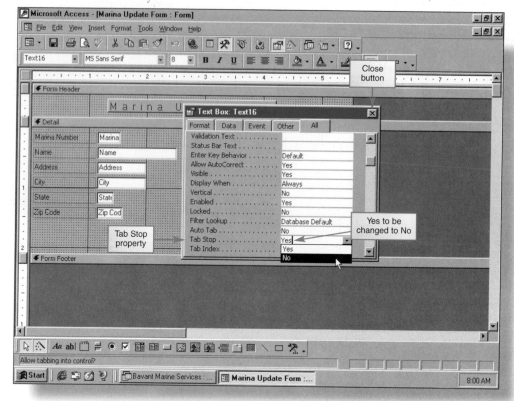

FIGURE 4-70

Other Ways

1. On File menu click Close

Closing and Saving a Form

To close a form, close the window using the window's Close button. Then indicate whether you want to save your changes. Perform the following step to close and save the form.

TO CLOSE AND SAVE A FORM

1 Click the window's Close button to close the window, and then click the Yes button to save the design of the form.

Opening a Form

To open a form, right-click a form in the Database window, and then click Open on the shortcut menu. The form will display and can be used to examine and update data. Perform the following steps to open the Marina Update Form.

TO OPEN A FORM

1 With the Forms object selected, right-click the Marina Update Form to display the shortcut menu. Click Open on the shortcut menu.

The form displays. It should look like the form shown in Figure 4-3 on page A 4.7.

Other Ways

1. Select form, click Open button on Database window toolbar
2. Double-click form

Using a Form

You use this form as you used the form in Project 3, with two differences. Access will not allow changes to the Total Amount, because Access calculates this amount automatically by adding the warranty and non-warranty amounts. The other difference is that this form contains combo boxes.

To use a combo box, click the arrow. Clicking the arrow in the Marina Type combo box produces a list of marina types (Figure 4-71). Clicking the arrow in the Technician Number combo box produces a list of numbers and the names of available technicians display as shown in Figure 4-3. In either case, you can type the appropriate value from the list you see on the screen or you can simply click the value in the list. With either method, the combo box helps you enter the correct value.

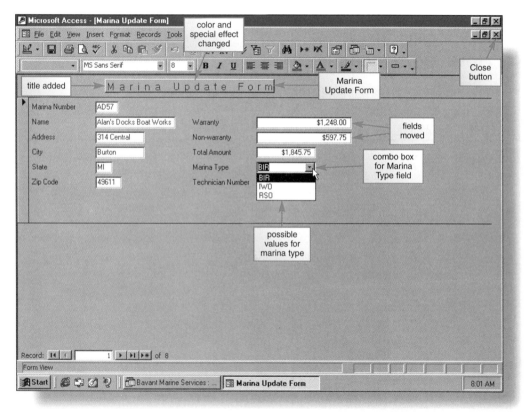

FIGURE 4-71

Closing a Form

To close a form, simply close the window containing the form. Perform the following step to close the form.

TO CLOSE A FORM

1 Click the Close button for the Form window.

More About

Quick Reference

For a table that lists how to complete the tasks covered in this book using the mouse, menu, shortcut menu, and keyboard, visit the Office 2000 Web page (www.scsite.com/off2000/qr.htm), and then click Microsoft Access 2000.

Form Design

Forms should be visually appealing and present data logically and clearly. Properly designed forms improve both the speed and accuracy of data entry. For more information, visit the Access 2000 Project 4 More About page (www.scsite.com/ac2000/more.htm) and click Form Design.

Form Design Considerations

As you design and create custom forms, keep in mind the following guidelines.

1. Remember that someone using your form may be looking at the form for several hours at a time. Forms that are cluttered or contain too many different effects (colors, fonts, frame styles, and so on) can become very hard on the eyes.
2. Place the fields in logical groupings. Fields that relate to each other should be close to one another on the form.
3. If the data that a user will enter comes from a paper form, make the screen form resemble the paper form as closely as possible.

Closing The Database

The following step closes the database by closing its Database window.

TO CLOSE A DATABASE

 Click the Close button for the Bavant Marine Services : Database window.

CASE PERSPECTIVE SUMMARY

In Project 4, you assisted the management of Bavant Marine Services by creating two custom reports and a data entry form. You created the first report from a query that used a calculated field. In the second report, you grouped records by technician number and displayed subtotal and grand total amounts. You created a custom form that used a calculated control and combo boxes.

Project Summary

In Project 4, you created two reports and a form. To create the reports, you learned the purpose of the various sections and how to modify their contents. You used grouping in a report. Then, you created and used a custom form. Steps and techniques were presented showing you how to move controls, create new controls, add combo boxes, and add a title. You changed the characteristics of various objects in the form. You also learned general principles to help you design effective reports and forms.

What You Should Know

Having completed this project, you now should be able to perform the following tasks:

- Add a New Field *(A 4.34)*
- Add a Title *(A 4.42)*
- Begin Creating a Form *(A 4.30)*
- Change a Tab Stop *(A 4.47)*
- Change the Can Grow Property *(A 4.15)*
- Change the Column Headings *(A 4.25)*
- Change the Format of a Field *(A 4.35)*
- Close a Database *(A 4.50)*
- Close a Form *(A 4.49)*
- Close and Save a Form *(A 4.48)*
- Close and Save a Report *(A 4.17, A 4.29)*
- Create a Report *(A 4.9)*
- Create a Query *(A 4.8)*
- Create a Second Report *(A 4.18)*
- Enhance a Title *(A 4.44)*
- Enlarge the Page Header Section *(A 4.25)*
- Modify the Form Design *(A 4.32)*
- Move and Resize Controls *(A 4.26)*
- Move to Design View and Dock the Toolbox *(A 4.13)*
- Open a Database *(A 4.7)*
- Open a Form *(A 4.48)*
- Place a Combo Box to Select Values from a List *(A 4.37)*
- Place a Combo Box to Select Values from a Related Table *(A 4.40)*
- Preview a Report *(A 4.29)*
- Print a Report *(A 4.17, A 4 29)*
- Remove Unwanted Controls *(A 4.23)*

Apply Your Knowledge

⊕ Project Reinforcement at www.scsite.com/off2000/reinforce.htm

1 Presenting Data in the Sidewalk Scrapers Database

Instructions: Start Access and open the Sidewalk Scrapers database from the Access Data Disk. See the inside back cover for instructions for downloading the Access Data Disk or see your instructor for information on accessing the files required for this book. Perform the following tasks.

1. Create the report shown in Figure 4-72. Sort the report by Customer Number.
2. Print the report.
3. Using the Form Wizard, create a form for the Customer table. Include all fields except Worker Id on the form. Use Customer Update Form as the title for the form.

4. Modify the form in the Design window to create the form shown in Figure 4-73. The form includes a combo box for the Worker Id field.
5. Print the form. To print the form, open the form, click File on the menu bar, and then click Print. Click Selected Record(s) as the Print Range. Click the OK button.

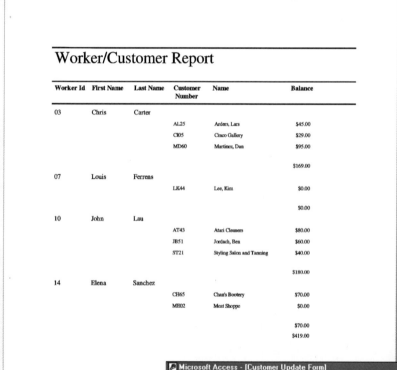

FIGURE 4-72

FIGURE 4-73

In the Lab

1 Presenting Data in the School Connection Database

Problem: The Booster's Club already has realized the benefits from the database of items and vendors that you created. The club must now prepare reports for auditors as well as the school board. The club greatly appreciates the validation rules that were added to ensure that data is entered correctly. They now feel they can improve the data entry process even further by creating custom forms.

FIGURE 4-74

Instructions: Open the School Connection database from the Access Data Disk. See the inside back cover for instructions for downloading the Access Data Disk or see your instructor for information on accessing the files required for this book. Perform the following tasks.

On Hand Value Report

Item Id	Description	On Hand	Cost	On Hand Value
BA02	Baseball Cap	15	$12.50	$187.50
CM12	Coffee Mug	20	$3.75	$75.00
DM05	Doormat	5	$14.25	$71.25
MN04	Mouse Pad	5	$9.10	$45.50
OR01	Ornament	25	$2.75	$68.75
PL05	Pillow	8	$13.50	$108.00
PN21	Pennant	22	$5.65	$124.30
PP20	Pen and Pencil Set	12	$16.00	$192.00
SC11	Scarf	17	$8.40	$142.80
WA34	Wastebasket	3	$14.00	$42.00

1. Create the On Hand Value Report shown in Figure 4-74 for the Item table. On Hand Value is the result of multiplying On Hand by Cost.
2. Print the report.
3. Create the Vendor/Items report shown in Figure 4-75. Profit is the difference between Selling Price and Cost.
4. Print the report.
5. Create the form shown in Figure 4-76. On Hand Value is a calculated control and is the result of multiplying On Hand by Cost. Include a combo box for Vendor Code.
6. Print the form. To print the form, open the form, click File on the menu bar, and then click Print. Click Selected Record(s) as the Print Range. Click the OK button.

Vendor/Items Report

Vendor Code	Name	Item Id	Description	Selling Price	Cost	Profit
AL	Alum Logo Inc.					
		BA02	Baseball Cap	$15.00	$12.50	$2.50
		MN04	Mouse Pad	$11.00	$9.10	$1.90
		SC11	Scarf	$12.00	$8.40	$3.60
GG	GG Gifts					
		CM12	Coffee Mug	$5.00	$3.75	$1.25
		OR01	Ornament	$4.00	$2.75	$1.25
		PP20	Pen and Pencil Set	$20.00	$16.00	$4.00
		WA34	Wastebasket	$15.00	$14.00	$1.00
TM	Trinkets 'n More					
		DM05	Doormat	$17.00	$14.25	$2.75
		PL05	Pillow	$15.00	$13.50	$1.50
		PN21	Pennant	$7.00	$5.65	$1.35

FIGURE 4-75

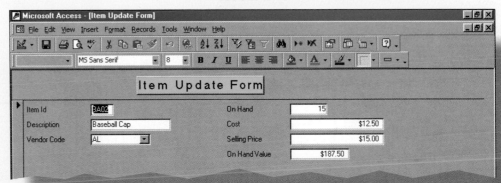

FIGURE 4-76

In the Lab

2 Presenting Data in the City Area Bus Company Database

Problem: The advertising sales manager already has realized several benefits from the database you created. The manager now would like to prepare reports from the database. He greatly appreciates the validation rules that were added to ensure that data is entered correctly. He now feels the data entry process can be improved even further by creating custom forms.

Instructions: Open the City Area Bus Company database from the Access Data Disk. See the inside back cover for instructions for downloading the Access Data Disk or see your instructor for information on accessing the files required for this book. Perform the following tasks.

1. Create the Advertising Income Report shown in Figure 4-77. Advertising Income is the sum of Balance and Amount Paid. Sort the report by Advertiser Id.
2. Print the report.
3. Create the Sales Rep/Advertiser report shown in Figure 4-78.
4. Print the report.
5. Create the form shown in Figure 4-79. Advertising Income is a calculated control and is the sum of Balance and Amount Paid. Ad Type and Sales Rep Number are combo boxes.

Sales Rep/Advertiser Report

Sales Rep Number	First Name	Last Name	Advertiser Id	Name	Ad Type	Amount Paid	Balance
24	Peter	Chou					
			AC25	Alia Cleaners	SER	$585.00	$85.00
			NO10	New Orient	DIN	$350.00	$150.00
			TM89	Tom's Market	RET	$500.00	$50.00
						$1,435.00	$285.00
29	Elvia	Ortiz					
			BB99	Bob's Bakery	RET	$1,150.00	$435.00
			CS46	Cara's Salon	SER	$660.00	$35.00
			HC11	Hilde's Cards & Gifts	RET	$500.00	$250.00
			MC34	Mom's Cookies	RET	$1,050.00	$95.00
						$3,360.00	$815.00
31	Pat	Reed					
			PJ24	Pajama Store	RET	$775.00	$0.00
			PP24	Pia's Pizza	DIN	$0.00	$50.00
						$775.00	$50.00
						$5,570.00	$1,150.00

FIGURE 4-78

Advertising Income Report

Advertiser Id	Name	City	Balance	Amount Paid	Advertising Income
AC25	Alia Cleaners	Crescentville	$85.00	$585.00	$670.00
BB99	Bob's Bakery	Richmond	$435.00	$1,150.00	$1,585.00
CS46	Cara's Salon	Cheltenham	$35.00	$660.00	$695.00
HC11	Hilde's Cards & Gifts	Crescentville	$250.00	$500.00	$750.00
MC34	Mom's Cookies	Crescentville	$95.00	$1,050.00	$1,145.00
NO10	New Orient	Manyunk	$150.00	$350.00	$500.00
PJ24	Pajama Store	Cheltenham	$0.00	$775.00	$775.00
PP24	Pia's Pizza	Richmond	$50.00	$0.00	$50.00
TM89	Tom's Market	Richmond	$50.00	$500.00	$550.00

FIGURE 4-77

In the Lab

FIGURE 4-79

6. Print the form. To print the form, open the form, click File on the menu bar, and then click Print. Click Selected Record(s) as the Print Range. Click the OK button.

3 Presenting Data in the Resort Rental Database

Instructions: Open the Resort Rentals database from the Access Data Disk. See the inside back cover for instructions for downloading the Access Data Disk or see your instructor for information on accessing the files required for this book Perform the following tasks.

1. Create the City Rental List shown in Figure 4-80. Sort the report in ascending order by city. Within city, the report should be sorted in ascending order by number of bedrooms and number of bathrooms. (*Hint*: Use a query to sort the data and base the report on the query.)
2. Print the report.
3. Create the Owner/Rental Units report shown in Figure 4-81 on the next page. Sort the data by city within each group.

City Rental List

City	Address	Bedrooms	Bathrooms	Sleeps	Weekly Rate
Gulf Breeze	956 First	2	2	6	$1,100.00
Gulf Breeze	783 First	3	3	8	$1,000.00
Hutchins	24 Plantation	1	1	2	$675.00
Hutchins	521 Ocean	2	1	4	$750.00
Hutchins	523 Ocean	2	2	6	$900.00
San Toma	684 Beach	1	1	3	$700.00
San Toma	123 Gulf	3	2	8	$1,300.00
San Toma	123 Second	3	3	10	$1,400.00
Shady Beach	278 Second	2	1	4	$1,000.00
Shady Beach	345 Coastal	2	2	5	$900.00

FIGURE 4-80

(continued)

In the Lab

Presenting Data in the Resort Rental Database *(continued)*

4. Print the report.
5. Create the form shown in Figure 4-82. Owner Id is a combo box.
6. Add the current date to the form. Place the date in the upper right corner of the Form Header section. (*Hint*: Use Help to solve this problem.)
7. Print the form. To print the form, open the form, click File on the menu bar, and then click Print. Click Selected Record(s) as the Print Range. Click the OK button.

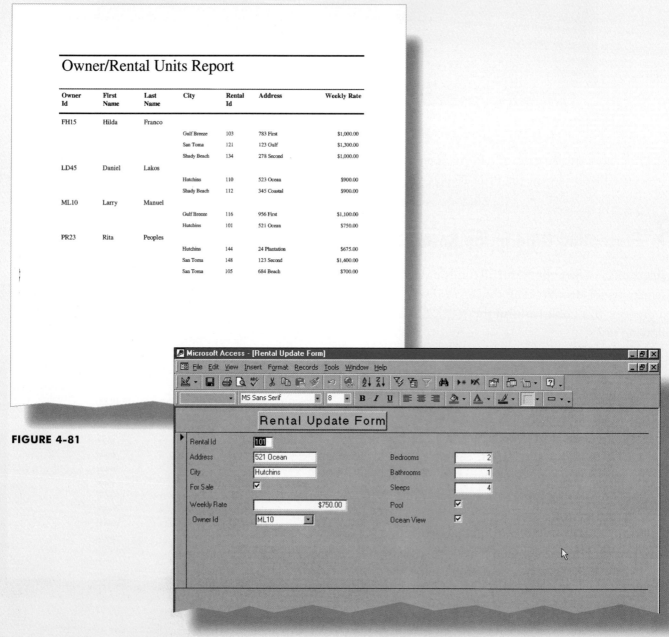

FIGURE 4-81

FIGURE 4-82

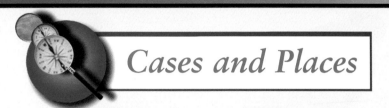

Cases and Places

The difficulty of these case studies varies:
▶ are the least difficult; ▶▶ are more difficult; and ▶▶▶ are the most difficult.

1 ▶ As a fund-raising project, the local college's Computer Science Club sells small computer accessories to students. Disks, disk cases, and mouse pads are some of the items the club sells from a small kiosk in the student computer lab. The club uses a database to keep track of their inventory and suppliers. The Computer Items database is on the Access Data Disk. Use this database and create the report shown in Figure 4-83. (*Hint:* Create a query and base the report on the query.) Print the report.

Supplier/Items Report

Name	Item Id	Description	Cost	Selling Price	Profit
Ergonomics Inc.					
	1663	Antistatic Wipes	$0.15	$0.25	$0.10
	2563	Desktop Holder	$3.85	$4.75	$0.90
Human Interfac					
	1683	CD Wallet	$3.45	$4.00	$0.55
	3923	Disk Cases	$2.20	$2.75	$0.55
	2593	Disks	$0.20	$0.75	$0.55
	6140	Zip Disk Wallet	$11.90	$14.00	$2.10
Mouse Trails					
	3953	Mouse Holder	$0.80	$1.00	$0.20
	5810	Mouse Pad-Logo	$3.45	$5.00	$1.55
	4343	Mouse Pad-Plain	$2.25	$3.00	$0.75

FIGURE 4-83

2 ▶ Using the database from Case Study 1 above, create the data entry form shown in Figure 4-84. Supplier code is a combo box. Inventory Value is a calculated field that is the result of multiplying the number of units on hand by the cost. Print the form.

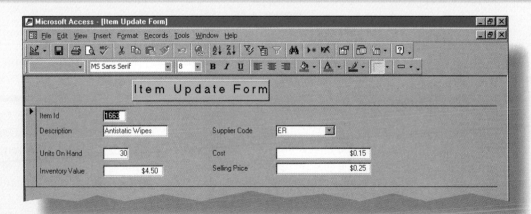

FIGURE 4-84

Cases and Places

3 ▶▶ Galaxy Books is a local bookstore that specializes in Science Fiction. The owner uses a database to keep track of the books she has in stock. The Galaxy Books database is on the Access Data Disk. Use this database to create a report similar to the one shown in Figure 4-74 on page A 4.53. Include the book code, book title, author, units on hand, and price fields. Use a calculated control called Stock Value that is the result of multiplying units on hand by price. Sort the report in ascending order by book title. Print the report. Create the report shown in Figure 4-85. The report groups books by publisher and displays the average book price for each publisher. Print the report.

Publisher/Books Report

Publisher Code	Publisher Name	Book Code	Title	Price	
BB	Bertrand Books				
		1019	Stargaze	$5.50	
		3495	Dark Wind	$4.95	
			Average Book Price		$5.23
PB	Pearless Books				
		128X	Comet Dust	$5.95	
		6517	Strange Alien	$8.95	
			Average Book Price		$7.45
SI	Simpson-Ivan				
		0488	Android Wars	$5.95	
		0533	Albert's Way	$4.75	
			Average Book Price		$5.35
VN	VanNester				
		1668	Robots R Us	$6.95	
		3859	No Infinity	$4.75	
		4889	The Galaxy	$6.75	
		7104	Secret Planet	$5.75	
			Average Book Price		$6.05

FIGURE 4-85

4 ▶▶ Using the database from Case Study 3, create a Book Update Form similar to the one shown in Figure 4-76 on page A 4.53. Use a calculated control called Stock Value that is the result of multiplying units on hand by price. Include a combo box for Publisher Code.

5 ▶▶▶ You are the treasurer for the Computer Science Club. Create a database to store information about the club's checking account. Include the check number, check payee, check amount, date written, and a code to indicate the expense category. Use expense categories such as supplies, food, meetings, and entertainment. Create and print a report that lists checks by expense category. In addition, create and print a form to help you update the database easily. Experiment with different styles.

Microsoft Access 2000

Enhancing Forms with OLE Fields, Hyperlinks, and Subforms

PROJECT 5

You will have mastered the material in this project when you can:

OBJECTIVES

- Use date, memo, OLE, and hyperlink fields
- Enter data in date fields
- Enter data in memo fields
- Enter pictures into OLE fields
- Enter Web page names into hyperlink fields
- Change the row and column spacing in tables
- Save table properties
- Create a form with a subform
- Move and resize fields on a form
- Change the styles and colors of labels
- Use special effects on forms
- Add a title to a form
- Use a form that contains a subform
- Use date and memo fields in a query
- Compact a database

Fingerprint Identification

Crime-Solving Data Gives FBI the Upper Hand

Automated fingerprint identification systems provide law enforcement officials around the country with technology for solving crimes. In the criminal justice system, hundreds of millions of fingerprint images have been added in the elaborate database tables filled with criminals' names, bodily characteristics, birth dates, and driver's license numbers, along with the nature of their crimes.

No two humans have the same patterns of swirls and ridges in their

fingerprints, so comparing these unique features has been the most powerful method of identifying people since Babylonians pioneered fingerprinting in 1700 B.C. The fingerprint identification technology is part of the growing field of biometrics, which identifies people based on physical characteristics. Manual comparisons of prints by looking through state and FBI files can take as long as three weeks, but computer database comparisons using search algorithms can make positive identifications in only two hours or less if a suspect is in custody.

The Federal Bureau of Investigation's Integrated Automated Fingerprint Identification System (IAFIS) is one of the largest of its kind, and the biggest single technology investment in FBI history. The system consists of a suite of powerful supercomputers, sophisticated image processing algorithms, and data management tools such as those available with Access 2000. The FBI system is capable of rapidly and accurately searching a national criminal database expected to grow to more than 400 million records by the year 2000. IAFIS is designed to be a rapid-response, paperless system that receives and processes electronic fingerprint images, criminal histories, and related data. Services include remote searches of crime scene fingerprints and remote access to fingerprint images.

Law enforcement officials get the prints when they arrest and book a suspect or when they obtain latent prints at the crime scene. If the subject has been apprehended, the officer rolls the suspect's fingers on a small glass plate connected to a computer. If the suspect has not been identified or apprehended, an evidence technician goes to the crime scene, uses special powders, chemicals, and lasers and lifts and photographs the print. In both cases, the fingerprints are displayed on the computer monitor, traced with a stylus to enhance the lines, scanned, and digitized. These images then are transmitted electronically to the FBI and added to the database.

The FBI receives more than 50,000 requests daily to query the database in an attempt to match prints with images stored in the database. The FBI's system is so elaborate it can handle requests to match partial, smudged, or faint prints.

IAFIS has been a success in helping the FBI nab nearly 3,000 fugitives a month by searching this database. San Francisco investigators cleared nearly 14 times more latent cases during their first year using this system as compared with the previous year.

Working hand in hand, the IAFIS and law enforcement community are apprehending many of the hundreds of thousands of fugitives on America's streets.

Microsoft Access 2000

Enhancing Forms with OLE Fields, Hyperlinks, and Subforms

PROJECT 5

C A S E   P E R S P E C T I V E

The management of Bavant Marine Services has found that it needs to maintain additional data on its technicians. Managers need to store the start date of each technician in the database. They also would like for the database to contain a description of the technician's specialties, the technician's picture, and the address of the technician's Web page.

They also would like to have a form created that incorporates some of the new fields along with some existing fields. In addition, the management would like for the form to contain the marina number, name, warranty amount, and non-warranty amount for the marinas of each technician. They would like to be able to display two or three marinas on the screen at the same time, as well as be able to scroll through all the marinas of a technician and be able to access his or her Web Page directly from the form. They will need queries that use the Start Date and Specialties fields as criteria. Finally, they are concerned the database is getting larger than necessary and would like to compact the database to remove any wasted space. You must help Bavant Marine Services make these changes.

Introduction

This project creates the form shown in Figure 5-1. The form incorporates the following features not covered in previous projects:

▶ New fields display in the form. The Specialties field allows the organization to store a paragraph describing the specialties of the technician. The Specialties entry can be only as long as the organization desires. The Picture field holds a photograph of the technician.

▶ The Web Page field enables the user to access the Technician's Web Page directly from the database.

▶ The form not only shows data concerning the technician, but also the technician's marinas. The marinas are displayed as a table on the form.

Project Five — Enhancing the Bavant Marine Services Forms

Before you create the form required by the management of Bavant Marine Services, you must change the structure of the Technician table to incorporate the four new fields: Start Date, Specialties, Picture, and Web Page. Each of these new fields uses a data type you have not encountered before. Then, you must fill in these new fields with the appropriate data. The manner in which this is achieved depends on the field type. After entering data in the fields, you are to create the form including the table of marina data. You will create queries to obtain the answer to two important questions that reference the new fields. Finally, you will compact the database, thus ensuring the database does not occupy more space than is required.

Microsoft Access 2000

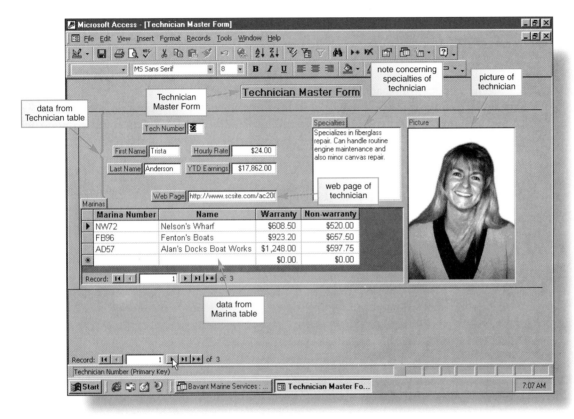

FIGURE 5-1

Opening the Database

Before you can modify the Technician table and create the form, you must open the database. Perform the following steps to complete this task.

TO OPEN A DATABASE

1. Click the Start button.

2. Click Open Office Document, and then click 3½ Floppy (A:) in the Look in box. Make sure the database called Bavant Marine Services is selected.

3. Click the Open button.

The database is open and the Bavant Marine Services : Database window displays.

More About

OLE Fields

OLE fields can store data such as Microsoft Word or Excel documents, pictures, sound, and other types of binary data created in other programs. For more information, visit the Access 2000 Project 4 More About page (www.scsite.com/ac2000/more.htm) and click OLE Fields.

Date, Memo, OLE, and Hyperlink Fields

The data to be added incorporates the following data types:

1. **Date (D)** — The field contains only valid dates.
2. **Memo (M)** — The field contains text that is variable in length. The length of the text stored in memo fields is virtually unlimited.
3. **OLE (O)** — The field contains objects created by other applications that support **OLE (Object Linking and Embedding)** as a server. Object Linking and Embedding is a special feature of Microsoft Windows that creates a special relationship between Microsoft Access and the application that created the object. When you edit the object, Microsoft Access returns automatically to the application that created the object.
4. **Hyperlink (H)** — This field contains links to other office documents or to Web Pages. If the link is to a Web Page, the field will contain the **Web page name**.

Adding Fields to a Table

You add the new fields to the Technician table by modifying the design of the table and inserting the fields at the appropriate position in the table structure. Perform the following steps to add the Start Date, Specialties, Picture, and Web Page fields to the Technician table.

 To Add Fields to a Table

1 If necessary, click Tables on the Objects bar. Right-click Technician, and then point to Design View on the shortcut menu.

The shortcut menu for the Technician table displays, and the Design View command is highlighted (Figure 5-2).

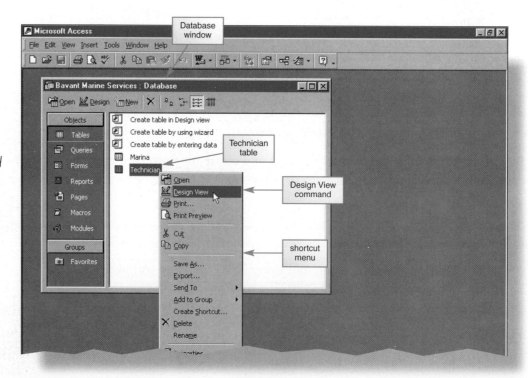

FIGURE 5-2

2 **Click Design View on the shortcut menu and then maximize the Microsoft Access – [Technician : Table] window. Point to the position for the new field (the Field Name column in the row following the YTD Earnings field).**

The Microsoft Access - Technician : Table] window displays (Figure 5-3).

3 **Click the position for the new field. Type** Start Date **as the field name, press the TAB key, select Date/Time as the data type, press the TAB key, type** Start Date **as the description, and then press the TAB key to move to the next field.**

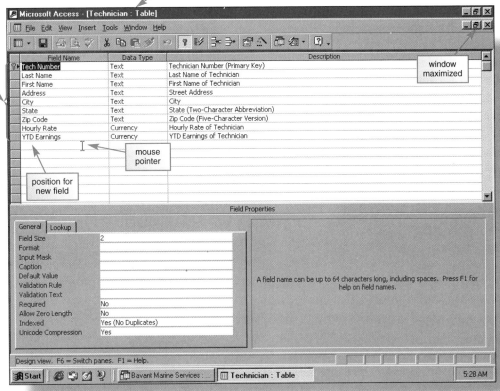

FIGURE 5-3

4 **Type** Specialties **as the field name, press the TAB key, select Memo as the data type, press the TAB key, type** Note Containing Details of Technician's Specialties **as the description, and then press the TAB key to move to the next field. Type** Picture **as the field name, press the TAB key, select OLE Object as the data type, press the TAB key, type** Picture of Technician **as the description, and then press the TAB key to move to the next field. Type** Web Page **as the field name, press the TAB key, select Hyperlink as the data type, press the TAB key, and type** Address of Technician's Web Page **as the description. Point to the Close button.**

The new fields are entered (Figure 5-4).

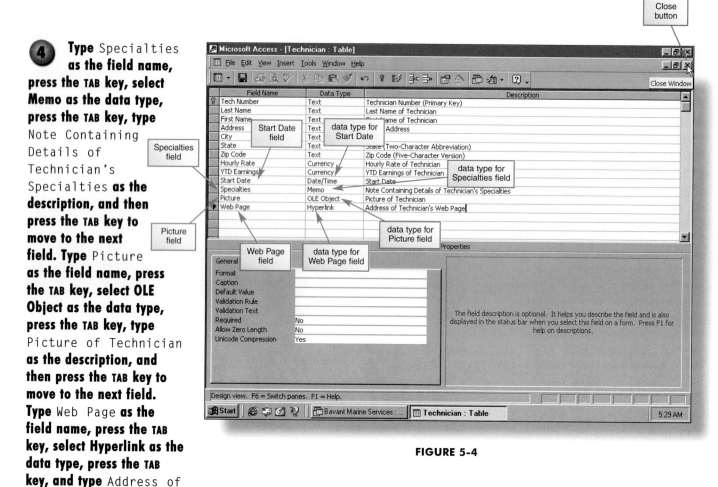

FIGURE 5-4

5 **Close the window by clicking its Close button. Click the Yes button in the Microsoft Access dialog box to save the changes.**

The new fields have been added to the structure.

Updating the New Fields

After adding the new fields to the table, the next task is to enter data into the fields. The manner in which this is accomplished depends on the field type. The following sections cover the methods for updating date fields, memo fields, OLE fields, and Hyperlink fields.

Updating Date Fields

To enter data in **date fields**, simply type the dates and include slashes (/). Perform the following steps to add the Start Dates for all three technicians using Datasheet view.

 To Enter Data in Date Fields

1 **With the Database window on the screen, right-click the Technician table. Point to Open on the shortcut menu.**

The shortcut menu displays, and the Open command is highlighted (Figure 5-5).

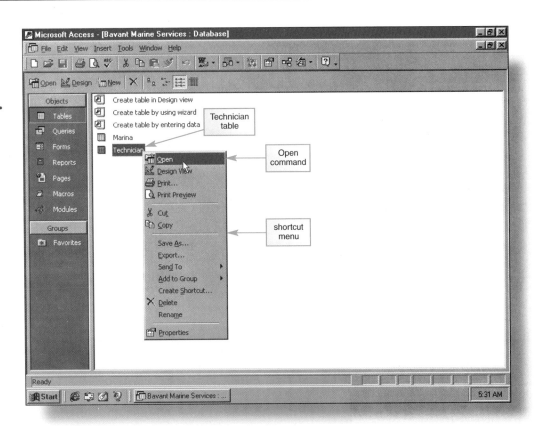

FIGURE 5-5

Microsoft Access 2000

2 Click Open on the shortcut menu and then, if necessary, maximize the window. Point to the right scroll arrow.

The Technician table displays in Datasheet view in the maximized window (Figure 5-6).

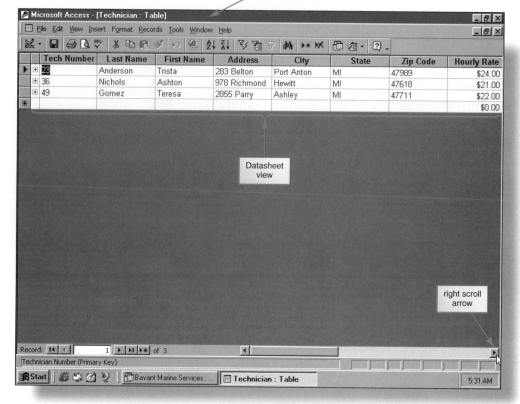

Microsoft Access - [Technician : Table]

	Tech Number	Last Name	First Name	Address	City	State	Zip Code	Hourly Rate
23	Anderson	Trista	283 Belton	Port Anton	MI	47989	$24.00
36	Nichols	Ashton	978 Richmond	Hewitt	MI	47618	$21.00
49	Gomez	Teresa	2855 Parry	Ashley	MI	47711	$22.00
								$0.00

Datasheet view

right scroll arrow

Record: 1 of 3

Technician Number (Primary Key)

FIGURE 5-6

3 Repeatedly click the right scroll arrow until the new fields display and then click the Start Date field on the first record (Figure 5-7).

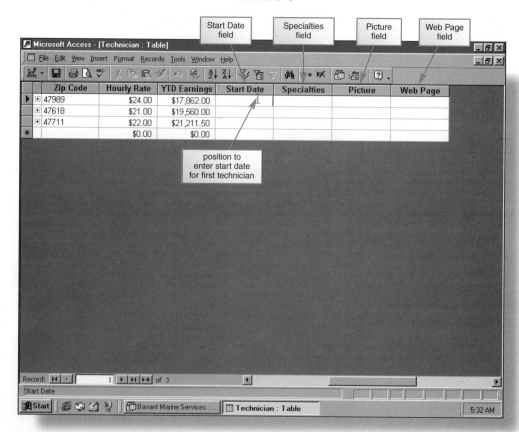

Microsoft Access - [Technician : Table]

Start Date field | Specialties field | Picture field | Web Page field

	Zip Code	Hourly Rate	YTD Earnings	Start Date	Specialties	Picture	Web Page
47989	$24.00	$17,862.00				
47618	$21.00	$19,560.00				
47711	$22.00	$21,211.50				
	$0.00	$0.00				

position to enter start date for first technician

Record: 1 of 3

Start Date

FIGURE 5-7

4 **Type** 9/9/1999 **as the date. Press the** DOWN ARROW **key. Type** 1/6/2000 **as the Start Date on the second record and then press the** DOWN ARROW **key. Type** 11/12/2000 **as the date on the third record.**

The dates are entered (Figure 5-8). If the dates do not display with four-digit years, click the Start menu, click Settings and then click Control Panel. Double-click Regional Settings, click the Date tab, and then change the short date style to MM/dd/yyyy. Click the OK button.

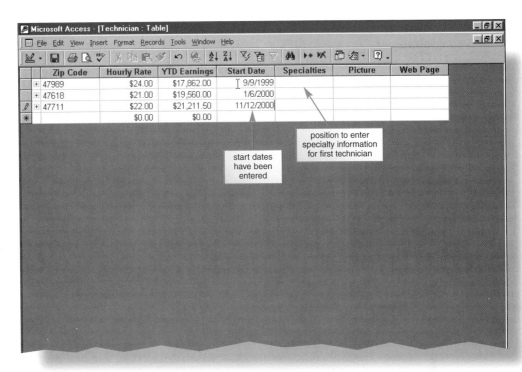

FIGURE 5-8

Updating Memo Fields

To **update a memo field,** simply type the data in the field. With the current spacing on the screen, only a small portion of the memo will display. To correct this problem, you will change the spacing later to allow more room for the memo. Perform the following steps to enter each technician's specialties.

 Steps **To Enter Data in Memo Fields**

1 **If necessary, click the right scroll arrow so that the Specialties field displays. Click the Specialties field on the first record. Type** Specializes in fiberglass repair. Can handle routine engine maintenance and also minor canvas repair. **as the entry.**

The last portion of the memo displays (Figure 5-9).

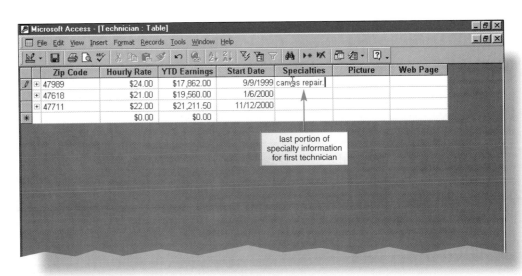

FIGURE 5-9

2 Click the Specialties field on the second record. Type Can handle all types of engine maintenance and repair. Can also do electrical work. **as the entry.**

3 Click the Specialties field on the third record. Type Specializes in electrical problems including electronics repair. Can also handle routine engine maintenance. **as the entry.**

All the Specialties are entered (Figure 5-10). The first portion of the specialty information for the first two technicians displays. Because the insertion point is still in the field for the third technician, only the last portion displays.

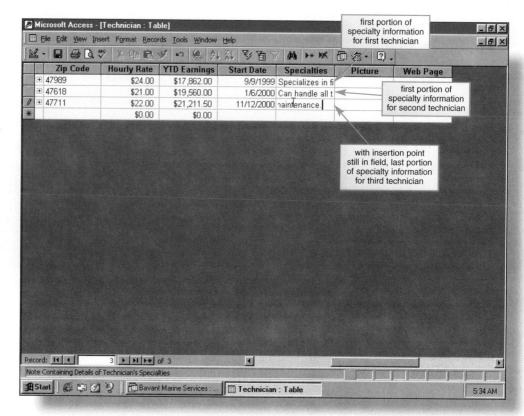

FIGURE 5-10

Changing the Row and Column Size

The Undo command cannot be used to reverse (undo) changes to the row and column size. To undo the changes to the sizes, close the datasheet without saving the changes. Once you have saved changes to row and column size, there is no automatic way to restore the original sizes.

Changing the Row and Column Size

Only a small portion of the information about the specialties displays in the datasheet. To allow more of the information to display, you can expand the size of the rows and the columns. You can change the size of a column by using the field selector. The **field selector** is the bar containing the field name. You position the mouse pointer on the right boundary of the column's field selector and then drag to change the size of the column. To change the size of a row, you use a record's **row selector**, which is the small box at the beginning of each record. You position the mouse pointer on the lower boundary of the record's row selector to select the record and then drag to resize the row.

The steps on the next page resize the column containing the Specialties field and the rows of the table so a larger portion of the Specialties field text will display.

Steps ## To Change the Row and Column Size

1 **Point to the line between the column headings for the Specialties and Picture columns.**

The mouse pointer changes to a two-headed horizontal arrow with a vertical crossbar, indicating you can drag the line to resize the column (Figure 5-11).

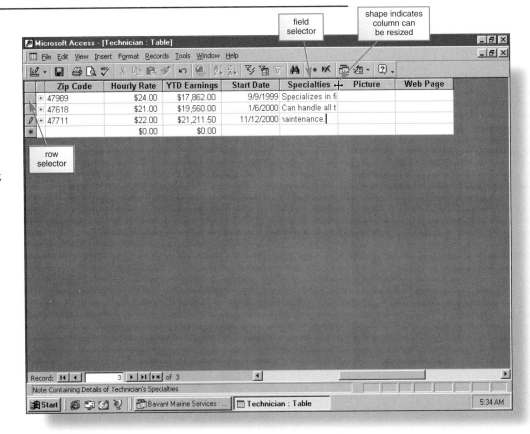

FIGURE 5-11

2 **Drag to the right to resize the Specialties column to the approximate size shown in Figure 5-12 and then point to the line between the first and second row selectors as shown in the figure.**

The mouse pointer changes to a two-headed arrow with a horizontal bar, indicating you can drag the line to resize the row.

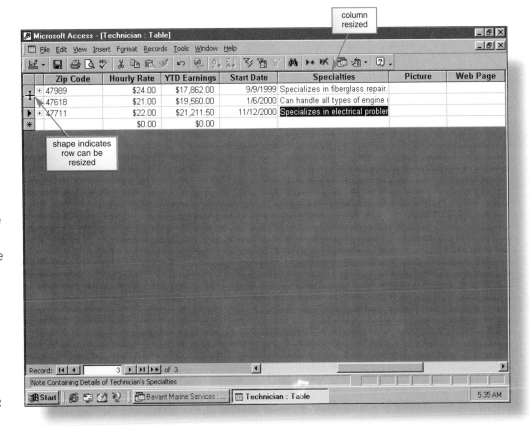

FIGURE 5-12

3 **Drag the edge of the row to approximately the position shown in Figure 5-13.**

All the rows are resized at the same time (Figure 5-13). The specialties now display in their entirety. The last row has a different appearance from the other two because it still is selected.

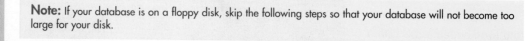

FIGURE 5-13

More About 2000

Updating OLE Fields

OLE fields can occupy a great deal of space. To save space in your database, you can convert a picture from Bitmap Image to Picture (Device Independent Bitmap). To make the conversion, right-click the field, click Bitmap Image Object, click Convert, and then double-click Picture.

Updating OLE Fields

To insert data into an OLE field, you will use the **Insert Object command** on the OLE field's shortcut menu. The Insert Object command presents a list of the various types of objects that can be inserted. Access then opens the corresponding application to create the object, for example, Microsoft Drawing. If the object already is created and stored in a file, as is the case with the photographs in this project, you simply insert it directly from the file.

Perform the following steps to insert pictures into the Picture field. The steps assume that the pictures are located in a folder called pictures on drive C:. If your pictures are located elsewhere, you will need to make the appropriate changes.

Note: If your database is on a floppy disk, skip the following steps so that your database will not become too large for your disk.

Steps To Enter Data in OLE Fields and Convert the Data to Pictures

1 **Ensure the Picture field displays. Right-click the Picture field on the first record. Point to Insert Object on the shortcut menu.**

The shortcut menu for the Picture field displays (Figure 5-14).

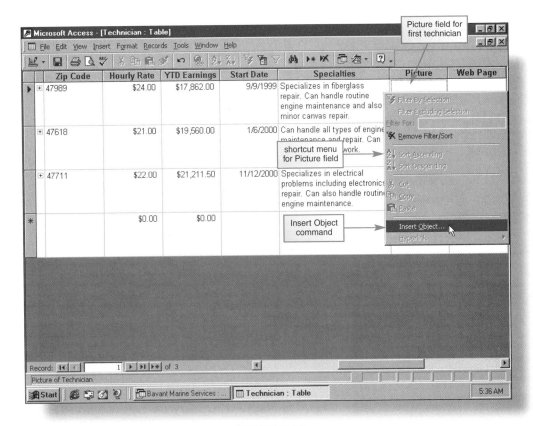

FIGURE 5-14

2 **Click Insert Object. Point to Create from File in the Insert Object dialog box.**

The Insert Object dialog box displays, and the Object Types display in the list box (Figure 5-15).

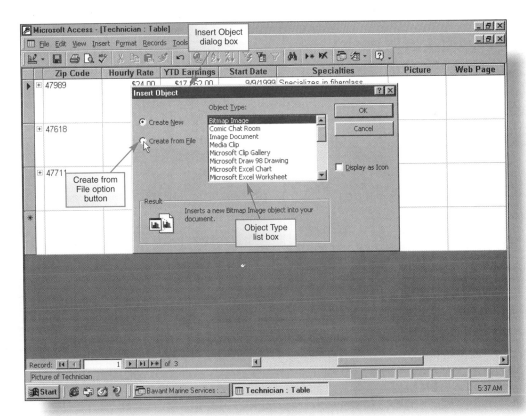

FIGURE 5-15

3 **Click Create from File. Type**
c:\pictures **in the File text box and then point to the Browse button. (If your pictures are located elsewhere, type the name and location of the folder where they are located instead of c:\pictures.)**

The Create from File option button is selected, and the location of the folder displays in the File text box (Figure 5-16).

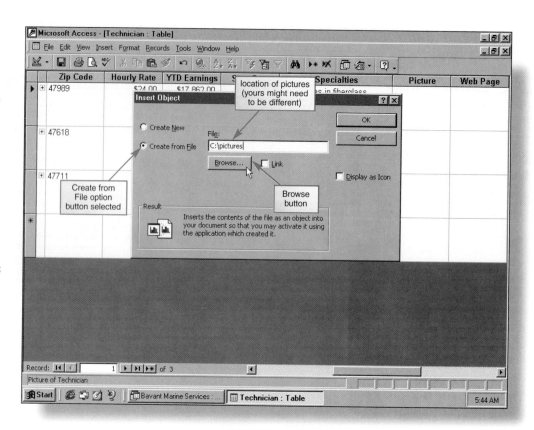

FIGURE 5-16

4 **Click the Browse button, and then point to pict1.**

The Browse dialog box displays (Figure 5-17). If you do not have the pictures, you will need to locate the folder in which yours are stored.

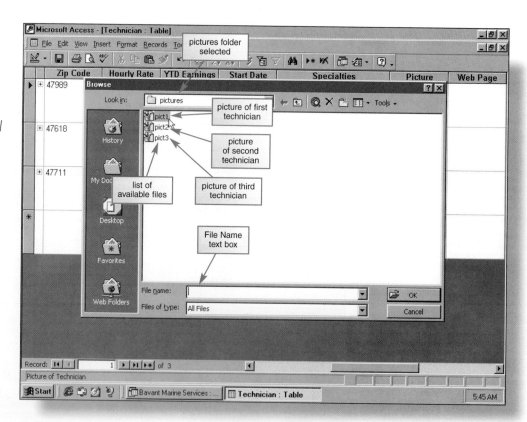

FIGURE 5-17

5 **Double-click pict1 and then point to the OK button.**

The Browse dialog box closes and the Insert Object dialog box displays (Figure 5-18). The name of the selected picture displays in the File text box.

6 **Click the OK button.**

7 **Insert the pictures into the second and third records using the techniques illustrated in Steps 1 through 6. For the second record, select the picture named pict2. For the third record, select the picture named pict3.**

The pictures are inserted.

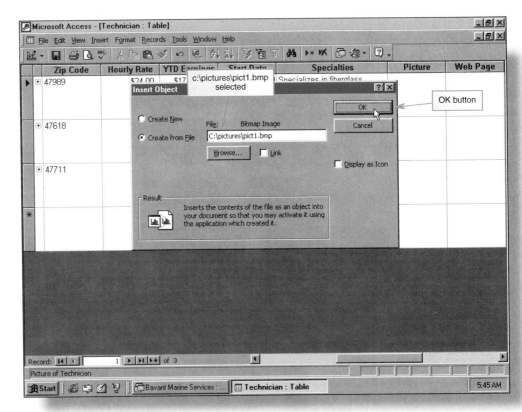

FIGURE 5-18

1. On Insert menu click Object

Updating Hyperlink Fields

To insert data into a Hyperlink field, you will use the **Hyperlink command** on the Hyperlink field's shortcut menu. You then edit the hyperlink. You can enter the Web page name for the appropriate Web Page or specify a file that contains the document to which you wish to link.

Perform the steps on the next page to insert data into the Web Page field.

Steps: To Enter Data in Hyperlink Fields

1 Be sure the Web Page field displays. Right-click the Web Page field on the first record, click Hyperlink on the shortcut menu, and then point to Edit Hyperlink.

The shortcut menu for the Web Page field displays (Figure 5-19).

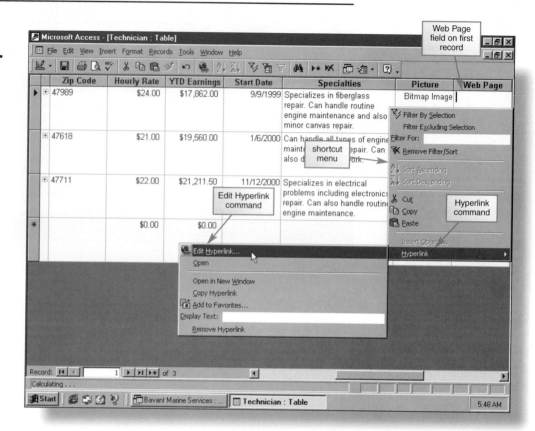

FIGURE 5-19

2 Click Edit Hyperlink. Type www.scsite.com/ac2000/tech1.htm in the Type the file or Web page name text box. Point to the OK button. (If you do not have access to the Internet, type a:\tech1.htm in the Type the file or Web page name text box instead of www.scsite.com/ac2000/tech1.htm as the Web page name.)

The Insert Hyperlink dialog box displays, and a list of Browsed Pages displays in the list box. Your list may be different (Figure 5-20).

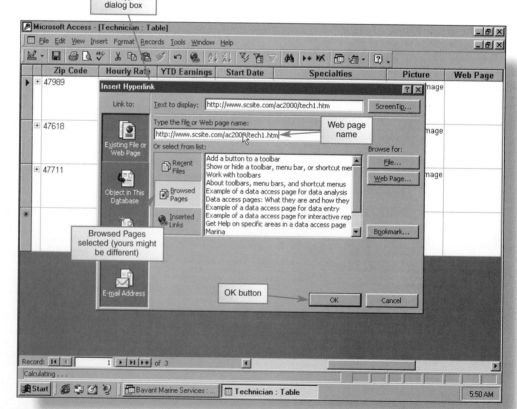

FIGURE 5-20

3 **Click the OK button. Use the techniques described in Steps 1 and 2 to enter Web page data for the second and third technicians. For the second technician, type** www.scsite.com/ac2000/tech2.htm **as the Web page name; and for the third, type** www.scsite.com/ac2000/tech3.htm **as the Web page name. (If you do not have access to the Internet, type** a:\tech2.htm **for the second technician and** a:\tech3.htm **for the third technician.)**

The Web page data is entered (Figure 5-21).

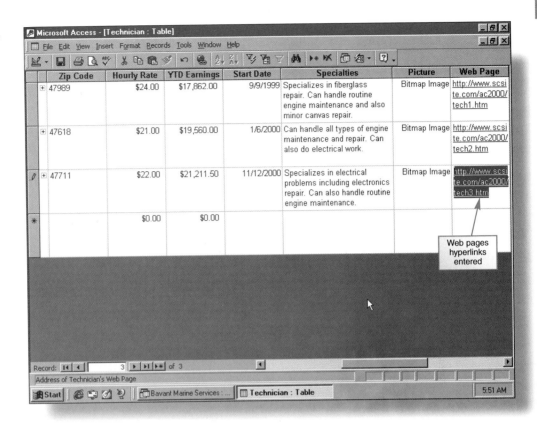

FIGURE 5-21

Saving the Table Properties

The row and column spacing are **table properties**. When changing any table properties, the changes apply only as long as the table is active *unless they are saved*. If they are saved, they will apply every time the table is opened. To save them, simply close the table. If any properties have changed, a Microsoft Access dialog box will ask if you want to save the changes. By answering Yes, you can save the changes.

Perform the steps on the next page to close the table and save the properties that have been changed.

Other **Ways**

1. On Insert menu click Hyperlink

Steps: To Close the Table and Save the Properties

1 **Close the table by clicking its Close button. Point to the Yes button.**

The Microsoft Access dialog box displays (Figure 5-22).

2 **Click the Yes button to save the table properties.**

The properties are saved.

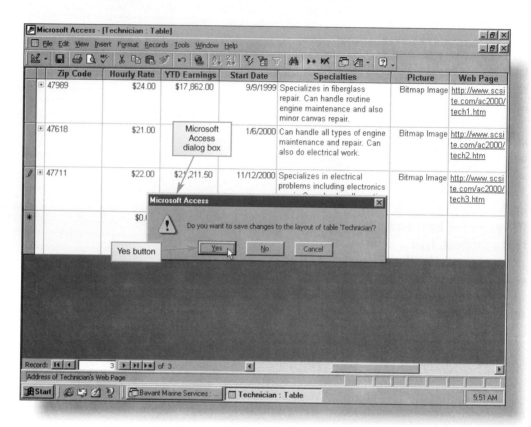

FIGURE 5-22

Although the pictures do not display on the screen, you can view them at any time. To view the picture of a particular technician, point to the Picture field for the technician, and then right-click to produce the shortcut menu. Click Bitmap Image Object on the shortcut menu, and then click Open. The picture will display. Once you have finished viewing the picture, close the window containing the picture by clicking its Close button. You also can view the Web Page for a technician, by clicking the technician's Web Page field.

Subforms

When you create forms with subforms, the tables for the main form and the subform must be related. The relationship must have been previously set in the Relationships window. To see if your tables are related, click the Relationships button. Relationships between tables display as lines connecting the tables.

Advanced Form Techniques

The form in this project includes data from both the Technician and Marina tables. The form will display data concerning one technician. It also will display data concerning the many marinas to which the technician is assigned. Formally, the relationship between technicians and marinas is called a **one-to-many relationship** (*one* technician services *many* marinas).

To include the data for the many marinas of a technician on the form, the marina data must display in a **subform**, which is a form that is contained within another form. The form in which the subform is contained is called the main form. Thus, the **main form** will contain technician data, and the subform will contain marina data.

Creating a Form with a Subform Using the Form Wizard

No special action is required to create a form with a subform if you use the Form Wizard. The Form Wizard will create both the form and subform automatically once you have selected the tables and indicated the general organization of your data. Perform the following steps to create the form and subform.

 To Create a Form with a Subform Using the Form Wizard

1 **With the Database window on the screen and the Forms object selected, right-click Create form by using Wizard and then point to Open on the shortcut menu.**

The shortcut menu displays (Figure 5-23).

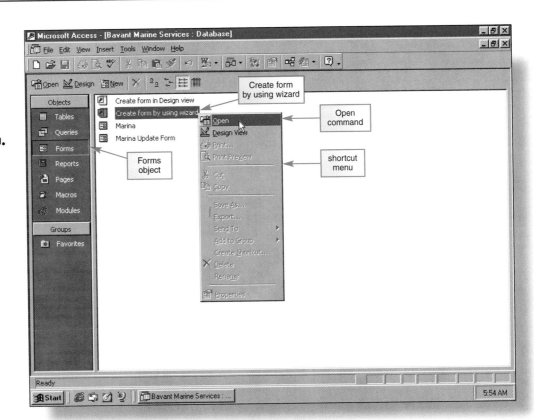

FIGURE 5-23

2 **Click Open on the shortcut menu and then click the Tables/ Queries arrow.**

The list of available tables and queries displays (Figure 5-24).

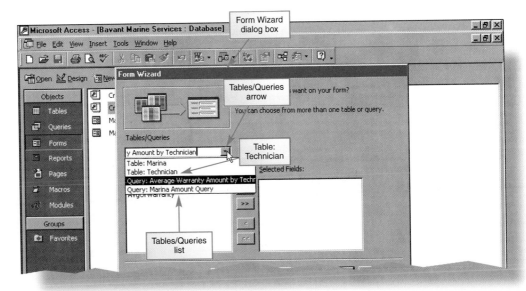

FIGURE 5-24

3 **Click Table: Technician. With the Tech Number field selected in the Available Fields box, click the Add Field button. Select the First Name, Last Name, Hourly Rate, YTD Earnings, Web Page, Specialties, and Picture fields by clicking the field and then clicking the Add Field button. Click the Table/Queries box arrow and then point to Table: Marina.**

The fields from the Technician table are selected for the form (Figure 5-25).

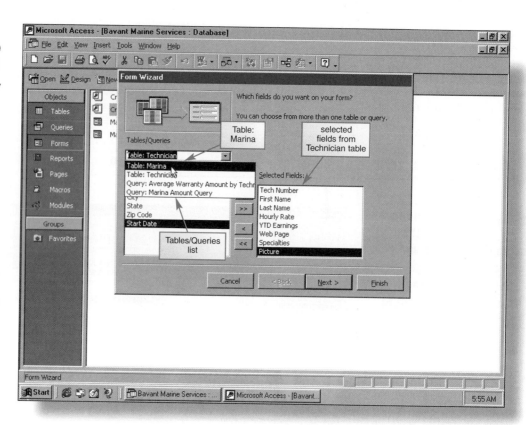

FIGURE 5-25

4 **Click Table: Marina. Select the Marina Number, Name, Warranty, and Non-warranty fields. Point to the Next button.**

All the fields are selected (Figure 5-26).

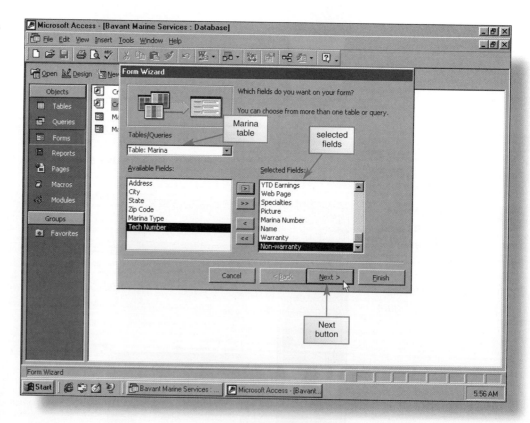

FIGURE 5-26

Click the Next button.

The Form Wizard dialog box displays, requesting how you want to view the data: by Technician or by Marina (Figure 5-27). The high-lighted selection, by Techni-cian, is correct. The box on the right indicates visually that the main organization is by Technician, with the Tech-nician fields listed at the top. Contained within the form is a subform that contains marina data.

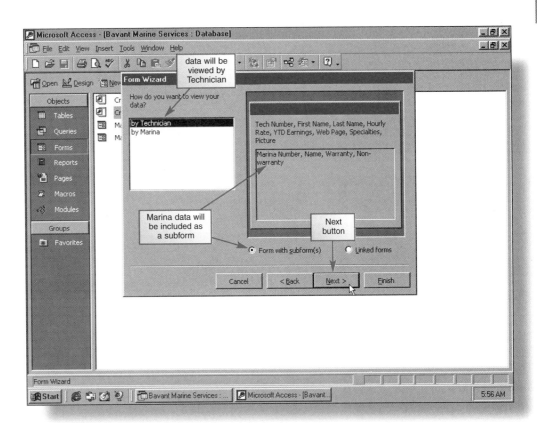

FIGURE 5-27

Click the Next button.

The Form Wizard dialog box displays, requesting the lay-out for the subform (Figure 5-28). This subform is to dis-play in Datasheet view.

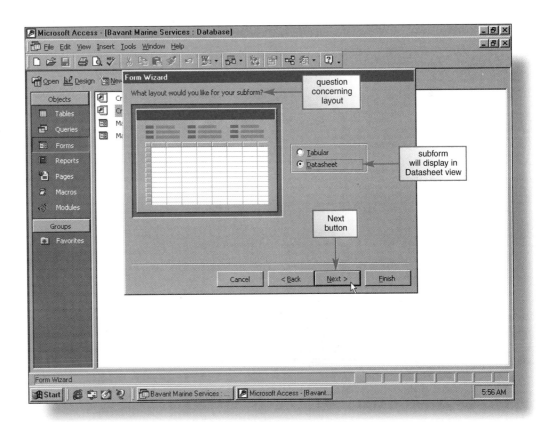

FIGURE 5-28

7 Be sure Datasheet is selected and then click the Next button. Ensure Standard style is selected.

The Form Wizard dialog box displays, requesting a style for the report, and Standard is selected (Figure 5-29).

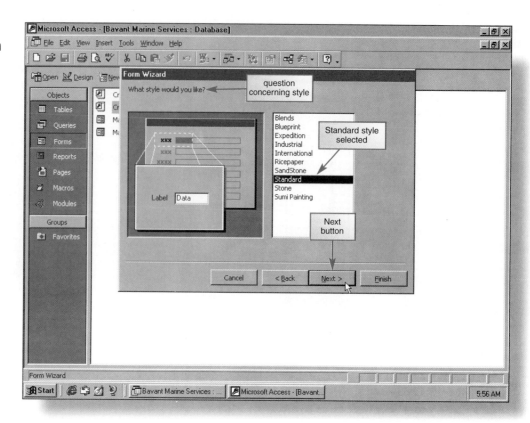

FIGURE 5-29

8 Click the Next button.

The Form Wizard dialog box displays (Figure 5-30). You use this dialog box to change the titles of the form and subform.

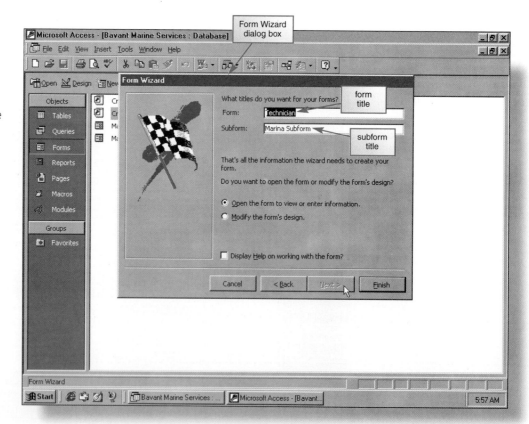

FIGURE 5-30

9 **Type** Technician Master Form **as the title of the form. Click the Subform text box, use the** DELETE **or** BACKSPACE **key to erase the current entry, and then type** Marinas **as the name of the subform. Point to the Finish button.**

The titles are changed (Figure 5-31).

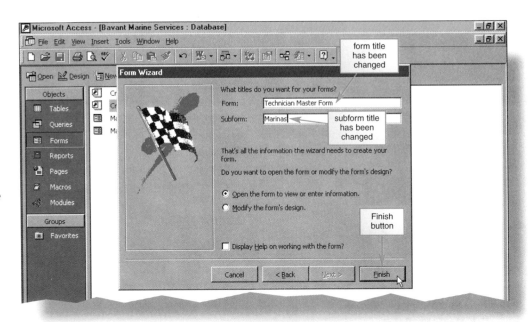

FIGURE 5-31

10 **Click the Finish button.**

The form displays (Figure 5-32).

11 **Close the form by clicking its Close button.**

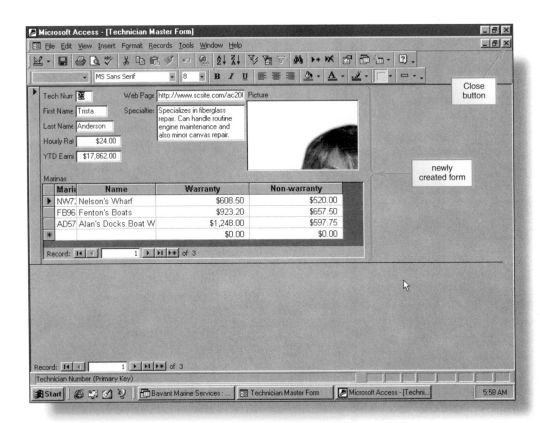

FIGURE 5-32

The form and subform now have been saved as part of the database and are available for future use.

Subform Design

To change the appearance of the subform, make sure the subform control is not selected, double-click inside the subform, right-click the form selector for the subform, click Properties, and then change the DefaultView property.

Modifying the Subform Design

The next task is to modify the spacing of the columns in the subform. The Marina Number column is so narrow that only the letters, Marin, display. Conversely, the Warranty column is much wider than needed. You can correct these problems by right-clicking the subform in the Database window and then clicking Design View. When the design of the subform displays, you then can convert it to Datasheet view. At this point, you resize each column by double-clicking the border to the right of the column name.

Perform the following steps to modify the subform design to improve the column spacing.

 To Modify the Subform Design

1 With the Forms object selected, right-click Marinas. Point to Design View on the shortcut menu.

The shortcut menu for the subform displays (Figure 5-33).

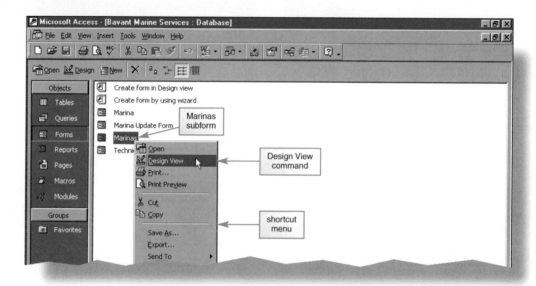

FIGURE 5-33

2 Click Design View on the shortcut menu. If the field list displays, point to its Close button (Figure 5-34).

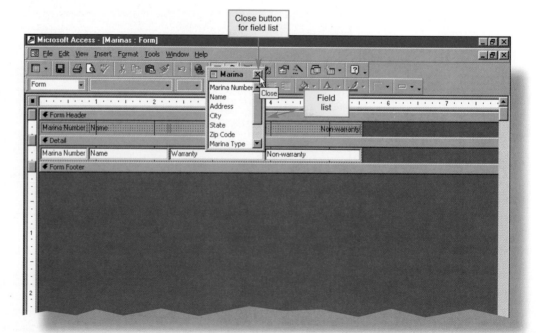

FIGURE 5-34

3 If the field list displays, click its Close button. Point to the View button on the toolbar (Figure 5-35).

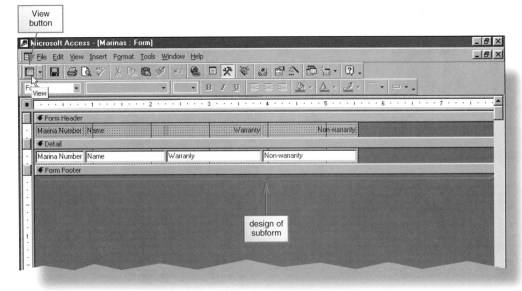

FIGURE 5-35

4 Click the View button to display the subform in Datasheet view. Resize each of the columns by pointing to the right edge of the field selector (to the right of the column name) and double-clicking. Point to the Close button.

The subform displays in Datasheet view (Figure 5-36). The columns have been resized. You also can resize each column by dragging the right edge of the field selector.

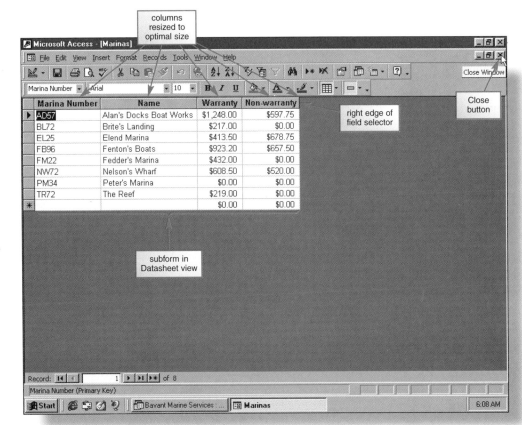

5 Close the subform by clicking its Close button.

The changes are made and saved.

FIGURE 5-36

Modifying the Form Design

The next step is to make several changes to the form. Various objects need to be moved or resized. The properties of the picture need to be adjusted so the entire picture displays. The appearance of the labels needs to be changed, and a title needs to be added to the form.

Right-click the form in the Database window and then click Design View to make these or other changes to the design of the form. If the toolbox is on the screen, make sure it is docked at the bottom of the screen.

Perform the following steps to begin the modification of the form design.

To Modify the Form Design

1 **Right-click Technician Master Form. Point to Design View on the shortcut menu.**

The shortcut menu for the form displays (Figure 5-37).

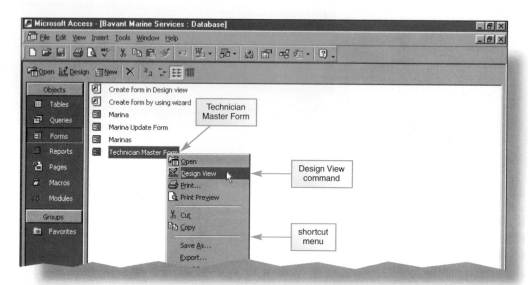

FIGURE 5-37

2 **Click Design View on the shortcut menu. If the toolbox does not display, click the Toolbox button on the toolbar. Make sure it is docked at the bottom of the screen as shown in Figure 5-38). If it is not, drag it to the bottom of the screen to dock it there. Maximize the window.**

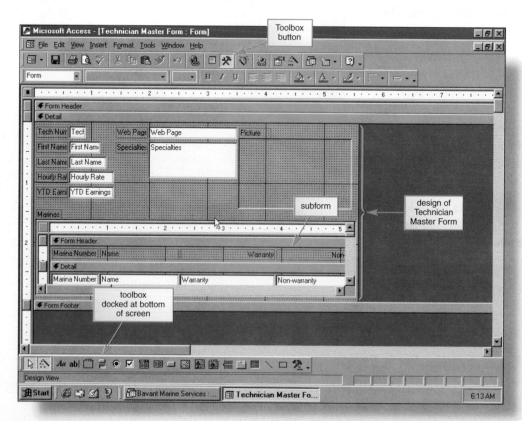

FIGURE 5-38

Moving and Resizing Fields

Fields on this form can be moved or resized just as they were in the form created in the previous project. First, click the field. To move it, move the mouse pointer to the boundary of the field so it becomes a hand, and then drag the field. To resize a field, drag the appropriate sizing handle. The following steps move certain fields on the form. They also resize the fields appropriately.

 Steps **To Move and Resize Fields**

1 **Click the Picture control, and then move the mouse pointer until the shape changes to a hand.**

The Picture control is selected, and sizing handles display (Figure 5-39).

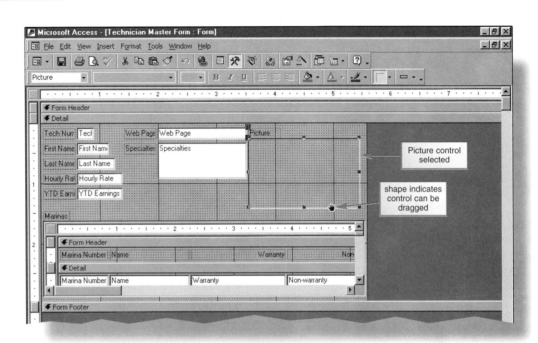

FIGURE 5-39

2 **Drag the Picture control to approximately the position shown in Figure 5-40 and then point to the sizing handle on the lower edge of the control.**

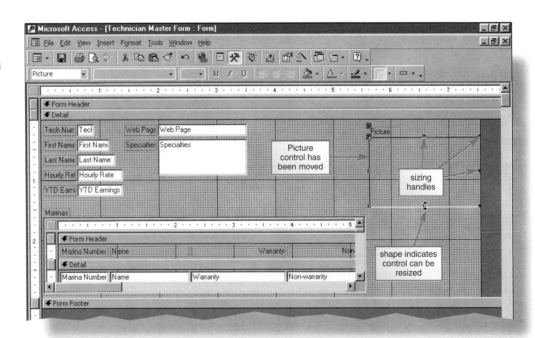

FIGURE 5-40

3 Drag the lower sizing handle to approximately the position shown in Figure 5-41 and then point to the sizing handle on the right edge of the control.

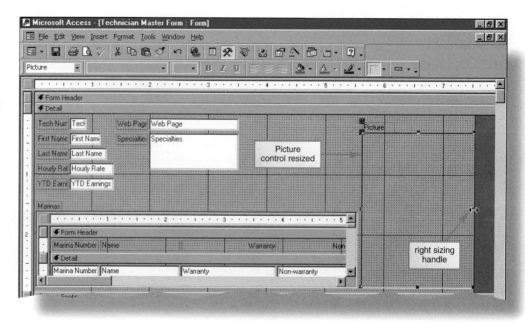

FIGURE 5-41

4 Resize the Picture control to the approximate size shown in Figure 5-42, and then move and resize the Specialties control to the approximate position and size shown in the figure.

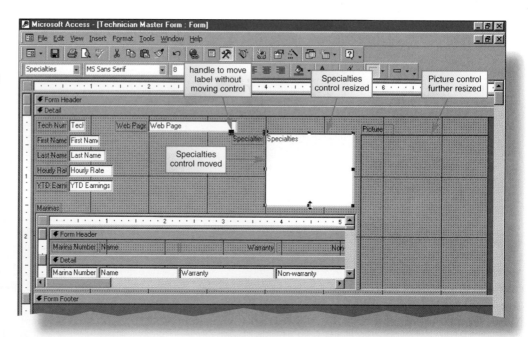

FIGURE 5-42

Moving Labels

To move a label independently from the field with which the label is associated, point to the large, **move handle** in the upper-left corner of the label. The shape of the mouse pointer changes to a hand with a pointing finger. By dragging this move handle, you will move the label without moving the associated field. Perform the step on the next page to move the label of the Specialties field without moving the field itself.

To Move a Label

1 **Click the label for the Specialties field and then drag the handle in the upper-left corner to the position shown in Figure 5-43.**

The shape of the mouse pointer changes to a hand with a pointing finger.

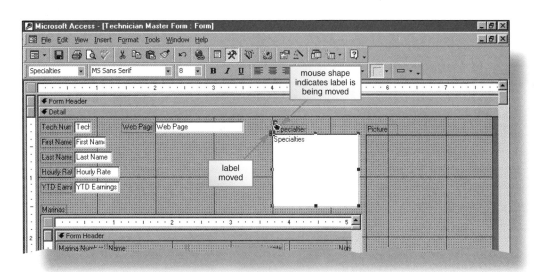

FIGURE 5-43

Resizing a Label

The label for the Specialties field has the last letter cut off. To resize a label, select the label by clicking it, and then drag the appropriate sizing handle. To resize a label to optimum size, select the label and then double-click the appropriate sizing handle. Perform the following steps to resize the label for the Specialties field by double-clicking the sizing handle on the right.

Steps **To Resize a Label**

1 **Ensure the label for the Specialties field is selected, and then point to the middle sizing handle on the right edge of the label.**

The shape of the mouse pointer changes to a two-headed arrow (Figure 5-44).

2 **Double-click the sizing handle to expand the label to the appropriate size.**

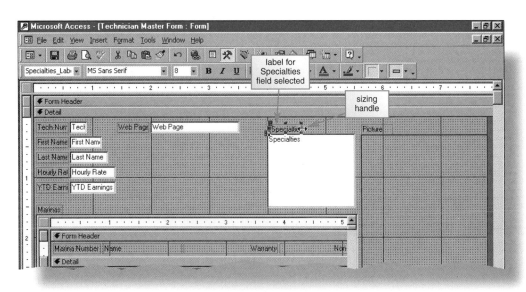

FIGURE 5-44

Moving Remaining Fields

The remaining fields on this form also need to be moved into appropriate positions. The following steps move these fields on the form.

 To Move Fields

1 Click the Web Page field, move the mouse pointer until the shape changes to a hand, and then drag the field to the position shown in Figure 5-45.

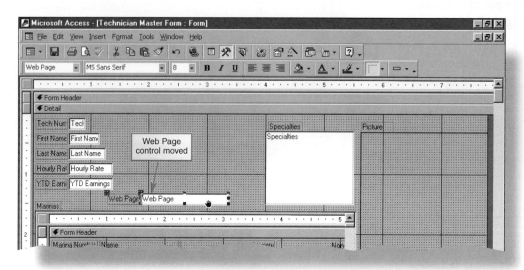

FIGURE 5-45

2 Drag the YTD Earnings, Hourly Rate, Last Name, First Name, and Tech Number fields to the positions shown in Figure 5-46.

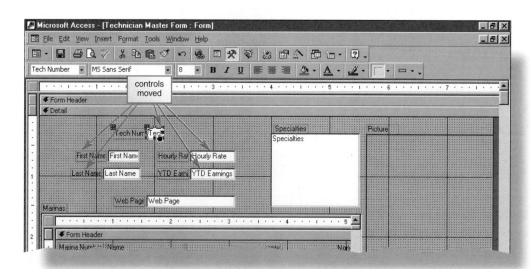

FIGURE 5-46

Changing Label Alignment

The labels for the Tech Number, First Name, Last Name, Hourly Rate, YTD Earnings, and Web Page fields illustrated in Figure 5-1 on page A 5.5 are **right-aligned**, that is, aligned with the right margin. Because the labels are currently left-aligned, the alignment needs to be changed. To change the alignment, right-click the label to display the shortcut menu, click Properties, and then scroll to display the Text Align property. Click Text Align. In the property sheet, you can select the appropriate alignment.

In some cases, you will want to make the same change to several objects, perhaps to several labels at one time. Rather than making the changes individually, you can select all the objects at once, and then make a single change. Perform the following steps to change the alignment of the labels.

 To Change Label Alignment

1 **If the label for the Tech Number field is not already selected, click it. Select the labels for the First Name, Last Name, Hourly Rate, YTD Earnings, and Web Page fields by clicking them while holding down the SHIFT key.**

The labels are selected (Figure 5-47).

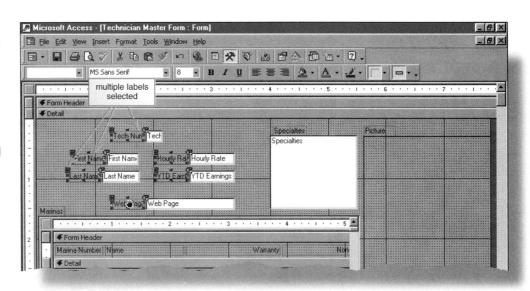

FIGURE 5-47

2 **Right-click the Web Page field. Point to Properties on the shortcut menu.**

The shortcut menu displays (Figure 5-48).

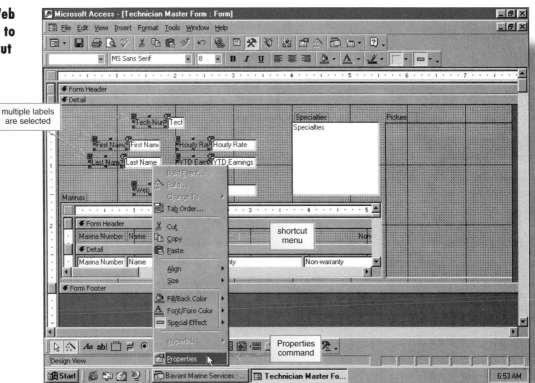

FIGURE 5-48

3 **Click Properties on the shortcut menu** and then click the down scroll arrow until the Text Align property displays. Click Text Align, and then click the Text Align arrow.

The Multiple selection property sheet displays (Figure 5-49). The Text Align property is selected and the list of available values for the Text Align property displays.

4 **Click Right to select right alignment for** the labels. Close the Multiple selection property sheet by clicking its Close button.

The alignment is changed.

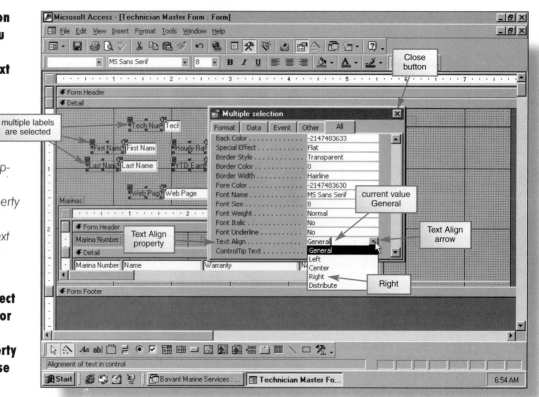

FIGURE 5-49

Resizing the Labels

To resize a label to optimum size, select the label by clicking it, and then double-click an appropriate sizing handle. Perform the following steps to resize the label for the Tech Number, First Name, Last Name, Hourly Rate, YTD Earnings, and Web Page fields just as you resized the label for the Specialties field earlier. The only difference is that you will double-click the sizing handles at the left edge of the labels instead of the right edge. You can resize them individually, but it is easier, however, to make sure they are all selected and then resize one of the labels. Access will automatically resize all the others as demonstrated in the steps on the next page.

Steps To Resize a Label

1 With all the labels selected, point to the handle on the left edge of the Tech Number label (Figure 5-50.

2 Double-click the middle sizing handle on the left edge of the Technician Number label to resize all the labels to the optimal size.

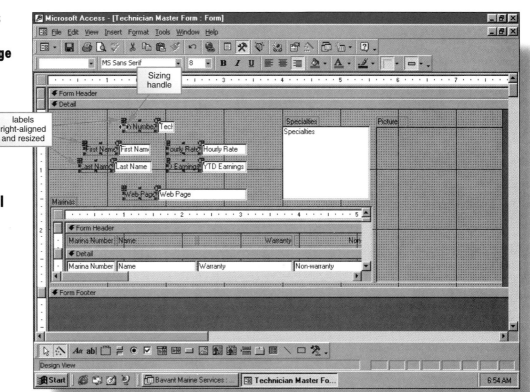

FIGURE 5-50

Changing the Size Mode of a Picture

The portion of a picture that displays as well as the way it displays is determined by the **size mode**. The possible size modes are as follows:

1. **Clip** — Displays only the portion of the picture that will fit in the space allocated to it.
2. **Stretch** — Expands or shrinks the picture to fit the precise space allocated on the screen. For photographs, usually this is not a good choice, because fitting a photograph to the allocated space can distort the image, giving it a stretched appearance.
3. **Zoom** — Does the best job of fitting the picture to the allocated space without changing the look of the picture. The entire picture will display and be proportioned correctly. Some white space may be visible either above or to the right of the picture, however.

Currently, the size mode is Clip, and that is the reason only a portion of the picture displays. To see the whole picture, use the shortcut menu for the picture to change the size mode to Zoom as shown in the steps on the next page.

 More About

Size Mode

The Clip setting for Size Mode is the most rapid to display, but may only show a portion of a picture. If your pictures have been created with a size such that the entire picture will display on the form with Clip as the setting for Size Mode, Clip is the best choice.

To Change the Size Mode of a Picture

1 **Right-click the Picture control to produce its shortcut menu, and then click Properties on the shortcut menu. Click the Size Mode property and then click the Size Mode box arrow. Point to Zoom.**

The Bound Object Frame: Picture property sheet displays (Figure 5-51). The list of Size Mode options displays.

2 **Click Zoom and then close the property sheet by clicking its Close button.**

The Size Mode is changed. The entire picture now will display.

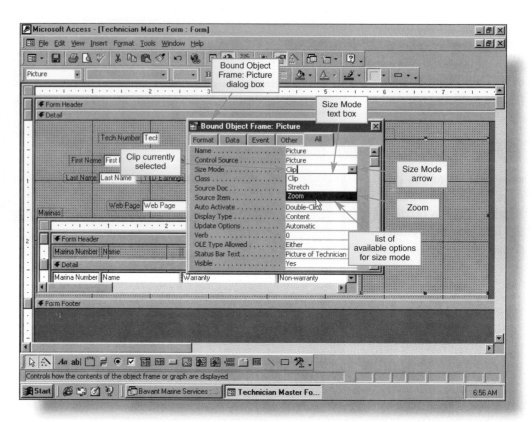

FIGURE 5-51

 **Colors of Labels**

There are two different colors you can change for many objects, including labels. Changing Fore Color (foreground) changes the color of the letters that appear in the label. Changing Back Color (background) changes the color of the label itself.

Changing the Special Effects and Colors of Labels

Access allows you to change a variety of the characteristics of the labels in the form. You can change the border style and color, the background color, the font, and the font size. You also can give the label **special effects**, such as raised or sunken. To change the special effects and colors (characteristics) of a label, perform the steps on the next page.

Steps To Change Special Effects and Colors of Labels

1 **Click the Tech Number label to select it. Then select each of the remaining labels by holding the SHIFT key down while clicking the label. Be sure to include the Marinas label for the subform. Right-click one of the selected labels and then point to Properties.**

All labels are selected (Figure 5-52). The shortcut menu displays.

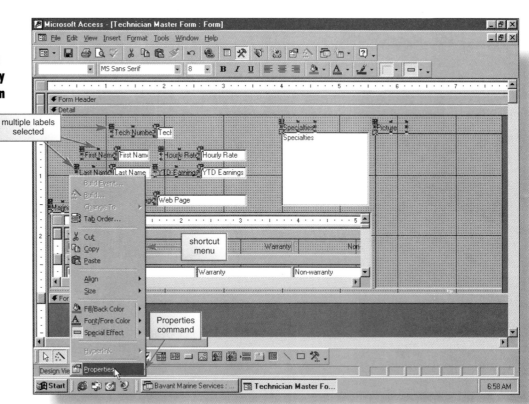

FIGURE 5-52

2 **Click Properties on the shortcut menu that displays. Click the Special Effect property and then click the Special Effect box arrow. Point to Raised.**

The Multiple selection property sheet displays (Figure 5-53). The list of values for the Special Effect property displays, and the Raised Special Effect property is highlighted.

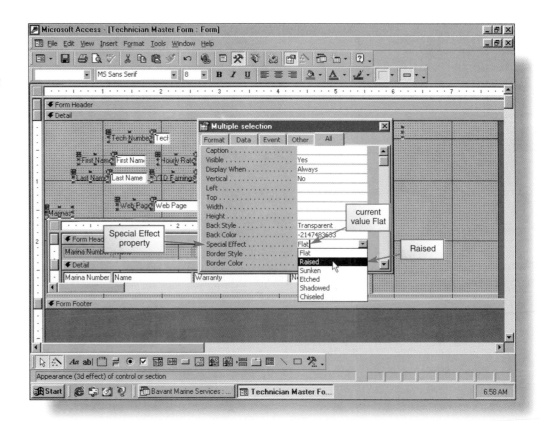

3 Click Raised. If necessary, click the down scroll arrow until the Fore Color property displays, and then click the Fore Color property. Point to the Build button (the button containing the three dots).

The Fore Color property is selected (Figure 5-54).

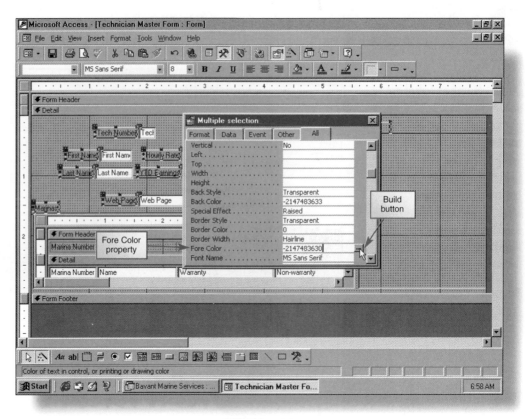

FIGURE 5-54

4 Click the Build button to display the Color dialog box, and then point to the color blue in row 4, column 5, as shown in Figure 5-55.

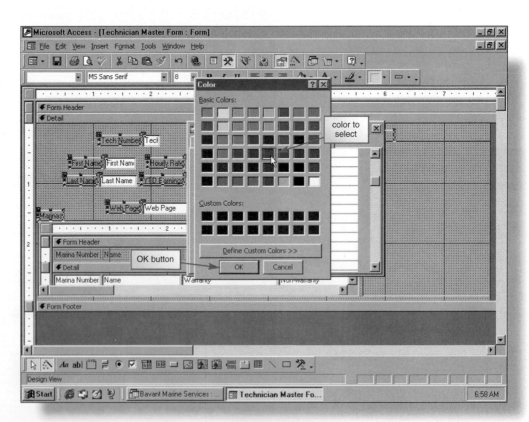

FIGURE 5-55

5 Click the color blue, and then click the OK button. Close the Multiple selection property sheet by clicking its Close button.

The changes to the labels are complete.

6 Click the View button to view the form.

The form displays (Figure 5-56). The fields have been moved and the appearance of the labels has been changed.

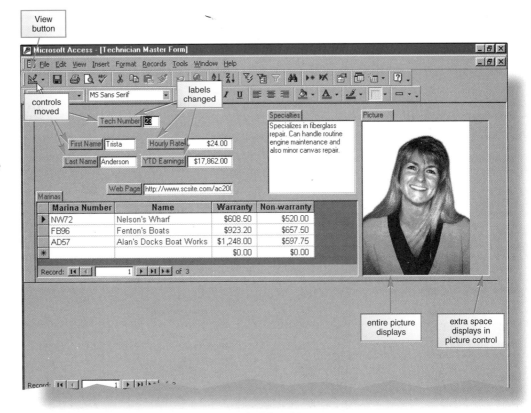

FIGURE 5-56

7 Click the View button a second time to return to the design grid.

The form design displays. Now that the size mode of the picture has been corrected, there is extra space on the right side of the picture, which can be corrected by resizing the picture a final time.

8 Click the Picture control to select it and then point to the right sizing handle (Figure 5-57).

9 Drag the right sizing handle to the left so that the size of the Picture control matches the size of the picture as shown in Figure 5-56.

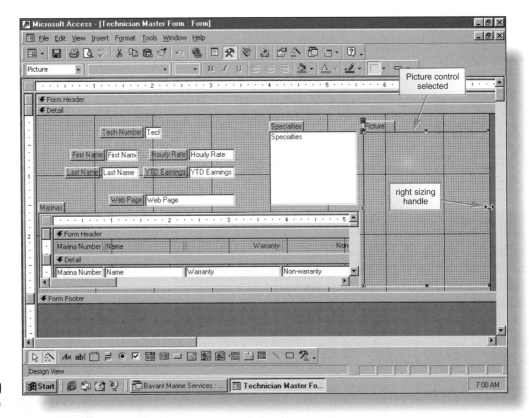

FIGURE 5-57

More About 2000

Form Headers

You may wish to add more than just a title to a form header. For example, you may wish to add a picture such as a company logo. To do so, click the Image button in the toolbox, click the position where you want to place the picture, and then select the picture to insert.

Adding a Form Title

Notice in Figure 5-1 on page A 5.5 that the form includes a title. To add a title to a form, add the title as a label in the Form Header section. To accomplish this task, first you will need to expand the size of the Form Header to accommodate the title by dragging the bottom border of the Form Header. Then, you can use the Label button in the toolbox to place the label. After placing the label, you can type the title in the label. Using the Properties command on the label's shortcut menu you can change various properties to improve the title's appearance, as well.

Perform the following steps to place a title on the form.

Steps **To Add a Form Title**

1 **Point to the line separating the Form Header section from the Detail section.**

The shape of the mouse pointer changes to a two-headed vertical arrow with a horizontal crossbar, indicating you can drag the line to resize the Form Header section (Figure 5-58).

FIGURE 5-58

2 **Drag the line to expand the size of the Form Header section to approximately the size shown in Figure 5-59. Point to the Label button in the toolbox as shown in the same figure.**

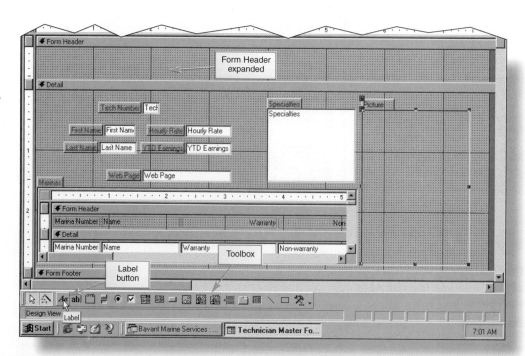

FIGURE 5-59

3 **Click the Label button and then position the mouse pointer as shown in Figure 5-60. The shape of the mouse pointer has changed, indicating you are placing a label.**

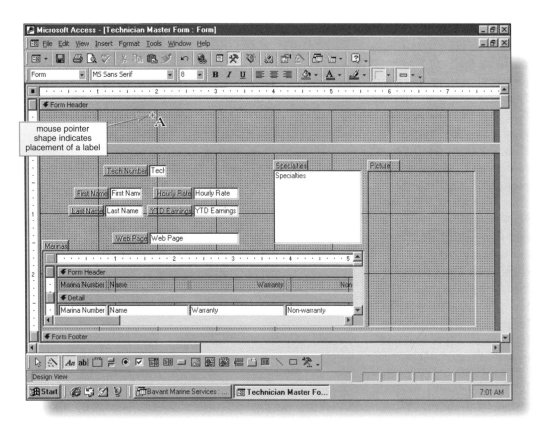

FIGURE 5-60

4 **Click the position shown in the figure to place the label on the form. Type** Technician Master Form **as the title. Click somewhere outside the rectangle containing the title to deselect the rectangle, and then right-click the rectangle containing the title. Click Properties on the shortcut menu that displays, click the Special Effect property, and then click the Special Effect box arrow. Point to Etched.**

The property sheet displays (Figure 5-61). The Etched Special Effect property is highlighted.

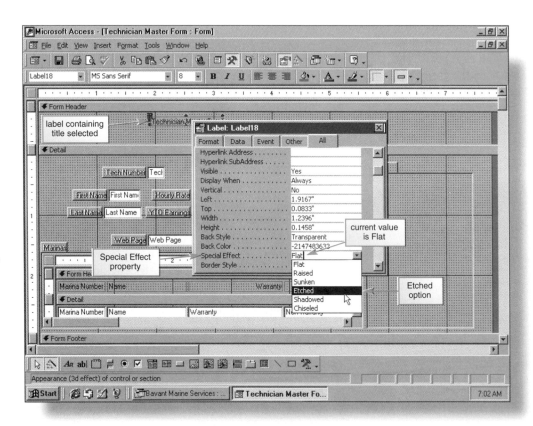

FIGURE 5-61

5 **Click Etched. Click the down scroll arrow so the Font Size property displays. Click the Font Size property, click the Font Size box arrow, and then click 12. If necessary, click the down scroll arrow to display the Font Weight property. Click the Font Weight property, click the Font Weight box arrow, and then click Bold. Close the property sheet by clicking its Close button. Resize the label to display the title completely in the larger font size. Move the label so that it is centered over the form.**

The Form Header is complete (Figure 5-62).

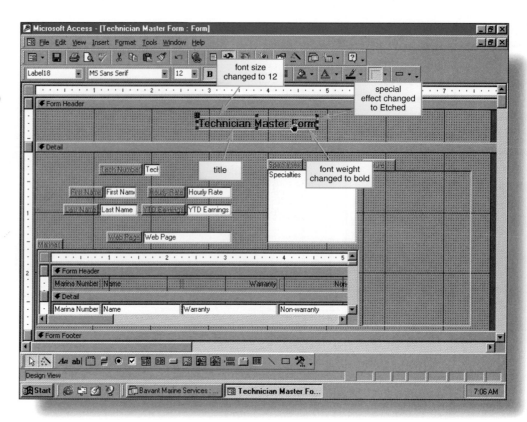

FIGURE 5-62

6 **Close the window containing the form. When asked if you want to save the changes to the design of the form, click Yes.**

The form is complete.

Viewing Data and Web Pages Using the Form

To use a form to view data, right-click the form in the Database window, and then click Open on the shortcut menu that displays. You then can use the navigation buttons to move among technicians or to move among the marinas of the technician currently displayed on the screen. By clicking the technician's Web Page field, you can display the technician's Web page. As soon as you close the window containing the Web page, Access returns to the form.

Perform the steps on the next page to display data using the form.

Steps To Use the Form to View Data and Web Pages

1 **If necessary, click Forms on the Objects bar. Right-click Technician Master Form and then click Open on the shortcut menu. Be sure the window containing the form is maximized. Point to the Next Record button for the Technician table.**

The data from the first record displays in the form (Figure 5-63).

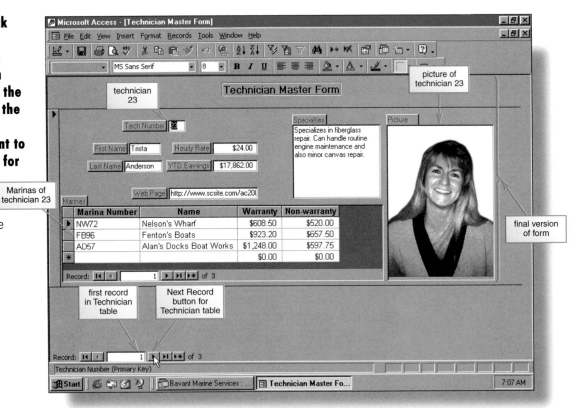

FIGURE 5-63

2 **Click the Next Record button to move to the second technician. Point to the Next Record button for the Marinas subform (the Next Record button in the set of navigation buttons immediately below the subform).**

*The data from the second record displays (Figure 5-64). (The records in your form may display in a different order.) If more marinas were included than would fit in the subform at a single time, Access would automatically add a **vertical scroll bar** to the Marinas subform. You can use either a scroll bar or the navigation buttons to move among marinas.*

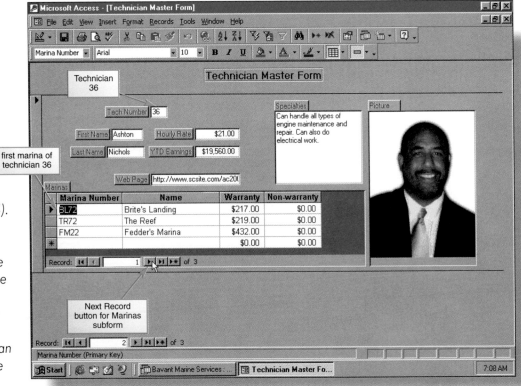

FIGURE 5-64

3 **Click the subform's Next Record button twice.**

The data from the third marina of technician 36 is selected (Figure 5-65).

FIGURE 5-65

4 **Point to the control for the technician's Web page (Figure 5-66).**

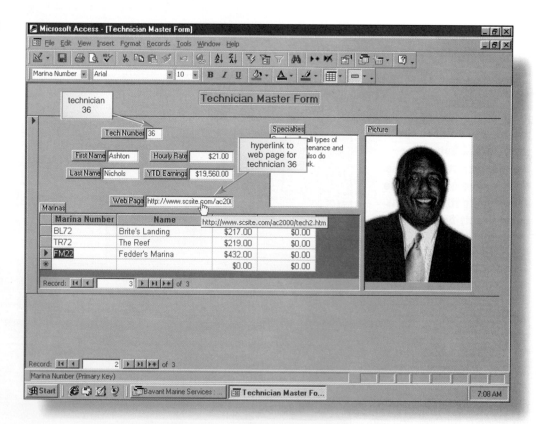

FIGURE 5-66

5 **Click the control for the technician's Web Page. If a dialog box displays in either this step or the next, follow the directions given in the dialog box.**

The technician's Web page displays (Figure 5-67).

6 **When you have finished viewing the technician's Web page, click the Close button to return to the form. Close the form by clicking its Close button.**

The form no longer displays.

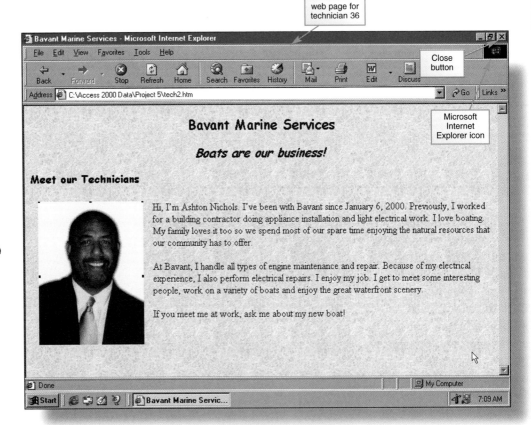

web page for technician 36

Close button

Microsoft Internet Explorer icon

FIGURE 5-67

The previous steps illustrated the way you work with a main form and subform, as well as how to use a hyperlink (the Web Page control in this form). Clicking the navigation buttons for the main form moves to a different technician. Clicking the navigation buttons for the subform moves to a different marina of the technician whose photograph displays in the main form. Clicking a hyperlink moves to the corresponding document or Web Page. The following are other actions you can take within the form:

1. To move from the last field in the main form to the first field in the subform, press the TAB key. To move back to the last field in the main form, press the CTRL+SHIFT+TAB keys.
2. To move from the last field in the subform to the first field in the next record's main form, press the CTRL+TAB keys.
3. To switch from the main form to the subform using the mouse, click anywhere in the subform. To switch back to the main form, click any control in the main form. Clicking the background of the main form will not cause the switch to occur.

Using Date and Memo Fields in a Query

To use date fields in queries, you simply type the dates including the slashes. To search for records with a specific date, you must type the date. You also can use **comparison operators**. To find all the technicians whose start date is prior to November 2, 2000, for example, you type the criterion <11/2/2000.

You also can use memo fields in queries. Typically, you will want to find all the records on which the memo field contains a specific word or phrase. To do so, you use wildcards. For example, to find all the technicians who have the word, electrical, in the Specialties field, you type the criterion, like *electrical*.

Perform the following steps to create and run queries that use date and memo fields.

Steps: To Use Date and Memo Fields in a Query

1 In the Database window, click **Tables** on the Objects bar, and then, if necessary, select the Technician table. Click the **New Object: AutoForm** button arrow on the toolbar. Click **Query**. Be sure **Design View** is highlighted, and then click the **OK** button.

2 Maximize the **Microsoft Access - [Query1 : Select Query]** window that displays. Resize the upper and lower panes and the Technician field list to the sizes shown in Figure 5-68. Double-click the **Tech Number, First Name, Last Name, Start Date, and Specialties** fields to include them in the query. Click the **Criteria** row under the Specialties field and then type `like *electrical*` as the criterion. Point to the **Run** button on the toolbar (Figure 5-68).

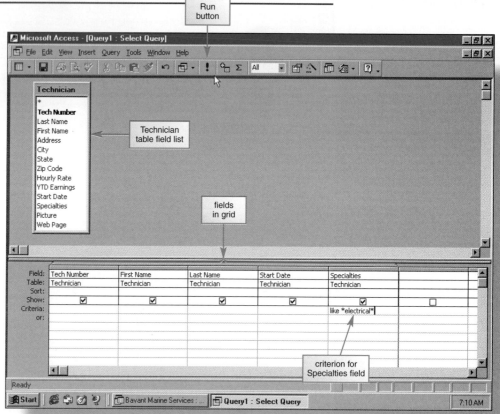

FIGURE 5-68

3 Click the Run button on the toolbar to run the query.

The results display in Datasheet view (Figure 5-69). Two records are included.

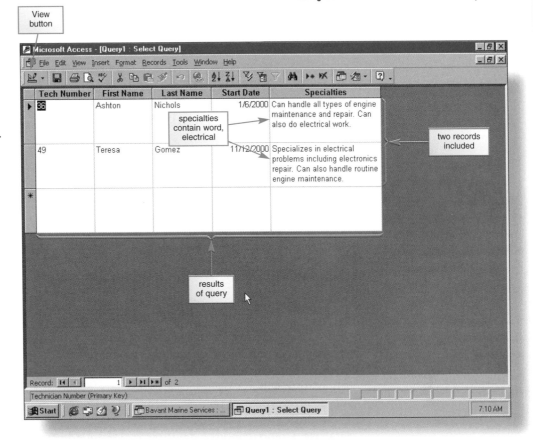

FIGURE 5-69

4 Click the View button to return to the Select Query window. Click the Criteria row under the Start Date field, and then type <11/2/2000 (Figure 5-70).

5 Click the Run button on the toolbar to run the query.

The result contains only a single row, because only one technician was hired before November 2, 2000 and has a specialty entry that contains the word, electrical.

6 Close the Select Query window by clicking its Close button. When asked if you want to save the query, click the No button.

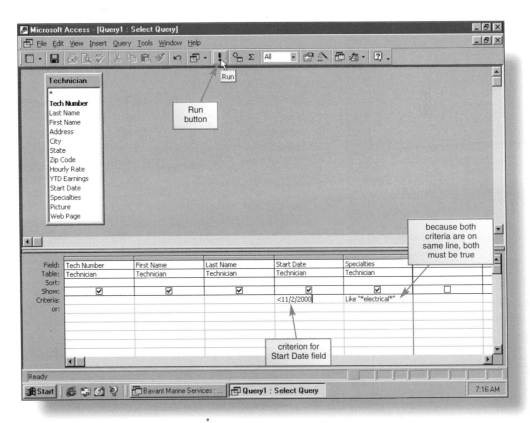

FIGURE 5-70

The results of the query are removed from the screen and the Database window again displays.

Closing the Database

The following step closes the database by closing its Database window.

TO CLOSE A DATABASE

 Click the Close button for the Bavant Marine Services : Database window.

Compacting a Database

As you add more data to a database, it naturally grows larger. Pictures will increase the size significantly. When you delete objects (for example, records, tables, forms, pictures), the space previously occupied by the object does not become available for additional objects. Instead, the additional objects are given new space, that is, space that was not already allocated. If you decide to change a picture, for example, the new picture will not occupy the same space as the previous picture, but instead it will be given space of its own.

In order to remove this wasted space from the database, you must **compact** the database. Compacting the database makes an additional copy of the database, one that contains the same data, but does not contain the wasted space that the original does. The original database will still exist in its unaltered form.

A typical three-step process for compacting a database is as follows:

1. Compact the original database (for example, Bavant Marine Services) and give the compacted database a different name (for example, Bavant Marine Services Compacted).
2. Assuming that the compacting operation completed successfully, use the delete feature of Windows to delete the original database (Bavant Marine Services).
3. Also assuming that the compacting operation completed successfully, use the rename feature of Windows to rename the compacted database (Bavant Marine Services Compacted) with the name of the original database (Bavant Marine Services).

Of course, if there is a problem in the compacting operation, you should continue to use the original database; that is, do not complete steps 2 and 3.

The operation can be carried out on a diskette, provided there is sufficient space available. If the database to be compacted occupies more than half the diskette, there may be not enough room for Access to create the compacted database. In such a case, you should first copy the database to a hard disk or network drive. (You can use whatever Windows technique you prefer for copying files in order to do so.) You can then complete the process on the hard disk or network drive.

Perform the steps on the next page to compact the Bavant Marine Services database after you have copied the database to a hard disk. If you have not copied the database to a hard disk, check with your instructor before completing these steps.

Steps **To Compact a Database**

1 Be sure the database is closed. Click Tools on the menu bar, click Database Utilities, and then point to Compact and Repair Database (Figure 5-71).

2 Click Compact and Repair Database. In the Database to Compact From, select the folder containing the Bavant Marine Services database on the hard disk, select the Bavant Marine Services database and then click the Compact button.

3 In the Compact Database Into dialog box, type Bavant Marine Services Compacted as the name of the database and then click the Save button.

The compacted database is stored with the name Bavant Marine Services Compacted.

4 Assuming the operation is completed successfully, delete the original database (Bavant Marine Services) and rename Bavant Marine Services Compacted as Bavant Marine Services.

The Bavant Marine Services database now is the compacted form of the original.

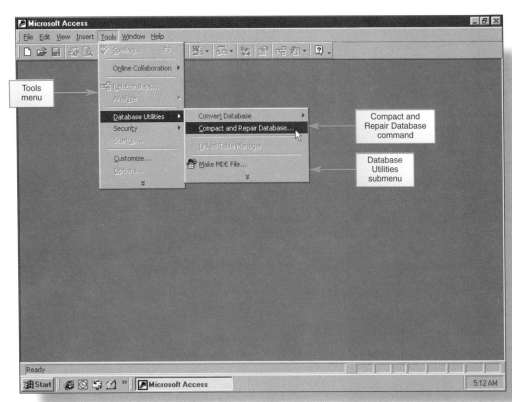

FIGURE 5-71

C A S E   P E R S P E C T I V E   S U M M A R Y

You have added the new fields requested by Bavant Marine Services to the Technician table in its database. You have updated the new fields and created a form incorporating some of the new fields. You have also included data about the marinas of the technician on this new form. In addition, you included a link to the technician's Web page on the form. You created queries for Bavant that included criteria based on the new fields. Finally, you compacted the database to remove any wasted space.

Project Summary

Project 5 introduced you to some additional field types. To maintain the additional data required at Bavant Marine Services, you needed to learn how to create and work with date, memo, OLE, and Hyperlink fields. You also learned how to use such fields in a form. You then learned how to build a form on a one-to-many relationship. One technician displayed on the form at the same time as the many marinas serviced by that technician. You learned how to use the form to view technician and marina data as well as to view the technician's Web Page. You saw how to use date and memo fields in queries to answer two important questions for the organization. Finally, you learned how to compact a database to remove any wasted space.

What You Should Know

Having completed this project, you now should be able to perform the following tasks:

▶ Add a Form Title *(A 5.40)*
▶ Add Fields to a Table *(A 5.6)*
▶ Change Label Alignment *(A 5.33)*
▶ Change Special Effects and Colors of Labels *(A 5.37)*
▶ Change the Row and Column Size *(A 5.12)*
▶ Change the Size Mode of a Picture *(A 5.36)*
▶ Close a Database *(A 5.48)*
▶ Close the Table and Save the Properties *(A 5.20)*
▶ Compact a Database *(A 5.49)*
▶ Create a Form with a Subform Using the Form Wizard *(A 5.21)*
▶ Enter Data in Date Fields *(A 5.9)*

▶ Enter Data in Hyperlink Fields *(A 5.18)*
▶ Enter Data in Memo Fields *(A 5.11)*
▶ Enter Data in OLE Fields and Convert the Data to Pictures *(A 5.15)*
▶ Modify the Form Design *(A 5.28)*
▶ Modify the Subform Design *(A 5.26)*
▶ Move Fields *(A 5.32)*
▶ Move and Resize Fields *(A 5.29)*
▶ Move Labels *(A 5.31)*
▶ Open a Database *(A 5.5)*
▶ Resize a Label *(A 5.31, A 5.35)*
▶ Use Date and Memo Fields in a Query *(A 5.45)*
▶ Use the Form to View Data and Web Pages *(A 5.43)*

Apply Your Knowledge

➕ Project Reinforcement at www.scsite.com/off2000/reinforce.htm

1 Enhancing the Sidewalk Scrapers Database

Instructions: Start Access. Open the Sidewalk Scrapers database from the Access Data Disk. See the inside back cover for instructions for downloading the Access Data Disk or see your instructor for information on accessing the files required for this book. Perform the following tasks.

1. Add the fields, Start Date and Notes, to the Worker table structure as shown in Figure 5-72.
2. Save the changes to the structure.
3. Add the data shown in Figure 5-73 to the Worker table. Adjust the row and column spacing for the table.
4. Print and then close the table.
5. Query the Worker table to find all workers who have a driver's license. Include the worker's first name, last name, and pay rate in the query. Print the query results. Do not save the query.
6. Use the Form Wizard to create a form with a subform for the Worker table. Include the Worker Id, First Name, Last Name, Pay Rate, Start Date, and Notes from the Worker table. Include the Customer Number, Name, Telephone, and Balance fields from the Customer table.
7. Modify the form design to create the form shown in Figure 5-74 on the next page.
8. Print the form. To print the form, open the form, click File on the menu bar, click Print, and then click Selected Record(s) as the Print Range. Click the OK button.

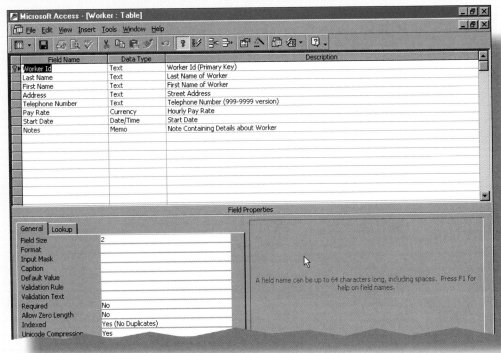

FIGURE 5-72

Data for Worker table		
WORKER ID	**START DATE**	**NOTES**
03	11/15/1999	Has driver's license. Can operate snowblower and pickup with snowplow attachment.
07	12/02/2000	Can operate snowblower. Available at all hours.
10	01/20/2001	Can work weekends only.
14	12/12/2000	Has driver's license. Can operate snowblower. Prefers to work in the early morning before 7 A.M.

FIGURE 5-73

(continued)

Apply Your Knowledge

➕ Project Reinforcement at www.scsite.com/off2000/reinforce.htm

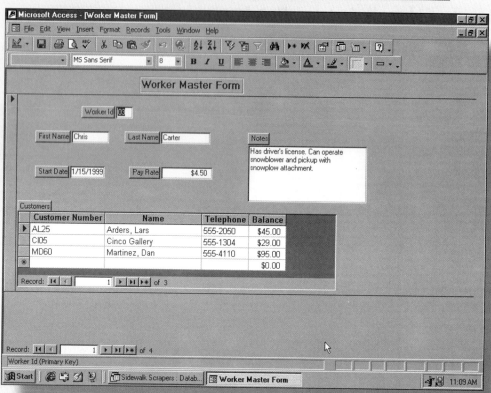

FIGURE 5-74

In the Lab

1 Enhancing the School Connection Database

Problem: The Booster's Club has found that the School Connection database needs to maintain additional data on vendors. They need to know the last date they placed an order with a vendor. They also would like to store some notes about each vendor's return policy as well as store the Web page name of each vendor's Web Page. The club requires a form that displays information about the vendor as well as the products the vendor sells.

Instructions: Open the School Connection database from the Access Data Disk. See the inside back cover of this textbook for instructions for downloading the Access Data Disk, or see your instructor for information on accessing the files required for this book. Perform the following tasks.

1. Add the fields, Last Order Date, Notes, and Web Page, to the Vendor table structure as shown in Figure 5-75 and then save the changes to the structure.

In the Lab

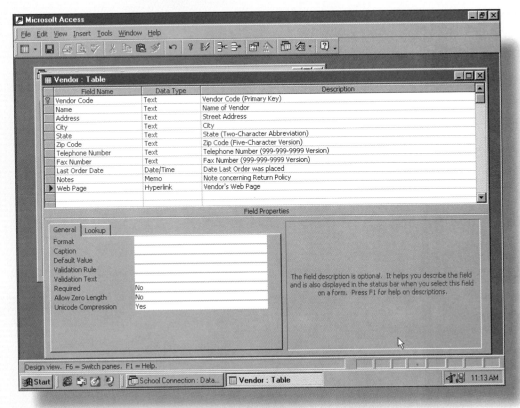

FIGURE 5-75

2. Add the data shown in Figure 5-76 to the Vendor table. Use the same hyperlink files that you used for the Technician table in this project. Adjust the row and column spacing for the table.
3. Print the table.
4. Create the form shown in Figure 5-77 on the next page for the Vendor table. Use Vendor Master Form as the name of the form and Items of Vendor as the name of the subform.
5. Print the form. To print the form, open the form, click File on the menu bar, click Print, and then click Selected Record(s) as the Print Range. Click the OK button.
6. Query the Vendor table to find all vendors that allow all unsold merchandise to be returned. Include the Vendor Code and Name in the query. Print the results. Do not save the query.

Data for Vendor table		
VENDOR CODE	LAST ORDER DATE	NOTES
AL	05/20/2001	Can return only those items ordered for the first time. Charges a fee.
GG	06/17/2001	Can return all unsold merchandise. No extra charges.
TM	08/24/2001	Can return all unsold merchandise. Charges a fee.

FIGURE 5-76

(continued)

In the Lab

Enhancing the School Connection Database (continued)

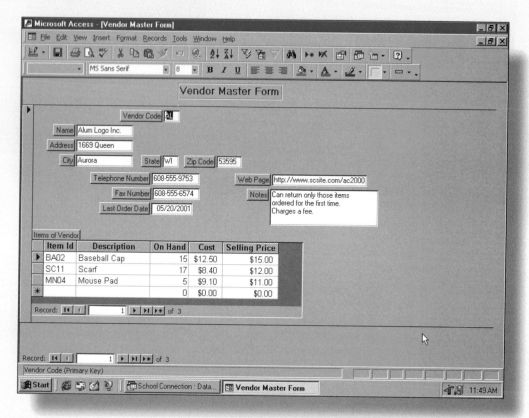

FIGURE 5-77

2 Enhancing the City Area Bus Company Database

Problem: The City Area Bus Company needs to maintain additional data on the advertising sales representatives. The company needs to maintain the date a sales rep started as well as some notes concerning the representative's abilities. They also would like to store a picture of the representative as well as a link to each representative's Web Page. The company wants you to create a form that displays advertising sales representative information and the advertisers for which they are responsible.

Instructions: Open the City Area Bus Company database from the Access Data Disk. See the inside back cover of this textbook for instructions for downloading the Access Data Disk, or see your instructor for information on accessing the files required for this book. Perform the following tasks.

1. Add the Start Date, Notes, Picture, and Web Page fields to the Sales Rep table as shown in Figure 5-78. Save the changes to the structure.

In the Lab

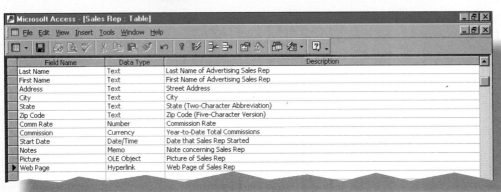

FIGURE 5-78

2. Add the data shown in Figure 5-79 to the Sales Rep table. Add pictures and hyperlinks for each representative. Use the same picture and hyperlink files that you used for the Technician table in this project. Pict1.bmp and pict3.bmp are pictures of females; pict2.bmp is of a male.

3. Print the table.

4. Create the form shown in Figure 5-80. Use Sales Rep Master Form as the name of the form and Advertiser Accounts as the name of the subform.

5. Add the current date to the form. (*Hint*: Use Microsoft Access Help to solve this problem.)

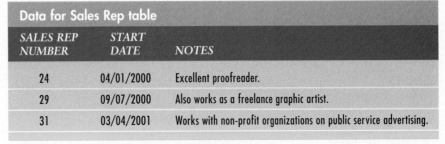

Data for Sales Rep table

SALES REP NUMBER	START DATE	NOTES
24	04/01/2000	Excellent proofreader.
29	09/07/2000	Also works as a freelance graphic artist.
31	03/04/2001	Works with non-profit organizations on public service advertising.

FIGURE 5-79

FIGURE 5-80

(continued)

In the Lab

Enhancing the City Area Bus Company Database *(continued)*

6. Print the form. To print the form, open the form, click File on the menu bar, click Print, and then click Selected Record(s) as the Print Range. Click the OK button.

7. Query the Sales Rep table to find all sales reps who also will work as freelance graphic artists. Include the Sales Rep Number, Last Name, and First Name in the query. Print the query results. Do not save the query.

8. Query the Sales Rep table to find all sales reps who started before 2001. Include the Sales Rep Number, Last Name, First Name, Commission, and Comm Rate in the query. Print the query results. Do not save the query.

3 Enhancing the Resort Rentals Database

Problem: The real estate company needs to maintain additional data on the owners. The company needs to maintain pictures of the owners as well as some notes concerning the owner's rental policies. The company wants you to create a form that displays owner information and the rental properties they own.

Instructions: Open the Resort Rentals database from the Access Data Disk. See the inside back cover of this textbook for instructions for downloading the Access Data Disk, or see your instructor for information on accessing the files required for this book. Perform the following tasks.

1. Add the fields, Picture and Notes, to the Owner table structure as shown in Figure 5-81. Save the changes to the structure.

2. Add the data shown in Figure 5-82 to the Owner table. Adjust the row and column spacing for the table, if necessary.

3. Print the table.

4. Create the form shown in Figure 5-83. Use Owner Master Form as the name of the form and Rental Properties as the name of the subform.

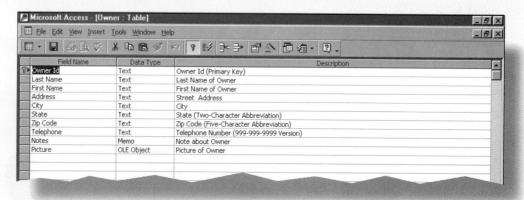

FIGURE 5-81

Data for Owner table

OWNER ID	NOTES
FH15	Has no pets policy. Will not rent to families with children under 12.
LD45	Will rent to families with children. Allows small pets only but requires $100 security deposit.
ML10	Has no smoking policy. Has no pets policy.
PR23	Will rent to families with children. Allows pets but requires $200 security deposit.

FIGURE 5-82

In the Lab

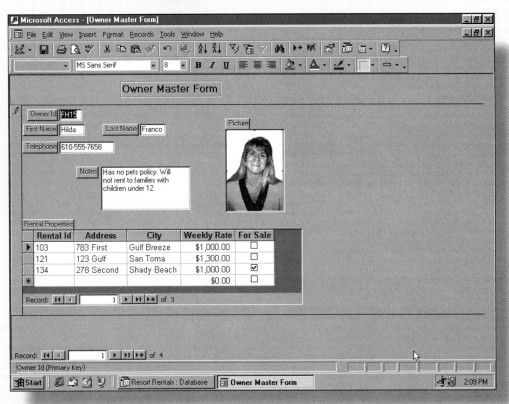

FIGURE 5-83

5. Print the form. To print the form, open the form, click File on the menu bar, click Print, and then click Selected Record(s) as the Print Range. Click the OK button.

6. Query the Owner table to find all owners who allow pets. Include the Owner Id, First Name, and Last Name in the query. Print the results. Do not save the query.

Cases and Places

The difficulty of these case studies varies:
▌ are the least difficult; ▌▌ are more difficult; and ▌▌▌ are the most difficult.

1 ▌ Use the Computer Items data-base on the Access Data Disk for this assignment. The Computer Club needs additional data on the suppliers. Add the fields and data shown in Figure 5-84 to the Sup-plier table. Adjust the row and col-umn spacing so that the complete notes about the supplier display. Print the Supplier table. Query the Supplier table to find all suppliers that offer volume discounts.

SUPPLIER CODE	LAST ORDER DATE	NOTES
ER	8/26/2001	Offers volume discounts when more than 12 items are ordered.
HI	9/1/2001	No discounts on any items.
MT	9/9/2001	Logo Mouse Pads are a special order. No discounts.

FIGURE 5-84

2 ▌ Create and print a Supplier Master Form for the Supplier table that is similar in format to Figure 5-77 on page A 5.54. The form should include all the fields from the Supplier table. The subform that displays should include all fields in the Item table except Supplier Code.

3 ▌▌ Use the Galaxy Books data-base on the Access Data Disk for this assignment. The bookstore owner needs additional data on the publishers. Add the fields and data shown in Figure 5-85 to the Pub-lisher table. Adjust the row and col-umn spacing so that the complete notes about the publisher display. Print the Publisher table. Query the database to find all publishers that will fill single orders.

PUBLISHER CODE	ORDER DATE	NOTES
BB	6/21/2001	Will fill single orders and special requests.
PB	6/30/2001	Will fill single orders on emergency basis only. Ships twice a week.
SI	6/15/2001	Has minimum order requirement of 25 books. Ships weekly.
VN	5/25/2001	Will fill single orders and special requests. Ships daily.

FIGURE 5-85

4 ▌▌ Create and print a Publisher Master Form for the Publisher table. The subform that displays should include all fields in the Book table except Year Published and Publisher Code. Be sure to include a form header and change the special effects and colors of the labels.

5 ▌▌▌ Enhance the Galaxy Books database by adding a summary description for each book. Make up your own summaries. Add a field to the Publisher table that will store a picture of the publisher's sales representative. Use the same picture files used for the Technician table in the project.

Microsoft Access 2000

P R O J E C T

6

Creating an Application System Using Macros, Wizards, and the Switchboard Manager

You will have mastered the material in this project when you can:

O B J E C T I V E S

- Use the Lookup Wizard to create a lookup field
- Use the Input Mask Wizard to create an input mask
- Update a field using an input mask
- Use a Lookup Wizard field
- Add a control for a single field to a report
- Add a calculated control to a report
- Add a control for a single field to a form
- Create a macro
- Add actions and comments to a macro
- Modify arguments in a macro
- Create a copy of a macro
- Run a macro
- Create a switchboard
- Modify switchboard pages
- Modify switchboard items
- Use a switchboard

Legal Concerns?

Hotlines Offer Speedy Counsel

What are your legal concerns? Do you need to prepare a contract for a job to be done? Are you involved in a dispute with a business partner? Have you been subpoenaed in a litigation? Will you be required to file a new small claims case? With any legal issue facing you for which you are not prepared or informed, you may ask if you have a place to turn for some plain and simple legal guidance. Knowledge of the law empowers you.

You know a lawyer can help you with these problems, but you fear the time and expense of hiring one will really stretch your resources. In response to

these concerns, legal hotlines have sprung up with the goal of providing quick, inexpensive advice. The more efficient hotline systems usually are staffed with experienced attorneys and paralegals who have access to powerful database application systems such as Access 2000 that help organize client information using forms and macros as you will do in this project.

A potential client calling the hotline provides basic information about the legal matter. The hotline staff member answering the telephone selects the client registration form in the database system and begins interviewing the client while simultaneously entering the answers in fields on the form.

Usually, the first field is the client's name. When the name is entered, the database system executes a macro, which is a series of actions designed to carry out a specific task. In this case, the macro searches the client table for a matching name. If a match is found, remaining fields in the registration form are filled in automatically with personal data from the client's previous record. If a match is not found, the hotline staff member interviews the client to obtain the required data.

A second macro is performed when the Social Security number is entered. While a client's last name may change, the Social Security number remains the same. Therefore, the last name macro might not retrieve the client's record if the client has used the hotline service previously using a different name, whereas the Social Security macro would find the record if the same number is used.

After this basic client data has been entered in the registration form, the database application system retrieves another form that includes a field for the name of the person or company causing the conflict. An attorney cannot represent a client if he or she previously has represented the opposing party in a similar case. Then, the database system executes a third macro to check the adverse party table for client conflicts.

If no conflict is found, the hotline worker continues to interview the caller about the case and record the facts and issues in memo fields. Many database application systems integrate with word   processing applications, so the attorney can generate a form letter that merges data from this initial client conversation with prewritten text that confirms the results of this telephone conversation.

With the installation and development of online and legal advice hotlines, trained law office staff are serving more clients and providing direct response at a fraction of the cost for services. Hotlines offer speedy counsel and solutions in an informal setting to resolve legal disputes and concerns.

Microsoft **Access 2000**

Microsoft Access 2000

Creating an Application System Using Macros, Wizards, and the Switchboard Manager

P R O J E C T

6

C A S E P E R S P E C T I V E

The management of Bavant Marine Services is pleased with the tables, forms, and reports that you have created thus far. They have additional requests, however. They now realize they should have included phone numbers for marinas in the database. They would like for you to add the phone number field to the Marina table, the Billing Summary report, and the Marina Update Form. They would like to be able to type only the digits in the phone number and then have Access format the number appropriately. If the user enters 6165552312, for example, Access will format the number as (616) 555-2312. Bavant is pleased with the Marina Type combo box you placed in the Marina Update form, which allows users to select a marina type from a list. They realized, however, that this combo box is not visible in Datasheet view. They would like for you to incorporate a similar feature in Datasheet view. Finally, they have heard about switchboard systems that enable users to click a button or two to open any form or table, preview any report, or print any report. They would like for you to create such a system for them because they believe this will increase employee productivity.

Introduction

In previous projects, you created tables, forms, and reports. Each time you wanted to use any of these, however, you had to follow the correct series of steps. To open the Marina Update Form in a maximized window, for example, first you must click Forms on the Objects bar in the Database window, and then right-click the correct form. Next, you had to click Open on the shortcut menu, and then finally click the Maximize button for the window containing the form.

All these steps are unnecessary if you create your own switchboard system, such as the one shown in Figure 6-1a. A **switchboard** is a form that includes buttons to perform a variety of actions. In this system, you just click a button — View Form, View Table, View Report, Print Report, or Exit Application — to indicate the action you wish to take. Other than Exit Application, clicking a button leads to another switchboard. For example, clicking the View Form button leads to the View Form switchboard as shown in Figure 6-1b. You then click the button that identifies the form you wish to view. Similarly, clicking the View Table button would lead to a switchboard on which you would click a button to indicate the table you wish to view. Thus, viewing any form, table, or report, or printing any report requires clicking only two buttons.

In this project, you will create the switchboard system represented in Figures 6-1a and 6-1b. Before doing so, you will create **macros**, which are collections of actions designed to carry out specific tasks, such as opening a form and maximizing the window containing the form. You can run the macros directly from the Database window. When you do, Access will execute the various steps, called **actions**, in the macro. You also can use the macros in the switchboard system. Clicking certain buttons in the switchboard system you create will cause the appropriate macros to be run.

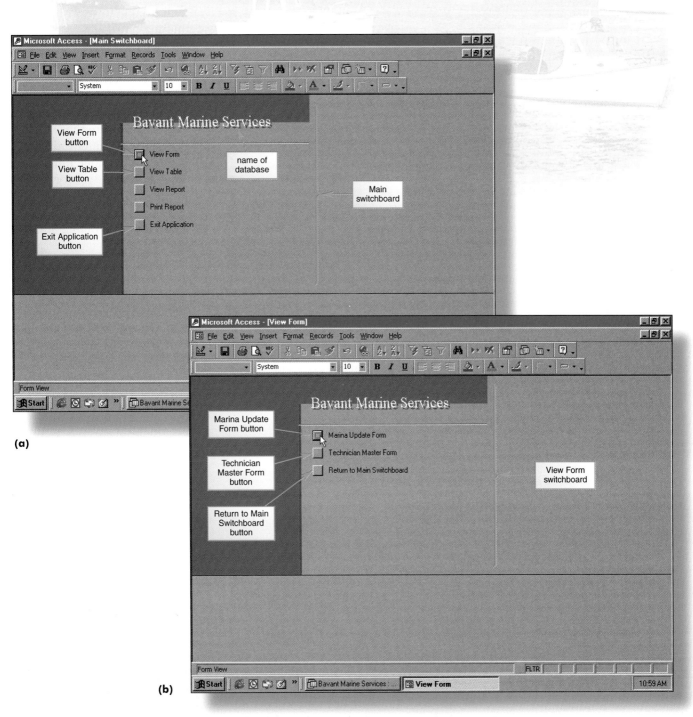

(a)

(b)

FIGURE 6-1

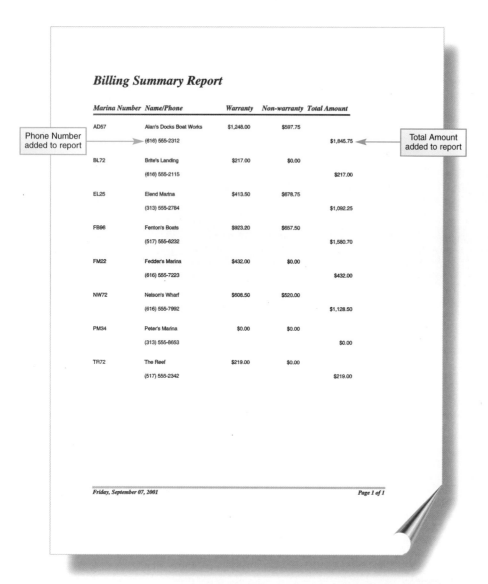

(a)

Before creating the switchboard system, you will make two changes to the Marina table. You will convert the data type of the Marina Type field to Lookup Wizard. By doing so, users will be able to select a marina type from a list just as they can when using the combo box on a form. You will also add the Phone Number field to the table and then use the Input Mask wizard to ensure that (1) users need to enter only the digits in the phone number and (2) Access will format the phone numbers appropriately. You will add the phone number to the Billing Summary Report (Figure 6-2a). In addition, you will add the total amount (warranty amount plus non-warranty amount) to the report. You also will add the phone number to the Marina Update Form (Figure 6-2b).

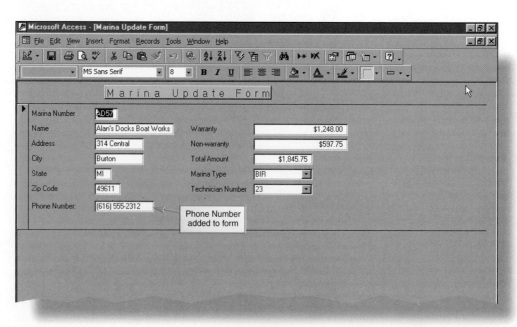

(b)

FIGURE 6-2

② **Click the row selector for the Marina Type field, and then press the INSERT key to insert a blank row. Click the Field Name column for the new field. Type** Phone Number **as the field name and then press the TAB key. Select the Text data type by pressing the TAB key. Type** Phone Number **as the description. Click the Input Mask text box, and then point to the Build button (the button containing three dots).**

The data is entered for the field and Build button displays in the Input Mask text box (Figure 6-9).

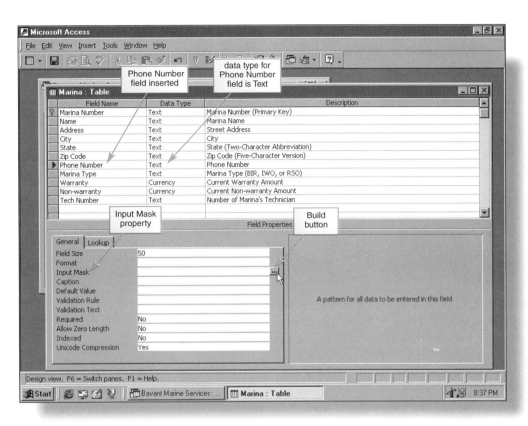

FIGURE 6-9

③ **Click the Build button, and ensure that Phone Number is selected. If a dialog box displays asking you to save the table, click Yes. Point to the Next button.**

The Input Mask Wizard dialog box displays (Figure 6-10). The dialog box contains several common input masks. The Phone Number input mask is highlighted.

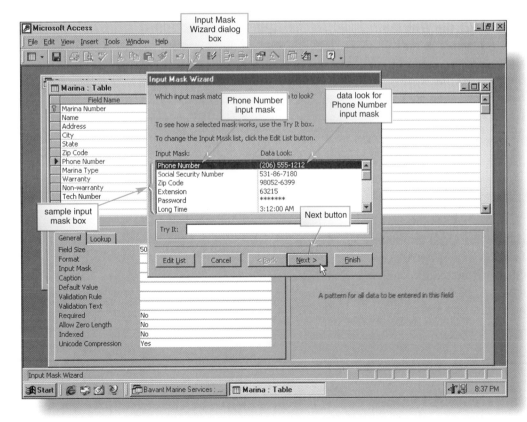

FIGURE 6-10

4 Click the Next button. You then are given the opportunity to change the input mask. Because you do not need to change it, click the Next button. Point to the With the symbols in the mask, like this option button.

The Input Wizard dialog box displays (Figure 6-11). You are asked to indicate whether the symbols in the mask (the parentheses and the hyphen) are to be stored in the database or not. Your dialog box may display different numbers in the examples.

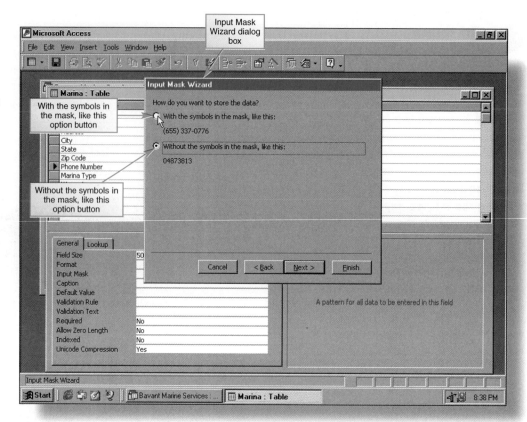

FIGURE 6-11

5 Click the With the symbols in the mask, like this option button, click the Next button, and then click the Finish button.

The input mask displays (Figure 6-12).

6 Close the Marina : Table window by clicking its Close button on the title bar. When the Microsoft Access dialog box displays, click the Yes button to save your changes.

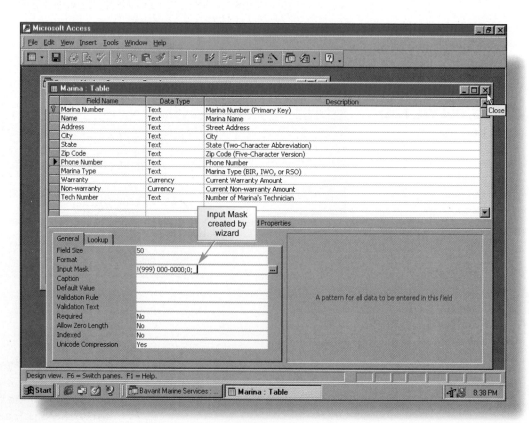

FIGURE 6-12

Entering Data Using an Input Mask

When entering data in a field that has an input mask, Access will insert the appropriate special characters in the proper positions. This means Access will insert the parentheses around the area code, the space following the second parenthesis, and the hyphen automatically in the Phone Number field. Perform the following steps to first resize the Phone Number field so that the entire heading displays and then add the phone numbers.

 To Enter Data Using an Input Mask

1 **If necessary, click the Tables object on the Objects bar. Right-click Marina and then click Open on the shortcut menu. Make sure the window is maximized, and then point to the right boundary of the field selector for the Phone Number field.**

The mouse pointer changes to a two-headed horizontal arrow with a vertical bar (Figure 6-13).

2 **Double-click the right boundary of the field selector to resize the field. Click the Phone Number field on the first record, and then type 6165552312 as the phone number.**

Access automatically inserts parentheses, a space, and a hyphen and displays underscores (_) as placeholders when you begin typing (Figure 6-14).

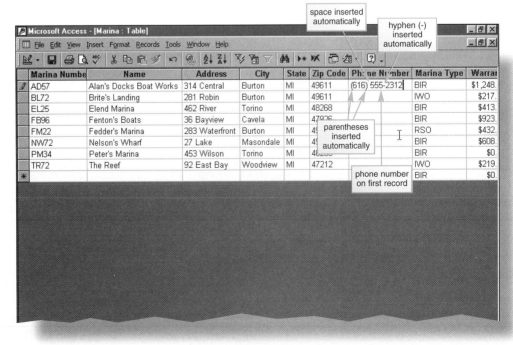

FIGURE 6-13

FIGURE 6-14

Microsoft **Access** 2000

3 Use the same technique to enter the remaining phone numbers as shown in Figure 6-15.

4 Close the window containing the datasheet by clicking its Close button. When asked if you want to save the changes to the layout (the resizing of the Phone Number column), click the Yes button.

FIGURE 6-15

Using a Lookup Wizard Field

You use a Lookup Wizard field just as you use a Combo box in a form. Click the arrow to display a list of available selections (see Figure 6-16). You can then click one of the items to select it from the list.

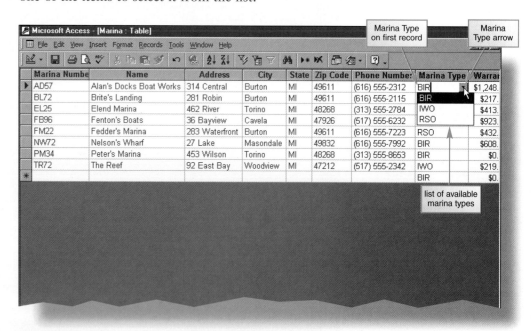

FIGURE 6-16

Modifying a Report

The Billing Summary Report shown in Figure 6-2 on page A 6.6 has two additional controls not present in the original version of the report. One of the additional controls contains the Phone Number field that you just added to the Marina table. The other is a calculated control. It displays the total amount, which is the sum of the warranty amount and the non-warranty amount.

Resizing and Moving Controls in a Report

Before adding the additional fields, you need to make changes to the size of the control for the Name field because currently it is not long enough to display all the names. In a previous project, the Name field was expanded after this report was created. You also need to resize and move the controls for the Warranty and Non-warranty fields to allow space to add the Total Amount field. Perform the following steps to resize and move the controls in the Billing Summary Report.

More About

Adding Controls

Even though a control is for a single field, you do not have to use a field list. You also can click the Text Box button on the toolbox, place the text box in the desired location on the report or form, and then type the name of the field in square brackets ([ ]).

To Resize and Move Controls in a Report

1 Click the Reports object in the Database window, right-click Billing Summary Report, and then point to Design View on the shortcut menu.

The Design View command on the shortcut menu is highlighted (Figure 6-17).

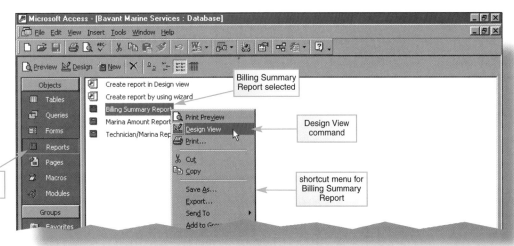

FIGURE 6-17

2 Click Design View. Click the Warranty control in the Page Header section to select the control. Hold down the SHIFT key, and then click the Non-Warranty control in the Page Header section, the Warranty control in the Detail section, and the Non-Warranty control in the Detail section to select all four controls simultaneously. Point to the left sizing handle for the Warranty control in the Page Header section.

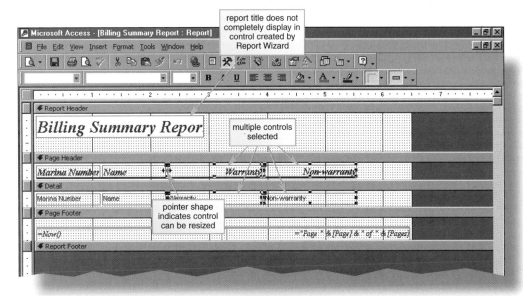

FIGURE 6-18

The report design displays (Figure 6-18). The report title does not completely display in the control, even though it displays correctly when you print or preview the report. (This is the way it was created by the report wizard. Yours may be different. If you would like for it to display completely in the report design, click the control and then drag the right-hand sizing handle.)

3 Drag the handle to the right to resize the controls to the approximate sizes shown in Figure 6-19.

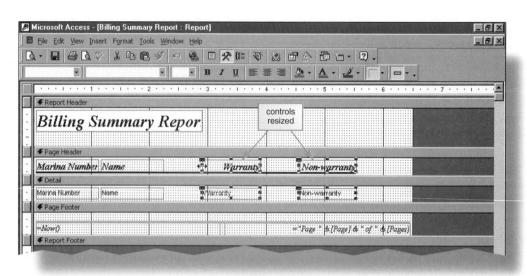

FIGURE 6-19

4 Click the Name control in the Page Header section. Hold down the SHIFT key, and then click the Name control in the Detail section to select both controls simultaneously. Point to the right sizing handle for the Name control in the Detail section.

The Name control in both the Page Header and Detail sections is selected (Figure 6-20).

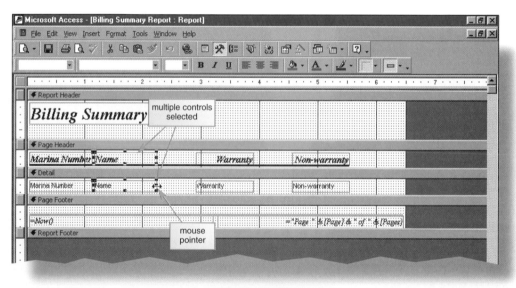

FIGURE 6-20

5 Drag the handle to the right to resize the controls to the approximate sizes shown in Figure 6-21.

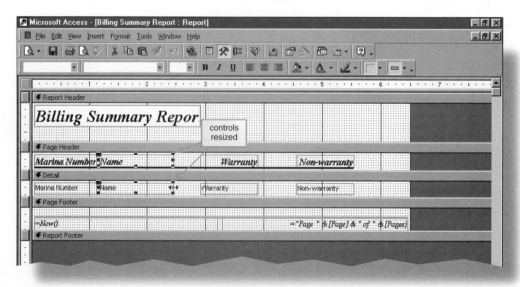

FIGURE 6-21

6 Select the Warranty controls in the Page Header and Detail sections. Point to the border of either control so that the mouse pointer changes shape to a hand and then drag the controls to the approximate position shown in Figure 6-22. Using the same process, move the Non-Warranty controls in the same sections into the approximate positions shown in the figure. Then drag the lower boundary of the Detail section to the position shown in the figure.

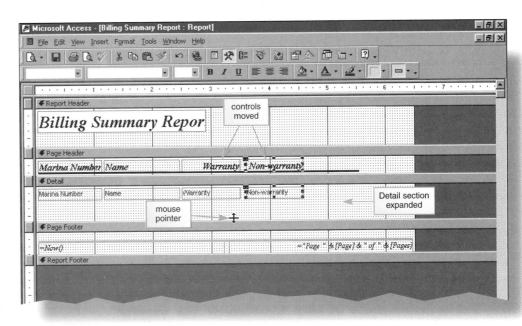

FIGURE 6-22

The Warranty and Non-warranty controls in the Page Header and Detail sections have been repositioned, and the Detail section resized (Figure 6-22).

Adding Controls to a Report

You can add controls to a report just as you added them to a form in Project 4 (pages A 4.34 and A 4.35). You can use either the toolbox or a field list to add various types of controls. If the control is for a single field, using the field list is usually an easier way to add the control. In this section you will add a control for the phone number field. You will also add a control that will display the total amount (warranty amount plus non-warranty amount). Perform the following steps to add the controls and also to make appropriate changes to the column headings.

More About 2000

Adding Controls

Instead of typing an expression in the text box, you can use the text box's Control Source property. Right-click the text box, click Properties, click Control Source, and then type the expression.

Steps To Add Controls to a Report

1 If the Field list does not already display, point to the Field List button on the Report Design toolbar (Figure 6-23).

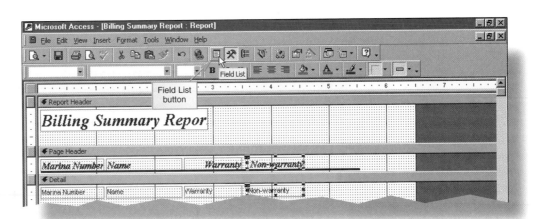

FIGURE 6-23

2 Click the Field List button, if necessary. Point to Phone Number in the Field list.

The Field list displays (Figure 6-24).

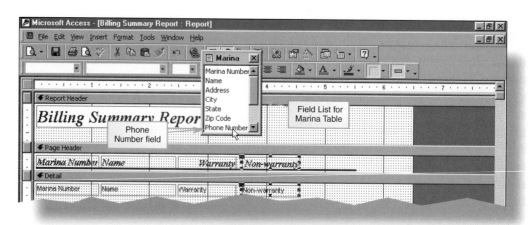

FIGURE 6-24

3 Drag the Phone Number field to the approximate position shown in Figure 6-25.

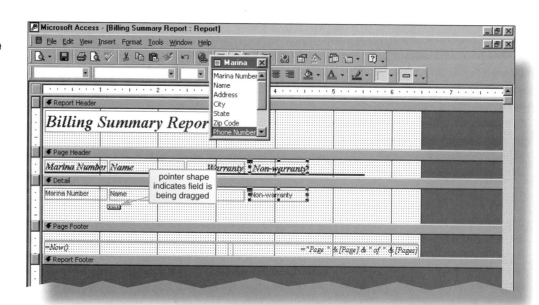

FIGURE 6-25

4 Release the mouse button to complete the placement of the field. Point to the label of the newly placed control (Figure 6-26).

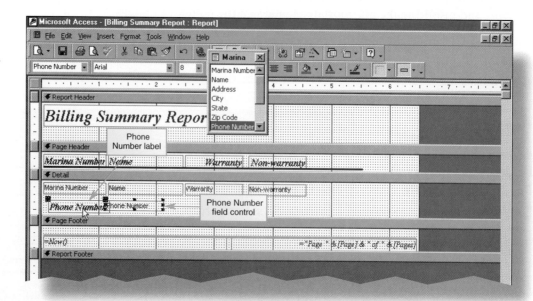

FIGURE 6-26

5 Click the label and then press the DELETE key to delete it. Click the Name control in the Page Header section to select it and then click immediately following the letter e to display an insertion point. Type /Phone to change the contents of the control to Name/Phone.

The contents of the control are changed (Figure 6-27).

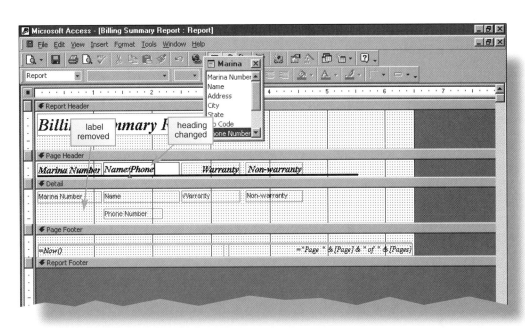

FIGURE 6-27

6 Close the Field list by clicking its Close button. Point to the Text Box button in the toolbox (Figure 6-28).

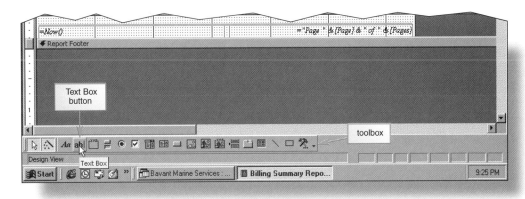

FIGURE 6-28

7 Click the Text Box button and then point to the approximate position shown in Figure 6-29.

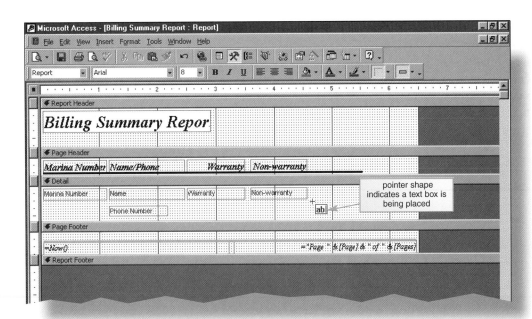

FIGURE 6-29

8 **Click the position shown in Figure 6-29, right-click the control, and then point to Properties on the shortcut menu.**

The shortcut menu for the control displays, and the Properties command is highlighted (Figure 6-30).

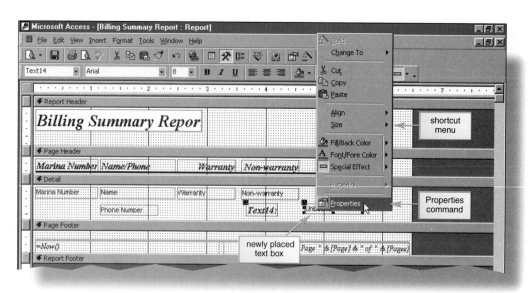

FIGURE 6-30

9 **Click Properties, click the Control Source property, and then type** =[Warranty]+[Non-warranty] **in the Control Source text box.**

The final portion of the expression displays in the Control Source text box (Figure 6-31).

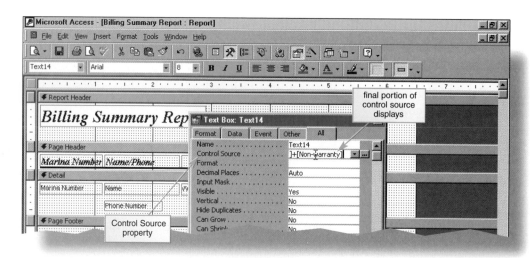

FIGURE 6-31

10 **Click the Format property, click the Format arrow, scroll down so that Currency displays, and then point to Currency (Figure 6-32).**

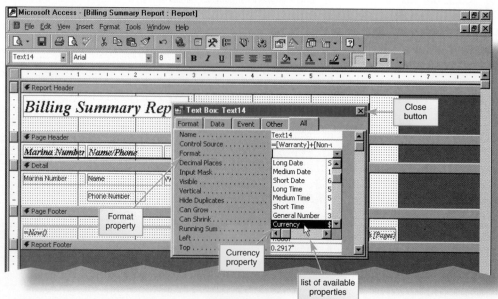

FIGURE 6-32

11 Click Currency to change the Format property. Close the property sheet by clicking its Close button, and then click the label for the text box to select it.

The label is selected (Figure 6-33).

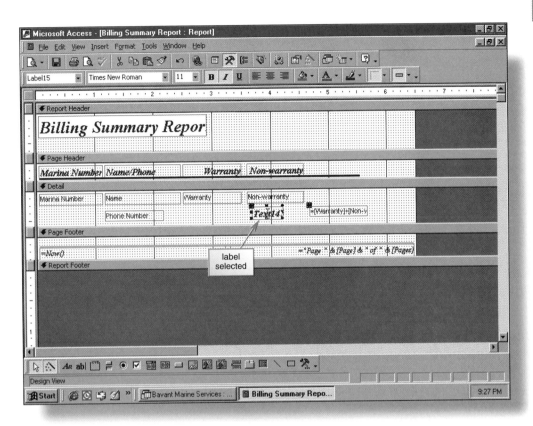

FIGURE 6-33

12 Press the DELETE key to delete the label, and then point to the Label button in the toolbox (Figure 6-34).

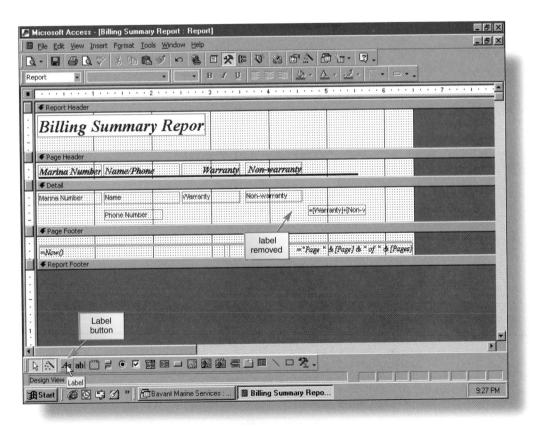

FIGURE 6-34

13 Click the Label button, and then move the pointer, whose shape changes to a small plus sign and label, to the approximate position shown in Figure 6-35.

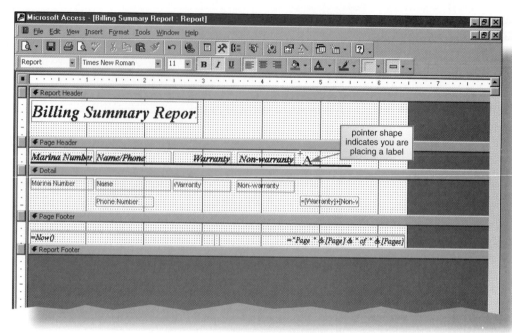

FIGURE 6-35

14 Click the position and then type

Total Amount **as the entry in the label.**

The label displays (Figure 6-36).

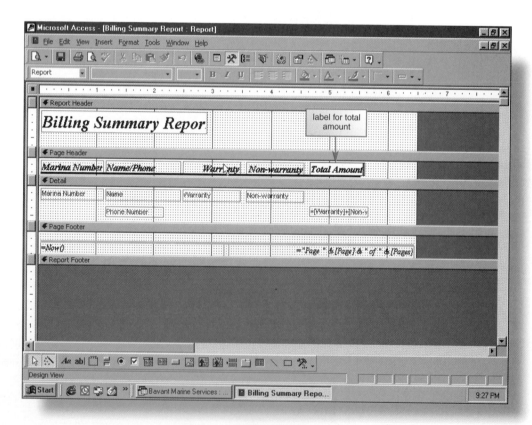

FIGURE 6-36

Previewing a Report

To view the report with sample data, preview the report by clicking the View button on the Report Design toolbar as illustrated in the steps on the next page.

Steps To Preview a Report

1 Point to the View button on the Report Design toolbar (Figure 6-37).

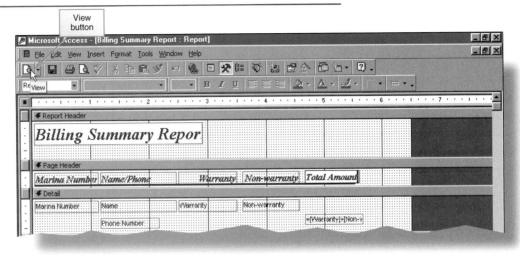

FIGURE 6-37

2 Click the View button to view the report.

The report displays (Figure 6-38). It looks like the one illustrated in Figure 6-2a.

3 Click the Close button to close the report. Click the Yes button in the Microsoft Access dialog box to save the changes to the report.

The report is closed, and the changes to the report are saved.

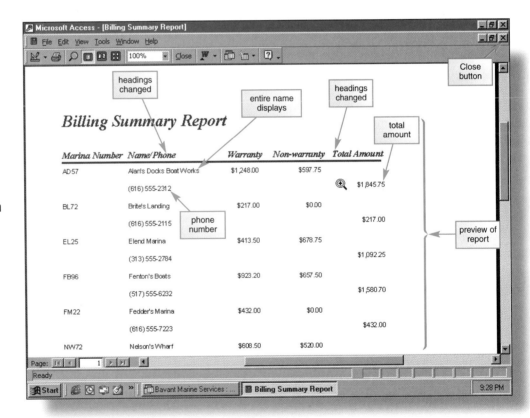

FIGURE 6-38

Modifying the Form

The Marina Update Form does not contain the Phone Number because there was no Phone Number field when the form was created. To incorporate this field in the form, you must perform the necessary steps to add it to the form.

Other Ways

1. Click Print Preview button on Report Design toolbar
2. On View menu click Print Preview

Adding Controls to a Form

You can add a control to a form by using the toolbox. If the control is for a single field, however, the easiest way to add the control is to use the field list, just as you did with the report. Perform the following steps to add a control for the Phone Number field.

 Steps **To Add a Control to a Form**

1 **Click the Forms object, right-click Marina Update Form, and then click Design View on the shortcut menu. Maximize the window. If the field list does not display, click the Field List button on the Form Design toolbar (see Figure 6-23). Point to Phone Number in the field list.**

The Microsoft Access - [Marina Update Form - Form] displays (Figure 6-39).

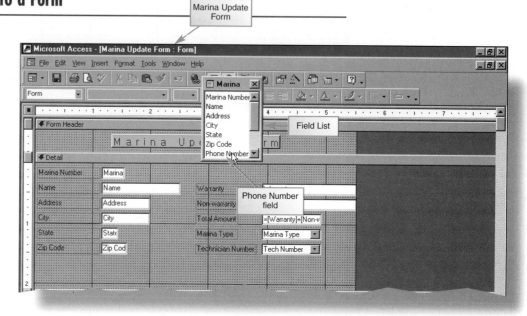

FIGURE 6-39

2 **Drag the Phone Number to the position shown in Figure 6-40.**

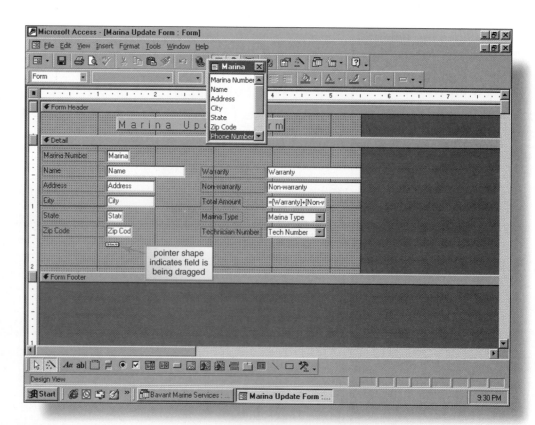

FIGURE 6-40

3 Release the mouse button to place the control. Point to the Move handle of the label for the Phone Number control.

The mouse pointer changes to a hand indicating the label can be moved (Figure 6-41).

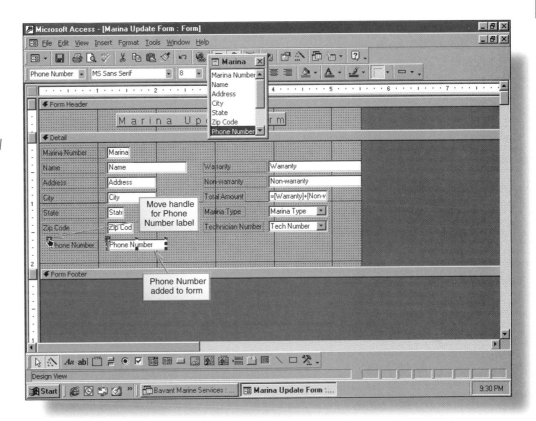

FIGURE 6-41

4 Drag the label so that it lines up with the labels above it.

The label is repositioned (Figure 6-42).

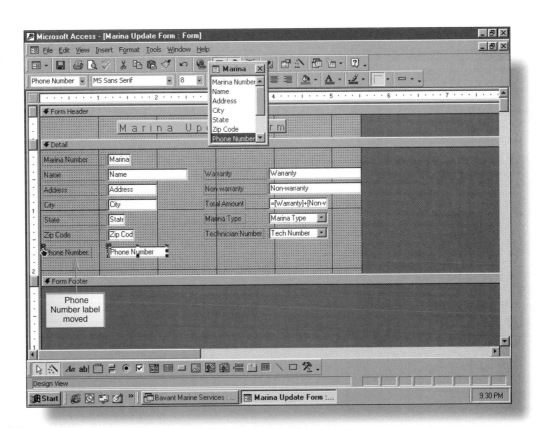

FIGURE 6-42

5 Point to the View button on the Form Design toolbar (Figure 6-43).

6 Click the View button to view the form.

The form displays. It looks like the one illustrated in Figure 6-2b.

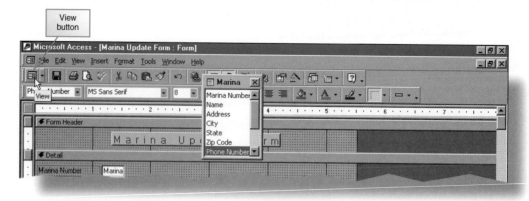

FIGURE 6-43

7 Click the Close button to close the form. Click the Yes button in the Microsoft Access dialog box to save the changes.

The form is closed and the changes are saved.

Changing the Tab Order

Users can repeatedly press the TAB key to move through the fields on a form. When you add new fields to a form, the resulting order in which the fields are encountered in this process may not be the most logical sequence. For example, on the Marina Update Form, an expected order to encounter the fields would be Marina Number, Name, Address, City, State, Zip Code, Phone Number, Warranty, Non-warranty, Marina Type, and Technician Number. This order skips the Total Amount field, because the total amount is automatically calculated from other fields. Because the Phone Number field was just added, however, it will not be encountered between Zip Code and Warranty, as you would like, but instead will be the last field encountered.

To change the **tab order**, that is, the order in which fields are encountered when tabbing through a form, ensure you are in Design view, and then use the Tab Order command on the View menu. When the Tab Order dialog box displays (Figure 6-44), click and drag the selected row(s) to change the tab order.

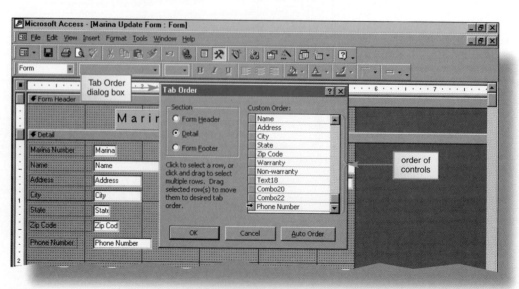

FIGURE 6-44

Creating and Using Macros

A **macro** consists of a series of actions that Access performs when the macro is run; therefore, you will need to specify the actions when you create the macro. The actions are entered in a special window called a **Macro window**. Once a macro is created, you can run it from the Database window by right-clicking the macro and then clicking Run on the shortcut menu. Macros also can be associated with items on switchboards. When you click the corresponding button on the switchboard, Access will run the macro. Whether a macro is run from the Database window or from a switchboard, the effect is the same: Access will execute the actions in the macro in the order in which they are entered.

In this project, you will create macros to open forms and maximize the windows; open tables in Datasheet view; open reports in preview windows; and print reports. As you enter actions, you will select them from a list box. The names of the actions are self-explanatory. The action to open a form, for example, is OpenForm. Thus, it is not necessary to memorize the specific actions that are available.

To create a macro, perform the following steps.

More *About*

Macros

The actions in a macro are executed when a particular event occurs. The event may be a user clicking Run on the macro's shortcut menu. It also may be clicking a button on a form or switchboard when the macro is associated with the button.

 To Create a Macro

1 **Click the Macros object and then point to the New button.**

The list of previously created macros displays (Figure 6-45). Currently, no macros exist.

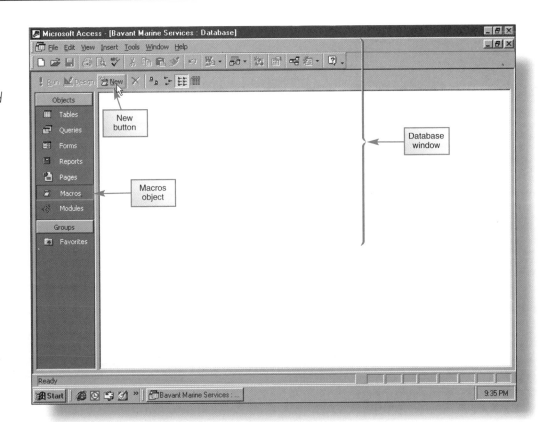

FIGURE 6-45

2 **Click the New button.**

The Microsoft Access – [Macro1: Macro] window displays (Figure 6-46).

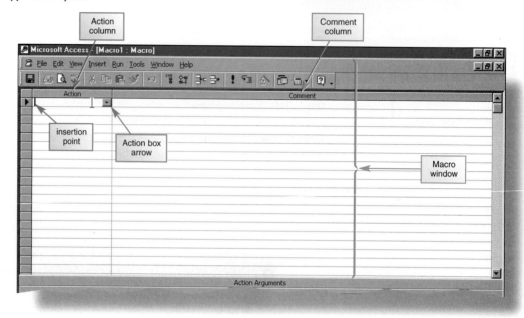

FIGURE 6-46

Other Ways

1. Click New Object: AutoForm button arrow on Database window toolbar, click Macro
2. On Insert menu click Macro

The Macro Window

The first column in the Macro window is the **Action column**. You enter the **actions** you want the macro to perform in this column (Figure 6-46). To enter an action, click the arrow in the Action column and then select the action from the list that displays. Many actions require additional information, called the **arguments** of the action. If you select such an action, the arguments will display in the lower portion of the Macro window and you can make any necessary changes to them.

The second column in the Macro window is the **Comment column**. In this column, you enter **comments**, which are brief descriptions of the purpose of the corresponding action. The actions, the arguments requiring changes, and the comments for the first macro you will create are illustrated in Table 6-1.

The macro begins by turning off the echo. This will eliminate the screen flicker that can be present when a form is being opened. The second action changes the shape of the mouse pointer to an hourglass to indicate that some process is taking place. The third action opens the form called Marina Update Form. The fourth action turns off the hourglass, and the fifth action turns the echo back on so the Marina Update Form will display.

Turning on and off the echo and the hourglass are not absolutely necessary. On computers with faster processors, you may not notice a difference between running a macro that includes these actions and one that does not. For computers with slower processors, however, these actions can make a noticeable difference, so they are included here.

Table 6-1	Specifications for First Macro		
ACTION	**ARGUMENT TO CHANGE**	**NEW VALUE FOR ARGUMENT**	**COMMENT**
Echo	Echo On	No	Turn echo off to avoid screen flicker
Hourglass			Turn on hourglass
OpenForm	Form Name	Marina Update Form	Open Marina Update Form
Hourglass	Hourglass On	No	Turn off hourglass
Echo			Turn echo on

Adding Actions to and Saving a Macro

To continue creating this macro, enter the actions. For each action, enter the action and comment in the appropriate text boxes, and then make the necessary changes to any arguments. When all the actions have been entered, close the macro, click the Yes button to save the changes, and then assign the macro a name. Perform the following steps to add the actions to, and save the macro.

 To Add Actions to and Save a Macro

1 **Click the box arrow in the first row of the Action column. Point to Echo.**

The list of available actions displays, and the Echo action is highlighted (Figure 6-47).

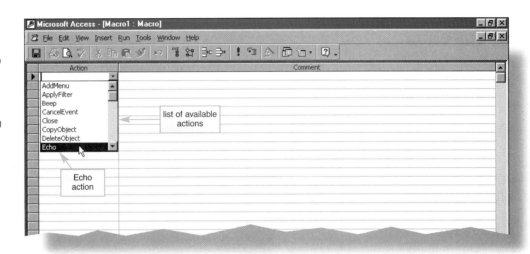

FIGURE 6-47

2 **Click Echo. Press the F6 key to move to the Action Arguments for the Echo action. Click the Echo On box arrow. Point to No.**

The arguments for the Echo action display (Figure 6-48). The list of values for the Echo On argument displays, and the No value is highlighted.

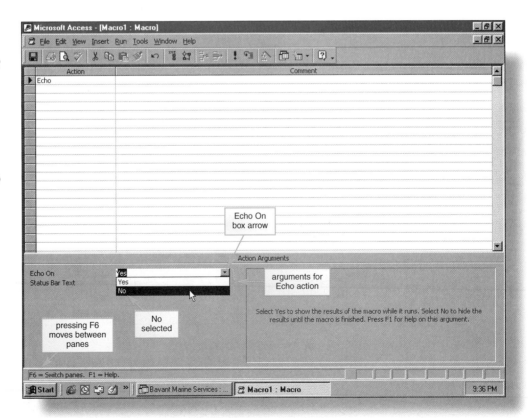

FIGURE 6-48

3 Click No. Press the F6 key to move back to Echo in the Action column. Press the TAB key. Type Turn echo off to avoid screen flicker in the Comment column and then press the TAB key.

The first action and comment are entered (Figure 6-49).

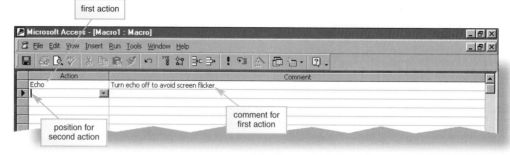

FIGURE 6-49

4 Select Hourglass as the action in the second row. Press the TAB key and then type Turn on hourglass as the comment in the second row. Press the TAB key and then select OpenForm as the third action. Press the F6 key to move to the Action Arguments and then click the Form Name box arrow. Point to Marina Update Form.

A list of available forms displays, and Marina Update Form is highlighted (Figure 6-50).

5 Click Marina Update Form, press the F6 key, press the TAB key, and then type Open Marina Update Form as the comment.

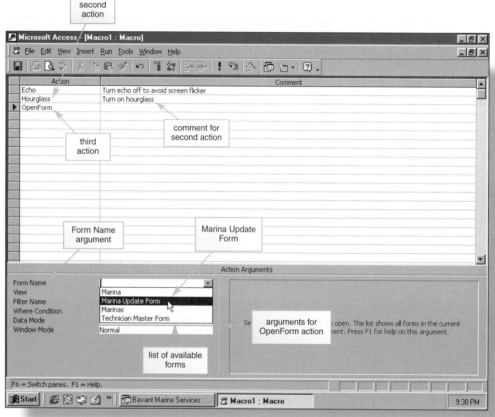

FIGURE 6-50

6 Select Hourglass as the fourth action. Change the Hourglass On argument to No, and then type Turn off hourglass as the comment.

7 Select Echo as the fifth action. Type Turn echo on as the comment.

The actions and comments are entered (Figure 6-51).

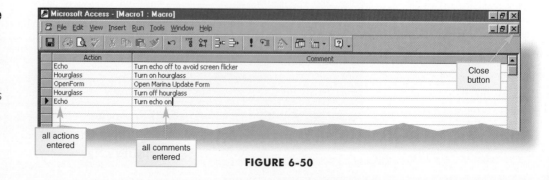

FIGURE 6-50

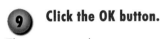

8 **Click the Close button for the Macro1: Macro window to close the macro, click the Yes button to save the macro, type** Open Marina Update Form **as the name of the macro, and then point to the OK button.**

The Save As dialog box displays (Figure 6-52).

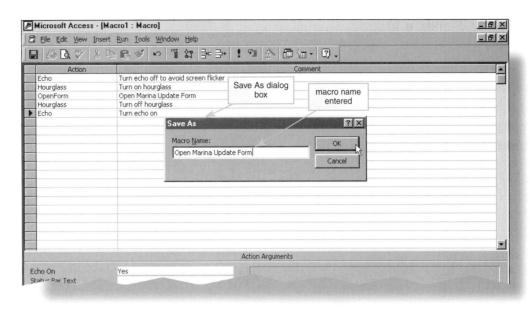

FIGURE 6-52

9 **Click the OK button.**

The actions and comments have been added to the macro, and the macro is saved.

Running a Macro

To **run a macro**, click the Macros object in the Database window, right-click the macro, and then click Run on the shortcut menu. The actions in the macro will execute. Perform the following steps to run the macro you just created and then close the form.

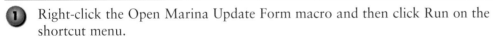

TO RUN A MACRO AND CLOSE A FORM

1 Right-click the Open Marina Update Form macro and then click Run on the shortcut menu.

2 Close the Marina Update Form by clicking its Close button.

The macro runs and the Marina Update Form displays. The window containing the form is maximized because the previous windows were maximized. The form no longer displays.

If previous windows had not been maximized, the window containing the form also would not be maximized. In order to ensure that the window containing the form is automatically maximized, you can include the Maximize action in your macro.

Modifying a Macro

To **modify a macro**, right-click the macro in the Database window, click Design View on the shortcut menu, and then make the necessary changes. To insert a new action, click the position for the action, or press the INSERT key to insert a new blank row if the new action is to be placed between two actions. Enter the new action, change the values for any necessary arguments, and then enter a comment.

The steps on the next page modify the macro just created, adding a new step to maximize the form automatically.

Other **Ways**

1. Click Macros on Objects bar, click macro name, click Run button

2. Click Macros on Objects bar, double-click macro name

To Modify a Macro

1 **Right-click the Open Marina Update Form macro, and then point to Design View on the shortcut menu.**

The shortcut menu displays, and the Design View command is highlighted (Figure 6-53).

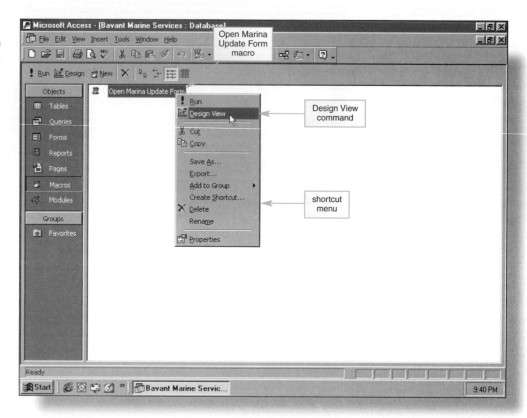

FIGURE 6-53

2 **Click Design View. Point to the row selector in the fourth row, which is directly to the left of the second Hourglass action.**

The Microsoft Access - [Open Marina Update Form : Macro] window displays (Figure 6-54).

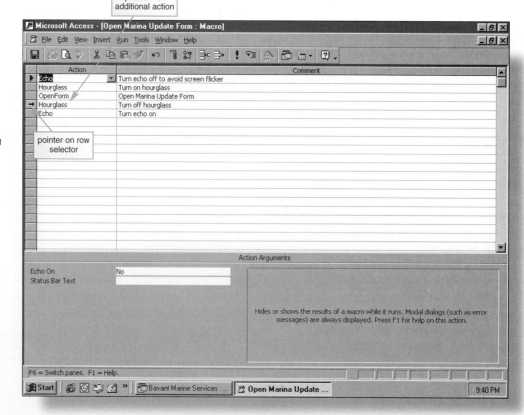

FIGURE 6-54

Click the row selector to select the row, and then press the INSERT key to insert a new row. Click the Action column on the new row, select Maximize as the action, and then type `Maximize the window` **as the comment.**

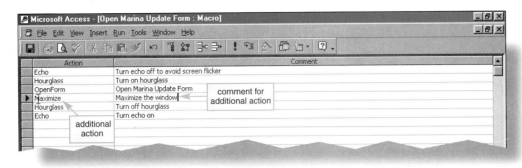

FIGURE 6-55

The new action is entered (Figure 6-55).

④ **Click the Close button, and then click the Yes button to save the changes.**

The macro has been changed and saved.

The next time the macro is run, the form not only will be opened, but the window containing the form also will be maximized automatically.

Errors in Macros

Macros can contain **errors**. For example, if you type the name of the form in the Form Name argument of the OpenForm action instead of selecting it from the list, you may type it incorrectly. Access then will not be able to execute the desired action. In that case, a Microsoft Access dialog box will display, indicating the error and solution as shown in Figure 6-56.

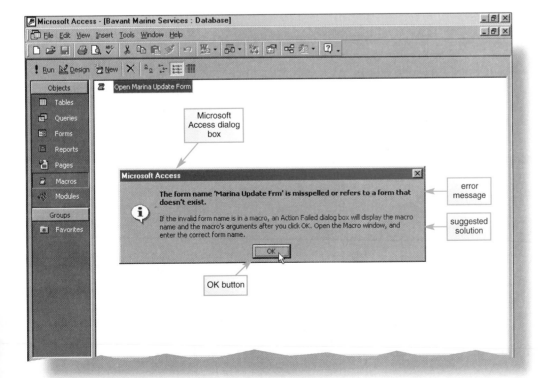

FIGURE 6-56

Other **Ways**

1. Click Macros on Objects bar, click Macro name, click Design on toolbar

More *About*

Inserting an Action

If you inadvertently press the DELETE key instead of the INSERT key when you are inserting a new line in a macro, you will delete the selected action from the macro. To return the deleted action to the macro, click the Undo button on the toolbar.

If such a dialog box displays, click the OK button. The Action Failed dialog box then displays (Figure 6-57). It indicates the macro that was being run, the action that Access was attempting to execute, and the arguments for the action. This information tells you which action needs to be corrected. To make the correction, click the Halt button, and then modify the design of the macro.

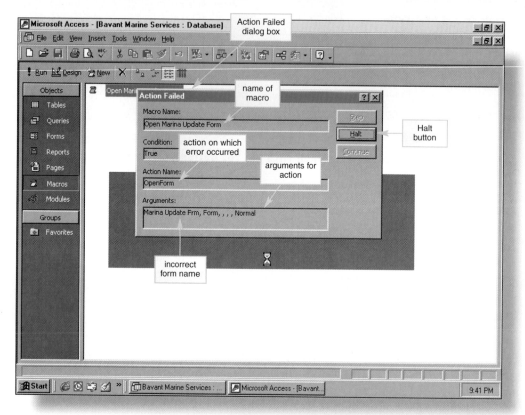

FIGURE 6-57

Additional Macros

The additional macros to be created are shown in Table 6-2. The first column gives the name of the macro, and the second column indicates the actions for the macro. The third column contains the values of the arguments that need to be changed, and the fourth column contains the comments.

Copying a Macro

When you wish to create a new macro, you often find there is an existing macro that is very similar to the one you wish to create. If this is the case, it is often simpler to use a copy of the existing macro and modify it instead of creating a new macro from scratch. The Open Technician Master Form macro you wish to create, for example, is very similar to the existing Open Marina Update Form macro. Thus, you can make a copy of the Open Marina Update Form macro, call it Open Technician Master Form, and then modify it to the new requirements by changing only the portion that differs from the original macro.

To make a copy of a macro, you use the clipboard. First copy the existing macro to the clipboard and then paste the contents of the clipboard. At that point, assign the new name to the macro.

TABLE 6-2	Specifications for additional macros		
MACRO NAME	ACTION	ARGUMENT(S)	COMMENT
Open Technician Master Form	Echo	Echo on: No	Turn echo off to avoid screen flicker
	Hourglass	Hourglass On: Yes	Turn on hourglass
	OpenForm	Form Name: Technician Master Form	Open Technician Master Form
	Maximize		Maximize the window
	Hourglass	Hourglass On: No	Turn off hourglass
	Echo	Echo on: Yes	Turn echo on
Open Marina Table	OpenTable	Table Name: Marina	Open Marina Table
		View: Datasheet	
	Maximize		Maximize the window
Open Technician Table	OpenTable	Table Name: Technician	Open Technician Table
		View: Datasheet	
	Maximize		Maximize the window
Preview Billing Summary Report	OpenReport	Report Name: Billing Summary Report	Preview Billing Summary Report
		View: Print Preview	
	Maximize		Maximize the window
Print Billing Summary Report	OpenReport	Report Name: Billing Summary Report	Print Billing Summary Report
		View: Print	
Preview Marina Amount Report	OpenReport	Report Name: Marina Amount Report	Preview Marina Amount Report
		View: Print Preview	
	Maximize		Maximize the window
Print Marina Amount Report	OpenReport	Report Name: Marina Amount Report	Print Marina Amount Report
		View: Print	
Preview Technician/ Marina Report	OpenReport	Report Name: Technician/Marina Report	Preview Technician/Marina Report
		View: Print Preview	
	Maximize		Maximize the window
Print Technician/ Marina Report	OpenReport	Report Name: Technician/Marina Report	Print Technician/Marina Report
		View: Print	

Incidentally, these same techiques will work for other objects as well. If you wish to create a new report that is similar to an existing report, for example, use the clipboard to make a copy of the original report, paste the contents, rename it, and then modify the copied report in whatever way you wish.

Perform the steps on the next page to use the clipboard to copy the Open Marina Update Form macro.

To Copy a Macro

1 **Ensure the Macros object is selected, right-click the Open Marina Update Form macro,** and then point **to Copy on the shortcut menu.**

The shortcut menu for the Open Marina Update Form macro displays, and the Copy command is high-lighted (Figure 6-58).

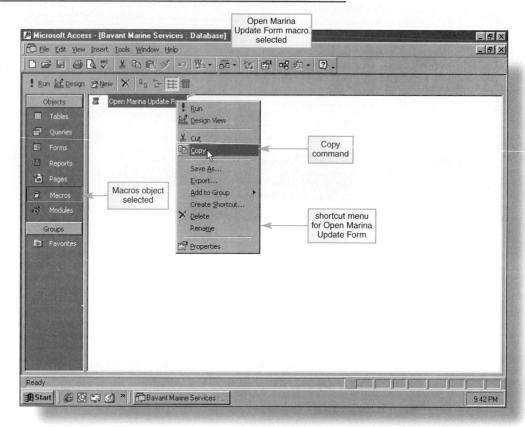

FIGURE 6-58

2 **Click Copy to copy the macro to the clipboard. Right-click any open area of the Database window, and then point to Paste on the shortcut menu.**

The shortcut menu displays, and the Paste command is highlighted (Figure 6-59).

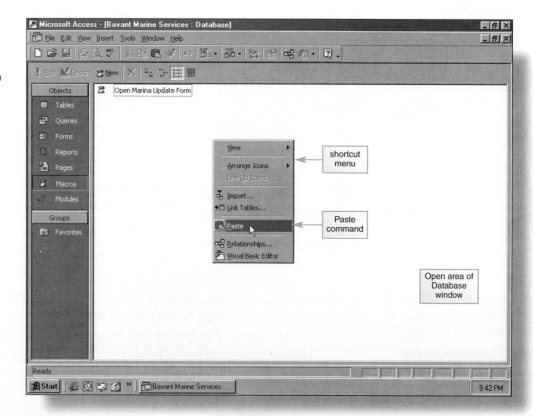

FIGURE 6-59

Click Paste on the shortcut menu, type Open Technician Master Form **in the Macro Name text box , and then point to the OK button.**

The Paste As dialog box displays, and the new macro name is entered in the text box (Figure 6-60).

 Click the OK button.

The new macro is copied and saved.

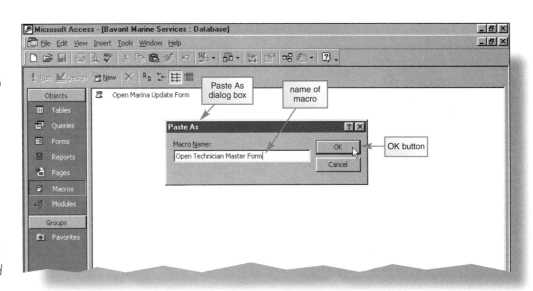

FIGURE 6-60

Modifying the Copied Macro

Once you have copied the macro, you can modify the copy to make any needed changes. The following steps modify the macro just copied by changing the Form Name argument for the OpenForm action to Technician Master Form.

Steps **To Modify the Copied Macro**

1 **Right-click the Open Technician Master Form macro, and then click Design View on the shortcut menu (Figure 6-61).**

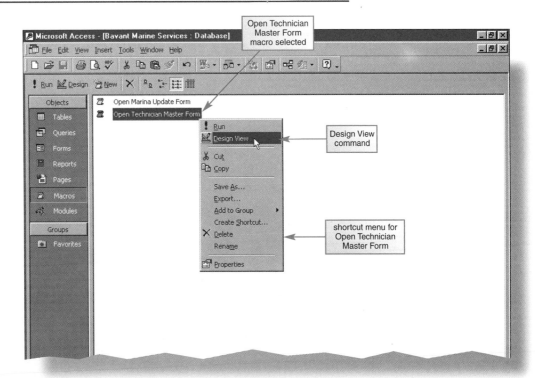

FIGURE 6-61

2 Click the row selector for the OpenForm action, click the Form Name argument, click the Form Name arrow, and then point to the Technician Master Form.

The macro displays in Design View. The OpenForm action is selected, the list of available forms displays, and Technician Master Form is highlighted (Figure 6-62).

3 Click Technician Master Form to change the Form Name argument. Click the Comment text box for the OpenForm action, delete the comment, and type `Open Technician Master Form` **as the new comment. Click the Close button for the Open Technician Master Form : Macro window and then click the Yes button to save the changes.**

The changes to the macro have been saved.

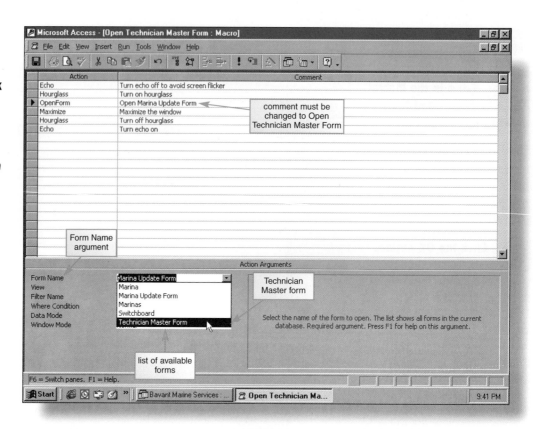

FIGURE 6-62

Macro Arguments

Some macros require a change to more than one argument. For example, to create a macro to preview or print a report requires a change to the Report Name argument and a change to the View argument. In Figure 6-63, the OpenReport action displays Billing Summary Report in the Report Name argument text box and Print Preview is highlighted in the View argument text box.

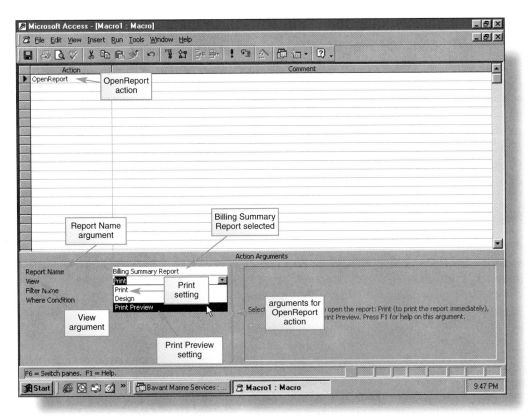

FIGURE 6-63

Creating Additional Macros

You can create additional macros using the same steps you used to create the first macro. You copy an existing macro and then modify the copied macro as needed. Perform the following step to create the additional macros illustrated in Table 6-2 on page A 6.6.

TO CREATE ADDITIONAL MACROS

 Using the same techniques you used to create the Open Marina Update Form macro (page A 6.27), create each of the macros described in Table 6-2.

The Open Technician Master Form, Open Marina Table, Open Technician Table, Preview Billing Summary Report, Print Billing Summary Report, Preview Marina Amount Report, Print Marina Amount Report, Preview Technician/Marina Report, and Print Technician/Marina Report macros are created.

Running the Macros

To run any of the other macros just as you ran the first macro, right-click the appropriate macro in the Database window and then click Run on the shortcut menu. The appropriate actions then are carried out. Running the Preview Billing Summary Report macro, for example, displays the Billing Summary Report in a maximized preview window.

Creating and Using a Switchboard

More About

Switchboards

A switchboard is considered a form and is run like any other form. A special tool is used to create it, however, called the Switchboard Manager. Although you can modify the design of the form by clicking Design on its shortcut menu, it is easier to use the Switchboard Manager for modifications.

A **switchboard** (see Figures 6-1a and 6-1b on page A 6.5) is a special type of form. It contains buttons you can click to perform a variety of actions. Buttons on the main switchboard can lead to other switchboards. Clicking the View Form button, for example, causes Access to display the View Form switchboard. Buttons also can be used to open forms or tables. Clicking the Marina Update Form button on the View Form switchboard opens the Marina Update Form. Still other buttons cause reports to be displayed in a preview window or print reports.

Creating a Switchboard

To create a switchboard, you use the Database Utilities command on the Tools menu and then click **Switchboard Manager**, which is an Access tool that allows you to create, edit, and delete switchboard forms for an application. If you have not previously created a switchboard, you will be asked if you wish to create one. Clicking the Yes button causes Access to create the switchboard. Perform the following steps to create a switchboard for the Bavant Marine Services database.

Steps To Create a Switchboard

 1 **With the Database window displaying,** click Tools on the menu bar, click Database Utilities on the Tools menu, and then point to Switchboard Manager.

and Tables at Objects column

The Tools menu displays (Figure 6-64). The Database Utilities submenu displays, and the Switchboard Manager command is highlighted.

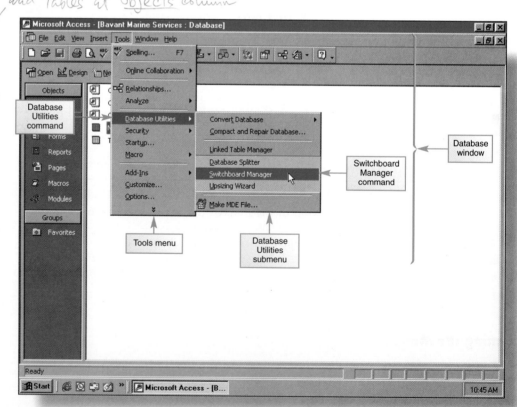

FIGURE 6-64

2 Click Switchboard Manager and then point to the Yes button.

The Switchboard Manager dialog box displays (Figure 6-65). The message indicates that no switchboard currently exists for this database and asks whether to create one.

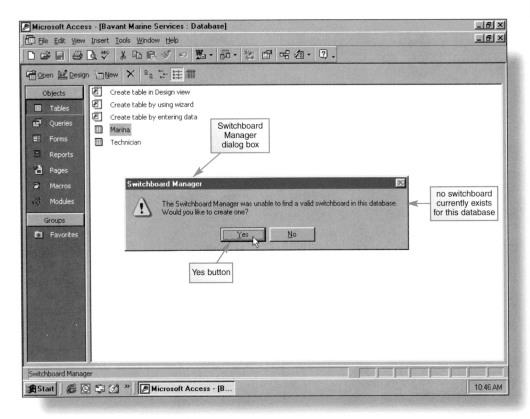

FIGURE 6-65

3 Click the Yes button to create a new switchboard. Point to the New button.

The Switchboard Manager dialog box displays and indicates there is only the Main Switchboard at this time (Figure 6-66).

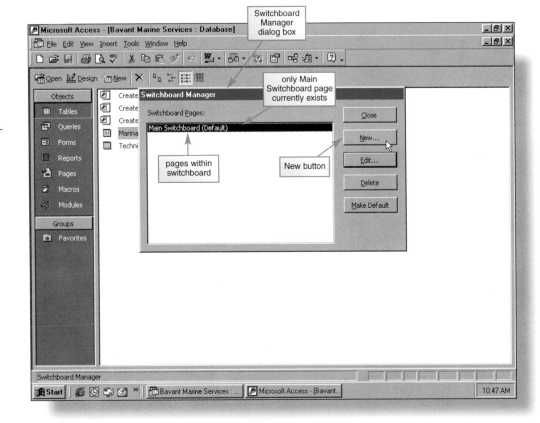

FIGURE 6-66

Creating Switchboard Pages

The next step in creating the switchboard system is to create the individual switchboards within the system. These individual switchboards are called the **switchboard pages**. The switchboard pages to be created are listed in the first column of Table 6-3. You do not have to create the Main Switchboard page because Access has created it automatically (Figure 6-66). To create each of the other pages, click the New button in the Switchboard Manager dialog box, and then type the name of the page.

TABLE 6-3 Specifications for Switchboard Pages and Items			
SWITCHBOARD PAGE	SWITCHBOARD ITEM	COMMAND	ARGUMENT
Main Switchboard	View Form	Go to Switchboard	Switchboard: View Form
	View Table	Go to Switchboard	Switchboard: View Table
	View Report	Go to Switchboard	Switchboard: View Report
	Print Report	Go to Switchboard	Switchboard: Print Report
	Exit Application	Exit Application	None
View Form	Marina Update Form	Run Macro	Macro: Open Marina Update Form
	Technician Master Form	Run Macro	Macro: Open Technician Master Form
	Return to Main Switchboard	Go to Switchboard	Switchboard: Main Switchboard
View Table	Marina Table	Run Macro	Macro: Open Marina Table
	Technician Table	Run Macro	Macro: Open Technician Table
	Return to Main Switchboard	Go to Switchboard	Switchboard: Main Switchboard
View Report	View Billing Summary Report	Run Macro	Macro: Preview Billing Summary Report
	View Marina Amount Report	Run Macro	Macro: Preview Marina Amount Report
	View Technician/Marina Report	Run Macro	Macro: Preview Technician/ Marina Report
	Return to Main Switchboard	Go to Switchboard	Switchboard: Main Switchboard
Print Report	Print Billing Summary Report	Run Macro	Macro: Print Billing Summary Report
	Print Marina Amount Report	Run Macro	Macro: Print Marina Amount Report
	Print Technician/Marina Report	Run Macro	Macro: Print Technician/ Marina Report
	Return to Main Switchboard	Go to Switchboard	Switchboard: Main Switchboard

Perform the steps on the next page to create the switchboard pages.

To Create Switchboard Pages

1 **Click the New button in the Switchboard Manager dialog box. Type** View Form **as the name of the new switchboard page. Point to the OK button.**

The Create New dialog box displays (Figure 6-67). The name of the new page is entered in the Switchboard Page Name text box.

2 **Click the OK button to create the View Form switchboard page.**

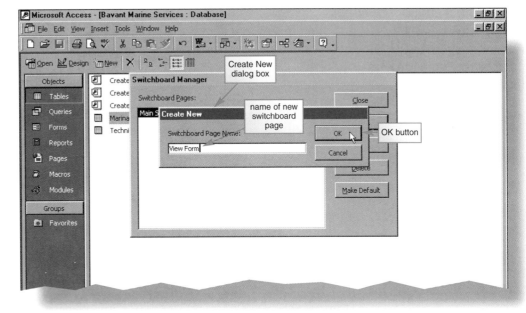

FIGURE 6-67

3 **Use the technique described in Step 1 and Step 2 to create the View Table, View Report, and Print Report switchboard pages.**

The newly created switchboard pages display in the Switchboard Manager dialog box in alphabetical order (Figure 6-68).

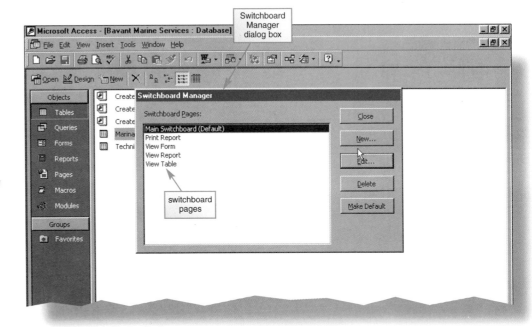

FIGURE 6-68

Modifying Switchboard Pages

You can **modify a switchboard page** by using the following procedure. Select the page in the Switchboard Manager dialog box, click the **Edit button**, and then add new items to the page, move existing items to a different position in the list of items, or delete items. For each item, you can indicate the command to be executed when the item is selected.

Perform the steps on the next page to modify the Main Switchboard page.

To Modify the Main Switchboard Page

1 **With the Main Switchboard (Default) page selected, point to the Edit button (Figure 6-69).**

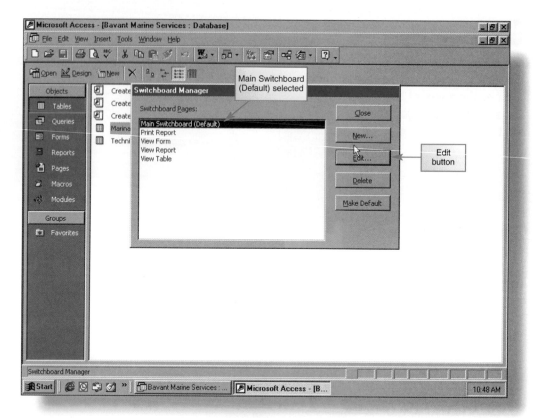

FIGURE 6-69

2 **Click the Edit button, and then point to the New button in the Edit Switchboard Page dialog box.**

The Edit Switchboard Page dialog box displays (Figure 6-70).

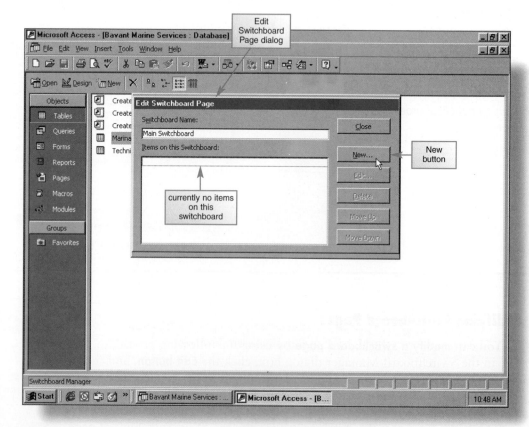

FIGURE 6-70

3 Click the New button, type View Form **as the text, click the Switchboard box arrow, and then point to View Form.**

The Edit Switchboard Item dialog box displays (Figure 6-71). The text is entered, the command is Go to Switchboard, the list of available switchboards displays, and the View Form switchboard is highlighted.

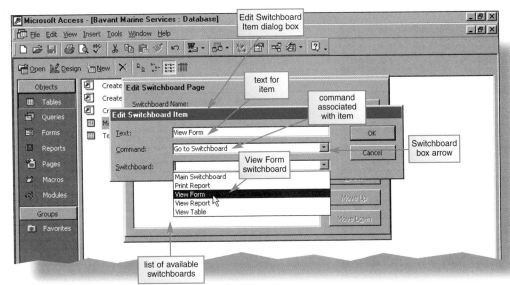

FIGURE 6-71

4 Click View Form, **and then click the OK button to add the item to the switchboard.**

5 Using the techniques illustrated in Steps 3 and 4, add the View Table, View Report, **and** Print Report **items to the** Main Switchboard **page. In each case, the command is** Go to Switchboard. **The names of the switchboards are the same as the name of the items. For example, the switchboard for the View Table item is called View Table.**

6 Click the New button, type Exit Application **as the text, click the Command box arrow, and then point to Exit Application.**

The Edit Switchboard Item dialog box displays (Figure 6-72). The text is entered, and the list of available commands displays, and the Exit Application command is highlighted.

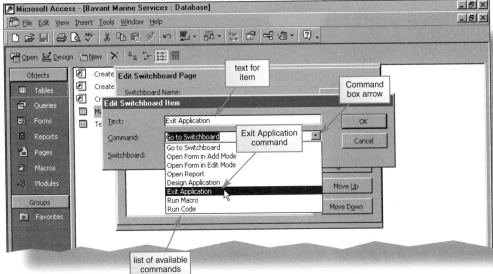

FIGURE 6-72

7 Click Exit Application, **and then click the OK button to add the item to the switchboard. Click the** Close **button in the Edit Switchboard Page dialog box to indicate you have finished editing the** Main Switchboard.

The Main Switchboard page now is complete. The Edit Switchboard Page dialog box closes, and the Switchboard Manager dialog box displays.

Modifying the Other Switchboard Pages

The other switchboard pages from Table 6-3 on page A 6.8 are modified in exactly the same manner you modified the Main Switchboard page. Perform the following steps to modify the other switchboard pages.

To Modify the Other Switchboard Pages

1 **Click the View Form switchboard page, and then point to the Edit button.**

The View Form page is selected (Figure 6-73).

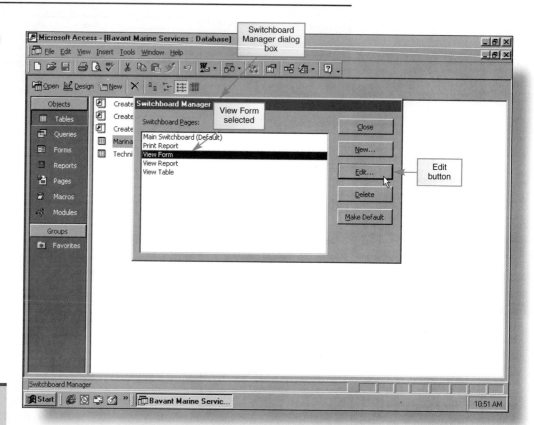

FIGURE 6-73

2 **Click the Edit button, click the New button to add a new item, type** Marina Update Form **as the text, click the Command box arrow, and then click Run Macro. Click the Macro box arrow, and then point to Open Marina Update Form.**

The Edit Switchboard Item dialog box displays (Figure 6-74). The text is entered and the command selected. The list of available macros displays, and the Open Marina Update Form macro is highlighted.

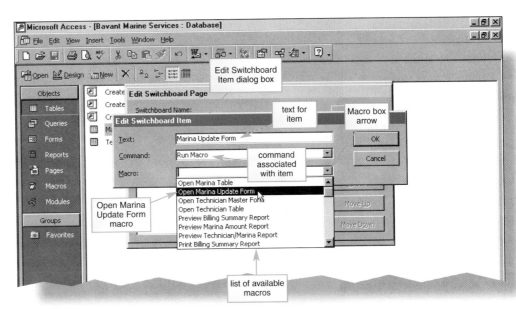

FIGURE 6-74

3 **Click Open Marina Update Form, and then click the OK button.**

The Open Marina Update Form item is added to the View Form switchboard.

4 **Click the New button, type** Technician Master Form **as the text, click the Command box arrow, and then click Run Macro. Click the Macro box arrow, click Open Technician Master Form, and then click the OK button.**

5 **Click the New button, type** Return to Main Switchboard **as the text, click the Command box arrow, and then click Go to Switchboard. Click the Switchboard box arrow, and then click Main Switchboard. Point to the OK button.**

The text is entered, and the command and switchboard are selected (Figure 6-75).

6 **Click the OK button. Click the Close button in the Edit Switchboard Page dialog box to indicate you have finished editing the View Form switchboard.**

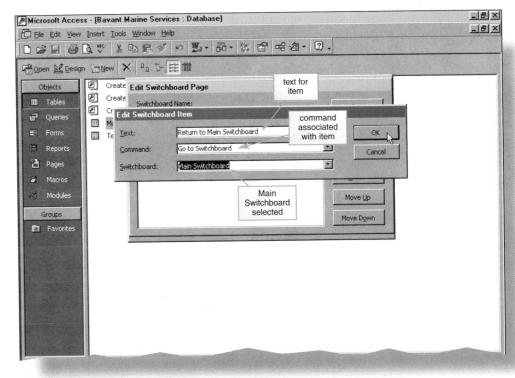

FIGURE 6-75

7 Use the techniques illustrated in Steps 1 through 6 to add the items indicated in Table 6-3 on page A 6.8 to the other switchboards. When you have finished, point to the Close button in the Switchboard Manager dialog box (Figure 6-76).

8 Click the Close button.

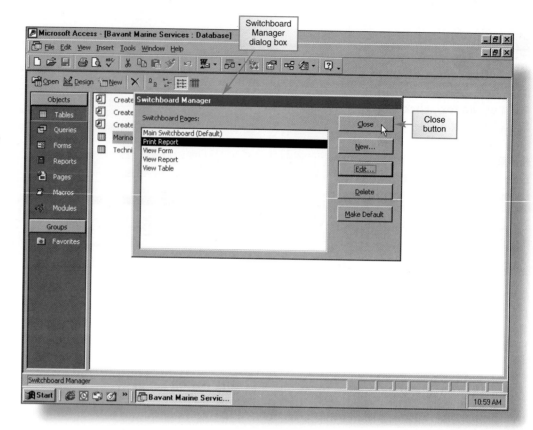

FIGURE 6-76

Displaying Switchboards

It is possible to have the switchboard display automatically when the database is opened. To do so, click Tools on the menu bar, and then click Startup. Click the Display Form box arrow, select the Switchboard form, and then click the OK button.

Closing a Switchboard

The button to close a switchboard is usually labeled Exit Application because a switchboard system is just a special type of application system. Clicking this button will not only close the switchboard, but will also close the database.

The switchboard is complete and ready for use. Access has created a form called Switchboard that you will run to use the switchboard. It also has created a table called Switchboard Items. *Do not modify this table.* It is used by the Switchboard Manager to keep track of the various switchboard pages and items.

Using a Switchboard

To use the switchboard, click the Forms object, right-click the switchboard, and then click Open on the shortcut menu. The main switchboard then will display. To take any action, click the appropriate buttons. When you have finished, click the Exit Application button. The switchboard will be removed from the screen, and the database will be closed. The steps on the next page illustrate opening a switchboard system for use.

To Use a Switchboard

1 **Click the Forms object, and then right-click Switchboard. Point to Open on the shortcut menu.**

The shortcut menu for Switchboard displays (Figure 6-77).

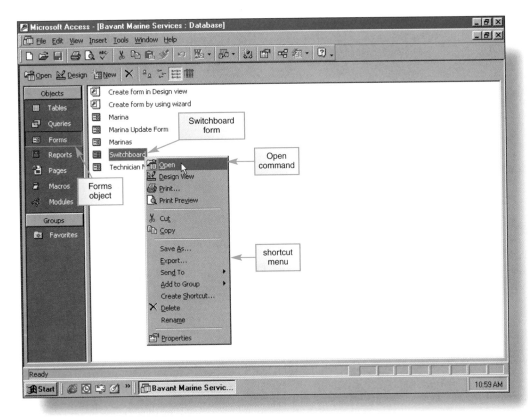

FIGURE 6-77

2 **Click Open.**

The Main Switchboard displays (Figure 6-78).

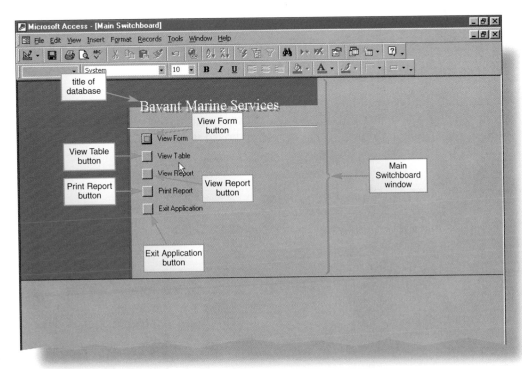

FIGURE 6-78

Quick Reference

For a table that lists how to complete the tasks covered in this book using the mouse, menu, shortcut menu, and keyboard, visit the Office 2000 Web page (www.scsite.com/off2000/qr.htm), and then click Microsoft Access 2000.

Click the View Form button to display the View Form switchboard page. Click the View Table button to display the View Table switchboard page. Click the View Report button to display the View Report switchboard page. Click the Print Report button to display the Print Report switchboard page. On each of the other switchboard pages, click the button for the form, table, or report you wish to view, or the report you wish to print. To return from one of the other switchboard pages to the Main Switchboard, click the Return to Main Switchboard button. To leave the switchboard system, click the Exit Application button.

If you discover a problem with the switchboard, click Tools on the menu bar, click Database Utilities, and then click Switchboard Manager. You can modify the switchboard system using the same techniques you used to create it.

Closing the Switchboard and Database

To close the switchboard and the database, click the Exit Application button. Perform the following step to close the switchboard.

TO CLOSE THE SWITCHBOARD AND DATABASE

 Click the Exit Application button.

The switchboard is removed from the screen. The database closes.

CASE PERSPECTIVE SUMMARY

In Project 6, you modified the Marina Type field, and you added the Phone Number field to the Marina table. You also added the Phone Number field to the Billing Summary Report and to the Marina Update Form. You added the total amount (warranty amount plus non-warranty amount) to the Billing Summary Report, and then you created the macros to be used in the switchboard system. Finally, you created a switchboard system for Bavant Marine Service.

Project Summary

In Project 6, you learned how to use the Lookup Wizard and the Input Mask Wizard. You added controls to both a report and a form. You created and used macros. Using Switchboard Manager, you created the switchboard, the switchboard pages, and the switchboard items. You also used the Switchboard Manager to assign actions to the buttons on the switchboard pages.

What You Should Know

Having completed this project, you now should be able to perform the following tasks:

- Add a Control to a Form *(A 6.24)*
- Add Actions to and Save a Macro *(A 6.29)*
- Add Controls to a Report *(A 6.17)*
- Close the Switchboard and Database *(A 6.43)*
- Create a Macro *(A 6.27)*
- Create a Switchboard *(A 6.40)*
- Create Additional Macros *(A 6.39)*
- Create Switchboard Pages *(A 6.43)*
- Copy a Macro *(A 6.36)*
- Enter Data Using an Input Mask *(A 6.13)*
- Modify a Macro *(A 6.36)*

- Modify the Copied Macro *(A 6.37)*
- Modify the Main Switchboard Page *(A 6.44)*
- Modify the Other Switchboard Pages *(A 6.46)*
- Open a Database *(A 6.7)*
- Open a Switchboard *(A 6.49)*
- Preview a Report *(A 6.23)*
- Resize and Move Controls in a Report *(A 6.15)*
- Run a Macro *(A 6.31)*
- Use a Switchoard *(A 6.49)*
- Use the Lookup Wizard *(A 6.8)*
- Use the Input Mask Wizard *(A 6.10)*

Apply Your Knowledge

1 Creating Macros and Modifying a Report for the Sidewalk Scrapers Database

Instructions: Start Access. Open the Sidewalk Scrapers database from the Data Disk. See the inside back cover of this book for instructions for downloading the Data Disk or see your instructor for information on accessing the files required for this book. Perform the following tasks.

1. Create a macro to open the Customer Update Form you created in Project 4. The macro should maximize the form automatically when it is opened.
2. Save the macro as Open Customer Update Form.
3. Create a macro to print the Worker/Customer Report you created in Project 4.
4. Save the macro as Print Worker/Customer Report.
5. Run the Print Worker/Customer Report macro, and then print the report.
6. Modify the Balance Due Report to include the Telephone Number as shown in Figure 6-79. (*Hint:* The horizontal line underneath the headings is a control that can be resized.)
7. Print the report.

Balance Due Report

Customer Number	Name	Telephone Number	Balance
AL25	Arders, Lars	555-2050	$45.00
AT43	Atari Cleaners	555-7410	$80.00
CH65	Chan's Bootery	555-0504	$70.00
CI05	Cinco Gallery	555-1304	$29.00
JB51	Jordach, Ben	555-0213	$60.00
LK44	Lee, Kim	555-5061	$0.00
MD60	Martinez, Dan	555-4110	$95.00
ME02	Meat Shoppe	555-7557	$0.00
ST21	Styling Salon and Tanning	555-6454	$40.00

Friday, September 07, 2001   *Page 1 of 1*

FIGURE 6-79

In the Lab

1 Creating an Application System for the School Connection Database

Problem: The Booster's Club is pleased with the tables, forms, and reports you have created. The club has some additional requests, however. First, they would like to be able to type only the digits in the Last Order Date field. They also would like to display the profit (selling price – cost) for an item on the Item Update Form. Finally, they would like an easy way to access the various tables, forms, and reports by simply clicking a button or two. This would make the database much easier to maintain and update.

Instructions: Open the School Connection database from the Data Disk. See the inside back cover of this book for instructions for downloading the Data Disk or see your instructor for information on accessing the files required for this book. Perform the following tasks.

1. Open the Vendor table in Design view and create an input mask for the Last Order Date field. Use the Short Date input mask. Save the change.
2. Modify the Item Update Form to create the form shown in Figure 6-80. The form includes a calculated control to display the profit (selling price – cost) on the item. Format the control as currency.

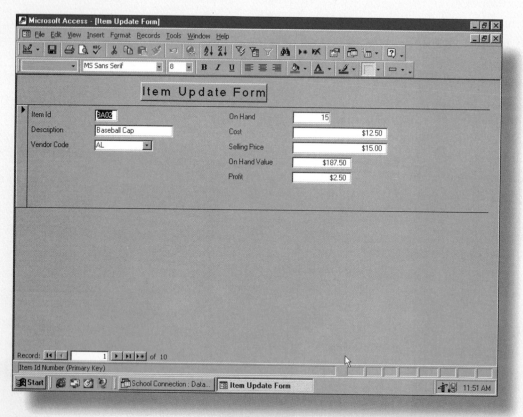

FIGURE 6-80

3. Save and print the form. To print the form, open the form, click File on the menu bar, and then click Print. Click Selected Record(s) as the Print Range. Click the OK button.

In the Lab

4. Create macros that will perform the following tasks:
   a. Open the Item Update Form
   b. Open the Vendor Master Form
   c. Open the Item Table
   d. Open the Vendor Table
   e. Preview the Inventory Report
   f. Preview the Vendor/Items Report
   g. Preview the On Hand Value Report
   h. Print the Inventory Report
   i. Print the Vendor/Items Report
   j. Print the On Hand Value Report

5. Create the switchboard for the School Connection database shown in Figure 6-81. Use the same design for your switchboard pages as the one illustrated in this project. For example, the View Form switchboard page should have three choices: Open Item Update Form, Open Vendor Master Form, and Return to Main Switchboard. Include all the forms, tables, and reports for which you created macros in Step 4.

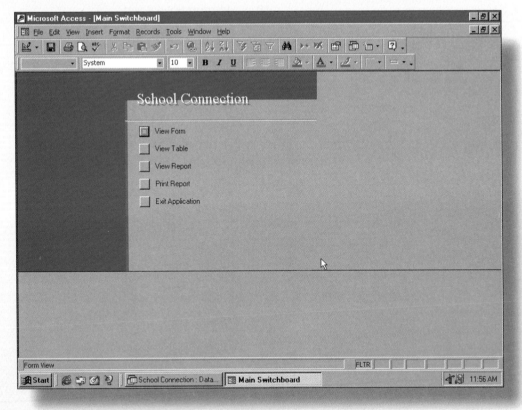

FIGURE 6-81

6. Run the switchboard and correct any errors.

In the Lab

2 Creating an Application System for the City Area Bus Company Database

Problem: The advertising sales manager is pleased with the tables, forms, and reports you have created. He has some additional requests, however. He finds that he needs to include the advertiser's phone number in the database. He also would like an easy way to access the various tables, forms, and reports by simply clicking a button or two.

Instructions: Open the City Area Bus Company database from the Data Disk. See the inside back cover of this book for instructions for downloading the Data Disk or see your instructor for information on accessing the files required for this book. Perform the following tasks.

1. Add the Telephone Number field to the Advertiser table. The field should follow the Zip Code field. Include an input mask for the field. Use the same input mask that was used for Bavant Marine Services.
2. Change the data type for the Ad Type field to a Lookup Wizard field. The values for the Ad Type field are DIN, RET, and SER.
3. Save the changes to the Advertiser table.
4. Open the Advertiser table in Datasheet view and resize the Telephone Number field. Enter the following data in the Telephone Number field:

Advertiser Id	Telephone Number
AC25	2165550987
BB99	3305559876
CS46	3305558765
HC11	3305557654
MC34	2165556543
NO10	3305555432
PJ24	2165554321
PP24	3305554455
TM89	3305558778

Save the changes to the layout of the table.

5. Modify the Advertiser Update Form to include the telephone number. Place the Telephone Number field below the Zip Code field. Be sure to align the Telephone Number label with the Zip Code label. Change the tab order for the form, so that the Telephone Number field immediately follows the Zip Code field and the Ad Type field follows the Telephone Number field. (*Hint:* Ad Type is a combo box control.)
6. Save and print the form. To print the form, open the form, click File on the menu bar and then click Print. Click Selected Record(s) as the Print Range. Click the OK button.
7. Modify the Advertiser Status Report to include the Telephone Number field as shown in Figure 6-82.

Advertiser Status Report

Advertiser Id	Name/Phone	Balance	Amount Paid
AC25	Alia Cleaners (216) 555-0987	$85.00	$585.00
BB99	Bob's Bakery (330) 555-9876	$435.00	$1,150.00
CS46	Cara's Salon (330) 555-8765	$35.00	$660.00
HC11	Hilde's Cards & Gifts (330) 555-7654	$250.00	$500.00
MC34	Mom's Cookies (216) 555-6543	$95.00	$1,050.00
NO10	New Orient (330) 555-5432	$150.00	$350.00
PJ24	Pajama Store (216) 555-4321	$0.00	$775.00
PP24	Pia's Pizza (330) 555-4455	$50.00	$0.00
TM89	Tom's Market (330) 555-8778	$50.00	$500.00

Friday, September 07, 2001 — *Page 1 of 1*

FIGURE 6-82

In the Lab

8. Print the report.
9. Create macros that will perform the following tasks:
   a. Open the Advertiser Update Form
   b. Open the Sales Rep Master Form
   c. Open the Advertiser Table
   d. Open the Sales Rep Table
   e. Preview the Advertiser Status Report
   f. Preview the Advertiser Income Report
   g. Preview the Sales Rep/Advertiser Report
   h. Print the Advertiser Status Report
   i. Print the Advertiser Income Report
   j. Print the Sales Rep/Advertiser Report
10. Create the switchboard for the City Area Bus Company database shown in Figure 6-83. Use the same design for your switchboard pages as the one illustrated in this project. For example, the View Form switchboard page should have three choices: Open Advertiser Update Form, Open Sales Rep Master Form, and Return to Main Switchboard. Include all the forms, tables, and reports for which you created macros in Step 9.

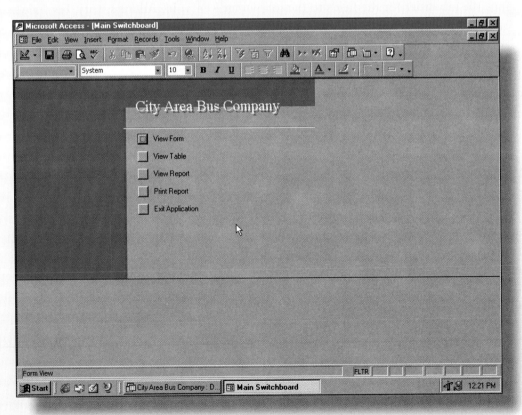

FIGURE 6-83

11. Run the switchboard and correct any errors.

In the Lab

3 Creating an Application System for the Resort Rentals Database

Problem: The real estate company is pleased with the tables, forms, and reports that you have created. The company has some additional requests, however. First, they want to add the sales price to the database. Then, they want an easy way to access the various tables, forms, and reports by simply clicking a button or two.

Instructions: Open the Resort Rentals database from the Data Disk. See the inside back cover of this book for instructions for downloading the Data Disk or see your instructor for information on accessing the files required for this book. Perform the following tasks.

1. Add a Sales Price field to the Rental Units table. Place the field after the For Sale field. Use currency as the data type. Save these changes.

2. Open the Rental Units table in Datasheet view and add the following data to the Sales Price field:

Rental Id	Sales Price
101	$150,000
134	$190,000
148	$165,000

3. Modify the Rental Update Form to create the form shown in Figure 6-84. The form includes the Sales Price field. Change the tab order for the fields to the following: Rental Id, Address, City, For Sale, Sales Price, Weekly Rate, Bedrooms, Bathrooms, Sleeps, Pool, Ocean View, Owner Id.

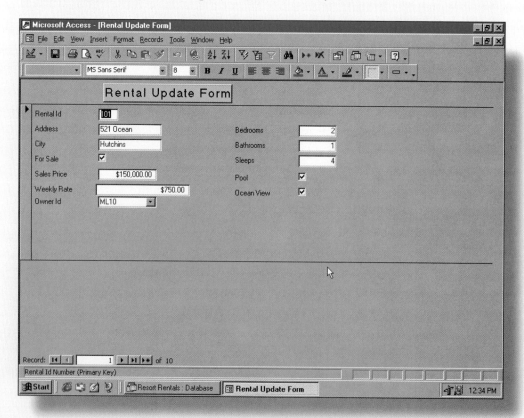

FIGURE 6-84

In the Lab

4. Save and print the form. To print the form, open the form, click File on the menu bar, and then click Print. Click Selected Record(s) as the Print Range. Click the OK button.

5. Add the Sales Price field to the Rental Properties subform you created in Project 5. If necessary, modify the Owner Master Form to ensure that the complete Sales Price field displays on the subform.

6. Save and print the form.

7. Create macros that will perform the following tasks:

a. Open the Rental Update Form
b. Open the Owner Master Form
c. Open the Rental Unit Table
d. Open the Owner Table
e. Preview the Available Rental Units Report

f. Preview the City Rental List
g. Preview the Owner/Rental Units Report
h. Print the Available Rental Units Report
i. Print the City Rental List
j. Print the Owner/Rental Units Report

8. Create the switchboard for the Resort Rentals database shown in Figure 6-85. Use the same design for your switchboard pages as the one illustrated in this project. For example, the View Form switchboard page should have three choices: Open Rental Update Form, Open Owner Master Form, and Return to Main Switchboard. Include all the forms, tables, and reports for which you created macros in Step 7.

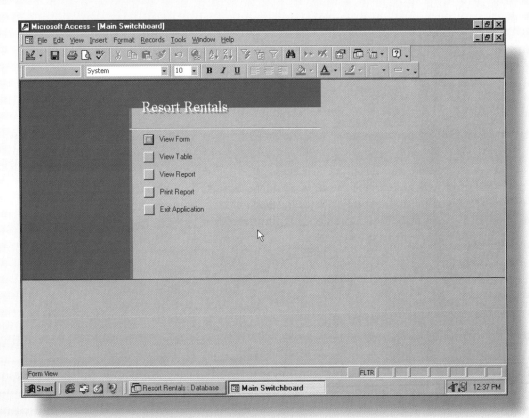

FIGURE 6-85

9. Run the switchboard and correct any errors.

Cases and Places

The difficulty of these case studies varies:
▶ are the least difficult; ▶▶ are more difficult; and ▶▶▶ are the most difficult.

1 ▶ Use the Computer Items database on the Access Data Disk for this assignment. Modify the Item Update Form that you created in Project 4 to include a calculated control called Profit. Profit is the result of subtracting Cost from Selling Price. Place the calculated control below the Selling Price field on the form. Be sure to format Profit as currency. The database includes a report, Inventory Report that contains the item number, description, units on hand, and cost. Modify this report to include a calculated control called On Hand Value. On Hand Value is the result of multiplying units on hand by cost. Be sure to format On Hand Value as currency.

2 ▶ Use the Computer Items database and create macros that will perform the following tasks:

a. Open the Item Update Form created in Project 4 and modified in Case Study 1
b. Open the Supplier Master Form created in Project 5
c. Open the Item Table
d. Open the Supplier Table
e. Preview the Inventory Report
f. Preview the Supplier/Items Report created in Project 4
g. Print the Inventory Report
h. Print the Supplier/Items Report

Create and run a switchboard that uses these macros.

3 ▶▶ Use the Galaxy Books database on the Access Data Disk for this assignment. Add a telephone number field to the Publisher table. Place the field after the Publisher Name field. Create an input mask for the Telephone Number field and the Last Order Date field. In Datasheet view, resize the Telephone Number field and enter the following telephone numbers:

Publisher Code	Telephone Number
BB	5125557654
PB	2135559854
SI	2155554329
VN	6105553201

4 ▶▶ Modify the Publisher Master Form that you created in Project 5 to include the Telephone Number field. Change the tab order so that Telephone Number is immediately after Publisher Name.

5 ▶▶▶ Create the appropriate macros to open all forms and tables in the Galaxy Books database. Create macros to preview and to print all reports in the database. Create a switchboard system for the database that uses these macros.

Microsoft Access 2000

Integrating Excel Worksheet Data into an Access Database

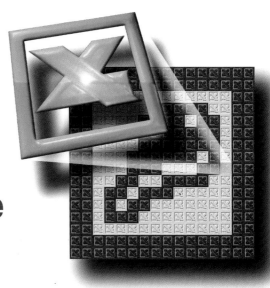

CASE PERSPECTIVE

Holton Clinic has been using Excel to automate a variety of tasks for several years. Employees at Holton have created several useful worksheets that have simplified their work tremendously. Along with the worksheets, they have created attractive charts for visual representation of the data.

When Holton decided it needed to maintain patient data, the familiarity with Excel led to the decision to maintain the data as an Excel worksheet. For a while, this seemed to work fine. As time passed, however, they began to question whether Excel was the best choice. Their counterparts at other clinics indicated that they were using Access to maintain patient data. Access had worked well for them. As the structure of their data became more complex, Access easily adapted to the increased complexity. They appreciated the power of the query and reporting features in Access. Finally, officials at Holton decided that they should follow the lead of the other clinics. They decided to convert their data from Excel to Access.

Introduction

It is not uncommon for people to use an application for some specific purpose, only to find later that another application may be better suited. For example, a clinic such as Holton Clinic might initially keep data in an Excel worksheet, only to discover later that the data would be better maintained in an Access database. Some common reasons for using a database instead of a worksheet are:

1. The worksheet contains a great deal of redundant data. Databases should be designed to eliminate redundant data.
2. The worksheet would need to be larger than Excel can handle. Excel has a limit of 16,384 rows. In Access, no such limit exists.
3. The data to be maintained consists of multiple interrelated items. For example, at Bavant Marine Services, they need to maintain data on two items, marinas and technicians, and these items are interrelated. A marina has a single technician and each technician services several marinas. The Bavant Marine Services database is a very simple one. Databases can easily contain thirty or more interrelated items.
4. You want to use the extremely powerful query and report capabilities of Microsoft Access.

Regardless of the reasons for making the change from a worksheet to a database, it is important to be able to make the change easily. In the not-too-distant past, converting data from one tool to another often could be a very difficult, time-consuming task. Fortunately, an easy way of converting data from Excel to Access is available.

Figures 1 and 2 illustrate the conversion process. The type of worksheet that can be converted is one in which the data is stored as a **list**, that is, a labeled series of rows in which each row contains the same type of data. For example, in the worksheet in Figure 1, the first row contains the labels, which are entries indicating the type of data found in the column. The entry in the first column, for example, is Patient Number, indicating that all the other values in the column are patient numbers. The entry in the second column is Last Name, indicating that all the other values in the column are last names. Other than the first row, which contains the labels, all the rows contain precisely the same type of data: a patient number in the first column, a last name in the second column, a first name in the third column, and so on.

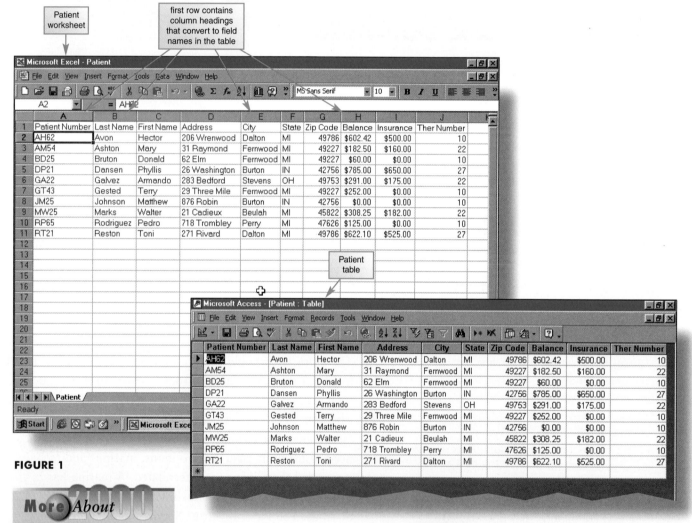

FIGURE 1

FIGURE 2

As the figures illustrate, the worksheet, shown in Figure 1, is copied to a database table, shown in Figure 2. The columns in the worksheet become the fields. The column headings in the first row of the worksheet become the field names. The rows of the worksheet, other than the first row, which contains the labels, become the records in the table. In the process, each field will be assigned the data type that seems the most reasonable, given the data currently in the worksheet.

The process of copying data to an Access database, referred to as **importing**, uses an Import Wizard. Specifically, if the data is copied from an Excel worksheet, the process will use the Import Spreadsheet Wizard. The wizard takes you through some basic steps, asking a few simple questions. Once you have answered the questions, the wizard will perform the conversion, creating an appropriate table in the database and filling it with the data from the worksheet.

Creating an Access Database

Before converting the data, you need to create the database that will contain the data. Perform the following steps to create the Holton Clinic database.

TO CREATE A NEW DATABASE

1. Click the Start button and then click New Office Document.

2. Click the General tab, make sure the Blank Database icon is selected, and then click the OK button.

3. Click the Save in box arrow and then click 3½ Floppy (A).

4. Type Holton Clinic as the filename and then click the Create button.

Importing an Excel Worksheet to an Access Database

To convert the data, you will use the Import Spreadsheet Wizard. In the process, you will indicate that the first row contains the column headings. These column headings will then become the field names in the Access table. In addition, you will indicate the primary key for the table. As part of the process, you can, if you desire, choose not to include all the fields from the worksheet in the resulting table. You should be aware that some of the steps might take a significant amount of time for Access to execute.

Steps   To Import an Excel Worksheet to an Access Database

1. **With the Holton Clinic database open, click File on the menu bar, click Get External Data on the File menu, and then point to Import. You may need to wait a few seconds for the entire menu to display.**

The Get External Data submenu data displays (Figure 3).

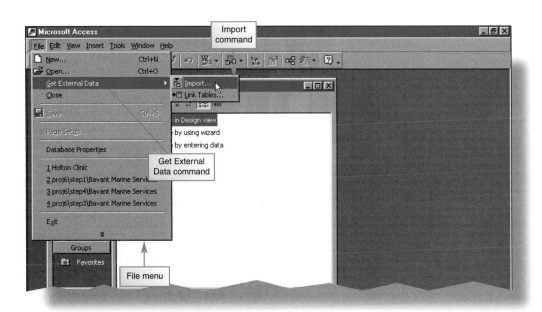

FIGURE 3

② **Click Import. Click the Files of type list arrow in the Import dialog box and then click Microsoft Excel. Select 3½ Floppy (A:) in the Look in drop-down list box. Make sure the Patient workbook is selected and then click the Open button.**

The Import Spreadsheet Wizard dialog box displays (Figure 4). It displays the list of worksheets in the Patient workbook. Currently, there is only one.

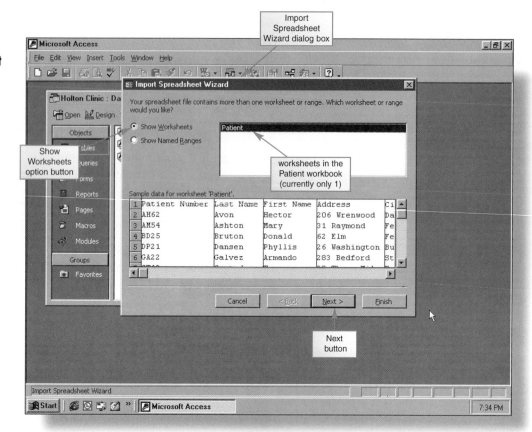

FIGURE 4

③ **Be sure the Patient worksheet is selected and then click the Next button.**

The Import Spreadsheet Wizard dialog box displays (Figure 5). It displays a portion of the worksheet that is being converted. In this dialog box you indicate that the first row of the worksheet contains the column headings. The wizard uses these values as the field names in the Access table.

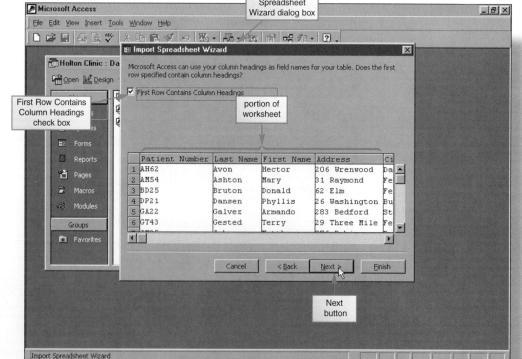

FIGURE 5

4 **Be sure First Row Contains Column Headings is selected (checked) and then click the Next button.**

The Import Spreadsheet Wizard dialog box displays asking whether the data is to be placed in a new table or in an existing table (Figure 6).

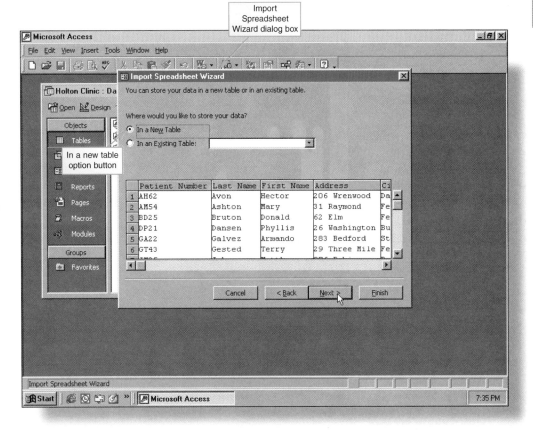

FIGURE 6

5 **Be sure that In a New Table is selected and then click the Next button.**

The Import Spreadsheet Wizard dialog box displays giving you the opportunity to specify field options (Figure 7). You can specify that indexes are to be created for certain fields. You also can specify that certain fields should not be included in the Access table.

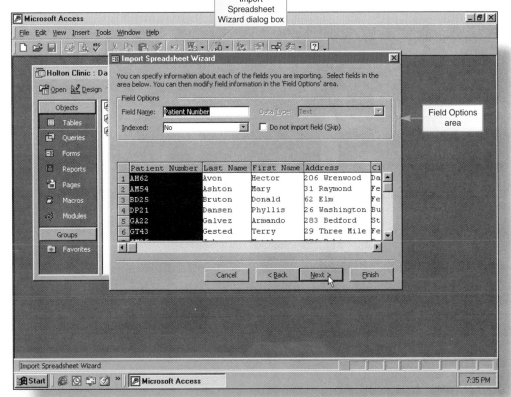

FIGURE 7

6 Click the Next button.

The Import Spreadsheet Wizard dialog box displays (Figure 8). Use this dialog box to indicate the primary key of the Access table. You can allow Access to add a special field to serve as the primary key as illustrated in the figure. You can choose an existing field to serve as the primary key. You also can indicate no primary key. Most of the time, one of the existing fields will serve as the primary key. In this worksheet, for example, the Patient Number serves as the primary key.

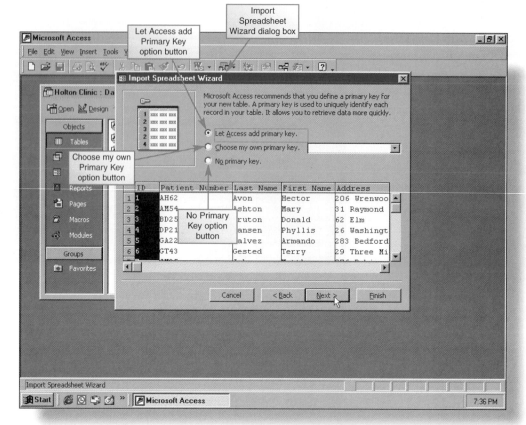

FIGURE 8

7 Click Choose my own Primary Key.

The Patient Number field, which is the correct field, will be the primary key. If some other field were to be the primary key, you could click the down arrow and select the other field from the list of available fields.

8 Click the Next button. Be sure Patient displays in the Import to Table text box.

The Import Spreadsheet Wizard dialog box displays (Figure 9). The name of the table will be Patient.

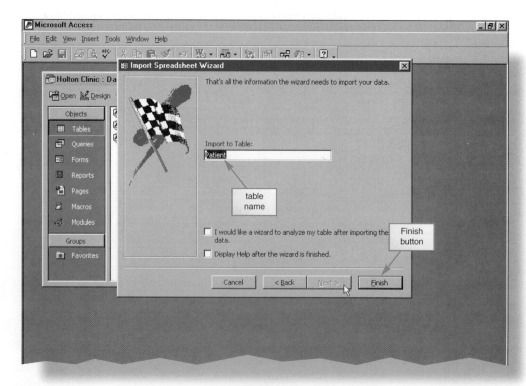

FIGURE 9

Click the Finish button.

The worksheet is converted into an Access table. When the process is completed the Import Spreadsheet Wizard dialog box displays (Figure 10).

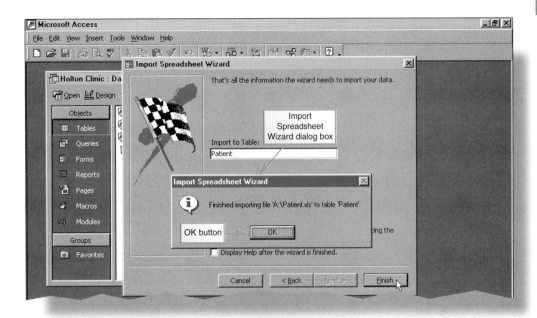

FIGURE 10

 Click the OK button.

The table has now been created (Figure 11).

 Close Access.

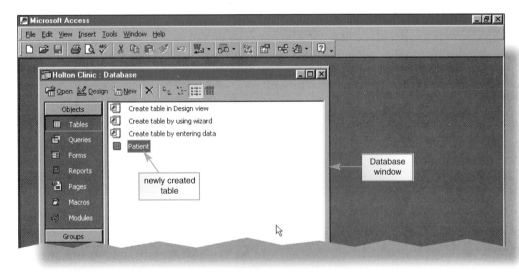

FIGURE 11

Using the Access Table

Once the Access version of the table has been created, you can treat it as you would any other table. After first opening the database containing the table, you can open the table in Datasheet view (Figure 2 on page AI 1.2). You can make changes to the data. You can create queries that use the data in the table.

By clicking Design View on the table's shortcut menu, you can view the table's structure and make any necessary changes to the structure. The changes may include changing field sizes and types, creating indexes, or adding additional fields. To accomplish any of these tasks, use the same steps you used in Project 3. In the Patient table shown in Figure 2, for example, the data type for the Balance and Insurance fields has been changed to Currency and the columns have all been resized to best fit the data.

Microsoft Certification

The Microsoft Office User Specialist (MOUS) Certification program provides an opportunity for you to obtain a valuable industry credential w proof that you have the Access 2000 skills required by employers. For more information, see Appendix D or visit the Shelly Cashman Series MOUS Web page at ww.scsite.com/ off2000/cert.htm.

Quick Reference

For a table that lists how to complete the tasks covered in this book using the mouse, menu, shortcut menu, and keyboard, visit the Office 2000 Web page (www.scsite. com/off2000/qr.htm), and then click Microsoft Access 2000.

Linking Versus Importing

When an external table or worksheet is imported, or converted, into an Access database, a copy of the data is placed as a table in the database. The original data still exists, just as it did before, but there is no further connection between it and the data in the database. Changes to the original data do not affect the data in the database. Likewise, changes in the database do not affect the original data.

It is also possible to **link** data stored in a variety of formats to Access databases. (The available formats include several other database management systems as well as a variety of non-database formats, including Excel worksheets.) With linking, the connection is maintained. To link data, select Link Tables rather than Import on the Get External Data submenu.

When an Excel worksheet is linked, for example, the worksheet is not stored in the database. Instead Access simply establishes a connection to the worksheet so you can view or edit the data in either Access or Excel. Any change made in either one will be immediately visible in the other. For example, if you would change an address in Access and then view the worksheet in Excel, you would see the new address. If you add a new row in Excel and then view the table in Access, the row would appear as a new record.

To identify that a table is linked to other data, Access places an arrow in front of the table (Figure 12). In addition, the Excel icon in front of the name identifies the fact that the data is linked to an Excel worksheet.

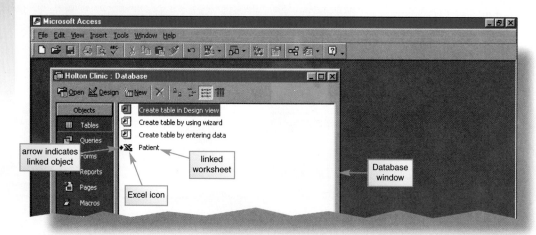

FIGURE 12

CASE PERSPECTIVE SUMMARY

You have now created a table in an Access database containing the same data that the users at Holton Clinic had previously placed in an Excel worksheet. To do so, you used the Import Spreadsheet Wizard. Now that the data has been converted the users at Holton can take advantage of any of the features of Access that they wish.

Integration Feature Summary

The Integration Feature covered the process of integrating an Excel worksheet into an Access database. To convert a worksheet to an Access table, you learned to use the Import Spreadsheet Wizard. Working with the wizard, you identified the first row of the worksheet as the row containing the column headings and you indicated the primary key. The wizard then created the table for you and placed it in a new database. You also saw that you could link data rather than import it.

In the Lab

1 Importing an Excel Worksheet

Problem: Literacy Educational Videos has been using Excel for a number of tasks. Literacy uses several worksheets to re-order videos, keep track of carrying costs, graph trends in video buying and maintain employee records. The company realizes that the employee data would be better handled in Access. The company management has asked you to convert its employee data to an Access database.

Instructions: Perform the following tasks:

1. Start Access and create a new database in which to store all the objects related to the employee data. Call the database Literacy Educational Videos.

2. Import the Employee worksheet shown in Figure 13 into Access. The worksheet is in the Literacy workbook on the Data Disk. See the inside back cover of this book for instructions for downloading the Data Disk or see your instructor for information on accessing the files required for this book. When the Import Spreadsheet Wizard dialog box displays, be sure the Employee worksheet is selected.

	A	B	C	D	E
1	Employee ID	Last Name	First Name	Dept Code	Pay Rate
2	132-90	Ortiz	Maya	ACC	10.50
3	282-36	Markwood	Martin	SHP	9.00
4	305-90	Nordsky	Luke	SHP	9.65
5	364-67	Chou	Rose	CSR	9.00
6	434-56	Radelton	Anne	ACC	10.90
7	575-45	Smith	Daniel	PUR	10.00
8	656-78	Pierce	Serena	CSR	8.30
9	680-11	Garrison	Chandra	PUR	9.80
10	745-89	Royce	LeVar	PUR	8.75
11	890-34	Suranov	Petra	SHP	7.80

FIGURE 13

3. Use Employee as the name of the Access table and Employee ID as the primary key.

4. Open the Employee table in Design view and change the data type for the Pay Rate field to Currency. Save the change to the table. Be sure to click Yes when a dialog box displays warning you that data may be truncated.

5. Open and print the Employee table

In the Lab

2 **Linking an Excel Worksheet**

Problem: The management of Literacy Educational Videos is pleased with the benefits they have derived from converting Employee data into an Access database. They now would like to be able to use the Query, Form, and Report features of Access for their inventory data yet still maintain the data in Excel worksheets.

Instructions: Perform the following tasks.

1. Open the Literacy Educational Videos database you created in In the Lab 1.
2. Link the Inventory Worksheet shown in Figure 14 to the database. The worksheet is in the Literacy workbook on the Data Disk. See the inside back cover of this book for instructions for downloading the Data Disk or see your instructor for information on accessing the files required for this book. When the Link Spreadsheet Wizard dialog box displays, be sure the Inventory worksheet is selected.

	A	B	C	D
1	Video ID	Title	Quantity	Price
2	A593	Learning to Read	8.00	79.95
3	A870	Reading is Fun	5.00	49.95
4	B673	Fun with Words	12.00	19.95
5	B693	ABC - Let's Read	22.00	29.95
6	C573	Follow the Words	10.00	24.95
7	C603	Down the Reading Trail	16.00	24.95
8	D933	Literacy and You	18.00	39.95
9	D963	Can You Read Yet?	3.00	39.95
10	E353	Spell It!	30.00	69.95
11	F820	The Most Important R	25.00	24.95
12	F940	Paint with Words	34.00	89.95
13	F950	Teaching Reading	10.00	29.95

FIGURE 14

3. Open the Inventory table in Access and resize the Title column so that the entire title displays.
4. Print the table.

Microsoft **Access 2000**

P R O J E C T

Microsoft Access 2000

Creating a Report
Using Design View

You will have mastered the material in this project
when you can:

O B J E C T I V E S

- Open a database
- Create additional tables
- Import data from an ASCII text file
- Change layout
- Relate several tables
- Create a Lookup Wizard field that uses a
  separate table
- Change join properties in a query
- Change field properties in a query
- Filter a query's recordset
- Create a parameter query
- Run a parameter query
- Create queries for reports
- Create a report
- Add fields to a report
- Add a subreport to a report
- Modify a subreport
- Move a subreport
- Add a date
- Add a page number
- Bold labels
- Change margins
- Create mailing labels
- Print mailing labels

Managing the Big Events

Successfully

Martians invading the earth? In 1938, Orson Welles's famous radio dramatization of the 1898 novel, *The War of the Worlds*, by H.G. Wells, caused widespread panic in the United States. Welles's version of the story had interrupted what appeared to be a live broadcast of dance music with a series of eyewitness news reports of Martian landings. Although at the time, the alarm of an entire nation was not thought to be entertaining, it was a vivid event in the memories of those who had experienced its reality.

This incident was a spoof, yet people loved hoaxes and trickery. Of note were the account of pelicans on the moon published in the *New York Sun* in 1834 and a mere few years later that century, the reporting of a bogus trans-Atlantic hot air balloon crossing, published as a news dispatch by Edgar Allen Poe, an avid practical jokester, who said, "I have great faith in fools; my friends call it self-confidence."

Into this climate of amusement and humbug strode a man who arguably was the all-time giant of American

THE GREATEST SHOW ON EARTH

entertainment. For 60 years, Phineas Taylor Barnum reigned as The Showman to the World. Barnum launched his famous mobile circus in 1871, publicized as the The Greatest Show on Earth. The Barnum circus promoted some of the more outrageous oddities America and the world have ever seen, most of them legitimate, others born of Barnum's abundant imagination and love for the prank.

After it became known that P.T. Barnum was a master of absurdities, crowds flocked to see the infamous sideshows. The public not only expected the unusual from him, but also required it. Barnum's name became a household word. As a master presenter, Barnum preceded each new attraction with a concentrated public relations campaign. The news media ate it up, and attendance under the Big Top soared. Barnum loved the sensational, and above all, he loved people. Now, more than 100 years later, the show of shows still goes on. You can visit the Barnum Museum online (www.barnum-museum.org).

In all likelihood, you may never have the opportunity to manage an event of such magnitude as a grand-scale Barnum circus. In your professional career, however, you are likely to oversee the day-to-day operations of a business or head a large corporation that requires you to keep the organization's data centralized and maintained. With the working knowledge you have gained thus far of the powerful database management capabilities of Access 2000, you have acquired many of the skills you will need.

In this project, the more advanced concepts and techniques of Access are presented that illustrate report design from scratch using the Report Design window, inserting page numbers on a report, and creating mailing labels using the Label Wizard. If this type of application had existed in the days of P.T. Barnum, he might have used an Access database to handle the vast amounts of information required to organize the acts, maintain inventories, monitor schedules, and keep records for such a huge undertaking. In this millennium, those who take advantage of using the right tools will find themselves equipped to mange the big events successfully.

Microsoft Access 2000

Creating a Report Using Design View

P R O J E C T

7

C A S E   P E R S P E C T I V E

The management of Bavant Marine Services has determined that they need to expand their database. They want to include information on open workorders; that is, uncompleted requests for service. These workorders are to be categorized by the requested type of service (for example, canvas repair). Once the workorders and service categories have been added to the database, they want a query created that enables them to find open workorders for all marinas, for a single marina, or for a range of marinas (for example, marinas whose number is between EL25 and FM22). Management also wants a report that lists for each technician, each of the technician's marinas along with all open workorders for the marina. Finally, they want to be able to produce mailing labels for the technicians. Your task is to fulfill these requests.

Introduction

This project creates the report shown in Figure 7-1a. This report is organized by technician. For each technician, it lists the number, first name, and last name. Following the technician number and name, it lists data for each marina served by the technician. The marina data includes the marina number, name, address, city, state, zip code, phone number, marina type, warranty amount, and non-warranty amount. It also includes any open workorders (requests for service) for the marina. For each such workorder, the report lists the location of the boat to be serviced, the category of service (for example, engine repair), a description of the problem, and the status of the request. Additional workorder data includes the estimated hours to rectify the problem, the hours spent so far, and the date of the next scheduled service for the workorder.

The project also creates mailing labels for the technicians. These labels, which are shown in Figure 7-1b, are designed to perfectly fit the type of labels that Bavant Marine Services has purchased.

Before creating the reports and labels, you must first add two tables to the Bavant Marine Services database. These tables help Bavant track open workorders.

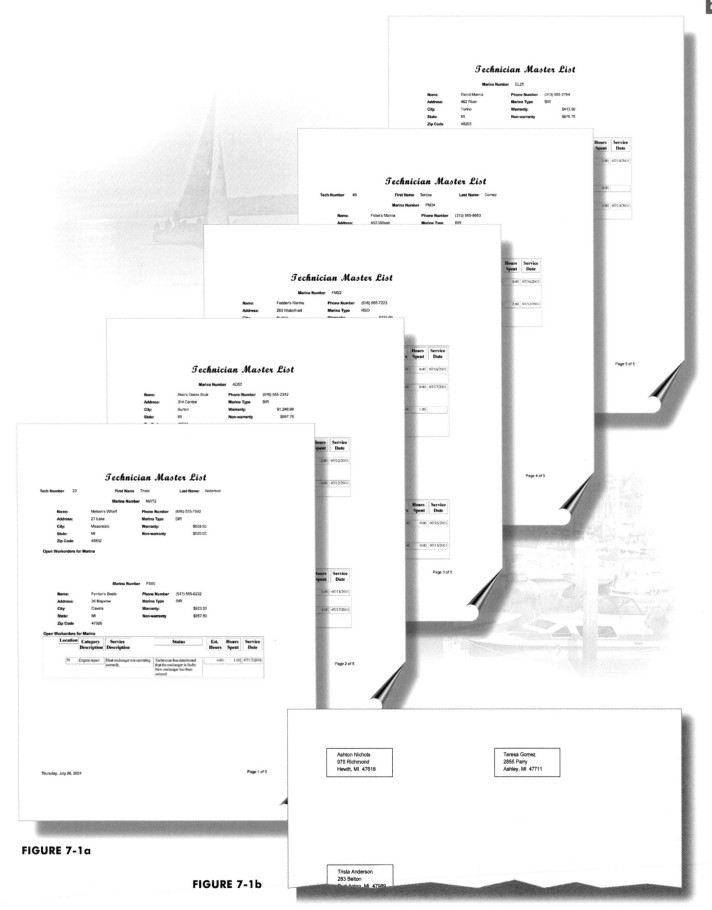

FIGURE 7-1a

FIGURE 7-1b

The first table, Category, is shown in Figures 7-2a and 7-2b. This table is used to categorize the open workorders. Figure 7-2a, which shows the structure of the table, indicates that there are two fields, Category Number (the primary key) and Category Description. Figure 7-2b shows the data in the table. The figure indicates, for example, that category 1 is routine engine maintenance, category 2 is engine repair, category 3 is air conditioning, and so on.

Category

NAME	TYPE	SIZE	DESCRIPTION
Category Number	Text	2	Category Number (Primary Key)
Category Description	Text	50	Description of Category

FIGURE 7-2a

Service Categories

CATEGORY NUMBER	CATEGORY DESCRIPTION
1	Routine engine maintenance
2	Engine repair
3	Air conditioning
4	Electrical systems
5	Fiberglass repair
6	Canvas installation
7	Canvas repair
8	Electronic systems (radar, GPS, autopilots, etc.)

FIGURE 7-2b

The second table, Open Workorders, is shown in Figures 7-3a and 7-3b. Figure 7-3a, the structure, indicates that the table contains a marina number and a location. The location, which is assigned by the marina, indicates the placement of the boat within the marina (for example, the number of the slip in which the boat is kept). The next field, Category Number, indicates the category of the service being requested. The Description field, a memo field, gives a description of the problem. The Status field, also a memo field, indicates the status of the request. The Total Hours (est) field gives an estimate of the total number of hours that will be required to satisfy the request. The Hours Spent field indicates how many hours already have been spent by a technician on the request. The final field, Next Service Date, indicates the next date scheduled for service related to this request.

Open Workorders

NAME	TYPE	SIZE	DESCRIPTION
Marina Number	Text	4	Marina Number (Portion of Primary Key)
Location	Text	6	Location (Remainder of Primary Key)
Category Number	Text	2	Category Number
Description	Memo	-	Description of Problem
Status	Memo	-	Status of Work Request
Total Hours (est)	Number	-	Estimate of Total Number of Hours Required
Hours Spent	Number	-	Hours Already Spent on Problem
Next Service Date	Date/Time	-	Date Scheduled for Next Service Related to Problem

FIGURE 7-3a

Open Workorders

MARINA	LOCATION	CATEGORY NUMBER	DESCRIPTION	STATUS	TOTAL HOURS (EST)	HOURS SPENT	NEXT SERVICE DATE
AD57	A21	3	Air conditioner periodically stops with code indicating low coolant level. Diagnose and repair.	Technician has verified the problem. Air conditioning specialist has been called.	4	2	7/12/2001
AD57	B14	4	Fuse on port motor blown on two occasions. Find cause and correct problem.	Open	2	0	7/12/2001
BL72	129	1	Oil change and general routine maintenance (check fluid levels, clean sea strainers, etc.)	Service call has been scheduled.	1	0	7/16/2001
BL72	146	2	Engine oil level has been dropping drastically. Find cause and repair.	Open	2	0	7/13/2001
EL25	11A	5	Open pockets at base of two stantions.	Technician has completed the initial filling of the open pockets. Will complete the job after the initial fill has had sufficient time to dry.	4	2	7/13/2001
EL25	15A	4	Electric-flush system will periodically not function. Find cause and repair.	Open	3	0	
EL25	43B	2	Engine overheating. Loss of coolant. Find cause and repair.	Open	2	0	7/13/2001
FB96	79	2	Heat exchanger not operating correctly.	Technician has determined that the exchanger is faulty. New exchanger has been ordered.	4	1	7/17/2001
FM22	A21	6	Canvas was severely damaged in windstorm. New canvas needs to be installed.	Open	8	0	7/16/2001
FM22	D14	8	Install new GPS and chart plotter	Scheduled	7	0	7/17/2001
FM22	D31	3	Air conditioning unit shuts down with HHH showing on the control panel.	Technician not able to repeat the problem. Air conditioning unit ran fine through multiple tests. Owner to notify technician if the problem repeats itself.	1	1	
PM34	56	8	Both speed and depth readings on data unit are significantly less than the owner thinks they should be.	Technician has scheduled appointment with owner to attempt to verify the problem.	2	0	7/16/2001
PM34	88	2	Engine seems to be making "clattering" (customer's description) noise.	Technician suspects problem with either propeller or shaft and has scheduled the boat to be pulled from the water for further investigation.	5	2	7/12/2001
TR72	B11	5	Owner had accident and left large gauge in forward portion of port side.	Technician has scheduled repair.	6	0	7/13/2001
TR72	B15	7	Canvas leaks around zippers in heavy rain. Install overlap around zippers to prevent leaks.	Overlap has been created, but still needs to be installed.	8	3	7/17/2001

FIGURE 7-3b

Figure 7-3b gives the data. For example, the first record shows that marina AD57 has requested service. The location of the boat to be serviced is slip A21. The service is in category 3 – Air Conditioning, as indicated in Figure 7-2a. The description of the problem is "Air conditioner periodically stops with code indicating low coolant level. Diagnose and repair." The status is "Technician has verified the problem. Air conditioning specialist has been called." (After verifying the problem, the technician evidently determined that the problem required a specialist.) The technician has estimated that 4 hours total will be required on the problem. So far, 2 hours of work already have been spent. The next service is scheduled for 7/12/2001.

If you examine the data in Figure 7-3b, you see that the Marina Number field cannot be the primary key. The first two records, for example, both have a marina number of AD57. Location also cannot be the primary key. The first and ninth records, for example, both have a location of A21. (Both marinas have slips numbered A21 and the boats in both slips currently require service.) Rather, the primary key is the combination of both of these fields.

It is possible for the primary key to be the combination of more than two fields. If marinas regularly placed requests to service boats that need service in more than one category, for example, Canvas Repair and Engine Repair, then the primary key would be a combination of the Marina Number, Location, and Category fields. In the Apply Your Knowledge exercise at the end of this project, you will create a table where the primary key is the combination of three fields.

Next you will create three queries. You first will create a query to join the Marina and Open Workorders tables. Then you will modify the join properties to ensure that all marinas display, even if they have no open workorders. You will modify the field properties of two of the fields and also filter the **recordset** (results) of the query. Then you will change the query to a **parameter query**, one that prompts the user for input when the query is run. Finally, you will create two queries that will be used in the report in Figure 7-1a on page A 7.5.

The report shown in Figure 7-1a contains a **subreport**, which is a report that is contained within another report. The subreport in the report in Figure 7-1a is the portion that lists the open workorders. You will create the report shown in the figure from scratch; that is, you will use Design view rather than the Report Wizard. You will create mailing labels for the technicians as shown in Figure 7-1b on page A 7.5.

You are to create the tables, queries, report, and mailing labels requested by the management of Bavant Marine Services.

Opening the Database

Before you complete the steps in this project, you must open the database. Perform the following steps to complete this task.

TO OPEN A DATABASE

1 Click the Start button.

2 Click Open Office Document on the Start menu and then click 3½ Floppy (A:) in the Look in box. Make sure the database called Bavant Marine Services is selected.

3 Click the Open button.

The database opens and the Bavant Marine Services : Database window displays.

Creating the Additional Tables

Before creating the queries, report, and mailing labels required by Bavant Marine Services, you need to create the two additional tables shown in Figures 7-2a, 7-2b, 7-3a, and 7-3b on pages A 7.6 and A 7.7.

Creating the New Tables

The steps to create the new tables are identical to those you have used in creating other tables. Perform the following steps to create the tables.

 To Create the New Tables

1 **Click the Tables** object. **Right-click Create table in Design view and then click Open on the shortcut menu. Enter the information for the fields in the Category table as indicated in Figure 7-2a. Close the window containing the table by clicking its Close button. Click the Yes button to save the changes. Type** Category **as the name of the table and then click the OK button.**

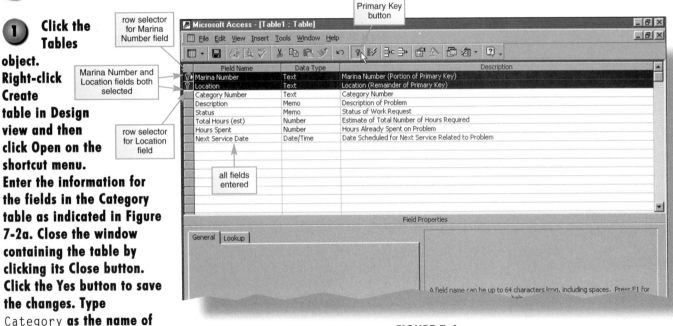

FIGURE 7-4

2 Right-click Create table in Design view and then click Open on the shortcut menu. Enter the information for the fields in the Open Workorders table as indicated in Figure 7-3a.

3 Click the row selector for the **Marina Number** field. Hold the SHIFT key down and click the row selector for the **Location** field so that both fields are selected. Click the Primary Key button on the toolbar.

The primary key consists of both the Marina Number field and the Location field (Figure 7-4).

4 **Close the window by clicking its Close button. Click the Yes button to save the table. Type** Open Workorders **as the name of the table and point to the OK button.**

The Save As dialog box displays (Figure 7-5).

5 **Click the OK button to save the table.**

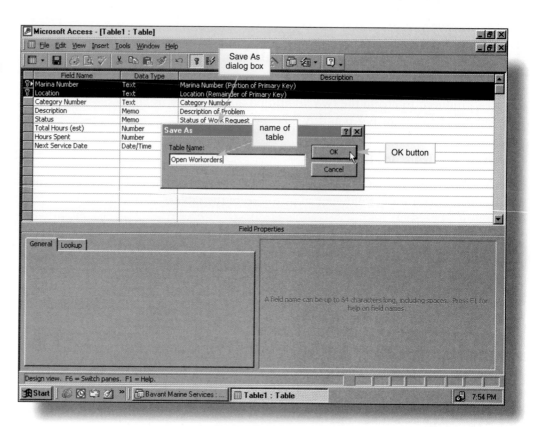

FIGURE 7-5

Importing Data

When importing text files, there are several options concerning how the data in the various fields are separated. For more information about importing data, visit the Access 2000 More About page (www.scsite.com/ac2000/more.htm) and then click Import Data.

Importing the Data

Now that the tables have been created, you need to add data to them. You either could enter the data, or if the data is already in electronic form, you could import the data. The data for the Category and Open Workorders tables are on your Access Data Disk as text files. Use the following steps to import the data.

TO IMPORT THE DATA

1 With the Bavant Marine Services database open, click File on the menu bar, click Get External Data and then click Import.

2 Click the Files of type box arrow in the Import dialog box and then click Text Files. Select 3½ Floppy (A:) in the Look in list. Make sure the Category text file is selected. Click the Import button.

3 Make sure the Delimited option button is selected and click the Next button. Click First Row Contains Field Names, make sure the Tab option button is selected, and then click the Next button again.

4 Click the In an Existing Table option button and select the Category table from the list. Click the Next button, click the Finish button, and then click OK.

5 Repeat Steps 1 through 4 to import the Workorders text file.

The data for the Category and Open Workorders tables are imported.

Changing the Layout

Now that the tables contain data, you need to adjust the column sizes. Perform the following steps to change the layouts of the tables.

 To Change the Layout

1 Right-click the Category table and then click Open on the shortcut menu. Double-click the right boundary of the field selector for each field to resize the columns to best fit the data.

2 Close the window containing the table. When asked if you want to save the changes to the layout, click the Yes button.

The changes to the layout for the Category table are saved.

3 Right-click the Open Workorders table and then click Open on the shortcut menu. Drag the lower boundary of the row selector for the first record to the approximate position shown in Figure 7-6. Resize the remaining columns as shown in Figure 7-6.

4 Close the window containing the table. When asked if you want to save the changes to the layout, click the Yes button.

The changes to the layout for the Open Workorders table are saved.

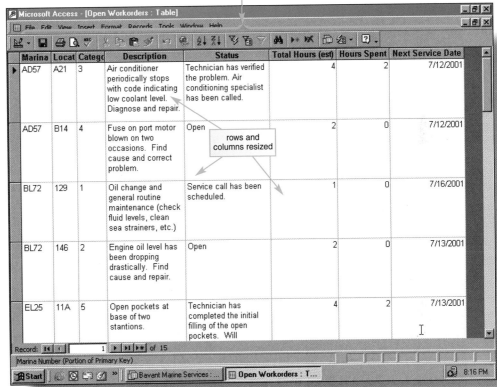

FIGURE 7-6

Relating Several Tables

Now that the tables have been created they need to be related to the existing tables. The Marina and Open Workorders tables are related through the Marina Number fields in both. The Category and Open Workorders tables are related through the Category Number fields in both. Perform the following steps to relate the tables.

TO RELATE SEVERAL TABLES

1️⃣ Close any open datasheet on the screen by clicking its Close button. Click the Relationships button on the toolbar. Right-click in the Relationships window and click Show Table on the shortcut menu. Click the Category table, click the Add button, click the Open Workorders table, click the Add button again, and then click the Close button. Resize the field boxes that display so all fields are visible.

2️⃣ Drag the Marina Number field from the Marina table to the Open Workorders table. Click Enforce Referential Integrity and then click the Create button.

3️⃣ Drag the Category Number field from the Category table to the Open Workorders table. Click Enforce Referential Integrity and then click the Create button.

4️⃣ Drag the Category and Open Workorders tables to the positions shown in Figure 7-7. Click the Close Window button and then click the Yes button to save the changes.

The relationships are created.

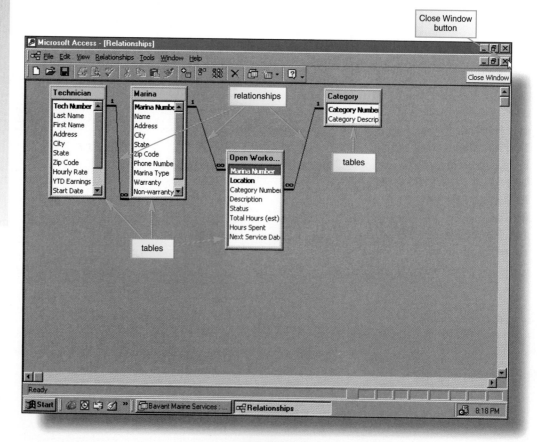

FIGURE 7-7

Creating a Lookup Wizard Field

The fact that the Open Workorders table is related to the Category table ensures that no workorder can be entered without a valid category number. It does not assist the users in knowing what category number to enter, however. To help the users who are entering data in Datasheet view, you will make the Category Number field in the Open Workorders table a Lookup Wizard field. In this case, the lookup would take place in the Category table. Perform the following steps to create a Lookup Wizard field.

 Steps To Create a Lookup Wizard Field

1 **If necessary, click the Tables object. Right-click Open Workorders, and then click Design View on the shortcut menu. Click the Data Type column for the Category Number field, click the box arrow, and then click Lookup Wizard.**

2 **If necessary, click the I want the lookup column to look up the values in a table or query button and then click the Next button. Be sure the Category table is selected and then click the Next button a second time. Click the Add All Fields button to add the Category Number and Category Description to the list of selected fields. Point to the Next button.**

The Lookup Wizard dialog box displays (Figure 7-8).

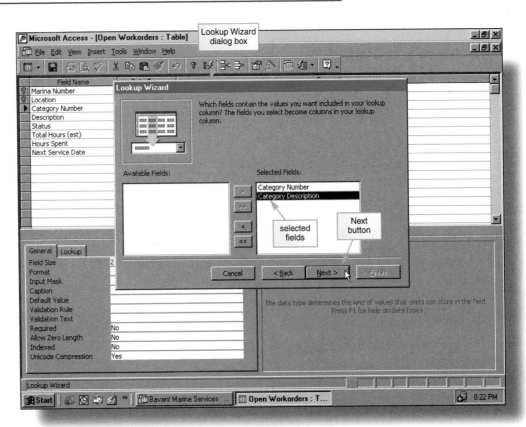

FIGURE 7-8

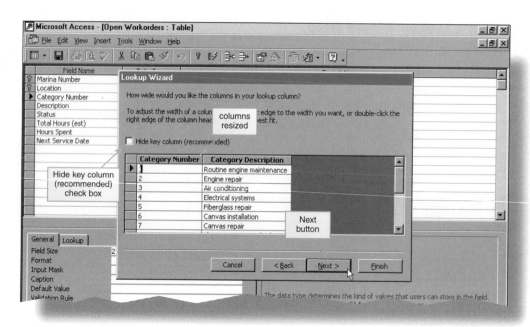

3 Click the Next button, click Hide key column (recommended) to remove the check mark. Resize each column to best fit the data by double-clicking the right-hand border of the column heading. Point to the Next button.

The Category Number column displays and the columns are resized (Figure 7-9).

FIGURE 7-9

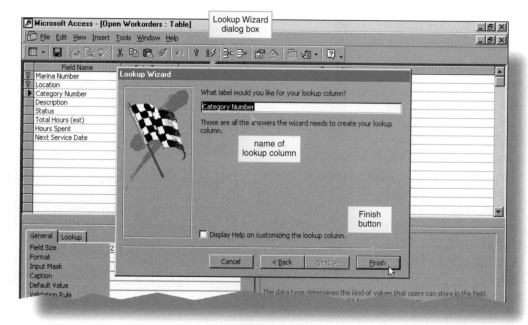

4 Click the Next button, be sure Category Number is selected in the list of available fields that displays and then click the Next button a second time.

5 Be sure Category Number is indicated as the label for the lookup column and then point to the Finish button.

The Lookup Wizard dialog box displays (Figure 7-10).

6 Click the Finish button to complete the definition of the Lookup Wizard field.

FIGURE 7-10

7 Click the Yes button to save the changes to the Category Number field. Close the window by clicking the Close Window button.

Creating Join Queries

Creating the required queries involves creating join queries. In the first query, the process also involves the modification of appropriate properties.

Creating a Query

Creating the initial query follows the same steps as in the creation of any query that joins tables. Perform the following steps to create a query that joins the Marina and Open Workorders tables.

 To Create a Query

1 If necessary, in the Database window, click Tables on the Objects bar, and then click Marina. Click the New Object: AutoForm button arrow on the Database window toolbar. Click Query. Be sure Design View is selected, and then click the OK button. If necessary, maximize the Query1 : Select Query window. Resize the upper and lower panes and the Marina field box so that all the fields in the Marina table display.

2 Right-click any open area in the upper pane, click Show Table on the shortcut menu, click the Open Workorders table, click the Add button, and then click the Close button in the Show Table dialog box. Resize the Open Workorders field box so that all the fields in the Open Workorders table display. Double-click the Marina Number and Name fields from the Marina table. Double-click the Location, Description, Status, Total Hours (est), and Hours Spent fields from the Open Workorders table.

The tables are related and the fields are selected (Figure 7-11).

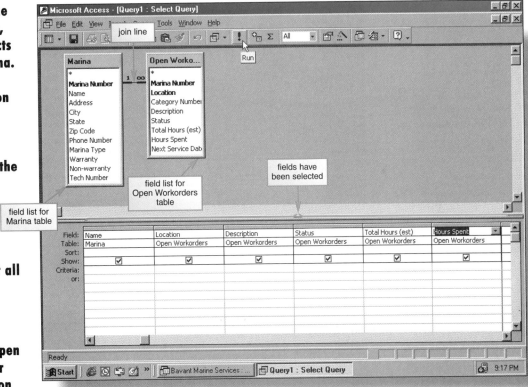

FIGURE 7-11

Changing Join Properties

Normally records that do not match will not display in the results of a join query. A marina for which there are no workorders, for example, would not display. In order to cause such a record to display, you need to change the **join properties**, the properties that indicate which records display in a join, of the query as in the following steps.

To Change Join Properties

1 Point to the middle portion of the join line (the portion of the line that is not bold) (Figure 7-12).

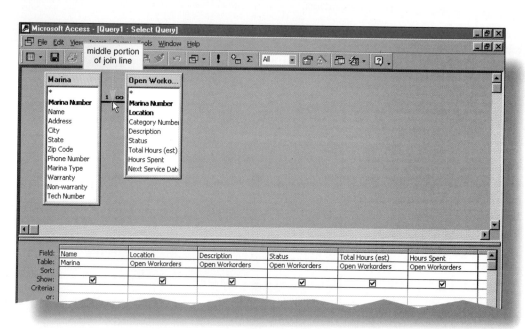

FIGURE 7-12

2 Right-click and then point to Join Properties on the shortcut menu (Figure 7-13). (If Join Properties does not display on your shortcut menu, you did not point to the appropriate portion of the join line.)

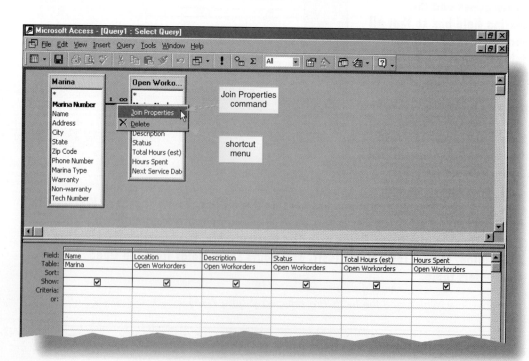

FIGURE 7-13

Click Join Properties on the shortcut menu and point to option button 2.

The Join Properties dialog box displays (Figure 7-14).

 Click option button 2 to include all records from the Marina table regardless of whether or not they match any open workorders. Click the OK button.

The join properties are changed.

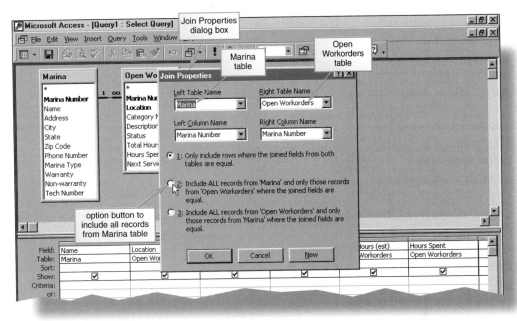

FIGURE 7-14

Changing Field Properties

You can change field properties within a query by using the Properties command and then changing the desired property in the field's property sheet. The following steps change the Format and Decimal Places properties to modify the way the contents of the Total Hours (est) and Hours Spent fields display. The steps also change the Caption properties so that the **captions** (column headings) are different from the field names.

Steps ## To Change Field Properties

 Right-click the Total Hours (est) column and then point to Properties on the shortcut menu (Figure 7-15).

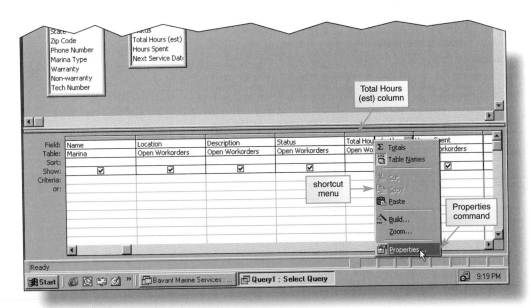

FIGURE 7-15

Click Properties. Be sure the Field Properties box displays. If the Query Properties box displays, close it and right-click in the column again. Click the Format property, click the arrow to display the list of available properties, and then select Fixed. Click the Decimal Places property and type 2 as the number of decimal places. Click the Caption property and then type Est Hours **as the caption.**

The changed properties display(Figure 7-16).

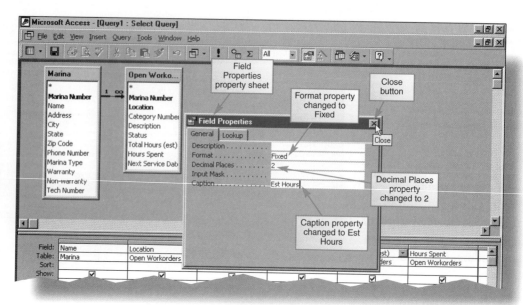

FIGURE 7-16

 Use the same technique to change the Format property for the Hours Spent field to Fixed, the number of decimal places to 2, and the caption to Spent Hours.

Running the Query and Changing the Layout

Perform the following steps to run the query and change the layout.

Steps **To Run the Query and Change the Layout**

1 **Click the Run button on the toolbar. Point to the lower boundary of the row selector for the first record.**

The results display (Figure 7-17). Marina NW72 displays, even though it has no open workorders. The captions for the Total Hours (est) and Hours Spent fields have been changed. Both fields display with precisely two decimal places.

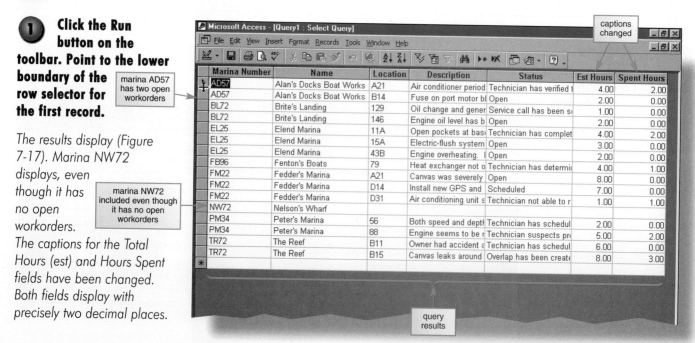

FIGURE 7-17

2 Drag the lower boundary of the row selector to the approximate position shown in Figure 7-18.

The complete memos display.

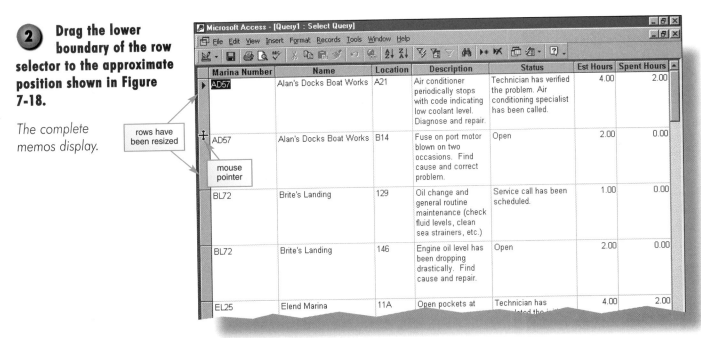

FIGURE 7-18

Filtering the Query's Recordset

You can filter the recordset (that is, the results) of a query just as you can filter a table. The following steps, for example, use Filter By Selection to restrict the records displayed to those on which the number of spent hours is 0.00.

Steps **To Filter a Query's Recordset**

1 Click the Spent Hours field on the second record to select 0.00 as the number of spent hours. Point to the Filter By Selection button (Figure 7-19).

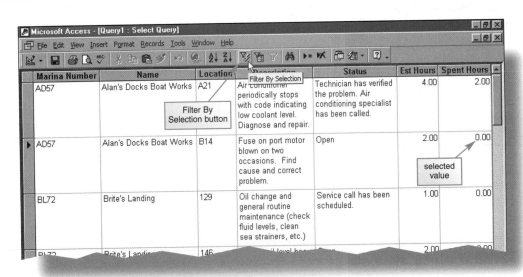

FIGURE 7-19

2 **Click the Filter By Selection button. Point to the Remove Filter button.**

Only those records on which the number of spent hours is 0.00 display (Figure 7-20). Nelson's Wharf, which had no open workorders, does not display because there was no value in the Spent Hours field.

3 **Click the Remove Filter button so that all records once again display. Close the Query by clicking its Close Window button. Click the Yes button to save the query. Type** `Work Orders by Marina` **as the name of the query and click the OK button.**

The query is saved.

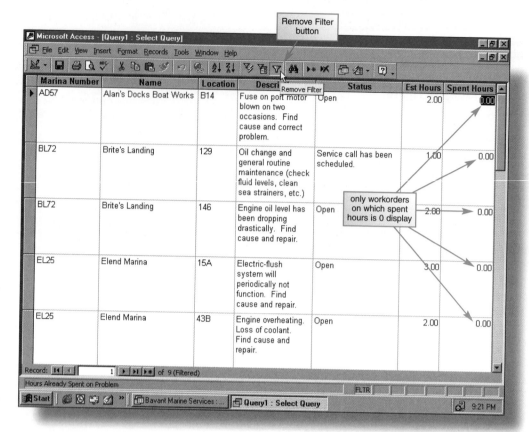

FIGURE 7-20

Parameter Queries

Parameter queries are especially useful in cases where the same query is run frequently with slight changes to one or more of the query's criteria. By using parameters rather than specific values, you can enter the values for the criterion as the query is run rather than having to change the query design. For more information about parameter queries, visit the Access 2000 More About page (www.scsite.com/ac2000/more.htm) and then click Parameter Queries.

Creating a Parameter Query

Rather than giving a specific criterion when you first create the query, there are occasions where you want to be able to enter part of the criterion when you run the query and then have the appropriate results display. For example, to display all the marinas located in Burton, you could enter Burton as a criterion in the City field. From that point on, every time you ran the query, only the marinas in Burton would display. If you wanted to display all the marinas in Glenview, you would need to create another query.

A better way is to allow the user to enter the city at the time the query is run. Thus a user could run the query, enter Burton as the city and then see all the marinas in Burton. Later, the user could run the same query, but enter Glenview as the city, and then see all the marinas in Glenview. In order to do this, you create a **parameter query**, a query that prompts for input whenever it is run. You enter a parameter, rather than a specific value as the criterion. You create one by enclosing a value in a criterion in square brackets (like you enclose field names), but where the value in the brackets does not match any field. For example, you could place [Enter city] as the criterion in the City field.

You can include more than one parameter in a query. At Bavant, they want to be able to enter a beginning and ending marina number and then display all the records in the Marina table for which the marina number is between the two values entered. If the user enters AA00 and ZZ99 as the beginning and ending numbers, the display will include all marinas. If the user enters BL72 as both the beginning number and the ending number, only those workorders for marina BL72 will display. If the user enters EL25 as the beginning number and FM22 as the ending number, only those workorders on which the marina number is between EL25 and FM22 will display.

In order to allow users to enter two values, there will be two values in the criterion enclosed in square brackets, that is, two parameters, as shown in the following steps.

Queries

If you create an expression in a query in which a field name enclosed in brackets is misspelled, Access will assume that the brackets contain a parameter. When you run the query, it will ask you for a value. If this happens, notice the name specified in the dialog box, check the spelling, and then make the necessary changes.

 To Create a Parameter Query

1 **In the Database window, click Queries on the Objects bar and then right-click Work Orders by Marina. Click Design View on the shortcut menu. If necessary, maximize the Work Orders by Marina : Select Query window.**

2 **Right-click the Criteria row under the Marina Number field and then point to Zoom (Figure 7-21).**

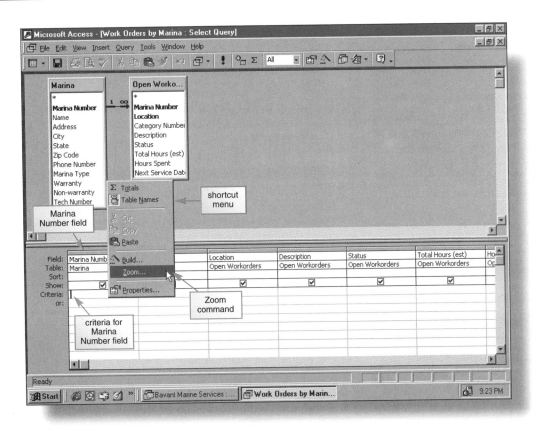

FIGURE 7-21

③ Click Zoom and then type Between [Beginning marina number] and [Ending marina number] **in the Zoom dialog box. Point to the OK button.**

The Zoom dialog box displays (Figure 7-22).

④ Click the OK button.

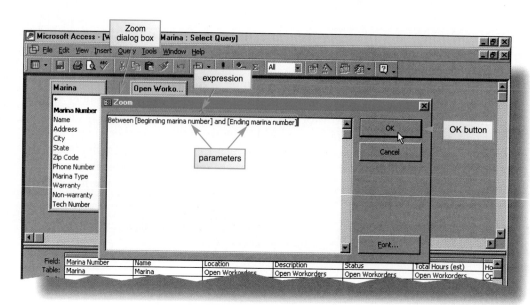

FIGURE 7-22

Running a Parameter Query

You run a parameter query similarly to any other query. The only difference is that when you do, you will be prompted for values for any parameter in the query; that is, the values for any expression enclosed in square brackets other than field names. For this query that means the values for both the beginning marina number and ending marina number. Once you have furnished these values, the appropriate results then will display. The following steps run the query from the query Design view. If you ran the query from the Database window, you would be prompted for the same parameter values.

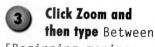 **To Run a Parameter Query**

① Click the Run button on the toolbar. Type AA00 **as the beginning marina number and then click the OK button. Type** ZZ99 **as the ending marina number (Figure 7-23). Point to the OK button.**

The Enter Parameter Value dialog box displays.

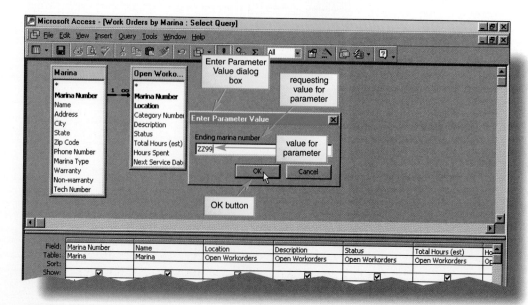

FIGURE 7-23

② **Click the OK button.**

All records display.

③ **Click the View button to return to Design view. Click the Run button. Type** BL72 **as the beginning marina number and then click the OK button. Type** BL72 **as the ending marina number and then click the OK button.**

Marina Number	Name	Location	Description	Status	Est Hours	Spent Hours
▶ BL72	Brite's Landing	129	Oil change and general routine maintenance (check fluid levels, clean sea strainers, etc.)	Service call has been scheduled.	1.00	0.00
BL72	Brite's Landing	146	Engine oil level has been dropping drastically. Find cause and repair.	Open	2.00	0.00

only records on which the marina number is BL72 display

Microsoft Access - [Work Orders by Marina : Select Query]

FIGURE 7-24

Only those workorders on which the marina number is BL72 display (Figure 7-24).

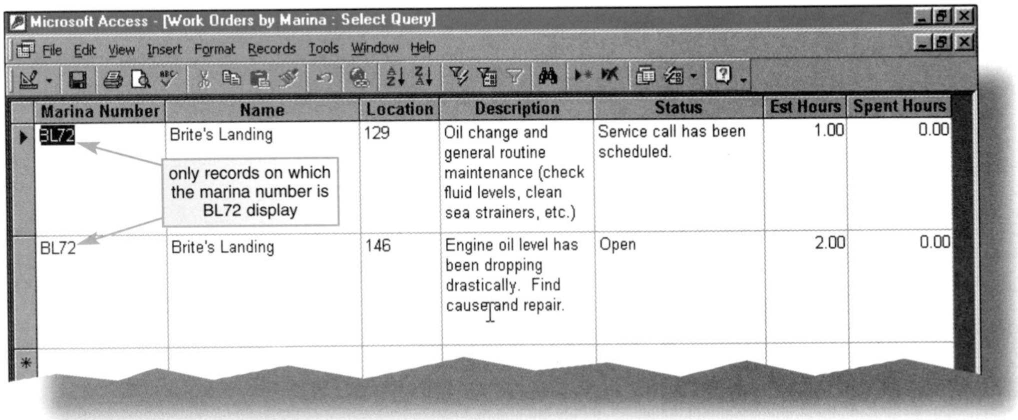

④ **Close the query by clicking its Close Window button. Click the Yes button to save the changes.**

Creating Queries for Reports

The report you will create requires two queries. The first query relates technicians and marinas and the second query relates categories and workorders. The following steps create the necessary queries.

TO CREATE THE QUERIES

① In the Database window, click Tables on the Objects bar, if necessary, and then click Technician. Click the New Object: Query button arrow on the Database window toolbar. (Yours may read New Object: AutoForm.) Click Query. Be sure Design View is selected, and then click the OK button. If necessary, maximize the Query1 : Select Query window. Resize the upper and lower panes and the Technician field box so that all the fields in the Technician table display.

② Right-click any open area in the upper pane, click Show Table on the shortcut menu, click the Marina table, click the Add button, and then click the Close button in the Show Table dialog box. Resize the Marina field box so that all the fields in the Marina table display. Double-click the Tech Number, First Name, and Last Name fields from the Technician table. Double-click the Marina Number, Name, Address, City, State, Zip Code, Phone Number, Marina Type, Warranty, and Non-warranty fields from the Marina table.

③ Close the query by clicking its Close Window button. Click the Yes button to save the query. Type Technicians and Marinas as the name of the query and then click the OK button.

④ Click Tables on the Objects bar, if necessary and then click Category. Click the New Object: Query button arrow on the Database window toolbar. Click Query. Be sure Design View is selected and then click the OK button. If necessary, maximize the Query1: Select Query window. Resize the upper and lower panes.

⑤ Right-click any open area in the upper pane, click Show Table on the shortcut menu, click the Open Workorders table, click the Add button and then click the Close button in the Show Table dialog box. Resize the Open Workorders field box so that all the fields in the Open Workorders table display. Double-click the Marina Number, Location, Category Description, Description, Status, Total Hours (est), Hours Spent, and Next Service Date fields.

⑥ Close the query by clicking its Close Window button. Click the Yes button to save the query. Type Workorders and Categories as the name of the query and then click the OK button.

The queries are saved.

Creating a Report

Creating the report shown in Figure 7-1a on page A 7.5 from scratch involves creating the initial report in Report Design view, adding the subreport, modifying the subreport separately from the main report, and then making the final modifications to the main report.

Creating the Initial Report

When you want to create a report from scratch, you begin with the same general procedure as when you want to use the Report Wizard to create the report. The difference is that you will select Design View rather than Report Wizard. Perform the following steps to create the initial version of the Technician Master List.

Steps **To Create the Initial Report**

① If necessary, in the Database window, click Queries on the Objects bar, and then click Technicians and Marinas. Click the New Object: Query button arrow on the Database window toolbar, and then click Report. Be sure Design View is selected and click the OK button.

② Dock the toolbox at the bottom of the screen, if necessary. Be sure the field box displays. If it does not, click the Field List button on the Report Design toolbar. Point to the lower boundary of the field box.

A blank report displays in Design view (Figure 7-25).

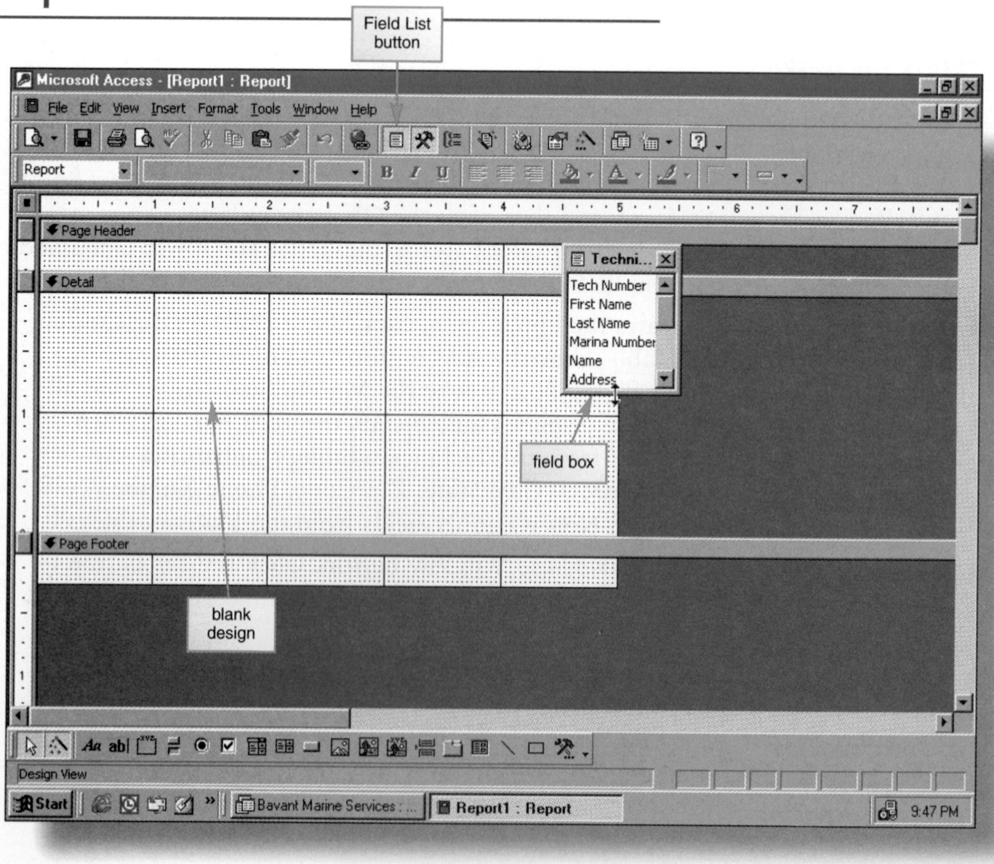

FIGURE 7-25

3 Drag the bottom boundary of the field box down so that all fields display. Move the field box to the lower-right corner of the screen by dragging its title bar. Right-click any open area of the Detail section of the report and then point to Sorting and Grouping on the shortcut menu.

The field box is moved and the shortcut menu displays (Figure 7-26).

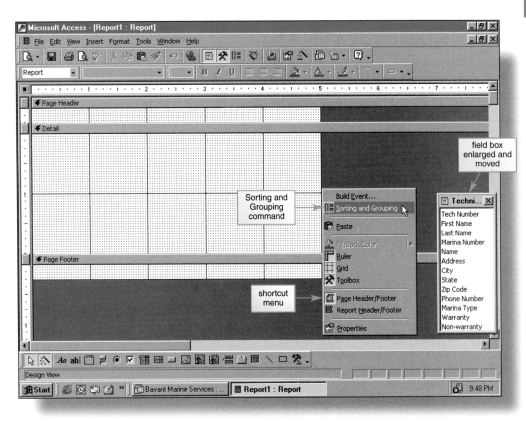

FIGURE 7-26

4 Click Sorting and Grouping, click the down arrow in the Field/Expression box, and then point to Tech Number.

The Sorting and Grouping dialog box displays (Figure 7-27). The list of available fields displays.

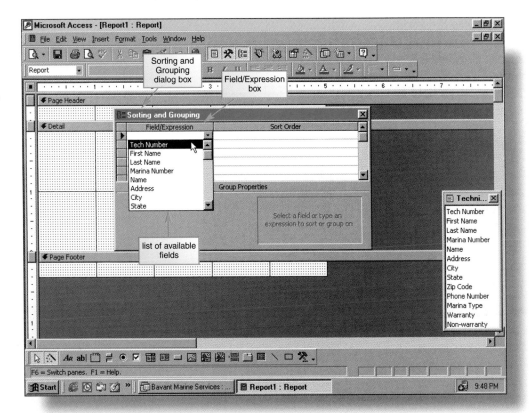

FIGURE 7-27

Microsoft Access 2000

5 Click Tech Number, click the Group Header property, click the Group Header box arrow, and then click Yes.

The Group Header property is changed from No to Yes (Figure 7-28). The group header for the Tech Number field displays.

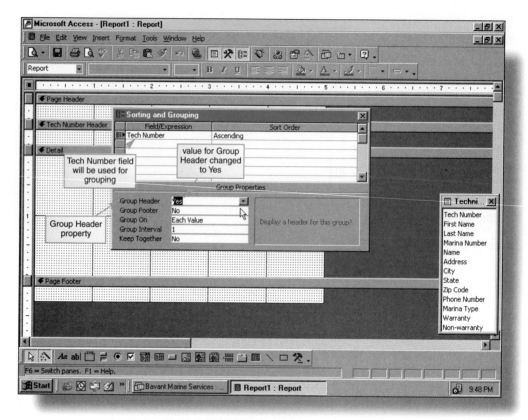

FIGURE 7-28

6 Close the Sorting and Grouping dialog box by clicking its Close button. Point to Tech Number in the field box (Figure 7-29).

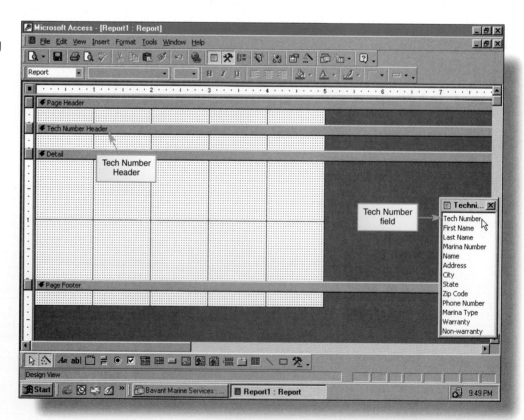

FIGURE 7-29

Adding the Fields

You can add the fields to the report by dragging them from the field list to the appropriate position on the report. The following steps add the fields to the report.

 To Add the Fields

1 **Drag the Tech Number field to the approximate position shown in Figure 7-30.**

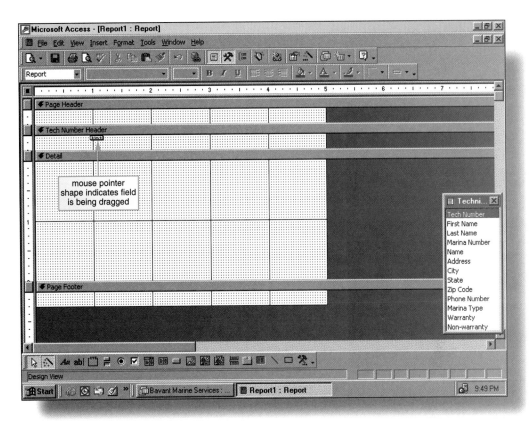

FIGURE 7-30

2 **Release the left mouse button to place the field. Use the same techniques to place the First Name and Last Name fields in the approximate positions shown in Figure 7-31. If any field is not in the correct position, drag it to its correct location. If you wish to move the control or the attached label separately, drag the large handle in the upper-left corner of the control or label.**

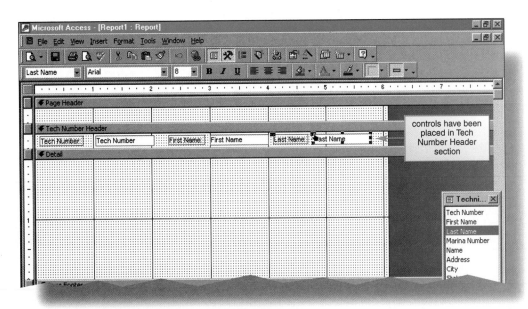

FIGURE 7-31

③ **Place the remaining fields in the positions shown in Figure 7-32 and point to the Close button in the field box.**

④ **Close the field box by clicking its Close button.**

The fields are placed. The field box no longer displays.

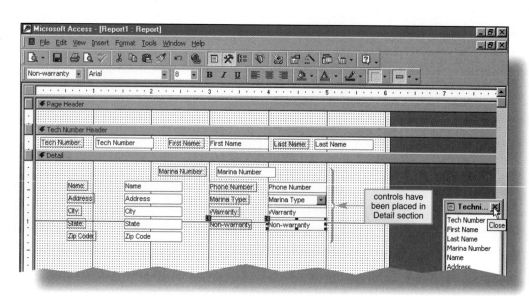

FIGURE 7-32

Saving the Report

Before proceeding with the next steps in the modification of the report, it is a good idea to save your work. Perform the following steps to save the current report.

Steps **To Save the Report**

① **Point to the Save button on the Report Design toolbar (Figure 7-33).**

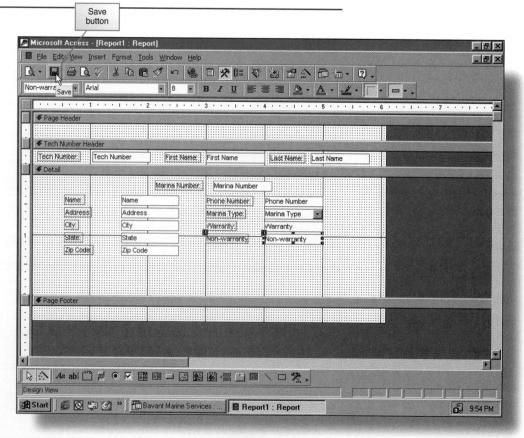

FIGURE 7-33

2 **Click the Save button and then type** Technician Master List **as the report name. Point to the OK button.**

The Save As dialog box displays (Figure 7-34).

3 **Click the OK button.**

The report is saved.

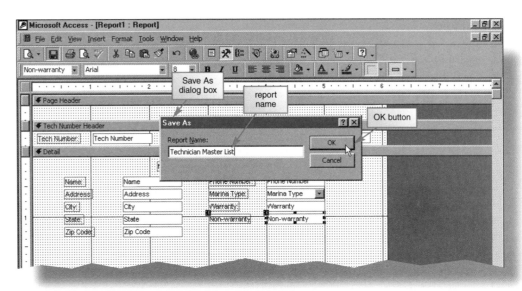

FIGURE 7-34

Adding a Subreport

To add a subreport to a report, you use the Subform/Subreport button in the toolbox. Provided the Control Wizards button is depressed, a wizard will guide you through the process of adding the subreport as in the following steps.

More About

Subreports

A main report can contain more than one subreport. If the main report is based on a table or query, each subreport must contain information related to the information in the main report.

Steps **To Add a Subreport**

1 **Be sure the Control Wizards button is depressed and point to the Subform/Subreport button in the toolbox (Figure 7-35).**

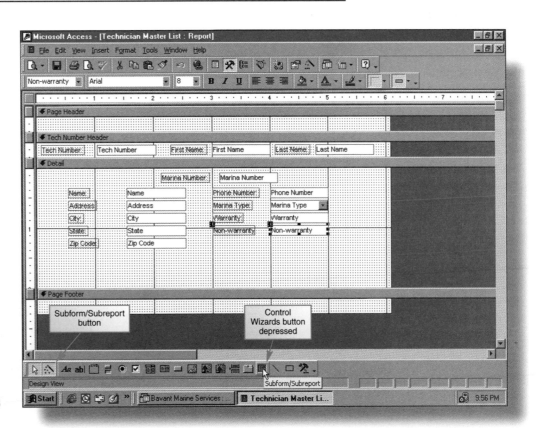

FIGURE 7-35

2 Click the
Subform/Subreport
button and move the
pointer, which has changed
to a plus sign with a
subreport, to the
approximate position
shown in Figure 7-36.

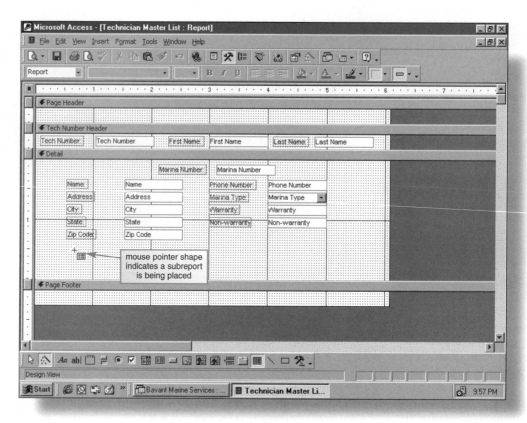

FIGURE 7-36

3 Click the position
shown in Figure
7-36. Be sure the Use
existing Tables and Queries
option button is selected
and then point to the Next
button.

*The SubReport Wizard dialog
box displays (Figure 7-37).*

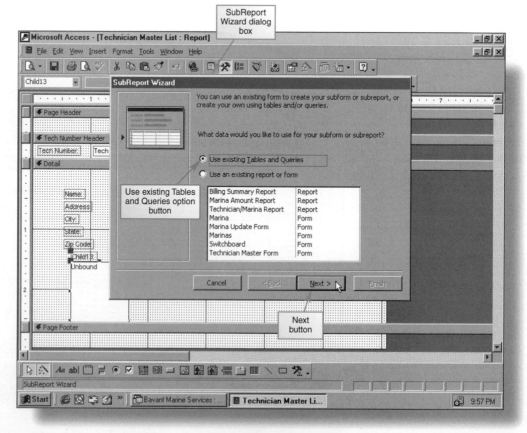

FIGURE 7-37

4 Click the Next button. Click the Tables/Queries box arrow and then point to Query: Workorders and Categories (Figure 7-38).

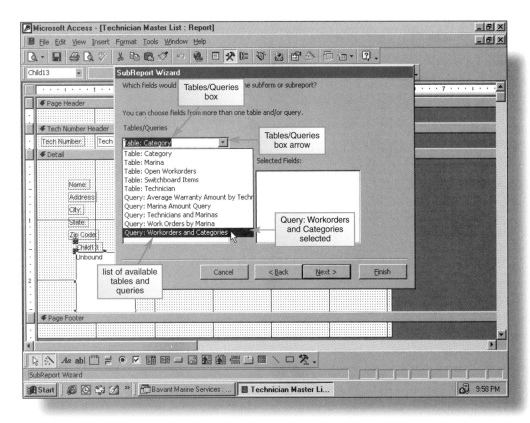

FIGURE 7-38

5 Click Query: Workorders and Categories, click the Add All Fields button, and then point to the Next button (Figure 7-39).

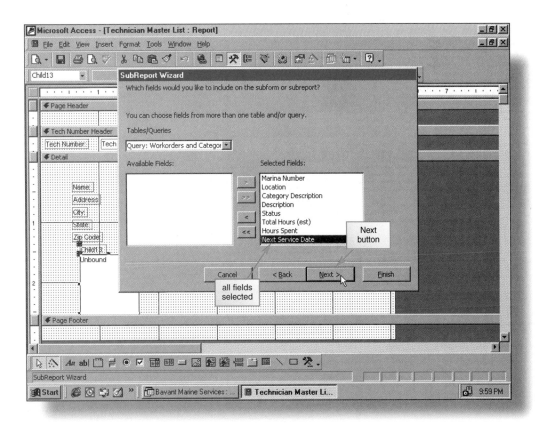

FIGURE 7-39

6 **Click the Next button. Be sure the Choose from a list option button is selected and then point to the Next button.**

The SubReport Wizard dialog box displays (Figure 7-40). You use this dialog box to indicate the fields that link the main report (referred to as "form" in the sentence) to the subreport (referred to as "subform"). If the fields have the same name, as they often will, you can simply select Choose from a list and then accept the selection Access already has made.

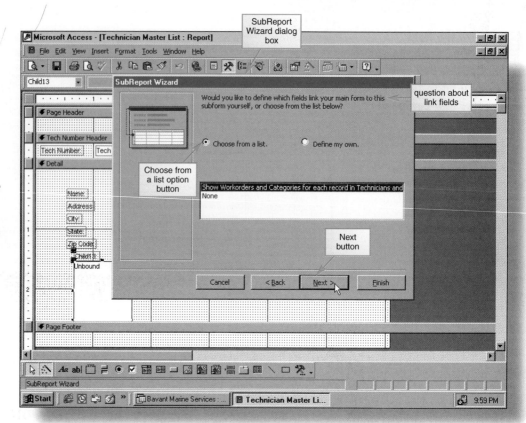

FIGURE 7-40

7 **Click the Next button. Type** Open Workorders for Marina **as the name of the subreport and then point to the Finish button (Figure 7-41).**

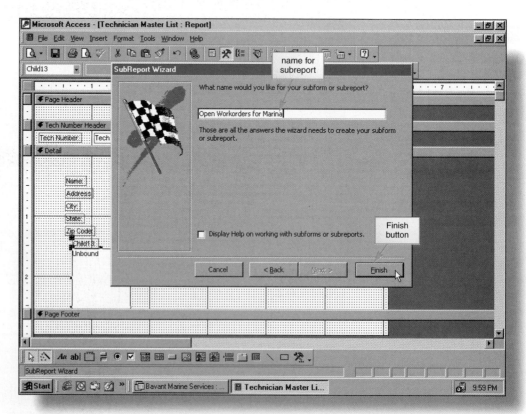

FIGURE 7-41

8 **Click the Finish button.**

The subreport is created and placed in the report design (Figure 7-42).

9 **Close the report design by clicking its Close Window button. Click the Yes button to save the changes.**

The report is saved. The Database window displays.

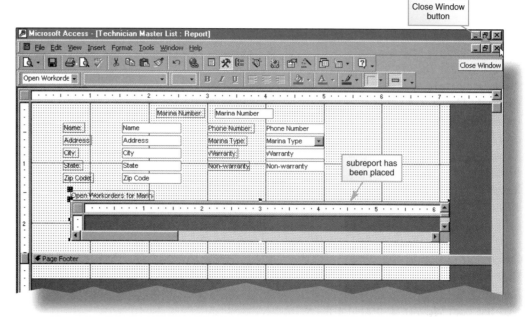

Close Window button

FIGURE 7-42

Modifying the Subreport

The subreport displays as a separate report in the Database window. It can be modified just like any other report. Perform the following steps to modify the subreport.

 To Modify the Subreport

More About

SubReports

A main report does not need to be based on a table or query. It can still contain one or more subreports. It simply serves as a container for the subreports, which then have no restrictions on the information they must contain.

1 **Be sure the Reports object is selected, right-click Open Workorders for Marina, and then click Design View on the shortcut menu that displays. Point to the lower boundary of the Report Header section. The font and style of your headings may be different.**

The design for the subreport displays (Figure 7-43).

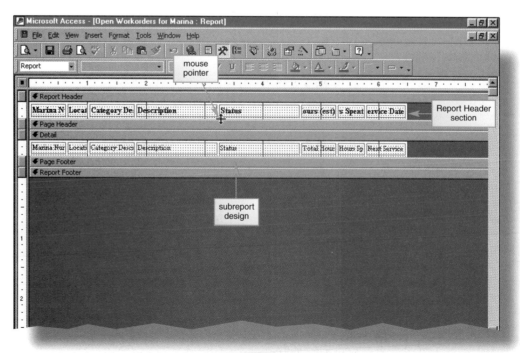

FIGURE 7-43

Microsoft **Access** 2000

2 Drag the lower boundary of the Report Header section to the approximate position shown in Figure 7-44. Delete the Marina Number controls from both the Report Header and Detail sections. Change the labels in the Report Header section to match those shown in the figure. The Font Name is Times New Roman, the Font Size is 10 and the Font Weight is Bold. (To extend a heading over two lines, press SHIFT+ENTER).

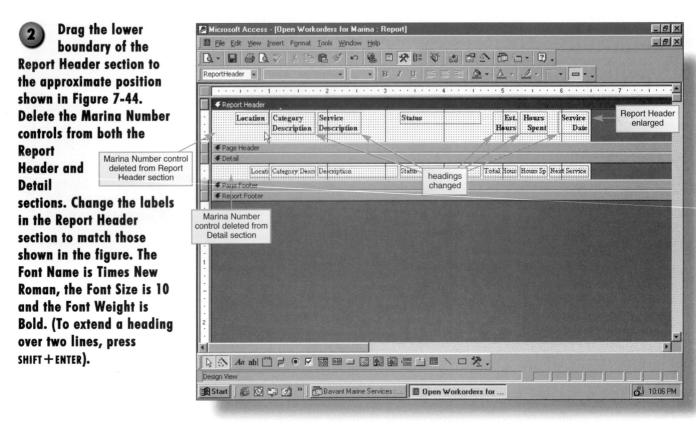

FIGURE 7-44

3 Point to the ruler in the position shown in Figure 7-45.

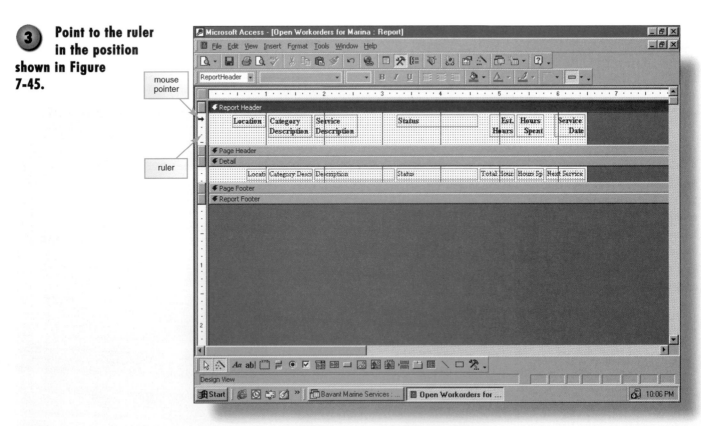

FIGURE 7-45

4 **Click the position shown in Figure 7-45.**

All the header labels are selected (Figure 7-46).

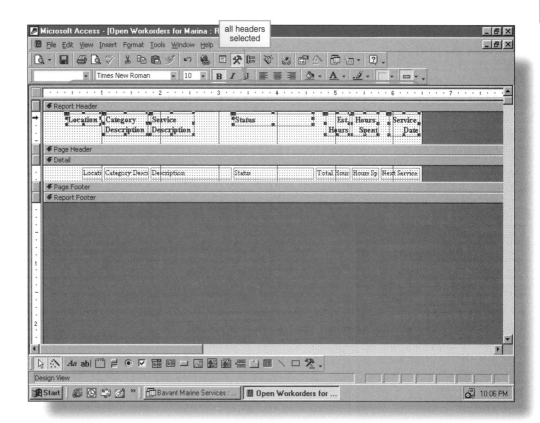

FIGURE 7-46

5 **Right-click any of the selected labels and then click Properties on the shortcut menu.**

The Multiple selection property sheet displays (Figure 7-47).

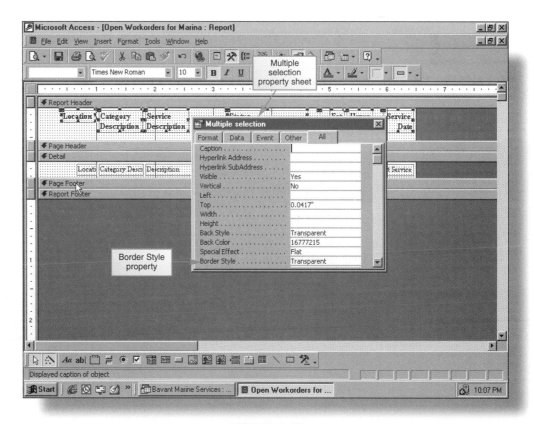

FIGURE 7-47

6 Click the Border Style property, click the Border Style box, and then click Solid. Click the down scroll arrow so that the Text Align property displays. Click the Text Align property, click the Text Align box arrow, and then point to Center.

The Multiple selection property sheet displays (Figure 7-48). The list of options for the Text Align property displays.

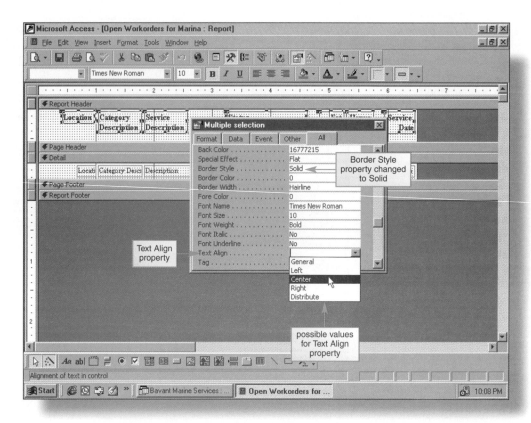

FIGURE 7-48

7 Click Center and then close the Multiple selection property sheet by clicking its Close button. Point to the ruler in the position shown in Figure 7-49.

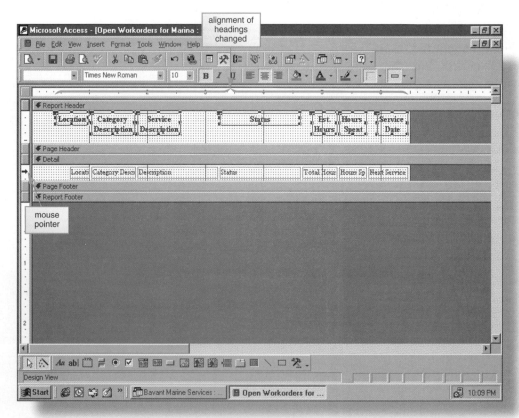

FIGURE 7-49

8 **Click the ruler in the position shown** in Figure 7-49 to select all the controls in the Detail section. Right-click any of the selected controls and then click Properties on the shortcut menu. Click the Border Style property, click the Border Style box arrow, and then click Solid. Point to the Close button for the Multiple selection property sheet.

The Border Style property is changed to Solid (Figure 7-50).

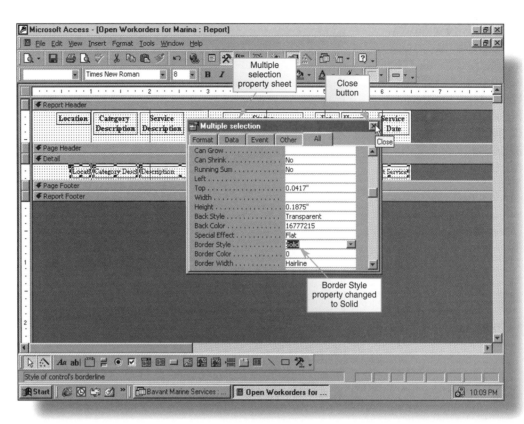

FIGURE 7-50

9 **Click the Close button. Click** anywhere outside the Detail section to deselect the controls. Click the Total Hours (est) control in the Detail section. Hold down the SHIFT key and then click the Hours Spent control in the Detail section. Right-click either of the selected controls and point to Properties on the shortcut menu (Figure 7-51).

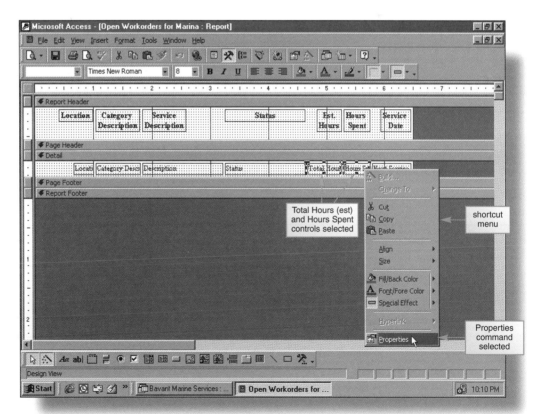

FIGURE 7-51

10 **Click Properties, click the Format property, click the Format box arrow, and then click Fixed. Click the Decimal Places property, click the Decimal Places box arrow, and then click 2. Point to the Close button.**

The format is changed to Fixed and the number of decimal places is changed to 2 (Figure 7-52).

11 **Click the Close button for the Multiple selection property sheet.**

12 **Right-click the Category Description control in the Detail section and click Properties on the shortcut menu. Click the Can Grow property, click the Can Grow box arrow, and then click Yes.**

The value for the Can Grow property has been changed to Yes. Category description will be spread over several lines.

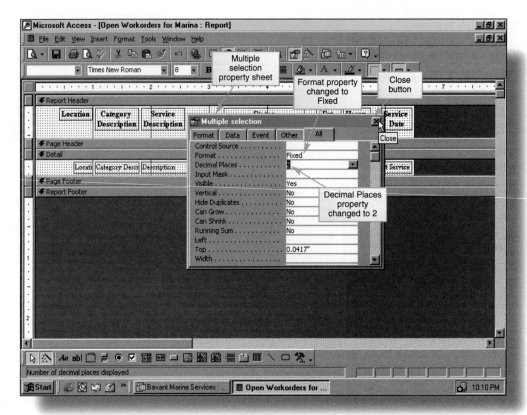

FIGURE 7-52

13 **Click the Close button for the property sheet and then close the subreport by clicking its Close Window button. Click the Yes button to save the changes.**

The changes are saved and the report is removed from the screen.

Moving the Subreport

To match the report shown in Figure 7-1a on page A 7.5, the subreport needs to be moved slightly to the left. The subreport can be dragged just like any other object in a report. Perform the following steps to move the subreport.

Steps: To Move the Subreport

1 Be sure the Reports object is selected, right-click Technician Master List, and then click Design View on the shortcut menu.

2 Drag the subreport to the position shown in Figure 7-53.

3 Click anywhere outside the subreport control to deselect it.

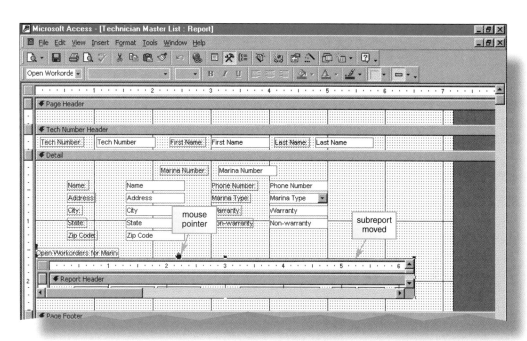

FIGURE 7-53

Adding a Date

To add a date to a report, use the Date and Time command on the Insert menu. When you do, you will be given a choice of a variety of date and time formats. After adding the date, you can drag it into the desired position. Perform the following steps to add the date.

More About

Adding a Date

After adding a date to a report, you can change the format used to display the date by right-clicking the date control and then selecting Properties on the shortcut menu. You then can select a format for the date and/or the time by changing the value for the Format property.

Steps: To Add a Date

1 Click Insert on the menu bar and then click Date and Time on the Insert menu. Be sure that Include Date is checked and that Include Time is not checked. Be sure the date format selected is the first of the three options. Point to the OK button.

The Date and Time dialog box displays (Figure 7-54).

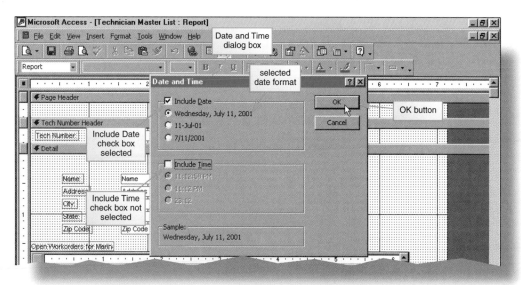

FIGURE 7-54

2 Click the OK button to add the date. Point to the boundary of the newly-added Date control away from any of the handles. The pointer shape changes to a hand as in Figure 7-55.

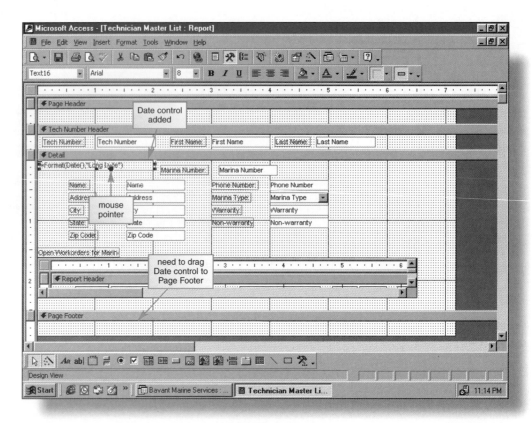

FIGURE 7-55

3 Drag the Date control to the position shown in Figure 7-56.

The date is added to the report.

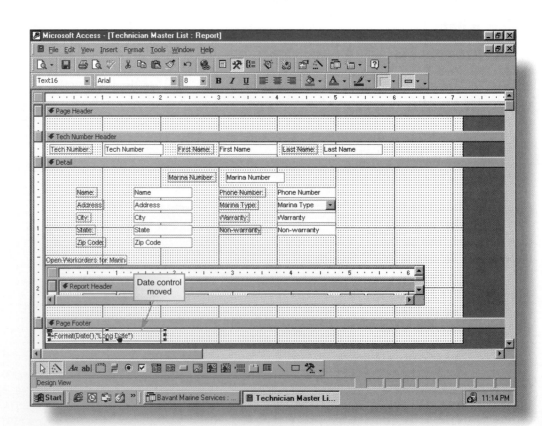

FIGURE 7-56

Adding a Page Number

To add a page number to a report, use the Page Numbers command on the Insert menu. When you do, you will be given a choice of a variety of page number formats and positions. Perform the following steps to add a page number.

 To Add a Page Number

1 Click Insert on the menu bar and then click Page Numbers on the Insert menu. Be sure Page N of M, Bottom of Page [Footer], Right alignment, and Show Number on First Page are selected and then point to the OK button.

The Page Numbers dialog box displays (Figure 7-57).

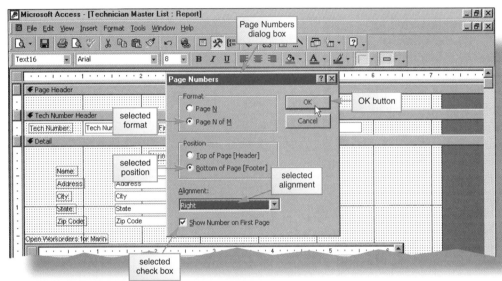

FIGURE 7-57

2 Click the OK button to add a page number. Drag the Page Number control to the position shown in Figure 7-58.

The page number is added.

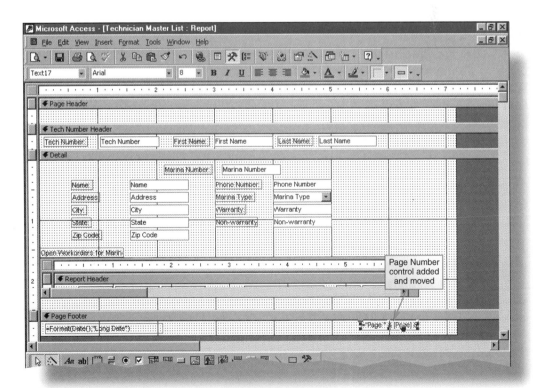

FIGURE 7-58

Bolding Labels

In the report shown in Figure 7-1a on page A 7.5, the labels are all bold. To bold the contents of one or more labels, change the Font Weight property to Bold. Perform the following steps to select all the labels and then change the Font Weight property.

 To Bold Labels

1 **Click the label for the Tech Number control to select it. Hold down the SHIFT key while selecting each of the other labels. Right-click any of the selected labels and point to Properties.**

The shortcut menu displays (Figure 7-59).

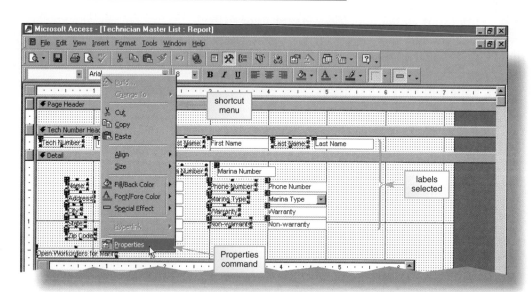

FIGURE 7-59

2 **Click properties. Click the down scroll arrow to display the Font Weight property. Click the Font Weight property and point to Bold in the list of available font weights.**

The Multiple selection property sheet displays (Figure 7-60) with the list of available font weights.

3 **Click Bold and then close the Multiple selection property sheet by clicking its Close button. Click somewhere outside the labels to deselect the labels.**

The labels are all bold.

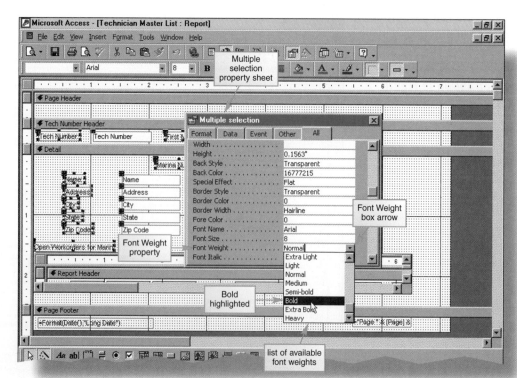

FIGURE 7-60

Adding a Title

A report title is added as a label. Assuming that the title is to display on each page, it should be added to the page header. (If it only is to display once at the beginning of the report, it instead would be added to the report header.) Perform the following steps to add a title to the page header.

 To Add a Title

1 **Point to the lower boundary of the page header.**

The pointer changes to a double-pointing arrow (Figure 7-61).

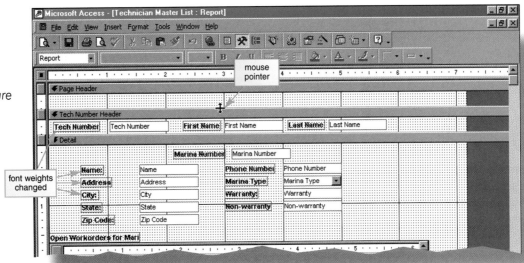

FIGURE 7-61

2 **Drag the lower boundary of the page header to the approximate position shown in Figure 7-62 and point to the Label button in the toolbox.**

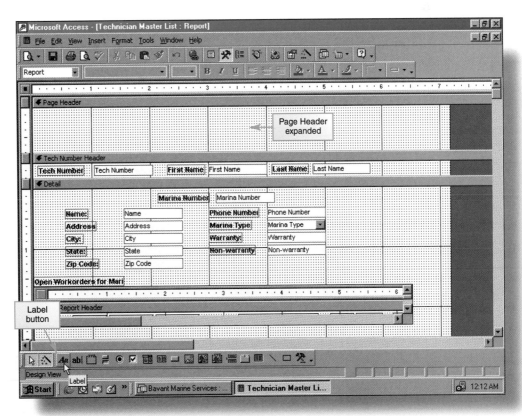

FIGURE 7-62

3 **Click the Label button and move the mouse pointer, which has changed to a plus sign with a label, to the position shown in Figure 7-63.**

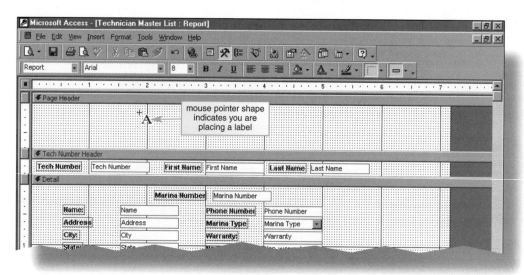

FIGURE 7-63

4 **Drag the pointer from the position shown in Figure 7-63 to the position shown in Figure 7-64.**

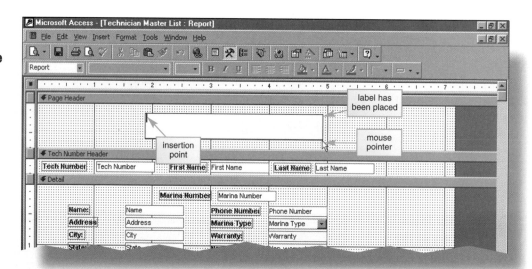

FIGURE 7-64

5 **Type** Technician Master List **as the title.**

The title is entered (Figure 7-65).

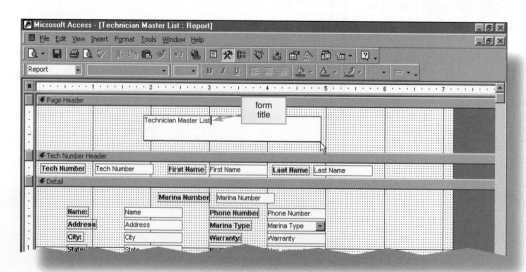

FIGURE 7-65

6 Click somewhere outside the label containing the title to deselect the label. Next, right-click the label containing the title. Click Properties on the shortcut menu. Click the down scroll arrow so that the Font Name property displays. Click the Font Name property, click the Font Name box arrow and scroll down until Script MT Bold displays. Point to Script MT Bold. If Script MT Bold does not display in your list of fonts, pick another font.

The Label: Label18 (your number may be different) property sheet displays (Figure 7-66) with the list of available fonts.

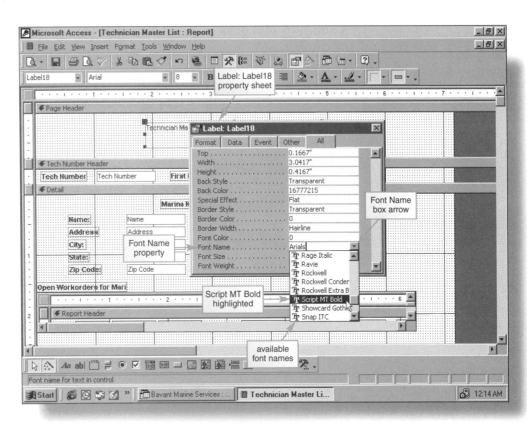

FIGURE 7-66

7 Click Script MT Bold (or another font if Script MT Bold is not in your list.) Click the Font Size property, click the Font Size box arrow, and then click 20 as the new font size. Click the down scroll arrow so that the Text Align property displays. Click the Text Align property, click the Text Align box arrow, and then click Distribute. Close the property sheet by clicking its Close button.

The format of the title is changed (Figure 7-67).

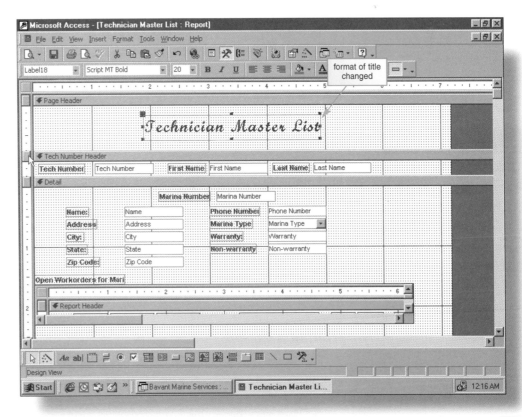

FIGURE 7-67

Margins

If you find you make the same changes to the margins on all your reports, you may wish to change the default margins. To do so, click Tools on the menu bar, click Options on the Tools menu, click the General tab, and then specify the desired margins.

Changing Margins

The report just created is slightly too wide to print across the width of the page. You could modify the report to decrease the width. If, however, you do not need to reduce it by much, it usually is easier to adjust the margins. To do so, use the Page Setup command as in the following steps, which reduces both the left and right margins to 0.5 inch.

 ## To Change the Margins

1 **Click File on the menu bar and then point to Page Setup on the File menu.**

The File menu displays (Figure 7-68)

2 **Click Page Setup. Be sure the Margins tab is selected. Change both the Left and Right margins to .5. Click the OK button.**

The margins are changed.

3 **Close the window containing the report design by clicking its Close Window button. Click the Yes button to save the changes.**

The completed report displays similarly to the one shown in Figure 7-1a on page A 7.5.

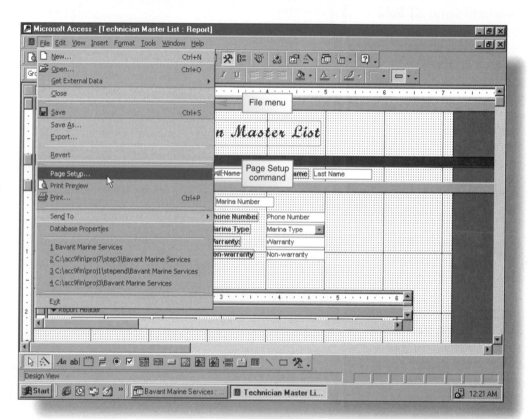

FIGURE 7-68

Printing a Report

To print a report, right-click the report in the Database window, and then click Print on the shortcut menu. Perform the steps on the next page to print the Technician Master List.

TO PRINT A REPORT

① If necessary, in the Database window, click the Reports object. Right-click Technician Master List.

② Click Print on the shortcut menu.

The report prints.

Mailing Labels

In order to print mailing labels, you create a special type of report. When this report prints, the data will display on the mailing labels all aligned correctly and in the order you specify.

Creating Labels

You create labels just as you create reports. There is a wizard, the Label Wizard, that assists you in the process. Using the wizard, you can specify the type and dimensions of the label, the font used for the label, and the contents of the label. Perform the following steps to create the labels.

More About

Mailing Labels

If you need to print labels that are not included in the list of available labels, you have two options. You can attempt to find labels in the list whose dimensions match your dimensions. You also can click the Customize button and specify precisely the dimensions you need.

 To Create Labels

① If necessary, in the Database window, click Tables on the Objects bar, and then click Technician. Click the New Object: Report button arrow on the Database window toolbar and then click Report. Click Label Wizard and then point to the OK button.

The New Report dialog box displays (Figure 7-69).

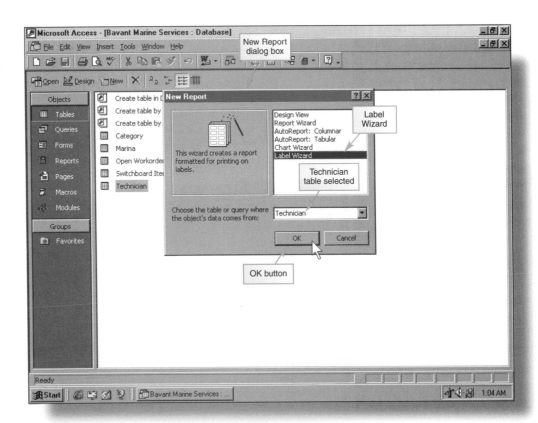

FIGURE 7-69

2 Click the OK button. Click English as the Unit of Measure and then click the Filter by manufacturer box arrow and point to Avery.

The Label Wizard dialog box displays (Figure 7-70) with the list of label manufacturers.

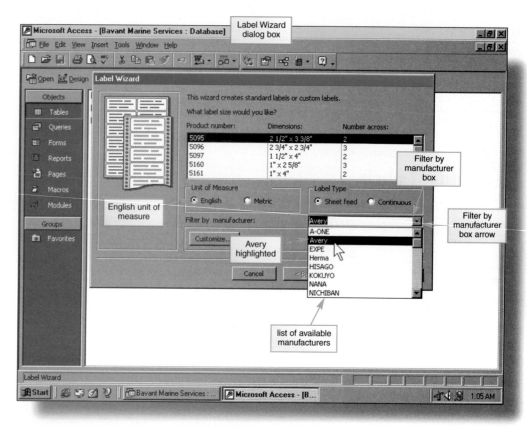

FIGURE 7-70

3 Click Avery. Be sure product number 5095 is selected and then point to the Next button.

The list of Avery labels displays (Figure 7-71).

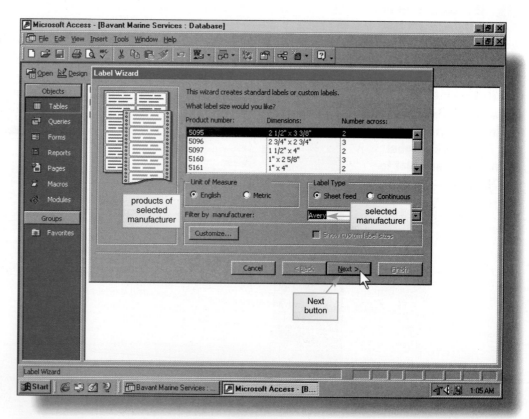

FIGURE 7-71

4 Click the Next button. Click the Next button a second time to accept the default font and color.

The Label Wizard dialog box displays asking for the contents of the mailing labels (Figure 7-72).

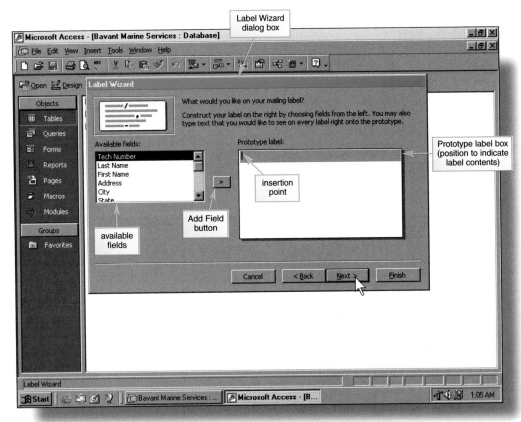

FIGURE 7-72

5 Select the First Name field, click the Add Field button, press the SPACEBAR, select the Last Name field, and then click the Add Field button. Click the second line in the label and then add the Address field. Click the third line of the label. Add the City field, type , (a comma), press the SPACEBAR, add the State field, press the SPACEBAR twice, and then add the Zip Code field. Point to the Next button.

The contents of the label are complete (Figure 7-73).

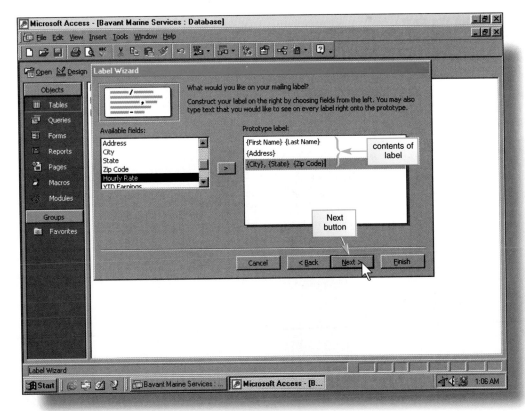

FIGURE 7-73

6 Click the Next button. Select the Zip Code field as the field to sort by and then click the Add Field button. Point to the Next button.

The Zip Code field is selected as the field to sort by (Figure 7-74).

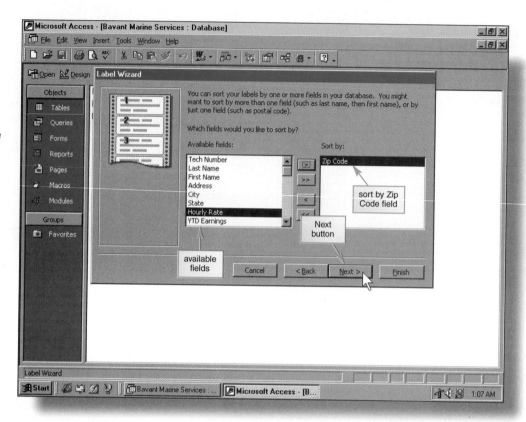

FIGURE 7-74

7 Click the Next button. Be sure the name for the report (labels) is Labels Technician and then point to the Finish button (Figure 7-75).

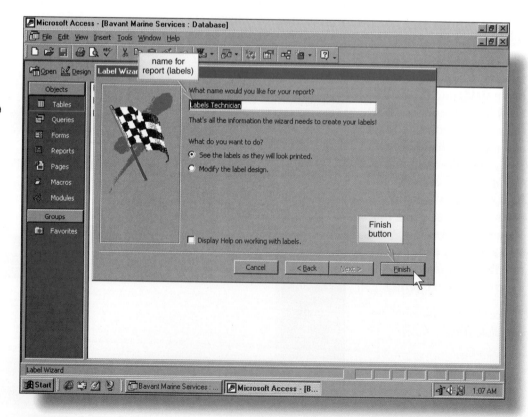

FIGURE 7-75

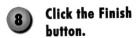

Click the Finish button.

The labels display (Figure 7-76) similarly to the ones in Figure 7-1b on page A 7.5.

9 **Close the window containing the labels by clicking its Close button.**

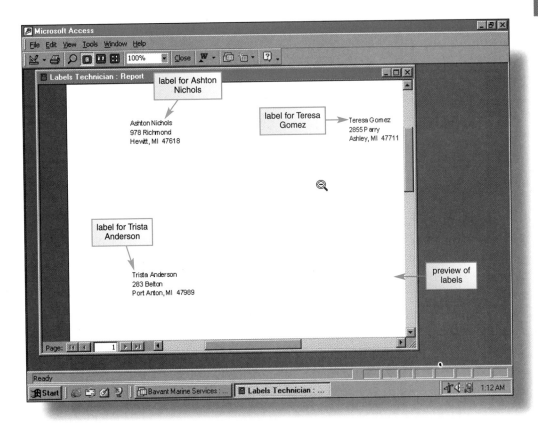

FIGURE 7-76

Printing the labels

To print the labels, right-click the label report in the Database window, and then click Print on the shortcut menu. Perform the following steps to print the labels just created.

TO PRINT LABELS

1 If necessary, in the Database window, click the Reports object. Right-click Labels Technician.

2 Click Print on the shortcut menu. If a warning message displays, click the OK button.

The labels print.

Closing the Database

The following step closes the database by closing its Database window.

TO CLOSE A DATABASE

1 Click the Close button for the Bavant Marine Services : Database window.

More About

Printing Labels

If you are printing labels on a dot-matrix or tractor-feed printer, you may have to make some changes to the page size in order to have the labels print correctly. To do so, click the Start button on the Windows desktop, click Settings, and then click Printers. Right-click your printer, click Properties, click the Paper tab, and then click the Custom icon. You can then make whatever changes might be necessary.

CASE PERSPECTIVE SUMMARY

In Project 7, you assisted the management of Bavant Marine Services by helping them add the Category and Open Workorders tables to their databases. You created a parameter query for them so they could examine easily the open workorders for any marinas in which they were interested. You created a detailed report that lists all technicians, marinas, and open workorders. Finally, you created mailing labels for the technicians at Bavant.

Project Summary

In Project 7, you added two new tables to the Bavant Marine Services database. You then related these new tables to the existing tables. You also created a Lookup Wizard field. You created a query in which you changed the join properties as well as some field properties. You transformed the query to a paramater query. You also created two queries to be used by the report. You then created the report from scratch, using Design view rather than the Report Wizard. In the report, you used grouping and also included a subreport. Finally, you created mailing labels for the Technician table.

What You Should Know

Having completed this project, you now should be able to perform the following tasks:

- Add a Date *(A 7.39)*
- Add a Page Number *(A 7.41)*
- Add a Subreport *(A 7.29)*
- Add a Title *(A 7.43)*
- Add the Fields *(A 7.27)*
- Bold Labels *(A 7.42)*
- Change Field Properties *(A 7.17)*
- Change Join Properties *(A 7.16)*
- Change the Layout *(A 7.11)*
- Change the Margins *(A 7.46)*
- Close a Database *(A 7.51)*
- Create a Lookup Wizard Field *(A 7.13)*
- Create a Parameter Query *(A 7.21)*
- Create a Query *(A 7.15, A 7.23)*
- Create Labels *(A 7.47)*

- Create the Queries *(A 7.15)*
- Create the Initial Report *(A 7.24)*
- Create the New Tables *(A 7.9)*
- Filter a Query's Recordset *(A 7.19)*
- Import the Data *(A 7.10)*
- Modify the Subreport *(A 7.33)*
- Move the Subreport *(A 7.38)*
- Open a Database *(A 7.8)*
- Print a Report *(A 7.47)*
- Print Labels *(A 7.51)*
- Relate Several Tables *(A 7.12)*
- Run a Parameter Query *(A 7.22)*
- Run the Query and Change the Layout *(A 7.18)*
- Save the Report *(A 7.28)*

Apply Your Knowledge

Project Reinforcement at www.scsite.com/off2000/reinforce.htm

1 Adding Tables to the Sidewalk Scrapers Database

Instructions: Start Access. Open the Sidewalk Scrapers database from the Access Data Disk. See the inside back cover for instructions for downloading the Access Data Disk or see your instructor for information on accessing the files required for this book. You will create two new tables for the Sidewalk Scrapers database. The Rate table contains information on the rate that each customer pays for snow removal service. The structure and data are shown for the Rate table in Figure 7-77. There is a one-to-one relationship between the Customer table and the Rate table. The Service table contains information on when the snow removal service was performed. Because this city receives lots of snow, snow removal can be done more than once in a single day. Therefore, for each record to be unique, the primary key for the Service table must be the combination of customer number, service date, and service time. There is a one-to-many relationship between the Customer table and the Service table. The structure and data for the Service table are shown in Figure 7-78. Perform the following tasks.

1. Create the Rate table using the structure shown in Figure 7-77. Use the name Rate for the table.
2. Import the Rates worksheet to the database. The worksheet is in the Scrapers workbook on your Access Data Disk. When the Import Spreadsheet Wizard dialog box displays, be sure the Rates worksheet is selected. Be sure to check First Row Contains Column Headings. Open the table in Datasheet view and resize the columns to best fit the data. Save the changes to the layout of the table.
3. Print the Rate table.

Structure of Rate table

FIELD NAME	DATA TYPE	FIELD SIZE	PRIMARY KEY?	DESCRIPTION
Customer Number	Text	4	Yes	Customer Number (Primary Key)
Rate	Currency			Rate Charged for Snow Removal

Data for Rate table

CUSTOMER NUMBER	RATE
AL25	$13.00
AT43	$14.00
CH65	$12.00
CI05	$11.00
JB51	$15.00
LK44	$20.00
MD60	$14.00
ME02	$16.00
ST21	$12.00

FIGURE 7-77

(continued)

Apply Your Knowledge

Project Reinforcement at www.scsite.com/off2000/reinforce.htm

Adding Tables to the Sidewalk Scrapers Database *(continued)*

4. Create the Service table using the structure shown in Figure 7-78. The primary key is the combination of the Customer Number, Service Date, and Service Time fields. Use the name Service for the table.

Structure of Service table

FIELD NAME	DATA TYPE	FIELD SIZE	PRIMARY KEY?	DESCRIPTION
Customer Number	Text	4	Yes	Customer Number (Portion of Primary Key)
Service Date	Date/Time		Yes	Date that Snow Removal was Performed (Portion of Primary Key)
Service Time	Date/Time		Yes	Time that Snow Removal was Performed (Portion of Primary Key)

5. Import the Services worksheet to the database. The worksheet is in the Scrapers workbook on your Access Data Disk. When the Import Spreadsheet Wizard dialog box displays, be sure the Services worksheet is selected. Be sure to check First Row Contains Column Headings. Open the table in Datasheet view and resize the columns to best fit the data. Save the changes to the layout of the table.
6. Print the Service table.
7. Click the Relationships button in the Database window, and add the Rate and Service tables to the Relationships window. Create a one-to-one relationship between the Customer table and the Rate table. Create a one-to-many relationship between the Customer table and the Service table. Print the Relationships window by making sure the Relationships window is open, clicking File on the menu bar, and then clicking Print Relationships.

Data for Service table

CUSTOMER NUMBER	SERVICE DATE	SERVICE TIME
AT43	01/04/2001	1:30:00 PM
AT43	01/05/2001	9:00:00 PM
CH65	01/04/2001	2:30:00 PM
CH65	01/04/2001	10:00:00 PM
CI05	01/04/2001	9:00:00 AM
CI05	01/04/2001	5:00:00 PM
JB51	01/05/2001	10:00:00 AM
LK44	01/05/2001	12:00:00 PM
MD60	01/05/2001	10:00:00 AM
ME02	01/04/2001	7:30:00 AM
ME02	01/04/2001	4:00:00 PM
ST21	01/04/2001	6:00:00 AM
ST21	01/04/2001	3:30:00 PM
ST21	01/05/2001	1:00:00 AM

FIGURE 7-78

8. Create a query that joins the Customer and Service tables. All records in the Customer table should display regardless of whether there is a matching record in the Service table. Display the Customer Number, Name, Service Date, and Service Time fields in the query results. Change the caption for Service Date to Snow Removal Date and the caption for Service Time to Snow Removal Time.
9. Run the query and print the results.
10. Filter the recordset to find only those customers who had snow removal performed on January 5, 2001.
11. Print the results.

In the Lab

1 Creating Queries, a Report, and Mailing Labels for the School Connection Database

Problem: The Booster's Club wants to track items that are being reordered from the vendor. The club must know when an item was ordered and how many were ordered. The club may place an order with a vendor one day and then find that they need to order more of the same item before the original order is filled. The club also wants to be able to query the database to find out whether an item is on order. Finally, they want a report that displays vendor information as well as information about the item and its order status.

Instructions: Open the School Connection database from the Access Data Disk. See the inside back cover for instructions for downloading the Access Data Disk or see your instructor for information on accessing the files required for this book. Perform the following tasks.

1. Create a table in which to store the reorder information using the structure shown in Figure 7-79. Create an input mask for the Date Ordered field in the format MM/dd/yyyy. Use the name Reorder for the table.

2. Add the data shown in Figure 7-79 to the Reorder table.

3. Add the Reorder table to the Relationships window and establish a one-to-many relationship between the Item and Reorder tables. Print the Relationships window by making sure the Relationships window is open, clicking File on the menu bar, and then clicking Print Relationships.

4. Open the Reorder table in Design view and change the Item Id field to a Lookup Wizard field. Both the Item Id and Description fields from the Item table should display.

5. Print the table.

6. Create a query that joins the Item, Reorder, and Vendor tables. The query should display all items in the Item table whether or not they are on reorder. Display the Item Id, Description, Date Ordered, Number Ordered, Cost, and Vendor Name fields. Change the caption for Number Ordered to On Order. Run the query and print the results.

Structure of Reorder table

FIELD NAME	DATA TYPE	FIELD SIZE	PRIMARY KEY?	DESCRIPTION
Item Id	Text	4	Yes	Item Id Number (Portion of Primary Key)
Date Ordered	Date/Time		Yes	Date Item Ordered (Remainder of Primary Key)
Number Ordered	Number			Number of Items Ordered

Data for Reorder table

ITEM ID	DATE ORDERED	NUMBER ORDERED
CM12	10/05/2001	25
DM05	09/10/2001	5
DM05	10/02/2001	10
MN04	09/12/2001	2
MN04	10/04/2001	2
PL05	09/12/2001	4
WA34	09/14/2001	5
WA34	09/22/2001	4

FIGURE 7-79

(continued)

In the Lab

Creating Queries, a Report, and Mailing Labels for the School Connection Database *(continued)*

7. Use filter by selection to display only those records where the vendor is Trinkets 'n More. Print the results.

8. Create a parameter query for the Reorder table. The user should be able to enter a beginning and ending item id. Display all fields in the query result. Run the query to find all records where the item id is between DM05 and PL05. Print the results.

9. Run the query again to find all records where item number is WA34. Print the results.

10. Create the report shown in Figure 7-80. The report uses the Vendors and Items query as the basis for the main report and the Reorder table as the basis for the subreport. Be sure to include the current date and page numbers on the report. Use the name Vendor Master Report for the report. The report is in the same style as that demonstrated in the project. The report contains clip art in the page header. To add clip art to the report, do the following:

   a. Click the Unbound Object Frame button in the toolbox, move the mouse pointer to the page header and click.

   b. When the Insert Object dialog box displays, make sure the Create New option button is selected. Click Microsoft Clip Gallery in the Object Type box and then click OK.

   c. Click the Pictures tab, click the Academic category, and then click the first clip art item in the second row. Click Insert Clip on the shortcut menu.

   d. Resize the picture to the appropriate size for the page header.

   e. Right-click the object, click Properties on the shortcut menu, and then change the Size Mode to Zoom.

11. Print the report.

12. Create mailing labels for the Vendor table. Use Avery labels 5095 and format the label with name on the first line, address on the second line, and city, state, and zip code on the third line. There is a comma and a space after the city and 2 spaces between the state and the zip code.

13. Print the mailing labels.

In the Lab

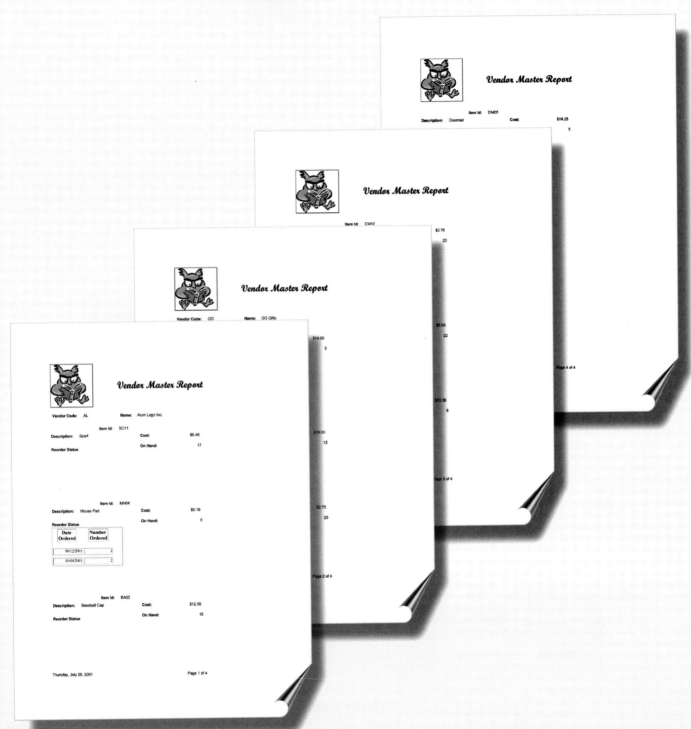

FIGURE 7-80

In the Lab

2 Creating Queries, a Report, and Mailing Labels for the City Area Bus Company Database

Problem: Advertisers contract with City Area Bus Company to advertise for one month. The same ad may run for several months or be replaced monthly with an ad of a different size or design. The advertising sales manager must track the active accounts for the current year and must be able to query the database for information on which advertisers currently have ads they want to display on the buses. The manager also needs a report that lists the sales rep, the accounts that the sales rep handles, and a list of the active ads.

Instructions: Open the City Area Bus Company database from the Access Data Disk. See the inside back cover for instructions for downloading the Access Data Disk or see your instructor for information on accessing the files required for this book. Perform the following tasks.

1. Create a table in which to store the active account information using the structure shown in Figure 7-81. Use the name Active Accounts for the table.

Structure of Active Accounts table				
FIELD NAME	DATA TYPE	FIELD SIZE	PRIMARY KEY?	DESCRIPTION
Advertiser Id	Text	4	Yes	Advertiser Id (Portion of Primary Key)
Ad Month	Text	3	Yes	Month that Ad Is to Run (Remainder of Primary Key)
Category Code	Text	1		Ad Category

FIGURE 7-81

2. Import the Accounts text file into the Active Accounts table. The text file is on your Data Disk. Be sure to check First Row Contains Column Headings. The data is in delimited format with each field separated by tabs.

3. Create the Category table shown in Figure 7-82. The Category table contains information on the ad category the advertiser has purchased.

Structure of Category table				
FIELD NAME	DATA TYPE	FIELD SIZE	PRIMARY KEY?	DESCRIPTION
Category Code	Text	1	Yes	Category Code (Primary Key)
Description	Text	50		Description of Ad Category

FIGURE 7-82

In the Lab

4. Import the Ad Categories text file into the Category table. The text file is on your Data Disk. Be sure to check the First Row Contains Column Headings box. The data is in delimited format with each field separated by tabs.

5. Open the Relationships window and establish a one-to-many relationship between the Advertiser table and the Active Accounts table and between the Category table and the Active Accounts table. Print the Relationships window by making sure the Relationships window is open, clicking File on the menu bar, and then clicking Print Relationships.

6. Open the Active Accounts table in Design view and change the Category Code field to a Lookup Wizard field.

7. Open the Active Accounts table in Datasheet view and resize the columns to best fit the data. Save the changes to the layout of the table.

8. Print the table.

9. Open the Category table in Datasheet view and resize the columns to best fit the data. Save the changes to the layout of the table.

10. Print the table.

11. Create a query that joins the Advertiser and the Active Accounts table. All Advertisers should display whether or not they have active accounts. Display the Advertiser Id, Name, Month, and Category Code fields. Run the query and print the results.

12. Filter the query results to find all accounts that will run ads during the month of June. Print the results.

13. Create the report shown in Figure 7-83. The report is grouped by Sales Rep Number and includes a subreport. It is in the same style as that demonstrated in the project. Be sure to include the current date and page numbers on the report. Use the name Sales Rep Master Report for the report. (Hint: Create queries for both the main report and the subreport.) Print the report.

14. Create mailing labels for the Advertiser table. Use Avery labels 5095 and format the label with name on the first line, address on the second line, and city, state, and zip code on the third line. There is a comma and a space after the city and 2 spaces between the state and the zip code. Print the mailing labels.

(continued)

In the Lab

Creating Queries, a Report, and Mailing Labels for the City Area Bus Company Database *(continued)*

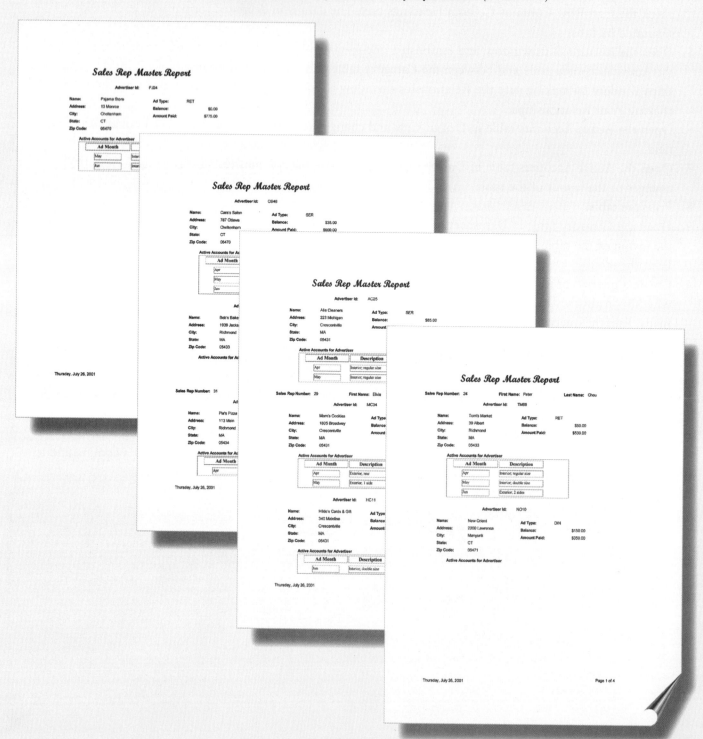

FIGURE 7-83

In the Lab

3 Creating Queries, a Report, and Mailing Labels for the Resort Rentals Database

Problem: The real estate company must keep track of the units that are rented and the individuals who rented the units. Units are rented a week at a time and rentals start on Saturday. They also need to be able to query the database to determine if a particular unit is rented. Finally, they need to prepare reports for the owners that display rental information.

Instructions: Open the Resort Rentals database from the Access Data Disk. See the inside back cover for instructions for downloading the Access Data Disk or see your instructor for information on accessing the files required for this book. Perform the following tasks.

1. Create the Active Rentals table using the structure shown in Figure 7-84. Use the name Active Rentals for the table. Use an input mask for the date in the form MM/dd/yyyy.

Structure of Active Rentals table				
FIELD NAME	DATA TYPE	FIELD SIZE	PRIMARY KEY?	DESCRIPTION
Rental Id	Text	3	Yes	Rental Id (Portion of Primary Key)
Start Date	Date/Time		Yes	Beginning Date of Rental (Remainder of Primary Key)
Length	Number			Length of Time in Weeks of Rental
Renter Id	Text	4		Id of Renter

FIGURE 7-84

2. Import the Rentals workbook into the Active Rentals table. The workbook is on the Access Data Disk. In the Import Spreadsheet Wizard dialog box, click the Show Named Ranges option button and select the Rentals range. Be sure to check First Row Contains Column Headings.

3. Create the Renter table using the structure shown in Figure 7-85. Use the name Renter for the table.

Structure of Renter table				
FIELD NAME	DATA TYPE	FIELD SIZE	PRIMARY KEY?	DESCRIPTION
Renter Id	Text	4	Yes	Renter Id (Primary Key)
First Name	Text	10		First Name of Renter
Last Name	Text	15		Last Name of Renter
Telephone Number	Text	12		Telephone Number (999-999-9999 version)

FIGURE 7-85

(continued)

In the Lab

Creating Queries, a Report, and Mailing Labels for the Resort Rentals Database *(continued)*

4. Import the Rentals workbook into the Renter table. The workbook is on the Access Data Disk. In the Import Spreadsheet Wizard dialog box, click the Show Named Ranges option button and select the Renters range. Be sure to check First Row Contains Column Headings.

5. Open the Relationships window and establish a one-to-many relationship between the Renter table and the Active Rentals table. Establish a one-to-many relationship between the Rental Unit table and the Active Rentals table. Print the Relationships window by making sure the Relationships window is open, clicking File on the menu bar, and then clicking Print Relationships.

6. Open the Active Rentals table in Design view and change the Renter Id field to a Lookup Wizard field. The Renter Id, First Name, and Last Name fields should display.

7. Open the Active Rentals table in Datasheet view, resize the columns to best fit the data, save the changes, and print the table.

8. Open the Renter table in Datasheet view, resize the columns to best fit the data, save the changes, and print the table.

9. Create a join query for the Rental Unit and Active Rentals tables. All rental units should display in the result regardless of whether the unit is rented. Display the Rental Id, Address, City, Weekly Rate, Start Date, and Length fields. Change the caption for the Length field to Weeks Rented. Run the query and print the results.

10. Filter the query results to find all rental units that rent for $1,000 per week. Print the results.

11. Create a parameter query to enter a start date. The query should display the rental id, start date, length, and the first and last name of the renter. Run the query to find all records where the start date is 12/1/2001. Print the results.

12. Run the query again to find all records where the start date is 11/24/2001. Print the results.

13. Create the report shown in Figure 7-86. The report includes a subreport. Group the report by owner id. Print the report.

14. Create mailing labels for the Owner table. Use Avery labels 5095 and format the label with first and last name on the first line, address on the second line, and city, state, and zip code on the third line. There is a comma and a space after the city and 2 spaces between the state and the zip code. Print the mailing labels.

In the Lab

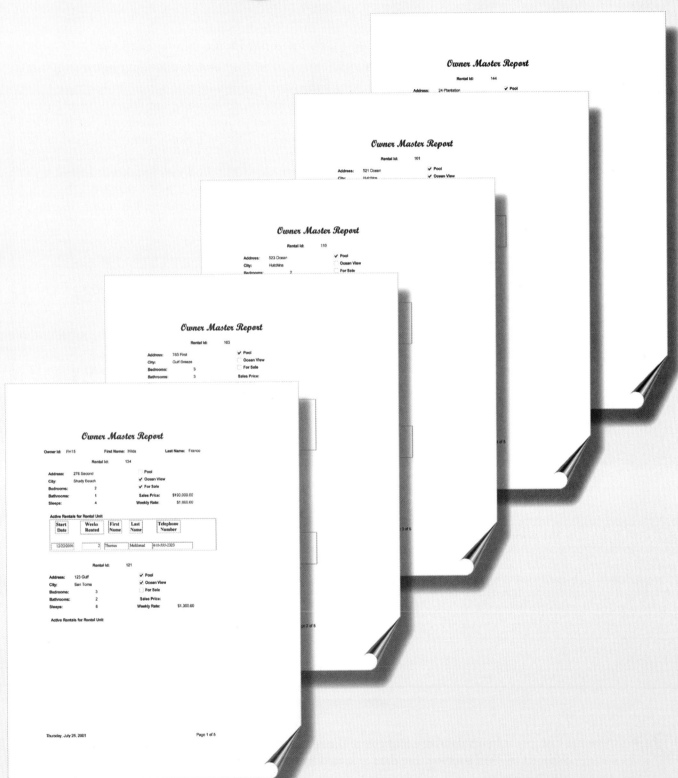

FIGURE 7-86

Cases and Places

The difficulty of these case studies varies:
▶ are the least difficult; ▶▶ are more difficult; and ▶▶▶ are the most difficult.

1 ▶ Use the Computer Items database on the Access Data Disk for this assignment. The Computer Club needs to add a table to the database that tracks the reorder status of items. The structure of the Reorder Status table and the data for the table are shown in Figure 7-87. There is a one-to-many relationship between the Item table and the Reorder Status table. The Item Id field in the Reorder Status table should be a Lookup Wizard field and the Reorder Date field should use the MM/dd/yyyy input mask. You may need to change the layout of the table. Print the Reorder Status table. Create a query that joins the Item, Reorder Status, and Supplier tables. Display the Item Id, Description, Reorder Date, Reorder Number, Cost, and Supplier Name fields. Include a calculated field, Reorder Cost, that is the result of multiplying Cost and Reorder Number.

Structure of Reorder Status table

FIELD NAME	DATA TYPE	FIELD SIZE	PRIMARY KEY?	DESCRIPTION
Item Id	Text	4	Yes	Item Id Number (Portion of Primary Key)
Reorder Date	Date/Time		Yes	Date Item was Reordered (Remainder of Primary Key)
Reorder Number	Number			Number of Items Ordered

Data for Reorder Status table

ITEM ID	DATE ORDERED	NUMBER ORDERED
1663	10/05/2001	10
1683	09/10/2001	12
1683	10/02/2001	5
5810	09/12/2001	4
5810	10/04/2001	2
6140	09/12/2001	2
6140	09/14/2001	5
3923	09/22/2001	4

FIGURE 7-87

2 ▶ Use the Computer Items database and create the report shown in Figure 7-88. The report groups the data by supplier. Within supplier, the data is sorted by item id. The report includes a subreport for the reorder information.

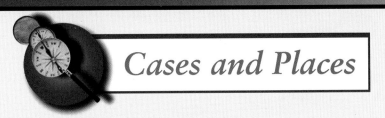

Cases and Places

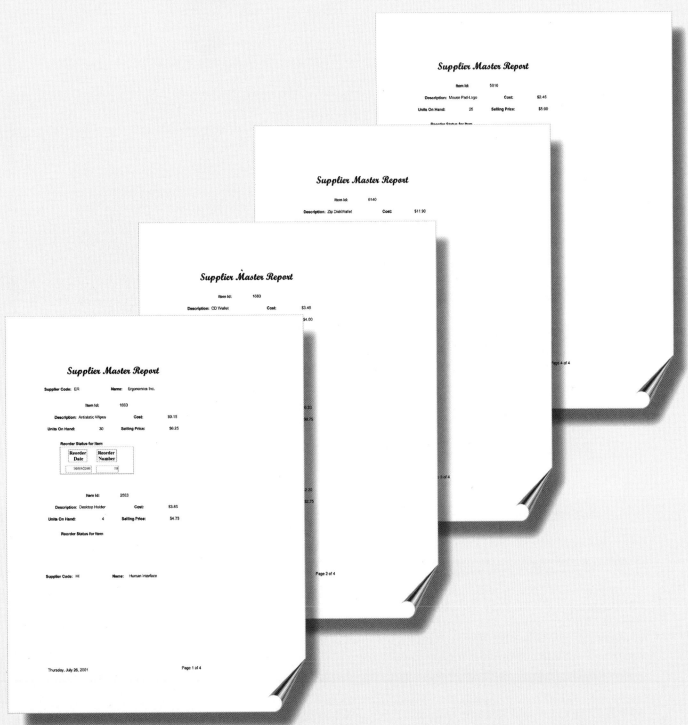

FIGURE 7-88

Cases and Places

3 ▶▶ Use the Galaxy Books database on the Access Data Disk for this assignment. The owner of the bookstore has several customers who have purchased books on the layaway plan. She wants to add data on these customers and the books they are buying to the database. Because a customer can purchase more than one book, the primary key for the Book Order table is the combination of the Customer Number and Book Code fields. The structure of the Book Order and Customer tables are shown in Figure 7-89. The data for the tables is in the Books workbook on the Access Data Disk. Update the Galaxy Books database to include these tables, establish the necessary relationships, modify the table designs to include Lookup Wizard fields, if appropriate, and print the tables.

Structure of Book Order table

FIELD NAME	DATA TYPE	FIELD SIZE	PRIMARY KEY?	DESCRIPTION
Book Code	Text	4	Yes	Book Code (Portion of Primary Key)
Customer Number	Text	3	Yes	Customer Ordering Book (Remainder of Primary Key)
Order Date	Date/Time			Date Ordered

Structure of Customer table

FIELD NAME	DATA TYPE	FIELD SIZE	PRIMARY KEY?	DESCRIPTION
Customer Number	Text	4	Yes	Customer Number (Primary Key)
Last Name	Text	15		Customer Last Name
First Name	Text	15		Customer First Name
Address	Text	15		Address
City	Text	10		City
State	Text	2		State
Zip Code	Text	5		Zip Code

FIGURE 7-89

4 ▶▶ Create a report for the Galaxy Books database that is similar in style to the report created for Bavant Marine Services. The report should group data by publisher and display the publisher code and name in the group header. For each publisher, display information about each book sorted in book code order and include a subreport for any book orders.

5 ▶▶▶ Use the Copy and Rename features of Windows to copy the Galaxy Books database and rename it as the Milky Way database. The owner of the bookstore is adding several new books that have multiple authors. For example, the authors of a new book, Asteroids and Meteors are H Brewster and G Chou. Modify the design of the Milky Way database to allow for multiple authors for a book.

Microsoft **Access 2000**

Microsoft Access 2000

Customizing Forms Using Visual Basic for Applications (VBA), Charts and PivotTable Objects

PROJECT 8

You will have mastered the material in this project when you can:

O
B
J
E
C
T
I
V
E
S

- Add command buttons to a form
- Modify VBA code associated with a command button
- Add a combo box to a form
- Use a combo box
- Modify the properties of a combo box
- Create a form using Design view
- Add a subform to a form
- Add a chart to a form
- Create a PivotTable form
- Use a PivotTable form

eCommerce

$111 billion in sales

Smart Shopping

Happy Buyers

Consumer e-commerce spending has increased steadily over the last few years and continues to soar. Americans comprise 44 percent of the of the Web population, spending more than $111 billion in 1999. On a regular basis, popular purchases include books, software, music, travel, hardware, clothing, and electronics. Auctions, prescription sales, holiday purchases, and grocery shopping are among many more goods and services selling via the World Wide Web.

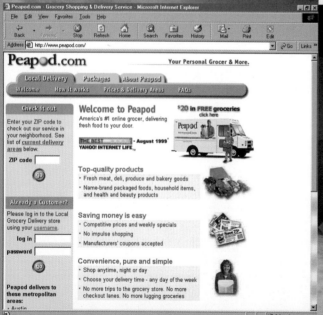

Industry experts speculate that Web surfers purchasing online could represent up to 20 percent of the grocery volume by 2003. From the convenience of their home computers, shopping in cyberspace has simplified this mundane task for many individuals in this fast-paced world. Consider that a trip to the grocery store requires 66 minutes on average. From hunting for a parking space to waiting in long checkout lines, the entire experience often is tiring and frustrating.

Using a service called Peapod, consumers in eight metropolitan areas of the United States from New York to San Francisco already are shopping regularly online. Entering data into Peapod Personal Grocer online forms, shoppers place their orders from work or home, day or night. With features such as Express Shop, you can locate all of your shopping items at once, or Personal Lists lets you organize your list into categories, making your shopping experience simple and relaxed.

Shoppers enter the store online, select, and then purchase items on their computers via forms and buttons. These forms and buttons are similar to the form and command button you will create in this Access 2000 project using advanced form techniques, the Form Design window, and an appropriate wizard. Forms allow users to place their orders, find items, create shopping lists, and then add the items to their shopping carts with a simple click of a button on the Web page.

Details such as the price and nutritional content of each item are kept in a database that is integrated with a billing system and a customer database. The products database is updated daily as prices change, new items are added to the stores' shelves, and unpopular items are removed. Produce prices change weekly.

A nutrition-conscious shopper can query the database to display a picture of the product, view its nutrition facts, and sort items by nutritional content. Selective shoppers instantly can compare prices in the database to find the best deals. Buyers can view items in their shopping carts, check subtotals any time to stay within budgets, redeem manufacturer and electronic coupons, and designate a delivery time.

Peapod delivers groceries to the customer's door. Deliveries are free for orders over $60. The driver accepts payment by check, credit card, or automatic debit from a checking account and even will return bags for recycling. Customers report top-quality products, competitive pricing, and convenience as their main reasons for using the Peapod service. The primary customer base consists of two-income families with children, individuals with disabilities, and the elderly. These groups find that the convenience of being able to order at any time and place gives them flexibility in their busy lifestyles, independence, and less stress.

Visit Peapod (www.peapod.com) on the Web to see America's #1 online grocer and how it works.

Microsoft Access 2000

Customizing Forms Using Visual Basic for Applications (VBA), Charts, and PivotTable Objects

PROJECT 8

CASE PERSPECTIVE

The management of Bavant Marine Services has three additional requests. First, they would like some improvements to the Marina Update Form. This includes placing buttons on the form for moving to the next record, moving to the previous record, adding a record, deleting a record, and closing the form. They also want users of the form to have a simple way of searching for a marina using the marina's name. They also would like an additional form, one that lists the number and name of technicians. This form should include a subform listing details concerning open workorders for each technician. It also should include two charts that graphically illustrate the number of hours spent by each technician in each of the service categories. Finally, they would like a PivotTable form that summarizes workorder data. Your task is to modify the Marina Update Form in accordance with their requests and to create the two additional forms.

Introduction

By including both command buttons and a combo box that allows users to search for marinas by name, you will enhance the Marina Update Form you created earlier (Figure 8-1). When clicked, a **command button** executes a command. For example, after creating the Next Record command button, clicking it will move to the next record.

When you add the command buttons and the combo box to the form, you will use appropriate Access wizards. The **wizards** create the button or the combo box to your specifications and place it on the form. They also create an event procedure for the button or the combo box. An **event procedure** is a series of steps that Access will carry out when an event, such as the clicking of a command button, occurs. For example, when you click the Delete Record button, the steps in the event procedure created for the Delete Record button will be executed. This procedure will cause the record to be deleted. Event procedures are written in a language called **Visual Basic for Applications**, or **VBA**, which is standard throughout Microsoft applications.

Generally, you do not need to be aware that these event procedures exist. Access creates and uses them automatically. Occasionally, you may wish to make changes to an event procedure. For example, without making changes, clicking the Add Record button clears the field contents on the form so you can enter a new record, yet, it would not produce an insertion point in the Marina Number field. You would be required to take special action, such as clicking the Marina Number field, before you could begin entering data. You can rectify this by making a change to the event procedure for the Add Record button.

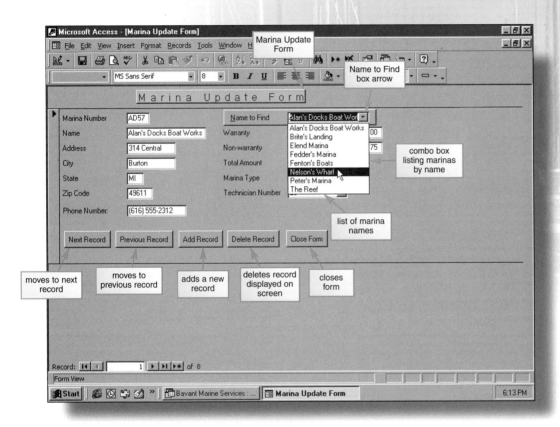

FIGURE 8-1

You also will create the form shown in Figure 8-2a on the next page and the PivotTable object in Figure 8-2b on the next page. The form in Figure 8-2a lists the Tech Number, First Name, and Last Name fields from the Technician table. It also contains a subform, which lists the Marina Number, Name, Location, Category Number, Total Hours (est), and Hours Spent for each workorder at any marina assigned to each technician. The form also contains two charts. In both charts, the bars represent the various service categories. The height of the bars in the left chart represents the total of the estimated hours. The height of the bars in the right chart represents the total of the hours spent.

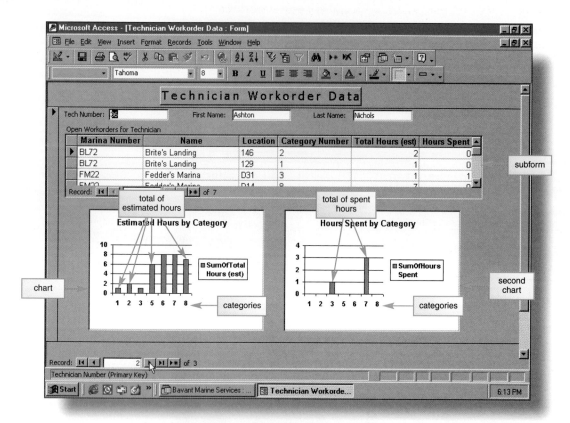

FIGURE 8-2a

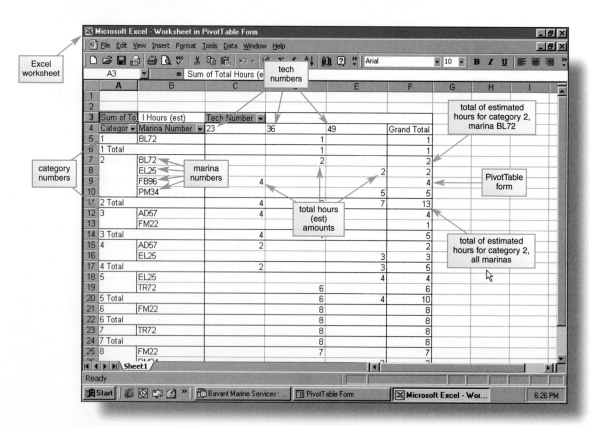

FIGURE 8-2b

The form in Figure 8-2b shows a **PivotTable** object, a special type of worksheet that allows you to summarize data in a variety of ways. To create a PivotTable form in Access, use the PivotTable Wizard. By clicking a button on this form, you can display the PivotTable object in Excel as shown in Figure 8-2b. You can then use Excel features to manipulate the PivotTable object.

The PivotTable object shown in Figure 8-2b shows the category numbers in the first column. The second column contains marina numbers. The next three columns contain the technician numbers. The final column contains totals.

Row 7 in the table, for example, indicates that for category 2 and marina BL72, technician 23 has 0 hours, technician 36 has 2 hours, and technician 49 has 0 hours, for a total of 2 hours. Row 8 indicates that for category 2 and marina EL25, technician 23 has 0 hours, technician 36 has 0 hours, and technician 49 has 2 hours, for a total of 2 hours. Row 11 indicates that for category 2, technician 23 has a total of 4 hours, technician 36 has a total of 2 hours, and technician 49 has a total of 7 hours, for a total of 13 hours.

One advantage to PivotTable forms is that they can be manipulated to change the way the data is summarized. You could interchange the Tech Number and Category Number fields so that the Tech Number field rather than the Category Number field would summarize the data as in the Figure 8-2b.

Project Eight — Using Advanced Form Techniques

You begin this project by adding the necessary command buttons to the Marina Update Form. Then, you add the combo box that allows users to find a marina using the marina's name. Next you will create a query that will be used in the form you will create. You then create the form from scratch using Design view. You will add a subform and two charts to this form. Finally, you will create a PivotTable form using Access.

Opening the Database

Before completing the tasks in this project, you must open the database. Perform the following steps to open the database.

TO OPEN A DATABASE

1. Click the Start button on the taskbar.
2. Click Open Office Document on the Start menu, and then click 3½ Floppy (A:) in the Look in box. If necessary, double-click the Access folder. Make sure the Bavant Marine Services database is selected.
3. Click the Open button.

The database opens and the Bavant Marine Services : Database window displays.

Enhancing the Form

You will enhance the form by adding command buttons and a combo box. The command buttons provide additional methods for performing common tasks. The combo box helps users to locate marinas easily.

Microsoft **Access 2000**

More About

Control Wizards

There are wizards associated with many of the controls. The wizards lead you through a series of dialog boxes that assist you in creating the control. To use the wizards, the Control Wizards button must be recessed. If not, you will need to specify all the details of the control without any assistance.

Adding Command Buttons to the Form

To add command buttons, you will use the Control Wizards button and Command Button button in the toolbox. Using the series of Command Button Wizard dialog boxes, you need to provide the action that should be taken when the button is clicked. Several categories of actions are available.

In the Record Navigation category, you will select the action Goto Next Record for one of the buttons. From the same category, you will select Goto Previous Record for another button. Other buttons will use the Add New Record and the Delete Record actions from the Record Operations category. The Close Form button will use the Close Form action from the Form Operations category.

Perform the following steps to add command buttons to move to the next record, move to the previous record, add a record, delete a record, and close the form.

 ## To Add Command Buttons to a Form

1 Click Forms on the Objects bar, right-click Marina Update Form, and then point to Design View on the shortcut menu.

The shortcut menu displays (Figure 8-3).

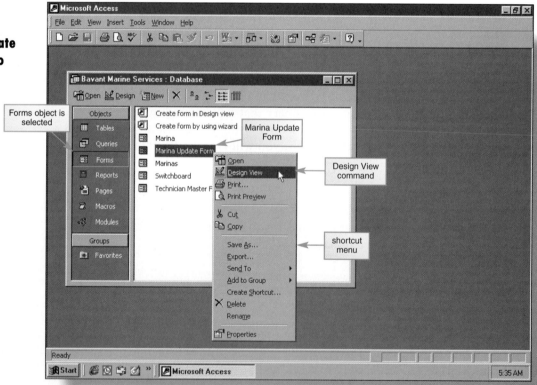

FIGURE 8-3

2 **Click Design View on the shortcut menu, and then, if necessary, maximize the window. Be sure the toolbox displays and is docked at the bottom of the screen. (If it does not display, click the Toolbox button on the Form Design toolbar. If it is not docked at the bottom of the screen, drag it to the bottom of the screen to dock it there.) If necessary, close the field box. Make sure the Control Wizards button is recessed, and then point to the Command Button button in the toolbox.**

The design of the form displays in a maximized window (Figure 8-4).

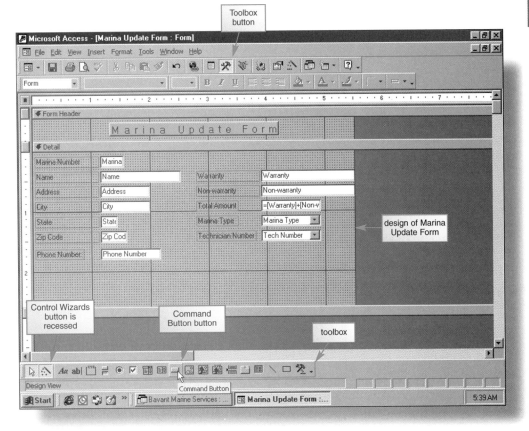

FIGURE 8-4

3 **Click the Command Button button and move the mouse pointer, whose shape has changed to a plus sign with a picture of a button, to the position shown in Figure 8-5.**

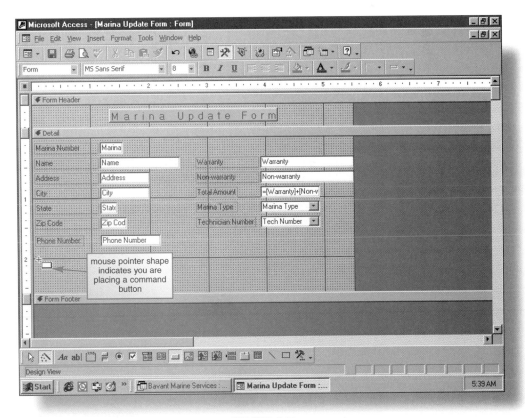

FIGURE 8-5

4 **Click the position shown in Figure 8-5. With Record Navigation selected in the Categories box in the Command Button Wizard dialog box, click Goto Next Record in the Actions box. Point to the Next button.**

The Command Button Wizard dialog box displays (Figure 8-6). Goto Next Record is selected as the action. A sample of the button displays in the Sample box.

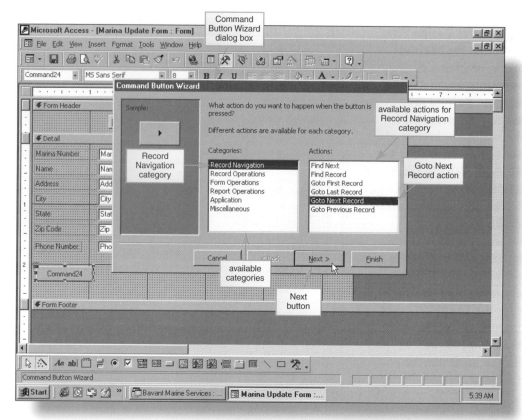

FIGURE 8-6

5 **Click the Next button. Point to the Text button.**

The next Command Button Wizard dialog box displays, asking what to display on the button (Figure 8-7). The button can contain either text or a picture.

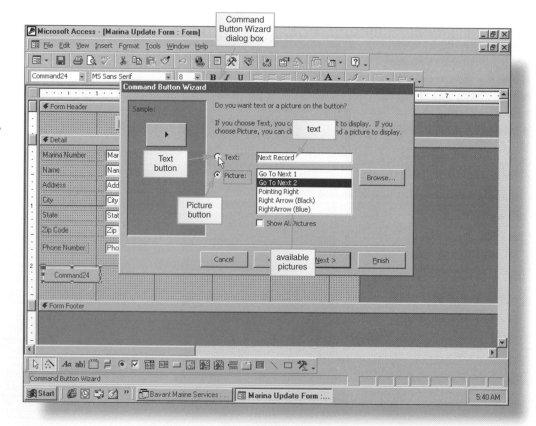

FIGURE 8-7

6 Click the Text button. Next Record is the desired text and does not need to be changed. Click the Next button, and then type Next Record as the name of the button. Point to the Finish button.

The name of the button displays in the text box (Figure 8-8).

7 Click the Finish button.

The button displays on the form.

8 Use the techniques in Steps 3 through 7 to place the Previous Record button directly to the right of the Next Record button. Click Goto Previous Record in the Actions box. The name of the button is Previous Record.

9 Place a button directly to the right of the Previous Record button. Click Record Operations in the Categories box. Add New Record is the desired action. Point to the Next button.

The Command Button Wizard dialog box displays with the selections (Figure 8-9).

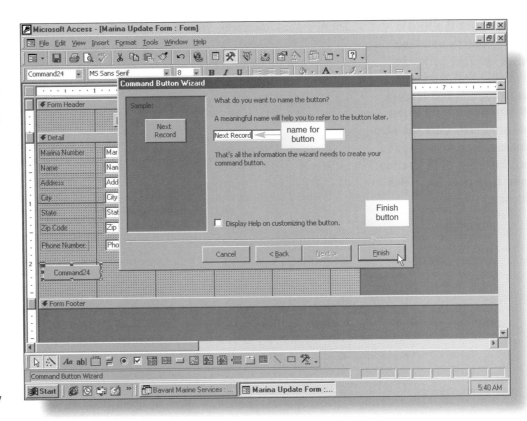

FIGURE 8-8

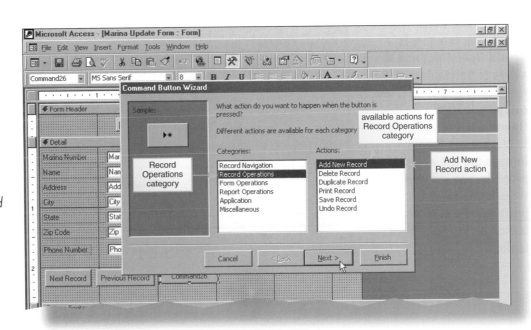

FIGURE 8-9

10 Click the Next button and then click the Text button to indicate that the button is to contain text (Figure 8-10). Add Record is the desired text. Click the Next button, type Add Record as the name of the button, and then click the Finish button.

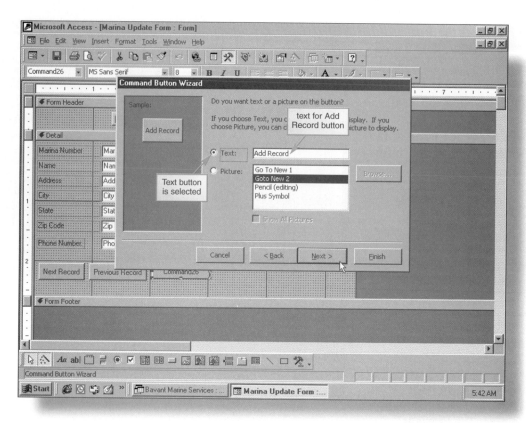

FIGURE 8-10

11 Use the techniques in Steps 3 through 7 to place the Delete Record and Close Form buttons in the positions shown in Figure 8-11. For the Delete Record button, the category is Record Operations and the action is Delete Record. For the Close Form button, the category is Form Operations and the action is Close Form. If your buttons are not aligned properly, you can drag them to the correct positions. Point to the View button on the Form View toolbar.

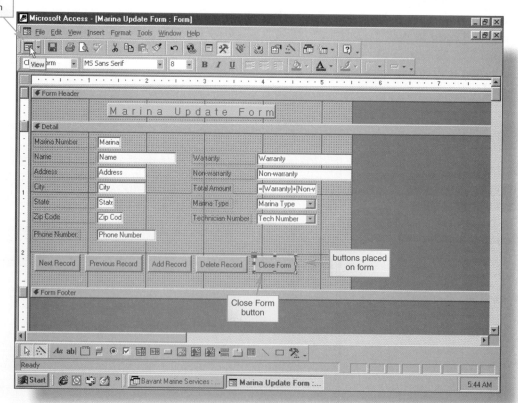

FIGURE 8-11

12 **Click the View button.**

The form displays with the added buttons (Figure 8-12).

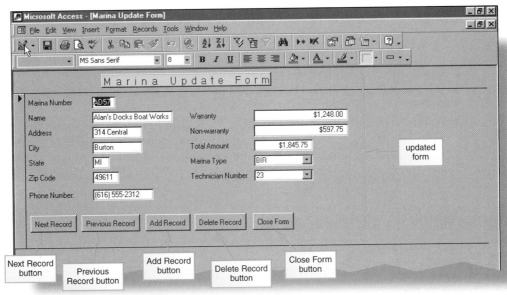

FIGURE 8-12

Using the Buttons

To move around on the form, you can use the buttons to perform the actions you specify. To move to the next record, click the Next Record button. Click the Previous Record button to move to the previous record. Clicking the Delete Record button will delete the record currently on the screen. You will get a message requesting you to verify the deletion before the record actually is deleted. Clicking the Close Form button will remove the form from the screen.

Clicking the Add Record button will clear the contents of the form so you can add a new record (Figure 8-13). Notice on the form in Figure 8-13 that an insertion point does not display. To begin entering a record, you will have to click the Marina Number field before you can start typing. To ensure that an insertion point displays in the field's text box when you click the Add Record button, you must change the focus. **Focus** is the ability to receive user input through mouse or keyboard actions. The Add Record button needs to update the focus to the Marina Number field.

More About

Focus

There is a visual way to determine which object on the screen has the focus. If a field has the focus, an insertion point will display in the field. If a button has the focus, a small rectangle will appear inside the button.

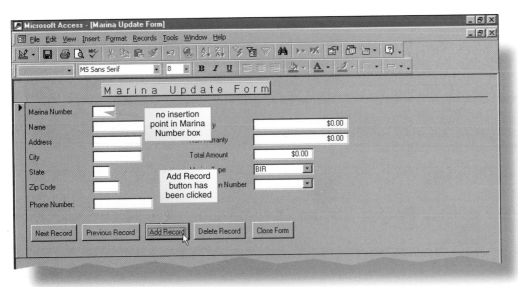

FIGURE 8-13

Modifying the Add Record Button

To display an insertion point automatically when you click the Add Record button, two steps are necessary using Visual Basic for Applications (VBA). First, you must change the name of the control for the Marina Number field to a name that does not contain spaces. Next, because Access automatically creates VBA code for the button, you must add a command to the VBA code. The added command will move the focus to the Marina Number field as soon as the button is clicked.

Perform the following steps to change the name of the Marina Number control to MarNumb and then add an additional command to the VBA code that will set the focus to MarNumb.

 To Modify the Add Record Button

1 **Click the View button on the toolbar to return to the design grid. Right-click the control for the Marina Number field (the white space, not the label), and then click Properties on the shortcut menu. If necessary, click the Name property, use the DELETE or BACKSPACE key to erase the current value, and then type** MarNumb **as the new name.**

The name is changed (Figure 8-14).

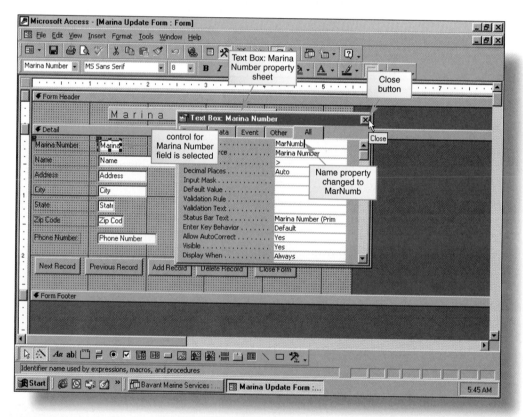

FIGURE 8-14

2 Click the Close button to close the Text Box: Marina Number property sheet. Right-click the Add Record button. Point to Build Event on the shortcut menu.

The shortcut menu displays (Figure 8-15).

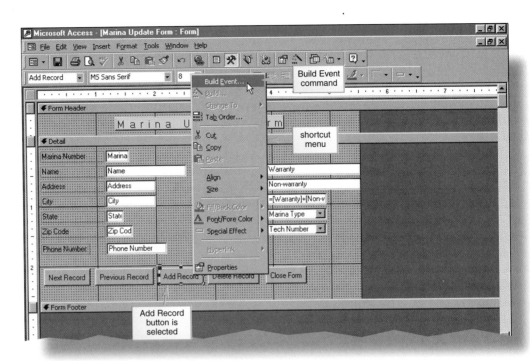

FIGURE 8-15

3 Click Build Event on the shortcut menu.

The VBA code for the Add Record button displays (Figure 8-16). The important line in this code is DoCmd, which stands for Do Command. Following DoCmd, is the command, formally called a method, that will be executed; in this case GoToRecord. Following GoToRecord are the arguments, which are items that provide information that will be used by the method. The only argument necessary in this case is acNewRec. This code indicates that Access is to move to the new record at the end of the table. This command will not set the focus to any particular field automatically, so an insertion point still will not be produced.

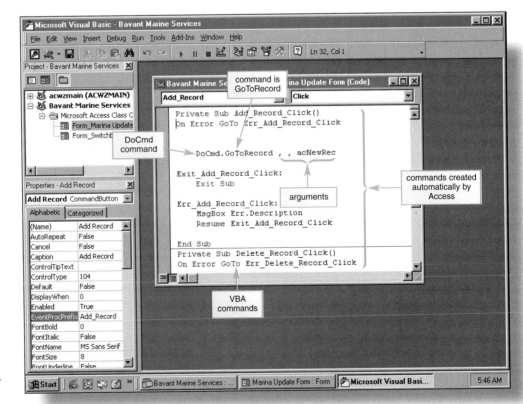

FIGURE 8-16

4 Press the DOWN ARROW key four times, press the TAB key, and type MarNumb. SetFocus as the additional command. Press the ENTER key.

The command is entered (Figure 8-17). While typing, a box may display indicating selections for the command. You may disregard this list. This command will set the focus in the control named MarNumb as soon as the previous command (GoToRecord) is executed.

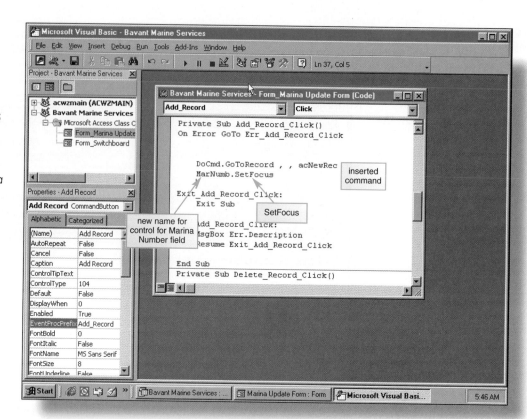

FIGURE 8-17

5 Close the window containing the VBA code. Click the View button on the toolbar and then click the Add Record button.

An insertion point displays in the Marina Number field (Figure 8-18).

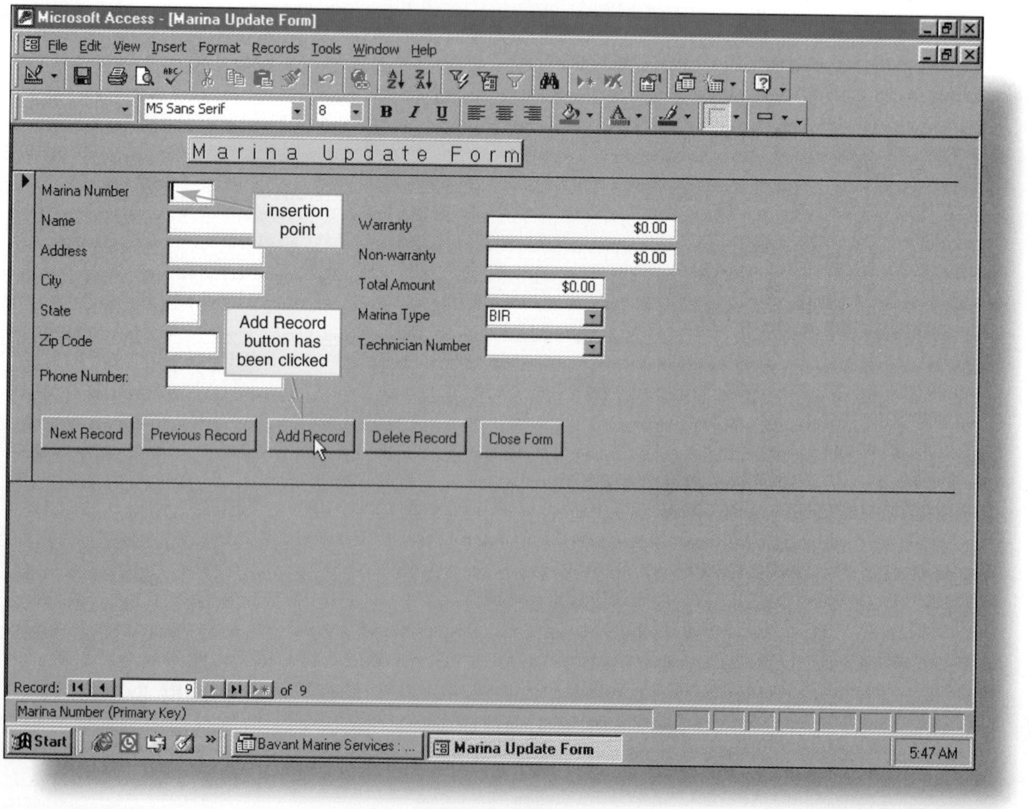

FIGURE 8-18

Creating and Using Combo Boxes

A **combo box**, such as the one shown in Figure 8-1 on page A 8.5, combines the properties of a **text box**, a box into which you can type an entry, and a **list box**, a box you can use to display a list. You could type the marina's name directly in the box or, you can click the Name to Find box arrow and Access will display a list of marina names. To select a name from the list, simply click the name.

Creating a Combo Box

To create a combo box, use the Combo Box button in the toolbox. The Combo Box Wizard then will guide you through the steps to create the combo box. Perform the following steps to place a combo box for marina names on the form.

More About

The Add Record Button

If your spelling was not consistent, you will get an error message when you click the Add Record button. To correct the problem, return to the form design. Check to make sure the name you gave to the Marina Number control and the name in the SetFocus command are both the same (MarNumb).

 Steps To Create a Combo Box

1 **Click the View button on the toolbar to return to the design grid. Make sure the Control Wizards button is recessed, and then point to the Combo Box button in the toolbox (Figure 8-19).**

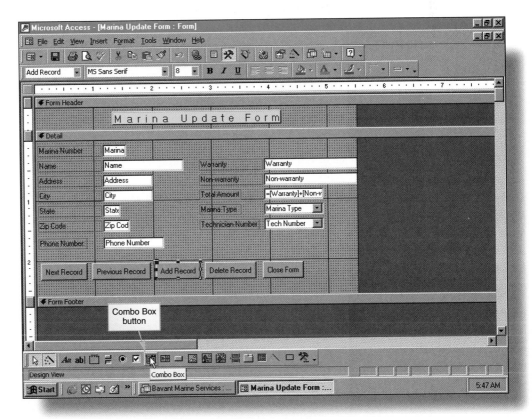

FIGURE 8-19

2 Click the Combo Box button and then move the mouse pointer, whose shape has changed to a small plus sign with a combo box, to the position shown in Figure 8-20.

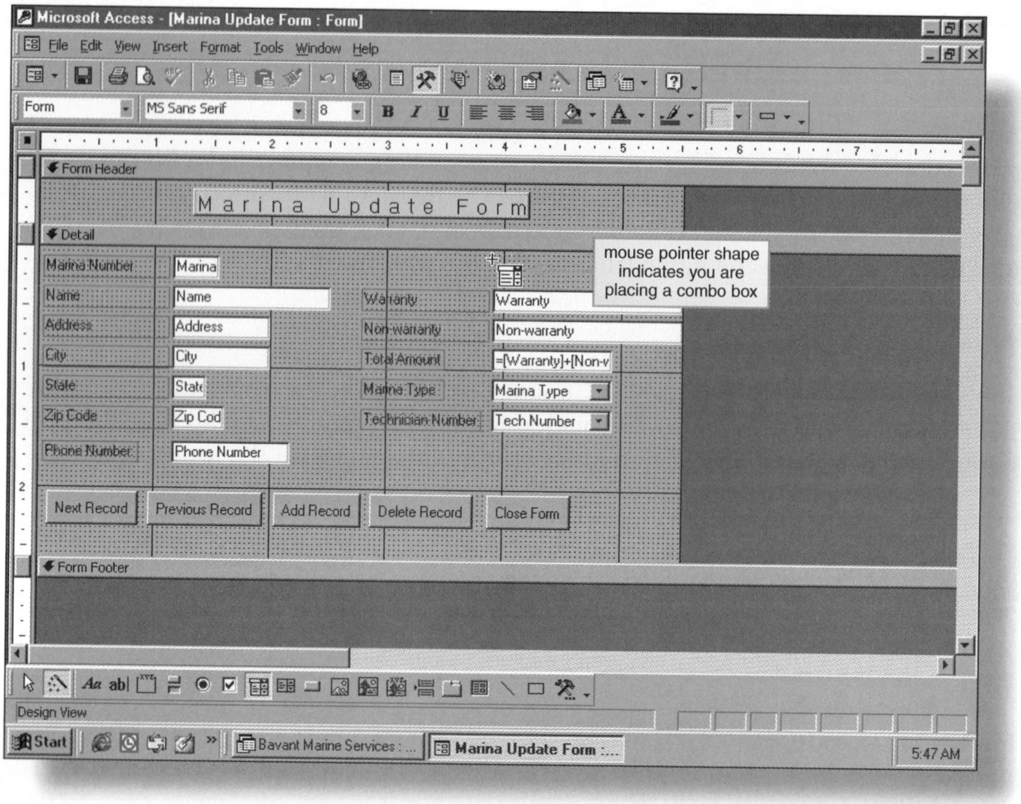

FIGURE 8-20

3 Click the position shown in Figure 8-20 to place a combo box. Click the Find a record on my form based on the value I selected in my combo box button. Point to the Next button.

The Combo Box Wizard dialog box displays, instructing you to indicate how the combo box is to obtain values for the list (Figure 8-21).

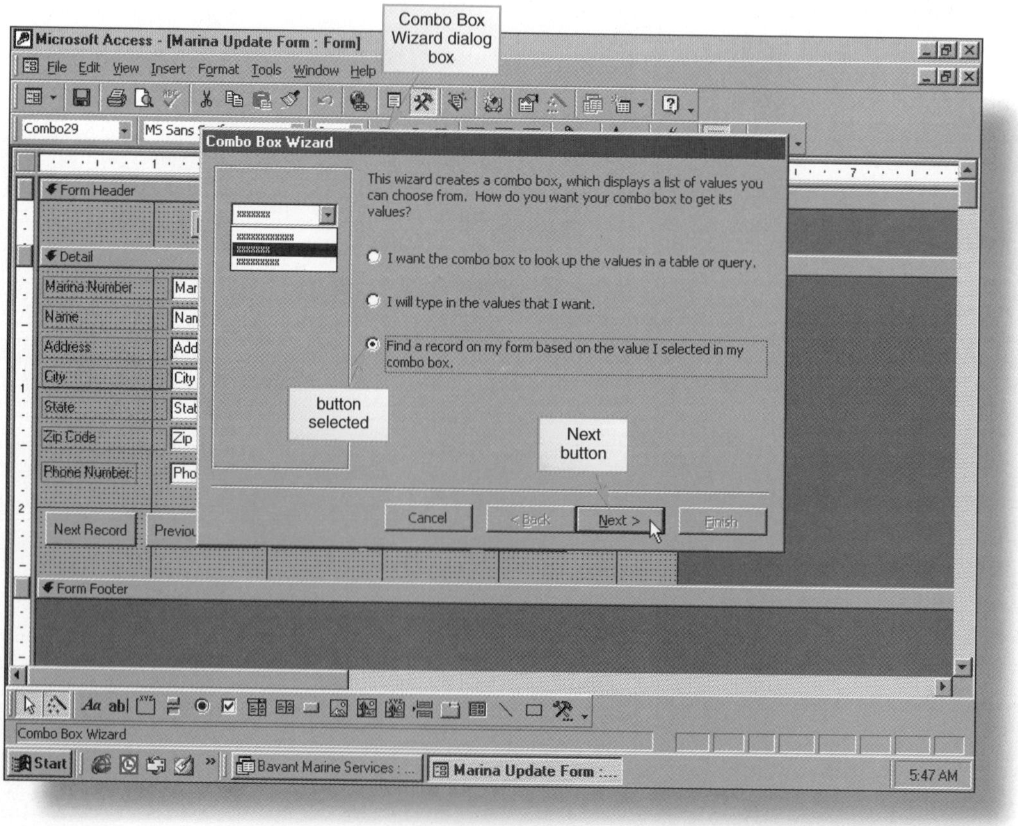

FIGURE 8-21

4 **Click the Next button, click the Name field, and then click the Add Field button to add Name as a field in the combo box. Point to the Next button.**

The Name field is added to the Selected Fields box (Figure 8-22).

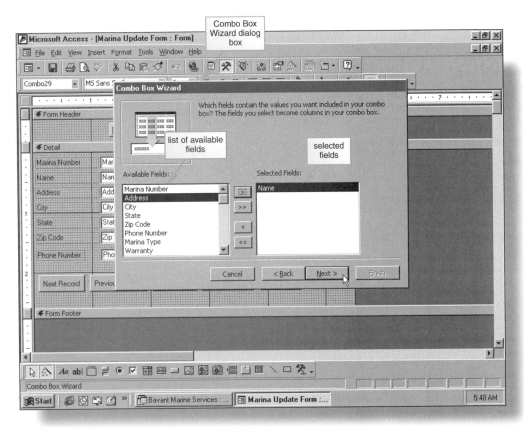

FIGURE 8-22

5 **Click the Next button. Point to the right edge of the column heading.**

The Combo Box Wizard dialog box displays (Figure 8-23), giving you an opportunity to resize the columns in the combo box.

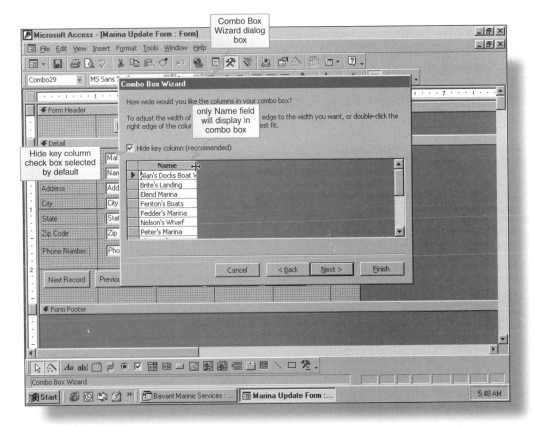

FIGURE 8-23

6 Double-click the right edge of the column heading to resize the column to the best fit. Click the Next button, and then type &Name to Find as the label for the combo box. Point to the Finish button.

The label is entered (Figure 8-24). The ampersand (&) in front of the letter N indicates that users can select the combo box by pressing the ALT+N keys.

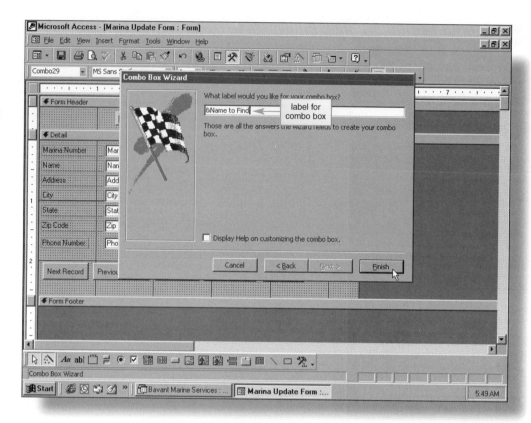

FIGURE 8-24

7 Click the Finish button. Click the label for the combo box. Point to the sizing handle on the right edge of the label.

The shape of the mouse pointer changes to a two-headed horizontal arrow, indicating that you can drag the right edge (Figure 8-25).

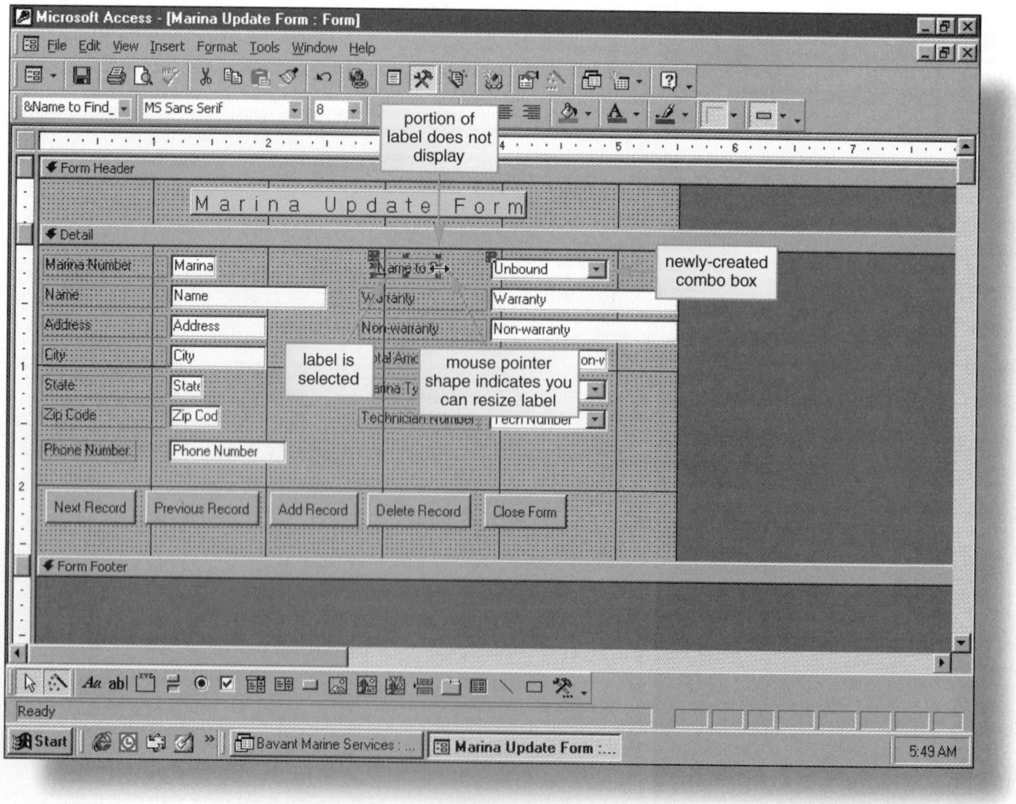

FIGURE 8-25

Double-click the handle so the entire label displays. Point to the View button on the toolbar.

The combo box is added and the label has been resized (Figure 8-26). The N in Name is underlined indicating that you can press the ALT+N keys to select the combo box.

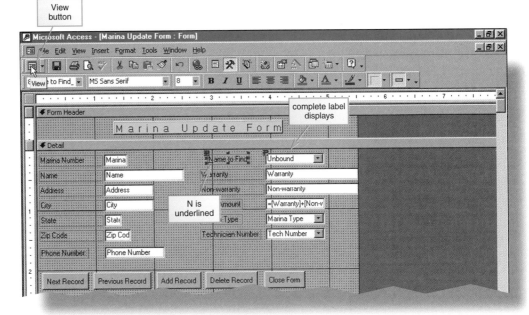

FIGURE 8-26

Using the Combo Box

Using the combo box, you can search for a marina in two ways. You either can click the combo box arrow to display a list of marina names and then select the name from the list by clicking it or, you can begin typing the name. Access will display automatically the name that begins with the letters you have typed. Once the correct name is displayed, select the name by pressing the TAB key. Regardless of the method you use, the data for the selected marina displays on the form once the selection is made.

The following steps first locate the marina whose name is Nelson's Wharf, and then use the Next Record button to move to the next marina.

Steps **To Use the Combo Box**

1 **Click the View button on the toolbar to display the form.**

The form displays (Figure 8-27).

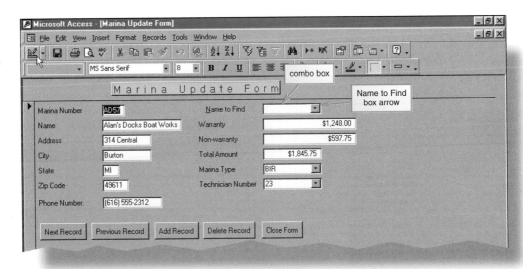

FIGURE 8-27

2 Click the Name to Find box arrow and then point to Nelson's Wharf.

The list of names displays (Figure 8-28).

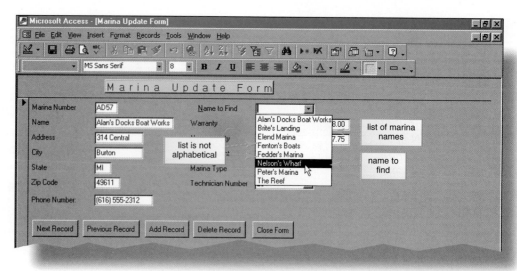

FIGURE 8-28

3 Click Nelson's Wharf.

The data for the marina whose name is Nelson's Wharf displays on the form (Figure 8-29).

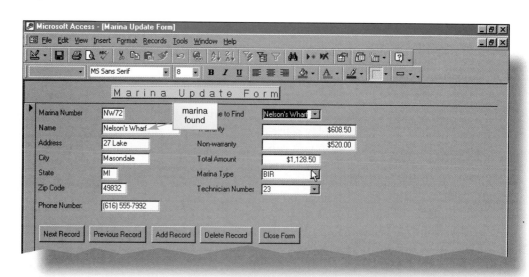

FIGURE 8-29

4 Click the Next Record button.

The data for the marina whose name is Peter's Marina displays on the form (Figure 8-30). The combo box still contains Nelson's Wharf.

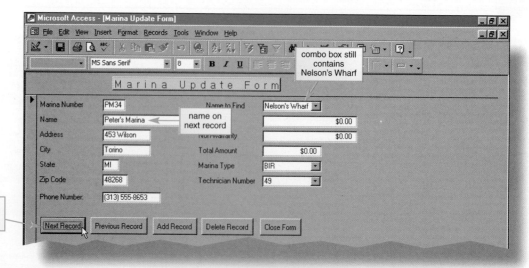

FIGURE 8-30

Issues with the Combo Box

Consider the following issues with the combo box. First, if you examine the list of names in Figure 8-28 on page A 8.22, you will see that they are not in alphabetical order (Fenton's Boats comes before Fedder's Marina). Second, when you move to a record without using the combo box, the name in the combo box does not change to reflect the name of the marina currently on the screen. Third, pressing the TAB key to move from field to field on the form should not move to the combo box.

Modifying the Combo Box

The following steps modify the query that Access has created for the combo box so the data is sorted by name. The modification to the On Current property will ensure that the combo box is kept current with the rest of the form; that is, it contains the name of the marina whose number currently displays in the Marina Number field. The final step changes the Tab Stop property for the combo box from Yes to No.

Perform the following steps to modify the combo box.

 ## To Modify the Combo Box

1 **Click the View button on the toolbar to return to the design grid. Right-click the Name to Find combo box (the white space, not the label), and then click Properties on the shortcut menu. Note the number of your combo box, which may be different from the one shown in Figure 8-31, this will be important later. Click the Row Source property, and then point to the Build button for the Row Source property.**

The Combo Box: Combo29 property sheet displays (Figure 8-31). The combo box number is 29 (Combo29). The Row Source property is selected. Depending on where you clicked the Row Source property, the value may or may not be highlighted.

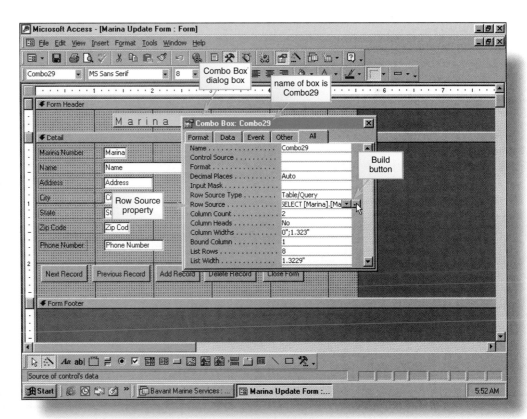

FIGURE 8-31

2 **Click the Build button. Point to the Sort row under the Name field.**

The SQL Statement : Query Builder window displays (Figure 8-32). This screen allows you to make changes just as you did when you created queries.

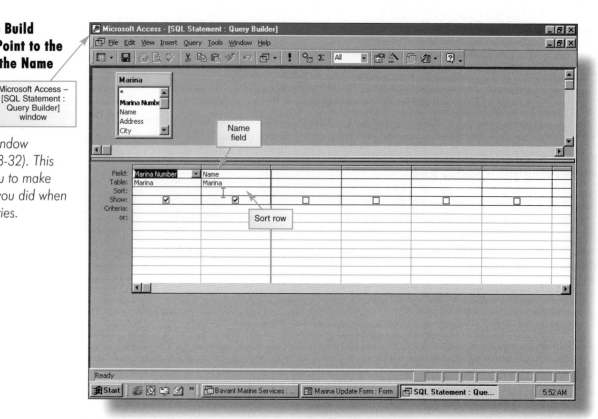

FIGURE 8-32

3 **Click the Sort row in the Name field, click the box arrow that displays, and then click Ascending. Point to the Close Window button for the SQL Statement : Query Builder window.**

The sort order is changed to Ascending (Figure 8-33).

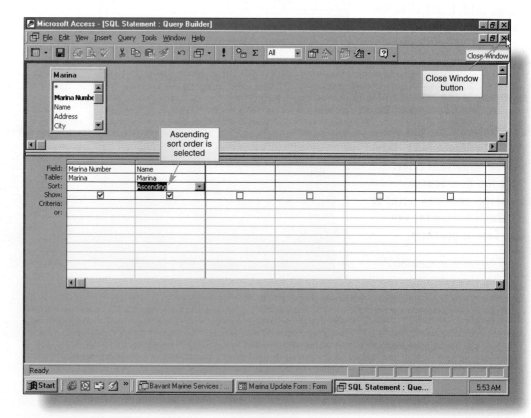

FIGURE 8-33

4 Close the SQL Statement : Query Builder window by clicking its Close Window button. Point to the Yes button in the Microsoft Access dialog box.

The Microsoft Access dialog box displays (Figure 8-34).

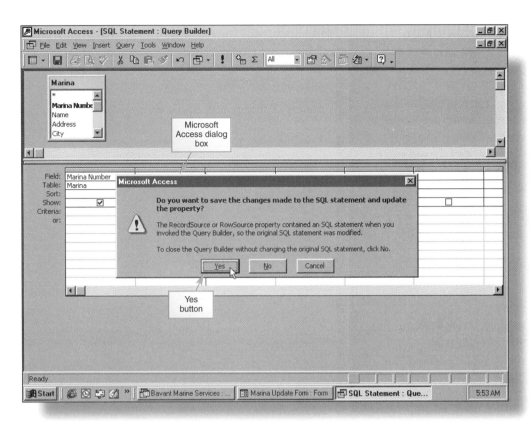

FIGURE 8-34

5 Click the Yes button to change the property, and then close the Combo Box: Combo29 property sheet. Point to the form selector, the box in the upper-left corner on the form (Figure 8-35).

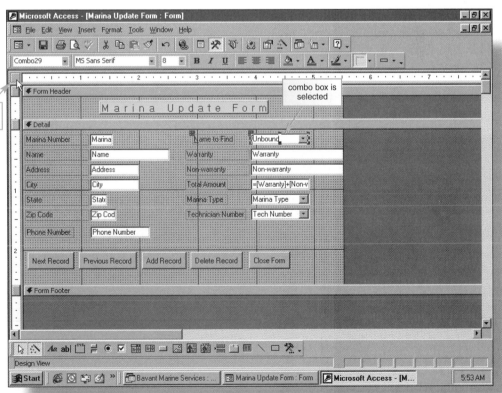

FIGURE 8-35

Microsoft Access 2000

6 Right-click the form selector, and then click Properties on the shortcut menu. Click the down scroll arrow on the Form property sheet until the On Current property displays, and then click the On Current property. Point to the Build button.

The Form property sheet displays (Figure 8-36).

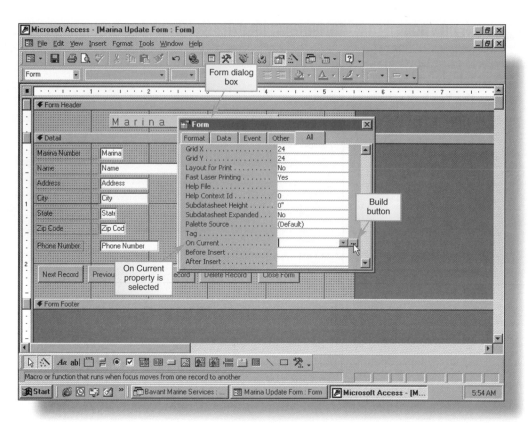

FIGURE 8-36

7 Click the Build button, click Code Builder, and then point to the OK button.

The Choose Builder dialog box displays (Figure 8-37). Code Builder is selected.

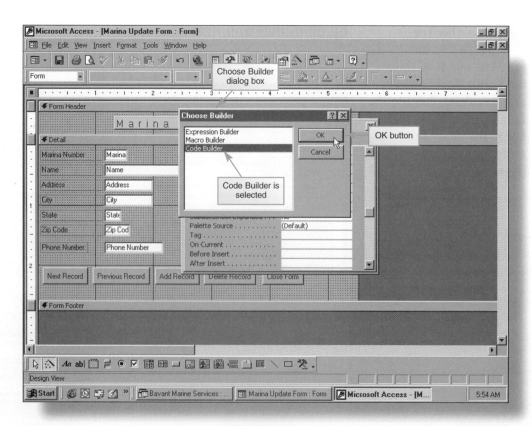

FIGURE 8-37

Click the OK button.

The code generated by Access for the form displays (Figure 8-38).

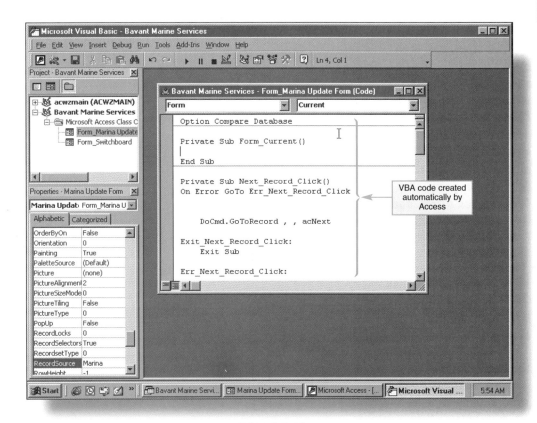

FIGURE 8-38

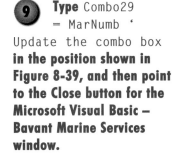

Type Combo29 = MarNumb '
Update the combo box **in the position shown in Figure 8-39, and then point to the Close button for the Microsoft Visual Basic – Bavant Marine Services window.**

This command assumes your combo box is Combo29. If yours has a different number, use your number in the command instead of 29. This command will update the contents of the combo box using the marina number currently in the MarNumb control. The portion of the command following the apostrophe is called a **comment,** *which describes the purpose of the command.*

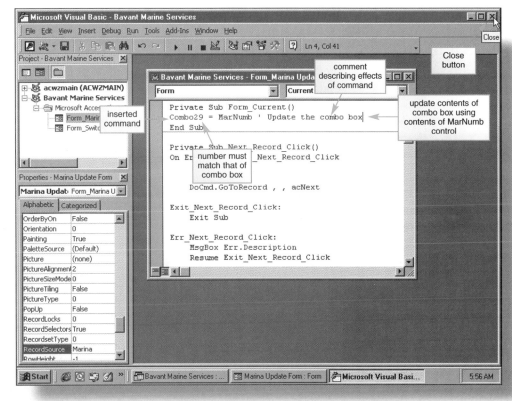

FIGURE 8-39

10 **Click the Close button, and then close the Form property sheet. Right-click the combo box, and then click Properties on the shortcut menu. Click the down scroll arrow until the Tab Stop property displays, click the Tab Stop property, click the Tab Stop box arrow, and then point to No (Figure 8-40).**

 11 **Click No, and then close the Combo Box: Combo29 property sheet.**

The modifications to the combo box are complete.

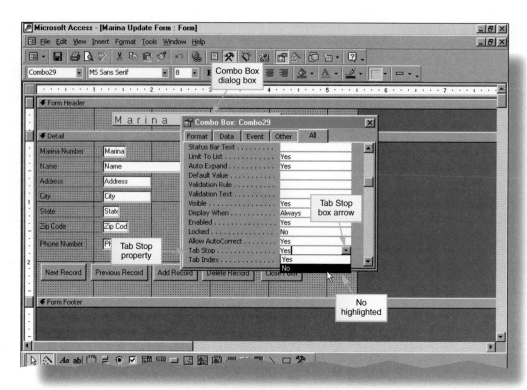

FIGURE 8-40

Using the Modified Combo Box

The problems with the combo box now are corrected. The search conducted in the following steps first looks for the marina whose name is Nelson's Wharf, and then moves to the next record in the table to verify that the combo box also will be updated. Perform the following steps to search for a marina.

Steps To Use the Combo Box to Search for a Marina

 1 **Click the View button on the toolbar to display the Marina Update Form, and then click the Name to Find box arrow.**

An alphabetical list of names displays (Figure 8-41).

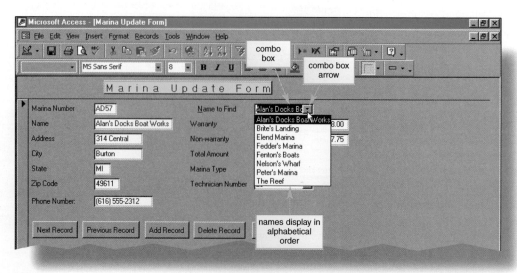

FIGURE 8-41

2 Click Nelson's Wharf, and then point to the Next Record button.

Marina NW72 displays on the form (Figure 8-42).

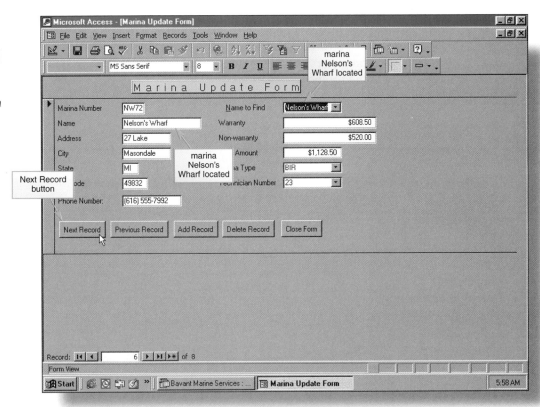

FIGURE 8-42

3 Click the Next Record button.

Marina PM34 displays on the form (Figure 8-43). The marina's name also displays in the combo box.

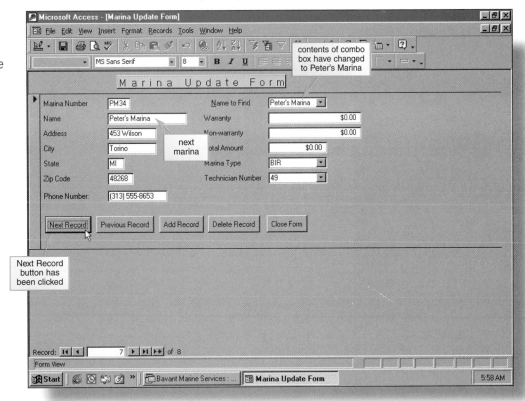

FIGURE 8-43

Placing a Rectangle

In order to emphasize the special nature of the combo box, you will place a rectangle around it. To do so, perform the following steps using the Rectangle button in the toolbox.

 ## To Place a Rectangle

1 **Click the View button on the toolbar to return to the design grid.**

2 **Point to the Rectangle button in the toolbox (Figure 8-44). Click the View button**

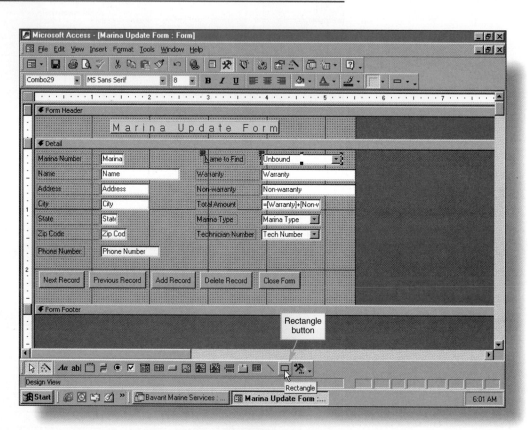

FIGURE 8-44

Click the Rectangle button in the toolbox and then move the pointer, whose shape has changed to a plus sign accompanied by a rectangle to the approximate position shown in Figure 8-45.

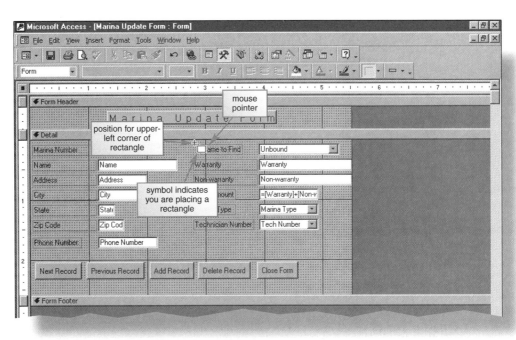

FIGURE 8-45

 With the pointer in the position shown in Figure 8-45, press and hold the left mouse button. Drag the pointer to the approximate position shown in Figure 8-46 and then release the left mouse button.

 Point to the border of the newly-created rectangle, right-click, and then click Properties on the shortcut menu. Change the value of the Special Effect property to Raised. If necessary, change the value of the Back Style property to Transparent, so that the combo box will display within the

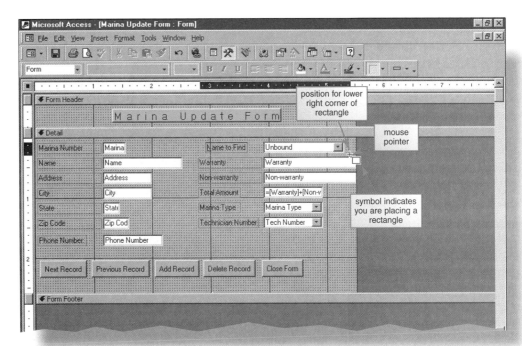

FIGURE 8-46

rectangle. (If the Back Style property were not changed, the rectangle would completely cover the combo box and the combo box would not be visible.)

 Close the Rectangle property sheet by clicking its Close button.

Closing and Saving a Form

To close a form, use the window's Close Window button. Then indicate whether you want to save your changes. Perform the following step to close and save the form.

TO CLOSE AND SAVE A FORM

1 Click the Close Window button to close the window, and then click the Yes button to save the design of the form.

Opening a Form

Right-click the form you want to open in the Database window, and then click Open on the shortcut menu. The form will display and can be used to examine and update data. Perform the following steps to open the Marina Update Form.

To Open a Form

1 **With the Forms object selected, right-click Marina Update Form to display the shortcut menu. Click Open on the shortcut menu.**

The form displays (Figure 8-47).

2 **Close the form by clicking the Close Form command button.**

The form no longer displays.

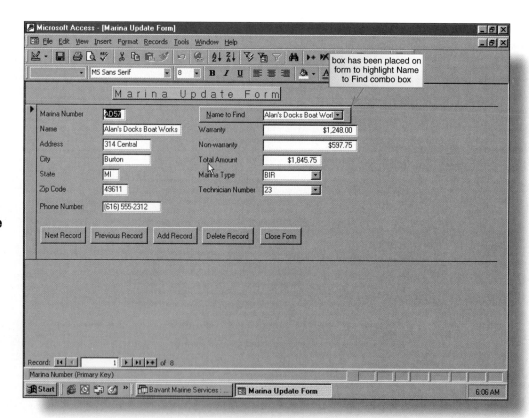

FIGURE 8-47

Creating a Form Using Design View

You have used the Form Wizard to create a variety of forms. You also can create a form without the wizard by using Design view. You will work with a blank form on which you can place all the necessary controls. In the form you create in this project, you will need to place a subform and two charts.

Creating a Query for the Subform

The subform is based on data in a query, so first you must create the query. Perform the following steps to create the query for the subform.

 To Create the Query for the Subform

1 In the Database window, click Tables on the Objects bar, and then click Marina. Click the New Object: AutoForm button arrow on the Database window toolbar. Click Query. Be sure Design View is selected, and then click the OK button. Maximize the Microsoft Access — [Query1 : Select Query] window. Resize the upper and lower panes and the Marina field box so that all the fields in the Marina table display.

2 Right-click any open area in the upper pane, click Show Table on the shortcut menu, click the Open Workorders table, click the Add button, and then click the Close button for the Show Table dialog box. Resize the Open Workorders field box so that all the fields in the Open Workorders table display. Double-click the Tech Number field.

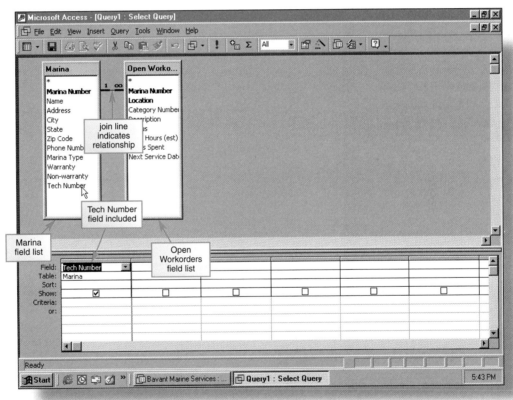

FIGURE 8-48

The tables are related and the Tech Number field is selected (Figure 8-48).

3 Double-click the Marina Number and Name fields from the Marina table. Double-click the Location, Category Number, Total Hours (est), and Hours Spent fields from the Open Workorders table.

 4 Right-click the Total Hours (est) field, click Properties, click the Caption property, and then type Est Hours as the caption. Change the caption for the Hours Spent field to Spent Hours. Click Ascending in the Sort: row for Tech Number and Marina Number.

 5 Close the query by clicking the Close Window button. Click the Yes button to save the query. Type Marinas and Workorders by Technician as the name of the query, and then point to the OK button.

The query is complete and the Save As dialog box displays (Figure 8-49).

 6 Click the OK button.

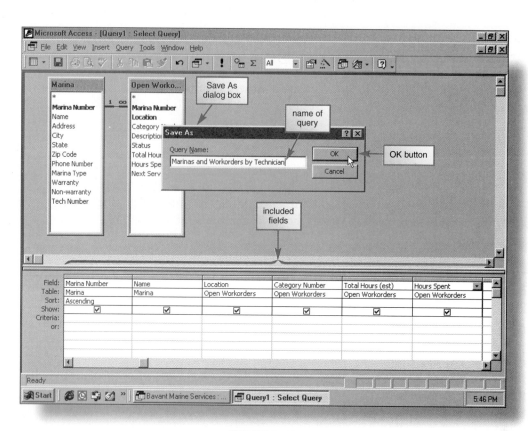

FIGURE 8-49

Creating the Form

When you want to create a form from scratch, you begin with the same general procedure as when you want to use the Form Wizard, except select Design View rather than Form Wizard. Perform the following steps to create the form.

TO CREATE THE FORM

1 If necessary, in the Database window, click Tables on the Objects bar, and then click Technician. Click the New Object: Query button arrow on the Database window toolbar. Click Form. Be sure Design View is selected, and then click the OK button.

2 Be sure the field list displays. (If it does not, click the Field List button on the toolbar.) Drag the Tech Number, First Name, and Last Name fields to the approximate positions shown in Figure 8-50. Move the attached labels for the First Name and Last Name fields to the positions shown in the figure by dragging their move handles. Point to the Close button in the field list box.

3 Close the field list box by clicking its Close button.

The field list no longer displays.

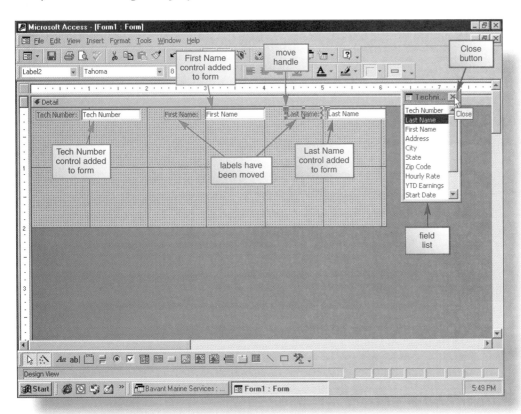

FIGURE 8-50

Placing a Subform

To place a subform on a form, you use the Subform/Subreport button in the toolbox. Provided the Control Wizards button is recessed, a wizard will guide you through the process of adding the subform as performed in the steps on the next page.

More About 2000

Subforms

A main form can contain more than one subform. If the main form is based on a table or query, each subform must contain information related to the information in the main form.

To Place the Subform

① Be sure the Control Wizards button is recessed, and then point to the Subform/Subreport button in the toolbox (Figure 8-51).

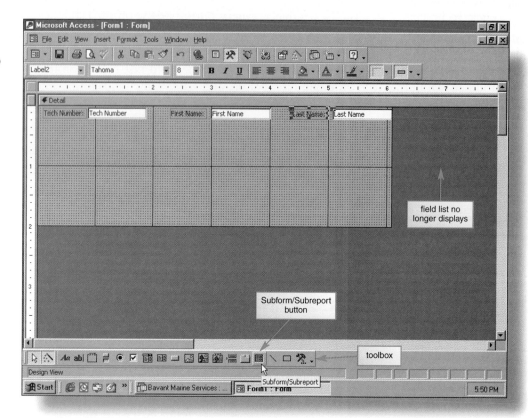

FIGURE 8-51

② Click the Subform/ Subreport button, and then move the mouse pointer to the approximate position shown in Figure 8-52.

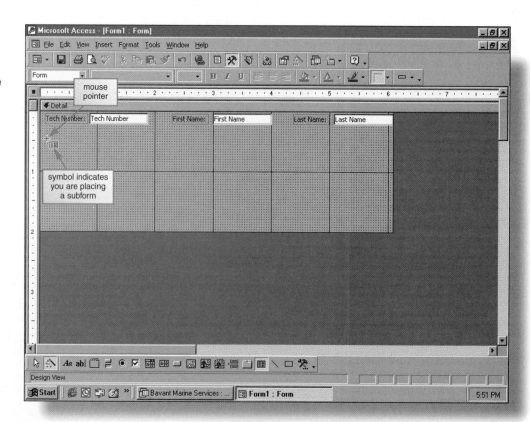

FIGURE 8-52

3 Click the position shown in Figure 8-52. Be sure the Use existing Tables and Queries button is selected and then point to the Next button.

The SubForm Wizard dialog box displays (Figure 8-53).

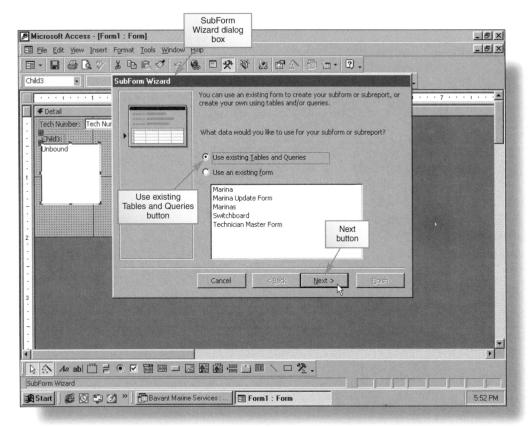

FIGURE 8-53

4 Click the Next button. Click the Tables/Queries box arrow and then click Query: Marinas and Workorders by Technician. Click the Add All fields button and then point to the Next button.

The Marinas and Workorders by Technician query is selected (Figure 8-54). All fields are selected.

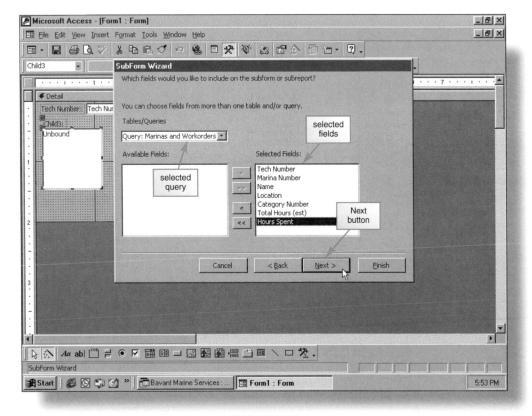

FIGURE 8-54

5 Click the Next button. Be sure the Choose from a list button is selected and then point to the Next button (Figure 8-55).

6 Click the Next button. Type Open Workorders for Technician as the name of the subform and then click the Finish button.

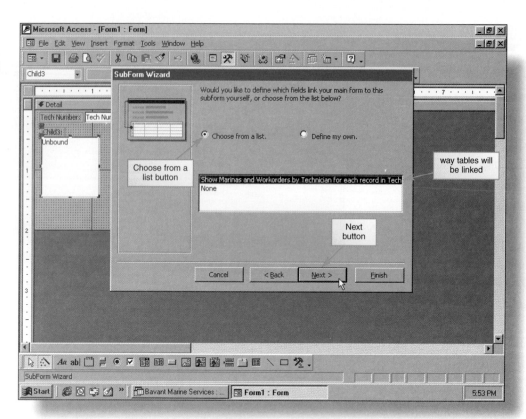

FIGURE 8-55

Closing and Saving the Form

To close a form, click the Close button. Then indicate whether you want to save your changes. Perform the following steps to close and save the form.

TO CLOSE AND SAVE A FORM

1 Close the form by clicking the Close button.

2 Click the Yes button to save the changes. Type Technician Workorder Data as the name of the form and then click the OK button.

Modifying the Subform

The next task is to modify the subform. The Tech Number field must be in the subform because it is used to link the data in the subform to the data in the main form, but it should not display. In addition, the remaining columns need to be resized to appropriate sizes. Perform the following steps to remove the Tech Number field and then resize the remaining columns.

Subforms

A main form does not need to be based on a table or query. If the main form is not based on a table or query, it can still contain one or more subforms. It simply serves as a container for the subforms, which then have no restrictions on the information they must contain.

PROJECT 8

Steps To Modify the Subform

1 In the Database window, click Forms on the Objects bar, right-click the Open Workorders for Technician form, and then click Design View on the shortcut menu.

2 Close the field box and maximize the window, if necessary. Click the Tech Number control in the Form Header section. Hold the SHIFT key down and click the Tech Number control in the Detail section.

Both controls are selected (Figure 8-56).

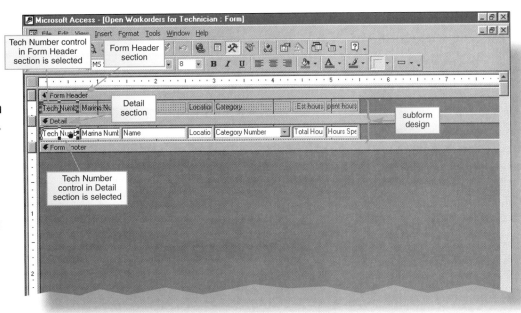

FIGURE 8-56

3 Press DELETE to delete the two Tech Number controls from both sections. Click the View button to display the form in Datasheet view. Point to the right boundary of the field selector for the Marina Number field.

The subform displays in Datasheet view (Figure 8-57). The Tech Number field has been removed. The mouse pointer has changed shape indicating that the Marina Number column can be resized.

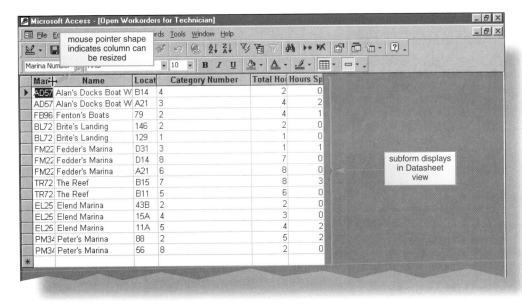

FIGURE 8-57

4 Double-click the right boundary of each of the field selectors to resize the fields to the best size. Close the subform by clicking the Close Window button. Click the Yes button to save the changes.

The subform has been changed.

Resizing the Subform

To resize the subform, click the subform and then drag the appropriate sizing handles as performed in the following steps.

 To Resize the Subform

1 **In the Database window, be sure the Forms object is selected, right-click the Technician Workorder Data form, and then click Design View on the shortcut menu.**

2 **Click the subform to select it. Drag the right sizing handle to the position shown in Figure 8-58 and then drag the lower sizing handle to the position shown in the figure.**

The subform is resized.

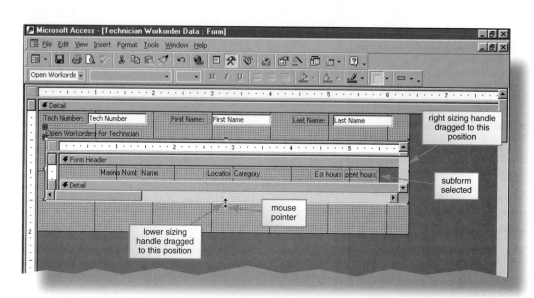

FIGURE 8-58

Inserting a Chart

To insert a chart, use the Chart command on the Insert menu. The Chart Wizard then will ask you to indicate the fields to be included on the chart and the type of chart you wish to insert. Perform the following steps to insert a chart.

 To Insert a Chart

1 **Click Insert on the menu bar and then point to Chart.**

The Insert menu displays (Figure 8-59).

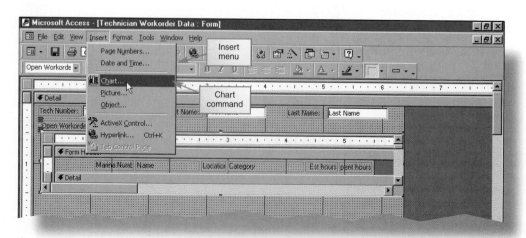

FIGURE 8-59

2 Click Chart and then move the pointer to the approximate position shown in Figure 8-60.

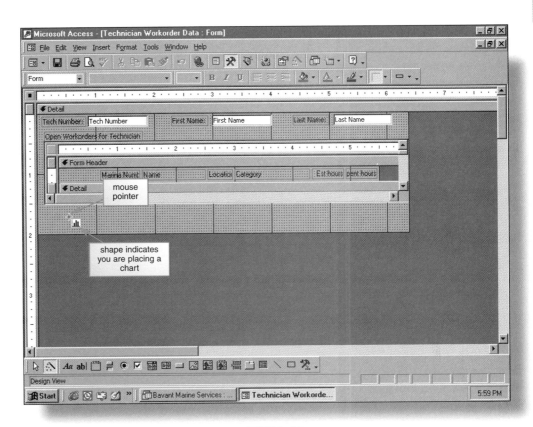

FIGURE 8-60

3 Click the position shown in Figure 8-60. Click the Queries button in the Chart Wizard dialog box, click the Marinas and Workorders by Technician query, and then click the Next button. Select the Category Number and Total Hours (est) fields by clicking them and then clicking the Add Field button. Point to the Next button.

The Chart Wizard dialog box displays (Figure 8-61). The fields for the chart have been selected.

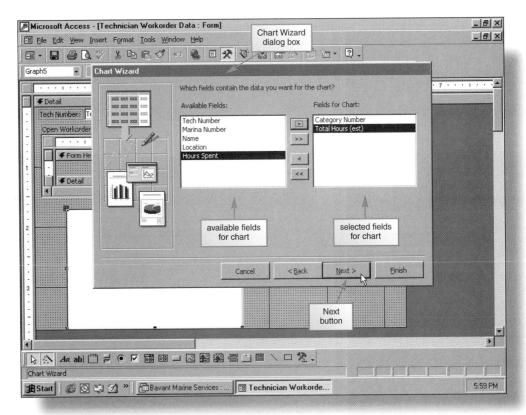

FIGURE 8-61

④ Click the Next button. Be sure the chart in the upper-left corner is selected and then point to the Next button.

The Chart Wizard dialog box displays (Figure 8-62). Use this box to select the type of chart you want to produce. A description of the selected chart type also displays in the dialog box.

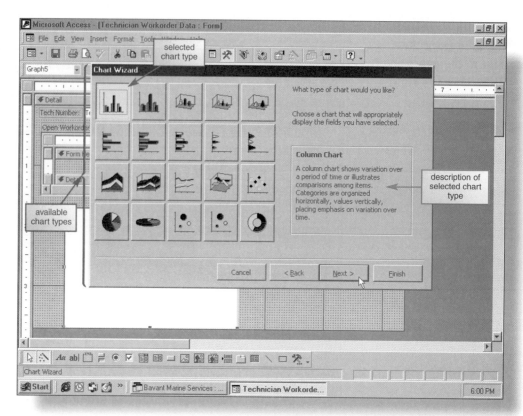

FIGURE 8-62

⑤ Click the Next button and then point to the Next button.

The Chart Wizard dialog box displays (Figure 8-63) indicating the x- and y-axis fields. You can click the Preview Chart button to confirm the layout of the chart.

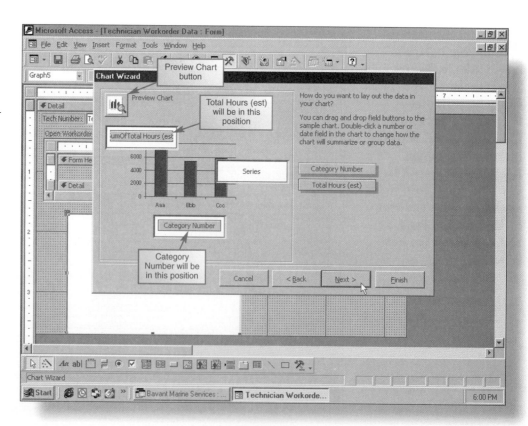

FIGURE 8-63

6 **Click the Next button and then point to the Next button.**

The Chart Wizard dialog box displays, indicating the fields that will be used to link the document and the chart (Figure 8-64). Linking the document and the chart ensures that the chart will accurately reflect the data for the correct technician who is currently displayed on the form.

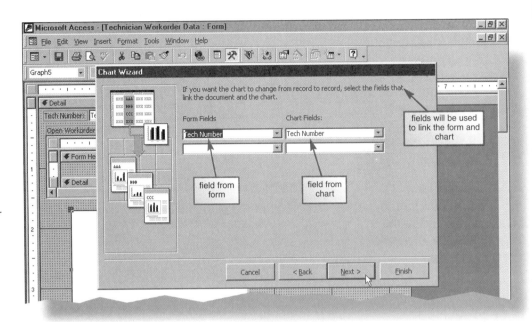

FIGURE 8-64

7 **Click the Next button. Type** Estimated Hours by Category **as the name of the chart and then click the Finish button.**

The sample chart displays on the design screen as a sample preview without using any of your data. You must display the chart in Form view to update the chart with actual data.

8 **Click the View button.**

The chart displays (Figure 8-65).

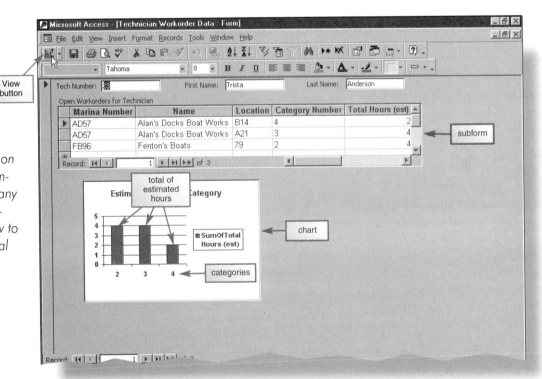

FIGURE 8-65

Across the bottom of the chart are categories (2, 3, and 4 for this technician). The height of the bars in the chart represents the total estimated hours. For category 2, for example, the bar has a height of 4 indicating the technician has a total of 4 estimated hours for services in category 2. The technician also has 4 hours in category 3 and 2 hours in category 4. None of the workorders for this technician involve any of the other categories. That is why no other categories display.

More About

Creating a Chart

In order to create a chart using the Chart Wizard, Microsoft Graph 2000 must be installed. It is also possible to create a chart, by adding a chart that has been created previously and stored in a separate file.

Inserting an Additional Chart

Inserting the second chart requires the same steps as inserting the first chart. The only differences are in the fields to be selected and the title for the chart. Perform the following steps to insert the second chart.

 To Insert an Additional Chart

1 **Click the View button to return to Design view. Point to the OK button in the Microsoft Access dialog box.**

The Microsoft Access dialog box displays (Figure 8-66). This message indicates that the chart is locked, that is, you cannot make any permanent changes to the data on the chart. (The chart data is calculated automatically from the current workorder data.)

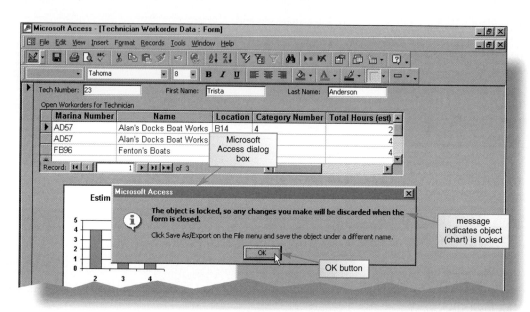

FIGURE 8-66

2 **Click the OK button. Use the techniques shown in the previous section to add a second chart at the position shown in Figure 8-67. In this chart, select Hours Spent rather than Total Hours (est) and type** Hours Spent by Category **as the name of the chart rather than Estimated Hours by Category.**

The chart is inserted.

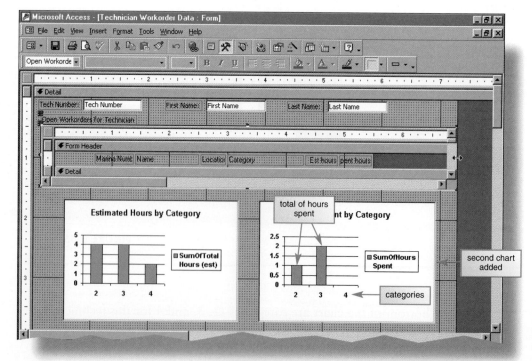

FIGURE 8-67

Adding a Title

The form in Figure 8-2a on page A 8.6 contains a title. To add a title to a form created in Design view, first click Form Header/Footer on the View menu to add a form header. Next, expand the form header to allow room for the title. You then can use the Label button in the toolbox to place the label in the form header and type the title in the label. Perform the following steps to add a title to the form.

More About

Charts

The use of charts in Access is not restricted to forms. You can also place a chart on a report or on a data access page. The steps involved in placing such charts are the same as those for placing charts on forms. For more information about charts, visit the Access 2000 More About page (www.scsite.com/ac2000/more.htm) and then click Charts.

 To Add a Title

1 **Click View on the menu bar and then click Form Header/Footer on the View menu. Drag the lower boundary of the form header so that the form header is approximately the size shown in Figure 8-68. Click the Label button in the toolbox and then point to the position shown in the figure.**

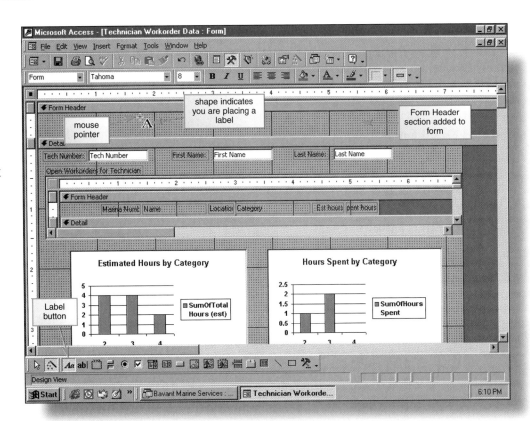

FIGURE 8-68

2 Click the position shown in the figure and then drag the pointer so that the label has the approximate size of the one shown in Figure 8-69. **Type** Technician Workorder Data **as the title. Click outside the label to deselect it, then right-click the label and click Properties on the shortcut menu. Change the value of the Font Size property to 14 and the value of the Text Align property to Distribute. Change the value of the Special Effect property to Raised. Close the Label property sheet and then click the View button. Point to the Next Record button.**

The completed form displays (Figure 8-69).

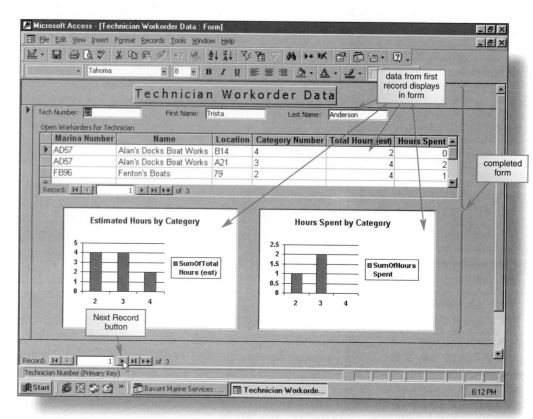

FIGURE 8-69

3 **Click the Next Record button.**

The second record displays on the form as was shown in Figure 8-2b on page A 8.6.

4 **Close the form by clicking the Close Window button. When the Microsoft Access dialog box containing a message indicating the object is locked displays, click the OK button. You will need to do this twice because there are two charts on the form. Click the Yes button to save the form.**

The form no longer displays.

PivotTable Objects

PivotTable objects, also called PivotTable lists, represent an important and flexible way of summarizing information. For more information about Pivot-Table lists and their use, visit the Access 2000 More About page (www.scsite.com/ac2000/more.htm) and then click PivotTable list.

Creating and Using PivotTable Forms

To create a PivotTable form in Access, you use the PivotTable Wizard. The wizard uses Excel to create the PivotTable object and Access to create a form in which it embeds the PivotTable object. To use the PivotTable form, open the form. If you simply want to view the data in its current format, you do not need to take any additional action. If you want to use the features of Excel to manipulate the PivotTable object, however, click the Edit PivotTable Object button. Provided you have access to Excel, the PivotTable form then will display in Excel as a worksheet that you can manipulate.

Creating a PivotTable Form

Creating a PivotTable form is similar to creating any other type of form. Rather than using Design view or the Form Wizard, however, you will use the PivotTable Wizard to create a PivotTable form as performed in the following steps.

 To Create a PivotTable Form

1 **Click Queries on the Objects bar, click Marinas and Workorders by Technician, click the New Object: AutoForm button arrow, and then click Form.**

2 **Click PivotTable Wizard and then point to the OK button.**

The New Form dialog box displays (Figure 8-70).

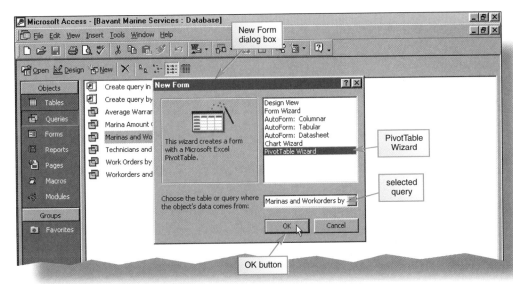

FIGURE 8-70

3 **Click the OK button and then point to the Next button.**

The PivotTable Wizard dialog box displays (Figure 8-71). This box contains a description of a PivotTable object and also a sample.

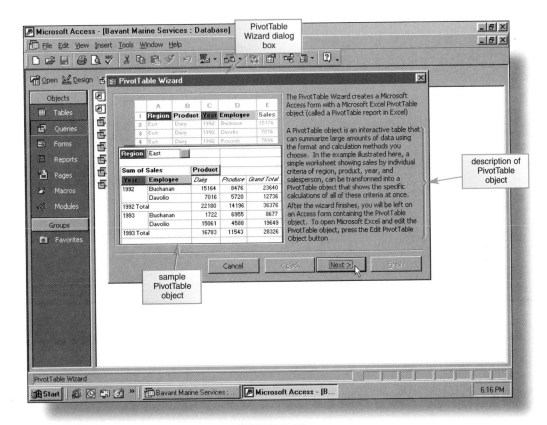

FIGURE 8-71

4 **Click the Next button. Add the Tech Number, Marina Number, Category Number, and Total Hours (est) fields to the PivotTable by selecting each one and then clicking the Add Field button. Point to the Next button.**

The PivotTable Wizard dialog box displays (Figure 8-72). The fields for the PivotTable object are selected.

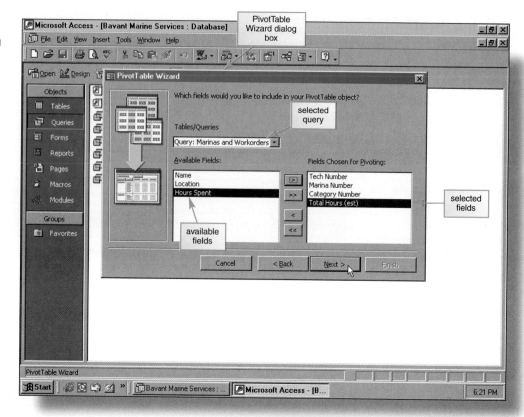

FIGURE 8-72

5 **Click the Next button. Point to the Layout button.**

The PivotTable Wizard dialog box displays (Figure 8-73). Use the Layout button to indicate the layout of the PivotTable object. Use the Options button to indicate other properties of the PivotTable object.

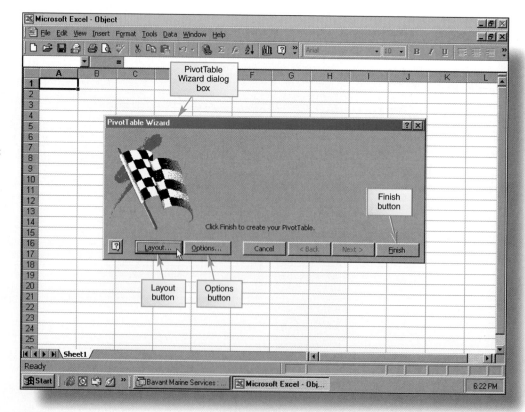

FIGURE 8-73

6 Click the Layout button. Drag the fields from the right-hand side of the PivotTable Wizard dialog box to the positions shown in Figure 8-74. Click the OK button.

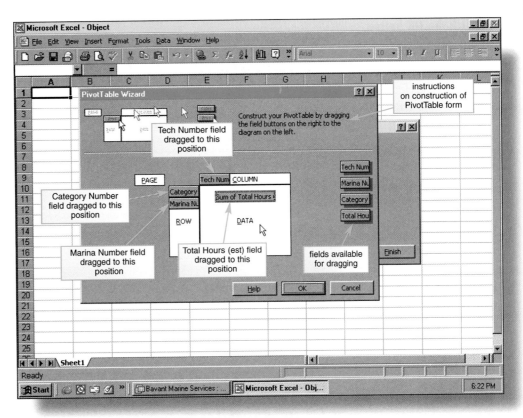

FIGURE 8-74

7 Click the Options button. Make sure your options match those shown in Figure 8-75 and then point to the OK button.

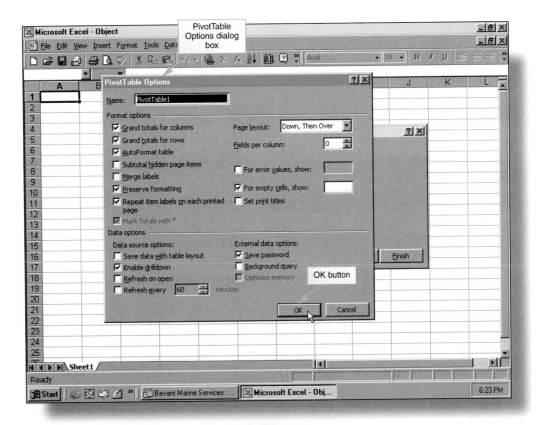

FIGURE 8-75

8 Click the OK button and then click the Finish button.

The completed PivotTable form displays (Figure 8-76).

9 Close the form by clicking the Close Window button. Click the Yes button to save the form. Type `Estimated Hours PivotTable` as the name of the form and then click the OK button.

The form is saved.

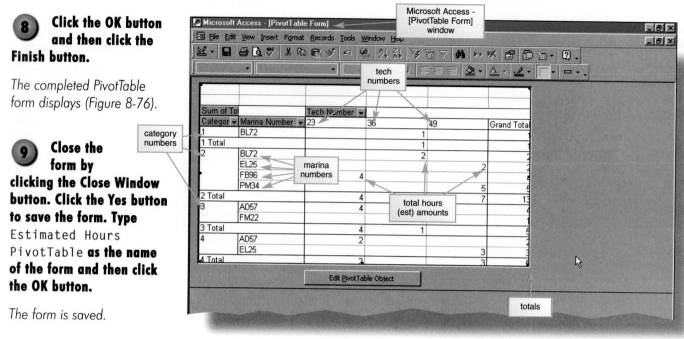

FIGURE 8-76

Using the PivotTable Form

To use the PivotTable form, perform the following steps.

 ## To Use the PivotTable Form

1 Click Forms on the Objects bar, right-click Estimated Hours PivotTable, and then click Open on the shortcut menu. Point to the Edit PivotTable Object button.

The PivotTable form displays (Figure 8-77).

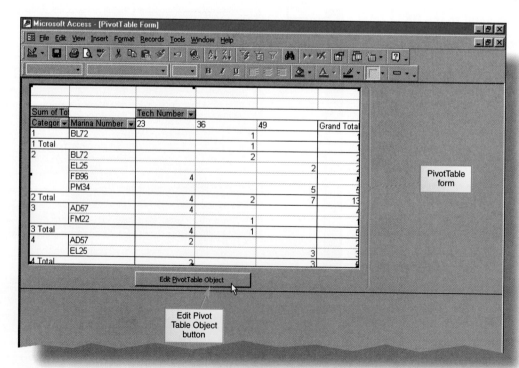

FIGURE 8-77

2 Click the Edit PivotTable Object button. If necessary, maximize the Microsoft Excel – Worksheet in PivotTable Form window. If necessary, remove the PivotTable toolbar from the screen by clicking the Close button.

The PivotTable form displays as an Excel worksheet (Figure 8-78). You now could use Excel to modify and analyze the PivotTable object.

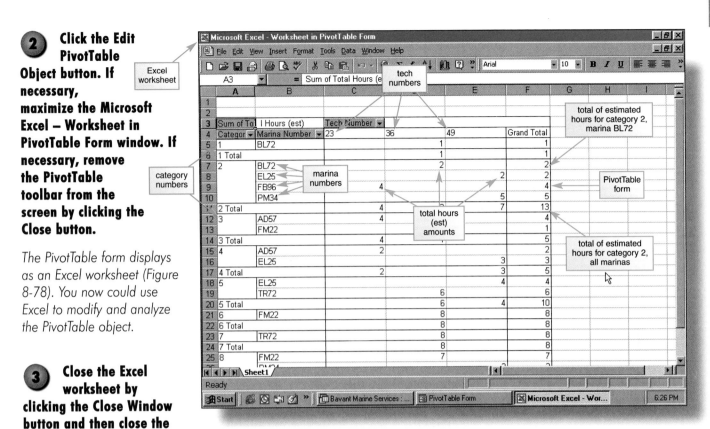

FIGURE 8-78

3 Close the Excel worksheet by clicking the Close Window button and then close the PivotTable form in Access by clicking the Close Window button.

The form no longer displays.

Closing the Database

The following step closes the database by closing its Database window.

TO CLOSE A DATABASE

1 Click the Close button for the Bavant Marine Services : Database window.

Pivot Table Objects

PivotTable objects can be used on data access pages, just as they can on forms. To place a PivotTable object on a data access page, use the Office PivotTable tool in the toolbox and follow the instructions.

C A S E P E R S P E C T I V E S U M M A R Y

In Project 8, you assisted the management of Bavant Marine Services by modifying the Marina Update Form to include special buttons and a combo box to be used to search for a marina based on the marina's name. You also created a form listing the number and name of technicians. The form included a subform listing details concerning open workorders for each technician as well as two charts that graphically illustrate the number of hours spent by the technician in each of the service categories. Finally, you created a PivotTable form that summarized the workorder data.

Project Summary

In Project 8, you learned how to add command buttons to a form and how to create a combo box to be used for searching. You learned how to create forms from scratch using Design view. You learned how to add a subform to a form and how to add charts to a form. Finally, you learned how to create and use a form containing a PivotTable object.

What You Should Know

Having completed this project, you now should be able to perform the following tasks:

▶ Add a Title *(A 8.45)*
▶ Add Command Buttons to a Form *(A 8.8)*
▶ Close a Database *(A 8.51)*
▶ Close and Save a Form *(A 8.32, A 8.38)*
▶ Create a Combo Box *(A 8.17)*
▶ Create a PivotTable Form *(A 8.47)*
▶ Create the Form *(A 8.35)*
▶ Create the Query for a Subform *(A 8.33)*
▶ Insert a Chart *(A 8.40)*
▶ Insert an Additional Chart *(A 8.44)*
▶ Modify the Combo Box *(A 8.23)*

▶ Modify the Subform *(A 8.39)*
▶ Modify the Add Record Button *(A 8.14)*
▶ Open a Database *(A 8.7)*
▶ Open a Form *(A 8.32)*
▶ Place a Rectangle *(A 8.30)*
▶ Place the Subform *(A 8.36)*
▶ Resize the Subform *(A 8.40)*
▶ Use the Combo Box *(A 8.21)*
▶ Use the Combo Box to Search for a Marina *(A 8.28)*
▶ Use the PivotTable Form *(A 8.51)*

Apply Your Knowledge

Project Reinforcement at www.scsite.com/off2000/reinforce.htm

1 Modifying Forms and Creating a PivotTable Form for the Sidewalk Scrapers Database

Instructions: Start Access. Open the Sidewalk Scrapers database from the Access Data Disk. See the inside back cover for instructions for downloading the Access Data Disk or see your instructor for information on accessing the files required for this book. Perform the following tasks.

1. Modify the Customer Update Form to create the form shown in Figure 8-79. The form includes command buttons and a combo box to search for customers by name. Be sure to sort the names in ascending order and update the combo box. The user should not be able to tab to the combo box. When the Add Record button is clicked, the insertion point should be in the Customer Number field.

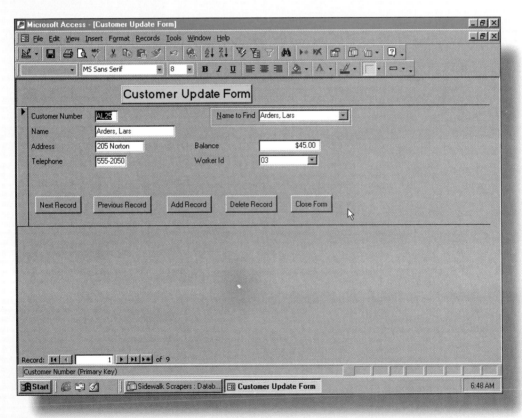

FIGURE 8-79

2. Save and print the form. To print the form, open the form, click File on the menu bar, click Print, and then click Selected Record(s) as the print range. Click the OK button.

Apply Your Knowledge

Project Reinforcement at www.scsite.com/off2000/reinforce.htm

3. Create the Balances by Worker PivotTable form shown in Figure 8-80. The table summarizes the customer balances by worker id.

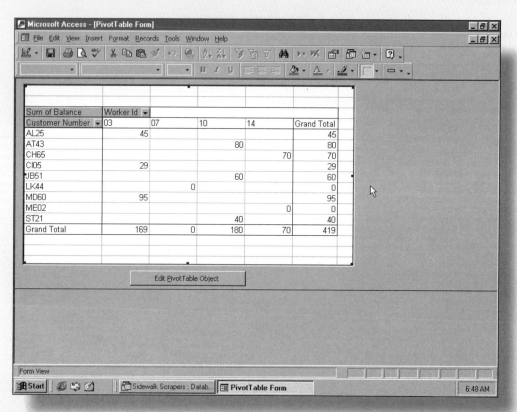

FIGURE 8-80

4. Print the Balances by Worker PivotTable form. To print the form, right-click the form in the Database window and then click Print on the shortcut menu.

In the Lab

1 Creating Advanced Forms and PivotTable Forms for the School Connection Database

Problem: The Booster's Club has three additional requests. First, they would like some improvements to the Item Update Form. This includes placing buttons on the form to make it easier to perform tasks such as adding a record and closing the form. They also want users of the form to have a simple way of searching for an item given its description. They also would like an additional form, one that lists the vendor code and name as well as any items that are on order with the vendor. The form should include a chart that graphically illustrates the total number ordered for each item. They also would like a PivotTable form that summarizes the reorder data.

Instructions: Start Access. Open the School Connection database from the Access Data Disk. See the inside back cover for instructions for downloading the Access Data Disk or see your instructor for information on accessing the files required for this book. Perform the following tasks.

1. Modify the Item Update Form to create the form shown in Figure 8-81. The form includes command buttons and a combo box to search for items by description. Be sure to sort the item description in ascending order and update the combo box. The user should not be able to tab to the combo box. When the Add Record button is clicked, the insertion point should be in the Item Id field.

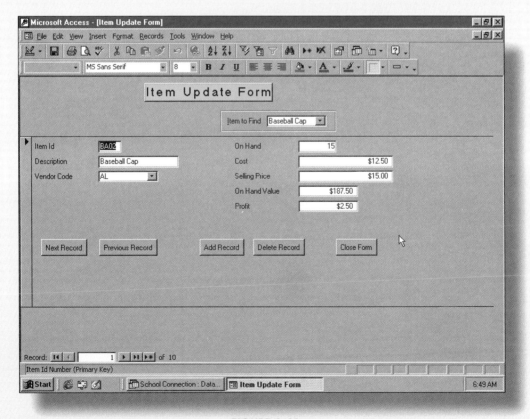

FIGURE 8-81

2. Print the form. To print the form, open the form, click File on the menu bar, click Print and then click Selected Record(s) as the print range. Click the OK button.

In the Lab

Creating Advanced Forms and PivotTable Forms for the School Connection Database *(continued)*

3. Create a query that joins the Item, Reorder, and Vendor tables. Display the Vendor Code, Name, Item Id, Description, Date Ordered, and Number Ordered fields. Save the query as Reorder Items by Vendor.

4. Create the Open Reorders by Vendor form shown in Figure 8-82. The subform uses the Reorder Items by Vendor query. Insert the graphic in the form header. (*Hint*: For help, see In the Lab 1 of Project 7.) The chart displays the item id on the x axis. The y axis shows the sum of the number ordered.

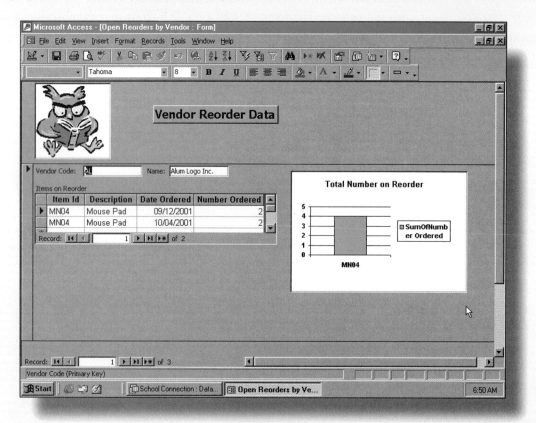

FIGURE 8-82

5. Open the Open Reorders by Vendor form and move to the record for GG Gifts. Print the form containing the data for GG Gifts. To print the form, open the form, click File on the menu bar, click Print, and then click Selected Record(s) as the print range. Click the OK button.

6. Create the Total Number Ordered PivotTable form shown in Figure 8-83. The PivotTable form summarizes the number of items on order by vendor.

In the Lab

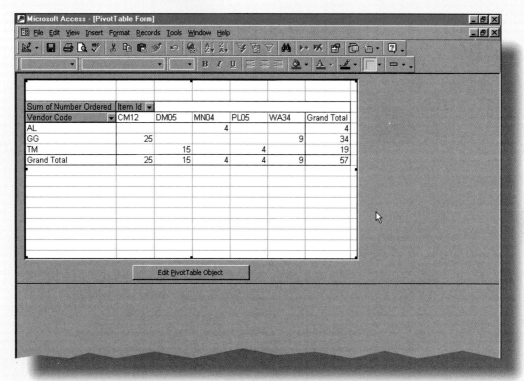

FIGURE 8-83

7. Print the Total Number Ordered PivotTable form. To print the form, right-click the form in the Database window and then click Print on the shortcut menu.

2 Creating Advanced Forms for the City Area Bus Company Database

Problem: The City Area Bus Company has two additional requests. First, they would like some improvements to the Advertiser Update Form. This includes placing buttons on the form to make it easier to perform tasks such as adding a record and closing the form. They also want users of the form to have a simple way of searching for an advertiser given its name. They also would like an additional form, one that lists the sales rep number and name as well as active account information. The form should include two charts that graphically illustrate the totals of amounts paid and balances by advertiser.

Instructions: Open the City Area Bus Company database from the Access Data Disk. See the inside back cover for instructions for downloading the Access Data Disk or see your instructor for information on accessing the files required for this book. Perform the following tasks.

1. Modify the Advertiser Update Form to create the form shown in Figure 8-84 on the next page. The form includes command buttons and a combo box to search for advertisers by name. Be sure to sort the name in ascending order and update the combo box. The user should not be able to tab to the combo box. When the Add Record button is clicked, the insertion point should be in the Advertiser Id field.

In the Lab

Creating Advanced Forms for the City Area Bus Company Database *(continued)*

FIGURE 8-84

2. Print the form. To print the form, open the form, click File on the menu bar, click Print, and then click Selected Record(s) as the print range. Click the OK button.

3. Create a query that joins the Active Accounts, Advertiser, Category, and Sales Rep tables. Display the Sales Rep Number, First Name, Last Name, Advertiser Id, Name, Description and Ad Month. Save the query as Active Accounts by Sales Rep.

4. Create the Sales Rep Account Data form shown in Figure 8-85. The subform uses the Active Accounts by Sales Rep query. The charts use data from the Advertiser table.

In the Lab

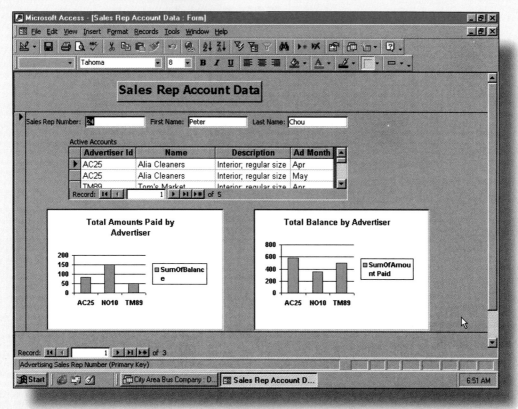

FIGURE 8-85

5. Open the Sales Rep Account Data form and move to the record for sales rep Elvia Ortiz. Print the record for Elvia Ortiz. To print the form, open the form, click File on the menu bar, click Print, and then click Selected Record(s) as the print range. Click the OK button.

In the Lab

3 Creating Advanced Forms and PivotTable Forms for the Resort Rentals Database

Problem: The real estate company has three additional requests. First, they would like some improvements to the Rental Update Form. This includes placing buttons on the form to make it easier to perform tasks such as adding a record, printing a record, and closing the form. They also want users of the form to have a simple way of searching for a rental unit given its address. They also would like an additional form, one that lists the owner id and name as well as any rentals. The form should include a chart that graphically illustrates the total number of weeks each unit is rented. They also would like a PivotTable form that summarizes the rental data.

Instructions: Open the Resort Rentals database from the Access Data Disk. See the inside back cover for instructions for downloading the Access Data Disk or see your instructor for information on accessing the files required for this book. Perform the following tasks.

1. Modify the Rental Update Form to create the form shown in Figure 8-86. The form includes command buttons and a combo box to search for rental units by address. Be sure to sort the addresses in ascending order and update the combo box. The user should not be able to tab to the combo box. When the Add Record button is clicked, the insertion point should be in the Rental Id field. The text for the buttons extends over two lines. To change the text, select the button, click to place the insertion point immediately after the first word, and then press SHIFT+ENTER. The First Record and Last Record buttons are Record Navigation buttons. The Print Record button is a Record Operations button.

FIGURE 8-86

In the Lab

2. Use the Next Record button and move to record eight. Click the Print Record button to print the record.
3. Create a query that joins the Active Rentals, Owner, Rental Unit, and Renter tables. Display the following fields: Owner Id, Rental Id, Address, City, Start Date, Length, and First Name and Last Name (of the renter). Sort the results in ascending order by the Rental Id field within the Owner Id field. Save the query as Active Rentals by Owner.
4. Create the form shown in Figure 8-87. The subform uses the Active Rentals by Owner query. The chart displays the rental id on the x axis and the total number of weeks rented on the y axis. Save the form as Owner Rental Data.

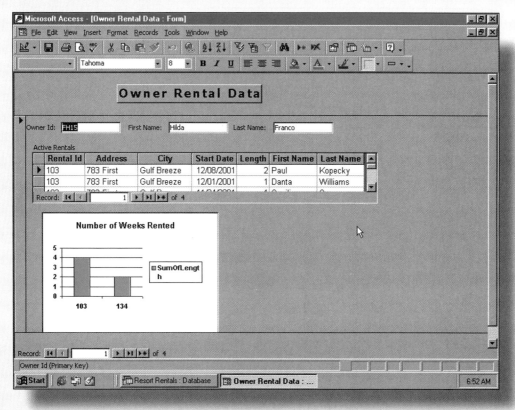

FIGURE 8-87

5. Open and print the form. To print the form, open the form, click File on the menu bar, click Print, and then click Selected Record(s) as the print range. Click the OK button.

In the Lab

Creating Advanced Forms and PivotTable Forms for the Resort Rentals Database *(continued)*

6. Create the Number of Weeks PivotTable form shown in Figure 8-88. The PivotTable form summarizes the number of weeks a unit is rented.

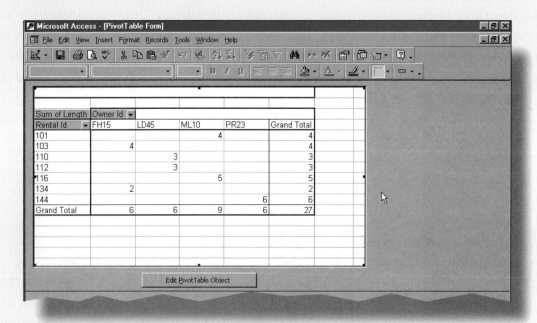

Microsoft Access - [PivotTable Form]

File Edit View Insert Format Records Tools Window Help

Sum of Length	Owner Id				
Rental Id	FH15	LD45	ML10	PR23	Grand Total
101			4		4
103	4				4
110		3			3
112		3			3
116			5		5
134	2				2
144				6	6
Grand Total	6	6	9	6	27

Edit PivotTable Object

FIGURE 8-88

7. Print the Number of Weeks PivotTable form. To print the form, right-click the form in the Database window, and then click Print on the shortcut menu.

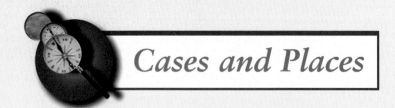

Cases and Places

The difficulty of these case studies varies:
▶ are the least difficult; ▶▶ are more difficult; and ▶▶▶ are the most difficult.

1 ▶ Open the Computer Items database on the Access Data Disk. Modify the Item Update Form to create the form shown in Figure 8-89. The form should incorporate the combo box and button features that were illustrated in the project.

Cases and Places

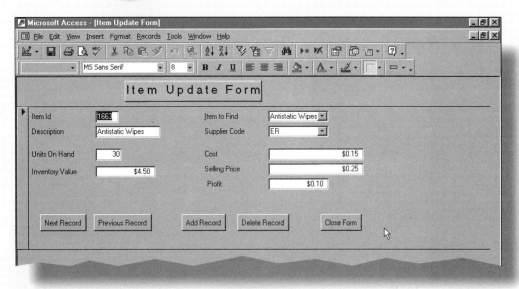

FIGURE 8-89

2 ▶ Use the Computer Items database and create the Open Reorders by Supplier form shown in Figure 8-90. The subform uses a query that joins the Item, Reorder Status, and Supplier tables. The chart graphically displays the total number of items ordered by supplier.

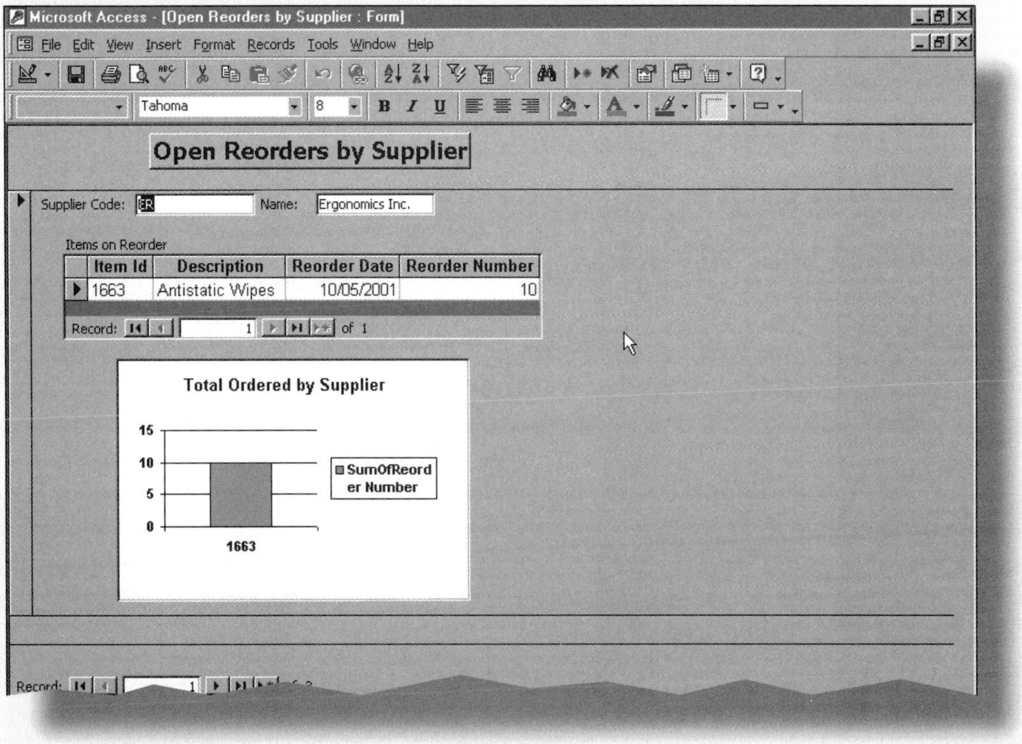

FIGURE 8-90

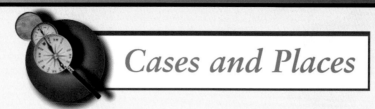

Cases and Places

3 ▶▶ Open the Galaxy Books database on the Access Data Disk. Modify the Book Update Form to create the form shown in Figure 8-91. The form should incorporate the combo box and button features that were illustrated in the project.

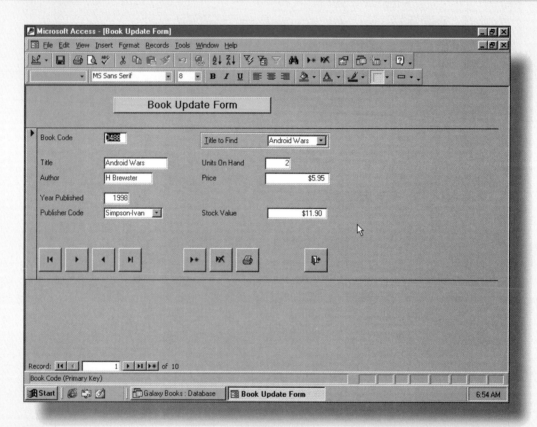

FIGURE 8-91

4 ▶▶ Create a form for the Galaxy Books database that includes a subform and a chart. The form should display the publisher code and name. The subform should include data about books on layaway. Display the book code, title, customer first and last name, and date placed on layaway in the subform. Include a chart that graphically displays the book codes and number of books for each publisher.

5 ▶▶▶ Create a PivotTable form for the Computer Items database that summarizes the number of items on order by supplier. Create a PivotTable form for the Galaxy Books database that summarizes the number of books on layaway by publisher.

Microsoft Access 2000

P R O J E C T

9

Administering a Database System

O B J E C T I V E S

You will have mastered the material in this project when you can:

- Convert a database to an earlier version of Access
- Use the Table Analyzer, Performance Analyzer, and Documenter
- Use an input mask
- Specify referential integrity options
- Set startup options
- Open a database in exclusive mode
- Set a password
- Encrypt a database
- Create a grouped data access page
- Preview a data access page
- Create and use a replica
- Synchronize a Design Master and a replica
- Create a new SQL query
- Include only certain fields
- Include all fields
- Use a criterion involving a Numeric field
- Use a criterion involving a Text field
- Use a compound criterion
- Use NOT in a criterion
- Use a computed field
- Sort the results
- Use built-in functions
- Use multiple functions in the same command
- Use grouping
- Restrict the groups that display
- Join tables
- Restrict the records in a join
- Join multiple tables

Raise the Fitness Bar

Interactive Workout Increases Motivation

Hey you! You on that bench press. Add five more pounds. And, by the way, where have you been for the past two weeks?

Imagine getting these messages from a piece of equipment at your local health club. That just might happen if your fitness center has FitLinxx installed on its machines.

The FitLinxx Interactive Fitness Network acts like a personal trainer. It monitors your workouts with a Personal Digital Assistant-sized personal computer and an optical sensor system attached to each piece of weight-stack equipment. As you work out, the system detects how much weight you are lifting, your range of motion, your lift speed, and other data on a form that resembles the forms you have created in projects in this book.

At the end of your workout, the FitLinxx network sends the data to a Microsoft Access or Microsoft SQL Server database. This database is connected to a touch-screen kiosk, so you can log in and obtain reports and graphs of your progress.

Fitness trainers traditionally use pencils and clipboards to track their clients' improvement; with FitLinxx they can log into their own computers, view a record of every workout, track trends, and create an individual's specific exercise plan. The system even tells the trainers which members have not been coming to the fitness center, and the trainers can send motivating e-mail messages to those people.

These fitness trainers perform activities related to the administration of the FitLinxx database. They help create database passwords, optimize database performance, and use add-in tools to help fitness center members optimize their exercise sessions. You will perform similar database administration actions in this project. You will replicate databases, use indexes and data type formats, set startup options, encrypt and decrypt a database, and convert an Access 2000 database to a previous version of Access.

FitLinxx is the brainchild of Keith Camhi and Andy Greenberg, who were friends at Cornell University and MIT where they studied physics, computer science, electrical engineering, and business. Camhi had joined a health club in 1991, and within six months was losing interest and thinking of quitting. He realized the value of exercise and wanted to continue the workouts, so he thought about why he was having the problem. He and Greenberg figured that software might help with the motivation factor.

They worked on a prototype system in Camhi's mother's basement beginning in 1993. A year later, they introduced a beta system in the New York Knicks basketball team's training center and a community center in Stamford, Connecticut, where FitLinxx is headquartered. Since then, they have installed their systems in more than 100 health clubs, YMCAs, and college gyms.

A subscription to the software runs about $10,000 annually, and a sensor and PDA for each piece of equipment cost about $2,000. The largest fitness centers spend from $40,000 to $250,000 to equip their entire facilities.

FitLinxx helps members achieve a safe, effective, and motivating workout. With these results, you can call the system your database workout buddy.

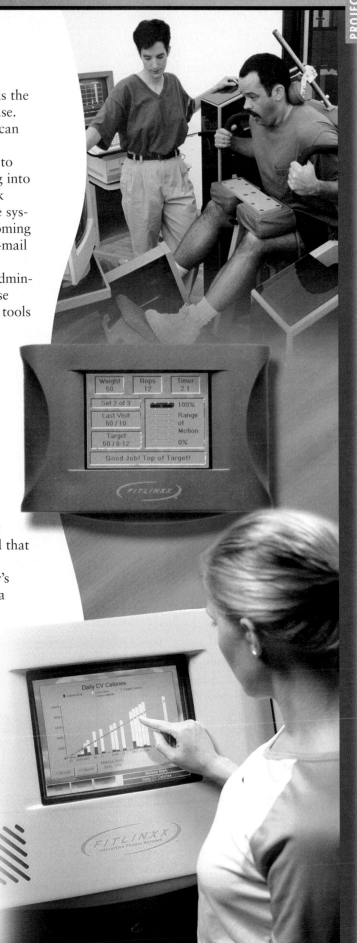

Microsoft Access 2000

Administering a Database System

Introduction

The management of Bavant Marine Services is so pleased with the work you have done for them that they have decided to put you in charge of administering their database system and have asked you to determine precisely what this would entail. You found many activities that the individual in charge of administering the database must perform. These include analyzing tables for possible duplication, analyzing performance to see where improvements could be made, and producing complete system documentation. You also determined that the administrator should specify necessary integrity constraints to make sure the data is valid. Security is another issue for the administrator, who should consider the use of both passwords and encryption to protect the database from unauthorized use. Bavant wants more users to have remote access to the database, so administration would include the creation of both data access pages and replicas. You also learned how important the language called SQL has become in a database environment and determined that the administrator should be familiar with the language and how it can be used.

Administering a database system encompasses a variety of activities (Figure 9-1). It can include conversion of a database to an earlier version. It usually includes such activities as analyzing tables for potential problems, analyzing performance to see if changes are warranted to make the system perform more efficiently, and documenting the various objects in the database. It also includes integrity issues; that is, taking steps to ensure that the data in the database is valid. These steps can include the creation of custom input masks and also the specification of referential integrity options. Securing the database through the use of passwords and encryption also is part of the administration of a database system as is the setting of startup options. Supporting remote users through data access pages and through replicas also falls in the category of administering a database. Replicas are duplicate copies of the database that could be used by individuals at remote sites and later synchronized with the actual database.

- Convert a database to an earlier version of Access
- Use the Table Analyzer
- Use the Performance Analyzer
- Use the Documenter
- Create a grouped Data Access page
- Use an Input Mask
- Specify Referential Integrity options
- Set Startup options
- Set a password
- Encrypt a database
- Create and use a replica
- Synchronize a Design Master and a replica
- Use SQL to query a database

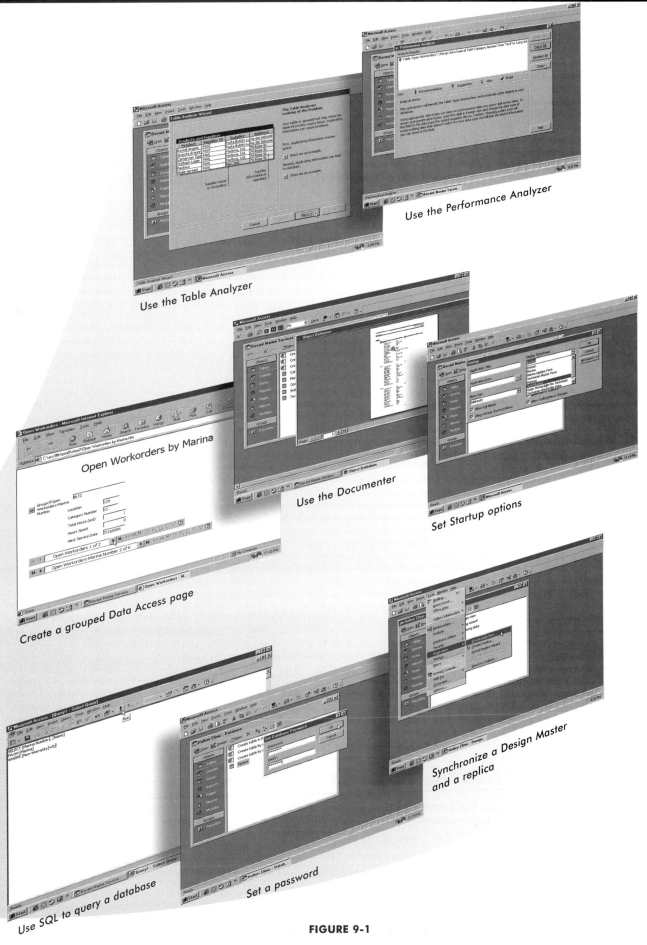

Use the Performance Analyzer

Use the Table Analyzer

Open Workorders by Marina

Use the Documenter

Set Startup options

Create a grouped Data Access page

Synchronize a Design Master and a replica

Use SQL to query a database

Set a password

FIGURE 9-1

SQL is an important language for querying and updating databases. It is the closest thing to a universal database language, because the vast majority of database management systems, including Access, use it in some fashion. Although many users will query and update databases through the query features of Access rather than SQL, those in charge of administering the database system should be familiar with this important language.

Microsoft Certification

The Microsoft Office User Specialist (MOUS) Certification program provides an opportunity for you to obtain a valuable industry credential - proof that you have the Access 2000 skills required by employers. For more information, see Appendix D or visit the Shelly Cashman Series MOUS Web page at www.scsite.com/off2000/cert.htm.

Project Nine — Administering a Database System

Begin this project by creating an Access 97 version of the database for a particular user who needs it. Next use three Access tools, the Table Analyzer, the Performance Analyzer, and the Documenter. Create a custom input mask and also specify referential integrity options. Set a startup option so that the Switchboard automatically displays when the database is opened. Then secure the database by setting a password and encrypting the database. Create a grouped data access page and also create a replica for remote users of the database. Next, turn to the SQL language and write several SQL commands to query the database in a variety of ways. You will use criteria involving number and text fields, compound criteria, and criteria involving NOT. You also will use a computed field, sort query results, use built-in functions, use grouping in a query, and join tables.

Opening the Database

Before completing the tasks in this project, you must open the database. Perform the following steps to complete this task.

Quick Reference

For a table that lists how to complete the tasks covered in this book using the mouse, menu, shortcut menu, and keyboard, visit the Office 2000 Web page (www.scsite.com/off2000/qr.htm), and then click Microsoft Access 2000.

TO OPEN A DATABASE

1 Click the Start button on the taskbar.

2 Click Open Office Document on the Start menu, and then click 3½ Floppy (A:) in the Look in box. Make sure the Bavant Marine Services database is selected.

3 Click the Open button.

The database opens and the Bavant Marine Services : Database window displays.

Using Microsoft Access Tools

Microsoft Access has a variety of tools that are useful in administering databases. These include tools to convert a database to an earlier version of Access, to analyze table structures, to analyze performance, and to create detailed documentation.

Converting a Database to an Earlier Version

Occasionally, you might encounter someone who needs to use your database, but who has the previous version of Access. Such a user cannot access the data directly. You need to convert the database to the earlier version in order for the user to access it. Once you have done so, the user can use the converted version. To convert the database, use the Convert Database command as in the following steps.

Steps: To Convert a Database to an Earlier Version

1 **Click Tools on the menu bar, click Database Utilities on the Tools menu, click Convert Database on the Database Utilities submenu, and then point to To Prior Access Database Version (Figure 9-2).**

2 **Click To Prior Access Database Version. Select 3 ½ Floppy (A:) in the Save in box. Type** Bavant Marine Services 97 **as the name of the file and then click the Save button.**

The Access 97 version of the database is created and available for use.

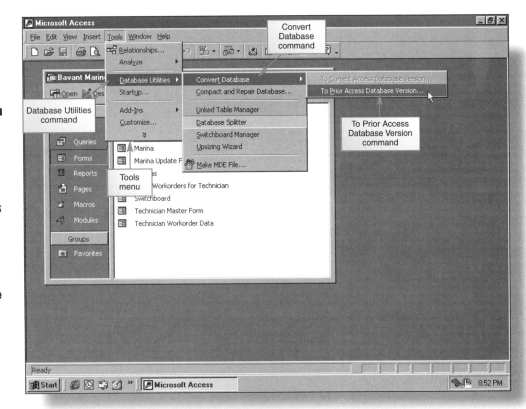

FIGURE 9-2

It is important to realize that any changes made in the converted version, will not be reflected in the original. Assuming the original version still is going to be used, the converted version should be used for retrieval purposes only. Otherwise, if you make changes they will display in one version and not the other, making your data inconsistent.

Using the Analyze Tool

Access contains an Analyze tool that performs three separate functions. It can be used to analyze tables, looking for potential redundancy (duplicated data) and to analyze performance. It will check to see if there is any way to make queries, reports, or forms more efficient and then make suggestions for possible changes. The final function of the analyzer is to produce detailed documentation of the various tables, queries, forms, reports, and other objects in the database.

Using the Table Analyzer

The Table Analyzer examines tables for **redundancy**, which is duplicated data. If found, Table Analyzer will suggest ways to split the table in order to eliminate the redundancy. Perform the steps on the next page to use the Table Analyzer.

More About

Redundancy

There is a special technique for identifying and eliminating redundancy, called normalization. For more information about normalization, visit the Access 2000 More About page (www.scsite.com/ac2000/more.htm) and then click Normalization.

To Use the Table Analyzer

1 **Click Tools on the menu bar, click Analyze on the Tools menu, and then point to Table (Figure 9-3).**

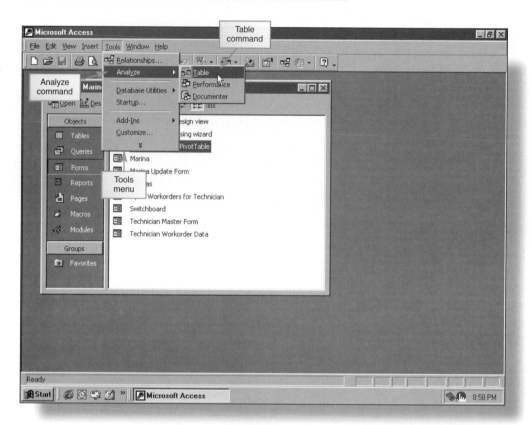

FIGURE 9-3

2 **Click Table and then point to the Next button.**

The Table Analyzer Wizard dialog box displays (Figure 9-4). The message indicates that tables may store duplicate information, which can cause problems.

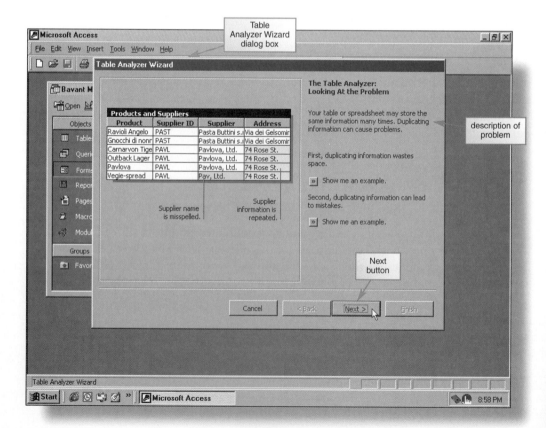

FIGURE 9-4

3 Click the Next button.

The Table Analyzer Wizard dialog box displays (Figure 9-5). The message indicates that the wizard will split the original table to remove duplicate information.

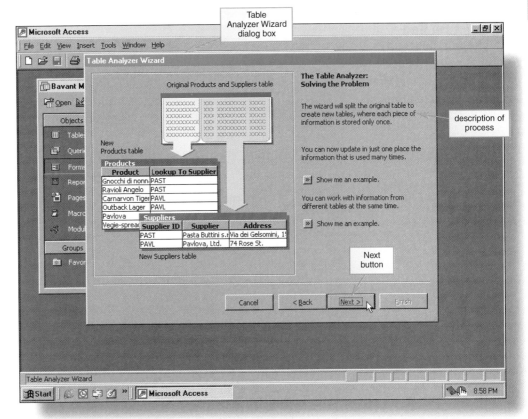

FIGURE 9-5

4 Click the Next button. Click the Marina table in the Tables box and then point to the Next button.

The Marina table is selected (Figure 9-6).

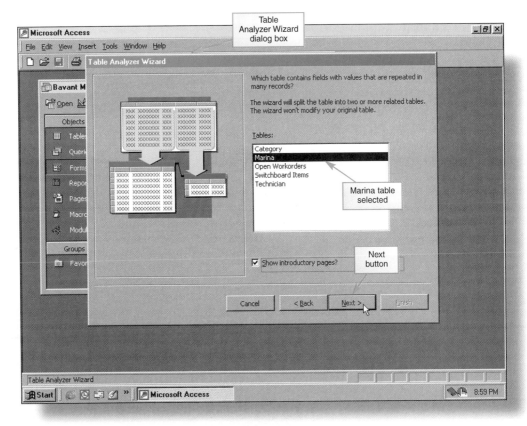

FIGURE 9-6

5 Click the Next button. Be sure the Yes, let the wizard decide button is selected and then point to the Next button (Figure 9-7).

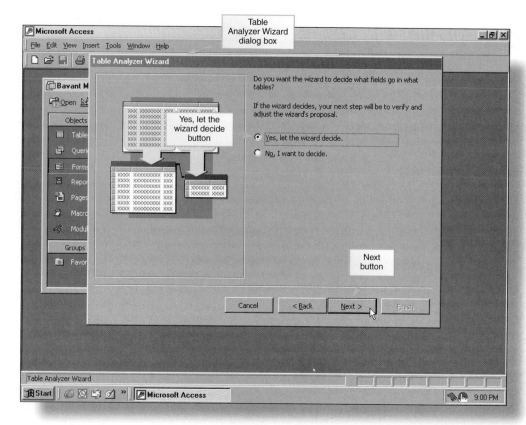

FIGURE 9-7

6 Click the Next button.

The Table Analyzer Wizard dialog box displays (Figure 9-8). It indicates duplicate information (for example, State, City, Zip Code). Your screen may be different.

7 Because the type of duplication identified by the analyzer does not pose a problem, click the Cancel button.

The structure is not changed.

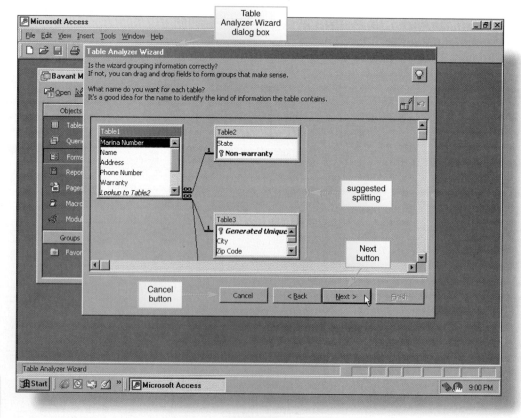

FIGURE 9-8

Other Ways

1. Click the Analyze button arrow on the Database window toolbar, click Analyze Table

Using the Performance Analyzer

The Performance Analyzer will examine the tables, queries, reports, forms, and other objects in your system, looking for changes that would improve the efficiency of your database. This could include changes to the way data is stored as well as changes to the indexes created for the system. Once it has finished, it will make recommendations concerning possible changes. Perform the following steps to use the Performance Analyzer.

Steps **To Use the Performance Analyzer**

1 **Click Tools on the menu bar, click Analyze on the Tools menu, and then point to Performance (Figure 9-9).**

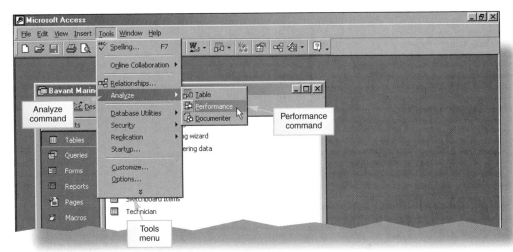

FIGURE 9-9

2 **Click Performance and then click the Tables tab. Point to the Select All button.**

The Performance Analyzer dialog box displays (Figure 9-10). The Tables tab is selected so that all the tables display.

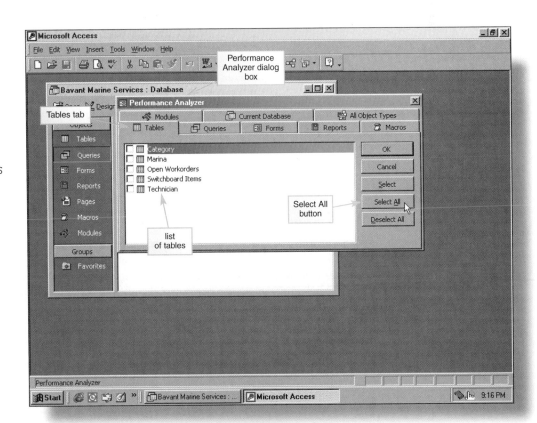

FIGURE 9-10

Microsoft **Access 2000**

 3 **Click the Select All button to select all tables. Click the Queries tab and then click the Select All button to select all queries. Click the OK button. Point to the Close button.**

The Performance Analyzer dialog box displays the results of its analysis (Figure 9-11). It indicates that you might consider changing the data type of the category number field from Text to Long Integer, which is an efficient number format, both for computations and data storage.

 4 **Click the Close button.**

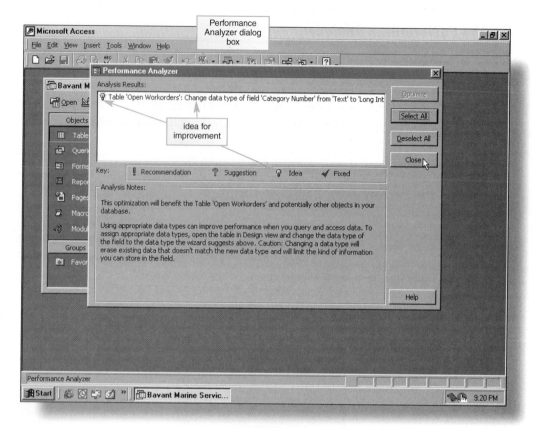

FIGURE 9-11

1. Click the Analyze button arrow on the Database window toolbar, click Analyze Performance

At this point, you can decide whether to follow the advice given by the Performance Analyzer. Because the Category Number field is used to relate tables (Category and Open Workorders), you cannot make the suggested change.

You also may decide to make a change to improve performance even though the Performance Analyzer did not indicate the change. If you have a query that is processing a large amount of data and the query is sorted on a particular field, you probably will want an index built on that field. If one does not already exist, you should create it.

 Data Types

Access provides several data types. In some cases, more than one data type might be appropriate. To select the best choice for your particular circumstance, you need to know the advantages and disadvantages associated with each of the possibilities. For more information, visit the Access 2000 More About page (www.scsite.com/ac2000/more.htm) and click Data Types.

Using the Documenter

The Documenter allows you to produce detailed documentation of the various tables, queries, forms, reports, and other objects in your database. Figure 9-12 shows a portion of the documentation for the Marina table. The complete documentation is much more lengthy than shown in the figure. In the actual documentation, all fields would have as much information displayed as the Marina Number field. In this documentation, only those items of interest are shown for the other fields.

Notice the documentation of the Phone Number includes the input mask. Notice also the documentation of the Marina Type field contains the default value, the description, and the row source associated with the Lookup information for the field. The documentation for both the Marina Type and Warranty fields contain validation rules and validation text.

The following steps use the Documenter to produce documentation for the Marina table.

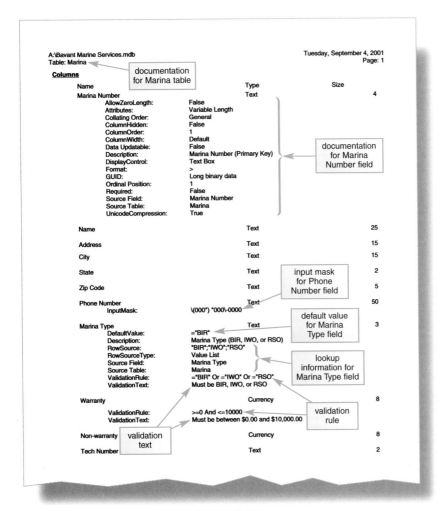

FIGURE 9-12

 To Use the Documenter

① **Click Tools on the menu bar, click Analyze on the Tools menu, and then click Documenter. Click the Tables tab, click the Marina check box, and then point to the OK button.**

The Documenter displays and the Marina table is selected (Figure 9-13).

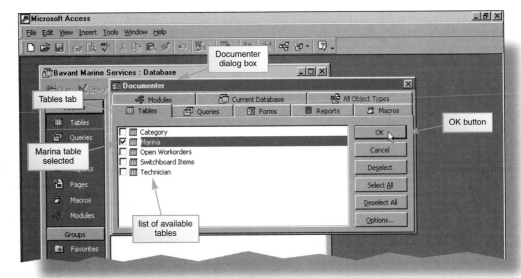

FIGURE 9-13

Click the OK button.

The documentation displays (Figure 9-14). (This may take a few minutes.) Your Object Definition window may display only a portion of the page. You can print the documentation by clicking the Print button. You also can save the documentation by using the Export command on the File menu.

 Click the Print button to print the documentation. Close the window by clicking its Close button. (If your window is in the position in Figure 9-14, drag the window to the left by dragging its Title bar. Once the Close button displays, click it.)

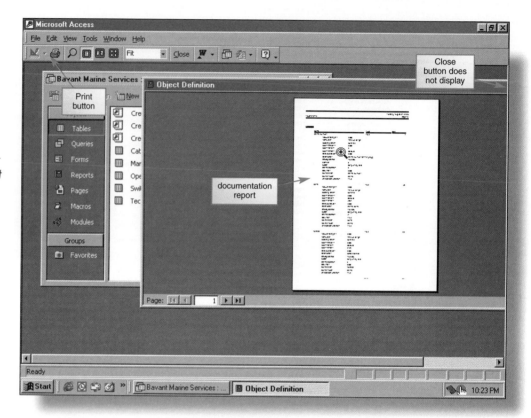

FIGURE 9-14

Integrity and Security Features

You have used several integrity features already, that is, features to ensure the data in the database is valid. These include creating validation rules and text, specifying relationships and referential integrity, using the Input Mask Wizard to create an input mask, and creating a Lookup Wizard field. In this section, you will create a custom input mask and also specify properties associated with referential integrity.

You also will use several security features, that is features that protect the database from unauthorized use. In this section, you will set startup options, set a password, and encrypt a database.

Using Input Masks

An input mask specifies how data is to be entered and how it will display. You already may have used the Input Mask Wizard to create an input mask. Using the wizard, you can select the input mask that meets your needs from a list. This is often the best way to create the input mask.

If the input mask you need to create is not similar to any in the list, you can create a custom input mask by entering the appropriate characters as the value for the Input Mask property. Use the symbols from Table 9-1.

For example, to indicate that marina numbers must consist of two letters followed by two numbers, you would enter LL99. The Ls in the first two positions indicate that the first two positions must be letters. Using L instead of a question mark indicates that the users must enter these letters; that is, they are not optional. With the question mark, they could leave these positions blank. Using 9 rather than 0 indicates that they could leave these positions blank; that is, they are optional. Finally, to ensure that any letters entered are converted to uppercase, you would use the > symbol at the beginning of the input mask. The complete input mask would be >LL99.

Perform the following steps to enter an input mask for the Marina Number field.

Table 9-1	Input Mask Symbols	
SYMBOL	TYPE OF DATA ACCEPTED	DATA ENTRY OPTIONAL
0	Digit (0 through 9) without plus (+) or minus (-) sign. Positions left blank display as zeros.	No
9	Digit or space without plus (+) or minus (-) sign. Positions left blank display as spaces.	Yes
#	Digit or space with plus (+) or minus (-) sign. Positions left blank display as spaces.	Yes
L	Letter (A through Z).	No
?	Letter (A through Z).	Yes
A	Letter or digit.	No
a	Letter or digit.	Yes
&	Any character or a space.	No
C	Any character or a space.	Yes
<	Converts any letters entered to lowercase.	Does not apply
>	Converts any letters entered to uppercase.	Does not apply
!	Characters typed in the input mask fill it from left to right.	Does not apply
\	Character following the slash is treated as a literal in the input mask.	Does not apply

To Use an Input Mask

1 **Click the Tables object, if necessary, to be sure the tables display. Right-click Marina and then click Design View on the shortcut menu. Maximize the window.**

2 **With the Marina Number field selected, click the Input Mask property and then type >LL99 as the value (Figure 9-15).**

3 **Close the window containing the design by clicking its Close button. When prompted to save the changes, click the Yes button.**

The changes are saved.

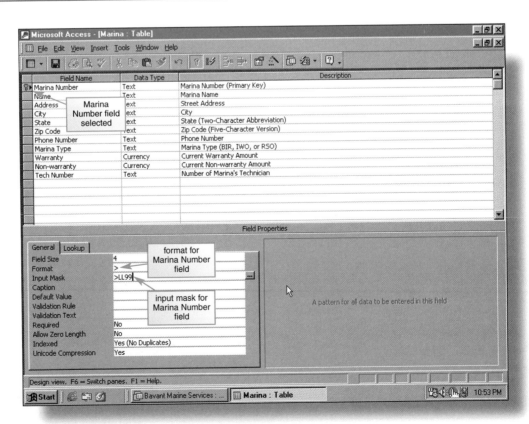

FIGURE 9-15

From this point on, anyone entering a marina number will be restricted to letters in the first two positions and numeric digits in the last two. Any letters entered in the first two positions will be converted to uppercase.

In Figure 9-15 on the previous page, the Marina Number field has both a custom input mask and a format. Technically, you do not need both. When the same field has both an input mask and a format, the format takes precedence. Because the format specified for the Marina Number field is the same as the input mask (uppercase), it will not affect the data.

More *About*

Referential Integrity

Referential integrity is an essential property for databases, but providing support for it proved to be one of the most difficult tasks facing the developers of relational database management systems. For more information, visit the Access 2000 More About page (www.scsite.com/ac2000/more.htm) and click Referential Integrity.

Specifying Referential Integrity Options

The property that ensures that the value in a foreign key must match that of another table's primary key is called referential integrity. When specifying referential integrity, there are two ways to handle deletion. In the relationship between marinas and open workorders, deletion of a marina for which open workorders exist, such as marina EL25, would violate referential integrity. Any open workorders for marina EL25 would no longer relate to any marina in the database. The normal way to avoid this problem is to prohibit such a deletion. The other option is to **cascade the delete**, that is, have Access allow the deletion but then automatically delete any workorders related to the deleted marina.

There also are two ways to handle update of the primary key. In the relationship between categories and open workorders, changing the category number for category 1 in the Category table from 1 to 11 would cause a problem. There are open workorders on which the category number is 1. These workorders no longer would relate to any existing category. The normal way of avoiding the problem is to prohibit this type of update. The other option is to **cascade the update**; that is, have Access allow the update but then make the corresponding change on any workorder on which the category number was 1 automatically.

The following steps specify cascade the delete for the relationship between marinas and open workorders. The steps also specify cascade the update for the relationship between categories and open workorders.

Steps To Specify Referential Integrity Options

1 **Point to the Relationships button** (Figure 9-16).

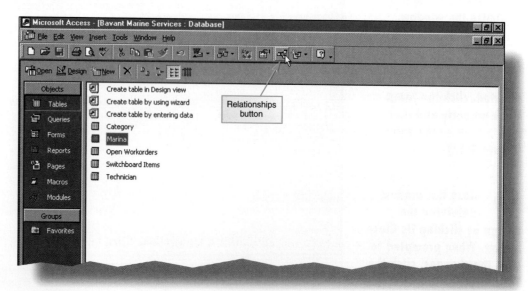

FIGURE 9-16

2 Click the Relationships button. (If the Relationships window displays a table named Category_1, right-click the line joining Category_1 and Open Workorders and click Delete on the shortcut menu. Click Yes to permanently delete the relationship from the database. Right-click the Category_1 table and then click Hide Table on the shortcut menu). Right-click the line joining the Marina and Open Workorders tables and then point to Edit Relationship on the shortcut menu.

The relationship between Marina and Workorders is selected (Figure 9-17).

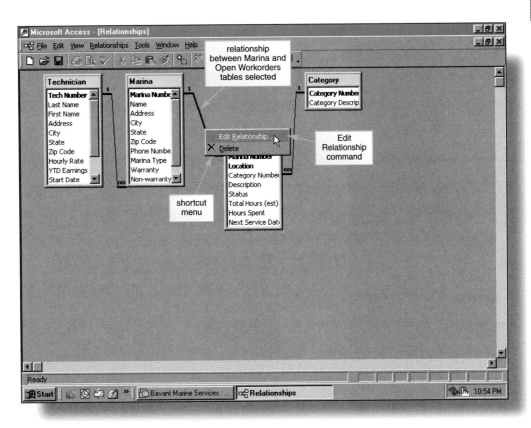

FIGURE 9-17

3 Click Edit Relationship on the shortcut menu. Click the Cascade Delete Related Records check box and then point to the OK button (Figure 9-18).

4 Click the OK button.

5 Right-click the line joining the Category and Open Workorders tables, click Edit Relationship on the shortcut menu, click the Cascade Update Related Records check box, and then click the OK button.

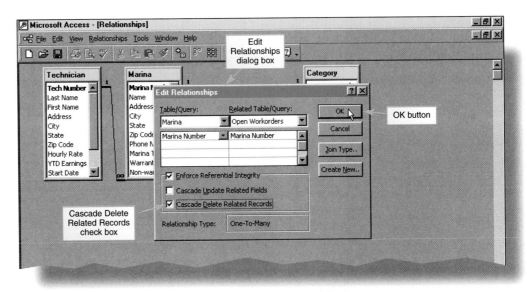

FIGURE 9-18

6 Click the Close Window button for the Relationships window. Click Yes to save the changes.

The relationships are saved.

Updating Tables with the Cascade Options

The Cascade options have a direct impact on updates to the database. The following steps first change a category number in the Category table from 1 to 11 and then delete marina EL25 from the Marina table. Because updates cascade in the relationship between the Category and Open Workorders tables, all workorders on which the category number was 1 automatically will have the category number changed to 11. Because deletes cascade in the relationship between the Marina and Open Workorders tables, all workorders for EL25 will be deleted.

To Update a Table with Cascade Options

1 **Open the Category table and change the category number on the first record to 11 (Figure 9-19). Press the TAB key twice.**

The change is made. Because the relationship between the Category and Open Workorders tables now allows for cascading the update, no error message displays.

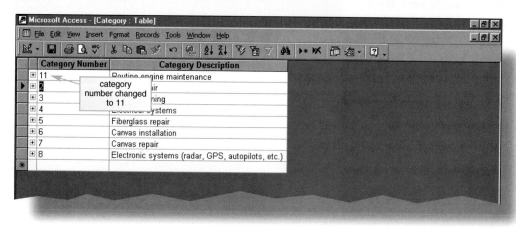

FIGURE 9-19

2 **Close the Category table and then open the Open Workorders table.**

The category number on the workorder for marina BL72, location 129 has been changed automatically to 11 (Figure 9-20).

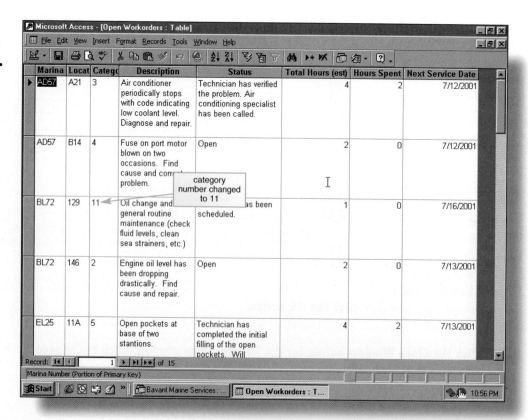

FIGURE 9-20

3 **Close the Open Workorders table. Open the Marina table and then click the record selector for marina EL25.**

Marina EL25 is selected (Figure 9-21).

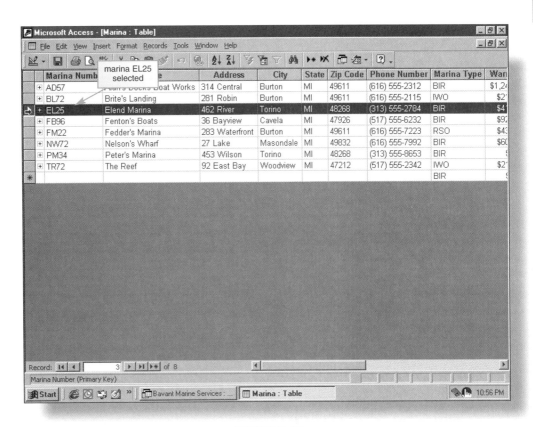

FIGURE 9-21

4 **Press the DELETE key to delete marina EL25 and then point to the Yes button.**

The Microsoft Access dialog box displays (Figure 9-22). It indicates that a record in a related table also will be deleted.

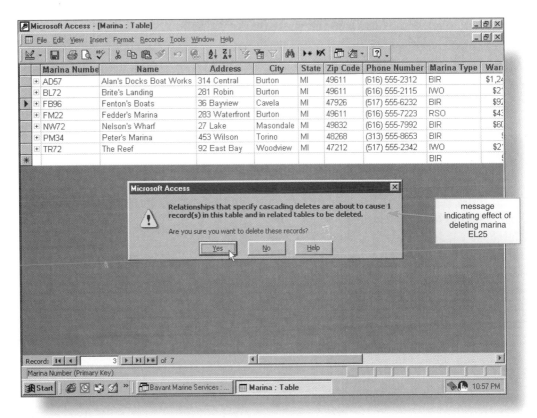

FIGURE 9-22

5 Click the Yes button. Close the Marina table and then open the Open Workorders table.

The workorder for marina EL25 (see Figure 9-20) has been deleted (Figure 9-23).

6 Close the Open Workorders table by clicking the Close Window button.

The table no longer displays.

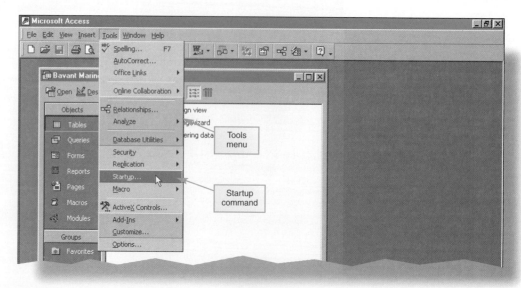

Marina	Locat	Categc	Description	Status	Total Hours (est)	Hours Spent	Next Service Date
AD57	A21	3	Air conditioner periodically stops with code indicating low coolant level. Diagnose and repair.	Technician has verified the problem. Air conditioning specialist has been called.	4	2	7/12/2001
AD57	B14	4	Fuse on port motor blown on two occasions. Find cause and correct problem.	Open	2	0	7/12/2001
BL72	129	11	Oil change and general routine maintenance (check fluid levels, clean sea strainers, etc.)	Service call has been scheduled.	1	0	7/16/2001
BL72	146	2	Engine oil level has been dropping drastically. Find	Open	2	0	7/13/2001
FB96	79	2	H operating correctly.	Technician has determined that the exchanger is faulty. New exchanger has	4	1	7/17/2001

workorder for marina EL25 deleted

FIGURE 9-23

Setting Startup Options

You can use the Startup command to set **startup options,** that is, actions that will be taken automatically when the database first is opened. Perform the following steps to use the Startup command to ensure that the switchboard displays automatically when the Bavant Marine Services database is opened.

 To Set Startup Options

1 Click the Restore button to return the Database window to its original size, if necessary. Click Tools on the menu bar and then point to Startup (Figure 9-24).

Tools menu

Startup command

FIGURE 9-24

② Click Startup, click
the Display
Form/Page box arrow, and
then point to Switchboard.

**② Click Startup, click
the Display
Form/Page box arrow, and
then point to Switchboard.**

*The Startup dialog box dis-
plays (Figure 9-25). The list
of available forms displays.
Your list may be sorted in a
different order.*

**③ Click Switchboard
and then click the
OK button.**

*The switchboard now will
display whenever the
database is opened.*

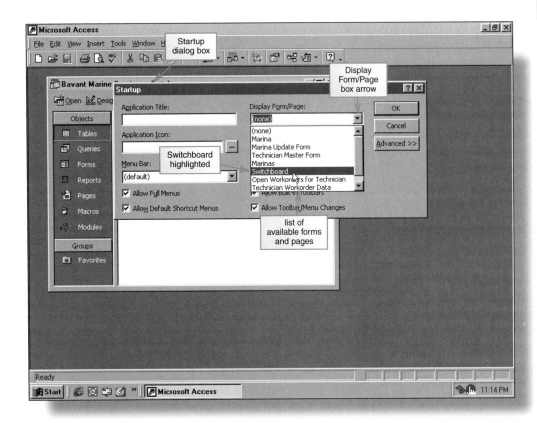

FIGURE 9-25

Setting Passwords

If you set a database password, users must enter the password before they can
open the database. The password is stored as part of the database so if you lose
or forget your password, you cannot open the database. Database passwords are
case-sensitive.

In order to set a password, the database must be open in exclusive mode. The
following steps open the Holton Clinic database in exclusive mode in preparation for
setting a password.

TO OPEN A DATABASE IN EXCLUSIVE MODE

① Close the Bavant Marine Services : Database window.

② Click the Open button on the Database toolbar.

③ If necessary, click 3½ Floppy (A:) in the Look in box. Make sure the Holton
Clinic database is selected.

④ Click the Open button arrow (not the button itself). Click Open Exclusive in
the menu that displays.

*The database opens in exclusive mode and the Holton Clinic : Database window
displays.*

Passwords

It is possible to set different
passwords for different users.
In addition, each password
can be associated with a
different set of privileges concerning accessing the database. For more information
concerning this use of passwords, visit the Access
2000 More About page
(www.scsite.com/ac2000/
more.htm) and click
Passwords.

To Set a Password

1 **Click Tools on the menu bar, click Security on the Tools menu, and then point to Set Database Password (Figure 9-26).**

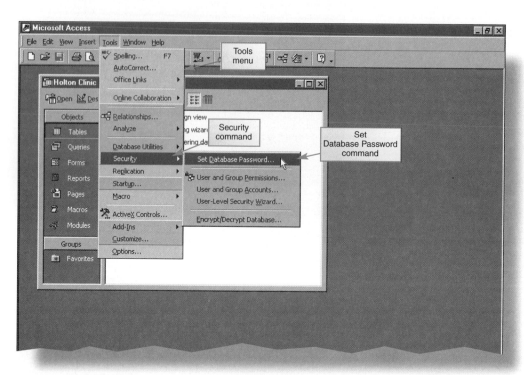

FIGURE 9-26

2 **Click Set Database Password. Type your password in the Password box. Asterisks, not the actual characters, appear as you type your password. Press the TAB key and then type your password again in the Verify box. Point to the OK button.**

The password is entered in both the Password box and the Verify box (Figure 9-27).

3 **Click the OK button.**

The password is changed.

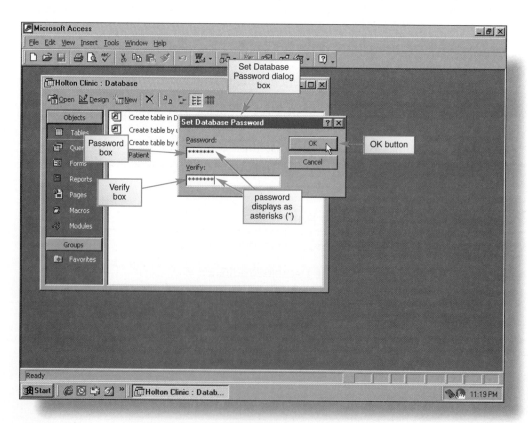

FIGURE 9-27

Now whenever a user opens the database, the user will be required to enter the password in the Password Required box (Figure 9-28).

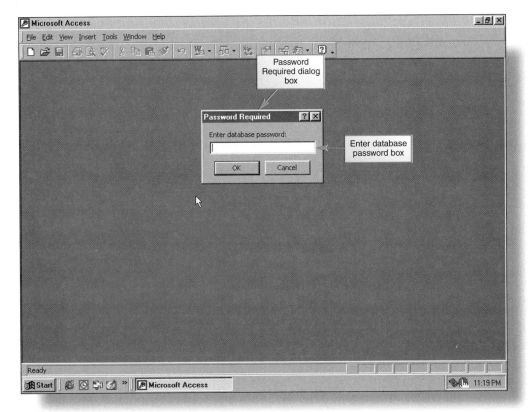

FIGURE 9-28

Encrypting a Database

Encryption refers to the storing of the data in the database in an encrypted (encoded) format. Any time a user stores or modifies data in the database, the Database Management System (DBMS) will encrypt the data before actually updating the database. Before a legitimate user retrieves the data via the DBMS, the data will be decrypted. The whole encryption process is transparent to a legitimate user, he or she is not even aware it is happening. If an unauthorized user attempts to bypass all the controls of the DBMS and get to the database through a utility program or a word processor, however, he or she will be able to see only the encrypted, and unreadable, version of the data.

In order to encrypt/decrypt a database, the database must be closed. Use the steps on the next page to encrypt a database using the Encrypt/Decrypt Database command.

Encryption

The encryption process requires Access to make an additional copy of the database, the encrypted version. Once the process is complete, the original will be deleted. During the process, however, there must be sufficient disk space available for both versions of the database. If there is not, the process will fail.

To Encrypt a Database

1 **Close the database by clicking the Holton Clinic : Database window Close button. Click Tools on the menu bar, click Security on the Tools menu, and then point to Encrypt/Decrypt Database (Figure 9-29).**

2 **Click Encrypt/Decrypt Database. If necessary, select 3½ Floppy (A:) in the Look in box. Select the Holton Clinic database, click OK, enter your password, and then click the OK button for the Password Required dialog box. Type** Holton Clinic Enc **as the file name in the File name box and then click the Save button.**

The database is encrypted and called Holton Clinic Enc.

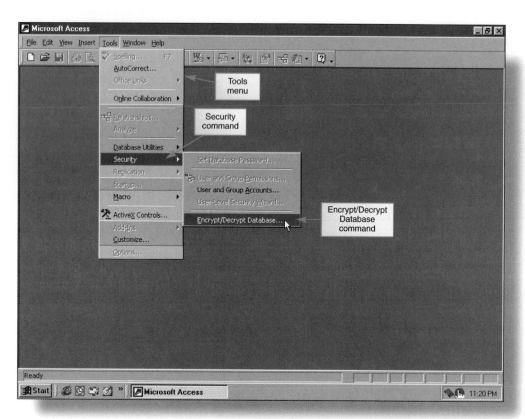

FIGURE 9-29

Removing a Password

If you no longer feel a password is necessary, you can remove it by using the Unset Database Password command as in the following steps.

Steps To Remove a Password

1 **Open Holton Clinic in exclusive mode (see the steps on page A 9.21). Enter your password when requested.**

2 **Click Tools on the menu bar, click Security on the Tools menu, and then point to Unset Database Password (Figure 9-30).**

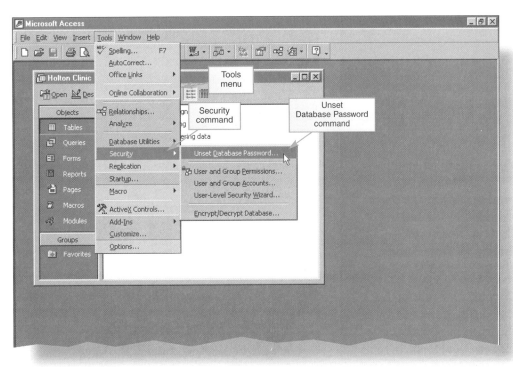

FIGURE 9-30

3 **Type the password and then point to the OK button.**

The Unset Database Password dialog box displays (Figure 9-31).

4 **Click the OK button.**

The password is removed.

5 **Close the Holton Clinic database.**

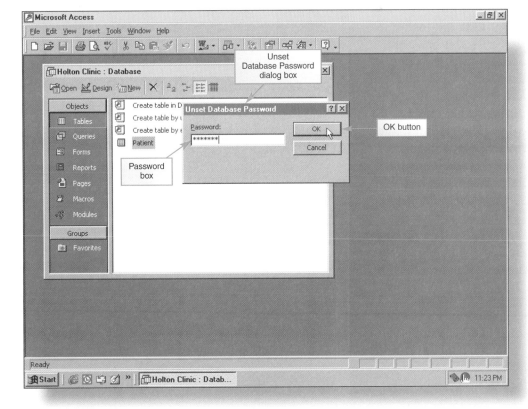

FIGURE 9-31

Creating a Grouped Data Access Page

Grouping means creating separate collections of records sharing some characteristics. You can group data in a data access page just as you can in a report. In the following steps, use the Page Wizard to identify the field to be used for grouping.

 Steps **To Create a Grouped Data Access Page**

① **Open the Bavant Marine Services** database. When the Main Switchboard window displays, close it by clicking its Close button.

② **Click Pages on the Objects bar** and maximize the Database window. Double-click Create data access page by using wizard.

③ **Click the Tables/ Queries box arrow** and then click the Open Workorders table. Click the Add Field button to add the Marina Number field to the list of selected fields. Add the Location, Category Number, Total Hours (est), Hours Spent, and Next Service Date to the list of selected fields by clicking the field and then clicking the Add Field button. Point to the Next button.

The Marina Number, Location, Category Number, Total Hours (est), Hours Spent, and Next Service Date fields are selected (Figure 9-32).

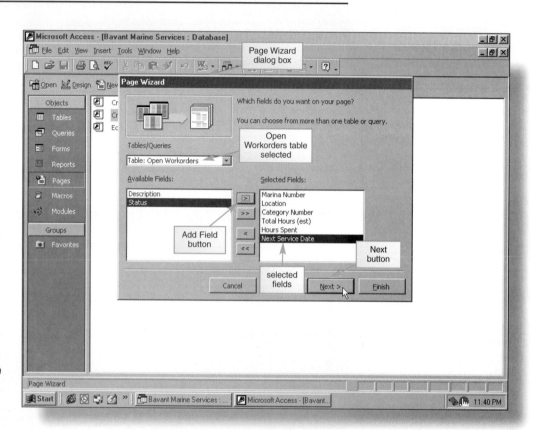

FIGURE 9-32

4 **Click the Next button and then point to the Next button.**

The Page Wizard dialog box displays, asking if you want to add grouping levels (Figure 9-33). The indicated grouping is by the Marina Number field, which is correct.

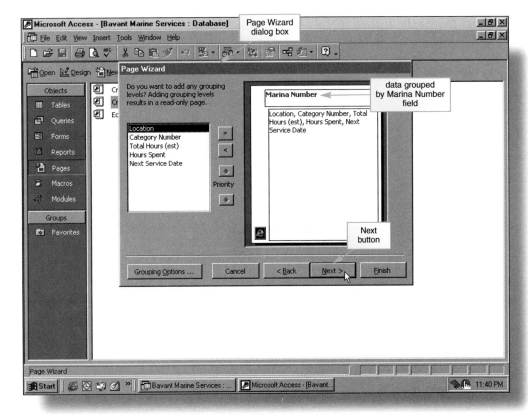

FIGURE 9-33

5 **Click the Next button. Click the 1 box arrow (the first sort box) and then select Location in the list. Point to the Next button.**

The Page Wizard dialog box displays (Figure 9-34). The Location field is selected as a sort key, meaning that the records within a group will be sorted by location.

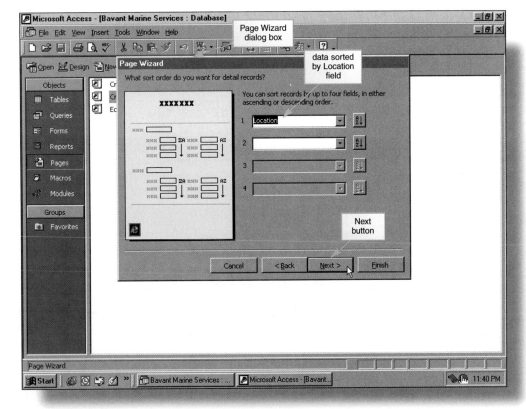

FIGURE 9-34

6 **Click the Next button. If necessary, type** Open Workorders **as the title for the page, and then point to the Finish button (Figure 9-35).**

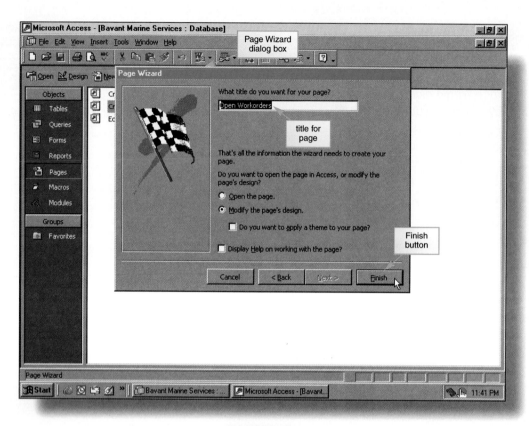

FIGURE 9-35

7 **Click the Finish button.**

The completed data access page displays (Figure 9-36).

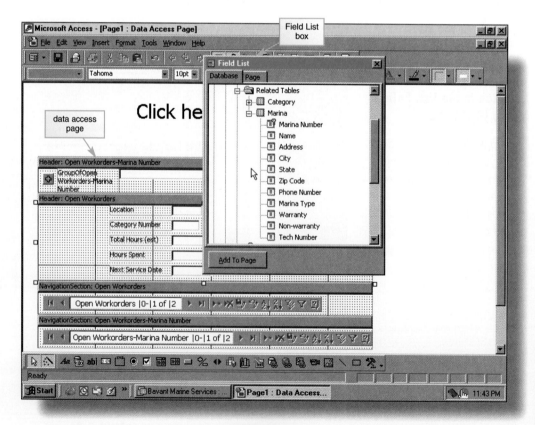

FIGURE 9-36

8 If the Field List box displays, close it by clicking the Close button. Maximize the Page1 : Data Access Page window, if necessary. Click anywhere in the portion of the screen labeled Click here and type title text and then type Open Workorders by Marina as the title text. Point to the Close Window button.

The title is changed (Figure 9-37).

9 Click the Close Window button. When asked if you want to save the changes, click the Yes button. Type Open Workorders by Marina as the name of the data access page and then click the Save button.

The page is saved.

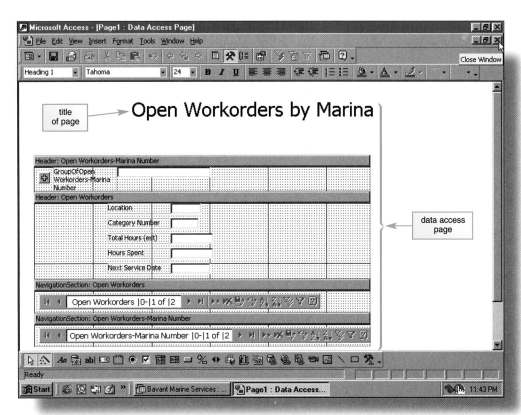

FIGURE 9-37

Previewing the Data Access Page

While in Access, you can preview what the page will look like in the browser by using Web Page Preview on the shortcut menu. Use the steps on the next page to preview the data access page that was just created.

Other Ways

1. On Insert menu click Page
2. On Objects bar click Pages, click New

To Preview the Data Access Page

 With the Database window displaying, click Pages on the Objects bar, right-click Open Workorders by Marina, and then point to Web Page Preview on the shortcut menu (Figure 9-38).

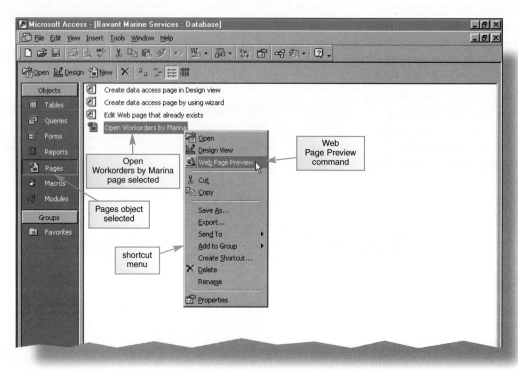

FIGURE 9-38

 Click Web Page Preview.

The page displays within Microsoft Internet Explorer (Figure 9-39). You can click the GroupOfOpen Workorders-Marina Number button to display the workorders of marina AD57, one at a time. The plus symbol will change to a minus symbol.

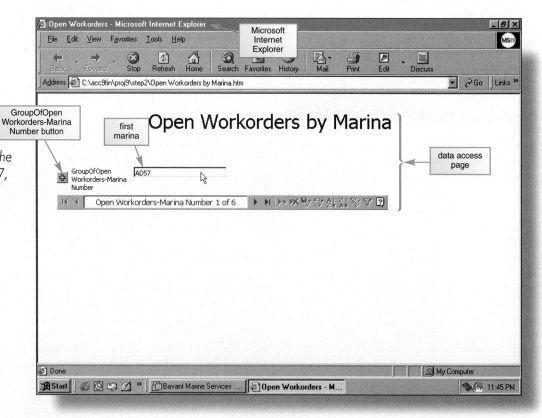

FIGURE 9-39

3 Click the GroupOfOpen Workorders-Marina Number button.

The first open workorder for marina AD57 displays (Figure 9-40). An extra navigation bar displays, indicating that this is the first of two workorders for the marina. The plus symbol changes to a minus symbol.

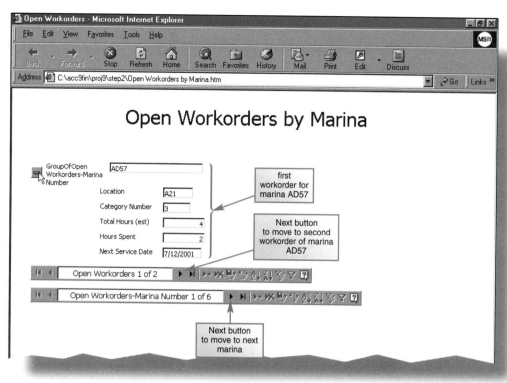

FIGURE 9-40

4 Click the Next button on the navigation bar for the workorders of the marina.

The second open workorder for marina AD57 displays (Figure 9-41).

5 Close the Open Workorders – Microsoft Internet Explorer window by clicking its Close button.

The data access page no longer displays.

6 Click the Close Window button for the Microsoft Access – [Bavant Marine Services : Database] window and then click the Close button for the Microsoft Access window.

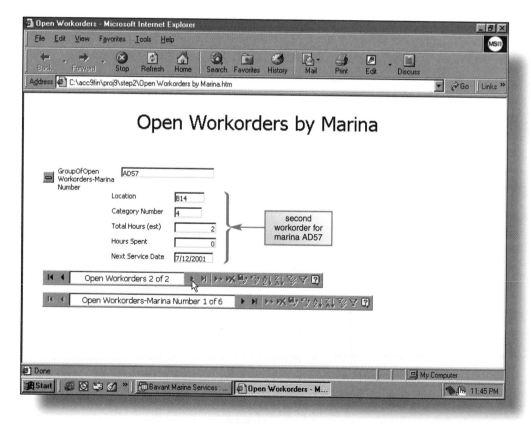

FIGURE 9-41

Replication

When many users are each using their own replicas there are potential problems in synchronizing the data. A user adding a workorder for a marina in one replica, while another user is deleting the same marina from a different replica would pose problems during synchronization. For more information concerning replication, visit the Access 2000 More About page (www.scsite.com/ac2000/more.htm) and click Replication.

Using Replication

Replication is the process of making multiple copies, called **replicas**, of a database. The original database is called the **Design Master**. The replicas then can be used at different locations. To make sure the Design Master reflects the changes made in the various replicas, the Design Master and the replicas will be **synchronized** periodically. This ensures that all databases reflect every change that has been made.

Creating a Replica

To create a replica, use the My Briefcase feature of Access. If this feature is installed, there is a My Briefcase icon on the Windows desktop. Drag the database to this icon to create a replica as in the following steps to make a replica of the Holton Clinic database. Check with your instructor to make sure the My Briefcase feature is installed before completing these steps.

TO CREATE A REPLICA

1. Use either My Computer or Windows Explorer to open a window for drive A:. Drag the Holton Clinic database from this window to the My Briefcase icon. If this is the first time you have used My Briefcase, you may see a dialog box explaining its use. Close the dialog box.

2. When the message indicating that Briefcase is making the database replica displays, asking if you want to continue, click the Yes button.

3. When the message asking if you want Briefcase to make a backup copy of your database displays, click the No button.

4. When the message asking if you want be able to make design changes in the original copy or the Briefcase copy displays, be sure that Original Copy is selected and then click the OK button.

5. Close any open windows.

The replica is created and placed in the My Briefcase folder.

Using a Replica

You can use a replica similar to any other database, except that you cannot change the structure of any of the objects in your database. Perform the following steps to add a record and change one of the names in the replica, which is stored in the My Briefcase folder.

Steps **To Use the Replica**

1 **Click the Start button on the taskbar, click Open Office Document on the Start menu, and then click My Briefcase in the Look in box. Make sure the Holton Clinic database is selected and then click the Open button.**

2 **Right-click Patient and then point to Open on the shortcut menu.**

The shortcut menu displays (Figure 9-42). The symbol in front of Patient indicates that it is a replica.

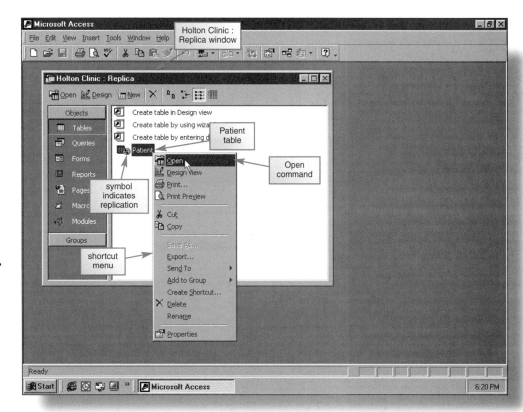

FIGURE 9-42

3 **Click Open, maximize the window, and then click the New Record button. Type the final record shown in Figure 9-43.**

FIGURE 9-43

4 Click the first name of patient number JM25, erase the current name, and then type Martin as the new name. Point to the Close Window button for the window containing the Patient table.

The changes are made (Figure 9-44).

5 Click the Close Window button.

The table no longer displays.

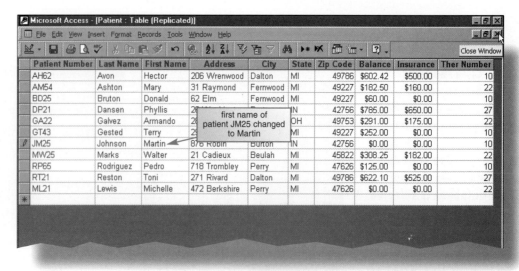

FIGURE 9-44

Synchronizing the Design Master and the Replica

Now that the replica has been updated, the data in both the Design Master and the replica no longer match. In order for them to match, the updates to the replica also must be made to the Design Master. Access will make these updates automatically, using a process called synchronization. Perform the following steps to synchronize the Design Master and the replica.

Steps **To Synchronize the Design Master and the Replica**

1 Close the Holton Clinic replica. Click Open on the toolbar, and then click 3½ Floppy (A:) in the Look in box. Make sure the Holton Clinic database is selected.

2 Click the Open button arrow (not the button itself). Click Open Exclusive in the menu that displays.

The database opens in exclusive mode and the Holton Clinic : Database window displays.

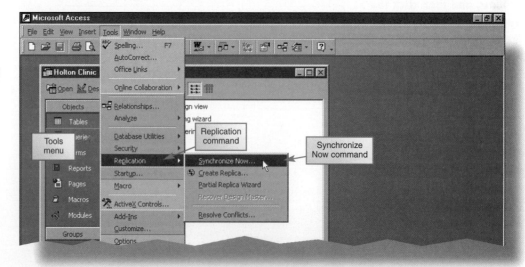

FIGURE 9-45

3 Click Tools on the menu bar, click Replication on the Tools menu, and then point to Synchronize Now on the Replication submenu (Figure 9-45).

4 Click Synchronize Now. Click the Directly with Replica button in the Synchronize Database 'Holton Clinic' dialog box and then click the OK button. When a message displays indicating that Access must close the database in order to perform the synchronization, click the Yes button.

The databases are synchronized. Access displays the message shown in Figure 9-46 when the process is complete.

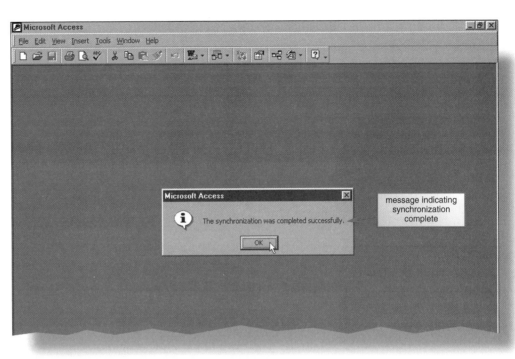

message indicating synchronization complete

FIGURE 9-46

5 Click the OK button.

The data in the replicated database (the Design Master) now incorporates the changes made earlier to the replica, as shown in Figure 9-47.

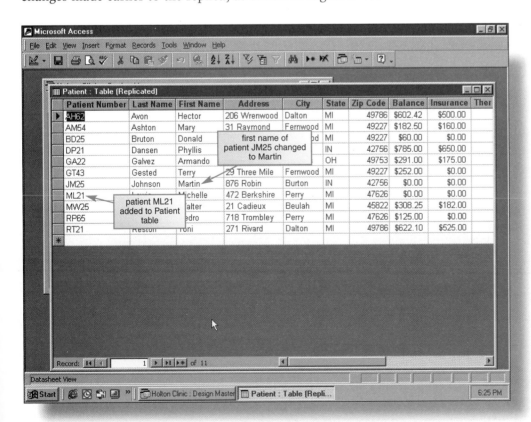

FIGURE 9-47

Microsoft **Access** 2000

More About

SQL

The American National Standards Institute (ANSI) has developed standards for SQL. These standards are continually reviewed and new and improved standards are periodically proposed and accepted. For more information concerning these standards, visit the Access 2000 More About page (www.scsite.com/ac2000/more.htm) and click SQL Standards.

S QL

This section examines **Structured Query Language** (**SQL**). Like creating queries in Design view, SQL furnishes users a way of querying relational databases. In SQL, you must type commands to obtain the desired resultsrather than making entries in the Design grid.

SQL was developed under the name SEQUEL at the IBM San Jose research facilities as the data manipulation language for IBM's prototype relational model DBMS, System R, in the mid-1970s. In 1980, it was renamed SQL to avoid confusion with an unrelated hardware product called SEQUEL. It is used as the data manipulation language for IBM's current production offerings in the relational DBMS arena, SQL/DS and DB2. Most relational DBMSs, including Access, use a version of SQL as a data manipulation language.

Creating a New SQL Query

Begin the creation of a new **SQL query**, which is a query expressed using the SQL language, just as you begin the creation of any other query in Access. The only difference is that you will use SQL view rather than Design view. Perform the following steps to create a new SQL query.

Steps To Create a New SQL Query

1 **Close the Holton Clinic database, if necessary. Open the Bavant Marine Services database. When the switchboard displays, close it by clicking the Close button.**

2 **Click Queries on the Objects bar and then click the New button. Be sure Design View is selected and then click the OK button. When the Show Table dialog box displays, click its Close button. Maximize the window.**

3 **Click the View button arrow and then point to SQL View (Figure 9-48).**

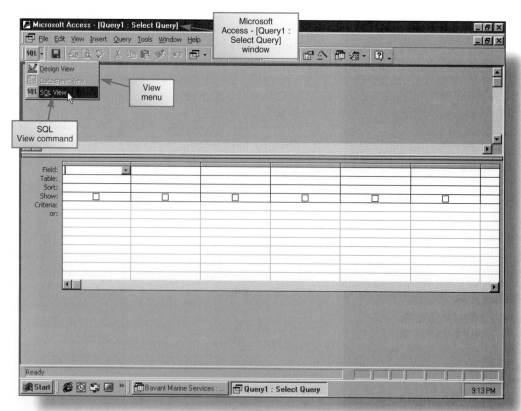

FIGURE 9-48

Click SQL View.

The Microsoft Access – [Query1 : Select Query] window displays in SQL view (Figure 9-49).

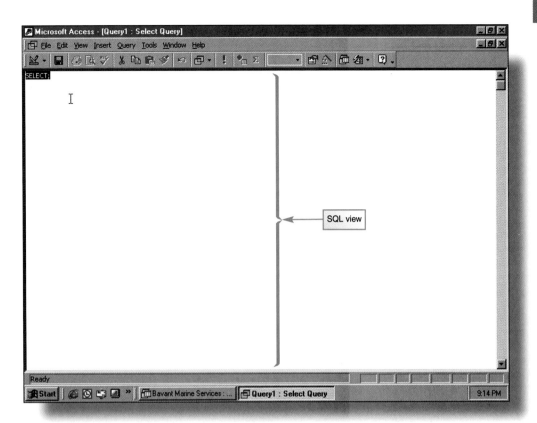

FIGURE 9-49

Other Ways

1. On View menu click SQL View

The basic form of an SQL expression is quite simple: SELECT-FROM-WHERE. After the SELECT, you list those fields you wish to display. The fields will display in the results in the order in which they are listed in the expression. After the FROM, you list the table or tables involved in the query. Finally, after the WHERE, you list any criteria that apply to the data you want to retrieve. The command ends with a semicolon (;).

There are no special format rules in SQL. In this text, you place the word FROM on a new line, then place the word WHERE, when it is used, on the next line. This makes the commands easier to read. Words that are part of the SQL language are entered in uppercase and others are entered in a combination of uppercase and lowercase. Because it is a common convention, and necessary in some versions of SQL, place a semicolon (;) at the end of each command.

Unlike some other versions of SQL, Access allows spaces within field names. There is a restriction, however, to the way such names are used in SQL commands. When a name containing a space displays in SQL, it must be enclosed in square brackets. For example, Marina Number must display as [Marina Number] because the name includes a space. On the other hand, City does not need to be enclosed in square brackets because its name does not include a space. In order to be consistent, all names in this text will be enclosed in square brackets. Thus, the City field would display as [City] even though the brackets are technically not required.

Including Only Certain Fields

To include only certain fields, list them after the word SELECT. If you want to list all rows in the table, you do not need to include the word WHERE. The steps on the next page list the number, name, warranty, and non-warranty amount of all marinas.

To Include Only Certain Fields

① **Type** SELECT [Marina Number], [Name], [Warranty], [Non-Warranty] **as the first line of the command. Press the ENTER key and then type** FROM [Marina]; **as the second line. Point to the Run button.**

The command is entered (Figure 9-50).

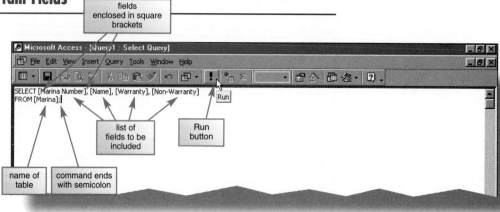

FIGURE 9-50

② **Click the Run button.**

The results display (Figure 9-51). Only the fields specified are included.

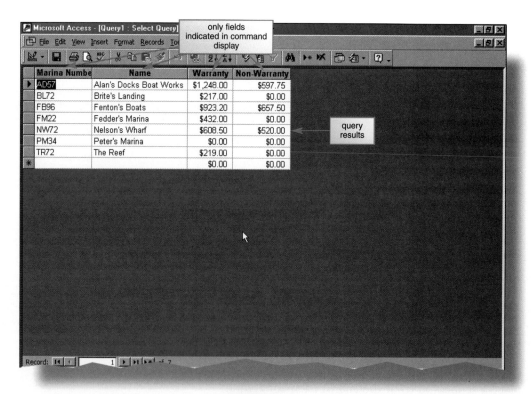

FIGURE 9-51

Preparing to Enter a New SQL Command

To enter a new SQL command, you could close the window, click the No button when asked if you want to save your changes, and then begin the process from scratch. A quicker alternative is to use the View button and select SQL View. You then will be returned to SQL view with the current command displaying. At that point, you could erase the current command and then enter a new one. (If the next command is similar to the previous one, it may be simpler to modify the current command rather than erasing it and starting over.)

Perform the following steps to prepare to enter a new SQL command.

To Prepare to Enter a New SQL Command

 Click the View button arrow and then point to SQL View (Figure 9-52).

Click SQL View.

The command once again displays in SQL view.

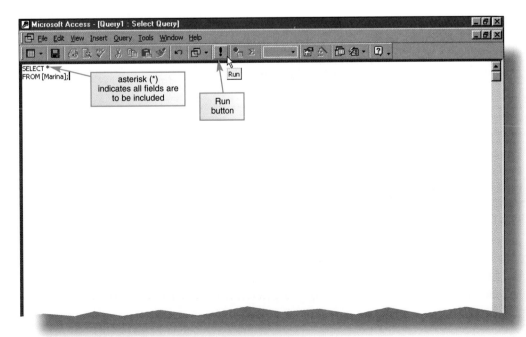

FIGURE 9-52

Other Ways

1. On View menu click SQL View

Including All Fields

To include all fields, you could use the same approach as in the previous steps; that is, list each field in the Marina table after the word SELECT. There is a shortcut, however. Instead of listing all the field names after SELECT, you can use the asterisk (*) symbol. This indicates that you want all fields listed in the order in which you described them to the system during data definition. To list all fields and all records in the Marina table, use the following steps.

 To Include All Fields

Select and delete the current SQL command. Type SELECT * **as the first line of the command. Press the ENTER key and then type** FROM [Marina]; **as the second line. Point to the Run button.**

The command is entered (Figure 9-53).

FIGURE 9-53

Microsoft Access 2000

2 **Click the Run button.**

The results display (Figure 9-54). All fields specified are included.

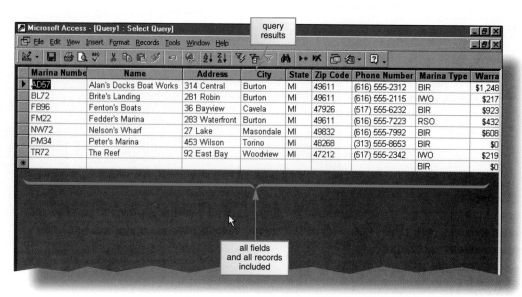

FIGURE 9-54

Using a Criterion Involving a Numeric Field

To restrict the records to be displayed, include the word WHERE followed by a criterion as part of the command. If the field involved is a Numeric field, you simply type the value. For example, to list the marina number of all marinas whose non-warranty amount is 0, you would type the condition [Non-Warranty]=0 as in the following steps.

Steps **To Use a Criterion Involving a Numeric Field**

 Click the View button arrow, click SQL View, and then select and delete the current SQL command.

2 **Type** SELECT [Marina Number], [Name] **as the first line of the command. Press the ENTER key and then type** FROM [Marina] **as the second line. Press the ENTER key and then type** WHERE [Non-Warranty]=0; **as the third line. Point to the Run button.**

The command is entered (Figure 9-55).

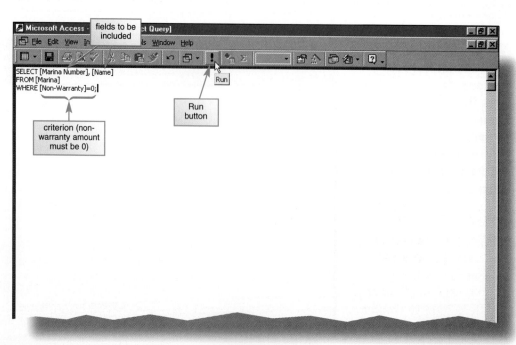

FIGURE 9-55

 **Click the Run button.**

The results display (Figure 9-56). Only those marinas for which the non-warranty amount is 0 are included.

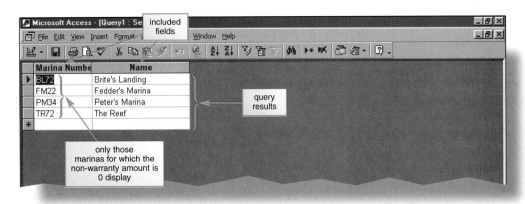

FIGURE 9-56

The criterion following the word WHERE in the preceding query is called a simple criterion. A **simple criterion** has the form: field name, comparison operator, then either another field name or a value. The possible comparison operators are shown in Table 9-2.

Using a Criterion Involving a Text Field

If the criterion involves a Text field, the value must be enclosed in single quotation marks. In the following example, all marinas located in Burton are listed; that is, all marinas for whom the value in the City field is Burton.

Table 9-2 Comparison Operators	
COMPARISON OPERATOR	**MEANING**
=	Equal to
<	Less than
>	Greater than
<=	Less than or equal to
>=	Greater than or equal to
<>	Not equal to

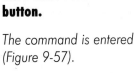 **To Use a Criterion Involving a Text Field**

 **Click the View button arrow, click SQL View, and then select and delete the current SQL command.**

 **Type** SELECT [Marina Number] **as the first line of the command. Press the ENTER key and then type** FROM [Marina] **as the second line. Press the ENTER key and then type** WHERE [City]='Burton'; **as the third line. Point to the Run button.**

The command is entered (Figure 9-57).

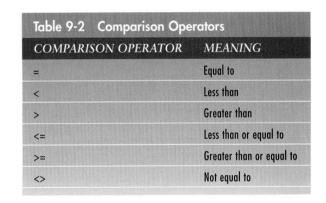

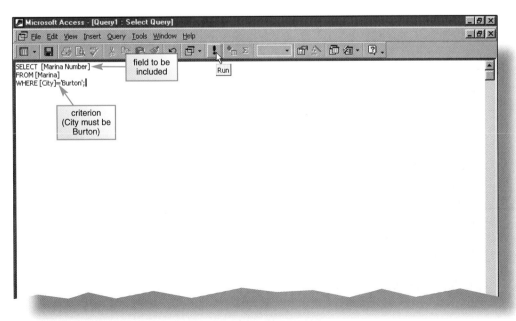

FIGURE 9-57

3 **Click the Run button.**

The results display (Figure 9-58). Only those marinas located in Burton are included.

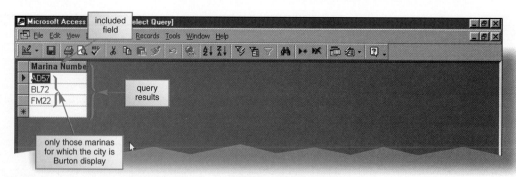

FIGURE 9-58

Using Compound Criteria

The criterion you have seen so far are called simple criterion. The next examples require compound criteria. **Compound criteria** are formed by connecting two or more simple criteria using AND, OR, and NOT. When connected by the word AND, all the simple criteria must be true in order for the compound criterion to be true. When connected by the word OR, the compound criteria will be true whenever any of the simple criterion is true. Preceding a criterion by NOT reverses the truth or falsity of the original criterion. If the original criterion is true, the new criterion will be false; if the original criterion is false, then the new one will be true.

The following steps use compound criteria to display the names of those marinas located in Burton and for whom the non-warranty amount is 0.

 To Use Compound Criteria

1 **Click the View button arrow, click SQL View, and then select and delete the current SQL command.**

2 **Type** SELECT [Name] **as the first line of the command. Press the ENTER key and then type** FROM [Marina] **as the second line. Press the ENTER key and then type** WHERE [City]='Burton' **as the third line. Press the ENTER key and then type** AND [Non-Warranty]=0; **as the fourth line. Point to the Run button.**

The command is entered (Figure 9-59).

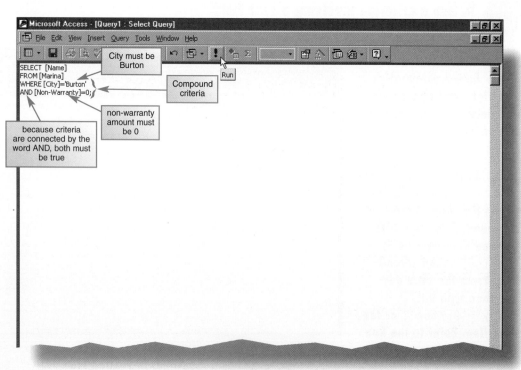

FIGURE 9-59

Click the Run button.

The results display (Figure 9-60). Only those marinas located in Burton and with a non-warranty amount of 0 are included.

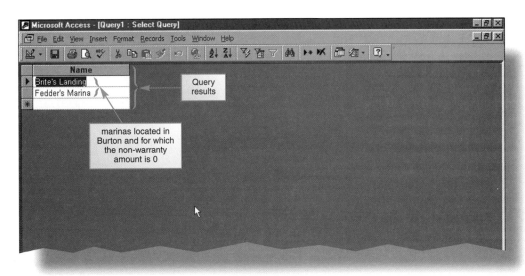

FIGURE 9-60

You use the same method to form compound criteria involving OR. Simply use the word OR instead of the word AND. In that case, the results would contain those records that satisfied either criterion.

Using NOT in a Criterion

To use NOT in a criterion, precede the criterion with the word NOT. Perform the following steps to list the names of the marinas not located in Burton.

 To Use NOT in a Criterion

Click the View button arrow, click SQL View, and then select and delete the current SQL command.

Type SELECT [Name] **as the first line of the command. Press the ENTER key and then type** FROM [Marina] **as the second line. Press the ENTER key and then type** WHERE NOT [City]='Burton'; **as the third line. Point to the Run button.**

The command is entered (Figure 9-61).

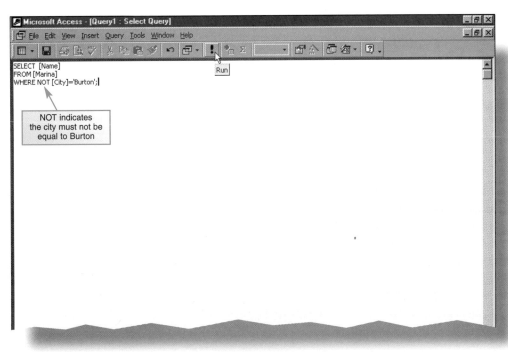

FIGURE 9-61

Click the Run button.

The results display (Figure 9-62). Only those marinas not located in Burton are included.

FIGURE 9-62

Using Computed Fields

Just as with queries created in Design view, you can include fields in queries that are not in the database, but that can be computed from fields that are. This type of field is called a **computed** or **calculated field**. Such computations can involve addition (+), subtraction (-), multiplication (*), or division (/). The query in the following steps includes the total amount, which is equal to the warranty amount plus the non-warranty amount.

To name the computed field, follow the computation with the word AS and then the name you wish to assign the field. The following steps assign the name Total Amount to the computed field and also list the Marina Number and Name for all marinas for which the non-warranty amount is greater than 0.

 To Use a Computed Field

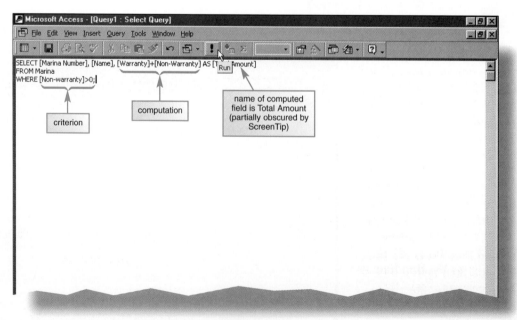

FIGURE 9-63

① **Click the View button arrow, click SQL View, and then select and delete the current SQL command.**

② **Type** SELECT [Marina Number], [Name], [Warranty]+ [Non-Warranty] AS [Total Amount] **as the first line of the command. Press the ENTER key and then type** FROM [Marina] **as the second line. Press the ENTER key and then type** WHERE [Non-Warranty]>0; **as the third line. Point to the Run button.**

The command is entered (Figure 9-63).

Click the Run button.

The results display (Figure 9-64). The total amount is calculated appropriately. Only those marinas with a non-warranty amount greater than 0 are included.

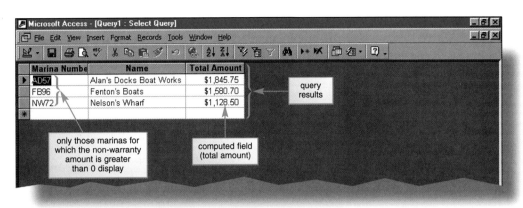

FIGURE 9-64

Sorting the Results

The field on which data is to be sorted is called a **sort key**, or simply a **key**. If the data is to be sorted on two fields, the more important key is called the **major sort key** (also referred to as the **primary sort key**) and the less important key is called the **minor sort key** (also referred to as the **secondary sort key**). To sort the output, you include the words ORDER BY, followed by the sort key. If there are two sort keys, the major sort key is listed first.

The following steps list the marina number, name, warranty amount, non-warranty amount, and technician number for all marinas. The data is to be sorted by technician number and within the marinas having the same technician number, the data is to be further sorted by warranty amount. This means that the Tech Number field is the major (primary) sort key and the Warranty field is the minor (secondary) sort key.

Sorting

In SQL, you can sort in descending order by following the sort key with DESC in the ORDER BY clause. If you have two sort keys, you could choose to sort one in descending order and the other in ascending order. For example, ORDER BY [Tech Number], [Warranty] DESC; would sort on ascending Tech Number and descending Warranty.

 To Sort the Results

 Click the View button arrow, click SQL View, and then select and delete the current SQL command.

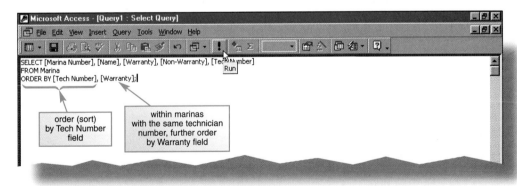

FIGURE 9-65

Type SELECT [Marina Number], [Name], [Warranty], [Non-Warranty], [Tech Number] **as the first line of the command. Press the ENTER key and then type** FROM [Marina] **as the second line. Press the ENTER key and then type** ORDER BY [Tech Number], [Warranty]; **as the third line. Point to the Run button.**

The command is entered (Figure 9-65). By default, the records will be sorted in ascending order.

3 **Click the Run button.**

The results display (Figure 9-66). The marinas are sorted ascending by the Tech Number field. Within the marinas of a particular technician, the results further are sorted by warranty amount.

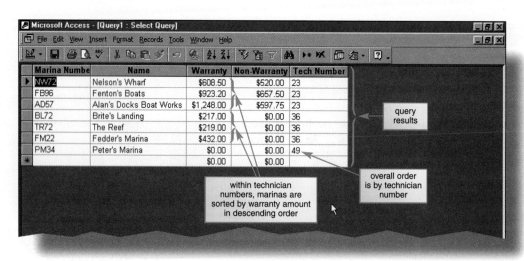

FIGURE 9-66

Using Built-In Functions

SQL has **built-in** functions (also called **aggregate** functions) to calculate the number of entries, the sum or average of all the entries in a given column, and the largest or smallest of the entries in a given column. In SQL, these functions are called COUNT, SUM, AVG, MAX, and MIN.

The following steps count the number of marinas assigned to technician 23. Perform these steps to use the COUNT function with an asterisk (*).

 To Use a Built-In Function

1 **Click the View button arrow, click SQL View, and then select and delete the current SQL command.**

2 **Type** SELECT COUNT(*) **as the first line of the command. Press the ENTER key and then type** FROM [Marina] **as the second line. Press the ENTER key and then type** WHERE [Tech Number]='23'; **as the third line. Point to the Run button.**

The command is entered (Figure 9-67).

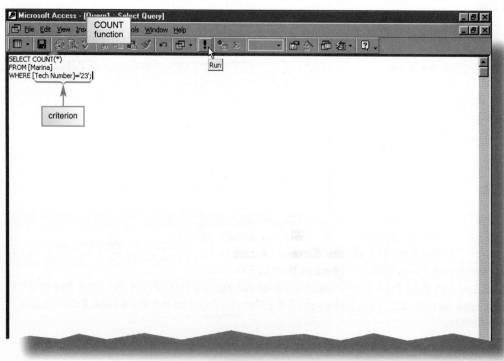

FIGURE 9-67

3 Click the Run button.

The results display (Figure 9-68). The heading Expr1000 is a default heading assigned by Access.

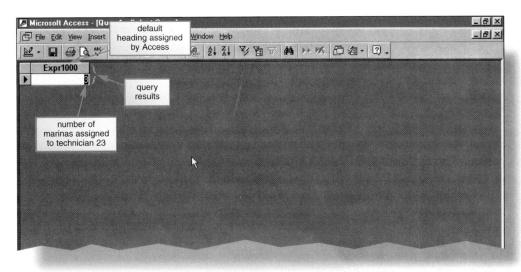

FIGURE 9-68

Using Multiple Functions in the Same Command

The only differences between COUNT and SUM, other than the obvious fact that they are computing different statistics, are that first, in the case of SUM, you must specify the field for which you want a total, rather than an asterisk (*), and second, the field must be numeric. You could not calculate a sum of names or addresses, for example. The following steps use both the COUNT and SUM functions to count the number of marinas and calculate the SUM (total) of their warranty amounts.

 To Use Multiple Functions in the Same Command

1 Click the View button arrow, click SQL View, and then select and delete the current SQL command.

2 Type SELECT COUNT(*), SUM([Warranty]) as the first line of the command. Press the ENTER key and then type FROM [Marina]; as the second line. Point to the Run button.

The command is entered (Figure 9-69).

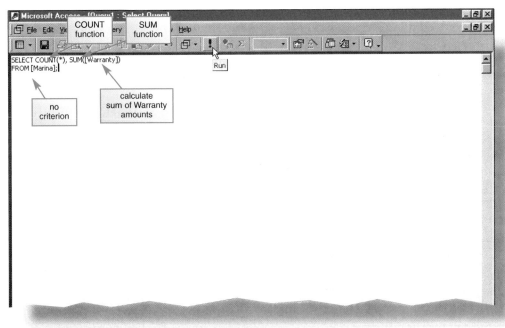

FIGURE 9-69

Microsoft **Access 2000**

3 **Click the Run button.**

The results display (Figure 9-70). The number of marinas (7) and the total of the warranty amounts ($3,647.70) both display.

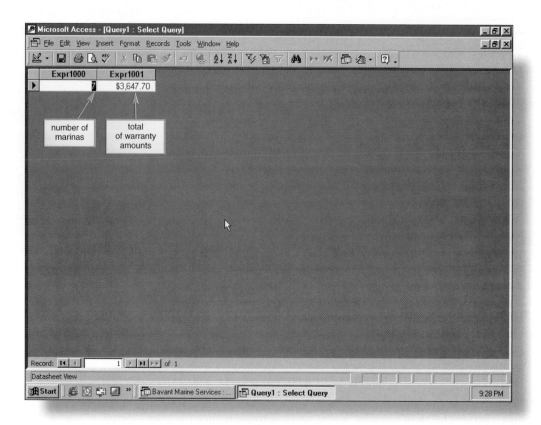

FIGURE 9-70

The use of AVG, MAX, and MIN is similar to SUM. The only difference is that a different statistic is calculated.

Using Grouping

Grouping means creating groups of records that share some common characteristic. In grouping workorders by marina number, for example, the workorders of marina AD57 would form one group, the workorders of marina BL72 would from a second, the workorders of marina FB96 would form a third, and so on.

The following steps calculate the totals of the Total Hours (est) and the Hours Spent fields for each marina. To calculate the totals, the command will include the SUM([Total Hours (est)]) and SUM([Hours Spent]). To get individual totals for each marina the command also will include the words GROUP BY followed by the field used for grouping, in this case Marina Number.

Including GROUP BY Marina Number will cause the workorders for each marina to be grouped together; that is, all workorders with the same marina number will form a group. Any statistics, such as totals, displaying after the word SELECT will be calculated for each of these groups. It is important to note that using GROUP BY does not imply that the information will be sorted. To produce the results in a particular order, you also should use ORDER BY as in the following steps.

Steps To Use Grouping

1 **Click the View button arrow, click SQL View, and then select and delete the current SQL command.**

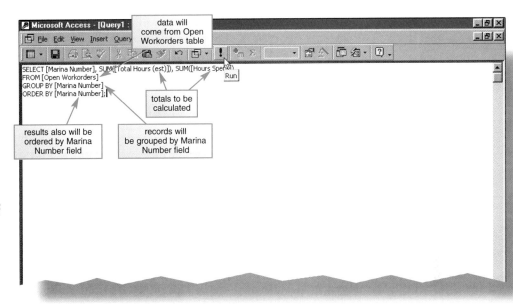

FIGURE 9-71

2 **Type** SELECT [Marina Number], SUM([Total Hours (est)]), SUM([Hours Spent]) **as the first line of the command. Press the ENTER key and then type** FROM [Open Workorders] **as the second line. Press the ENTER key and then type** GROUP BY [Marina Number] **as the third line. Press the ENTER key and then type** ORDER BY [Marina Number]; **as the fourth line. Point to the Run button.**

The command is entered (Figure 9-71).

3 **Click the Run button.**

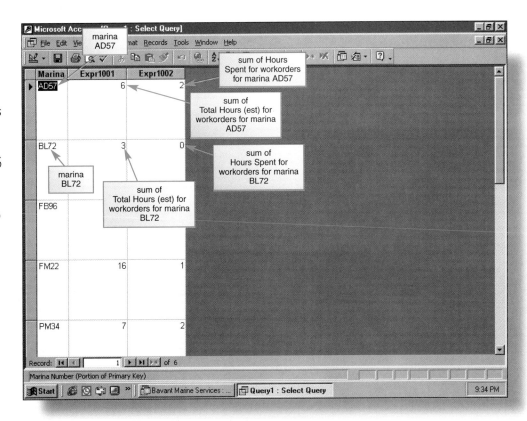

The results display (Figure 9-72). The first row represents the group of workorders for marina AD57. For these workorders, the sum of the Total Hours (est) amounts is 6 and the sum of the Hours Spent amounts is 2. The second row represents the group of workorders for marina BL72. For these workorders, the sum of the Total Hours (est) amounts is 3 and the sum of the Hours Spent amounts is 0.

FIGURE 9-72

When rows are grouped, one line of output is produced for each group. The only things that may be displayed are statistics calculated for the group or fields whose values are the same for all rows in a group. For example, it would make sense to display the marina number, because all the workorders in the group have the same marina number. It would not make sense to display the start date, because the start date will vary from one row in a group to another. SQL could not determine which start date to display for the group.

Restricting the Groups that Display

In some cases you only want to display certain groups. For example, you may wish to display only those marinas for which the sum of Total Hours (Est) is greater than 6. This restriction does not apply to individual rows, but rather to groups. Because WHERE applies only to rows, it is not possible to accomplish the kind of selection you have here. Fortunately, the word HAVING groups in a similar way as WHERE groups rows. Use the following steps to restrict the groups that display using the word HAVING.

 To Restrict the Groups that Display

1 Click the View button arrow and then click SQL View.

2 Move the insertion point to the beginning of the fourth line (ORDER BY [Marina Number];) and click. Press the ENTER key, click the beginning of the new blank line and then type HAVING SUM([Total Hours (est)])>6 **as the fourth line. Point to the Run button.**

The command is entered (Figure 9-73).

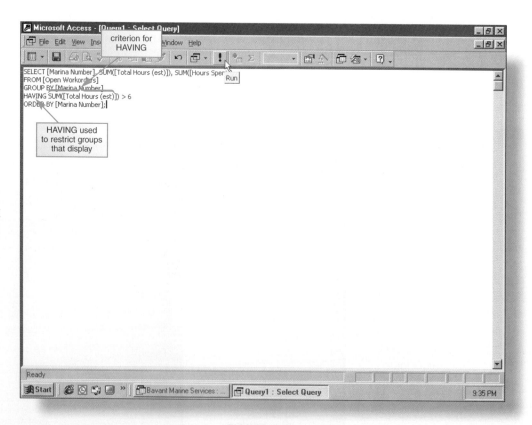

FIGURE 9-73

③ Click the Run button.

The results display (Figure 9-74). Only those groups for which the sum of the Total Hours (est) is greater than 6 display.

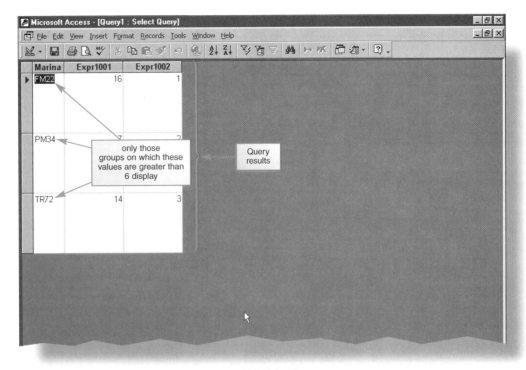

FIGURE 9-74

Joining Tables

Many queries require data from more than one table. Just as with creating queries in Design view, it is necessary to be able to **join** tables, that is, to find rows in two tables that have identical values in matching fields. In SQL this is accomplished through appropriate criteria following the word WHERE.

If you wish to list the Marina Number, Name, Location, Category Number, Total Hours (est), and Hours Spent fields for all workorders, you need data from both the Open Workorders and Marina tables. The Marina Number field is in both tables, the Name field is only in the Marina table, all other fields are only in the Open Workorders table. You need to access both tables in your SQL command, as follows:

1. After the word SELECT, you indicate all fields you want displayed.
2. After the word FROM, you list all tables involved in the query.
3. After the word WHERE, you give the criterion that will restrict the data to be retrieved to only those rows from the two tables that match.

There is a problem, however. The matching fields are both called Marina Number. There is a field in Marina called Marina Number, as well as a field in Open Workorders called Marina Number. In this case, if you only enter Marina Number, it will not be clear which table you mean. It is necessary to **qualify** Marina Number; that is, to specify which field in which table you are referring to. You do this by preceding the name of the field with the name of the table, followed by a period. The Marina Number field in the Open Workorders table is [Open Workorders].[Marina Number]. The Marina Number field in the Marina table is [Marina].[Marina Number].

Perform the steps on the next page to list the Marina Number, Name, Location, Category Number, Total Hours (est), and Hours Spent fields for all workorders.

More About

Join

There are different types of joins that can be implemented in SQL. For example, in joining marinas and workorders in such a way that a marina will display even if it has no open workorders, you would need to perform a type of join called an outer join. For more information, visit the Access 2000 More About page (www.scsite.com/ac2000/more.htm) and click Joins in SQL.

Steps: To Join Tables

1 Click the View button arrow, click SQL View, and then select and delete the current SQL command.

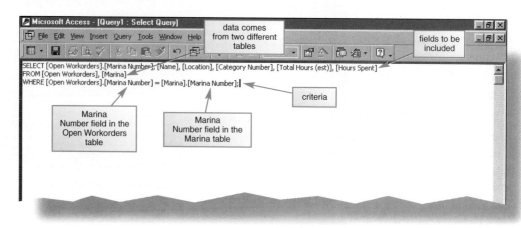

FIGURE 9-75

2 Type `SELECT [Open Workorders].[Marina Number], [Name], [Location], [Category Number], [Total Hours (est)], [Hours Spent]` as the first line of the command. Press the **ENTER** key and then type `FROM [Open Workorders], [Marina]` as the second line. Press the **ENTER** key and then type `WHERE [Open Workorders].[Marina Number]=[Marina].[Marina Number];` as the third line.

The command is entered (Figure 9-75).

3 Click the Run button.

The results display (Figure 9-76). They include the appropriate data from both the Open Workorders table and the Marina table.

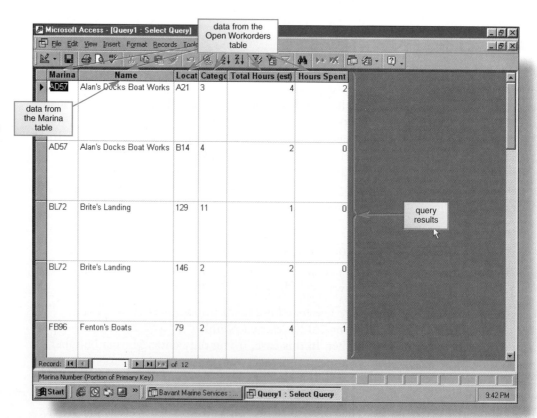

FIGURE 9-76

Note that whenever there is potential ambiguity, you must qualify the fields involved. You can qualify other fields as well, even if there is no confusion. For example, rather than [Name], you could have typed [Marina].[Name] to indicate the Name field in the Marina table. Some people prefer to qualify all fields and this is not a bad approach. In this text, you only will qualify fields when it is necessary to do so.

Restricting the Records in a Join

You can restrict the records to be included in a join by creating a compound criterion. The criterion will include the criterion necessary to join the tables along with a criterion to restrict the records. The criteria will be connected with AND. Perform the following steps to list the Marina Number, Name, Location, Category Number, Total Hours (est), and Hours Spent fields for all workorders on which the hours spent amount is greater than 0.

 To Restrict the Records in a Join

1 **Click the View button arrow and then click SQL View.**

2 **Click immediately after the semicolon on the third line. Press the BACKSPACE key to delete the semicolon. Press the ENTER key and then type** AND [Hours Spent]>0; **as the third line.**

The command is entered (Figure 9-77).

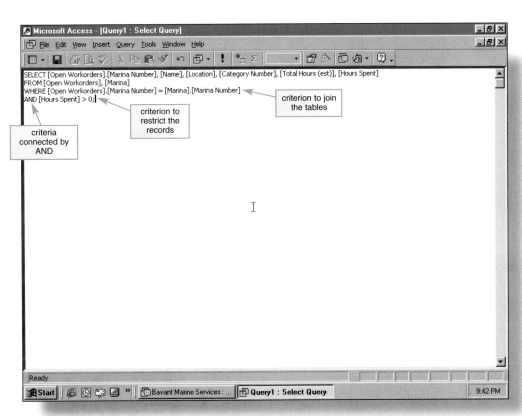

FIGURE 9-77

3 **Click the Run button.**

The results display (Figure 9-78). Only those workorders for which the hours spent amount is greater than 0 display.

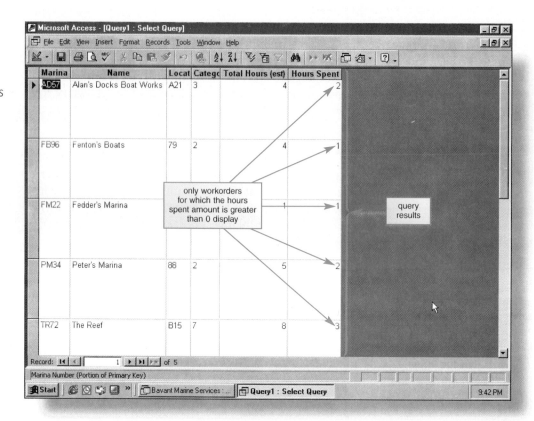

FIGURE 9-78

Joining Multiple Tables

In some cases, you will need data from more than two tables. The following steps include all the data from the previous query together with the category description, which is found in the Category table. Thus, the Category table also must be included in the query as well as a condition relating the Category and Open Workorders tables. The condition to do so is [Open Workorders].[Category Number] = [Category].[Category Number]. The following steps produce the desired results.

Steps To Join Multiple Tables

1 **Click the View button arrow, click SQL View, and then select and delete the current SQL command.**

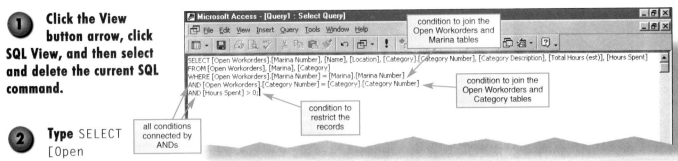

FIGURE 9-79

2 **Type** SELECT [Open Workorders].[Marina Number], [Name], [Location], [Category].[Category Number], [Category Description], [Total Hours (est)], [Hours Spent] **as the first line of the command. Press the ENTER key and then type** FROM [Open Workorders], [Marina], [Category] **as the second line. Press the ENTER key and then type** WHERE [Open Workorders].[Marina Number]= [Marina].[Marina Number] **as the third line. Press the ENTER key and then type** AND [Open Workorders].[Category Number]=[Category].[Category Number] **as the fourth line. Press the ENTER key and then type** AND [Hours Spent]>0; **as the fifth line.**

The command is entered (Figure 9-79).

3 **Click the Run button. Reduce the size of the Category Description column so that all columns display.**

The results display (Figure 9-80).

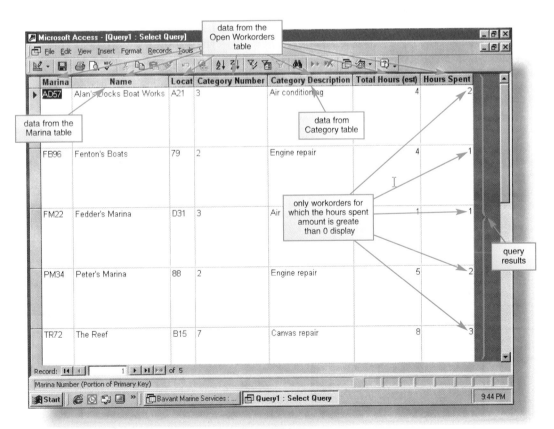

FIGURE 9-80

To create an SQL command that joins data from more than two tables, follow these steps:

1. List all the columns to be included after the word SELECT. If the name of any column appears in more than one table, qualify it by preceding the column name with the table name.

2. List all the tables involved in the query after the word FROM.

3. Take the tables involved one pair at a time, put the condition that relates the tables after the word WHERE. Join these conditions with AND. If there are any other conditions, include them after the word WHERE and connect them to the others with the word AND.

Closing The Query

The following step closes the query by closing the Query Datasheet window.

TO CLOSE A QUERY

 Click the Close Window button for the Microsoft Access – [Query1 : Select Query] window and then click No.

Comparison with Access-Generated SQL

When you create a query in Design view, Access automatically creates a corresponding SQL command that is similar to the commands you have created. The Access query shown in Figure 9-81, for example, includes the Marina Number and Name. There is a criterion in the City field (Burton), but the City field will not display in the results. The View menu displays in the figure.

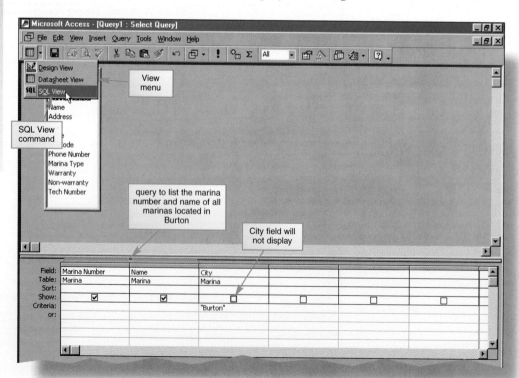

FIGURE 9-81

The corresponding SQL query is shown in Figure 9-82. It is very similar to the queries you have entered, but there are three slight differences. First, the fields are qualified (Marina.[Marina Number] and Marina.Name), even though they do not need to be. There only is one table involved in the query, so no qualification is necessary. Second, the Name field is not enclosed in square brackets. It is legitimate not to enclose it in square brackets because there are no spaces or other special characters in the field name. Finally, there are extra parentheses in the criteria around the criteria that follow the word WHERE.

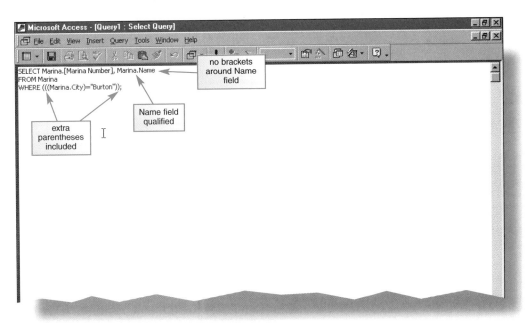

FIGURE 9-82

Both the style used by Access and the style you have been using are legitimate. The choice of style is a personal preference.

Closing the Database

The following step closes the database by closing its Database window.

TO CLOSE A DATABASE

 Click the Close button for the Bavant Marine Services : Database window.

CASE PERSPECTIVE SUMMARY

In Project 9, you assisted the management of Bavant Marine Services by becoming the administrator of their database system. You converted their database to a prior version of Access for a user who needed to query the database and did not have the current version. You analyzed both tables and performance and also produced important documentation. You also specified important integrity constraints involving an input mask and referential integrity. You made sure the database was secure by setting a password and also by encrypting the database. You created a grouped data access page for access to the data via the Internet. You also created a replica of the database for use by a remote user and then synchronized that replica with the Design Master. You also learned about the importance of SQL and used it in several queries.

Project Summary

In Project 9, you learned how to create an Access 97 version of the database. You used the Table Analyzer, the Performance Analyzer, and the Documenter. You created a custom input mask and also specified referential integrity options. You ensured that the Switchboard automatically displays when the database is opened by setting startup options. You set a password and encrypted the database. You also created a grouped data access page. You created a replica for remote users of the database, updated the replica, and synchronized the replica with the Design Master. You wrote several SQL commands to query the database. You used criteria involving both Number and Text fields, compound criteria, and criteria involving NOT. You also used a computed field, sorted query results, and used built-in functions. You used grouping in a query and also joined tables.

What You Should Know

Having completed this project, you now should be able to perform the following tasks:

- Close a Database (A 9.57)
- Close a Query (A 9.56)
- Convert a Database to an Earlier Version (A 9.7)
- Create a Grouped Data Access Page (A 9.26)
- Create a New SQL Query (A 9.36)
- Create a Replica (A 9.32)
- Encrypt a Database (A 9.24)
- Include All Fields (A 9.39)
- Include Only Certain Fields (A 9.38)
- Join Multiple Tables (A 9.55)
- Join Tables (A 9.52)
- Open a Database (A 9.6)
- Open a Database in Exclusive Mode (A 9.21)
- Prepare to Enter a New SQL Command (A 9.39)
- Preview the Data Access Page (A 9.30)
- Remove a Password (A 9.25)
- Restrict the Groups that Display (A 9.50)
- Restrict the Records in a Join (A 9.53)
- Set a Password (A 9.22)
- Set Startup Options (A 9.20)

- Sort the Results (A 9.45)
- Specify Referential Integrity Options (A 9.16)
- Synchronize the Design Master and the Replica (A 9.34)
- Update a Table with Cascade Options (A 9.18)
- Use a Built-In Function (A 9.46)
- Use Compound Criteria (A 9.42)
- Use a Computed Field (A 9.44)
- Use a Criterion Involving a Numeric Field (A 9.40)
- Use a Criterion Involving a Text Field (A 9.41)
- Use the Replica (A 9.33)
- Use an Input Mask (A 9.15)
- Use Grouping (A 9.49)
- Use Multiple Functions in the Same Command (A 9.47)
- Use NOT in a Criterion (A 9.43)
- Use the Documenter (A 9.13)
- Use the Performance Analyzer (A 9.11)
- Use the Table Analyzer (A 9.8)

Apply Your Knowledge

Project Reinforcement at www.scsite.com/off2000/reinforce.htm

1 Administering the Sidewalk Scrapers Database

Instructions: Start Access. Open the Sidewalk Scrapers database from the Access Data Disk. See the inside back cover for instructions for downloading the Access Data Disk or see your instructor for information on accessing the files required for this book. Perform the following tasks.

1. Use the Table Analyzer to analyze the Customer table. On your own paper, list the results of the analysis.
2. Use the Performance Analyzer to analyze all the tables and queries in the Sidewalk Scrapers database. On your own paper, list the results of the analysis.
3. Use the Documenter to produce documentation for the Rate table. Print the documentation.
4. Create a custom input mask for the Customer Number field in the Customer table. The first two characters of the customer number must be uppercase letters and the last two characters must be digits. No position may be blank. On your own paper, list the input mask that you created.
5. Open the Relationships window and edit the relationship between the Customer table and the Worker table. Cascade the update so that any changes made to the Worker Id field in the Worker table will result in a change in the Worker Id field in the Customer table. Save the changes to the layout of the Relationships window.
6. Open the Worker table in Datasheet view and change the worker id for worker 10 from 10 to 20. Close the table.
7. Print the Customer table.
8. Use SQL to create a query that joins the Customer table and the Service table. Include the Customer Number, Name, Service Date, and Service Time fields in the query results. Run the query and print the results.
9. Return to the SQL window, highlight the SQL command you used in Step 8 above and click Copy on the Query Design toolbar.
10. Start Microsoft Word, create a new document, type your name at the top of the document, and then click Paste on the Standard toolbar.
11. Print the Word document containing the SQL command.
12. Close Word and Access.

In the Lab

1 Administering the School Connection Database

Problem: The Booster's Club has placed you in charge of administering their database system. A database administrator must perform activities such as analyzing the performance of the DBMS, specifying integrity constraints, protecting the database from unauthorized use, creating data access pages, and using SQL.

Instructions: Start Access. Open the School Connection database from the Access Data Disk. See the inside back cover for instructions for downloading the Access Data Disk or see your instructor for information on accessing the files required for this book. Perform the following tasks.

1. Use the Performance Analyzer to analyze all the tables and queries in the School Connection database. On your own paper, list the results of the analysis.
2. Use the Documenter to print the documentation for the Reorder table.
3. Vendor Code is a field in both the Item and Vendor tables. Create an input mask for the Vendor Code field in both tables. On your own paper, list the input mask that you created.
4. Edit the relationship between the Reorder table and the Item table so that an item may be deleted from the Item table and then automatically deleted from the Reorder table.
5. Edit the relationship between the Vendor table and the Item table so that a change to the Vendor Code field in the Vendor table will result in the same change to the Vendor Code field in the Item table.
6. Open the Vendor table and change the vendor code for Trinkets 'n More to TR.
7. Print the Item table.
8. Open the Item table and delete item PL05.
9. Print the Item table and the Reorder table.
10. Create the grouped data access page for the Reorder table shown in Figure 9-83. Print the data access page for the record shown in Figure 9-83. To print the page, preview the page and then click Print on the File menu in the Microsoft Internet Explorer window.

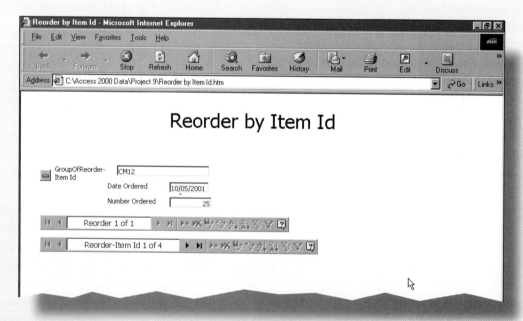

FIGURE 9-83

In the Lab

11. Open Microsoft Word, create a new document, and then type your name at the top. With both Access and Word open on the desktop, create the queries in Steps 12 through 15 in SQL. For each query, run the query, print the query results and copy the SQL command to the Word document. To copy the SQL command, highlight the command, click Copy on the Query Design toolbar, switch to Word, and then click Paste on the Standard toolbar.

12. Find all records in the Item table where the difference between the cost of the item and the selling price of the item is less than $2.00. Display the item id, description, cost, and selling price.

13. Join the Reorder table and the Item table. Display the item id, description, number ordered, cost, and total cost (cost * number ordered). Be sure to name the computed field, Total Cost.

14. Join the Item and Reorder tables. Display the item id, description, and number ordered for all items where the number ordered is less than 5.

15. Find the total number of reordered items for each item. Display the item id and total number reordered.

16. Print the Word document that includes the 4 SQL commands used above.

2 Administering the City Area Bus Company Database

Problem: The City Area Bus Company has placed you in charge of administering their database system. A database administrator must perform activities such as analyzing the performance of the DBMS, specifying integrity constraints, protecting the database from unauthorized use, creating data access pages, and using SQL.

Instructions: Open the City Area Bus Company database from the Access Data Disk. See the inside back cover for instructions for downloading the Access Data Disk or see your instructor for information on accessing the files required for this book. Perform the following tasks.

1. Use the Performance Analyzer to analyze all the tables and queries in the City Area Bus Company database. On your own paper, list the results of the analysis.

2. Use the Documenter to print the documentation for the Category table.

3. Sales Rep Number is a field in both the Advertiser and the Sales Rep tables. Create an input mask for the Sales Rep Number field in both tables. On your own paper, list the input mask that you created.

4. Edit the relationship between the Active Accounts and the Advertiser tables so that an advertiser may be deleted from the Advertiser table and then automatically deleted from the Active Accounts table.

5. Edit the relationship between the Sales Rep and the Advertiser tables so that a change to the Sales Rep Number field in the Sales Rep table will result in the same change to the Sales Rep Number field in the Advertiser table.

6. Open the Sales Rep table and then change the sales rep number for Pat Reed to 46.

7. Print the Advertiser table.

8. Open the Advertiser table and then delete advertiser HC11.

9. Print the Advertiser and the Active Accounts tables.

10. Create the grouped data access page for the Active Accounts table shown in Figure 9-84 on the next page. Print the data access page for the record shown in Figure 9-84. To print the page, preview the page and then click Print on the File menu in the Microsoft Internet Explorer window.

(continued)

Administering the City Area Bus Company Database *(continued)*

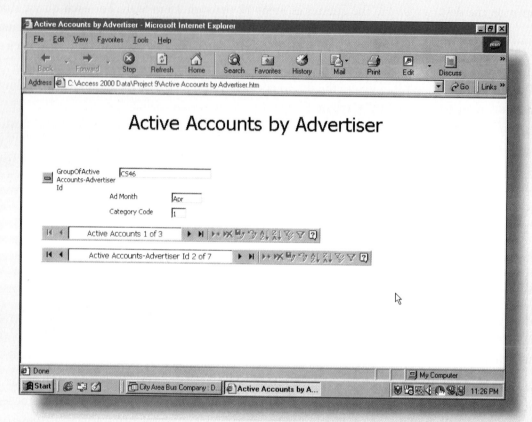

FIGURE 9-84

11. Open Microsoft Word, create a new document, and then type your name at the top. With both Access and Word open on the desktop, create the following queries in SQL. For each query, run the query, print the query results and copy the SQL command to the Word document. To copy the SQL command, highlight the command, click Copy on the Query Design toolbar, switch to Word, and then click Paste on the Standard toolbar.

12. Display the Advertiser Id, Name, City, and State fields for all advertisers. Sort the records in ascending order by city within state.

13. Display the Advertiser Id, Name, City, and Balance fields for all advertisers that are not located in the city of Crescentville. Sort the records in ascending order by city.

14. Display the sales rep's First Name and Last Name, Advertiser Id, Name, and Description fields for all active accounts that are running ads during the month of April.

15. Display the advertiser id, name, and total amount (balance + amount paid) for all records where the advertiser is located in MA.

16. Group the active accounts by advertiser id and count the number of months for which the advertiser has ads.

17. Print the Word document that includes the five SQL commands used in Steps 12 through 16.

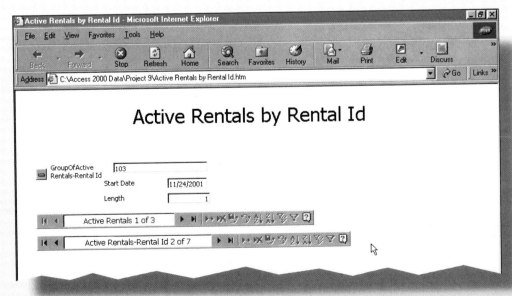

In the Lab

3 Administering the Resort Rentals Database

Problem: The Resort Rentals company has placed you in charge of administering their database system. A database administrator must perform activities such as analyzing the performance of the DBMS, specifying integrity constraints, protecting the database from unauthorized use, creating data access pages, and using SQL.

Instructions: Open the Resort Rentals database from the Access Data Disk. See the inside back cover for instructions for downloading the Access Data Disk or see your instructor for information on accessing the files required for this book. Perform the following tasks.

1. Use the Performance Analyzer to analyze all the tables and queries in the Resort Rentals database. On your own paper, list the results of the analysis.
2. Use the Documenter to display the documentation for the Active Rentals table. Print page 1 of the Documenter by click Print on the File menu, and then clicking the Pages button. Enter 1 in both the From and To boxes.
3. Renter Id is a field in both the Renter and the Active Rentals tables. Create an input mask for the Renter Id field in both tables. On your own paper, list the input mask that you created.
4. Edit the relationship between the Rental Unit and the Active Rentals tables so that a rental unit may be deleted from the Rental Unit table and then automatically deleted from the Active Rentals table.
5. Edit the relationship between the Renter and the Active Rentals tables so that a change to the renter id in the Renter table will result in the same change to the renter id in the Active Rentals table.
6. Open the Renter table and then change the renter id for Stephanie Taber to R007.
7. Print the Active Rentals table.
8. Open the Rental Unit table and then delete rental id 112.
9. Print the Rental Unit and the Active Rentals tables.
10. Create the grouped data access page for the Active Rentals table shown in Figure 9-85. Print the data access page for the record shown in Figure 9-85. To print the page, preview the page and then click Print on the File menu in the Microsoft Internet Explorer window.

FIGURE 9-85

(continued)

In the Lab

Administering the Resort Rentals Database *(continued)*

11. Open Microsoft Word, create a new document, and type your name at the top. With both Access and Word open on the desktop, create the following queries in SQL. For each query, run the query, print the query results and copy the SQL command to the Word document. To copy the SQL command, highlight the command, click Copy on the Query Design toolbar, switch to Word, and then click Paste on the Standard toolbar.

12. Display and print the rental address, renter first name and last name, and total amount owed (weekly rate * length) for all active rentals.

13. Display and print the average weekly rate by city.

14. Display and print the owner's first and last name, the rental address, and the weekly rate for all rental units that have an ocean view. (*Hint*: Search Yes/No fields by using True and False as the criterion.)

15. Display and print the rental id, rental address, start date, length, and renter first and last name for all active rentals.

16. Display and print the rental data for all rental units that either are in Shady Beach or San Toma.

17. Print the Word document that includes the five SQL commands used in Steps 12 through 16.

Cases and Places

The difficulty of these case studies varies:
▶ are the least difficult; ▶▶ are more difficult; and ▶▶▶ are the most difficult.

1 ▶   Open the Computer Items database on the Access Data Disk. Perform the following database administration tasks and answer the questions about the database.

    a. Run the Table Analyzer on all tables and describe the results of the analysis.

    b. Run the Performance Analyzer on all tables and queries and describe the results of the analysis.

    c. Set a password for the Computer Items database. Why did you choose that particular password? What will happen if you try to open the Computer Items database and cannot remember your password?

    d. Create an Access 97 version of the Computer Items database.

    e. Encrypt the database. What is the purpose of encryption?

    f. Modify the startup options so that the switchboard opens automatically when the database is opened.

2 ▶   Use the Computer Items database and create a grouped data access page for the Reorder Status table. Print the grouped data access page. Edit the relationship between the Supplier table and the Items table to cascade the update between the two tables. Edit the relationship between the Reorder Status and the Item tables to cascade the delete between the two tables. Change the Supplier Code for Human Interface to HF. Delete the item with Item Id 1663. Print the Item, Supplier, and Reorder Status tables.

3 ▶▶   Use the Computer Items database for this assignment. Create and run the following SQL queries. Print the query results, copy the SQL commands to a Word document, and then print the Word document.

    a. Find the total cost (units on hand * cost) of all items.

    b. Find the average cost by supplier.

    c. Display the item id, description, reorder data, reorder number, and vendor name for all items that are on reorder.

    d. Display the item id, description, cost, and selling price of all items where the difference between the selling price and cost is more than $1.50.

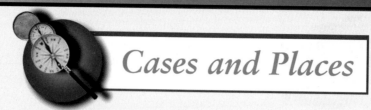

Cases and Places

4 ▶▶ Use the Galaxy Books database on the Access Data Disk for this assignment. Create custom input masks for the Book Code and Customer Number fields. Be sure to use the input mask in all tables that include either field. Create a grouped data access page for the Book table that groups records by author. Print the grouped data access page. Edit the relationship between the Publisher table and the Book table to cascade the update between the two tables. Edit the relationship between the Book Order and the Book tables to cascade the delete between the two tables. Change the Publisher Code for Pearless Books to PR. Delete the book, No Infinity. Print the Book, Publisher, and Book Order tables. Create and run the following SQL queries. Print the query results, copy the SQL commands to a Word document, and then print the Word document.

    a. Display and print all the customer data. Sort the data in ascending order by city within state.

    b. Display and print the book title, price, date ordered, customer first name, and last name for all books that are on order.

    c. Display and print the book code, title, price, publication year, and publisher name for all books that cost more than $6.00.

    d. Display and print all the data for books that were not written by E Dearling.

    e. Display and print all the data for books that are published by VanNester and cost less than $6.00.

    f. Display and print the total cost of inventory and the average book price for each publisher.

5 ▶▶▶ Replicate the Galaxy Books database. Use the replica and add yourself as a customer. Select a book to purchase and add the data to the Book Order table. Synchronize the master and the replica. Use the master to print the updated tables.

Microsoft **Access 2000**

Microsoft Access 2000

Using Access Data in Other Applications

CASE PERSPECTIVE

Bavant Marine Services has determined that it needs to export (copy) some of the data in its database to other formats. Bavant users proficient in Microsoft Excel want to use its powerful what-if features to analyze data concerning open workorders. Other users want the workorder data to be placed in a Microsoft Word document. They will use Word to add other items to the document, format the document in the appropriate fashion, and then print it. The results will form a key portion of an important presentation that they need to make in the near future. Bavant also wants to be able to e-mail one of the Microsoft Access reports included in the database to several users. Upon investigating the best way to accomplish this, Bavant determined they need to create a snapshot of the database. The snapshot, which is stored in a separate file, then can be sent to anyone who has the Snapshot Viewer. Your task is to help Bavant Marine Services export the data to Microsoft Excel and Microsoft Word as well as create a snapshot of the report.

Introduction

Exporting is the process of copying database objects to another database, a spreadsheet, or some other format so that another application can use the data. There are different ways to export data. The two more common ways are to use the Export command on the File menu, which you will use to export a query to a Microsoft Excel worksheet (Figure 1a on the next page), and to use drag-and-drop, which you will use to export the query to a Microsoft Word document (Figure 1b on the next page).

Microsoft Access allows you to export database objects to many different destinations including another Microsoft Access database. In addition, you can export to other databases such as dBASE and Paradox and to spreadsheet programs such as Lotus. With Access, you can export to an HTML document and to a Rich Text Format file (.rtf), which then can be opened in many word processing and desktop publishing programs.

You also can automate the process so the user can run a macro or click a button in a switchboard to export the database object to a selected format. To create such a macro, use the TransferDatabase action in the macro and then fill in the arguments appropriately. After doing so, you then could associate the running of the macro with an item on one of the pages in your switchboard.

There are occasions when you want to send a report to a user via e-mail. It would be prohibitive to send the whole database to the other user, just so the user could print or view a single report. In addition, doing so would require the other user to have Microsoft Access installed. A better way is to create a snapshot of the report. A **snapshot** is a special file that contains the report exactly as it displays when printed. You will use the Export command to create a snapshot of a report. The other user then can use the Snapshot Viewer (Figure 1c on the next page) to view or print the report.

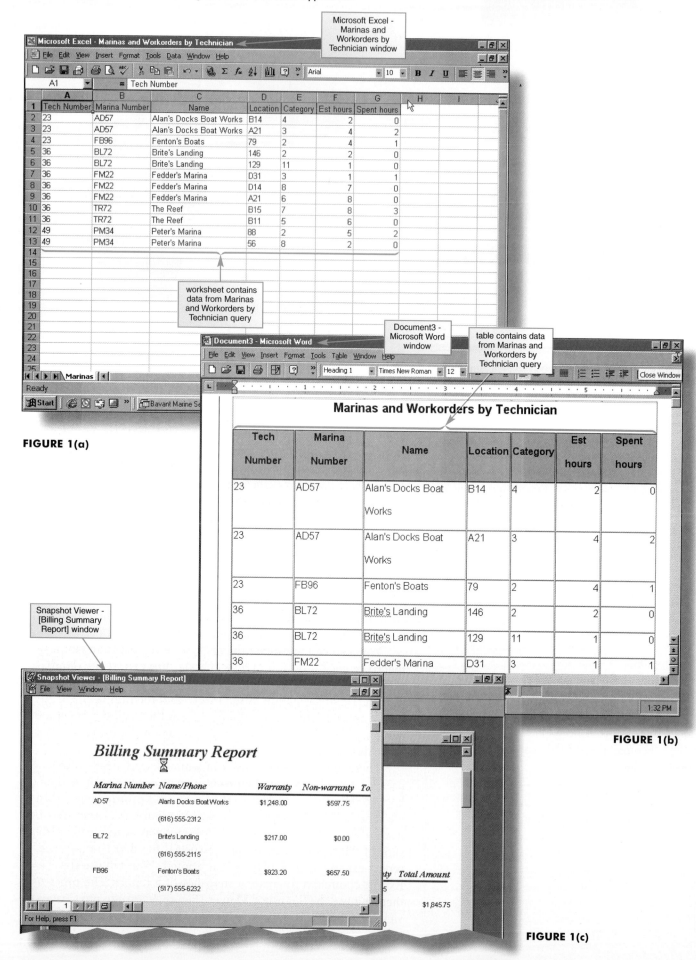

FIGURE 1(a)

Microsoft Excel - Marinas and Workorders by Technician window

worksheet contains data from Marinas and Workorders by Technician query

Document3 - Microsoft Word window

table contains data from Marinas and Workorders by Technician query

Marinas and Workorders by Technician

Tech Number	Marina Number	Name	Location	Category	Est hours	Spent hours
23	AD57	Alan's Docks Boat Works	B14	4	2	0
23	AD57	Alan's Docks Boat Works	A21	3	4	2
23	FB96	Fenton's Boats	79	2	4	1
36	BL72	Brite's Landing	146	2	2	0
36	BL72	Brite's Landing	129	11	1	0
36	FM22	Fedder's Marina	D31	3	1	1

Snapshot Viewer - [Billing Summary Report] window

Billing Summary Report

Marina Number	Name/Phone	Warranty	Non-warranty	To...
AD57	Alan's Docks Boat Works (616) 555-2312	$1,248.00	$597.75	
BL72	Brite's Landing (616) 555-2115	$217.00	$0.00	
FB96	Fenton's Boats (517) 555-6232	$923.20	$657.50	

Total Amount

$1,845.75

FIGURE 1(c)

FIGURE 1(b)

1:32 PM

Opening the Database

Before carrying out the steps in this project, you first must open the database. To do so, perform the following steps.

TO OPEN A DATABASE

1 Click the Start button.

2 Click Open Office Document and then click 3½ Floppy (A:) in the Look in box. If necessary, click the Bavant Marine Services database name.

3 Click the Open button.

4 Close the Switchboard by clicking its Close button.

The database opens and the Bavant Marine Services : Database window displays.

Using the Export Command to Export Data to Excel

One way to export data to Excel, as well as to a variety of other formats, is to select the data to be exported and then select the Export command on the File menu. Once you have selected the command, indicate the file type, for example, Microsoft Excel 97-2000, and then click the Save button. For some of the formats, including Excel, you can select Save formatted, in which case the export process will attempt to preserve as much of the Access formatting of the data as possible. You also can select Autostart so that the application receiving the data will be started automatically once the data is exported. The resulting data then will display in the application.

Perform the following steps to use the export command to export the Marinas and Workorders by Technician query to Excel.

More About

Exporting

The process of exporting records from a table is identical to that of exporting records from a query. Simply select the Tables object and then the table containing the records to be exported before selecting the Export command. All records and all fields from the table then will be exported.

 Steps **To Use the Export Command to Export Data to Microsoft Excel**

1 **If necessary, click Queries on the Objects bar, click the Marinas and Workorders by Technician query, click File on the menu bar, and then point to Export.**

The File menu displays (Figure 2).

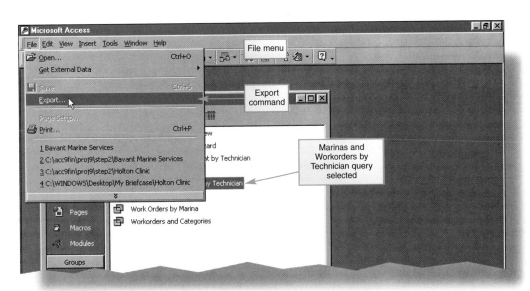

FIGURE 2

2 **Click Export. Click the Save in box arrow and then click 3 ½ Floppy (A:). Click the Save as type box arrow and then point to Microsoft Excel 97-2000 in the Save as type list.**

The Save as type list displays. The Save in box on your screen should display 3 ½ Floppy (A:) (Figure 3).

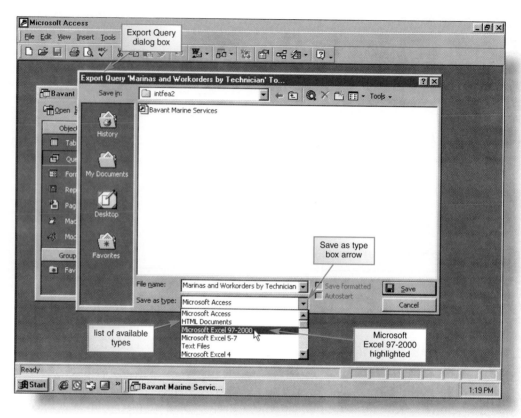

FIGURE 3

3 **Click Microsoft Excel 97-2000 in the Save as type list. Click the Save formatted check box and then click the Autostart check box. Point to the Save button.**

Save formatted and Autostart both are selected (Figure 4).

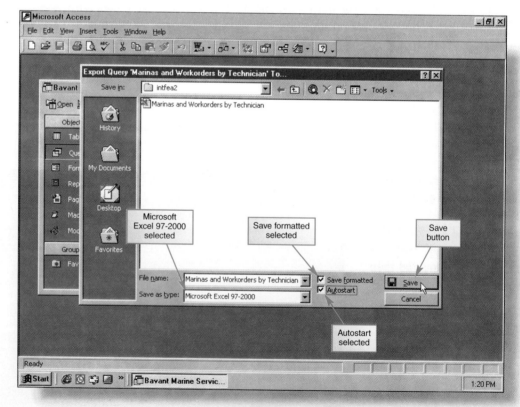

FIGURE 4

4 **Click the Save button.**

The worksheet displays (Figure 5). It contains the data from the Access query.

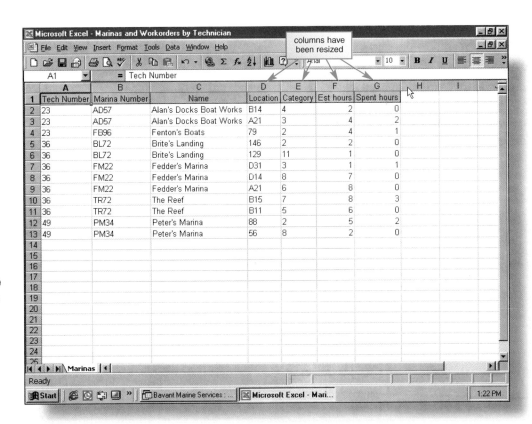

FIGURE 5

5 **Resize each column to best fit the data by double-clicking the right-hand edge of the column heading.**

The columns are resized (Figure 6).

6 **Close the window containing the worksheet and then click the Yes button to save the changes to the column sizes. If you see a message asking if you would like to overwrite the file with the latest Excel format, click Yes. Quit Excel by clicking its Close button.**

The worksheet no longer displays.

FIGURE 6

More *About*

Drag-and-Drop

You can use drag-and-drop to export data to Excel just as you can to Word. Be sure Excel is running rather than Word. Drag the table or query from the database window in Access to the Excel worksheet. The records will be converted to rows in the worksheet and the fields will be converted to columns.

Using Drag-and-Drop to Export Data to Word

When using the Export command, Microsoft Word is not one of the available file types. You would need to select one of the file types that can be imported into Word, export from Access to the selected file type, and then import the file that is created into Word. A simpler way to export to Word is to use the drag-and-drop method. In this method, both Access and Word must be open simultaneously. You then drag the object to be imported from Access to the Word document. Perform the following steps to export the Marinas and Workorders by Technician query to Word using the drag-and-drop method.

 To Use Drag-and-Drop to Export Data to Word

① **Click the Start button, click Programs, and then click Microsoft Word. Click the Bavant Marine Services button on the taskbar. Point to the Restore button in the Microsoft Access window.**

Microsoft Access displays (Figure 7) while Microsoft Word also is running. In the figure, the Tables object is selected. Your screen may have a different object selected.

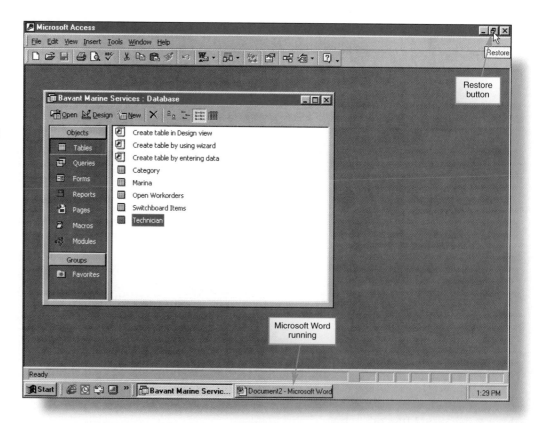

FIGURE 7

2 Click the Restore button so that Access does not occupy the full screen. Click the Queries object, if necessary. Point to the icon for the Marinas and Workorders by Technician query.

Both Word and Access display (Figure 8).

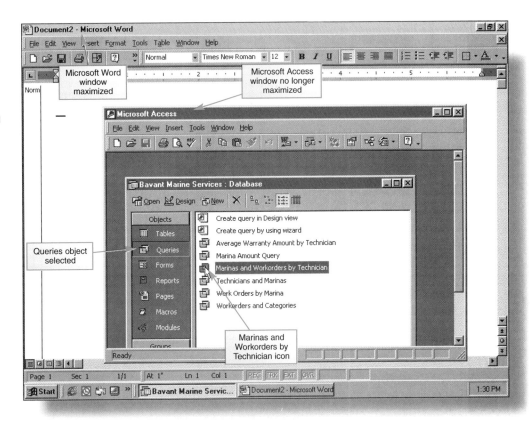

FIGURE 8

3 Drag the query to the upper-left corner of the document (Figure 9).

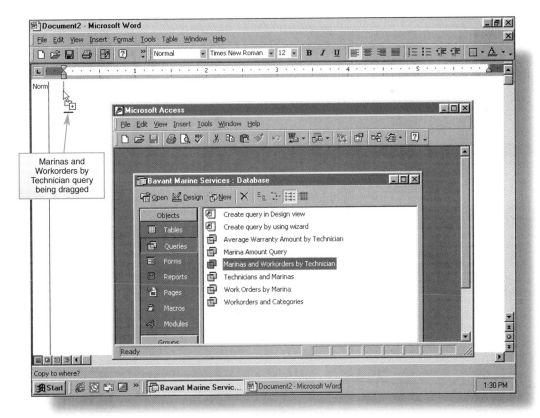

FIGURE 9

Step 4

Release the left mouse button.

The data from the query is inserted in the Word document (Figure 10). The title of the query displays in bold font at the top of the document. The data is inserted as a Word table.

Step 5

Close the window containing the document by clicking its Close button. Click the Yes button when asked if you want to save the changes. Be sure the file name entered is Marinas and Workorders by Technician. Click the Save in box arrow and then click 3½ Floppy (A:). Click the Save button.

The document is saved.

Step 6

Quit Word by clicking its Close button.

Microsoft Word no longer displays.

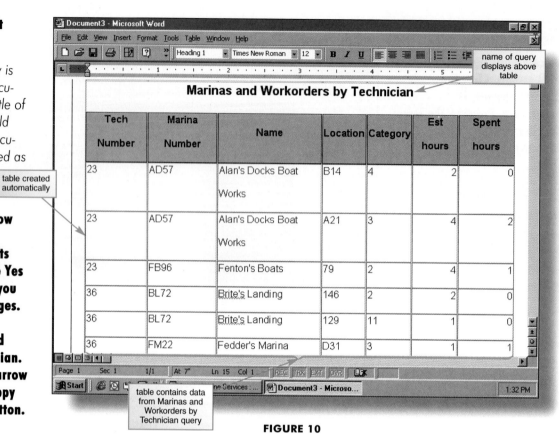

FIGURE 10

Using the Export Command to Create a Snapshot

If you want to send a report to someone via e-mail, the simplest way is to create a snapshot of the report. The snapshot is stored in a separate file with an extension of .snp. This file contains all the details of the report, including fonts, effects (for example, bold or italic), and graphics. In other words, the contents of the snapshot file look precisely like the report. The snapshot file can be viewed by anyone having the Snapshot Viewer; Access is not required. You can use the Snapshot Viewer to e-mail the snapshot; the recipient can use the Snapshot Viewer to view or print the snapshot.

To create a snapshot, use the Export command on the File menu as in the following steps.

Steps | To Use the Export Command to Create a Snapshot

① Maximize the Microsoft Access window. Click Reports on the Objects bar, right-click the Billing Summary Report, and then click Print Preview on the shortcut menu. Click File on the menu bar and then point to Export.

A preview of the Billing Summary Report displays (Figure 11).

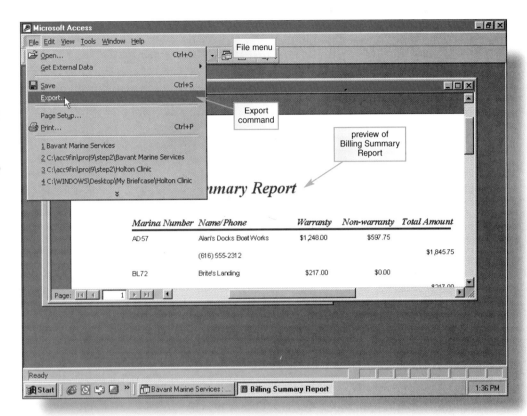

FIGURE 11

② Click Export and then click the Save as type box arrow. Be sure Autostart is checked. Point to Snapshot Format (Figure 12).

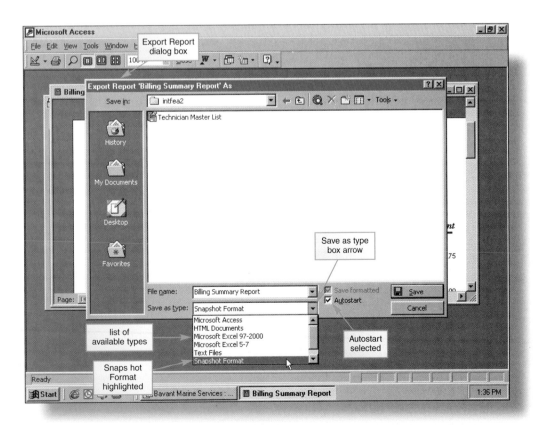

FIGURE 12

3   **Click Snapshot Format. Click the Save in box arrow and then click 3 ½ Floppy (A:). Click the Save button.**

The snapshot of the report displays in the Snapshot Viewer (Figure 13).

4   **Close the Snapshot Viewer by clicking its Close button.**

The Snapshot Viewer no longer displays.

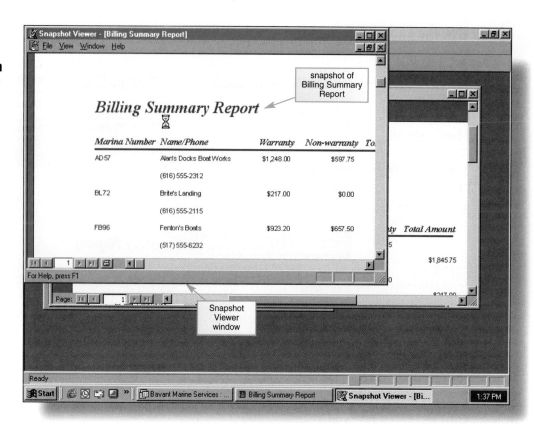

FIGURE 13

You can use the Snapshot Viewer to e-mail the snapshot to other users. The other users can use the Snapshot Viewer to view the report online or print the report.

Closing the Database

The following step closes the database by closing its Database window.

TO CLOSE A DATABASE

1   Click the Close button in the Billing Summary Report window. Click the Close button in the Bavant Marine Services : Database window.

Integration Feature Summary

In this Integration Feature, you learned to use the Export command to export data to a Microsoft Excel worksheet. You also learned to use the drag-and-drop feature to export data to a Microsoft Word document. Finally, you learned to use the Export command to create a snapshot of a report.

What You Should Know

Having completed this Integration Feature, you now should be able to perform the following tasks:

- Close a Database *(AI 2.10)*
- Open a Database *(AI 2.3)*
- Use Drag-and-Drop to Export Data to Word *(AI 2.6)*
- Use the Export Command to Create a Snapshot *(AI 2.9)*
- Use the Export Command to Export Data to Excel *(AI 2.3)*

More About 2000

Microsoft Certification

The Microsoft Office User Specialist (MOUS) Certification program provides an opportunity for you to obtain a valuable industry credential - proof that you have the Access 2000 skills required by employers. For more information, see Appendix D or visit the Shelly Cashman Series MOUS Web page at www.scsite.com/off2000/cert.htm.

Apply Your Knowledge

Project Reinforcement at www.scsite.com/off2000/reinforce.htm

1 Exporting Data from the Booster's Club Database to Other Applications

Problem: The Booster's Club wants to be able to export some of the data in the Access database to other applications. Specifically, they want to export the Reorder Items by Vendor query for further processing in Excel. They also want to use the On Hand Value query in a Word document that they need to prepare.

Instructions: Start Access. Open the School Connection database from the Access Data Disk. See the inside back cover for instructions for downloading the Access Data Disk or see your instructor for information on accessing the files required for this book. Perform the following tasks.

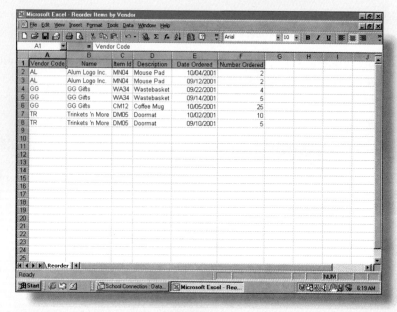

FIGURE 14

1. Export the Reorder Items by Vendor query to Excel as shown in Figure 14. If you see the message File error, some number formats may have been lost, click OK.
2. Resize the columns to best fit the data as shown in Figure 14.
3. Print the Excel worksheet.
4. Use drag-and-drop to place the On Hand Value query in a Word document.
5. Print the Word document.

2 Creating a Snapshot

Problem: The Booster's Club has received several requests from people outside the school district who want to start a similar club. To help these individuals, the Booster's Club wants to be able to e-mail sample reports.

Instructions: Start Access. Open the School Connection database from the Access Data Disk. See the inside back cover for instructions for downloading the Access Data Disk or see your instructor for information on accessing the files required for this book. Perform the following tasks.

FIGURE 15

1. Preview the Vendor/Items Report shown in Figure 15 and then export the report as a snapshot.
2. Print the report that displays in the Snapshot Viewer.

Microsoft Access 2000

APPENDIX A
Microsoft Access 2000 Help System

Using the Access Help System

This appendix shows you how to use the Access Help system. At any time while you are using Access, you can interact with its Help system and display information on any Access topic. It is a complete reference manual at your fingertips.

The two primary methods of obtaining Help are using the Office Assistant and the Microsoft Access Help window. Which one you use will depend on your preference. As shown in Figure A-1, you access either form of Help by pressing the F1 key, clicking Microsoft Access Help on the Help menu, or clicking the Microsoft Access Help button on the Database window toolbar. Access responds in one of two ways:

1. If the Office Assistant is turned on, then the Office Assistant displays with a balloon (lower-right side in Figure A-1).
2. If the Office Assistant is turned off, then the Microsoft Access Help window displays (lower-left side in Figure A-1).

Table A-1 on the next page summarizes the eight categories of Help available to you. Because of the way the Access Help system works, please review the rightmost column of Table A-1 if you have difficulty activating the desired category of Help.

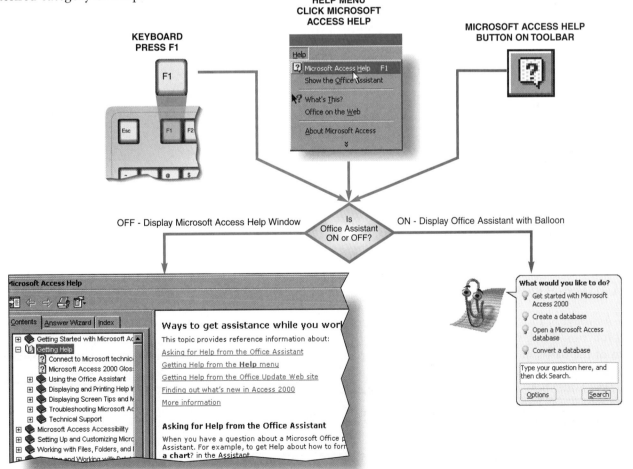

FIGURE A-1

Table A-1   Access Help System

TYPE	DESCRIPTION	HOW TO ACTIVATE	TURNING THE OFFICE ASSISTANT ON AND OFF
Answer Wizard	Similar to the Office Assistant in that it answers questions that you type in your own words.	Click the Microsoft Access Help button on the toolbar. If necessary, maximize the Help window by double-clicking its title bar. Click the Answer Wizard tab.	If the Office Assistant displays, right-click it, click Options on the shortcut menu, click Use the Office Assistant to remove the check mark, click the OK button.
Contents sheet	Groups Help topics by general categories. Use when you know only the general category of the topic in question.	Click the Microsoft Access Help button on the toolbar. If necessary, maximize the Help window by double-clicking its title bar. Click the Contents tab.	If the Office Assistant displays, right-click it, click Options, click Use the Office Assistant to remove the check mark, click the OK button.
Detect and Repair	Automatically finds and fixes errors in the application.	Click Detect and Repair on the Help menu.	
Hardware and Software Information	Shows Product ID and allows access to system information and technical support information.	Click About Microsoft Access on the Help menu and then click the appropriate button.	
Index sheet	Similar to an index in a book. Use when you know exactly what you want.	Click the Microsoft Access Help button on the toolbar. If necessary, maximize the Help window by double-clicking its title bar. Click the Index tab.	If the Office Assistant displays, right-click it, click Options, click Use the Office Assistant to remove the check mark, click the OK button.
Office Assistant	Answers questions that you type in your own words, offers tips, and provides Help for a variety of Access features.	Click the Microsoft Access Help button on the toolbar or double-click the Office Assistant icon. Some dialog boxes also include the Microsoft Access Help button.	If the Office Assistant does not display, close the Microsoft Access Help window and click Show the Office Assistant on the Help menu
Office on the Web	Used to access technical resources and download free product enhancements on the Web.	Click Office on the Web on the Help menu.	
Question Mark button and What's This? command	Used to identify unfamiliar items on the screen.	In a dialog box, click the Question Mark button and then click an item in the dialog box. Click What's This? on the Help menu, and then click an item on the screen.	

The best way to familiarize yourself with the Access Help system is to use it. The next several pages show examples of how to use the Help system. Following the examples is a set of exercises titled Use Help that will sharpen your Access Help system skills.

The Office Assistant

The **Office Assistant** is an icon that displays in the Access window (lower-right-side of Figure A-1 on page A A.1). It has a dual function. First, it will respond with a list of topics that relate to the entry you make in the text box at the bottom of the balloon. The entry can be in the form of a word, phrase, or question written as if you were talking to a human being. For example, if you want to learn more about saving a file, in the balloon text box, you can type save, save a file, how do I save a file, or anything similar. The Office Assistant responds by displaying a list of topics from which you can choose. Once you choose a topic, it displays the corresponding information.

Second, the Office Assistant monitors your work and accumulates tips during a session on how you might better do your work. You can view the tips at any time. The accumulated tips display when you activate the Office Assistant balloon. Also, if at any time you see a light bulb above the Office Assistant, click it to display the most recent tip.

You may or may not want the Office Assistant to display on the screen at all times. You can hide it, and then show it at a later time. You may prefer not to use the Office Assistant at all. In this case, you use the Microsoft Access Help window (lower-left side of Figure A-1 on page A A.1). Thus, not only do you need to know how to show and hide the Office Assistant, but you also need to know how to turn the Office Assistant on and off.

Showing and Hiding the Office Assistant

When Access is first installed, the Office Assistant displays in the Access window. You can move it to any location on the screen. You can click it to display the Office Assistant balloon, which allows you to request Help. If the Office Assistant is on the screen and you want to hide it, you click the **Hide the Office Assistant command** on the Help menu. You also can right-click the Office Assistant to display its shortcut menu and then click the **Hide command** to hide it. When the Office Assistant is hidden, then the **Show the Office Assistant command** replaces the Hide the Office Assistant command on the Help menu. Thus, you can show or hide the Office Assistant at any time.

Turning the Office Assistant On and Off

The fact that the Office Assistant is hidden does not mean it is turned off. To turn the Office Assistant off, it must be displaying in the Access window. You right-click it to display its shortcut menu (right side of Figure A-2). Next, click Options. Invoking the **Options command** causes the Office Assistant dialog box to display (left side of Figure A-2).

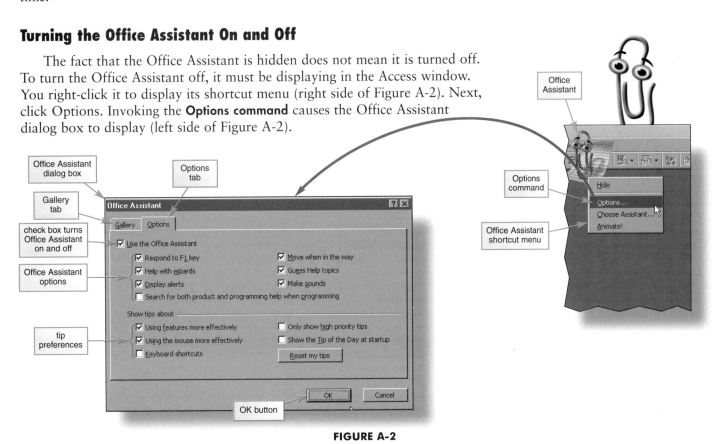

FIGURE A-2

The top check box in the Options sheet determines whether the Office Assistant is on or off. To turn the Office Assistant off, remove the check mark from the **Use the Office Assistant check box** and then click the OK button. As shown in Figure A-1 on page A A.1, if the Office Assistant is off when you invoke Help, then the Microsoft Access Help window displays instead of the Office Assistant. To turn the Office Assistant on at a later time, click the Show the Office Assistant command on the Help menu.

Through the Options command on the Office Assistant shortcut menu, you can change the look and feel of the Office Assistant. For example, you can hide the Office Assistant, turn the Office Assistant off, change the way it works, choose a different Office Assistant icon, or view an animation of the current one. These options also are available by clicking the Options button that displays in the Office Assistant balloon (Figure A-3 on the next page).

The **Gallery sheet** in the Options dialog box (Figure A-2) allows you to change the appearance of the Office Assistant. The default icon is the paper clip (Clippit). You can change it to a bouncing red happy face (The Dot), a robot (F1), a professor (The Genius), the Microsoft Office logo (Office Logo), the earth (Mother Nature), a cat (Links), or a dog (Rocky).

Using the Office Assistant

As indicated earlier, the Office Assistant allows you to enter a word, phrase, or question and then it responds by displaying a list of topics from which you can choose to display Help. The following steps show how to use the Office Assistant to obtain Help on resizing columns.

Steps **To Use the Office Assistant**

1 If the Office Assistant is not turned on, click Help on the menu bar and then click Show the Office Assistant. Click the Office Assistant. When the Office Assistant balloon displays, **type** how do i resize columns **in the text box immediately above the Options button. Point to the Search button.**

The Office Assistant balloon displays as shown in Figure A-3. Your balloon may display different items.

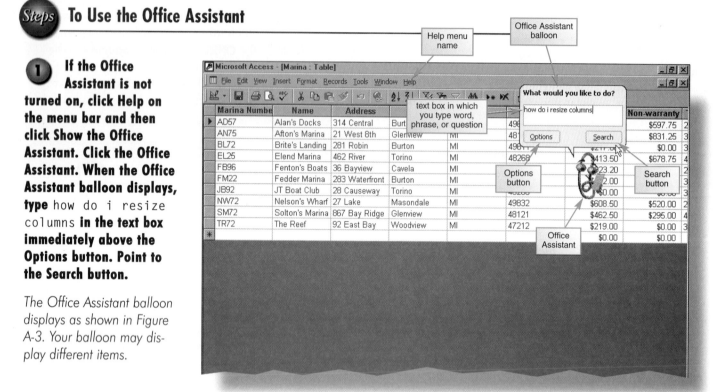

FIGURE A-3

2 Click the Search button. When the Office Assistant balloon redisplays, point to the topic, Resize a column in Datasheet view (Figure A-4).

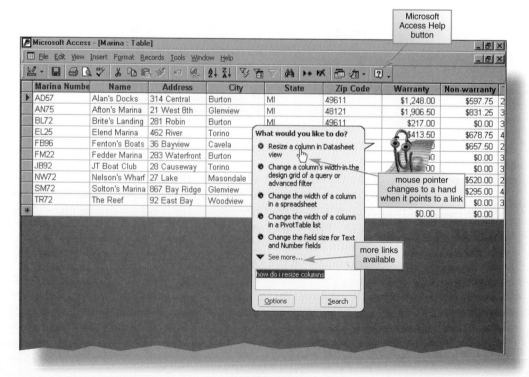

FIGURE A-4

3 **Click the topic, Resize a column in Datasheet view. If necessary, move or hide the Office Assistant so you can view all of the text in the Microsoft Access Help window.**

The Microsoft Access Help window displays with information on how to resize a column (Figure A-5).

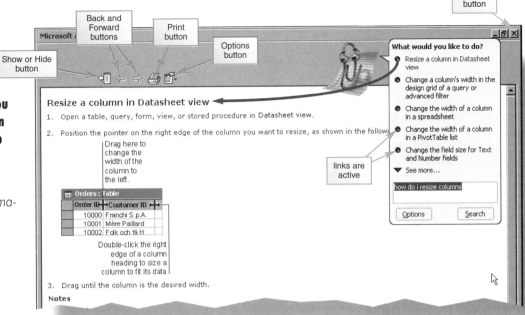

FIGURE A-5

When the Microsoft Access Help window displays, you can read or print it. To print the information, click the Print button on the Microsoft Access Help toolbar. Table A-2 lists the function of each button on the Microsoft Access Help toolbar. To close the Microsoft Access Help window shown in Figure A-5, click the Close button on the title bar.

Table A-2	Microsoft Access Help Toolbar Buttons	
BUTTON	**NAME**	**FUNCTION**
or	Show or Hide	Displays or hides the Contents, Answer Wizard, and Index tabs
	Back	Displays the previous Help topic
	Forward	Displays the next Help topic
	Print	Prints the current Help topic
	Options	Displays a list of commands

Other Ways

1. If Office Assistant is turned on, on Help menu click Microsoft Access Help, or click Microsoft Access Help button on toolbar to display Office Assistant balloon

The Microsoft Access Help Window

If the Office Assistant is turned off and you click the Microsoft Access Help button on the toolbar, the **Microsoft Access Help window** displays (Figure A-6). This window contains three tabs on the left side: Contents, Answer Wizard, and Index. Each tab displays a sheet with powerful look-up capabilities. Use the Contents sheet as you would a table of contents in the front of a book to look up information on various topics. The Answer Wizard sheet answers your queries the same as the Office Assistant. You use the Index sheet in the same way as an index in a book to look up information in Help.

Click the tabs to move from sheet to sheet. The five buttons on the toolbar, Show or Hide, Back, Forward, Print, and Options are described in Table A-2.

In addition to clicking the Microsoft Access Help button on the toolbar, you also can click the Microsoft Access Help command on the Help menu or press the F1 key to display the Microsoft Access Help window to gain access to the three sheets. To close the Microsoft Access Help window, click the Close button in the upper-right corner on the title bar.

Using the Contents Sheet

The **Contents sheet** is useful for displaying Help when you know the general category of the topic in question but not the specifics. The following steps show how to use the Contents sheet to obtain information on designing databases.

TO OBTAIN HELP USING THE CONTENTS SHEET

1 With the Office Assistant turned off, click the Microsoft Access Help button on the toolbar (Figure A-4 on page A A.4).

2 When the Microsoft Access Help window displays, click the Maximize button to maximize the window. If necessary, click the Show button to display the tabs.

3 Click the Contents tab. Double-click the Creating and Working with Databases book on the left side of the window.

4 Click the About designing a database subtopic below the Creating and Working with Databases book.

Access displays Help on the subtopic, About designing a database (Figure A-6).

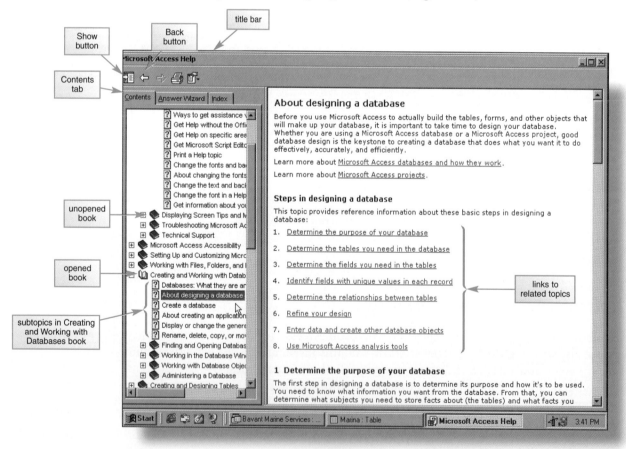

FIGURE A-6

Once the information on the subtopic displays, you can read it as you scroll through, or you can click the Print button to obtain a hard copy. If you decide to click another subtopic on the left or a link on the right, you can get back to the Help page shown in Figure A-6 by clicking the Back button.

Each topic in the Contents list is preceded by a book icon or question mark icon. A **book icon** indicates subtopics are available. A **question mark icon** means information on the topic will display if you double-click the topic. The book icon opens when you double-click the book (or its title) or click the plus sign (+) to the left of the book icon.

Using the Answer Wizard Sheet

The **Answer Wizard sheet** works like the Office Assistant in that you enter a word, phrase, or question and it responds with topics from which you can choose to display Help. The following steps show how to use the Answer Wizard sheet to obtain Help on naming a field.

TO OBTAIN HELP USING THE ANSWER WIZARD SHEET

1 With the Office Assistant turned off, click the Microsoft Access Help button on the toolbar (Figure A-4 on page A A.4).

2 When the Microsoft Access Help window displays, click the Maximize button to maximize the window. If necessary, click the Show button to display the tabs.

3 Click the Answer Wizard tab. Type how do i name a field in the What would you like to do? text box on the left side of the window. Click the Search button.

Access displays Help on Guidelines for naming fields, controls, and objects (Figure A-7).

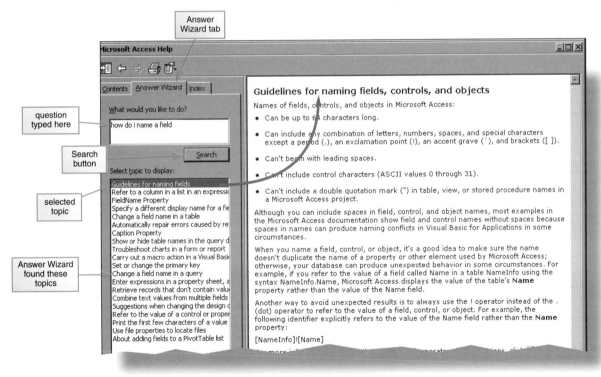

FIGURE A-7

If the topic, Guidelines for naming fields, does not include the information you are searching for, click another topic in the list. Continue to click topics until you find the desired information.

Using the Index Sheet

The third sheet in the Microsoft Access Help window is the Index sheet. Use the **Index sheet** to display Help when you know the keyword or the first few letters of the keyword you want to look up. The steps on the next page show how to use the Index sheet to obtain Help on databases.

TO OBTAIN HELP USING THE INDEX SHEET

1 With the Office Assistant turned off, click the Microsoft Access Help button on the toolbar (Figure A-4 on page A A.4).

2 When the Microsoft Access Help window displays, click the Maximize button to maximize the window. If necessary, click the Show button to display the tabs.

3 Click the Index tab. Type database in the Type keywords text box on the left side of the window. Click the Search button.

4 When a list of topics displays in the Choose a topic list box, click Databases: What they are and how they work. When the Help topic displays, click the graphic as indicated.

A second Microsoft Access Help window displays with Help about the topic, Databases: What they are and how they work (Figure A-8).

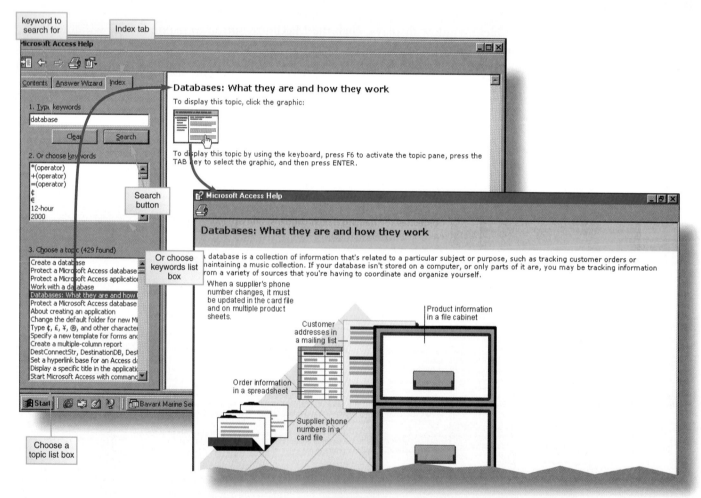

FIGURE A-8

You can click each of the page numbers at the bottom of the second Help window to learn more about databases. In the Choose a topic list box on the left side of the window, you can click another topic to display additional Help.

An alternative to typing a keyword in the Type keywords text box is to scroll through the Or choose keywords list box (the middle list box on the left side of the window). When you locate the keyword you are searching for, double-click it to display Help on the topic. Also in the Or choose keywords list box, the Access Help system displays other topics that relate to the new keyword. As you begin typing a new keyword in the Type keywords text box, Access jumps to that point in the middle list box. To begin a new search, click the Clear button.

What's This? Command and Question Mark Button • A A.9

APPENDIX A

What's This? Command and Question Mark Button

Use the What's This command on the Help menu or the Question Mark button in a dialog box when you are not sure what an object on the screen is or what it does.

What's This? Command

You use the **What's This? command** on the Help menu to display a detailed ScreenTip. When you invoke this command, the mouse pointer changes to an arrow with a question mark. You then click any object on the screen, such as a button, to display the expanded ScreenTip for that object. For example, after you click the What's This? command on the Help menu and then click the Database Window button on the Datasheet toolbar, a description of the button displays (Figure A-9). You can print the ScreenTip by right-clicking it and then clicking Print Topic on the shortcut menu.

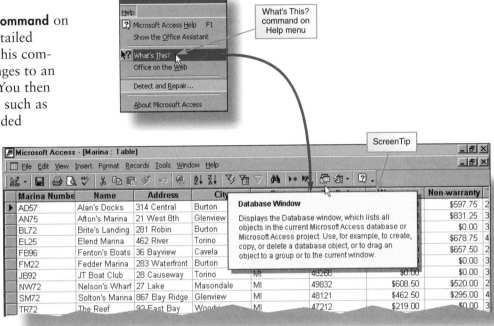

FIGURE A-9

Question Mark Button

Similarly to the What's This? command, the **Question Mark button** displays a ScreenTip. You use the Question Mark button with dialog boxes. It is located in the upper-right corner on the title bar of dialog boxes, next to the Close button. For example, in Figure A-10, the New Report dialog box displays on the screen. If you click the Question Mark button and then click the text box arrow, an explanation of the text box displays. You can print the ScreenTip by right-clicking it and then clicking Print Topic on the shortcut menu.

If a dialog box does not include a Question Mark button, press the SHIFT+ F1 keys. This combination of keys will change the mouse pointer to an arrow with a question mark. You then can click any object in the dialog box to display the ScreenTip.

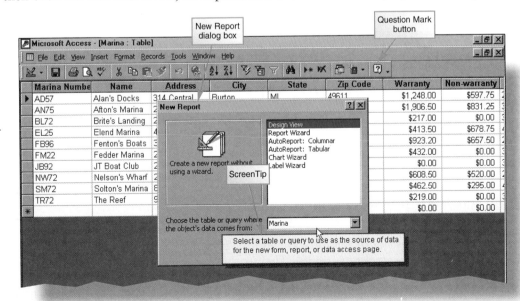

FIGURE A-10

Office on the Web Command

The **Office on the Web command** on the Help menu displays a Microsoft Web page containing up-to-date information on a variety of Office-related topics. To use this command, you must be connected to the Internet. Once the page displays, you can click the Access link on the left side of the window and then click the Assistance link (Figure A-11). The Access Assistance Web page contains several links, such as Knowledge Base Articles about Access and Frequently Asked questions about Access.

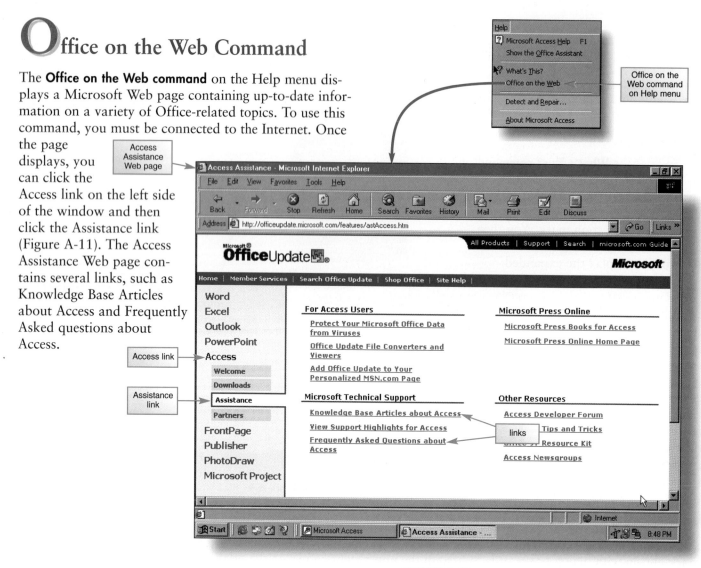

FIGURE A-11

Other Help Commands

Two additional commands available on the Help menu are Detect and Repair and About Microsoft Access.

Detect and Repair Command

Use the **Detect and Repair command** on the Help menu if Access is not running properly or if it is generating errors. When you invoke this command, the Detect and Repair dialog box displays. Click the Start button in the dialog box to initiate the detect and repair process.

About Microsoft Access Command

The **About Microsoft Access command** on the Help menu displays the About Microsoft Access dialog box. The dialog box lists the owner of the software and the product identification. You need to know the product identification if you call Microsoft for assistance. The two buttons below the OK button are the System Info button and the Tech Support button. The **System Info button** displays system information, including hardware resources, components, software environment, and applications. The **Tech Support button** displays technical assistance information.

Use Help

1 Using the Office Assistant

Instructions: Perform the following tasks using the Access Help system.

1. If the Office Assistant is turned on, click it to display the Office Assistant balloon. If the Office Assistant is not turned on, click Help on the menu bar and then click Show the Office Assistant.
2. Right-click the Office Assistant and then click Options on the shortcut menu. Click the Options tab in the Office Assistant dialog box and review the different options for the Office Assistant. Click the Question Mark button and display ScreenTips for the first two check boxes. Print the ScreenTips and hand them in to your instructor. Close the Office Assistant dialog box.
3. Click the Office Assistant and then type what data types should i use in the text box at the bottom of the balloon. Click the Search button.
4. Click What data type should I use for a field in my table? in the Office Assistant balloon. Maximize the Microsoft Access Help window. Read and print the information. Click the link to display a summary of field data types. Print the information. Hand in the printouts to your instructor. Use the Back button to return to the original page.
5. Click the Close button in the Microsoft Access Help window.
6. Click the Office Assistant. If it is not turned on, click Show the Office Assistant on the Help menu. Search for the topic, deleting a record. Click the Delete a record in Datasheet or Form view link. When the Microsoft Access Help window displays, maximize the window. Read and print the information. Click the referential integrity link. Print the information on referential integrity. Close the Microsoft Access Help window.

2 Expanding on the Access Help System Basics

Instructions: Use the Access Help system to understand the topics better and answer the questions listed below. Answer the questions on your own paper, or hand in the printed Help information to your instructor.

1. Right-click the Office Assistant. If it is not turned on, click Show the Office Assistant on the Help menu. When the shortcut menu displays, click Options. Click Use the Office Assistant to remove the check mark, and then click the OK button.
2. Click the Microsoft Access Help button on the toolbar. Maximize the Microsoft Access Help window. If the tabs are hidden on the left side, click the Show button. Click the Index tab. Type toolbar in the Type key-words text box. Click the Search button. Click About toolbars. Print the information. Click the Hide button, and then click the Show button. Click the two links below More information. Read and print the information for each link. Close the Microsoft Access Help window. Hand in the printouts to your instructor.
3. Press the F1 key. Click the Answer Wizard tab. Type printing in the What would you like to do? text box, and then click the Search button. Click Preview a report. Read through the information that displays. Print the information. Click the two links. Read and print the information for both.
4. Click the Contents tab. Click the plus sign (+) to the left of the Working with Data book. One at a time, click the first two subtopics below the Working with Data book. Read and print each one. Close the Microsoft Access Help window. Hand in the printouts to your instructor.
5. Click Help on the menu bar and then click What's This? Click the New button on the Database window tool-bar. Right-click the ScreenTip and then click Print Topic on the shortcut menu. Click the Open command on the File menu. When the Open dialog box displays, click the Question Mark button on the title bar. Click the Cancel button. Right-click the ScreenTip and then click Print Topic. Close the Microsoft Access Help window. Hand in the printouts to your instructor.

APPENDIX B
Publishing Office Web Pages to a Web Server

With a Microsoft Office 2000 program, such as Word, Excel, Access, or PowerPoint, you use the Save as Web Page command on the File menu to save the Web page to a Web server using one of two techniques: Web folders or File Transfer Protocol. A **Web folder** is an Office 2000 shortcut to a Web server. **File Transfer Protocol (FTP)** is an Internet standard that allows computers to exchange files with other computers on the Internet.

You should contact your network system administrator or technical support staff at your ISP to determine if their Web server supports Web folders, FTP, or both, and to obtain necessary permissions to access the Web server. If you decide to publish Web pages using a Web folder, you must have the Office Server Extensions (OSE) installed on your computer. OSE comes with the Standard, Professional, and Premium editions of Office 2000.

Using Web Folders to Publish Office Web Pages

If you are granted permission to create a Web folder (shortcut) on your computer, you must obtain the URL of the Web server, and a user name and possibly a password that allows you to access the Web server. You also must decide on a name for the Web folder. Table B-1 explains how to create a Web folder.

Office adds the name of the Web folder to the list of current Web folders. You can save to this folder, open files in the folder, rename the folder, or perform any operations you would to a folder on your hard disk. You can use your Office program or Windows Explorer to access this folder. Table B-2 explains how to save to a Web folder.

Using FTP to Publish Office Web Pages

When publishing a Web page using FTP, you first add the FTP location to your computer and then you can save to it. An **FTP location**, also called an **FTP site**, is a collection of files that resides on an FTP server. In this case, the FTP server is the Web server.

To add an FTP location, you must obtain the name of the FTP site, which usually is the address (URL) of the FTP server, and a user name and a password that allows you to access the FTP server. You save and open the Web pages on the Web server using the name of the FTP site. Table B-3 explains how to add an FTP site.

Office adds the name of the FTP site to the FTP locations in the Save As and Open dialog boxes. You can open and save files on this FTP location. Table B-4 explains how to save using an FTP location.

Table B-1 Creating a Web Folder

1. Click File on the menu bar and then click Save As; or click File on the menu bar and then click Open.
2. When the Save As dialog box or the Open dialog box displays, click the Web Folders shortcut on the Places Bar along the left side of the dialog box.
3. Click the Create New Folder button.
4. When the first dialog box of the Add Web Folder wizard displays, type the URL of the Web server and then click the Next button.
5. When the Enter Network Password dialog box displays, type the user name and, if necessary, the password in the respective text boxes and then click the OK button.
6. When the last dialog box of the Add Web Folder wizard displays, type the name you would like to use for the Web folder. Click the Finish button.
7. Close the Save As or the Open dialog box.

Table B-2 Saving to a Web Folder

1. Click File on the menu bar and then click Save As.
2. When the Save As dialog box displays, type the Web page file name in the File name text box. Do not press the ENTER key.
3. Click Web Folders shortcut on the Places Bar along the left side of the dialog box.
4. Double-click the Web folder name in the Save in list.
5. When the Enter Network Password dialog box displays, type the user name and password in the respective text boxes and then click the OK button.
6. Click the Save button in the Save As dialog box.

Table B-3 Adding an FTP Location

1. Click File on the menu bar and then click Save As; or click File on the menu bar and then click Open.
2. In the Save As dialog box, click the Save in box arrow and then click Add/Modify FTP Locations in the Save in list; or in the Open dialog box, click the Look in box arrow and then click Add/Modify FTP Locations in the Look in list.
3. When the Add/Modify FTP Locations dialog box displays, type the name of the FTP site in the Name of FTP site text box. If the site allows anonymous logon, click Anonymous in the Log on as area; if you have a user name for the site, click User in the Log on as area and then type the user name. Type the password in the Password text box. Click the OK button.
4. Close the Save As or the Open dialog box.

Table B-4 Saving to an FTP Location

1. Click File on the menu bar and then click Save As.
2. When the Save As dialog box displays, type the Web page file name in the File name text box. Do not press the ENTER key.
3. Click the Save in box arrow and then click FTP Locations.
4. Double-click the name of the FTP site you want to save to.
5. When the FTP Log On dialog box displays, type your user name and password and then click the OK button.
6. Click the Save button in the Save As dialog box.

APPENDIX C
Resetting the Access Menus and Toolbars

In Microsoft Access 2000, you can personalize toolbars and menus. You can change the toolbar or toolbars that display by clicking View on the menu bar, clicking Toolbars, and then clicking the toolbars you want to display. You also can change the buttons that display on a particular toolbar by clicking the More Buttons button (see Figure C-1). In addition, Access personalizes the commands on the menus based on their usage. Each time you start Access, the toolbars and menus display in the same settings as the last time you used the application. The following steps show how to reset the menus and toolbars to their installation settings. In the steps, the Bavant Marine Services: Database window is open. You do not need to open a database to reset the menus and toolbars.

 To Reset My Usage Data and Toolbar Buttons

① Click View on the menu bar and then point to Toolbars. Point to Customize on the Toolbars submenu.

The View menu and Toolbars submenu display (Figure C-1).

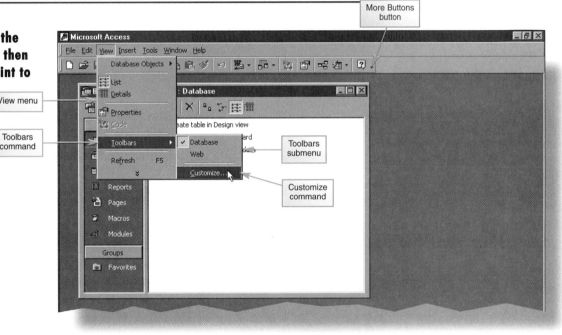

FIGURE C-1

② Click Customize. When the Customize dialog box displays, click the Options tab. Point to the Reset my usage data button.

The Customize dialog box displays as shown in Figure C-2.

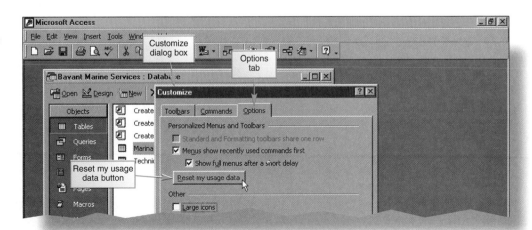

FIGURE C-2

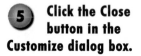 **Click the Reset my usage data button. When the Microsoft Access dialog box displays explaining the function of the Reset my usage data button, click the Yes button. In the Customize dialog box, click the Toolbars tab.**

The Toolbars sheet displays (Figure C-3).

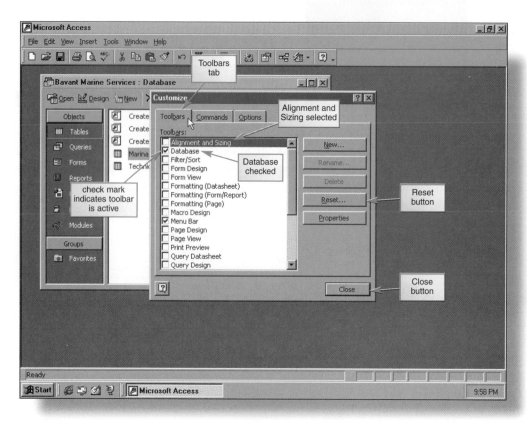

FIGURE C-3

4 **Click Database in the Toolbars list and then click the Reset button. When the Microsoft Access dialog box displays asking you if you are sure you want to reset the Database toolbar, click the OK button. Repeat the process for any other toolbar you want to reset.**

5 **Click the Close button in the Customize dialog box.**

The toolbars display as shown in Figure C-4.

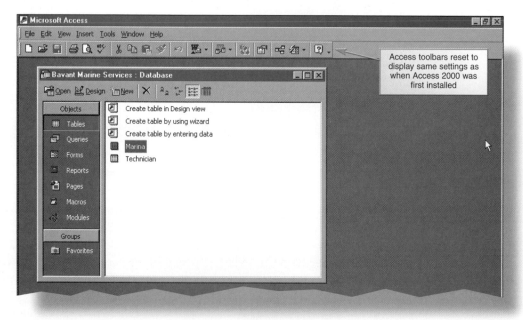

FIGURE C-4

Steps 3 and 4 display or remove any buttons that were added or deleted through the use of the Add or Remove Buttons button on the More Buttons menu.

APPENDIX D

Microsoft Office User Specialist Certification Program

The Microsoft Office User Specialist (MOUS) Certification Program provides a framework for measuring your proficiency with the Microsoft Office 2000 applications, such as Word 2000, Excel 2000, Access 2000, and PowerPoint 2000. Three levels of certification are available — Master, Expert, and Core. The three levels of certification are described in Table D-1.

Table D-1 Three Levels of MOUS Certification			
LEVEL	*DESCRIPTION*	*REQUIREMENTS*	*CREDENTIAL AWARDED*
Master	Indicates that you have a comprehensive understanding of Microsoft Office 2000	Pass all FIVE of the required exams: Microsoft Word 2000 Expert Microsoft Excel 2000 Expert Microsoft PowerPoint 2000 Core Microsoft Access 2000 Core Microsoft Outlook 2000 Core	Candidates will be awarded one certificate for passing all five of the required Microsoft Office 2000 exams: Microsoft Office User Specialist: Microsoft Office 2000 Master
Expert	Indicates that you have a comprehensive understanding of the advanced features in a specific Microsoft Office 2000 application	Pass any ONE of the Expert exams: Microsoft Word 2000 Expert Microsoft Excel 2000 Expert	Candidates will be awarded one certificate for each of the Expert exams they have passed: Microsoft Office User Specialist: Microsoft Word 2000 Expert Microsoft Office User Specialist: Microsoft Excel 2000 Expert
Core	Indicates that you have a comprehensive understanding of the core features in a specific Microsoft Office 2000 application	Pass any ONE of the Core exams: Microsoft Word 2000 Core Microsoft Excel 2000 Core Microsoft PowerPoint 2000 Core Microsoft Access 2000 Core Microsoft Outlook 2000 Core	Candidates will be awarded one certificate for each of the Core exams they have passed: Microsoft Office User Specialist: Microsoft Word 2000 Microsoft Office User Specialist: Microsoft Excel 2000 Microsoft Office User Specialist: Microsoft PowerPoint 2000 Microsoft Office User Specialist: Microsoft Access 2000 Microsoft Office User Specialist: Microsoft Outlook 2000

Why Should You Get Certified?

Being a Microsoft Office User Specialist provides a valuable industry credential — proof that you have the Office 2000 applications skills required by employers. By passing one or more MOUS certification exams, you demonstrate your proficiency in a given Office application to employers. With nearly 80 million copies of Office in use around the world, Microsoft is targeting Office certification to a wide variety of companies. These companies include temporary employment agencies that want to prove the expertise of their workers, large corporations looking for a way to measure the skill set of employees, and training companies and educational institutions seeking Microsoft Office teachers with appropriate credentials.

The MOUS Exams

You pay $50 to $100 each time you take an exam, whether you pass or fail. The fee varies among testing centers. The Expert exams, which you can take up to 60 minutes to complete, consist of between 40 and 60 tasks that you perform online. The tasks require you to use the application just as you would in doing your job. The Core exams contain fewer tasks, and you will have slightly less time to complete them. The tasks you will perform differ on the two types of exams.

How Can You Prepare for the MOUS Exams?

The Shelly Cashman Series® offers several Microsoft-approved textbooks that cover the required objectives on the MOUS exams. For a listing of the textbooks, visit the Shelly Cashman Series MOUS Web page at www.scsite.com/off2000/cert.htm and then click the Shelly Cashman Series Office 2000 Microsoft-Approved MOUS Textbooks link (Figure D-1). After using any of the books listed in an instructor-led course, you will be prepared to take the MOUS exam indicated.

How to Find an Authorized Testing Center

You can locate a testing center by calling 1-800-933-4493 in North America or visiting the Shelly Cashman Series MOUS Web page at www.scsite.com/off2000/cert.htm and then clicking the Locate an Authorized Testing Center Near You link (Figure D-1). At this Web page, you can look for testing centers around the world.

Shelly Cashman Series MOUS Web Page

The Shelly Cashman Series MOUS Web page (Figure D-1) has more than fifteen Web pages you can visit to obtain additional information on the MOUS Certification Program. The Web page (www.scsite.com/off2000/cert.htm) includes links to general information on certification, choosing an application for certification, preparing for the certification exam, and taking and passing the certification exam.

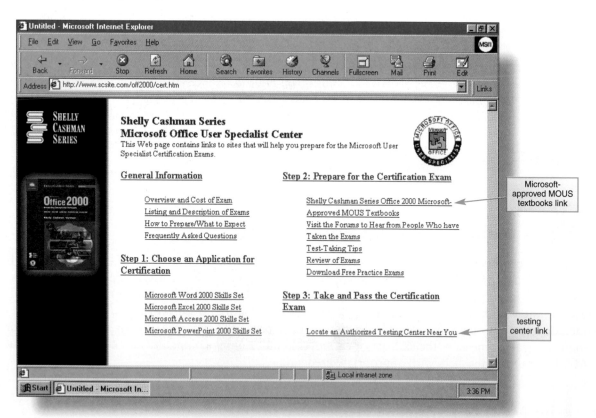

FIGURE D-1

Microsoft Access 2000 User Specialist Certification Map

This book has been approved by Microsoft as courseware for the Microsoft Office User Specialist (MOUS) program. After completing the projects and exercises in this book, students will be prepared to take the Core level Microsoft Office User Specialist Exam for Microsoft Access 2000. Table D-2 lists the skill sets, activities, and page number where the activity is discussed in the book for the Core level Microsoft Office User Specialist Exam for Microsoft Access 2000. You should be familiar with each of the activities if you plan to take the Microsoft Access 2000 Core examination. Table D-3 on the next page lists the skill sets, activities, and page number where the activity is discussed in the book for the Proposed Expert level Microsoft Office User Specialist Exam for Microsoft Access 2000.

Table D-2 Microsoft Access 2000 MOUS Core Skill Sets, Activities, and Map

SKILL SETS	ACTIVITIES	PAGE NUMBERS
Planning and designing databases	Determine appropriate data inputs for your database	A 1.52
	Determine appropriate data outputs for your database	A 1.53
	Create table structure	A 1.15, A 1.34
	Establish table relationships	A 3.38
Working with Access	Use the Office Assistant	A 1.49
	Select an object using the Objects Bar	A 1.39, A 1.48, A 2.6
	Print database objects (tables, forms, reports, queries)	A 1.31, A 1.48, A 2.12
	Navigate through records in a table, query, or form	A 1.27, A 1.41
	Create a database (using a Wizard or in Design view)	A 1.9
Building and modifying tables	Create tables by using the Table Wizard	A 1.13
	Set primary keys	A 1.14, A 1.17
	Modify field properties	A 3.16, A 3.28
	Use multiple data types	A 1.14
	Modify tables using Design view	A 3.16
	Use the Lookup Wizard	A 6.7
	Use the Input Mask Wizard	A 6.10
Building and modifying forms	Create a form with the Form Wizard	A 4.31, A 5.21
	Use the Control Toolbox to add controls	A 4.34, A 4.37, A 4.43
	Modify format properties (font, style, font size, color, caption, etc.) of controls	A 4.36, A 4.45, A 5.42
	Use form sections (headers, footers, detail)	A 4.43, A 5.40
	Use a calculated control on a form	A 4.34
Viewing and organizing information	Use the Office Clipboard	A 6.36
	Switch between object views	A 1.42, A 3.11
	Enter records using a datasheet	A 1.21, A 1.28

Table D-2 Microsoft Access 2000 MOUS Core Skill Sets, Activities, and Map

SKILL SETS	ACTIVITIES	PAGE NUMBERS
Viewing and organizing information (con't)	Enter records using a form	A 3.8
	Delete records from a table	A 1.29, A 3.14, A 3.26
	Find a record	A 3.9
	Sort records	A 2.26, A 3.43
	Apply and remove filters (filter by form and filter by selection)	A 3.13, A 3.14
	Specify criteria in a query	A 2.17, A 2.19, A 2.21, A 2.24, A 3.26
	Display related records in a subdatasheet	A 3.42
	Create a calculated field	A 2.36
	Create and modify a multi-table select query	A 2.32, A 2.34
Defining relationships	Establish relationships	A 3.38
	Enforce referential integrity	A 3.38
Producing reports	Create a report with Report Wizard	A 1.43, A 4.9, A 4.19
	Preview and print a report	A 1.48
	Move and resize a control	A 4.27, A 6.16
	Modify format properties (font, style, font size, color, caption, etc.)	A 4.16, A 6.20
	Use the Control Toolbox to add controls	A 6.21
	Use report sections (headers, footers, detail)	A 4.14, A 4.25
	Use a calculated control in a report	A 6.20
Integrating with other applications	Import data to a new table	AI 1.3
	Save a table, query, form as a Web page	AW 1.1
	Add hyperlinks	A 5.6, A 5.18
Using Access tools	Print database relationships	A 3.41
	Backup and restore a database	A 3.6
	Compact and repair a database	A 5.48

Table D-3 Microsoft Access 2000 MOUS
Proposed Expert Skill Sets, Activities, and Map

SKILL SETS	ACTIVITIES	PAGE NUMBERS
Building and modifying tables	Set validation text	A 3.31
	Define data validation criteria	A 3.28
	Modify an input mask	A 6.10, A 9.15
	Create and modify Lookup fields	A 6.7, A 7.13
	Optimize data type usage (double, long, int, byte, etc.)	A 9.12
Building and modifying forms	Create a form in Design view	A 8.35
	Insert a graphic on a form	A 8.56
	Modify control properties	A 4.16, A 5.36, A 5.37, A 5.38, A 8.14, A 8.33
	Customize form sections (headers, footers, detail)	A 4.43, A 5.40,
	Modify form properties	A 4.45, A 5.33,
	Use the subform control and synchronize forms	A 5.26, A 8.36
	Create a switchboard	A 6.40
Refining queries	Apply filters (filter by form and filter by selection) in a query's recordset	A 7.19
	Create a totals query	A 2.38
	Create a parameter query	A 7.20
	Specify criteria in multiple fields (AND vs. OR)	A 2.24, A 2.25
	Modify query properties (field formats, caption, input masks, etc.)	A 7.17
	Create an action query (update, delete, insert)	A 3.23, A 3.26
	Optimize queries using indexes	A 3.48, A 9.12
	Specify join properties for relationships	A 7.16
Producing reports	Insert a graphic on a report	A 7.56
	Modify report properties	A 4.15, A 7.26
	Create and modify a report in Design view	A 7.24
	Modify control properties	A 4.15, A 6.20, A 7.35
	Set section properties	A 4.15
	Use the subreport control and synchronize reports	A 7.29
Defining relationships	Establish one-to-one relationships	A 7.12
	Establish many-to-many relationships	A 7.12
	Set Cascade Update and Cascade Delete options	A 9.17
Utilizing Web capabilities	Create hyperlinks	A 5.6, A 5.18
	Use the group and sort features of data access pages	A 9.26
	Create a data access page	AW 1.3
Using Access tools	Set and modify a database password	A 9.22
	Set startup options	A 9.20
	Use Add-ins (Database Splitter, Analyzer, Link Table Manager)	A 9.8, A 9.11
	Encrypt and decrypt a database	A 9.24
	Use simple replication (copy for a mobile user)	A 9.32
	Run macros using controls	A 6.49
	Create a macro using the Macro Builder	A 6.29
	Convert a database to a previous version	A 9.7
Data integration	Export database records to Excel	AI 2.3
	Drag and drop tables and queries to Excel	AI 2.6
	Present information as a chart (MS Graph)	A 8.40
	Link to existing data	AI 1.3

Index

Microsoft Access 2000 Quick Reference Summary

In Microsoft Access 2000, you can accomplish a task in a number of ways. The following table provides a quick reference to each task presented in this textbook. You can invoke the commands listed in the MENU BAR and SHORTCUT MENU columns using either the mouse or keyboard.

Microsoft Access 2000 Quick Reference Summary

TASK	PAGE NUMBER	MOUSE	MENU BAR	SHORTCUT MENU	KEYBOARD SHORTCUT
Add Clip Art	A 7.56	Unbound Object Frame button	Insert | Object		
Add Chart	A 8.40		Insert | Chart		
Add Combo Box	A 4.37	Combo Box button			
Add Command Button	A 8.9	Command Button button			
Add Date	A 7.39		Insert | Date and Time		
Add Field	A 3.17	Insert Rows button	Insert | Rows	Insert Rows	INSERT
Add Fields Using Field List	A 7.27	Drag field			
Add Label	A 4.43	Label button			
Add Page Number	A 7.41		Insert | Page Number		
Add Record	A 1.21, A 1.28	New Record button	Insert | New Record	New Record	
Add Rectangle	A 8.30	Rectangle button			
Add Subform	A 8.36	Subform / Subreport button			
Add Subreport	A 7.29	Subform / Subreport button			
Add Switchboard Item	A 6.44	New button			
Add Switchboard Page	A 6.43	New button			
Add Table to Query	A 2.32	Show Table button	Query | Show Table	Show Table	
Add Text Box	A 4.34	Text Box button			
Apply Filter	A 3.13	Filter by Selection or Filter by Form button	Records | Filter | Filter by Selection or Records | Filter | Filter by Form	Filter by Selection or Filter For:	
Calculate Statistics	A 2.40	Totals button	View | Totals	Totals	
Change Field Properties in Query	A 7.17	Properties button	View | Properties	Properties	
Change Group of Records	A 3.23	Query Type button arrow | Update Query	Query | Update Query	Query Type | Update Query	

(continued)

MICROSOFT ACCESS 2000 QUICK REFERENCE SUMMARY

Microsoft Access 2000 Quick Reference Summary (continued)

TASK	PAGE NUMBER	MOUSE	MENU BAR	SHORTCUT MENU	KEYBOARD SHORTCUT
Change Join Properties in Query	A 7.16		View	Join Properties	Join Properties	
Change Margins	A 7.41		File	Page Setup	Margins tab		
Change Property	A 4.16	Properties button	View	Properties	Properties	
Change Referential Integrity Options	A 9.16		Relationships	Edit Relationship	Edit Relationship	
Clear Query	A 2.16		Edit	Clear Grid		
Close Database	A 1.25	Close button	File	Close		
Close Form	A 1.38	Close button	File	Close		
Close Query	A 2.14	Close button	File	Close		
Close Table	A 1.25	Close button	File	Close		
Collapse Subdatasheet	A 3.42	Expand indicator (–)			
Compact a Database	A 5.48		Tools	Database Utilities	Compact and Repair		
Convert Database to Earlier Version	A 9.7		Tools	Database Utilities	Convert Database		
Copy Object to Clipboard	A 6.36	Copy button	Edit	Copy	Copy	CTRL+C
Create Calculated Field	A 2.36			Zoom	SHIFT+F2
Create Data Access Page	AW 1.3	New Object button arrow	Page	Insert	Page		
Create Database	A 1.9	Start button	New Office Document	File	New		CTRL+N
Create Form	A 1.37, A 4.31	New Object button arrow	AutoForm	Insert	Form		
Create Form Using Design View	A 8.35	Double-click Create Form in Design View	Insert	Form	Design View		
Create Index	A 3.48	Indexes button	View	Indexes		
Create Input Mask	A 6.10	Input Mask text box			
Create Labels	A 7.47	New Object button arrow	Report	Label Wizard	Insert	Report	Label Wizard		
Create Lookup Wizard Field	A 6.8	Text arrow	Lookup Wizard			
Create Macro	A 6.27	New Object button arrow	Macro	Insert	Macro		
Create Pivot Table	A 8.47	New Object button arrow	Form	PivotTable Wizard	Insert	Form	PivotTable Wizard		
Create Query	A 2.6	New Object button arrow	Query	Insert	Query		
Create Replica	A 9.32		Tools	Replication	Create Replica		

Microsoft Access 2000 Quick Reference Summary *(continued)*

TASK	PAGE NUMBER	MOUSE	MENU BAR	SHORTCUT MENU	KEYBOARD SHORTCUT
Create Report	A 1.43	New Object button arrow | Report	Insert | Report		
Create Report Using Design View	A 7.24	Double-click Create Report in Design View	Insert | Report | Design View		
Create Snapshot	AI 2.9		File | Export	Export	
Create SQL Query	A 9.36	View button arrow | SQL View	View | SQL View	SQL View	
Create Switchboard	A 6.40		Tools | Database Utilities | Switchboard Manager		
Create Table	A 1.14	Tables object | Create table in Design view or Create table by using Wizard	Insert | Table		
Default Value	A 3.31	Default Value box			
Delete Field	A 1.19, A 3.19	Delete Rows button	Edit | Delete Rows	Delete Rows	DELETE
Delete Group of Records	A 3.26	Query Type button arrow | Delete Query	Query | Delete Query	Query Type | Delete Query	
Delete Record	A 3.14	Delete Record button	Edit | Delete Record	Delete Record	DELETE
Display Field List	A 7.24	Field List button	View | Field List		
Encrypt Database	A 9.24		Tools | Security | Encrypt/Decrypt Database		
Exclude Duplicates	A 2.29	Properties button	View | Properties | Unique Values Only	Properties | Unique Values Only	
Exclude Field from Query Results	A 2.20	Show check box			
Expand Subdatasheet	A 3.42	Expand indicator (+)			
Export Data Using Drag-and-Drop	AI 2.6	Drag object to desired application			
Export Data Using Export Command	AI 2.3		File | Export	Export	
Field Size	A 1.17, A 3.16	Field Size text box			
Field Type	A 1.16	Data Type arrow | appropriate type, appropriate letter			
Filter Query's Recordset	A 7.19	Filter by Selection or Filter by Form button	Records | Filter | Filter by Selection or Records | Filter | Filter by Form	Filter by Selection or Filter For:	
Format	A 3.33	Format box			
Import Worksheet	AI 1.3		File | Get External Data | Import	Import	
Include All Fields in Query	A 2.15	Double-click asterisk			

(continued)

Microsoft Access 2000 Quick Reference Summary *(continued)*

TASK	PAGE NUMBER	MOUSE	MENU BAR	SHORTCUT MENU	KEYBOARD SHORTCUT
Include Field in Query	A 2.10	Double-click field in field list box			
Key Field	A 1.17	Primary Key button	Edit | Primary Key	Primary Key	
Link Worksheet	AI 1.3		File | Get External Data | Link Tables	Link Tables	
Modify Switchboard Page	A 6.44, A 6.46	Edit button			
Move Control	A 4.33	Drag control		Properties | All tab | Top and Properties | All tab | Left	
Move to Design View	A 5.39	View button	View | Design View	Design View	
Move to First Record	A 1.27	First Record button			CTRL+UP ARROW
Move to Last Record	A 1.27	Last Record button			CTRL+DOWN ARROW
Move to Next Record	A 1.27	Next Record button			DOWN ARROW
Move to Previous Record	A 1.27	Previous Record button			UP ARROW
Open Database	A 1.26	Start button | Open Office Document	File | Open Database		CTRL+O
Open Form	A 3.7	Forms object | Open button		Open	Use arrow keys to move highlight to name, then press ENTER key
Open Table	A 1.21	Tables object | Open button		Open	Use arrow keys to move highlight to name, then press ENTER key
Preview Table	A 1.31	Print Preview button	File | Print Preview	Print Preview	
Print Relationships	A 3.38		File | Print Relationships		
Print Report	A 1.48	Print button	File | Print	Print	CTRL+P
Print Results of Query	A 2.12	Print button	File | Print	Print	CTRL+P
Print Table	A 1.31	Print button	File | Print	Print	CTRL+P
Quit Access	A 1.25	Close button on title bar	File | Exit		ALT+F4
Relationships (Referential Integrity)	A 3.38	Relationships button	Tools | Relationships	Relationships	
Remove Control	A 4.24	Cut button	Edit | Cut	Cut	DELETE
Remove Filter	A 3.14	Remove Filter button	Records | Remove Filter/Sort	Remove Filter/Sort	
Remove Password	A 9.25		Tools | Security | Unset Database Password		
Resize Column	A 3.21, A 5.13	Drag right boundary of field selector	Format | Column Width	Column Width	

Microsoft Access 2000 Quick Reference Summary *(continued)*

TASK	PAGE NUMBER	MOUSE	MENU BAR	SHORTCUT MENU	KEYBOARD SHORTCUT
Resize Control	A 5.29	Drag sizing handle	View | Properties | All tab | Width and View | Properties | All tab | Height	Properties | All tab | Width and Properties | All tab | Height	
Resize Row	A 5.13	Drag lower boundary of row selector	Format | Row Height	Row Height	
Resize Section	A 4.43	Drag section boundary	View | Properties | All tab | Height	Properties | All tab | Height	
Restructure Table	A 3.16	Tables object | Design button		Design View	
Return to Design View	A 2.12	View button	View | Design View		
Run Query	A 2.11	Run button	Query | Run		
Save Form	A 1.38	Save button	File | Save		CTRL+S
Save Query	A 2.42	Save button	File | Save		CTRL+S
Save Table	A 1.19	Save button	File | Save		CTRL+S
Search for Record	A 3.9	Find button	Edit | Find		CTRL+F
Select Fields for Report	A 1.45	Add Field button or Add All Fields button			
Set Password	A 9.22		Tools | Security | Set Database Password		
Set Startup Options	A 9.20		Tools | Startup		
Sort Data in Query	A 2.26	Sort row | arrow | type of sort			
Sort Records	A 3.43	Sort Ascending or Sort Descending button	Records | Sort | Sort Ascending or Sort Descending	Sort Ascending or Sort Descending	
Specify Sorting and Grouping in Report	A 7.25	Sorting and Grouping button	View | Sorting and Grouping	Sorting and Grouping	
Switch Between Form and Datasheet Views	A 1.42, A 3.11	View button	View | Datasheet View		
Synchronize Design Master and Replica	A 9.34		Tools | Replication | Synchronize Now		
Update Hyperlink Field	A 5.18		Insert | Hyperlink	Hyperlink | Edit Hyperlink	CTRL+K
Update OLE Field	A 5.15		Insert | Object	Insert Object	
Use AND Criterion	A 2.24				Type criteria on same line
Use Documenter	A 9.13	Analyze button arrow | Documenter	Tools | Analyze | Documenter		
Use OR Criterion	A 2.25				Type criteria on separate lines
Use Performance Analyzer	A 9.11	Analyze button arrow | Analyze Performance	Tools | Analyze | Performance		

Microsoft Access 2000 Quick Reference Summary *(continued)*

TASK	PAGE NUMBER	MOUSE	MENU BAR	SHORTCUT MENU	KEYBOARD SHORTCUT
Use Table Analyzer	A 9.8	Analyze button arrow | Analyze Table	Tools | Analyze | Table		
Validation Rule	A 3.30	Validation Rule box			
Validation Text	A 3.30	Validation Text box			